TRAGIC YEARS

1860-1865

VOLUME TWO

A DOCUMENTARY HISTORY
OF THE AMERICAN CIVIL WAR BY

Paul M. Angle AND Earl Schenck Miers

1960

SIMON AND SCHUSTER · NEW YORK

FIRST PRINTING

Acknowledgement is gratefully made to the following for permission to quote from the books indicated:

American Heritage Publishing Company—*The Hanging of John Brown* by Boyd B. Stutler, copyright 1955.

Appleton-Century-Crofts, Inc.—*Lincoln in the Telegraph Office* by David Homer Bates, copyright 1907; *Under the Old Flag* by James Harrison Wilson, copyright 1912.

Brandt & Brandt—*John Brown's Body* by Stephen Vincent Benét, Rinehart & Company, Inc., copyright 1927, 1928 by Stephen Vincent Benét; renewed 1955, 1956 by Rosemary Carr Benét.

Thomas Y. Crowell Company—*South After Gettysburg: The Letters of Cornelia Hancock, 1863–1868,* copyright 1958 by Henrietta Stratton Jaquette.

Dodd, Mead & Company—*Lincoln and the Civil War,* edited by Tyler Dennett, copyright 1939.

Harvey S. Ford, Esquire—*The Memoirs of a Volunteer* by John Beatty, edited by Harvey S. Ford, copyright 1946.

Georgetown University Press—*John Dooley, Confederate Soldier,* edited by Joseph T. Durkin, copyright 1945.

Harcourt, Brace & Company—*Sherman, Fighting Prophet* by Lloyd Lewis, copyright 1932.

Houghton Mifflin Company—*An Autobiography* by Charles Francis Adams, copyright 1916; *The Education of Henry Adams* by Henry Adams, copyright 1906; *A Cycle of Adams Letters,* edited by Worthington C. Ford, copyright 1920; *Europe and the American Civil War* by Donaldson Jordan and Edwin J. Pratt, copyright 1931; *Diary of Gideon Welles,* copyright 1911; *The Life of Lyman Trumbull* by Horace White, copyright 1913.

Indiana University Press—*Grant and Lee* by J. F. C. Fuller, copyright 1957; *The Generalship of Ulysses S. Grant* by J. F. C. Fuller, copyright 1929; *With Sherman to the Sea* by Theodore F. Upson, edited by Oscar Osburn Winther, copyright 1943.

Little Brown & Company—*Meade's Headquarters, 1863–1865, Letters of Colonel Theodore Lyman from the Wilderness to Appomattox,* edited by George R. Agassiz, copyright 1922.

Longmans, Green & Company, Inc.—*Inside Lincoln's Cabinet: The Civil War Diaries of Salmon P. Chase,* edited by David Donald, copyright 1954; *Lincoln's Secretary: A Biography of John G. Nicolay* by Helen Nicolay, copyright 1949.

Louisiana State University Press—*Brokenburn: The Journal of Kate Stone,* edited by John Q. Anderson, copyright 1955; *Doctors in Gray: The Confederate Medical Service* by H. H. Cunningham, copyright 1958; *Behind the Lines in the Southern Confederacy* by Charles W. Ramsdell, copyright 1944; *The Plain People of the South* by Bell Irvin Wiley, copyright 1943.

McCowat-Mercer Press—*Cleburne and His Command* by Irving A. Buck, copyright 1908.

The Macmillan Company—*A History of the Southern Confederacy* by Clement Eaton, copyright 1954.

The Ohio Historical Society—*The Diary and Letters of Rutherford Birchard Hayes,* edited by Charles R. Williams, copyright 1922.

Oxford University Press—*Inside the Confederate Government: The Diary of Robert Garlick Hill Kean,* edited by Edward Younger, copyright 1957.

G. P. Putnam's Sons—*Letters of Ulysses S. Grant* by Jesse Grant Cramer, copyright 1912.

Charles Scribner's Sons—*War Years with Jeb Stuart* by W. W. Blackford, copyright 1945; *The Emergence of Lincoln* by Allan Nevins, copyright 1950.

University of Chicago Press—*The Civil War: A Soldier's View* by Col. G. F. R. Henderson, edited by Jay Luvaas, copyright 1958; *The Journal of Benjamin Moran, 1857–1865,* edited by Sarah Agnes Wallace and Frances Elma Gillespie, copyright 1948.

University of North Carolina Press—*Two Soldiers: The Campaign Diaries of Thomas J. Key, C. S. A. and Robert J. Campbell, U. S. A.,* edited by William A. Cate, copyright 1938; *I Rode with Stonewall* by Henry Kyd Douglas, copyright 1940.

University of South Carolina Press—*Mason Smith Family Letters, 1860–1868,* edited by Daniel E. H. Smith, Alice R. H. Smith and Arney R. Childs, copyright 1950.

University of Texas Press—*This Infernal War: The Confederate Letters of Sgt. Edwin H. Fay,* edited by Bell Irvin Wiley, copyright 1958.

LIBRARY OF CONGRESS CATALOG CARD NUMBER: 60–8012
MANUFACTURED IN THE UNITED STATES OF AMERICA
BY KINGSPORT PRESS, INC., KINGSPORT, TENN.

CONTENTS

VOLUME TWO

1864

CONTENTS

1865

1863

CONTINUED

CHAPTER 23

MISSISSIPPI HIGH JINKS: VICKSBURG

L ATE IN JANUARY 1863, Oliver P. Morton, Governor of Indiana, telegraphed Lincoln: "It is important that I see you for a few hours, but I cannot leave long enough to go to Washington. Can you meet me in Harrisburg?"

Morton believed that he had collected evidence of a conspiracy among Democratic politicians in Ohio, Indiana and Illinois to form a Northwest Confederacy, cast aside New England as an abolitionist's wilderness, and join with the South. Perhaps Lincoln never called Morton—as some said he did—"the skeerdest man I know of"; but, in any event, the President replied calmly:

"I think it would not do for me to meet you at Harrisburg. It would be known, and would be misconstrued a thousand ways. Of course if the whole truth could be told and accepted as the truth, it would do no harm, but that is impossible."

I

Governor Morton sent a courier to see Lincoln. Essential to the success of any Northwest Confederacy, the Governor stressed, was control of the Mississippi. Lincoln doubtless held his temper, though he might have inquired why a campaign against Vicksburg had been weeks in planning if he were not aware of the river's importance. Sherman's failure in December to take the city by frontal assault had increased Southern defiance and emboldened the Butternuts. Again, Lincoln didn't need Morton to tell him these facts of political life. His hope was that something of a happier nature would occur with the spirited bride-

groom, General John A. McClernand, now at Vicksburg to command his own troops.

What transpired principally was a clash of personalities, with Sherman declaring that he essayed the role of peacemaker between a huffy Admiral Porter and an arrogant McClernand. Eventually the admiral and the two generals agreed to put aside their own quarrels and concentrate upon the Confederates with an unexpected adventure into Arkansas. In McClernand's name, a glowing victory was claimed:[1]

HDQRS. ARMY OF THE MISSISSIPPI,
POST ARKANSAS, Jan. 12, 1863.

SOLDIERS OF THE ARMY OF THE MISSISSIPPI: I congratulate you. Within seven days you have sailed 250 miles, from Vicksburg to this Post, borne upon numerous transports, from time to time furnished with fuel cut by you from the forest. With ranks thinned by former battles and disease you have waded and cut your way through miles of swamps and timber in advancing to the attack. You have stormed the defenses of the enemy's position which both nature and art had combined to render extraordinarily strong, capturing after three and a half hours' hard fighting the whole hostile force opposed to you, numbering 7,000 men, together with 8,000 stand of arms, 20 cannon, and a large amount of commissary, quartermaster's, and ordnance stores.

A success so complete in itself has not hitherto been achieved during the war. It is an important step toward the restoration of our national jurisdiction and unity over the territory on the right bank of the Mississippi River. It reflects honor upon your courage and patriotism. It will challenge the grateful acclaim of your country.

Your and my only cause of regret is the loss of the brave men who have fallen or been wounded in the defense of a just and sacred cause. All honor to them! Their names and their memory will be cherished in the hearts of their countrymen.

Soldiers, let this triumph be but the precursor of still more important achievements. Win for the Army of the Mississippi an imperishable renown. Surmount all obstacles, and relying on the God of Battles wrest from destiny and danger the homage of still more expressive acknowledgments of your unconquerable constancy and valor.

By order of Maj. Gen. John A. McClernand, commanding Army of the Mississippi:

A. SCHWARTZ,
Major and Acting Assistant Adjutant-General

A somewhat different account of the battle was contained in the report of Brigadier General Thomas J. Churchill, the Confederate commander along the lower Arkansas and White Rivers:[2]

RICHMOND, VA., May 6, 1863

GENERAL: On the morning of the 9th of January I was informed by my pickets stationed at the mouth of the cut-off that the enemy, with his gunboats, followed by his fleet of seventy or eighty transports, were passing into the Arkansas River. It now became evident that their object was to attack the Arkansas Post. I immediately made every arrangement to meet him, and ordered out the whole force under my command, numbering about 3,000 effective men, to take position in some lower trenches about 1¼ miles below the fort. The Second Brigade, under Colonel Deshler, and the Third, under Colonel Dunnington, occupied the works, while the First Brigade, under Colonel Garland, was held in reserve.

Three companies of cavalry, under command of Captains Denson, Nutt, and Richardson, were sent in advance to watch the movements of the enemy. During the night the enemy effected a landing about 2 miles below, on the north side of the river.

The following day about 9 o'clock the gunboats commenced moving up the river and opened fire upon our position. Having but one battery of field pieces, of 6 and 12 pounders, I did not return their fire. It was here that I expected the co-operation of the guns from the fort, but owing to some defect in the powder they were scarcely able to throw a shell below the trenches much less to the fleet. About 2 o'clock P.M., discovering that I was being flanked by a large body of cavalry and artillery, I thought it advisable to fall back under cover of the guns of the fort to an inner line of intrenchments.

The enemy advanced cautiously, and as they approached our lines were most signally repulsed. They made no further attempt that evening to charge our works, and I employed the balance of the time till next morning in strengthening my position and completing my intrenchments. Discovering that a body of the enemy had occupied some cabins in our old encampment, I ordered Col. R. Q. Mills with his regiment to drive them from the position, which he did most successfully, capturing several prisoners. Just before dark Admiral Porter moved up with several of his iron-clads to test the metal of our fort. Colonel Dunnington, who commanded the fort, was ready in an instant to receive him. The fire opened and the fight lasted near two hours, and finally the gunboats were compelled to fall back in a crippled condition.

Our loss was slight; that of the enemy much heavier. During the night I received a telegraphic dispatch from you, ordering me "to hold out till help arrived or until all dead," which order was communicated to brigade commanders, with instructions to see it carried out in spirit and letter. Next morning I made every disposition of my forces to meet the enemy in the desperate conflict which was soon to follow. . . . It was near 12 o'clock before the enemy got fully into position, when he commenced moving upon my lines simultaneously by land and water. Four iron-clads opened upon the fort, which responded in gallant style with its three guns.

After a continuous fire of three hours they succeeded in silencing every gun we had with the exception of one small 6-pounder Parrott gun which was on the land side. Two boats passed up and opened a cross-fire upon the fort and our lines; still we maintained the struggle. Their attack by land was less successful; on the right they were repulsed twice in attempting to storm our works, and on the left were driven back with great slaughter in no less than eight different charges. To defend this entire line of rifle pits I had but one battery of small field pieces, under command of Captain Hart, to whom great credit is due for the successful manner in which they were handled, contending, as he did, with some fifty pieces in his front. The fort had now been silenced about an hour, most of the field pieces had been disabled, still the fire raged furiously along the entire line, and that gallant band of Texans and Arkansians having nothing to rely upon now save their muskets and bayonets, still disdained to yield to the overpowering foe of 50,000 men, who were pressing upon them from almost every direction. Just at this moment, to my great surprise, several white flags were displayed in the Twenty-fourth Regiment Texas Dismounted Cavalry, First Brigade, and before they could be suppressed the enemy took advantage of them, crowded upon my lines, and not being prevented by the brigade commander from crossing, as was his duty, I was forced to the humiliating necessity of surrendering the balance of the command. My great hope was to keep them in check until night, and then, if re-enforcements did not reach me, cut my way out. No stigma should rest upon the troops. It was no fault of theirs; they fought with a desperation and courage yet unsurpassed in this war, and I hope and trust that the traitor will yet be discovered, brought to justice, and suffer the full penalty of the law. My thanks are due to Colonels Anderson and Gillespie for the prompt measures taken to prevent the raising of the white flag in their regiments. In the Second Brigade, commanded by the gallant Deshler, it was never displayed.

So McClernand gave one version of the capture of the Arkansas Post and Churchill another; Sherman told a story that flattered neither McClernand nor Churchill, and by Porter's account the Navy had done most of the effective fighting. Meanwhile McClernand turned to the political arena, advising his neighbor from Springfield that the Emancipation Proclamation had been a sad mistake. McClernand had been talking to "a gentleman of the first respectability just arrived from the rebel army" who had been speaking with officers in that army "formerly my warm personal and political friends," and McClernand advised his old Springfield neighbor, "These officials desire the restoration of peace and are represented to be willing to wheel their columns into the line of that policy. They admit that the South West and the North West are geographically and commercially identified."

The old Springfield neighbor in this instance was Abraham Lincoln, who held an opinion of his own concerning the usefulness of the Emancipation Proclamation:[3]

EXECUTIVE MANSION,
WASHINGTON, January 8, 1863

MAJOR GENERAL MCCLERNAND

MY DEAR SIR Your interesting communication by the hand of Major Scates is received. I never did ask more, nor ever was willing to accept less, than for all the States, and the people thereof, to take and hold their places, and their rights, in the Union, under the Constitution of the United States. For this alone have I felt authorized to struggle; and I seek neither more nor less now. Still, to use a coarse, but an expressive figure, broken eggs can not be mended. I have issued the emancipation proclamation, and I can not retract it.

After the commencement of hostilities I struggled nearly a year and a half to get along without touching the "institution"; and when finally I conditionally determined to touch it, I gave a hundred days fair notice of my purpose, to all the States and people, within which time they could have turned it wholly aside, by simply again becoming good citizens of the United States. They chose to disregard it, and I made the peremptory proclamation on what appeared to me to be a military necessity. And being made, it must stand. As to the States not included in it, of course they can have their rights in the Union as of old. Even the people of the states included, if they choose, need not to be hurt by it. Let them adopt systems of apprenticeship for the colored people, conforming substantially to the most approved plans of gradual emancipation; and, with the aid they can have from the general government, they may be nearly as well off, in this respect, as if the present trouble had not occurred, and much better off than they can possibly be if the contest continues persistently.

As to any dread of my having a "purpose to enslave, or exterminate, the whites of the South," I can scarcely believe that such dread exists. It is too absurd. I believe you can be my personal witness that no man is less to be dreaded for undue severity, in any case.

If the friends you mention really wish to have peace upon the old terms, they should act at once. Every day makes the case more difficult. They can so act, with entire safety, so far as I am concerned.

I think you would better not make this letter public; but you may rely confidently on my standing by whatever I have said in it. Please write me if any thing more comes to light. Yours very truly

A. LINCOLN

II

When later in January McClernand again wrote Lincoln, he had a new complaint—Grant had reduced him to a corps commander and he, McClernand, knew that Halleck was to blame for this mischief. Lincoln replied in part: "You are now doing well—well for the country, and well for yourself—much better than you could possibly be, if engaged in open war with Gen. Halleck. Allow me to beg, that for your sake, for my sake, & for the country's sake, you give your whole attention to the better work."

What Lincoln said between the lines was that Grant had taken personal command of the campaign against Vicksburg. On a bleak day, toward the end of January, Grant reached Young's Point, about seven miles above the fortified city on the river bluffs. He did not exaggerate the problems that confronted him:[4]

The real work of the campaign and siege of Vicksburg now began. The problem was to secure a footing upon dry ground on the east side of the river from which the troops could operate against Vicksburg. The Mississippi River, from Cairo south, runs through a rich alluvial valley of many miles in width, bound on the east by land running from eighty up to two or more hundred feet above the river. On the west side the highest land, except in a few places, is but little above the highest water. Through this valley the river meanders in the most tortuous way, varying in direction to all points of the compass. At places it runs to the very foot of the bluffs. After leaving Memphis, there are no such highlands coming to the water's edge on the east shore until Vicksburg is reached.

The intervening land is cut up by bayous filled from the river in high water—many of them navigable for steamers. All of them would be, except for overhanging trees, narrowness and tortuous course, making it impossible to turn the bends with vessels of any considerable length. Marching across this country in the face of an enemy was impossible; navigating it proved equally impracticable. The strategical way according to the rule, therefore, would have been to go back to Memphis; establish that as a base of supplies; fortify it so that the storehouses could be held by a small garrison, and move from there along the line of railroad, repairing as we advanced, to the Yallabusha, or to Jackson, Mississippi. At this time the North had become very much discouraged. Many strong Union men believed that the war must prove a failure. The elections of 1862 had gone against the party which was for the prosecution of the war to save the Union if it took the last man and the last dollar. Voluntary enlistments had ceased throughout the greater part of the North, and the draft had been resorted to to fill up our ranks. It was my judgment at the time that to make a backward movement as long as that from Vicksburg to Memphis, would be interpreted, by many of those yet full of hope for the preservation of the Union, as a defeat, and that the draft would be resisted, desertions ensue and the power to capture and punish deserters lost. There was nothing left to be done but to *go forward to a decisive victory*. This was in my mind from the moment I took command in person at Young's Point.

The winter of 1862–3 was a noted one for continuous high water in the Mississippi and for heavy rains along the lower river. To get dry land, or rather land above the water, to encamp the troops upon, took many miles of river front. We had to occupy the levees and the ground immediately behind. This was so limited that one corps, the 17th, under General McPherson, was at Lake Providence, seventy miles above Vicksburg.

It was in January the troops took their position opposite Vicksburg. The water was very high and the rains were incessant. There seemed no possibility of a land movement before the end of March or later, and it would not do to lie idle all this time. The effect would be demoralizing to the troops and injurious to their health. Friends in the North would have grown more and more discouraged, and enemies

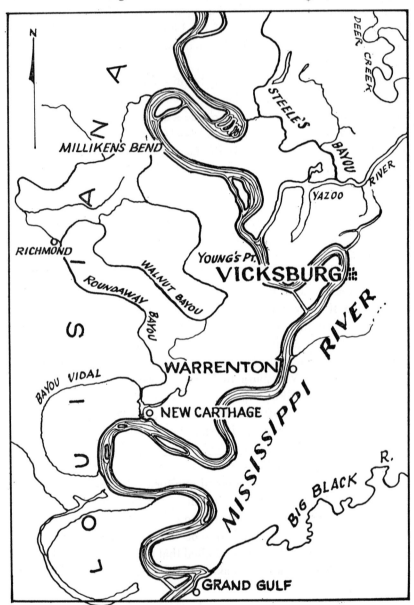

VICKSBURG: THE RIVER APPROACHES

in the same section more and more insolent in their gibes and denunciation of the cause and those engaged in it.

One who could testify to how the flood waters of the Mississippi complicated Grant's problems was the reporter Sylvanus Cadwallader:[5]

For a few weeks after we arrived at Young's Point a large proportion of the dead were buried in a strip of bottom land laying between the river bank and the levee. As the water rose to the level of the river bank, in some places, this bottom was converted into a mud hole and quagmire, until teams that were still contriving to drag through to the transports for supplies would often strike the end of the box or coffin and heave it clear out of the ground. Generally these were buried a second time, a little deeper. For another period thereafter, the dead were buried in the side of the levee (there being no other dry ground for miles), until the levee was literally honeycombed by such excavations.

On one occasion the father of a dead soldier came from the north with a metallic casket, disinterred the remains of his son who had died of smallpox from the bank, and left the empty box on the side of the levee. That night one of the negro roustabouts on the *Magnolia* * brought this discarded smallpox coffin to the lower deck of the vessel and used it to sleep in for fully a week before he was detected. Singularly the contagion did not spread, but fumigations were in order for a while.

At Brokenburn, a large cotton plantation about thirty miles northwest of Vicksburg, young Kate Stone recorded the discomforts produced by the presence of Grant and his Yankees:[6]

Jan. 25: Sunday. After three weeks of silence let me think of what has happened. The Yankees, after an absence of more than a week employed in taking Arkansas Post, have returned in large force, have invested Vicksburg, and are cutting another ditch across the point above DeSoto, or it may be deepening the first ditch. My Brother, Mr. Hardison, Dr. Waddell, and several other Louisiana gentlemen were in Vicksburg when the boats came in sight, and they had great trouble

---

* Grant's headquarters boat.

regaining their horses, just missing several encounters with scouting bands.

My Brother started off this morning with the best and strongest of the Negroes to look for a place west of the Ouachita. Only the old and sickly with the house servants are left here. He is sure we will all be forced to leave this place as the enemy intend going into camp at the Bend, and in the event of their defeat at Vicksburg which is certain, will lay this whole country waste, sending out bands of Negroes and soldiers to burn and destroy. My Brother thinks we had better leave at once, and we will commence packing tomorrow. The Negroes did so hate to go and so do we. . . .

Jan. 26: Preparing to run from the Yankees, I commit my book to the bottom of a packing box with only a slight chance of seeing it again.

March 2: Saturday [Monday] I think. We have not had an almanac for more than a year, and so I can only guess at the time until someone better posted comes along. The Yankees have not visited us yet, and so after more than a month's concealment I take my book out to write again.

The soldiers have been all around us but not on the place. At first we were frightened, expecting them all the time and preparing to start for the hills beyond the Macon, the Mecca for most of the refugee-ing planters. Mamma had all the carpets taken up and the valuable clothes and everything but the furniture sent away or ready to send when My Brother came back from Delhi, where he left the Negroes waiting until they could be shipped on the train. Such a crowd was there that it will be several days before they can get off.

He gave such a disheartening account of the roads—they are impassable for anything but a six-mule team—that he and Mamma concluded it was impossible to move at this time and we would await further developments here. Mamma has had the house put in order, and we are again comfortable. I am so glad for I dreaded going into the back country, where we would never see or hear anything among total strangers, and to leave our pleasant home most probably to be destroyed by the Yankees, and we may be able to protect it if we are here. . . .

March 3: Last night it was reported that the Yankees were at Dr. Devine's, and we looked for them here today. My Brother and Mr. Hardison, who is conscript agent, went out early this morning to stay in the woods until nightfall, as they do not want to be captured and ornament a Yankee prison. It is My Brother's last day at home too, and we can see nothing of him because of those horrid Yankees. The fear of his imprisonment alone reconciles us to his departure. We are in hourly dread of his being taken. We will feel safe only when he is across the river again. . . .

Johnny who has been out scouting reports the Yankees at Rescue, the adjoining place, yesterday hunting horses and Negroes, and today they are scattered all through the lower neighborhood on the same quest. This band is said to be Kansas Jayhawkers, the very offscourings of the Northern Army. They say they will take by force all Negroes, whether they wish to go or not. A great number of Negroes have gone to the Yankees from this section. Mr. Watson and his father-in-law, Mr. Scott, living, I think, on Eagle Lake near Richmond got up one morning and found every Negro gone, about seventy-five, only three little girls left. The ladies actually had to get up and get breakfast. They said it was funny to see their first attempt at milking. Mr. Matt Johnson has lost every Negro off one place and a number from the other places. Keene Richards has lost 160 from Transylvania and fifty of them are reported dead. The Negroes at work on the canal have what they call black measles, and it is very fatal to them.

III

During those winter months along the flooded Mississippi, the campaign against Vicksburg followed neither military rule, rhyme nor reason. Grant's problem was to find a way—any way—to break through the natural obstacles of swamp, water and forest protecting the city; the schemes advanced—and tried—to achieve this end multiplied from week to week, and sometimes from day to day. The river in 1863 made a big bend in front of Vicksburg, and the purpose of the canal to which Kate Stone referred was to channel across this bend of land so that Union gunboats could approach the city out of range of the massed batteries. The canal failed; and names like Lake Providence and Yazoo Pass in newspaper headlines indicated bayous and complicated systems of waterways that were explored in an effort to get below the city, land troops, and swing back upon Vicksburg's defenses.

With flood waters permitting gunboats to sail in areas ordinarily unnavigable in a canoe, Admiral Porter was entranced by the possibilities. Among all the plans proposed for getting at Vicksburg through the back door, Porter's stood apart for dash and originality. Grant, believing that anything was better than idleness, sent troops under Sherman to co-operate in an expedition unique in naval history, as Porter cheerfully testified:[7]

When the fleet came to the pass into which it was to turn, after having ascended the Yazoo, the entrance could scarcely be made out, so dense was the growth of the overhanging bushes and trees, but these the men cut away with cutlasses and axes, and a pass wide enough for three vessels abreast, showed itself, lined out by heavy trees, and through this the gun-boats followed one another in line, their leadsmen singing out in melodious song, "quarter less three." There was no more channel here than elsewhere, as the water overflowed every place alike, but there was a long, straight pass opening through the forest, about 170 feet wide, which was, no doubt, a road cut through the woods for hauling cotton to some landing.

It was a novel scene. Thousands of crows flew from their perches, and broke the silence of the forest with their discordant notes, no doubt wondering what could have caused those great "mudturtles" to invade their hitherto inaccessible abode, where for centuries they had reared their young and digested their plunder without interruption.

On went the gun-boats, officers and sailors alike, delighted with the romantic scenery, which baffled description; every heart was cheered with the hope that the long sought for road to Vicksburg had been found, and that the great prize would soon be in their hands. Now and then, a stray tree as much as three feet in diameter would be found standing in the middle of the channel as if to dispute the way. The vessels might have passed on either side, but the desire to try the strength of these outlying sentinels proved so great that the flagship "Cincinnati" would run into them with her strong, broad bow, and topple them over, a feat rendered possible by the softening action of the water upon the earth about their roots. The vessels in the rear were told to haul them out of the way. This was good practice, and came into play before the expedition had proceeded many miles. It was all fair sailing at first, but became rough work in the end.

After some ten miles of easy progress through the woods, the fleet arrived at Black Bayou, a place about four miles long, leading into Deer Creek—and here the plain sailing ended. The gun-boats, being too wide to pass between the trees, had to go to work and knock them down, and pull them up by the roots. The line of vessels was broken, and each went to work to make her way through the tangle as best she

could. Saws and axes now came into use, and every means was resorted to for clearing the way. The narrow tugs and the mortar floats
had no difficulty in getting along, but the wider iron-clads were, for a
time, brought to a stand. The open roadway had vanished, and the pilot
confessed his ignorance of this locality. There was plenty of water,
and the stentorian voice of the leadsman was still heard singing out
"quarter less three!"

There is nothing that will daunt the American sailor but a lee shore
and no sea room. There was plenty of sea room here, but no room to
pass between the tangle. The obstruction was passed, after working
twenty-four hours consecutively, and that four miles overcome, leaving
a good road for those coming after, but a number of trees were moved
away, Titans of the forest that had reigned there for a century or more.

Sherman had arrived at Black Bayou with part of his force, another
part had started to march over from a point twenty miles above the
Yazoo River, on the Mississippi, following a ridge of land not inun-
dated. The part of the Army embarked had been transported in small
stern-wheel steamers, which being very narrow, succeeded in passing
between the trees with only the loss of a few smoke-stacks. From Black
Bayou, the gun-boats turned again into Steele's Bayou, a channel just
one foot wider than the vessels, and here came the tug of war, such
as no vessels ever encountered before. The keel of the skiff was the
largest thing that had ever floated in waters now bearing vessels of
600 tons burthen. These had to break through bridges spanning this
muddy ditch, pass through the smoke and fire of burning cotton-bales
(which the enemy set in a blaze as soon as the fleet was discovered),
and work on, at the rate of half a mile an hour, through lithe willows
growing in the middle of the stream, which at intervals was choked up
with rafts that had been there for years. The pilot proved to be a fraud;
he had never seen the place before.

This bayou was bordered on both sides with overhanging trees,
whose Briarean arms would cling around the passing vessels and
sweep away boats and smoke-stacks, while the limbs of decayed trees
would fall upon the decks, smashing skylights to pieces, and injuring
the people.

It was dreadful to witness the infatuation of the Confederate Government agents, who, riding about on horseback, were setting fire to
the cotton far and near. They must have imagined the expedition sent
to gather cotton—a purpose never thought of.

Houses were often consumed with the cotton piles, and everything

betokened a Moscow affair. It was the cotton of the Confederate government, and they were allowed to burn it. It was the Confederate sin-
ews of war they were destroying; they were burning up their cash with
which they had expected to carry on the struggle.

The leaders of the expedition soon saw they were discovered; the
move was certainly known in Vicksburg, and the whole Confederacy
would be at work to defeat this measure. . . . The expedition hurried
on to get into the Rolling Fork, and thence into the Sunflower, whence
it could reach the Yazoo above Haines' Bluff. It seemed insane to proceed, there were so many dreadful obstacles in the way, yet no one apparently minded them. The work was hard on the sailors, nevertheless
they only made a lark of it.

Vicksburg was never so aroused as on hearing of the raid right into
the heart of her preserves. The expedition had struck that city's store-
house: here were the fleshpots that would make any people glad; cattle, corn, "hog and hominy" enough to subsist a great Army.

*Porter was ahead of Sherman's troops, with his gunboats stuck in wil-
low withes and an armed Confederate force soon appearing to contest
his escape. By courier the admiral dispatched to the general "somewhere in the bayous" an urgent plea:*

*"Dear Sherman: Hurry up, for Heaven's sake. I never knew how
helpless an ironclad could be steaming around through the woods
without an army to back her."*

Porter continued his tale of how not to fight in an ironclad:[8]

As night came on, the gun-boats were ordered to unship their rudders and drop down with the current; and, the water now running
rapidly into the bayou, owing to the cut at Delta—which was overflowing the whole country—the vessels bumped along at double the rate
they had ascended, bounding from tree to tree, and bringing down the
dead branches on the decks, to the destruction of everything around
—boats were smashed, and more or less injury done to everything.

As the gun-boats departed, the enemy . . . kept the fleet under
fire without the latter being able to fire more than an occasional gun
until nightfall, when it was found necessary to tie up. A watch of
armed men and all the howitzers were put ashore in preparation for
emergencies.

In the night the patrolling parties captured two of the enemy's officers and some men, who stated that two batteries had been landed,

and three thousand sharpshooters, and that they were quite satisfied they would capture the gun-boats in twenty-four hours. They were not aware that an army was with the fleet; they took this for a raid of gun-boats only, and, as one of them remarked, "a crazy one at that."

At daylight the fleet started down stream again, stern foremost, hoping to meet the army by noon, but at 8 A.M., they were surrounded by sharpshooters, who kept up such a fire that it was almost impossible for any one to show himself on deck. The riflemen on board, lying behind defences, kept up a brisk fire whenever they saw a curl of smoke. The howitzers were kept at work from behind the deck-houses, and the mortars, which were fired with small charges, landed their shells in amongst the enemy, and kept them at a distance. Now and then a mortar shell, landing at the foot of a tree behind which was a sharpshooter, would overthrow the tree as it exploded—making trees unsafe as a protection. Still, the sharpshooters increased in numbers, when, suddenly, the fleet had to come to a stand. Eight or ten large trees, some three feet in diameter, had been felled right across their track, from either side of the bayou, thus completely blocking the way, and the loud cheers of the Confederates as they rang through the woods showed they thought their prey entrapped.

The officers and men of the fleet, undaunted by this state of things, went to work to surmount the difficulty and remove the trees. Five hundred armed men were put on shore, and took to the trees to meet the enemy's sharpshooters, while howitzers and mortars kept up a rapid fire which was more than the enemy cared to face.

The working party from the vessels commenced operations below the banks, out of reach of the enemy's fire, and by using hawsers, tackles, and that powerful adjunct, steam, in six hours the trees were all removed, and the fleet went on its way down rejoicing.

Sherman had heard the firing, and had pushed on to get to the aid of the gun-boats. In the meantime, the enemy had landed more infantry —there were about four thousand in all. Pemberton, at Vicksburg, was well posted in all that was going on, and was determined to leave nothing undone to capture the venturesome fleet.

Again the fleet came to a stand-still, but this time only two large trees had been felled. The crews of the vessels commenced the work of removal, when a large body of Confederate troops were seen advancing directly through the woods upon the steamers, while the sharpshooters in redoubled numbers opened fire on the fleet from behind trees not more than fifty yards distant.

The working parties were called on board to defend the vessels, but before they could get to their arms, there was a rattle of musketry in the woods, a cheering of the crews, and a rapid retreat by the Confederates. They had fallen in with the head of Sherman's column, which was a great surprise to them, and after one or two volleys, they broke and fled back to their steamers. Sherman arrived just in the nick of time. Whether the gun-boats could have held their own under the circumstances is impossible to say. They were well prepared for a brave fight, and from behind the banks they could have mown down the enemy as they rushed on, but it was better as it was, and they were not subjected to the trial. . . . No set of people were ever so glad to see the soldiers as the men of that fleet were to see Sherman and his Army; and, as the gallant general rode up to the gun-boats, he was received with the warmest cheers he ever had in his life.

IV

Cries arose that the Union forces under Grant were hopelessly stuck in the mud before Vicksburg. To judge the situation at first hand, Secretary of War Stanton sent Charles A. Dana as a special emissary from Washington. Sylvanus Cadwallader described a threatened crisis:[9]

Gen. Grant had been apprized by friends of Mr. Dana's visit and its probable object. A conference of Staff officers was held, the situation was explained by Rawlins, and a line of procedure agreed upon. The paramount object was to keep Mr. Dana quiet until Grant could work out his campaign. Several of the staff could scarcely be restrained from open manifestations of their hostility, but wiser counsel prevailed. Col. Duff, chief of artillery, pronounced him a government spy, and was more inclined to throw him in the river, than to treat him with common civility. But Rawlins took a sensible, practical view of the situation, and said: "I am surprised, Col. Duff, at your discourteous and unmilitary remarks. Mr. Dana is the First Assistant Secretary of War,* and an official representative of the government. He should not be left in a moment's doubt as to the cordiality of his reception. He is entitled to as much official recognition as Mr. Stanton, or any other high

---

* Previously Dana, as editor of the New York *Tribune,* had stanchly supported Stanton as Cameron's successor in the War Department, one of the many points of disagreement between Dana and Greeley. When finally publisher and editor parted, Dana said: "While he was for peace I was for war . . . and there was a spirit that was not his spirit—that he did not like."

public functionary. I shall expect you to see that a tent is always pitched alongside Gen. Grant's, for Mr. Dana's use as long as he remains at headquarters—that sentries are placed in front of it—that orderlies are detailed for his service—and a place at mess-table specially reserved for him."

A suitable horse and equipments were provided for Mr. Dana's use and the entire staff, including Col. Duff, were properly deferential. Dana was not long in becoming an enthusiastic admirer of Gen. Grant's military ability, and remained his staunch friend till the war ended. Thus again was imminent danger averted by the wisdom and tact of Rawlins, and Grant spared to become the greatest military chieftain his generation produced.

Dana's own story bore out Cadwallader's claims:[10]

As soon as I arrived at Milliken's Bend, on April 6th, I had hunted up Grant and explained my mission. He received me cordially. Indeed, I think Grant was always glad to have me with his army. He did not like letter writing, and my daily dispatches to Mr. Stanton relieved him from the necessity of describing every day what was going on in the army. From the first neither he nor any of his staff or corps commanders evinced any unwillingness to show me the inside of things. In this first interview at Milliken's Bend, for instance, Grant explained to me so fully his new plan of campaign—for there was now but one—that by three o'clock I was able to send an outline of it to Mr. Stanton. From that time I saw and knew all the interior operations of that toughest of tough jobs, the reopening of the Mississippi.

The new project, so Grant told me, was to transfer his army to New Carthage, and from there carry it over the Mississippi, landing it at or about Grand Gulf; to capture this point, and then to operate rapidly on the southern and eastern shore of the Big Black River, threatening at the same time both Vicksburg and Jackson, and confusing the Confederates as to his real objective. If this could be done he believed the enemy would come out of Vicksburg and fight.

The first element in this plan was to open a passage from the Mississippi near Milliken's Bend, above Vicksburg, to the bayou on the west side, which led around to New Carthage below. The length of navigation in this cut-off was about thirty-seven miles, and the plan was to take through with small tugs perhaps fifty barges, enough, at least, to transfer the whole army, with artillery and baggage, to the other side of the Mississippi in twenty-four hours. If necessary, troops were to be transported by the canal, though Grant hoped to march them by the road along its bank. Part of McClernand's corps had already reached New Carthage overland, and Grant was hurrying other troops forward. The canal to the bayou was already half completed, thirty-five hundred men being at work on it when I arrived.

The second part of the plan was to float down the river, past the Vicksburg batteries, half a dozen steamboats protected by defenses of bales of cotton and wet hay; these steamboats were to serve as transports of supplies after the army had crossed the Mississippi.

Perhaps the best evidence of the feasibility of the project was found in the fact that the river men pronounced its success certain. General Sherman, who commanded one of the three corps in Grant's army, and with whom I conversed at length upon the subject, thought there was no difficulty in opening the passage, but that the line would be a precarious one for supplies after the army was thrown across the Mississippi. Sherman's preference was for a movement by way of Yazoo Pass, or Lake Providence, but it was not long before I saw in our daily talks that his mind was tending to the conclusion of General Grant. As for General Grant, his purpose was dead set on the new scheme. Admiral Porter cordially agreed with him.

In early February the Union ram, Queen of the West, *had run past the Vicksburg batteries, giving Grant his idea for transporting his army below the city via the same route. Julia Grant arrived to be with the general on the appointed night. James H. Wilson, an aide on Grant's staff, described the scene:*[11]

On the night of the first passage Grant with his staff and family moved down the river on his headquarters steamboat to a favorable point of observation just beyond the range of the enemy's guns and witnessed the whole extraordinary pageant. The fleet started after dark, between nine and ten o'clock, but before it got abreast of the enemy's guns all engines were stopped and all lights concealed, and for a few minutes it was hoped that the rapid current might carry the boats by unperceived, but this hope was fallacious. By the time they were abreast of the upper part of the bend, where the river was narrowest, the enemy discovered them and opened fire upon them with all the guns they could bring to bear. A small outhouse near the water was set on fire, lighting up the whole river and the opposite shore.

The roar of the heavy guns both from the batteries and the fleet was incessant and impressive, but without starting the engines the fleet drifted by and out of danger, lighted in its lower course by the transport which had been set on fire, abandoned by the crew, and burned to the water's edge.

It was an anxious hour for all, and especially for me. It was a brilliant moonlight night, and during the firing the point opposite the front of the city, as well as the surface of the river, in this bend only eight hundred yards wide, were further lighted up by the burning buildings on the banks. The roar of the enemy's heavy guns, twenty-five in number, from six-inch to ten-inch caliber, was deafening, and the whole scene was grand and awe-inspiring. One of the Grant children sat on my knees with its arms around my neck, and as each crash came, it nervously clasped me closer, and finally became so frightened that it was put to bed. Mrs. Grant sat by the General's side with the other children near, while the staff and clerks looked on in silence and wonder, if not in doubt. It was not till after midnight that the roar of artillery ceased and silence rested on the scene, and it was not till the next morning that the details became fully known. . . .

Dana witnessed the passage of the batteries:[12]

Just before ten o'clock on the night of April 16th the squadron cast loose its moorings. It was a strange scene. First a mass of black things detached itself from the shore, and we saw it float out toward the middle of the stream. There was nothing to be seen except this big black mass, which dropped slowly down the river. Soon another black mass detached itself, and another, then another. It was Admiral Porter's fleet of ironclad turtles, steamboats, and barges. They floated down the Mississippi darkly and silently, showing neither steam nor light, save occasionally a signal astern, where the enemy could not see it.

The vessels moved at intervals of about two hundred yards. First came seven ironclad turtles and one heavy armed ram; following these were two side-wheel steamers and one stern-wheel, having twelve barges in tow; these barges carried the supplies. Far astern of them was one carrying ammunition. The most of the gunboats had already doubled the tongue of land which stretches northeasterly in front of Vicksburg, and they were immediately under the guns of nearly all the Confederate batteries, when there was a flash from the upper forts, and then for an hour and a half the cannonade was terrific, raging incessantly along the line of about four miles in extent. I counted five hundred and twenty-five discharges. Early in the action the enemy put the torch to a frame building in front of Vicksburg to light up the scene and direct his fire.

About 12:45 A.M. one of our steamers, the *Henry Clay*, took fire, and burned for three quarters of an hour. The *Henry Clay* was lost by being abandoned by her captain and crew in a panic, they thinking her to be sinking. The pilot refused to go with them, and said if they would stay they would get her through safe. After they had fled in the yawls, the cotton bales on her deck took fire, and one wheel became unmanageable. The pilot then ran her aground, and got upon a plank, on which he was picked up four miles below.

The morning after Admiral Porter had run the Vicksburg batteries I went with General Grant to New Carthage to review the situation. We found the squadron there, all in fighting condition, though most of them had been hit. Not a man had been lost.

Porter explained why the maneuver had succeeded:[13]

The danger to the vessels was more apparent than real. Their weak points on the sides were mostly protected by heavy logs which prevented many shot and shells going through the iron. Some rents were made but the vessels stood the ordeal bravely and received no damage calculated to impair their efficiency.

The management of the vessels on this occasion was virtually in the hands of the pilots, who handled them beautifully and kept them in line at the distance apart ordered.

The enemy's shot was not well aimed; owing to the rapid fire of shells, shrapnel, grape and canister from the gun-boats, the sharpshooters were glad to lay low, and the men at the great guns gave up in disgust when they saw the fleet drift on apparently unscathed.

V

Elsewhere Mississippians were experiencing a different kind of shock. On the morning Porter's fleet moved below Vicksburg a one-time teacher of music and greengrocer named Benjamin H. Grierson set off at Grant's bidding on a series of lightning-fast cavalry raids. Some seventeen hundred horse soldiers rode with Grierson into the heart of enemy country. In late April the Jackson, Mississippi, Appeal told this story:[14]

From various sources we have particulars of the enemy's movements from the north line of Mississippi, through the eastern portion of the State, almost to the Louisiana line. The route chosen for his daring dash was through the line of counties lying between the Mobile and Ohio, and New Orleans, Jackson and Great Northern Railroads, in which, as they anticipated, there was no organized force to oppose them.

The penetration of an enemy's country, however, so extensively, will be recorded as one of the gallant feats of the war, no matter whether the actors escape or are captured. The expedition, we learn, was under command of Col. Grierson, of Illinois, who has already acquired considerable reputation as a dashing leader in West Tennessee. He boasted that he had no fears of his ability to extricate his command from the dangerous position it seemed to be in, but gave no indication as to the route he should take to get out of the country. . . . After crossing Leaf river, the bridges behind them were burned. Last night, it appears to be authentically reported, they camped near Westville, in the southern part of Simpson county. Whether they will move thence to Natchez, *via* Monticello and Holmesville, can only be conjectured; but we still incline to the opinion so confidently expressed some days ago, on first being advised of their presence at Newton, that Baton Rouge will be their haven, if undisturbed.* The crossing of Pearl river is the only natural difficulty they will encounter, and as we have no doubt they are advised as to the facilities they can secure at the different prominent fords, we presume they will act accordingly. Monticello and Holmesville may expect a visit.

The damage to the Southern railroad extends over a distance of four and a half miles, commencing a mile west of Newton, and running east. Two bridges, each about 150 feet long, seven culverts and one cattle gap, constitute the injury done. . . . Twenty freight cars were burned at Newton, and the depot buildings and two commissary buildings. The telegraph wire was taken down for miles, and cut in pieces. In many instances the wire was rolled up and put into ditches and pools. But few poles were destroyed. We can hear of but little outrage having been committed upon the persons of non-combatants or upon their property, except by the seizure of every good horse, and of the necessary forage and provisions. They had to depend upon the country for these. . . . The safe at the railroad depot was broken

---

* The editor guessed correctly.

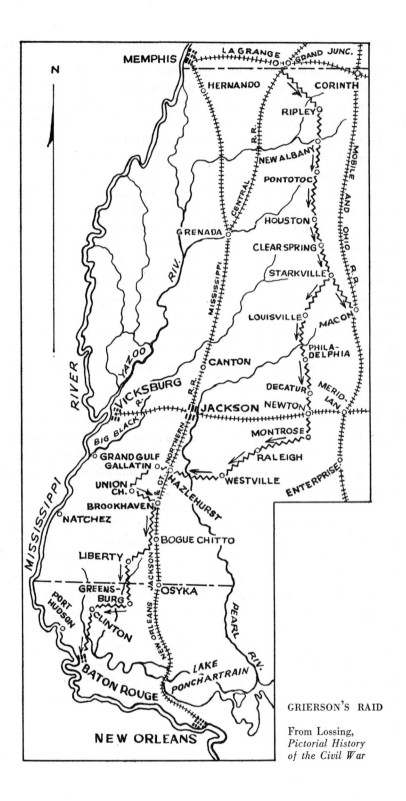

GRIERSON'S RAID

From Lossing,
*Pictorial History
of the Civil War*

open and the funds abstracted. The money was returned, however, by their commanding officer, with the exception of fifteen hundred dollars that, it was claimed, some of the men had stolen. The main body of the party in the movement upon Enterprise was halted at Hodge's residence, about five miles out, where they remained several hours. A detachment was sent to take the place [Company B, Seventh Illinois], and they advanced with the greatest confidence. Fortunately, the Thirty-fifth Alabama, under Lieutenant-Colonel Goodman, arrived about the same time and met the advancing party as they were approaching the bridge. As our men were about to open fire a flag of truce was raised, when a parley ensued and a demand for a surrender was made. Colonel G. was expecting reinforcements every moment and asked time to consider. The Yankees then fell back and, Colonel Loring arriving with the Twelfth Louisiana, Colonel Scott, and the Seventh Kentucky, Major Bell, pursuit was commenced, when it was found the advance had fallen back to the main body and all had gone. A fruitless effort to come up with them was made some miles further, but they had evidently become alarmed and feared an encounter.

At Doctor Hodge's the main body halted several hours. . . . Some of them entered the doctor's enclosure and required his daughters to furnish them provisions, which was done to the extent of cooked articles on hand. The rose bushes and flower beds of the young ladies were also sadly despoiled by the unwelcome visitors, but beyond this our informant says they did no damage, nor did they insult the ladies. The doctor was absent.

The Columbus, Mississippi, Republic *drew a bitter conclusion from the success of Grierson and his Yankee raiders:*[15]

The past week has been an eventful one. The boldest, and we may say one of the most successful, raids of cavalry that has been known since the war began, has been made (we say it with shame) through the very center of Mississippi, and at the time of this writing we fear have escaped without the loss of a man. We are almost inclined to believe the words of a correspondent, that the manhood of Mississippi had gone to the wars; women only were left, although some of them wore the garb of men. We do not know where the responsibility rests, but wherever it is, if it is not a fit and proper subject for court martial, we are afraid there are none. . . . It is reported that between four and five thousand federal cavalry started on this raid. They divided; some fifteen hundred, or perhaps a few more, stopped and gave Colonel Barteau battle, while the remainder, three thousand strong, marched directly south, scouring the country, from eight to ten miles wide, leaving the railroad, south of West Point, on their left. They encamped one night within twenty-five miles of this place. They destroyed the hospital at Okolona and a few other buildings, passing south through Houston, Siloam and Starkville, to within one mile of Macon, and thence south to Newton Station, on the Southern road, which we learn they destroyed. We can learn of no serious damage done or any ill treatment to the inhabitants personally. Their main objects seem to have been to examine the country and robbery—taking horses, mules and a few negroes.

At Starkville they robbed the inhabitants of horses, mules, negroes, jewelry and money; went into the stores and threw their contents (principally tobacco) into the street or gave it to the negroes; caught the mail boy and took the mail, robbed the postoffice, but handed back a letter from a soldier to his wife, containing $50.00, and ordered the postmaster to give it to her. Doctor Montgomery was taken prisoner and kept in camp all night, six miles from town, and allowed to return home next morning, after relieving him of his watch and other valuables. Hale & Murdock's hat wagon, loaded with wool hats, passing through at the time was captured. They gave the hats to the negroes and took the mules. Starkville can boast of better head covering for its negroes than any other town in the state.

They left quite a number of broken down horses all along their route, supplying themselves as they went. They stated that they were not destroying property; that they were gentlemen.

VI

While Grierson and his raiders disrupted Confederate communications, Grant pushed on. To reach the crossing point from Louisiana to Mississippi that he had selected, the next obstacle to overcome was the Confederate bastion at Grand Gulf called Bald Head, which, set on a promontory at the bend of the river, enabled its gunners to sight for miles along the Mississippi. Porter believed that Grand Gulf was too strong for a direct assault; Grant, convinced that the admiral overestimated the strength of the rebel batteries, ordered the attack. The battle raged for five and a half hours. Porter never forgot its flaming intensity:[16]

When the troops arrived at the point abreast of Bald Head, and the soldiers on the transports were ready to land as soon as the batteries should be silenced, Admiral Porter got under way with the squadron and commenced the attack at 8 A.M., on the 29th of April, 1863.

The "Pittsburg," "Louisville," "Mound City," and "Carondelet" attacked the lower batteries, while the "Benton," "Tuscumbia," and "Lafayette" attacked Bald Head battery, the two former as close as they could get, and the "Lafayette" lying in an eddy four hundred yards above the fort where she could enfilade it.

As the vessels approached the works the enemy opened fire and in ten minutes the battle was raging all along the line. The fight was severely contested, and it was not until three hours after the first gun was fired, that the enemy deserted his guns at the lower batteries, and then only after the "Lafayette" had been ordered from her first position to reinforce the gun-boats below.

In the meantime the flag-ship "Benton," and the "Tuscumbia" were doing their best to silence the upper battery, getting close *under* the guns and endeavoring to knock off their muzzles, when they were run out to fire. The current was so strong, however, that it was impossible to keep the two vessels in position and they sheered about very much. In one of these sheers, a shot entered the "Benton's" pilot house, disabled the wheel and cut Pilot Williams' foot nearly off. Though the brave pilot never left his post it was impossible to manage the vessel and she was accordingly run into the bank to repair damages.

The gun-boats at the lower batteries had been signalled to double up on Bald Head, the "Lafayette" to resume her old position, and the "Pittsburg," Volunteer-Lieutenant Hoel, arrived opportunely to take the "Benton's" place. During the time the latter vessel was out of action—twenty-five minutes—the "Pittsburg" lost six killed and had twelve wounded.

After all the vessels concentrated their fire on Bald Head, there was less resistance, although the Confederates still stood to their guns. When the battle had lasted more than five hours, General Grant, who from a tug up the river, was looking on, made signal to the Admiral that he wished to communicate, and the "Benton" joined him two miles above the forts. The Confederates had now ceased firing, but the gun-boats maintained their position around Bald Head, occasionally firing a shell to keep the enemy out of the works.

When General Grant went on board the flag-ship, he decided that it would be too hazardous to attempt to land troops, as it did not appear that the guns in the enemy's works were dismounted and the gunners would therefore jump to their batteries again, open on the unprotected transports and destroy many of the troops. For the same reason the general concluded not to send the transports past the batteries with the soldiers on board but to march the latter around by land. In this he was quite right, as afterwards appeared.

As there was no longer any object in keeping the gun-boats under the batteries, all but the "Lafayette" were recalled, and the latter was left in her old position to keep the enemy from reoccupying the works and repairing damages. This duty Commander Walke effectually performed, firing a shell every five minutes into the works until darkness set in.

The engagement was fought under great disadvantages; the current around the promontory of Bald Head ran with great rapidity, and it was as much as the gun-boats could do to stem it. Clumsy vessels at best, the ironclads would frequently be turned completely round, presenting their weak points to the enemy, of which the expert Confederate gunners were not slow to take advantage, and seldom missed their mark so close were the vessels to the forts. The light armor plates of most of the vessels offered but an imperfect resistance to the heavy missiles of the enemy, and, in consequence, the list of killed and wounded in the squadron was large.

Porter offered harrowing statistics to show the damage his river fleet had suffered—eighty-one hits on the Tuscumbia, *forty-five on the* Lafayette, *forty-seven on the flagship* Benton, *as examples. The admiral concluded: "Then came the melancholy duty of burying the dead, who were followed mournfully to their graves by their messmates and friends." Meanwhile Grant accepted the failure of the assault in good spirit and revised his plans to take advantage of an unexpected opportunity:*[17]

When the troops debarked, the evening of the 29th, it was expected that we would have to go to Rodney, about nine miles below, to find a landing; but that night a colored man came in who informed me that a good landing would be found at Bruinsburg, a few miles above Rodney, from which point there was a good road leading to Port Gibson some twelve miles in the interior. The information was found correct, and our landing was effected without opposition.

Sherman had not left his position above Vicksburg yet. On the morning of the 27th I ordered him to create a diversion by moving his corps up the Yazoo and threatening an attack on Haines' Bluff.

My object was to compel Pemberton to keep as much force about Vicksburg as I could, until I could secure a good footing on high land east of the river. The move was eminently successful and, as we afterwards learned, created great confusion about Vicksburg and doubts about our real design. Sherman moved the day of our attack on Grand Gulf, the 29th, with ten regiments of his command and eight gunboats which Porter had left above Vicksburg.

He debarked his troops and apparently made every preparation to attack the enemy while the navy bombarded the main forts at Haines' Bluff. This move was made without a single casualty in either branch of the service. On the first of May Sherman received orders from me (sent from Hard Times the evening of the 29th of April) to withdraw from the front of Haines' Bluff and follow McPherson with two divisions as fast as he could.

I had established a depot of supplies at Perkins' plantation. Now that all our gunboats were below Grand Gulf it was possible that the enemy might fit out boats in the Big Black with improvised armament and attempt to destroy these supplies. McPherson was at Hard Times with a portion of his corps, and the depot was protected by a part of his command. The night of the 29th I directed him to arm one of the transports with artillery and send it up to Perkins' plantation as a guard; and also to have the siege guns we had brought along moved there and put in position.

The embarkation below Grand Gulf took place at De Shroon's, Louisiana, six miles above Bruinsburg, Mississippi. Early on the morning of 30th of April McClernand's corps and one division of McPherson's corps were speedily landed.

When this was effected I felt a degree of relief scarcely ever equalled since. Vicksburg was not yet taken it is true, nor were its defenders demoralized by any of our previous moves. I was now in the enemy's country, with a vast river and the stronghold of Vicksburg between me and my base of supplies. But I was on dry ground on the same side of the river with the enemy. All the campaigns, labors, hardships and exposures from the month of December previous to this time that had been made and endured, were for the accomplishment of this one object.

Grant now was sixty miles south of Vicksburg. He moved swiftly toward Port Gibson, and at a point about five miles west of that place collided with a force of Missourians and Mississippians under General John S. Bowen. The Battle of Thompson's Hill, bitter and brief, served notice that the Yankees were across the river to stay. Grant pushed through Port Gibson to Grand Gulf. Once more confronted with unexpected circumstances, he readjusted his plans:[18]

When I reached Grand Gulf May 3d I had not been with my baggage since the 27th of April and consequently had had no change of underclothing, no meal except such as I could pick up sometimes at other headquarters, and no tent to cover me. The first thing I did was to get a bath, borrow some fresh underclothing from one of the naval officers and get a good meal on the flag-ship. Then I wrote letters to the general-in-chief informing him of our present position, dispatches to be telegraphed from Cairo, orders to General Sullivan commanding above Vicksburg, and gave orders to all my corps commanders. About twelve o'clock at night I was through my work and started for Hankinson's ferry, arriving there before daylight. While at Grand Gulf I heard from Banks, who was on the Red River, and who said that he could not be at Port Hudson before the 10th of May and then with only 15,000 men. Up to this time my intention had been to secure Grand Gulf, as a base of supplies, detach McClernand's corps to Banks and co-operate with him in the reduction of Port Hudson.

The news from Banks forced upon me a different plan of campaign from the one intended. To wait for his cooperation would have detained me at least a month. The reinforcements would not have reached ten thousand men after deducting casualties and necessary river guards at all high points close to the river for over three hundred miles. The enemy would have strengthened his position and been reinforced by more men than Banks could have brought. I therefore determined to move independently of Banks, cut loose from my base, destroy the rebel force in rear of Vicksburg and invest or capture the city.

Grand Gulf was accordingly given up as a base and the authorities at Washington were notified. I knew well that Halleck's caution would lead him to disapprove of this course; but it was the only one that gave any chance of success. The time it would take to communicate with Washington and get a reply would be so great that I could not be interfered with until it was demonstrated whether my plan was practicable. Even Sherman, who afterwards ignored bases of supplies other than what were afforded by the country while marching through four States of the Confederacy with an army more than twice as large as mine at this time, wrote me from Hankinson's ferry, advising me of the impossibility of supplying our army over a single road. He urged me to "stop all troops till your army is partially supplied with wagons, and then act as quick as possible; for this road will be jammed, as sure as life." To this I repied: "I do not calculate upon the possibility of supplying the army with full rations from Grand Gulf. I know it will be impossible without constructing additional roads. What I do expect is to get up what rations of hard bread, coffee and salt we can, and make the country furnish the balance." We started from Bruinsburg with an average of about two days' rations, and received no more from our own supplies for some days; abundance was found in the mean time. A delay would give the enemy time to reinforce and fortify.

VII

Grant was in camp now at Hankinson's Ferry, whence Charles A. Dana wrote a cheerful letter to a young relative:[19]

All of a sudden it is very cold here. Two days ago it was hot like summer, but now I sit in my tent in my overcoat, writing, and thinking if I only were at home instead of being almost two thousand miles away.

Away yonder, in the edge of the woods, I hear the drum-beat that calls the soldiers to their supper. It is only a little after five o'clock, but they begin the day very early and end it early. Pretty soon after dark they are all asleep, lying in their blankets under the trees, for in a quick march they leave their tents behind. Their guns are all ready at their sides, so that if they are suddenly called at night they can start in a moment. It is strange in the morning before daylight to hear the bugle and drums sound the reveille, which calls the army to wake up. It will begin perhaps at a distance and then run along the whole line, bugle after bugle and drum after drum taking it up, and then it goes from front to rear, farther and farther away, the sweet sounds throbbing and rolling while you lie on the grass with your saddle for a pillow, half awake, or opening your eyes to see that the stars are all bright in the sky, or that there is only a faint flush in the east, where the day is soon to break.

Living in camp is queer business. I get my meals in General Grant's mess, and pay my share of the expenses. The table is a chest with a double cover, which unfolds on the right and the left; the dishes, knives and forks, and caster are inside. Sometimes we get good things, but generally we don't. The cook is an old negro, black and grimy. The cooking is not as clean as it might be, but in war you can't be particular about such things.

The plums and peaches here are pretty nearly ripe. The strawberries have been ripe these few days, but the soldiers eat them up before we get a sight of them. The figs are as big as the end of your thumb, and the green pears are big enough to eat. But you don't know what beautiful flower gardens there are here. I never saw such roses; and the other day I found a lily as big as a tiger lily, only it was a magnificent red.

The apparent calm was deceptive. Grant, like a panther tensing for a spring, moved his headquarters to Rocky Springs on May 7. Grant knew where he would strike—the state capital at Jackson, thus getting astride the railroad that supplied Vicksburg. Pemberton thought he divined Grant's intentions, and guessed wrong.

Some critics of John C. Pemberton would have said that guessing wrong was one of his chief traits, but at the base of all criticisms of "Old Pem" was the fact that he was one of those Southern generals who carried the heavy burden of being Northern-born. Pemberton's first war service had been in Charleston where his refusal to permit trading with the enemy in cotton had earned him a reputation as an "unfeeling brute," but that great student of character, Rhett of the Charleston Mercury, *had called Pemberton "a thorough soldier" although "not a 'popular man.'" The Vicksburg paper at least had been happy to see Pemberton take command, and had rejoiced that at last Mississippians no longer were "to be put off" with "one-horse Generals."*

Moods had shifted since then—most of all since Grant had started to change his campaign whenever the fancy took him. No one was more aware of the confusion that consumed Pemberton than Samuel H. Lockett, chief engineer of Vicksburg's defenses:[20]

. . . General Pemberton first thought that Grant would turn north from Port Gibson and try to force a passage across Big Black River at one of the ferries. He accordingly sent about a brigade each to Hankinson's, Hall's, and Baldwin's ferries, and ordered field-works to be thrown up at these crossings. . . .

At last General Pemberton became convinced that General Grant's intention was to march up the east bank of the Big Black River, to

strike the railroad at or near Edwards's depot, and thus cut his communications with Jackson. To prevent this, and at the same time to
defeat Grant, if possible, he concentrated all of his forces at Edwards's
depot, excepting General Forney's division which was left in Vicksburg,
and General Smith's which was posted at and near the railroad bridge.
On the 12th of May, under the orders of General Pemberton, I went to
Edwards's depot to put the Confederate forces in position upon the
ground selected for them to occupy, covering all the approaches from
the south and east. The army here assembled consisted of three divisions: Bowen's on the right, Loring's in the center, and C. L. Stevenson's on the left, numbering about 18,000 men. Some slight field-works
had been thrown up at favorable points. The position was naturally a
strong one, on high ground, with the cultivated valley of Baker's Creek
in its front. Here General Pemberton wished to wait to be attacked by
Grant. There can be no doubt that if he had been allowed to do so a
desperate and bloody battle would have been fought on that ground, the
issue of which might have been different from that of the two unfortunate engagements which did actually occur. The army remained
at Edwards's depot from the 13th to the 15th. During this time General
Pemberton received numerous dispatches from President Davis, and
from General J. E. Johnston, who had recently arrived at Jackson. I
saw, or heard read, most of these dispatches. They were very conflict-
ing in their tenor, and neither those of Mr. Davis nor those of General
Johnston exactly comported with General Pemberton's views. He then
made the capital mistake of trying to harmonize instructions from his
superiors diametrically opposed to each other, and at the same time
to bring them into accord with his own judgment, which was adverse
to the plans of both. . . .

*Grant's great advantage was not only that he knew whither he was
going, but also that Washington couldn't possibly argue the decision beforehand. By May twelfth a Federal column approached Raymond,
eighteen miles west of Jackson, where a small Confederate force offered brisk, if hopeless, opposition. Sylvanus Cadwallader drew a picture of another type of difficulty Grant's forces encountered:*[21]

That afternoon and night refugee "contrabands" came swarming into
our lines by hundreds. They were of all ages, sexes and conditions, and
came on foot, on horses and mules, and in all manner of vehicles,
from the typical southern cart, to elegant state carriages and barouches.

Straw collars and rope harness alternated with silver plate equipments, till the moving living panorama became ludicrous beyond description.

The runaway darkies who had made sudden and forcible requisition upon their old masters for these varied means of transportation, generally loaded their wagons and carriages with the finest furniture left in the mansions when their owners had abandoned them at our approach. Feather beds and tapestried upholstery seemed to possess a peculiar charm and value to the dusky runaways. A black boy named Jerry, probably fourteen years old, who came to headquarters at that time, was taken by Rawlins as a body servant, and attended him till the war ended. On settling in Washington City in 1865, Rawlins kept him in his family, gave him quite a fair education, and had no more sincere mourner at his funeral than this faithful black boy Jerry.

Another boy named Willis attached himself in the same capacity to Col. Duff and remained with him till his expiration of service at City Point. He then became mine by adoption, as he claimed; but he certainly adopted me instead of my adopting him; and would doubtless be with me today,* had not Count Saldatankoff of the Grand Duke Alexis' retinue during his visit to the U. S. over a quarter of a century ago, taken an especial fancy to him and prevailed on Willis to accompany him to Russia.

"Cad" witnessed another side of Grant:[22]

The night of May 12th was spent by me on an army cot in Col. Duff's tent. About midnight, or soon thereafter, Gen. Grant came into the tent alone, in the dark, and requested a drink of whiskey. Col. Duff drew a canteen from under his pillow and handed it to him. The general poured a generous potation into an army tin cup and swallowed it with great apparent satisfaction. He complained of extraordinary fatigue and exhaustion as his excuse for needing the stimulant, and took the second, if not the third drink, before retiring.

A light was struck upon his entrance, so that he knew of my presence; but he made his request, and drank the whiskey in an ordinary manner, as if it was a matter of fact procedure which required no particular apology. His stay in the tent did not exceed twenty or thirty minutes. He

* Cadwallader's reminiscences were written "very near to the close of a busy life"; notations on the manuscript by General James H. Wilson are dated February, 1905.

sat on the edge of Duff's cot, facing mine, and apparently addressed himself to me as much as to Duff.

This was the first time I ever saw Gen. Grant use any spirituous liquor, and I was a little surprised by his openness in asking for it, and drinking it, before me. My intercourse with him to that time had been casual or accidental rather than intimate and confidential as it afterwards became; yet there was nothing evinced in word or behavior, from which I could infer that he desired the slightest secrecy or concealment concerning the object of his midnight call. The occurrence was never mentioned by me, excepting perhaps to Rawlins, until after the close of the rebellion. I think Col. Duff did suggest to me after the general's exit from the tent, that in view of Grant's reputation for excessive drinking, and his peculiar surroundings at the time, the affairs of state as well as my personal interests, might be best promoted by discreet silence, inasmuch as the general did not know that anyone occupied the tent with him until concealment was out of the question.

But I put a different construction upon his indifference, which was fully borne out by after events. The general knew that Gov. Oglesby * had left nearly a half barrel of whiskey in the joint care of Col. Duff and myself on taking his departure from headquarters a few days before. I also subsequently learned that Duff had catered to Grant's inordinate desire for stimulants long before this, and continued to do so till his "muster-out" at City Point. Rawlins suspected him of doing so, but had no positive proof of the fact for more than a year after this. Duff did not rise from his cot during Grant's stay that night, but lay stretched out at full length, except when he half rose on one elbow to join the General in his drinks, and to volunteer "success to our campaign, and confusion to the Whole Confederacy." But little was said by Grant in response to these sentiments, beyond an expression of satisfaction at what he had thus far accomplished, and a cheerful hope and belief that Vicksburg would soon be ours.

VIII

Whatever the brand of whisky Duff served, it was not clouding Grant's judgment. One who could testify to that fact was General Joseph E. Johnston, whom Richmond ordered from Tennessee to Mississippi in the prayerful hope that he could avert a Confederate disaster. John-

* Should read Yates; Oglesby was not elected governor of Illinois until late 1864.

ston reached the state capital on the thirteenth of May; the news that he received was hardly cheering:[23]

I arrived in Jackson at nightfall, exhausted by an uninterrupted journey of four days, undertaken from a sickroom; in consequence of which Major Mims, chief quartermaster of the department, the first officer who reported to me, found me in bed. He informed me, among other military occurrences, that two brigades had marched into the town an hour or two before. Brigadier-General Gregg, their senior officer, reported to me soon after that he had been ordered from Port Hudson to Raymond by General Pemberton, but had been driven from that place the day before by the Federal Seventeenth Corps; and, in obedience to the general's instructions for such an event, had fallen back to Jackson, accompanied by Brigadier-General W. H. T. Walker, whom he had met on the way, marching to join him with his brigade. The latter had just come from General Beauregard's department [South Carolina, Georgia, and Florida]. There were about six thousand men in the two brigades.

He said further that Colonel Wirt Adams, of the cavalry, had informed him that General Pemberton's forces were at Edwards's depot, 20 miles from Vicksburg, and his headquarters at Bovina, 8 miles from that place; that the Seventeenth Corps (McPherson's) had moved that day from Raymond to Clinton 9 or 10 miles from Jackson, on the road to Vicksburg. He added that General Maxey's brigade from Port Hudson was expected in Jackson next day. I had passed General Gist's during that day, on its way from Charleston. The arrival of these troops, and, as I hoped, 3000 from Tennessee, would increase the force in Jackson to near 15,000 men. The most important measure to be executed then was the junction of these reënforcements with the army. For that object, an order in writing was sent without delay to General Pemberton by Captain Yerger, who volunteered to bear it, to move to Clinton at once and attack a Federal corps there, the troops in Jackson to coöperate; to beat that detachment and establish communication, that he might be reënforced. It was delivered at Bovina early next morning, and General Pemberton replied promptly that he "moved at once with his whole available force"; but in the ride of ten or twelve miles to his camp at Edwards's depot he determined to disobey my order, and on his arrival assembled a council of war, which he informed of that intention, and consulted upon the measure to be substituted for the movement to Clinton. It was decided to move southward to a point on the road by which General Grant's forces had advanced, which would have made it impossible for the troops then in Jackson and other expected reënforcements to join Pemberton's army.

Grant, reaching Jackson, recalled, "I slept that night in the room that Johnston was said to have occupied the night before." Sylvanus Cadwallader supplied other details of the Federal occupation of the capital of Jefferson Davis' home state:[24]

As soon as the fire of the Confederate batteries was silenced, Fred Grant (a stout, good-natured son of the General who accompanied the army all through the campaign) and myself, started for the Capitol at full speed to secure the large Confederate flag which waved from a staff on the roof. We supposed ourselves far in advance of anyone connected with the Union army. We dismounted hurriedly in front of the building, ran upstairs till we reached those leading from the garret to the roof, where we met a ragged, muddy, begrimed cavalryman descending with the coveted prize under his arm. To say that our disappointment was extreme but mildly expresses the state of our feelings. We were beaten and compelled to admit that to the victor belongs the spoils.

I pushed on to the Bowman House, then the principal hotel in the city, and found its office and corridors filled with Confederate officers and soldiers, some of whom were wounded and disabled men from convalescent hospitals; others who were doubtless bummers, skulkers and deserters who fell out of the Confederate ranks as Johnston's army retreated across the river; and a large concourse of townspeople and civilians who chanced to be there from other parts of the state. I ran the gauntlet of unfriendly observation; secured a room at once; and wrote dispatches for the Chicago *Times,* with scarcely a moment's relaxation, till Gen. Grant's courier was ready to take the road for Grand Gulf, with government dispatches, announcing his victories at the capital of Mississippi.

Grant and staff arrived at the Bowman House soon after I did, which diverted attention from me. . . . Many calls were made upon him by citizens asking for guards to protect their private property, some of which perhaps were granted, but by far the greater number were left to the tender mercies of Confederate friends.

Gen. Sherman was charged with the provost duty of the city and was directed to remain with his corps till all the public property used

by the Confederacy had been destroyed and its usefulness as a great
Confederate railroad center put past the possibility of being speedily
re-established. Foundries, machine-shops, warehouses, factories, arsenals and public stores were fired as fast as flames could be kindled.
Many citizens fled at our approach, abandoning houses, stores, and all
their personal property, without so much as locking their doors.

The negroes, poor whites—and it must be admitted—some stragglers and bummers from the ranks of the Union army—carried off
thousands of dollars worth of property from houses, homes, shops and
stores, until some excuse was given for the charge of "northern vandal-
ism," which was afterward made by the South. The streets were filled
with people, white and black, who were carrying away all the stolen
goods they could stagger under, without the slightest attempt at concealment, and without let or hindrance from citizens or soldiers. Of course
this was mainly stopped as soon as Sherman had fairly and formally
assumed control of affairs; but the era of stealing and plundering lasted
through the evening and night of the 14th, I believe. In addition to
destruction of property by Gen. Sherman's orders, the convicts of the
penitentiary, who had been released by their own authorities, set all
the buildings connected with that prison on fire, and their lurid flames
added to the holocaust elsewhere prevailing. . . .

CHAPTER 24

SEESAW: VICKSBURG AND GETTYSBURG

O N MAY 15, 1863, Grant moved out of Jackson, Mississippi. Now that he was securely wedged between Confederate armies under Johnston and Pemberton, Grant proposed to lose no time in disposing of each in detail. Soon his blue-clad columns were marching back toward Vicksburg, seeking to find Pemberton for the kill.

In Richmond, Virginia, there were grave conflicts of heart and mind. War Clerk Jones wrote in his diary on May 15:

"Gens. Lee, Stuart and French were all at the War Department today. Lee looked thinner, and a little pale. Subsequently he and the Secretary of War were long closeted with the President."

Mounting Confederate disasters in Mississippi weighed heavily in the gloomy speculations of Richmond. If the situation worsened in the West, should Lee detach part of his forces in an effort to rescue Pemberton? Lee responded in character—passionately a Virginian. The best way—the only way—that Lee saw to help Pemberton was by creating a diversion in the East. Moreover, Virginia's proud defenders weren't going to be of much assistance anywhere unless they could obtain food, shoes, horses, forage. Lee thought he knew exactly where he could find these provisions. The magic word that he mentioned was Pennsylvania.

I

*Lee hurried back to his base at Culpeper, where, as he should have
expected, Longstreet disagreed with the plan of invasion. To save
Pemberton and ease the strain on Virginia, in Longstreet's opinion,
Lee should help Bragg stand off Rosecrans in Tennessee. Lee shook his
head. Bragg like Pemberton must take comfort from the strike into
Pennsylvania.*

*Nonetheless misgivings gnawed at Lee. "We should not conceal from
ourselves," he wrote Davis, "that our resources in men are constantly
diminishing, and the disproportion in this respect between us and our
enemies, is steadily augmenting." Burnside's arrest of Vallandigham
had encouraged many Confederates to believe that Lincoln and his
cronies were quaking in their boots at the growing force of Copperhead
opposition to the war. Lee apparently had indulged in the same wishful
thinking, for his letter to Jefferson Davis continued:[1]*

Nor do I think we should, in this connection, make nice distinctions
between those who declare for peace unconditionally and those who
advocate it as a means of restoring the Union, however much we may
prefer the former.

We should bear in mind that the friends of peace at the North must
make concessions to the earnest desire that exists in the minds of their
countrymen for a restoration of the Union, and that to hold out such
an inducement is essential to the success of their party.

Should the belief that peace will bring back the Union become general, the war would no longer be supported, and that, after all, is what
we are interested in bringing about. When peace is proposed to us, it
will be time enough to discuss its terms, and it is not the part of pru-
dence to spurn the proposition in advance, merely because those who
wish to make it believe, or affect to believe, that it will result in bringing
us back into the Union. We entertain no such apprehensions, nor doubt
that the desire of our people for a distinct and independent national
existence will prove as steadfast under the influence of peaceful measures as it has shown itself in the midst of war.

If the views I have indicated meet the approval of Your Excellency,
you will best know how to give effect to them. Should you deem them
inexpedient or impracticable, I think you will nevertheless agree with
me that we should at least carefully abstain from measures or expressions that tend to discourage any party whose purpose is peace.

This was "Butternut talk," pure and simple, comforting alike to Peace Democrats and wearied, worried Confederates. If Davis failed to respond to Lee's somewhat crafty suggestions, perhaps two items for May 19 in the diary of War Clerk Jones explained why:[2]

A despatch from Gen. Johnston says a battle has been fought between Pemberton and Grant, between Jackson and Vicksburg, Mississippi. Pemberton was *forced back*. That is all we know yet. . . .

The President is too ill again to come to the Executive Office. His messenger, who brought me some papers this morning, says he is in a "decline." I think he has been ill every day for several years, but this has been his most serious attack. No doubt he is also worried at the dark aspects in his own State—Mississippi.

Grant's army had collided with Pemberton's at the Battle of Champion's Hill on May 16. The Rebels, dug in along a ridge with a ravine and creek protecting one flank and a narrow belt of timber screening the other, in Grant's phrase "commanded all the ground in range." The fighting was opened by troops under Brigadier General Alvin P. Hovey, an Indiana lawyer who had taught himself as much about war as most West Pointers learned. He threw his troops in waves up the hill, trying to gain a foothold on the ridge, and his boys seemed to melt away under the broiling Mississippi sun. That morning Sergeant Charles L. Longley had eaten a "hasty and slender breakfast" as he awaited "a pregnant day." Hours went by as Longley and his comrades in the Twenty-fourth Iowa wondered if Hovey had forgotten them. Longley needn't have fretted; his turn was coming:[3]

. . . The grim chorus of battle has been nearing, rising and swelling on the air until its angry roar seems to have filled the earth; then, at a little after twelve comes the dreaded and impatiently expected command, "Fall in.". . . The lines are formed and dressed with an absolute sense of relief. See them now, stretching away to the length of nine companies of about forty-five men each, and prolonged by the rest of the brigade on the right. Now we are advancing over rough ground, but steadily touching elbows, while the warming blood begins to be felt bounding through the veins and throbbing at the temples. Now we pass through the first brigade, lying at the foot of the long wooded hill, and for the first time begin to hear the wicked *zipping* of the hostile lead. Soon it tells its errand—the first man falls. . . .

Onward and upward you go; thicker and faster falls the hissing hail.
At last the timber grows larger and you begin to locate the flaming line
whence the trouble comes. Suddenly the added elevation brings into
view a battery, and at the same instant the horrid howling of grape and

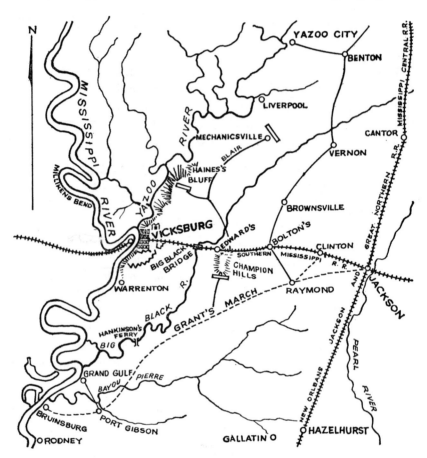

VICKSBURG: THE APPROACHES FROM SOUTH AND EAST

From Lossing, *Pictorial History of the Civil War*

canister is about us. A halt is made and the Enfields of the 24th add
their clamor to the hell of sound, and their missiles to the many that
make the very air writhe. The more accustomed eye now detects here
and there a gray-clad enemy marking their line at but a few rods distant. You note one, perhaps, striving to find shelter behind a slender
tree—he is reloading, and, hastily withdrawing his rammer, un-
covers the upper part of his body—instantly you aim and fire, and when

he falls backward, throwing the useless gun over his head, you forget that other bullets than your own have sped and scream aloud in the very frenzy of self-congratulation.

At this moment, while every human instinct is carried away by a torrent of passion, while kill, KILL, KILL, seems to fill your heart and be written over the face of all nature—at this instant you hear a command (it may have come from the clouds above, you know not) to "Fix bayonets, forward, charge!" and away you go with a wild yell in which all mouths join. . . .

Their backs are toward you—they fly—the line becomes a crowd—you pause only to fire—from one end of the regiment to the other the leaden hail converges upon that fated band; you see them plunging down in all directions, and shout with unnatural glee. They pass through the Rebel battery, and that too is swept with the besom of destruction. As it runs parallel with the line, a full artillery team catches the eye just long enough to see a leader fall and the six horses almost stand on end as they go over and down in struggling confusion—now the battery itself is ours, and fairly won, and cheer follows cheer!

What next? Alas, there is no leader, Wilds is wounded, and so is Wright. . . . You had seen no one fall but enemies since your own work began. But so it is; they, with brave Carbee, Johnson, Lawrence, and many more. Confusion reigns. . . . There comes a new line of gray. Its head of column is already in our rear. See that orderly sergeant in advance making the ins and outs of the fence he is following. Shoot at him? Yes; and all the rest while you may, for now they halt, front, and enfilade that road with a fire that patters in the dust like the big drops of a summer shower and makes the wounded wretches lying there writhe again in impotent agony and terror.

Grant understood this battle, as critical and as desperate as any he would ever fight:[4]

From Raymond there is a direct road to Edward's station, some three miles west of Champion's Hill. There is one also to Bolton. From this latter road there is still another, leaving it about three and a half miles before reaching Bolton and leads direct to the same station. It was along these two roads that three divisions of McClernand's corps, and Blair of Sherman's, temporarily under McClernand, were moving. Hovey of McClernand's command was with McPherson, farther north on the road from Bolton direct to Edward's station. The middle road

comes into the northern road at the point where the latter turns to the
west and descends to Baker's Creek; the southern road is still several
miles south and does not intersect the others until it reaches Edward's
station. Pemberton's lines covered all these roads, and faced east.
Hovey's line, when it first drove in the enemy's pickets, was formed
parallel to that of the enemy and confronted his left.

By eleven o'clock the skirmishing had grown into a hard-contested
battle. Hovey alone, before other troops could be got to assist him, had
captured a battery of the enemy. But he was not able to hold his position and had to abandon the artillery. McPherson brought up his
troops as fast as possible, Logan in front, and posted them on the right
of Hovey and across the flank of the enemy. Logan reinforced Hovey
with one brigade from his division; with his other two he moved farther
west to make room for Crocker, who was coming up as rapidly as the
roads would admit. Hovey was still being heavily pressed, and was calling on me for more reinforcements. I ordered Crocker, who was now
coming up, to send one brigade from his division. McPherson ordered
two batteries to be stationed where they nearly enfiladed the enemy's
line, and they did good execution.

From Logan's position now a direct forward movement carried him
over open fields, in rear of the enemy and in a line parallel with them.
He did make exactly this move, attacking, however, the enemy through
the belt of woods covering the west slope of the hill for a short distance.
Up to this time I had kept my position near Hovey where we were the
most heavily pressed; but about noon I moved with a part of my staff by
our right around, until I came up with Logan himself. . . .

Grant's composure was no pose. S. H. M. Byers saw him that day:[5]

We were in that most trying position of soldiers, for regulars even—
being fired on without permission to return the shots. We were standing two files deep, bearing as patiently as we could not a heavy, but a
steady fire from infantry, while an occasional cannon-ball tore up the
turf in front or behind us. A good many men were falling, and the
wounded were being borne to the rear of the brigade, close to an old
well, whose wooden curb seemed to offer the only protection from bullets on the exposed line. "Colonel, move your men a little by the left
flank," said a quiet, though commanding voice. On looking round, I
saw immediately behind us Grant, the commander-in-chief, mounted on
a beautiful bay mare, and followed by perhaps a half dozen of his staff.

For some reason he dismounted, and most of his officers were sent off, bearing orders, probably, to other quarters of the field. It was Grant under fire. . . . He now stood leaning complacently against his favorite steed, smoking—as seemed habitual with him—the stump of a cigar. . . . In front of us was an enemy; behind us, and about us, and liable to overcome and crush us, were his reinforcements. For days we had been away from our base of supplies, and marching inside the enemy's lines. What if Grant should be killed, and we be defeated here—in such a place, and at such a time? I am sure everyone who recognized him wished him away; but there he stood—clear, calm, and immovable.

What manner of man was Grant? Pondering this question, Byers watched a comrade with a fractured leg being helped to the rear:

. . . His cries of pain attracted the attention of Grant, and I noticed the half-curious, though sympathizing shades, that crossed his quiet face as the bleeding soldier seemed to look toward him for help. Men have often asked if Grant were personally brave in battle. Bravery, like many other human qualities, is comparative. . . . Where duty was, imposed or assumed, Grant feared not to stand . . . He was eminently and above all things a cool man, and that, I take it, was, in the exciting times in which he lived, the first great key to his success. . . . He was called a born soldier, but was, in fact, nothing of the kind. He was simply a man of correct methods and a fixed will. The same methods and the same will would have led men to call him a born railway director, or a born anything to which he had once in good earnest turned his hand. As a young soldier he had lacked opportunity. He lived in a land where neither soldiers nor poets were wanted. There were no wars, no romances, and little history. If he had tried business a little as a farmer, a tanner, a surveyor, or what not, it was not in good earnest. It was a makeshift for the occasion. The war was Grant's opportunity, and he was at the age and had the disposition to seize it. But his military renown was not of luck alone. It was earned blow by blow.

One of the hardest blows—Champion's Hill—soon mounted to its climax, and Byers was in the thick of that action:

We had not waited many minutes at the meadow when an orderly dashed up to Grant, and handed him a communication. Then followed an order to move rapidly to the left, and into the road. The fire grew heavier, and the air seemed too hot to be borne. "Forward!" came a second order, all along the line—"Forward! double quick!" Everybody shouted "double quick," as the noise was becoming terrific. We had forgotten to fix bayonets! what forgetfulness! and again the screaming was, "Fix bayonets! fix bayonets!" I had been selected by the colonel, just as we entered the road, to act as sergeant major, and I now ran behind and along the line, shouting at the top of my voice, "Fix bayonets!" The orders were not heard, and we were charging the enemy's position with bare muskets. A moment more and we were at the top of the ascent, and among thinner wood and larger trees. The enemy had fallen back a few rods, forming a solid line parallel with our own; and now commenced, in good earnest, the fighting of the day. For half an hour we poured the hot lead into each others' faces. We had forty rounds each in our cartridge-boxes, and, probably, nine-tenths of them were fired in that half hour. For me it was the first real "stand up and fight," as the boys called it, of my life. Of skirmishes, I had seen many, and had been under fire; but this was a real battle, and what Grant himself might have called the "business." I tried to keep cool, and determined to fire no shot without taking aim; but a slight wound in the hand ended my coolness, and the smoke of the battle soon made aim-taking mere guessing. One rebel officer I noticed, through the smoke, directly in front of me on horseback. That was my mark, and I must have fired twenty times at him before his form disappeared. I remember how, in the midst of it all, a young lad—he could not have been more than sixteen—came running up to me, and weeping, cried: "My regiment—my regiment is gone—has run! What shall I do?" "Here's the place," I said, "pitch in!" and pitch in he did. He was of metal, that boy, and kept his place with the bravest veteran in the line. Hotter and hotter grew the fight, and soon this same boy cried: "Look —look behind us," and sure enough, the regiment to our left had disappeared, and we were flanked.

"Stop! halt! surrender!" cried a hundred rebels, whose voices seem to ring in my ears to this very day. But there was no stopping, and no surrender. We ran, and ran manfully. It was terribly hot, a hot afternoon under a Mississippi sun, and an enemy on flank and rear, shouting and firing. The grass, the stones, the bushes, seemed melting under the shower of bullets that was following us to the rear. We tried to halt, and tried to form. It was no use. Again we ran, and harder, and farther, and faster. We passed over the very spot where, half an hour before, we left Grant leaning on his bay mare and smoking his cigar. Thank

God! he was gone. The dead were still there, and the wounded called pitiably to us to halt and help them as we ran headlong to the rear. Like ten thousand starving and howling wolves the enemy pursued, closer and closer, and we scarcely dared look back to face the fate that seemed certain. Grant had seen it all, and in less time than I can tell it a line of cannon had been thrown across our path, which as soon as we had passed, belched grape-shot and canister into the faces of our pursuers. They stopped, they turned, and they, too, ran, and left their dead side by side with our own. Our lines, protected by the batteries, rallied and followed, and Champion hills was won, and with it was won the door to Vicksburg. . . .

Byers overstated the situation. Considerable fighting still faced Grant before the door to Vicksburg would be open to him. In fact, the Union general left the field at Champion's Hill nourishing a bitter grievance:[6]

McClernand, with two divisions, was within a few miles of the battle-field long before noon, and in easy hearing. I sent him repeated orders by staff officers fully competent to explain to him the situation. These traversed the wood separating us, without escort, and directed him to push forward; but he did not come. It is true, in front of McClernand there was a small force of the enemy and posted in a good position behind a ravine obstructing his advance; but if he had moved to the right by the road my staff officers had followed the enemy must either have fallen back or been cut off. Instead of this he sent orders to Hovey, who belonged to his corps, to join on to his right flank. Hovey was bearing the brunt of the battle at the time. To obey the order he would have had to pull out from the front of the enemy and march back as far as McClernand had to advance to get into battle, and substantially over the same ground. Of course I did not permit Hovey to obey the order of his immediate superior.

We had in this battle about 15,000 men absolutely engaged. This excludes those that did not get up, all of McClernand's command except Hovey. Our loss was 410 killed, 1,814 wounded and 187 missing. Hovey alone lost 1,200 killed, wounded and missing—more than one-third of his division.

Had McClernand come up with reasonable promptness, or had I known the ground as I did afterwards, I cannot see how Pemberton could have escaped with any organized force. As it was he lost over three thousand killed and wounded and about three thousand captured in battle and in pursuit.

II

Pemberton reported the number of Confederates engaged at Cham-
pion's Hill at 17,400 and his casualties at 3,624. That night he fell back
to the Big Black River, and after a sharp struggle here, crossed the
bridge and gained the security of his prepared defenses. His official
report told of his conflict behind the scenes with Johnston:[7]

. . . About noon of the eighteenth May, whilst engaged in an inspection of the intrenchments, with Major Lockett, my Chief Engineer, and
several of my General officers, the enemy was reported to be advancing
by the Jackson road. Just at this moment the following communication
was received by courier:

"CAMP BETWEEN LIVINGSTON AND BROWNSVILLE,
       "May 17, 1863
"LIEUTENANT-GENERAL PEMBERTON:
"Your dispatch of to-day, by Captain Henderson, was received. If
Haines' Bluff is untenable, Vicksburg is of no value, and cannot be held.
If, therefore, you are invested in Vicksburg, you must ultimately sur-
render. Under such circumstances, instead of losing both troops and
place, we must, if possible, save the troops. If it is not too late,
evacuate Vicksburg and its dependencies, and march to the north-east.
    "Most respectfully,
       "Your obedient servant,
"(Signed)   J. E. JOHNSTON,
                                                           "*General*"

The evacuation of Vicksburg! It meant the loss of the valuable stores
and munitions of war collected for its defence; the fall of Port Hudson;
the surrender of the Mississippi River, and the severance of the Confederacy.

These were mighty interests, which, had I deemed the evacuation
practicable, in the sense in which I interpreted General Johnston's instructions, might well have made me hesitate to execute them. I believed
it to be in my power to hold Vicksburg. I knew and appreciated the
earnest desire of the government and of the people that it should be
held. I knew, perhaps better than any other individual, under all the
circumstances, its capacity for defence.

As long ago as the seventeenth of February last, in a letter addressed
to his Excellency the President, I had suggested the possibility of the
investment of Vicksburg by land and water, and for that reason the

necessity of ample supplies of ammunition, as well as of subsistence, to stand a siege. My application met his favorable consideration, and additional ammunition was ordered. With proper economy of subsistence and ordnance stores, I knew that I could stand a siege. I had a firm reliance on the desire of the President and of General Johnston to do all that could be done to raise a siege. I felt that every effort would be made, and I believed it would be successful. With these convictions in my own mind, I immediately summoned a council of war, composed of all my General officers. I laid before them General Johnston's communication, but desired them to confine the expression of their opinions to the question of practicability. Having obtained their views, the following communication was addressed to General Johnston:

> "HEADQUARTERS DEPARTMENT OF MISSISSIPPI
> "AND EAST LOUISIANA,
> "VICKSBURG, May 18, 1863

"GENERAL J. E. JOHNSTON:

"GENERAL: I have the honor to acknowledge receipt of your communication in reply to mine, by the hands of Captain Henderson. In a subsequent letter of same date as this letter, I informed you that the men had failed to hold the trenches at Big Black Bridge, and that, as a consequence, Snyder's Mills was directed to be abandoned.

"On the receipt of your communication, I immediately assembled a council of war of the General officers of this command, and having laid your instructions before them, asked the free expression of their opinions as to the practicability of carrying them out. The opinion was unanimously expressed that it was impossible to withdraw the army from this position with such *morale* and material as to be of further service to the Confederacy. While the council of war was assembled, the guns of the enemy opened on the works, and it was at the same time reported that they were crossing the Yazoo River at Brandon's Ferry, above Snyder's Mills. I have decided to hold Vicksburg as long as is possible, with the firm hope that the government may yet be able to assist me in keeping this obstruction to the enemy's free navigation of the Mississippi River. I still conceive it to be the most important point in the Confederacy.

"Very respectfully,
"Your obedient servant,

"J. C. PEMBERTON,
"*Lieutenant-General*"

On May 19 Grant ordered an assault which, in an optimistic view, he declared "resulted in securing more advanced positions for all our troops where they were fully covered from the fire of the enemy." What, really, Grant was gleaning he probably didn't care to admit. Could he take Vicksburg by a direct assault? He calculated the risks— and the stakes:[8]

The 20th and 21st were spent in strengthening our position and in making roads in rear of the army, from Yazoo River or Chickasaw Bayou. Most of the army had now been for three weeks with only five days rations issued by the commissary. They had an abundance of food, however, but began to feel the want of bread. I remember that in passing around to the left of the line on the 21st, a soldier, recognizing me, said in rather a low voice, but yet so that I heard him, "Hard tack." In a moment the cry was taken up all along the line, "Hard tack! Hard tack!" I told the men nearest to me that we had been engaged ever since the arrival of the troops in building a road over which to supply them with everything they needed. The cry was instantly changed to cheers. By the night of the 21st all the troops had full rations issued to them. The bread and coffee were highly appreciated.

I now determined on a second assault. Johnston was in my rear, only fifty miles away, with an army not much inferior in numbers to the one I had with me, and I knew he was being reinforced. There was danger of his coming to the assistance of Pemberton, and after all he might defeat my anticipations of capturing the garrison if, indeed, he did not prevent the capture of the city. The immediate capture of Vicksburg would save me sending the reinforcements which were so much wanted elsewhere, and would set free the army under me to drive Johnston from the State. But the first consideration of all was—the troops believed they could carry the works in their front, and would not have worked so patiently in the trenches if they had not been allowed to try.

The attack was ordered to commence on all parts of the line at ten o'clock A.M. on the 22d with a furious cannonade from every battery in position. All the corps commanders set their time by mine so that all might open the engagement at the same minute. The attack was gallant, and portions of each of the three corps succeeded in getting up to the very parapets of the enemy and in planting their battle flags upon them; but at no place were we able to enter. . . .

General McClernand claimed otherwise. At 11:15 A.M. his courier brought Grant a note:[9]

GENERAL,

I am hotly engaged with the enemy. He is massing on me from the right and left. A vigorous blow by McPherson would make a diversion in my favor.

At noon McClernand sent Grant another message:

GENERAL,

We are hotly engaged with the enemy. We have part possession of two forts, and the Stars and Stripes are floating over them. A vigorous push ought to be made all along the line.

"I did not see the success he reported," Grant said; still, Grant sent the reinforcements and at 3:15 P.M. McClernand dispatched another message.

GENERAL,

I have received your dispatches in regard to Gen. Quinby's division and Gen. MacArthur's. As soon as they arrive I will press the enemy with all possible dispatch, and doubt not that I will force my way through. I have lost no ground. My men are in two of the enemy's forts, but they are commanded by rifle pits in the rear. Several prisoners have been taken who intimate that the rear is strong. At this moment I am hard pressed.   J. A. McC.

Sylvanus Cadwallader claimed that he witnessed McClernand's troops in action on that twenty-second of May:[10]

As McClernand's advance neared the rebel works, it came into plain view from my place of shelter. It had been so mercilessly torn to pieces by Confederate shot and shell that it had lost nearly all resemblance to a line of battle, or the formation of a storming column. Officers and men were rushing ahead pell-mell without much attention to alignment. The small number in sight could no longer be mown down by artillery, as the guns of the forts could not be depressed sufficiently.

When they crossed the deep ditch in front of the earthworks and began to ascend the glacis, they were out of musketry range for the same reason, excepting from one or two salients within reach. A straggling line, continually growing thinner and weaker, finally reached the summit, when all who were not instantly shot down were literally pulled over the rebel breastworks as prisoners. One stand of our colors was planted half way up the embankment and remained there till they could crawl away covered by darkness. I cannot pretend to say how much time was consumed in what I have been describing. But it seemed to me hours before firing subsided enough to warrant my crossing the field and returning to headquarters.

I then learned that McClernand signalled Gen. Grant that he had carried the rebel works on his front—asked for reinforcements to hold them—and also requested the attack to be vigorously pressed at all points, to prevent concentration on him. Grant was somewhat incredulous, and had the dispatch repeated, fearing some mistake in its transmission. He then ordered Quinby's brigade lying near McClernand's right to be moved to his support at once. This was done quickly as possible.

But instead of using Quinby as a support to his own troops, McClernand ordered them to the front in the forlorn hope of retrieving the fortunes of the day, and attempted to make a second assault, with some of his own demoralized troops on Quinby's flank. One of his Colonels flatly refused to obey this order and declared that he would take the consequences of his disobedience rather than lead his men to certain death. . . . I remember distinctly that I gave to Grant and Rawlins the first complete account of its failure—stated that I was within plain view of the rebel earthworks—that McClernand never gained a footing inside of them—and that the small number of his men who actually reached the crest, or scrambled over it, were there yet as prisoners. I was questioned closely concerning it; and shall never forget the fearful burst of indignation from Rawlins, and the grim glowering look of disappointment and disgust which settled down on Grant's usually placid countenance, when he was convinced of McClernand's duplicity, and realized its cost in dead and wounded.

III

Clearly, Grant had approached the breaking point with McClernand. Bitter charges and countercharges remained to be exchanged, and when shortly thereafter Grant relieved McClernand of his command, stinging protests would be addressed to the Governor of Illinois, influential politicians in Washington, and the President. But McClernand, shrewd politician though he was, should have realized that he was involved in a losing argument. Grant had success on his side.

True, after the failure of the assault on May 22 Grant must call his

*situation anything but a complete success. Except at perhaps fatal cost,
he was not going to oust Pemberton from Vicksburg by conventional
methods.*

*Grant's Vicksburg campaign continued to be without parallel in
American history. Lieutenant Cyrus E. Dickey wrote to his sister in
Ottawa, Illinois:*[11]

> HEADQUARTERS,
> 2ND BRIGADE, 6TH DIVISION,
> 17TH CORPS,
> WALNUT HILLS, NEAR VICKSBURG
> May 29, 1863

MY DEAR SISTER,

This evening closes the tenth day of our siege of Vicksburg. I am
sitting in my booth, made of a tent fly, concealed by clippings from a
cane-brake, and located on the eastern slope of a ridge 500 yards from
the enemy. . . . General Grant has ridden out to McPherson's quarters and I am sitting up to wait for him. Things are remarkably quiet.
An occasional shell from one of our gunboats, or from a battery, breaks
the stillness of the night, then a long silence, and another gun.

I have been over to the picket lines for an hour tonight; the lines of
the picket are so close together that the sentries talk together in ordinary tones and spend the whole night in "poking jokes" at each other,
and they are not much disposed to deal in compliments. We have them
thoroughly invested, and unless a stray force attacks us in the rear, we
will keep them caged until they surrender. Our brigade has made two
assaults upon the works, but were both times repulsed with heavy loss;
the first was on the 19th the second on the 22nd.

. . . We are apt to go into almost any kind of a fight any day, or
any hour. . . . There is a part, at least, of the 6th Texas in our Vicksburg pen and I have hopes of capturing our cousin alive.

> INCONVENIENTLY NEAR THE REBEL
> WORKS, IN VIEW OF VICKSBURG
> June 17th 1863

MY DEAR SISTER,

It will be one month tomorrow since we invested this rebel Sebastapol,
and still it holds out against us.

For the first week I looked daily for a surrender; for the next two
weeks we daily expected an attack in our rear; for the past week new

reenforcements have been rapidly arriving, we feel secure against all outside assaults. The excitement attending the commencement of our intimate relations with the Vicksburg garrison has worn away, and we have settled down to our work as quietly and regularly as if we were hoeing corn or drawing bills in chancery. We are drawing closer day by day in regular approaches. General Ransom got a battery in position last night, so close that I threw a clod of dirt into the rebel entrenchments from it. The rebels do not submit to this quietly. They have been throwing 9-inch shells from mortars at us all day today, several of which have exploded very uncomfortably close to our quarters.

I have gathered up about a peck of fragments that fell close to our tent, yesterday and today.

Our brigade has been exceedingly fortunate during the siege, having lost about a dozen men since the charges of the 22d.

This is a queer phase of war to us all; the ground around Vicksburg is a network of ravines running parallel to the rebel works. Our troops are occupying these ravines, have terraced the slopes, and dug caves for tents. During a bombardment from the enemy these caves are at a premium. The timid boys who have not dug caves for themselves try to buy out others who have dug their holes. Good caves today run up to $250 this afternoon, but are at a discount this evening since the line has become quiet.

Private Francis W. Tupper, Fifteenth Illinois Cavalry, gave his parents an unretouched picture of what life could be like "in the ditches" before Vicksburg:[12]

Some two weeks ago I went out into the trench and tried my hand at sharpshooting. The men are mostly detailed for this work, but I went into an advanced place where no one went—only those that volunteered.

One of the boys gave me his gun, but I couldn't see any heads in sight above their works, yet I could hear balls whistle over, every minute, and some of them very close. At last we discovered that they had a hole through the embankment about two feet from the top, and by knowing where it was, and looking sharp, you could see the sky beyond it. I fired a few times to get the range. The boys told me where my shots struck. After that every time we couldn't see through the hole we would all fire and the firing from the hole soon ceased. There are several such places along the line, and I am told that at one of them the rebs have had over a dozen men killed. We also have a lookout and sharpshooter post, on the highest point of the ridge, the lookout is 20 or 25 feet high, and is built of heavy timber and protects a man on three sides and has three loop-holes in it. Hole #1 has five large bullet holes in the exposed side of it; this was named "Coonskin Tower," I believe, in honor of one of our men that used it.* The outside is more than spotted full of holes. An ingenious plan was devised to watch their operations and not be exposed at the loopholes, which was for the time being closed up. A looking-glass was put up on top, and to the back side of the tower. You could just stand in the tower and look into the glass and see all that was to be seen of their operations. They soon discovered this and commenced firing at it and broke it all to smash after about 100 rounds had been fired at it. It was in the morning when I was there, and the sun shone just right. I had an excellent view of their works: . . . their yellow flags,† the court house and part of the town, the river, and in the distance the Louisiana shore. At one battery we had two 9-inch guns and two Parrots 30-pounders, the first two are from the gun-boats and are smooth, the latter are siege-pieces and rifled. They all sighted nearly as fine as a rifle, and they can put a shot right where they want it every time. You can see the balls plainly from these pieces as they go screaming through the air, and see them when they strike, they make the dust fly at a terrible rate sometimes. The army is a great place for jokes and they always have a joke no matter what the circumstances are.

Our 6th Missouri regiment is in the trenches opposite the rebel 6th Missouri, and the boys call them the "bogus six" to distinguish them from ours. At night firing ceases as a general thing, except at or near their forts where we will not allow them to come out. At the other points on the line they post their pickets outside of the works and ours are advanced and posted near them. They have great times talking together. They know every regiment of ours that has ever been in a fight and are always asking where they are and they also know the numbers of the regiments that have fought them the hardest.

* "Coonskin" was Lieutenant Henry C. Foster, Company B, Twenty-third Indiana Volunteers, who built his tower from railroad iron and cross-ties. A contemporary said: "Learned in backwoods lore, he knew how to construct the genuine pioneer log-cabin." Height was what Coonskin wanted, and in time he was able to look down into the Confederate parapets, giving credence to the report that he was the "terror" among all Yankee sharpshooters.
† In the Civil War, hospitals flew yellow flags.

The reporters make some big yarns out of whole cloth. They stay mostly on the boats at the landing, eight or ten miles off. They fill a whole column and have it headed with large type about something that no one here would cross the road to see. They send to their respective papers for publication any report they may hear without ascertaining whether it is true or not. That is the way Vicksburg and other places come to be captured so often.

We have on our table a 3-inch shot weighing 8¼ pounds, which was dug up three-quarters of a mile beyond our camp. We use it for a paper-weight and ornament. Some of the rebel ladies that have had to come to us for rations lately don't feel exactly comfortable while here after they are informed that such rebel messengers pass over camp repeatedly. . . .

I have just seen a sketch by Frank Leslie's artist which shows the manner in which the secesh ladies make their appearance here at our office to get an order on the commissary for rations. In case the picture is published I can inform you that it is a facsimile of the scene. The commissary's quarters represented in the picture is just on the left of us. When we came here we had nothing to eat and the soldiers ate up everything the folks had for ten miles around. They are now of necessity compelled to come here and ask for something to live upon, and they have also discovered that they have the best success when the youngest and best-looking one in the family comes to plead their case and they have some very handsome women here. They are well educated and were rich before their niggers ran away. If I was to meet them in Illinois I should think they were born and brought up there. . . .

IV

Besieged Vicksburg had only one hope—relief from Johnston—but by late May Pemberton knew that the hope was vain:[13]

. . . Two couriers had arrived from General Johnston on the twenty-eighth and twenty-ninth, respectively. The former brought eighteen thousand caps, the latter twenty thousand, and the following dispatch, the first received since the eighteenth:

"May 25, 1863

"LIEUTENANT-GENERAL PEMBERTON:

"My last note was returned by the bearer. Two hundred thousand caps have been sent. It will be continued as they arrive. Bragg is sending a division; when it comes I will move to you. Which do you think the best route? How and where is the enemy encamped? What is your force?

"(Signed)   J. E. Johnston"

The two hundred thousand caps mentioned in the above dispatch were captured by the enemy. I dispatched the following in reply: "Your dispatch of twenty-fifth received this morning, with twenty thousand caps; Fontaine yesterday with eighteen thousand. No messenger from you since the eighteenth. I have eighteen thousand men to man the lines and river-front; no reserves. I do not think you should move with less than thirty or thirty-five thousand men, and then, if possible towards Snyder's Mills, giving me notice of the time of your approach. The enemy encompasses my lines from right to left flank, occupying all roads. He has three corps: Sherman on my left; McPherson, centre; McClernand on my right; Hurlbut's division from Memphis, and Ellett's marine brigade (the last afloat). Enemy has made several assaults. My men are in good spirits, awaiting your arrival. Since investment we have lost about one thousand men, many officers. You may depend on my holding the place as long as possible. On the twenty-seventh we sunk one of their best iron-clad gunboats."

On the thirtieth, I again dispatched as follows: "Scouts report the enemy to have withdrawn most of his forces from our right yesterday, leaving Hall's Ferry road open, I apprehend, for a movement against you. I expect this courier to return to me."

The meat ration having been reduced one-half, that of sugar, rice, and beans, was largely increased. It was important, above all things, that every encouragement should be given to the troops. With this object in view, I ordered the impressment of chewing-tobacco, and its issue to the troops. This had a very beneficial influence. The enemy kept steadily at work, day and night, and, taking advantage of the cover of the hills, had run his parallels up to within seventy-five yards of our works. He was also mining at different points, and it required the active and constant attention of our engineers to repair at night the damage inflicted upon our works during the day, and to meet his different mines by countermining. Orders were issued to prepare thunderbarrels and petards for the defence of near points, and every precaution taken to check the enemy in his operations, and to delay them as far as possible. On the seventh of June, the following dispatch was sent to General Johnston: "I am still without information from you later than your dispatch of twenty-fifth. The enemy continues to intrench his position around Vicksburg. I have sent out couriers to you almost daily. The same men are constantly in the trenches, but are still in good spirits, expecting your approach. The enemy is so vigilant that it is impossible to obtain reliable information. When may I expect you to move, and in what direction? My subsistence may be put down for about twenty days." On the tenth, I again dispatched as follows: "The enemy bombards day and night from seven mortars on opposite side of peninsula. He also keeps up constant fire on our lines with artillery and sharpshooters. We are losing many officers and men. I am waiting most anxiously to know your intentions. Have heard nothing of you or from you since twenty-fifth of May. I shall endeavor to hold out as long as we have anything to eat. Can you not send me a verbal message by a courier crossing the river above or below Vicksburg, and swimming across again opposite Vicksburg?" Again, on the twelfth, I dispatched as follows: "Courier Walker arrived this morning, with caps. No message from you. Very heavy firing yesterday from mortars and on lines." About this time our provisions, particularly of meat, having become exhausted, General Stevenson was instructed to impress all the cattle in the city, and the Chief Commissary directed to sell only one ration per diem to any officer. He was also instructed to issue for bread equal portions of rice and flour—four ounces each. About the thirteenth, Captain Saunders arrived from Jackson, via Steele's Bayou, with two hundred thousand percussion-caps, and a day or two subsequently I received the following dispatch from General Johnston:

"May 29, 1863

"I am too weak to save Vicksburg; can do no more than attempt to save you and your garrison. It will be impossible to extricate you unless you co-operate, and we make mutually supporting movements. Communicate your plans and suggestions, if possible."

Meanwhile, within Vicksburg, men, women and children shared the terrors of the siege, praying that Johnston would soon come to their rescue. Among them was one whom George W. Cable described simply as "a young lady of New Orleans." In time "a betrothed lover came suddenly from a neighboring state . . . and bore her away, a happy bride. . . . In the south, those days, all life was romantic. Theirs was full of adventure. At length they were shut up in Vicksburg." So the "young lady of New Orleans" watched the war approach the city—in

January, when "paper is a serious want"; in February, when "an egg is a rare and precious thing"; in March, when "the slow shelling of Vicksburg goes on all the time, and we have grown indifferent"; in April, when "the owner of the house suddenly returned and notified us that he intended to bring his family back; didn't think there'd be any siege." In late May both the "young lady from New Orleans" and her landlord realized how far wrong they had guessed:[14]

May 28th: "We are utterly cut off from the world, surrounded by a circle of fire. Would it be wise like the scorpion to sting ourselves to death? The fiery shower of shells goes on day and night. H——'s occupation, of course, is gone, his office closed. Every man has to carry a pass in his pocket. People do nothing but eat what they can get, sleep when they can, and dodge the shells. There are three intervals when the shelling stops, either for the guns to cool or for the gunners' meals, I suppose—about eight in the morning, the same in the evening, and at noon. In that time we have both to prepare and eat ours. Clothing cannot be washed or anything else done. On the 19th and 22nd, when the assaults were made on the lines, I watched the soldiers cooking on the green opposite. The half-spent balls coming all the way from those lines were flying so thick that they were obliged to dodge at every turn. At all the caves I could see from my high perch, people were sitting, eating their poor suppers at the cave doors, ready to plunge in again. As the first shell again flew they dived, and not a human being was visible. The sharp crackle of the musketry-firing was a strong contrast to the scream of the bombs. I think all the dogs and cats must be killed or starved, we don't see any more pitiful animals prowling around."

Friday, June 5th: In the cellar.

"Wednesday evening H—— said he must take a little walk, and went while the shelling had stopped. He never leaves me alone for long, and when an hour had passed without his return I grew anxious; and when two hours, and the shelling had grown terrific, I momentarily expected to see his mangled body. All sorts of horrors fill the mind now, and I am so desolate here; not a friend. When he came he said that passing a cave where there were no others near, he heard groans, and found a shell had struck above and caused the cave to fall in on the man within. He could not extricate him alone, and had to get help and dig him out. He was badly hurt, but not mortally, and I felt fairly sick from the suspense. . . ."

June 7th: In the cellar.

"There is one thing I feel especially grateful for, that amid these horrors, we have been spared that of suffering for water. The weather has been dry a long time, and we hear of others dipping up the water from the ditches and mud-holes. This place has two large underground cisterns of good cool water, and every night in my subterranean dressing-room a tub of cold water is the nerve-calmer that sends me to sleep in spite of the roar. . . ."

June 9th: "The churches are a great resort for those who own no caves. People fancy they are not shelled so much, and they are substantial and the pews good to sleep in. . . ."

June 13th: "Shells burst just over the roof this morning. Pieces tore through both floors down into the dining-room. The entire ceiling of that room fell in a mass. We had just left it. Every piece of crockery on the table was smashed up. The 'Daily Citizen' to-day is a foot and a half long and six inches wide. The editorial says, '. . . The undaunted Johnston is at hand.'"

June 18th: "To-day the 'Citizen' is printed on wall paper; therefore has grown a little in size. It says, 'But a few days more and Johnston will be here'; also that 'Kirby Smith has driven Banks from Port Hudson'; and that 'the enemy are throwing incendiary shells in.'"

June 20th: "The gentleman who took our cave came yesterday to invite us to come to it, because he said, 'It's going to be very bad today!' I don't know why he thought so. We went, and found his own and another family in it; sat outside and watched the shells till we concluded the cellar was as good a place as that hill-side. I fear the want of good food is breaking down H——. I know from my own feelings of weakness, but mine is not an American constitution, and has a recuperative power that his has not."

June 21st: "I had gone upstairs to-day during the interregnum to enjoy a rest on my bed and read the reliable items in the 'Citizen' when a shell burst right outside the window in front of me. Pieces flew in, striking all round me, tearing down masses of plaster that came tumbling over me. When H—— rushed in I was crawling out of the plaster, digging it out of my eyes and hair. When he picked up a piece large as a saucer beside my pillow, I realized my narrow escape. The window-frame began to smoke, and we saw the house was on fire. H——— ran for a hatchet and I for water, and we put it out. Another [shell] came crashing near, and I snatched up my comb and brush and ran down here. It has taken all afternoon to get the plaster out of my hair, for my hands were rather shaky. . . ."

June 25th: "A horrible day. The most horrible yet to me, because I've lost my nerve. We were all in the cellar when a shell came tearing through the roof, burst upstairs, tore up that room, and the pieces coming through both floors down into the cellar. One of them tore open the leg of H———'s pantaloons. This was tangible proof the cellar was no place of protection from them. . . ."

Mrs. W. W. Lord and her four children were among the unhappy horde who "literally lived in the dens and caves of the earth." She remembered that, when she had heard the news of Johnston's evacuating Jackson and of Pemberton's moving toward the Big Black River, she had accepted the two movements as "parts of a great plan . . . to surround Grant's army." Now, "sadly undeceived," she lived on numbly:[15]

. . . Imagine one of these Vicksburg hills in the very heart of the city—caves underlay even the very heart of it and intersecting each other reaching again to the front, forming in that way several passages and fire openings. In this cave were gathered 8 families besides other single persons . . . The firing began to be very steady and severe and the whole hill shook—a large piece of earth fell upon Mrs. McRoas's little daughter and almost killed her . . . You can imagine our feelings all shut up in this cave—the horrible shells roaring and bursting all around us and the concussion making our heads feel like they would burst. Poor Mrs. Gunn with her little baby only ten days old!

The next day, Friday, the most terrible battle took place between our batteries and the gunboats,—but we were successful, by the mercy of God, and drove them back. The same day a shell burst at the opening and almost closed it. Mr. Ford and Mr. Merriam were standing almost at the place—such screaming and rushing you never heard. Mr. Merriam exclaimed, "Great God! Out of these caves, out of these caves!"

. . . I have not been undressed now for nearly two weeks and we all live on the plainest food. . . . the children bear themselves like little heroes. At night when the balls begin to fly like pigeons over our tent and I call them to run to the caves, they spring up, even to little Louli, like soldiers, slip on their shoes without a word and run up the hill to the cave.

Mrs. Lord described her cave:

. . . Imagine to yourself in the first place a good sized parapet, about 6 feet high, a path cut through, and then the entrance to the cave —this is secured strong with boards; it is dug the height of a man and about 40 feet under the hill. It communicates with the other cave which is about the same length opening out on the other side of the hill,—this gives us a good circulation of air. . . . I have a little closet dug for provisions, and niches for flowers, lights and books—inside just by the little walk is our eating table with an arbor over it and back of that our fireplace and kitchen with table &c. In the valley beneath is our tent and back of it the tents of the generals. This is quite picturesque and attractive to look at but Oh! how wearisome to live.

Even in these surroundings of common suffering, according to the Vicksburg Daily Citizen, *that great foe of the Southern cause—the extortioner—was not to be denied his pound of flesh:*[16]

If aught would appeal to the heart of stone of the extortioner with success, the present necessities of our citizens would do so. It is needless to attempt to disguise from the enemy of our people that our wants are great. . . . We are satisfied that there are numerous persons within our city who have bread secreted, and are doling it out, at exorbitant prices, to those who had not the foresight or means at their command to provide for the exigencies now upon us. A rumor has reached us that parties in our city have been, and are now, selling flour at $5 per pound! molasses at $10 per gallon! and corn at $10 per bushel! We have not as yet proved the facts upon the parties accused, but this allusion to the subject may induce some of our citizens to ascertain whether such prices have been paid, and to whom; and if so, may a brand not only be placed upon their brows, but seared into their very brains, that humanity may scorn and shun them as they would the portals of hell.

The great historian of the old river, Sam Clemens, added his chapter on "Vicksburg during the trouble"—perhaps the best, most perceptive

*chapter on the subject ever written. Sam found a couple who had lived
through the siege and let them tell the story:*[17]

A week of their wonderful life there would have made their tongues
eloquent forever perhaps; but they had six weeks of it, and that wore
the novelty all out; they got used to being bombshelled out of home and
into the ground; the matter became commonplace. After that, the
possibility of their ever being startlingly interesting in their talks about
it was gone. What the man said was to this effect:

It got to be Sunday all the time. Seven Sundays in the week—to us,
anyway. We hadn't anything to do, and time hung heavy. Seven Sundays, and all of them broken up at one time or another, in the day or in
the night, by a few hours of the awful storm of fire and thunder and
iron. At first we used to shin for the holes a good deal faster than we
did afterward. The first time I forgot the children, and Maria fetched
them both along. When she was all safe in the cave she fainted. Two or
three weeks afterward, when she was running for the holes, one morning, through a shell-shower, a big shell burst near her and covered her
all over with dirt, and a piece of iron carried away her game-bag of
false hair from the back of her head. Well, she stopped to get that game-
bag before she shoved along again! Was getting used to things already,
you see. We all got so that we could tell a good deal about shells; and
after that we didn't always go under shelter if it was a light shower. Us
men would loaf around and talk; and a man would say, "There she
goes!" and name the kind of shell it was from the sound of it, and go
on talking—if there wasn't any danger from it. If a shell was bursting
close over us, we stopped talking and stood still; uncomfortable, yes,
but it wasn't safe to move. When it let go, we went on talking again, if
nobody was hurt—maybe saying, "That was a ripper!" or some such
commonplace comment before we resumed; or, maybe, we would see a
shell poising itself away high in the air overhead. In that case, every
fellow just whipped out a sudden "See you again, gents!" and shoved.
Often and often I saw gangs of ladies promenading the streets, looking
as cheerful as you please, and keeping an eye canted up watching the
shells; and I've seen them stop still when they were uncertain about
what a shell was going to do, and wait and make certain; and after
that they sa'ntered along again, or lit out for shelter, according to the
verdict. Streets in some towns have a litter of pieces of paper, and odds
and ends of one sort or another lying around. Ours hadn't; they had
iron litter. Sometimes a man would gather up all the iron fragments

and unbursted shells in his neighborhood, and pile them into a kind of monument in his front yard—a ton of it, sometimes. No glass left; glass couldn't stand such a bombardment; it was all shivered out. Windows of the houses vacant—looked like eyeholes in a skull. *Whole* panes were as scarce as news.

We had church Sundays. Not many there, along at first; but by and by pretty good turnouts. I've seen service stop a minute, and everybody sit quiet—no voice heard, pretty funeral-like then—and all the more so on account of the awful boom and crash going on outside and overhead; and pretty soon, when a body could be heard, service would go on again. Organs and church music mixed up with a bombardment is a powerful queer combination—along at first. Coming out of church, one morning, we had an accident—the only one that happened around me on a Sunday. I was just having a hearty hand-shake with a friend I hadn't seen for a while, and saying, "Drop into our cave to-night, after bombardment; we've got hold of a pint of prime wh—" Whisky, I was going to say, you know, but a shell interrupted. A chunk of it cut the man's arm off, and left it dangling in my hand. And do you know the thing that is going to stick the longest in my memory, and outlast everything else, little and big, I reckon, is the mean thought I had then? It was, "the whisky *is saved.*" And yet, don't you know, it was kind of excusable; because it was as scarce as diamonds, and we had only just that little; never had another taste during the siege.

Sometimes the caves were desperately crowded, and always hot and close. Sometimes a cave had twenty or twenty-five people packed into it; no turning-room for anybody; air so foul, sometimes, you couldn't have made a candle burn in it. A child was born in one of those caves one night. Think of that; why, it was like having it born in a trunk.

Twice we had sixteen people in our cave; and a number of times we had a dozen. Pretty suffocating in there. We always had eight; eight belonged there. Hunger and misery and sickness and fright and sorrow, and I don't know what all, got so loaded into them that none of them were ever rightly their old selves after the siege. They all died but three of us within a couple of years. One night a shell burst in front of the hole and caved it in and stopped it up. It was lively times, for a while, digging out. Some of us came near smothering. After that we made two openings—ought to have thought of it at first.

Mule meat? No, we only got down to that the last day or two. Of course it was good; anything is good when you are starving.

This man had kept a diary during—six weeks? No, only the first six days. The first day, eight close pages; the second, five; the third, one —loosely written; the fourth, three or four lines; a line or two the fifth and sixth days; seventh day, diary abandoned; life in terrific Vicksburg having now become commonplace and matter of course.

V

For Grant's soldiers, cooped up "in the ditches" before Vicksburg, the days dragged slowly. But generals also were depressed by the tedium of the siege, as William Ward Orme could testify:[18]

> BRIGADE HEADQUARTERS
> CAMP 2½ MILES S. OF VICKSBURG
> June 20th 1863—
> Saturday night

MY DEAR GOOD WIFE—

On account of the delay in forwarding letters from here I have not written for two days— Since I wrote you the other day I received your nice letter of the 9th— How glad I was to hear from you & of your safe arrival at home;—that home at which before very long I hope to arrive safe & sound myself— Once more there, my dear Nannie, I pledge you never again to leave you, our dear sweet children and our happy happy homestead.— O! for its cool recesses and shady trees, now! for its comforts & luxuries—

This is an awful hot country here full of bugs of all sorts.— The heat is very oppressive indeed— Yesterday morning I was taken with a slight attack of bilious diarrhea, but it wore off without proving serious; and this evening I am as well as usual. We have blackberries here in abundance; they are nice & ripe.— Peaches will be ripe in four or five days.

I am now suffering terribly from the effects of mosquitos & other bugs— I am full of bites all over. There is a small insect about the size of a pin's point which bites its way into the flesh & makes a very sore place— This insect is called a "chicker" or "jigger."— We are all suffering from its depredations. They are much worse than the "wood tick"— I have to stop after every sentence I write to scratch myself & drive off the bugs.— . . .

. . . I have no news to send you from here. We are still closely investing the city and digging our way nearer to the enemy's forts every night.— This morning at four O'Clock a general cannonade

opened all around the line; and the enemy replied throwing their shell
in every direction, but doing no damage to us— Our cannonade was
kept up for about four hours.— I don't know what the prospect of a
surrender is— The rebels hold out well, & it may be a month before
they give up, or it may be a week.— So you see there is nothing new
& everything is comparatively quiet & dull.—

Kiss the children for me very often— Tell Willy & Berny they each
owe me a letter— I think I wrote them last. Lucy's letter will come soon
tell her. Remember me to all friends & much love to Fanny & your
mother.—

Keep me in constant remembrance & be assured dear Nannie of my
increasing love for you & home—

Your devoted husband
Wm. W. O.

*No one chafed more than Grant under the strain of the siege. Toward
mid-June his hope for ending the ordeal rested in a scheme to tunnel
under the Vicksburg defenses and blow them into eternity. Major Andrew Hickenlooper, Grant's chief engineer, explained how a trap was
set:*[19]

The general plan of conducting the work with flying-sap by night
and deepening and widening by day was pushed forward with the utmost energy until June 22d, when the head of the sap * reached the
outer ditch surrounding the fort. A few days previous an order had
been issued for all men in the corps having a practical knowledge of
coal-mining to report to the chief engineer. Out of those reporting
thirty-six of the strongest and most experienced were selected and
divided into two shifts for day and night duty, and each shift was divided into three reliefs. On the night of the 22d these men, properly
equipped with drills, short-handled picks, shovels, etc., under the immediate command of Lieutenant Russell of the 7th Missouri and Sergeant Morris of the 32d Ohio, commenced the mining operations by
driving a gallery, four feet in width by five feet in height, in at right
angles to the face of the parapet of the fort. Each relief worked an
hour at a time, two picking, two shoveling, and two handing back the
grain-sacks filled with earth, which were deposited in the ditch

* A sap-roller, used to protect the diggers against the enfilading fire of the
enemy, was a wicker casing, five feet in diameter and ten feet in length, com-
pactly filled with cotton.

until they could be carried back. The main gallery was carried in 45 feet, and then a smaller gallery extended in on the same line 15 feet, while from the end of the main gallery two others were run out on either side at angles of 45 degrees for a distance of 15 feet. The soil through which this gallery was driven was a reddish clay of remarkable tenacity, easily cut and requiring but little bracing. So rapidly was this work executed that on the morning of the 25th the miners commenced depositing the powder, 800 pounds at the extreme end of the main gallery and 700 pounds at the end of each of the lateral galleries, making a total of 2,200 pounds. From each of these deposits there were laid two strands of safety fuse,—obtained, as was the powder, from the navy,—this duplication being made to cover the possible contingency of one failing to burn with the desired regularity and speed. These six strands were cut to exactly the same length, and having been carefully laid, the earth, which had been previously removed in grain-sacks, was carried back and deposited in the most compact manner possible, and well braced by heavy timbers, beyond the junction point of the three galleries. From this point out to the entrance it was more loosely packed in. The Confederate garrison, surmising the object in view, were active in efforts to thwart the purpose of the Union forces by throwing hand-grenades and rolling shells with lighted fuses over their parapet down into the trench in front of the fort. They also countermined in hopes of tapping the gallery. So near were they to the attainment of this object that during the last day the miners could distinctly hear the conversation and orders given in the counter-mine.

The powder was brought up in barrels and kept in the main sap at a safe distance from the enemy's hand-grenades and shells, and there opened and placed in grain-sacks, each one of which contained about 25 pounds. These were taken upon the backs of the miners, who made the run over the exposed ground during the intervals between the explosion of the enemy's shells; and so well timed were these movements that, although it required nearly one hundred trips with the dangerous loads, all were landed in the mine without a single accident.

The commanding general having been advised on the day previous that the work would be completed before 3 P.M. of the 25th, general orders were issued directing each corps commander to order up the reserves and fully man the trenches, and immediately following the explosion to open with both artillery and musketry along the entire twelve miles of investing line; under cover of which the assaulting columns, composed of volunteers from the 31st and 45th Illinois, preceded by ten picked men from the pioneer corps under charge of the chief engineer, were to move forward and take possession of the fort. For an hour or two previous to the time of the explosion the scene from "Battery Hickenlooper," where General Grant and his subordinate commanders had taken their positions, was one of the most remarkable ever witnessed. As far as the eye could reach to the right and left could be seen the long winding columns of blue moving to their assigned positions behind the besiegers' works. Gradually as the hour of 3 approached the booming of artillery and incessant rattle of musketry, which had been going on day and night for thirty days, suddenly subsided, and a deathlike and oppressive stillness pervaded the whole command. Every eye was riveted upon that huge redoubt standing high above the adjoining works. At the appointed moment it appeared as though the whole fort and connecting outworks commenced an upward movement, gradually breaking into fragments and growing less bulky in appearance until it looked like an immense fountain of finely pulverized earth, mingled with flashes of fire and clouds of smoke, through which could occasionally be caught a glimpse of some dark objects,—men, gun-carriages, shelters, etc. Fire along the entire line instantly opened with great fury, and amidst the din and roar of 150 cannon and the rattle of 50,000 muskets the charging column moved forward to the assault. . . .

With that assaulting column went Wilbur F. Crummer of the Forty-fifth Illinois, who remembered:[20]

. . . When the smoke and dust had cleared away partly, a great saucer-shaped crater was seen, where before was the A-shaped Fort Hill. It was large enough to hold about 60 or 80 men. The 23rd Indiana and the 45th Illinois were in the trenches ready to charge; the command was given before the dust had fully settled; the 23rd Indiana charging to the left of the crater to the top of the works; the 45th Illinois up and into the crater. The enemy had come up behind the big pile of earth thrown out by the explosion, and as we went into the crater, they met us with a terrible volley of musketry, but on the boys went, up and over the embankment with a cheer, the enemy falling back a few paces to an inner or second line of breastworks, where are placed cannon loaded with grape and canister, and these cannon belched forth their death-dealing missiles, in addition to the heavy musketry fire, with such telling effect that many of the brave boys fall to rise no more; the line wavers, staggers, and then falls back into the crater. The enemy charge on us, but we repel them at the west bank of the crater; and a hand-to-hand conflict rages for hours; hand grenades and loaded shells are lighted and thrown over the parapet as you would play ball. These shells and hand grenades carry death, as many as a dozen men being killed and wounded at one explosion. . . . Many a brave hero laid down his life in that death hole, or, as we most appropriately called it, "Fort Hell.". . .

We fought at close range with the enemy over that embankment of earth, many of the men receiving bayonet wounds. . . . What a terrible sacrifice it was to hold that little piece of ground. It probably was all right to have made the charge into the crater after the explosion and try to make a breech inside the enemy's lines, but it was a serious mistake, either of Gen. Grant or Gen. McPherson, to cause that crater to be held for over 48 hours with the loss of brave men every hour. I remember, upon returning to the trenches, after having been relieved in the crater, of passing Gen. John A. Logan, surrounded by some of his aid-de-camp, and as they bore past him some wounded hero, he broke forth with vehemence, saying: "My God! they are killing my bravest men in that hole.". . . The crater was at last given up and we resumed the ordinary duties of everyday life in the trenches and in camp.

VI

Grant's troops settled back to the tedium of life in the ditches before the besieged city. Meanwhile there were persistent rumors from the East that Lee's Army of Northern Virginia had crossed the Potomac and was invading Maryland and Pennsylvania.

The reports were true. On June 22 Ewell's corps had crossed in two columns at Shepherdstown and Williamsport, converged at Hagerstown and struck up the valley toward Chambersburg, Pennsylvania. On the twenty-fourth A. P. Hill's corps crossed a mile above Shepherdstown; and Longstreet moved up to follow.

In the sleepy town of Gettysburg the Reverend Dr. Michaels Jacobs taught mathematics and chemistry at little Pennsylvania College. The mine that Grant had exploded under Fort Hill, or the agony with which Wilbur Crummer's comrades died as they tried to wrest that crater from the rebels, were part of a fantastic military seesaw that historians

*would comprehend long years afterward; what Professor Jacobs re-
membered on June twenty-six was a sudden disruption in his academic
life:*[21]

The advance guard of the enemy, consisting of 180 to 200 cavalry,
rode into Gettysburg at 3¼ P.M., shouting and yelling like so many
savages from the wilds of the Rocky Mountains; firing their pistols, not
caring whether they killed or maimed man, woman, or child; and rush-

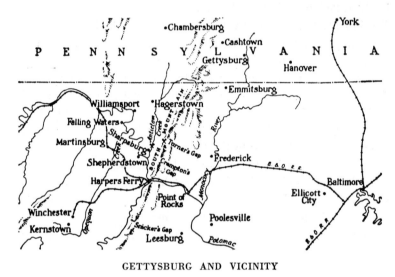

GETTYSBURG AND VICINITY

From *Atlas of American History*

ing from stable to stable in search of horses, the most of which, however, had fortunately a few hours before been sent forward to Hanover
and York.

This advance party was soon followed by 5,000 infantry, being General Gordon's brigade of Early's division of Ewell's corps. Most of the
men were exceedingly dirty, some ragged, some without shoes, and
some surmounted by the skeleton of what was once an entire hat, affording unmistakable evidence that they stood in great need of having
their scanty wardrobe replenished; and hence the eagerness with which
they inquired after shoe, hat, and clothing stores, and their disappointment when they were informed that goods of that description were not
to be had in town; and it ought not to have surprised us that they actually took shoes and hats from the persons of some of our Franklin
county cousins whom they considered more able to endure the loss

than we, whilst they permitted us to escape that infliction. Being wet
from the rain which had fallen during the most of the day, and considerably heated by a long march, there was found, by a person near
them as they passed, to have been more truth than fiction in the remark
of a friend, that "the air was filled with the filthy exhalations from their
bodies." Whether this was a judgment dictated by prejudice or not, it
was difficult for us to recognize, in the great body of them, the character
previously heralded in our community by a lady sympathizer, of "chiv-
alrous Southerners, all from the first families of the South." But we
do not intend to reproach them for not presenting a better appearance;
they doubtless did the best they could, and had come a long journey for
the express purpose of supplying their pressing wants.

General Early, who accompanied this brigade and remained in town
over Friday night, demanded of the authorities of our borough 1,200
pounds of sugar, 600 pounds of coffee, 60 barrels of flour, 1,000 pounds
of salt, 7,000 pounds of bacon, 10 barrels of whisky, 10 barrels of
onions, 1,000 pairs of shoes, and 500 hats, amounting in value to
$6,000; or, in lieu thereof, $5,000 cash. To this demand Messrs.
D. Kendlehart and A. D. Buehler, as representatives of the town council, replied in substance, that it was impossible to comply with their
demands; that the goods were not in town or within reach; that the
borough had no funds, and the council had no authority to borrow
either in the name of the borough or county; and that, as we were at
the mercy of the General and his men, they could search, and take from
citizens and the empty stores whatsoever they might be able to find.
No attempt was made to enforce the requisition, and but few of the
houses of citizens were robbed. Whether this forbearance was owing
to the evident fact that he was outwitted by our citizens, or from his
generosity to our apparent poverty, we will permit our York friends
to judge, to whom he is reported to have replied, when, as a reason
why he should not insist on the enforcement of the large demand he
had made of them, they reminded him of his leniency towards us,
"Why, gentlemen, there was nothing there to take." Be it so: Gettysburg escaped; and York paid a premium of $28,000. During the eve-
ning of Friday, however, the Rebels burned the railroad bridge and
a few cars, took from the few articles that our merchants had not sent
away such as suited them, and divested the taverns and liquor stores
of their liquors. Besides this, they did not do much damage in the town.
In the country, however, they treated the farmers less gently. They
there re-enacted their old farce of professing to pay for what they took

by offering freely their worthless "Confederate" scrip; which, they
said, would, in a few days, be better than our own currency. In the town
they obtained but little booty, because all the valuables of the Bank,
and nearly all those of the merchants, had been previously sent for
safety to Philadelphia. This proved a great disappointment to them;
and they acknowledged that, for this time, they had been too slow in
their movements. They consequently hurried forward, that night and
the next morning, towards Hanover and York. A portion of them passed
through Hanover at 11 A.M., reaching the Northern Central Railroad
at Hanover Junction, early in the afternoon, whilst another portion
went to East Berlin, and on the next day, Sunday, reached York.

Our citizens, with a few exceptions, kept at a respectful distance
from them during their stay amongst us, avoiding as much as possible
communicating any information which might prove advantageous to
them; so much so, that they said: "It is a very strange thing that you
people know so little."

CHAPTER 25

FATEFUL JULY

O N June 16, 1863, Lincoln had written to his wife, who was visiting in Philadelphia: "It is a matter of choice with yourself whether you come home. There is no reason why you should not, that did not exist when you went away. As bearing on the question of your coming home, I do not think the raid into Pennsylvania amounts to anything at all."

A week later "the raid" had proved the precursor of a full-scale invasion. On June 27 residents of Philadelphia read an ominous proclamation:

"CITIZENS OF PHILADELPHIA: Prepare to defend your homes. The traitors who have spread desolation in the southern counties of your State, and carried into captivity free men and women, because they were black and under your protection, approach your city. Their strategy is sufficiently well understood to make it certain that their object is Philadelphia. Do the citizens of the Quaker City expect more favorable treatment at their hands than others? Arise now in your might; shake off your apathy, meet the enemy and drive him back, that you may deserve the blessings of a home. To stand idly now would invite suspicion either of treachery or cowardice. I urge upon the citizens of Philadelphia that they close all places of manufacture by noon, and all other places of business at three o'clock P.M. of each day, devoting the remainder of the day to military organization and instruction. Let companies of from sixty to a hundred men each be rapidly organized, and having chosen their officers, stand ready at a moment's notice. There is not a moment to be lost, and therefore let us not squander away valuable time.

N. J. T. Dana, *Major-Gen. Commanding.*"

I

Marching his troops through the abundant farm lands of Pennsylvania, Confederate General Richard S. Ewell was delighted by the scene around him. "It's like a hole of blubber to a Greenlander," he wrote home. On Sunday, June 22, Gettysburg had not yet seen a rebel, but Sallie Robbins Broadhead, a schoolteacher in the village, filled her diary with disquieting news:[1]

The report now is that a large [Rebel] force is in the mountains about eighteen miles away, and a call is made for a party of men to go out and cut down trees to obstruct the passages of the mountains.

About fifty, among them my husband, started.

I was very uneasy lest they might be captured, but they had not gone halfway when the discovery was made that it was too late; that the Rebels were on this side of the mountain, and coming this way. Our men turned back, uninjured, though their advance, composed of a few men, was fired upon. About seventy of the Rebels came within eight miles, and then returned by another road to their main force.

They stole all the horses and cattle they could find, and drove them back to their encampment.

We did not know but that the whole body would be down upon us, until eleven o'clock, when a man came in and said that he had seen them, and that they had recrossed. I shall now retire, and sleep much better than I had expected an hour since.

Another resident of Gettysburg, Tillie Alleman, remembered:[2]

. . . It was amusing to behold the conduct of the colored people of the town. Gettysburg had a goodly number of them. They regarded the Rebels as having an especial hatred toward them, and believed that if they fell into their hands, annihilation was sure.

These folks mostly lived in the southwestern part of town, and their flight was invariably down Breckenridge Street and Baltimore Street, and toward the woods on and around Culp's Hill.

I can see them yet; men and women with bundles as large as old-fashioned feather ticks slung across their backs, almost bearing them to the ground. Children also, carrying their bundles, and striving in vain to keep up with their seniors. The greatest consternation was depicted on all their countenances as they hurried along; crowding, and running against each other in their confusion; children stumbling,

falling, and crying. Mothers, anxious for their offspring, would stop
for a moment to hurry them up, saying:

"Fo' de Lod's sake, you chillen, cum right long quick! If dem Rebs
dun kotch you, day tear you all up." These terrible warnings were
sure to have the desired effect; for, with their eyes open wider than
ever, they were not long in hastening their steps.

*On the other side of town thirteen-year-old Billy Bayly was having the
time of his life, running horses into the foothills where the Rebs couldn't
find them:*[3]

Along the wood-bordered ridge which constituted the west boundary
of the farm we could see soldiers moving at a rapid pace in an easterly
direction—the general direction in which we were going. The afternoon being cloudy and dark, with rain still falling, made it impossible
for us to distinguish uniforms, and we knew not whether the soldiers
were friends or foes. But we took no chance and rode off at a John
Gilpin rate, I using my coat and shoes forcibly to urge "Nellie" to more
rapid motion. One of my uncles living in the vicinity and other neighbors had ridden up to the barn while father was saddling the horses,
but seeing the "Rebs," as they supposed, only a quarter of a mile distant, hastily fled leaving us to follow. As we were well mounted, we
soon overtook the party and remained with them three or four days.

Our first purpose was to go toward Harrisburg, but fearing the enemy had cut us off in that direction, we turned toward Hanover.

On crossing one of the roads radiating from Gettysburg, I noticed a
horseman coming over the hill toward us and being anxious for information about the enemy, I hung back and let my party go on, having every
confidence in the fleetness of my mount. The horseman, covered with
a rubber poncho splashed with mud, rode up to where my horse was
standing, and I recognized him as a recruit in Bell's Cavalry whom I
knew, so I said, "Hello, Bill! What's up?"

Bill replied, "If you don't get out of here pretty quick you'll find
out what's up. The Rebel Cavalry chased me out of town about fifteen
minutes ago, and must now be close on my heels."

My desire for information not being satisfied however, I said, "But
where is the rest of your company?"

"Oh hell," said the trooper, "I don't know; they ran long before I
did. But you git or you'll be got." And away he rode toward Harrisburg
and I after my party.

Our riding party continued for about fifteen miles, and darkness approaching, concluded that the Rebels would not overtake us that night so we put up with a farmer who fed us abundantly, and I was tired enough to sleep soundly regardless of what the morrow might bring forth.

II

Lincoln, who had doubted from the start whether Hooker could "keep tavern" for an entire army, faced the truth that Chancellorsville had revealed. On June 27—that Saturday when Philadelphians were being roused to defend their city—the command of the Army of the Potomac was given to Pennsylvania-born George G. Meade, whose childhood playmates had included George B. McClellan and John C. Pemberton. Some described this West Pointer as a quiet man without much sense of humor; others insisted that in Meade's case still water ran deep. Next day none could deny the manly tone of Meade's address to his army:[4]

By direction of the President of the United States, I hereby assume command of the Army of the Potomac. As a soldier, in obeying this order—an order totally unexpected and unsolicited—I have no promises or pledges to make. The country looks to this army to relieve it from the devastation and disgrace of the hostile invasion. Whatever fatigues and sacrifices we may be called upon to undergo, let us have in view constantly the magnitude of the interests involved, and let each man determine to do his duty, leaving to an all-controlling Providence the decision of the contest. It is with just diffidence that I relieve, in the command of this army, an eminent and accomplished soldier, whose name must ever appear conspicuous in the history of its achievements; but I rely upon the hearty support of my companions in arms to assist me in the discharge of the duties of the important trust which has been confided to me.

GEORGE G. MEADE
Major-General Commanding

As the Army of the Potomac marched toward Gettysburg under a new chief, at Cashtown, only eight miles away, Lee set up temporary quarters and wondered what had happened to Jeb Stuart. After the affair at Brandy Station in early June, Lee had reason to expect results from Jeb. A surprise raid of the Yankees at Brandy Station had caught Stuart and his officers at a dance and cost 523 Confederate casualties. The Richmond *Examiner had sneered—"If the war was a tournament, invented and supported for the pleasure of a few vain and weak-headed officers, these disasters might be dismissed with compassion." Cut to the quick, Stuart listened perfunctorily to orders to screen the movements of Hill and Longstreet, then to join Ewell and act as "the eyes" of the army. On that twenty-seventh of June when Philadelphians read an ominous proclamation and Hooker stepped down from command, Stuart rested on the shores of the Potomac at Rockville, Maryland. Lieutenant Colonel W. W. Blackford remembered:*[5]

. . . A long wagon train of a hundred and fifty wagons appeared on the road slowly approaching from the direction of Washington, and a detail from Hampton's brigade was at once sent to capture it, which I accompanied. Galloping full tilt into the head of the train, we captured a small guard and a lot of gayly dressed quartermasters, and over half the wagons, before they could turn round; but then those beyond took the alarm, turned and fled as fast as their splendid mule teams could go. After them we flew, popping away with our pistols at such drivers as did not pull up, but the more we popped the faster those in front plied the whip; finally, coming to a sharp turn in the road, one upset and a dozen or two others piled up on top of it, until you could see nothing but the long ears and kicking legs of the mules sticking above the bags of oats emptied from the wagons upon them. . . . Half a dozen wagons had made the turn . . . and after them two or three of us dashed. It was as exciting as a fox chase for several miles, until when the last was taken I found myself on a hill in full view of Washington. . . . Here was a godsend to our poor horses, for every wagon was loaded with oats intended for Meade's army and it did one's heart good to see the way the poor brutes got on the outside of those oats. . . .

Stuart's horsemen returned to Rockville. Girls cheered them and cut buttons from their uniforms for souvenirs. While Lee waited at Cashtown, eager to learn whither Meade had taken the Army of the Potomac, Stuart continued to play hare and hounds with detachments of the Yankee cavalry protecting railroads and supply convoys.

Meanwhile Pickett's division, the rearmost of Lee's army, reached Chambersburg, Pennsylvania. Private John E. Dooley railed in his journal against the "dashing" Stuart who had left "our infantry and

*artillery unguarded in flank and rear" and had stripped "our cautious
Lee of sufficient force to explore the exact position of his enemy."
Pickett's boys were protecting "the spoils of our invasion, which with
very frail guards were being constantly sent across the Potomac." For
Dooley the situation was discomfiting:[6]*

In and around the town of Chambersburg we found the people very
sullen and maliciously disposed, and not a few maledictions were
hurled at us from garret windows by croaking croans; and many young
but frowning brows and pouting lips we saw in doorways and even on
the sidewalks. But our boys laughed cheerfully, and when contempt
and scorn were shewn them answered by jests and witticisms rather
than with the bayonet, as often did those Yankee ruffians in our Southern Cities. . . . Here any where may be seen young ladies in silks
padding along the pavement without *shoes or stockings*. Such sights are
worthy of note as manifesting one of the peculiar customs of this *race
of people*, if indeed it be not a peculiarity arising from the war. . . .
We know how straight into the very jaws of destruction and death leads
this road of Gettysburg; and none of us are yet aware that a battle is
before us; still there pervades our ranks a solemn feeling, as if some
unforeseen danger was ever dropping darksome shadows over the road
we unshrinkingly tread.

III

*On July 1 Lee agreed that General Henry Heth could take his division
to Gettysburg in the hope of securing shoes for the barefooted men of
the Third Corps. On the Chambersburg Pike, about a mile and a half
from the village near a sluggish little stream called Willoughby Run,
Yankee vedettes were encountered. So, unexpectedly, began one of
the world's classic battles. Thus war overtook Tillie Alleman:[7]*

We were having our regular literary exercises on Friday afternoon,
at our Seminary, when the cry reached our ears. Rushing to the door,
and standing on the front portico we beheld a dark, dense mass, moving toward town. Our teacher, Mrs. Eyster, at once said:
"Children, run home as quickly as you can."
It did not require repeating. I am satisfied some of the girls did not
reach their homes before the Rebels were in the streets.
As for myself, I had scarcely reached the front door, when, on looking up the street, I saw some of the men on horseback. I scrambled in,

slammed shut the door, and hastening to the sitting room, peeped out between the shutters.

Already at home, Sallie Robbins Broadhead remembered:[8]

I had just put my bread in the pans when the cannons began to fire . . . About ten o'clock the shells began to "fly around quite thick," and I took my child and went to the house of a friend up town. As we passed up the street we met wounded men coming in from the field. When we saw them, we, for the first time, began to realize our fearful situation, and anxiously to ask, "Will our army be whipped?" Some said there was no danger of that yet, and pointed to Confederate prisoners who began to be sent through our streets to the rear.

Such a dirty, filthy set, no one ever saw. They were dressed in all kinds of clothes, of all kinds and no kind of cuts. Some were barefooted and a few wounded. Though enemies, I pitied them. I, with others, was sitting at the doorstep bathing the wounds of some of our brave soldiers, and became so much excited as the artillery galloped through the town, and the infantry hurried out to reinforce those fighting, that for a time we forgot our fears and our danger.

Young Billy Bayly was up on a ridge outside Gettysburg, picking rasp-berries with two chums:[9]

. . . The discharge of a cannon . . . made us jump, as it seemed to be just beyond the bushes concealing us. This was instantly followed by a rapid succession of discharges, and we three boys broke for the open and back to the blacksmith's shop. . . . The blacksmith's shop was deserted by all but its owner; his anvil was silent and his forge dead . . . so we perched ourselves on the topmost rail of the road fence and drank in the melody of the battle.

But our gallery seats, although good for the whole show, began to have features of discomfort when we noticed up the road, coming over the nearest hill, great masses of troops and clouds of dust; how the first wave swelled into successive waves, gray masses with the glint of steel as the sun struck the gun barrels, filling the highway, spreading out into the fields, and still coming on and on, wave after wave, billow after billow. We waited not until we could "see the whites of their eyes" but until they were a few hundred yards between us and the advance column, and then we departed. . . .

*Among the first Union casualties was General John F. Reynolds, who
was shot through the back of the head by a Rebel sharpshooter. Yankee
cavalry under General John Buford and a corps under General Abner
Doubleday managed at first to throw back the Rebels at Willoughby
Run. Meanwhile General Oliver Otis Howard reached Gettysburg,
climbed to the top of an observatory, and "with maps and field glasses"
looked down on the battle:*[10]

. . . Wadsworth's infantry, Buford's cavalry and one or two batteries were nearest, and their fighting was manifest. Confederate prisoners were just then being sent to the rear in large groups from Seminary Ridge down the street past my post of observation. . . .

Under my order Osborn's batteries were placed on Cemetery Ridge.
. . . General Steinwehr's division I put on the same heights near the
Baltimore Pike. Dilger's Ohio Battery preceded the corps, and soon
after Wheeler's, the two pacing through the town at a trot, to take their
places on the right of the First Corps. Schurz ordered General Schim-
melfennig (who had Schurz's division now) to advance briskly
through Gettysburg and form on the right of the First Corps in two
lines. Shortly after that the first division under Barlow arrived by the
Emmitsburg Road proper, and advanced through the town on the right
of the third division. I rode with Barlow through the city and out to
what is now Barlow Hill.

The firing at the front was now severe and an occasional shell burst
over our heads or among the houses. When I think of this day, I shall
always recall one incident which still cheers my heart: it was that a
young lady, after all other persons had disappeared for safety, remained behind on her porch and waved her handkerchief at the soldiers
as they passed. . . . How heartily they cheered her!

*Meade had reached Taneytown, about thirteen miles south of Gettys-
burg. Around two o'clock the first reports reached him and "he rode
at a rapid gallop." Meanwhile at Cashtown, Lee heard the sound of
battle and hurried forward. His immediate plan was to avoid a major
engagement until his entire army had reached the vicinity. By luck a
courier overtook Ewell, who was marching the Second Corps from
Fayetteville to Cashtown, and wheeled him around toward Gettysburg.
More or less the power of Federal troops had been split in two, with
Doubleday's First Corps occupying the Rebels along Willoughby Run
and Howard's Eleventh Corps fighting along Seminary Ridge. A railroad cut drew both armies toward the bitterest, climactic contest of*

the day. In the thickest of the fray were "those damned black-hatted fellows," the Iron Brigade. Sergeant George Eustice remembered:[11]

It must have been about noon when I saw a little old man coming up in the rear of Company F. In regard to the peculiarities of his dress, I remember he wore a swallowed-tailed coat with smooth brass buttons. He had a rifle on his shoulder. We boys began to poke fun at him as soon as he came amongst us, as we thought no civilian in his senses would show himself in such a place. . . . Bullets were flying thicker and faster, and we hugged the ground about us as close as we could. Burns got behind a tree and surprised us all by not taking a double-quick to the rear. He was as calm and collected as any veteran.

Bret Harte immortalized old John Burns, standing firm with the Iron Brigade:[12]

'Twas but a moment, for that respect
Which clothes all courage their voices checked;
And something the wildest could understand
Spake in the old man's strong right hand,
And his corded throat, and the lurking frown
Of his eyebrows under his old bell-crown;
Until, as they gazed, there crept an awe
Through the ranks in whispers, and some men saw,
In the antique vestments and long white hair,
The Past of the Nation in battle there;
And some of the soldiers since declare
That the gleam of his old white hat afar,
Like the crest plume of the brave Navarre,
That day was their oriflamme of war.

Yet an old man's courage does not win battles. Charles Coffin, reporting for the Boston Journal, *understood how Ewell's forces, deploying on the York Road, won the day for Lee:*[13]

. . . The [Rebel] batteries were wheeled into position and opened on the Union forces. Weiderick's battery in the cemetery replied. . . .

"I sent again to General Slocum, stating that my right flank was attacked; that it was in danger of being turned, and asking him if he was coming up," said General Howard. . . . But General Slocum did not move. . . .

Sickles was too far off to render assistance. Meanwhile Ewell was pressing on towards the college. Another division of Rebels under General Pender came in from the southwest, and began to enfold the left of Howard's line. . . .

An hour passed of close, desperate fighting. It wanted a quarter to four. Howard, confronted by four times his own force, was still holding his ground, waiting for Slocum. Another messenger rode to the Two Taverns [Slocum's fieldquarters on the Baltimore Pike], urging Slocum to advance.

"I must have reinforcements!" was the message Howard received from Doubleday on the left. "You must reinforce me!" was the word from Wadsworth in the center.

"Hold out a little longer, if possible; I am expecting General Slocum every moment" was Howard's reply. Still another dispatch was sent to the Two Taverns, but General Slocum had not moved. The Rebel cannon were cutting Wadsworth's line. Pender was sweeping round Doubleday; Ewell was enclosing Schurz [part of Howard's own Eleventh Corps]. Sickles was five miles distant, advancing as fast as he could. . . . For six hours the ground had been held against a greatly superior force.

Major Howard, the general's brother, a member of his staff, dashed down the pike in search of Slocum, with a request that he move at once and send one division to the right and the other to the left of Gettysburg. Slocum declined to go up to the front himself and take any responsibility, as he understood that General Meade did not wish to bring on a general engagement. He was willing, however, to send forward his troops as General Howard desired, and issued his orders accordingly. . . .

But before the divisions of the Twelfth Corps could get in motion, the Confederates had completely enfolded both flanks of Howard's line. The order to retreat was given. . . . The enemy pressed on with cheers. . . .

Sallie Broadhead hated what she saw—"The town was full of filthy rebels." Tillie Alleman was more struck by the terrible consequences of a battle:[14]

The first wounded soldier whom I met had his thumb tied up. This I thought was dreadful, and told him so.

"Oh," said he, "this is nothing; you'll see worse than this before long."

Soon two officers carrying their arms in slings made their appearance, and I more fully began to realize that something terrible had taken place.

Now the wounded began to come in greater numbers. Some limping, some with their heads and arms in bandages, some crawling, others carried on stretchers or brought in ambulances. Suffering, cast down and dejected, it was a truly pitiable gathering. Before night the barn was filled with shattered and dying heroes of this day's struggle.

That evening Beckie Weikert, the daughter at home, and I went out to the barn to see what was transpiring there. Nothing before in my experience had ever paralleled the sight we then and there beheld. There were the groaning and the crying, the struggling and dying, crowded side by side, while attendants sought to aid and relieve them as best they could.

We were so overcome by the sad and awful spectacle that we hastened back to the house weeping bitterly.

As we entered the basement or cellar-kitchen of the house, we found many nurses making beef tea for the wounded. Seeing that we were crying . . . they at once endeavored to cheer us by telling funny stories, and ridiculing our tears. They soon dispelled our terror and caused us to laugh so much that many times when we should have been sober minded we were not; the reactions having been too sudden for our overstrung nerves.

Ewell led the Confederate pursuit of the fleeing Yankees. Tired obviously from handling his new artificial limb, depressed in mind and spirit, surrounded by joyous soldiers toasting their victory with wine pilfered from Gettysburg cellars, Ewell decided to wait until morning to renew the battle. The Federals escaped into Cemetery Ridge beyond the town, falling exhausted among the tombstones. Frank Aretas Haskell, who served with the Iron Brigade as aide-de-camp to General Gibbon, had learned that the night before a battle was not a time for generals and their staff officers to sleep:[15]

. . . This war makes strange confusion of night and day! . . . At midnight Gen. Meade and staff rode by Gen. Gibbon's headquarters, on their way to the field; and in conversation with Gen. Gibbon, Gen. Meade announced that he had decided to assemble the whole army before Gettysburg, and offer the enemy battle there. The Second Corps would move at the earliest daylight, to take up its position.

At three o'clock, A.M., of the second of July, the sleepy soldiers of
the Corps were aroused; before six the Corps was up to the field, and
halted temporarily by the side of the Taneytown Road, upon which it
had marched, while some movements of the other troops were being
made, to enable it to take position in the order of battle. The morning
was thick and sultry, the sky overcast with low, vapory clouds. As we
approached all was astir upon the crests near the Cemetery, and the
work of preparation was speedily going on. Men looked like giants
there in the mist, and the guns of the frowning batteries so big that it
was a relief to know that they were our friends.

. . . The line of battle as it was established, on the evening of
the first, and morning of the second of July was in the form of the letter
"U," the troops facing outwards, and the "Cemetery," which is at the
point of the sharpest curvature of the line, being due South of the town
of Gettysburg. "Round Top," the extreme left of the line, is a small,
woody, rocky elevation, a very little West of South of the town, and
nearly two miles from it. . . . A short distance North . . . is a
smaller elevation called Little Round Top. . . . Near the right of the
line is a small, woody eminence, named Culp's Hill. . . .

On arriving upon the field, Gen. Meade established his headquarters at a shabby little farmhouse on the left of the Taneytown Road,
the house nearest the line, and a little more than five hundred yards in
the rear of what became the center of the position of the Second Corps,
a point where he could communicate readily and rapidly with all parts
of the army. The advantages of the position, briefly, were these: the
flanks were quite well protected by the natural defences there, Round
Top up the left, and a rocky, steep, untraversable ground up the right.
Our line was more elevated than that of the enemy, consequently our
artillery had a greater range and power than theirs. On account of
the convexity of our line, every part of the line could be reinforced by
troops having to move a shorter distance than if the line were straight;
further, for the same reason, the line of the enemy must be concave,
and, consequently, longer, and with an equal force, thinner and so
weaker than ours. Upon those parts of our line which were wooded,
neither we nor the enemy could use artillery; but they were so strong
by nature, aided by art, as to be readily defended by a small, against
a very large, body of infantry. When the line was open, it had the advantage of having open country in front, consequently, the enemy here
could not surprise, as we were on a crest, which besides the other advantages that I have mentioned, had this: the enemy must advance to

the attack up an ascent, and must therefore move slower, and be, before coming upon us, longer under our fire, as well as more exhausted. These and some other things, rendered our position admirable—for a defensive battle.

IV

Longstreet liked nothing about the Confederate situation. With Meade up on those heights, Lee faced Fredericksburg in reverse. Common sense to Longstreet would be to move Lee's right to the left of Meade, putting the Army of Northern Virginia between Meade and Washington, "and thus force him to attack us in such position as we might select." Longstreet, full of arguments proving how foolhardy it was to fight here, recalled them all long years afterward—and also the strange mood that had fallen upon Lee:[16]

General Lee was impressed with the idea that by attacking the Federals he could whip them in detail. I reminded him that if the Federals were there in the morning, it would be proof that they had their forces well in hand, and that with Pickett in Chambersburg and Stuart out of reach we should be somewhat in detail. He, however, did not seem to abandon the idea of attack on the next day. He seemed under a subdued excitement, which occasionally took possession of him when "the hunt was up," and threatened his severe equipoise. The sharp battle fought by Hill and Ewell on that day had given him a taste of victory. . . .

On the morning of the second, I went to General Lee's headquarters and renewed my views against making an attack. He seemed resolved, however, and we discussed the probable results. We observed the position of the Federals and got a general idea of the nature of the ground. About sunrise General Lee sent Colonel Venable, of his staff, to General Ewell's headquarters, ordering him to make a reconnaissance of the ground in his front with a view of making the main attack on his left. A short time afterward he followed Colonel Venable in person. He returned about nine o'clock and informed me that it would not do to have Ewell open the attack. He finally determined that I should make the main attack on the extreme right. It was fully eleven o'clock when General Lee arrived at this conclusion and ordered the movement.

Under overcast skies, with a mizzling effort at rain, the morning wore on. Haskell watched the waiting Union soldiers—"Some loitered, some

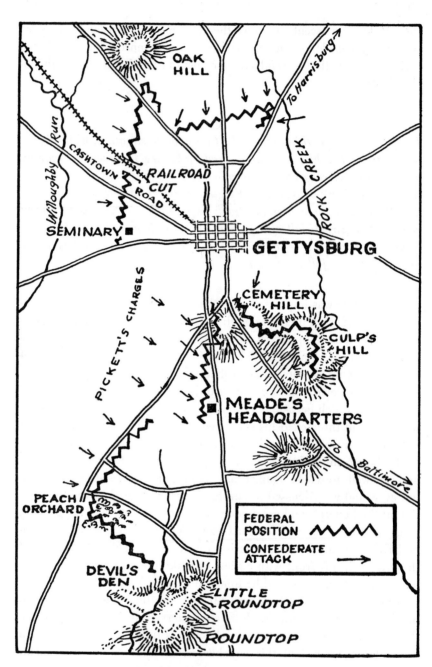

THE GETTYSBURG BATTLEFIELD

went to sleep on the ground, some, a single man, carrying twenty can-
teens slung over the shoulder, went for water. Some made a fire and
boiled a dipper of coffee. Some with knees cocked up enjoyed the sol-
dier's peculiar solace, a pipe of tobacco." In town Sallie Broadhead
could not hide her amusement at her husband, going into the garden to
pick "a mess of beans, though stray bullets from sharpshooters or others
whizzed about his head in a way I would not have liked. He persevered
until he had picked all, for he declared the Rebels should not have
one." Young Billy Bayly, tasting high adventure, helped conceal a
deserter on the farm—"He was added to the cherry picking brigade and
broke off branches and threw them down to his late comrades in arms."
Poor Tillie Alleman faced a grimmer experience:[17]

During the early part of the forenoon my attention was called to
numerous rough boxes which had been placed outside the garden fence.
Ominous and dismal as was the sight presented, it nevertheless did not
prevent some of the soldiers from passing jocular expressions. One of
the men near by, being addressed with the remark that there was no
telling how soon he would be put in one of them, replied:

"I will consider myself very lucky if I *get* one."

This forenoon another incident occurred which I shall ever remember. While the infantry were passing, I noticed a poor, worn-out soldier
crawling along on hands and knees. An officer yelled at him, with curs-
ing, to get up and march. The poor fellow said he could not, whereupon
the officer, raising his sword, struck him down three or four times. The
officer passed on, little caring what he had done. Some of his comrades
at once picked up the prostrate form and carried the unfortunate man
into the house. After several hours of hard work the sufferer was
brought back to consciousness. He seemed quite a young man, and
was suffering from sunstroke received on the forced march. As they
were carrying him in, some of the men who had witnessed this act of
brutality remarked:

"We will mark that officer for this."

It is a pretty well established fact that many a brutal officer fell in
battle, from being shot other than by the enemy.

Lee's plan was for Longstreet to attack on the right as quickly as pos-
sible; and for Ewell, on the extreme left opposite Culp's Hill, to assault
when he heard Longstreet's guns. The morning passed; then one
o'clock, two o'clock. Pickett's division had not come up, a source of

fretfulness to Longstreet, who with a force of hardly 13,000 men be-
lieved that "the proposition for our inferior forces to assault and drive
out the masses of troops on the heights was a very problematical one."
Colonel James Freemantle of the Coldstream Guards, serving as an
observer with Lee's army, judged that the time was about two o'clock:[18]

. . . General Longstreet advised me if I wished to have a good view
of the battle to return to my tree of yesterday. I did so, and remained
there with Lawly and Captain Schreibert [of the Prussian Army] during the rest of the afternoon. But until four forty-five P.M. all was
profoundly still and we began to doubt whether a fight was coming off
today at all. At that time, however, Longstreet suddenly commenced
a heavy cannonade on the right. Ewell immediately took it up on the
left. The enemy replied with at least equal fury. . . . A dense smoke
rose for six miles . . . [and] so soon as the firing began, General Lee
joined Hill just below our tree, and he remained there nearly all the
time looking through his field glasses—sometimes talking to Hill and
sometimes to Colonel Long of his staff. But generally he sat quite alone
on the stump of a tree. . . . When the cannonade was at its height, a
Confederate band of music, between the cemetery and ourselves, began
to play polkas and waltzes, which sounded very curious accompanied
by the hissing and bursting of shells.

Meanwhile across the 1,400 yards that separated the two armies, a
Union general, Dan Sickles, headstrong, rash, an egotistic product of
the hard school of Tammany politics, decided he knew more about
war than Meade. The ground in front of him, strewn in places with
boulders, he described as "unfit for infantry, impracticable for artil-
lery"; if Lee planted enough guns along the higher ground of the Em-
mitsburg Road, then Gettysburg could become another Chancellors-
ville! So reasoned Sickles, who might have been a presidential
candidate had he not killed a man for an affair with Mrs. Sickles. He
decided to move within reach of the Emmitsburg Road. Astonished,
Frank Haskell described what followed:[19]

It was magnificent to see those ten thousand or twelve thousand men
—they were good men—with their batteries, and some squadrons of
cavalry upon the left flank . . . sweep steadily down the slope, across
the valley, and up the next ascent toward their destined position! . . .
The Third Corps now became the absorbing object of interest of all

eyes. The Second Corps took arms, and the 1st Division of this Corps was ordered to be in readiness to support the Third Corps, should circumstances render support necessary. The Third Corps was the extreme left of our line, as it advanced, and if the enemy was assembling to the West of Round Top with a view to turn our left, as we had heard, there would be nothing between the left flank of the corps and the enemy, and the enemy would be square upon its flank by the time it had attained the road. So when this advance line came near the Emmitsburg Road, and we saw . . . the smoke of some guns, and we heard the reports away to Sickles' left, anxiety became an element in our interest in these movements. The enemy opened slowly at first, and from long range; but he was square upon Sickles' left flank.

General Caldwell pulled back the first division of the Second Corps to the woods at the west slope of Round Top, thus attempting to cover Sickles in flank and rear. A reserve corps came up the Baltimore Pike, heading to the support of Caldwell. Another corps came up and halted on the Baltimore Pike. As Haskell said, "the plot thickened":

. . . The enemy seem to be fearfully in earnest this time. And what is more ominous than the thunder or the shot of his advancing guns . . . far to Sickles' left, appear the long lines and the columns of the Rebel infantry, now unmistakably moving out to the attack. The position of the Third Corps becomes at once one of great peril, and it is probable that its commander by this time began to realize his true situation. All was astir now on our crest. Generals and their Staffs were galloping hither and thither—the men were all in their places, and you might have heard the rattle of ten thousand ramrods as they drove home and "thugged" upon the little globes and cones of lead. As the enemy was advancing upon Sickles' flank, he commenced a change, or at least a partial one, of front, by swinging back his left and throwing forward his right, in order that his lines might be parallel to those of his adversary, his batteries meantime doing what they could to check the enemy's advance; but this movement was not completely executed before new Rebel batteries opened upon Sickles' right flank—his former front—and in the same quarter appeared the Rebel infantry also.

Now came the dreadful battle picture, of which we for a time could be but spectators. Upon the front and right flank of Sickles came sweeping the infantry of Longstreet and Hill. Hitherto there had been skirmishing and artillery practice—now the battle began; for amid the heavier smoke and larger tongues of flame of the batteries, now began to appear the countless flashes, and the long fiery sheets of the muskets, and the rattle of the volleys, mingled with the thunder of the guns. We see the long gray lines come sweeping upon Sickles' front, and mix with the battle smoke; now the same colors emerge from the bushes and orchards upon his right, and envelope his flank in the confusion of the conflict. O, the din and the roar, and these thirty-thousand Rebel wolf cries! What a hell is there down that valley!

Through the Peach Orchard, the Wheat Field—names that by night-fall would forever be inscribed in blood in American history—came the howling Rebels who would make July 2, 1863, "Longstreet's great-est day." Haskell watched mutely:[20]

These ten or twelve thousand men of the Third Corps fight well, but it soon becomes apparent that they must be swept from the field, or perish there where they are doing so well, so thick and overwhelming a storm of Rebel fire involves them. It was fearful to see, but these men, such as ever escape, must come from that conflict as best they can. To move down and support them with other troops is out of the question, for this would be to do as Sickles did, to relinquish a good position, and advance to a bad one. There is no other alternative—the Third Corps must fight itself out of its position of destruction! . . .

The Rebel, as anticipated, tries to gain the left of the Third Corps, and for this purpose is now moving into the woods at the west of Round Top. We knew what he would find there. No sooner had the enemy gotten a considerable force into the woods mentioned, in the attempted execution of his purpose, than the roar of the conflict was heard there also. The Fifth Corps and the First Division of the Second were there at the right time, and promptly engaged him; and there, too, the battle soon became general and obstinate.

Now the roar of battle has become twice the volume that it was before, and its range extends over more than twice the space. The Third Corps has been pressed back considerably, and the wounded are streaming to the rear by hundreds, but still the battle there goes on, with no considerable abatement on our part. The field of actual conflict extends now from a point to the front of the left of the Second Corps, away down to the front of Round Top, and the fight rages with the greatest fury. The fire of artillery and infantry and the yells of the

Rebels fill the air with a mixture of hideous sounds. When the First Division of the Second Corps first engaged the enemy, for a time it was pressed back somewhat, but under the able and judicious management of Gen. Caldwell, and the support of the Fifth Corps, it speedily ceased to retrograde, and stood its ground; and then there followed a time, after the Fifth Corps became well engaged, when from appearances we hoped the troops already engaged would be able to check entirely, or repulse the further assault of the enemy. . . .

Private John W. Plummer, sent to support the left of the beleaguered Third Corps, found that men in battle act strangely:[21]

We were marched up there about a quarter of a mile, and ordered to lie down in front of the batteries, as the shot and shell were coming over pretty plentifully. From there we could look all over the field, see our lines, the rebel lines, and their batteries very plainly. As I saw our men fall back, rally, and fall back again, skedaddlers rushing to the rear in squads, I never felt so bad in my life. I thought sure the day was gone for us, and felt that I would prefer to die there, rather than live and suffer the disgrace and humiliation a defeat of our army there would entail on us; and if ever I offered a sincere prayer in my life, it was then, that we might be saved from defeat. We all felt bad, but resolved, when our chance came, to do our best to retrieve the fortunes of the day, hardly expecting to come out of the conflict unharmed. Our turn soon came. We were ordered forward against the enemy, who were then within musket range of us; and if any ever were willing and anxious to go forward into what we all could see was a deadly place, our boys were. We had two open fields to advance over, while the rebels were coming down over another open field, and the Third corps falling back before. We went forward on a run, and with a yell, till about half way across the second field, when we were ordered, for some unaccountable reason to us, to halt, and the bullets were coming like hail-stones, and whittling our boys like grain before the sickle. "Why don't they let us charge?" cried all of us. "Why do they stop us here to be murdered?" Every one seemed anxious to go forward, and some run way out ahead and beckoned for us to come on. We have always believed that a determined charge would break any line, and that more would be accomplished and less life lost, than by lying down and firing two or three hours. We felt that we could check and force them to retreat, and we wanted to go against them with a vengeance and get over the deadly ground as soon as possible. We were halted again when across the second field; and though by this time few were left, we were just as anxious to go forward. We were almost together, and the rebels had nearly flanked the right of the regiment. But what surprised me most was to see some of the rebels, not fifty yards from us, standing out openly and loading and firing as deliberately as though they were in no danger whatever. Ah! there is no mistake but what some of those rebels are just as brave as it is possible for human beings to be. . . .

The afternoon shadows lengthened, the battle roared on, and then with a sense of shock both North and South realized that the key to the entire field, the Round Tops, had been ignored. How close the Rebels came to winning this prize lived in the memory of William Colvin Oates, who led the Fifteenth Alabama up those rocky slopes:[22]

I now ordered my regiment to drive the Federals from the ledge of rocks and from the hill. My men advanced about halfway to the enemy's position, but the fire was so destructive that my line wavered like a man trying to walk against a strong wind, and then slowly, doggedly, gave back a little; then, with no one on the left or right of me, to stand there and die was sheer folly; either to advance or retreat became a necessity.

I again ordered the advance . . . I passed through the line waving my sword, shouting, "Forward, men, to the ledge!" and was promptly followed by the command in splendid style. . . . Five times they rallied and charged us, twice coming so near that some of my men had to use the bayonet. . . . It was our time now to deal death. . . .

Colonel W. F. Perry of the Forty-eighth Alabama thought that "the view was imposing. Little Round Top, crowned with artillery, resembled a volcano in eruption; while a hillock near Devil's Den resembled a smaller one." Perry's line emerged from a woods:

A sheet of flame burst from the rocks less than fifty yards away. A few scattering shots in the beginning gave warning in time for my men to fall down, and thus largely to escape the effect of the main volley. They doubtless seemed to the enemy to be all dead, but the volley of the fire which they immediately returned proved that they were very much alive. . . . Before the enemy had time to load their guns a decision was made. Leaping over the prostrate line before me, I shouted the order, "Forward!" and started for the rocks. The response was a bound, a yell, and a rush, and in ten seconds my men were pouring into the Den, and the enemy were escaping from the opposite side. . . . In the charge the left wing of the regiment struck the hill on which the artillery were stationed, and the center and right swept into the rocks east of it. Major George W. Carey led the left wing up the hill, and bounding over the rocks on its crest, landed among the artillery-men ahead of the line, and received their surrender. . . . The Major a few moments later found me near the foot of the hill, completely prostrated by heat and excessive exertion.

To the little band of the Twentieth Maine fell the brunt of saving the Round Tops for the Union. For Captain Howard L. Prince the sight of those hostile slopes was etched on his memory:[23]

The front surged backward and forward like a wave. At times our dead and wounded were in front of our line, and then by a superhu-man effort our gallant lads would carry the combat forward beyond their prostrate forms. Continually the gray lines crept up by squads under protecting trees and boulders, and the firing became at closer and closer range. And even the enemy's line essayed to reach around the thin front of blue that stretched out in places in single rank and could not go much farther without breaking. So far had they extended, that their bullets passed beyond and into the ranks farther up the hill, and Captain Woodward, commanding the Eighty-third, sent his adjutant to ask if the Twentieth had been turned. . . . Meanwhile the brigade in front of the hill was hard pushed to hold its own, and the heavy roar of musketry in the fitful lulls of our guns came to the anxious ears of our commander and told too plainly what would be the result if our line gave way. Not a man in that devoted band but knew that the safety of the brigade, and perhaps of the army, depended on the steadfastness with which that point was held, and so fought on and on, with no hope of assistance, but not a thought of giving up. Already nearly half of the little force is prostrate. The dead and the wounded clog the footsteps of the living.

The countercharges of the Twentieth Maine broke the Rebel attack; Oates described the retreat: "We ran like a herd of wild cattle." Many times that day on those slopes an exhausted Ziba B. Graham of the

Sixteenth Michigan turned his head and saw the Third Corps in the peach orchard and the wheat field:

We could see line after line of Longstreet's men forming and advancing; also the close contact, the repulses, the fierce havoc of artillery, the close range of the musketry, the break of the lines, the gallant unbroken line still pushing forward, the gradual pressure upon Sickles, his stubborn falling back, the hand-to-hand conflict in the wheatfield where the gallant Fourth Michigan fought so stubbornly, and where their brave and noble Colonel Jefferds lost his life by a bayonet thrust, still holding to the flag. All this and more passed before our eyes. So fierce was our own fight that we could spare no men to take off the field our own wounded. I engaged part of my time in securing from them the ammunition they had not used.

On Cemetery Ridge, Haskell now discovered that a battle raged furiously:[24]

All senses for the time are dead but the one of sight. The roar of the discharges and the yells of the enemy all pass unheeded; but the impassioned soul is all eyes, and sees all things, that the smoke does not hide. How madly the battery men are driving home the double charges of canister in those broad-mouthed Napoleons, whose fire seems almost to reach the enemy. How rapidly these long, bluecoated lines of infantry deliver their file fire down the slope.

But there is no faltering—the men stand nobly to their work. Men are dropping dead or wounded on all sides, by scores and by hundreds, and the poor mutilated creatures, some with an arm dangling, some with a leg broken by a bullet, are limping and crawling towards the rear. They make no sound of complaint or pain, but are as silent as if dumb and mute. . . . The fire all along our crest is terrific, and it is a wonder how anything human could have stood before it, and yet the madness of the enemy drove them on, clear up to the muzzle of the guns, clear up to the lines of our infantry—but the lines stood right in their places. Gen. Hancock and his Aides rode up to Gibbon's Division under the smoke. Gen. Gibbon, with myself, was near, and there was a flag dimly visible, coming toward us from the direction of the enemy.

"Here, what are these men falling back for?" said Hancock.

The flag was no more than fifty yards away, but it was the head of

a Rebel column, which at once opened fire with a volley. . . . The
1st Minn. . . . the less than three hundred that are left out of fifteen
hundred that it has had, swings around upon the enemy, gives them a
volley in their faces, and advances upon them with the bayonet. . . .

Such fighting as this cannot last long. It is now near sundown, and
the battle has gone on wonderfully long already. But if you will stop to
notice it, a change has occurred. The Rebel cry has ceased, and the
men of the Union begin to shout there, under the smoke, and their lines
to advance. See, the Rebels are breaking! They are in confusion in all
our front! The wave has rolled upon the rock, and the rock has smashed
it. Let us shout, too!

First upon their extreme left the Rebels broke, where they had almost pierced our lines; thence the repulse extended rapidly to their
right. They hung longest about Round Top . . . but in a space of time
incredibly short, after they first gave signs of weakness, the whole force
of the Rebel assault along the whole line, in spite of waving red flags,
and yells, and the entreaties of officers, and the pride of the chivalry,
fled like chaff before the whirlwind, back down the slope, over the
valley, across the Emmitsburg Road, shattered, without organization
in utter confusion, fugitive into the woods, and victory was with the
arms of the Republic.

v

*Fields beautiful this morning and desolate now—in the last glimmer-
ing light of that second of July Haskell noted the "haversacks, yawning
with the rations the owners will never call for; canteens of cedar of
the Rebel men of Jackson, and of cloth-covered tin of the men of the
Union; blankets and trousers, and coats and caps, and some are blue
and some are gray; muskets and ramrods, and bayonets, and swords,
and scabbards and belts, some bent and cut by the shot or shell;
broken wheels, exploded caissons, and limber-boxes, and dismantled
guns, and all of these are sprinkled with blood; horses, some dead, a
mangled heap of carnage, some alive, with a leg shot clear off, or other
frightful wounds, appealing to you with almost more than brute gaze
as you pass; and last, but not least numerous, many thousands of men
. . . sleeping the last sleep." The wounded Sickles ordered a special
casket made for his amputated leg so that he could carry it with pride
to Washington; and General Birney, who took over his command,
whispered to a lieutenant, "I wish I were already dead!" Sallie Broadhead could not sleep; she washed a few pieces for her child and fretted*

*over rumors that the Rebels would shell the town in the morning. Billy
Bayly was tempted to steal the scabbards of two officers who slept at
the farm, but then "feared for the rest of the family."*

*For Meade it had been a long day. Earlier to Colonel Thomas Raf-
ferty, who fought under Sickles, Meade had seemed "utterly worn out
and hollow-eyed. Anxiety and want of sleep were evidently telling on
him." Later, when a shell frightened his horse, Meade had clung to the
runaway, and, in the testimony of Henry Tremain of Sickles' staff,
"was apparently ingloriously and temporarily carried from the front
at the formal opening of the furious engagement of July 2, 1863." But
now that day had ended, at least in a draw for Meade, and he called
his generals to a council of war. Haskell's portrait of Meade, with his
Romanish face, large nose, white forehead and wide, bespectacled
eyes, was sympathetic; "His fibres are all of the long and sinewy kind."
Yet for General John Gibbon the meeting produced an uneasy mood:*[25]

I had never been a member of a council of war before (nor have I
since) and did not feel very confident that I was properly a member of
this one; but I was engaged in the discussion and found myself (Warren being asleep) the junior member in it. By the customs of war the
junior member votes first, as on courts-martial; and when Butterfield
read off his question, the substance of which was: "Should the army
remain in its present position or take up some other?" he addressed
himself first to me. To say "Stay and fight" would be to ignore the objections made by General Newton [an officer of engineers, who had
argued "this was no place to fight a battle"], and I therefore answered
somewhat in this way: "Remain here, and make such correction in our
position as may be deemed necessary, but take no step which even
looks like retreat." The question was put to each member and his answer taken down, and when it came to Newton who was first in rank, he
voted pretty much the same way I did, and we had some playful sparring as to whether he agreed with me or I with him; the rest voted to
remain.

The next question put by Butterfield was: "Should the army attack
or await the attack of the enemy?" I voted not to attack, and all the
others voted substantially the same way; and on the third question,
"How long shall we wait?" I voted "Until Lee moves." The answer to
this last question showed the only material variation in the opinion of
the members.

When the meeting was over, General Meade said, quietly but decidedly, "Such then is the decision" and certainly he said nothing which produced a doubt in my mind as to his being in accord with the members of the council.

The night, sultry and starless, stretched on; the slopes between the contending armies flickered with the twinkling lanterns of the litter-bearers. Then daylight—the work of the ambulance corps has been suspended—and General George Pickett tries to explain what this day must mean to him in a letter to his wife:[26]

. . . A summons came from Old Peter, and I immediately rode to the top of the ridge where he and Marse Robert were making a reconnaissance of Meade's position. "Great God!" said Old Peter as I came up. "Look, General Lee, at the insurmountable difficulties between our line and that of the Yankees—the steep hills, the tiers of artillery, the fences, the heavy skirmish line—and then we'll have to fight our infantry against their batteries. Look at the ground we'll have to charge over, nearly a mile of that open ground there under the rain of their canister and shrapnel."

"The enemy is there, General Longstreet, and I am going to strike him," said Marse Robert in his firm, quiet, determined voice.

About 8 o'clock I rode with them along our line of prostrate infantry. They had been told to lie down to prevent attracting attention, and though they had been forbidden to cheer they voluntarily arose and lifted in reverential adoration their caps to our beloved commander as we rode slowly along. Oh, the responsibility for the lives of such men as these! Well, my darling, their fate and that of our beloved Southland will be settled ere your glorious brown eyes rest on these scraps of penciled paper—your Soldier's last letter, perhaps. . . .

I closed my letter to you a little before three o'clock and rode up to Old Peter for orders. I found him like a great lion at bay. I have never seen him so grave and troubled. For several minutes after I had saluted him he looked at me without speaking. Then in an agonized voice, the reserve all gone, he said:

"Pickett, I am being crucified at the thought of the sacrifice of life which this attack will make. I have instructed Alexander to watch the effect of our fire upon the enemy, and when it begins to tell he must take the responsibility and give you your orders, for I can't."

While he was yet speaking a note was brought to me from Alexander. After reading it I handed it to him, asking if I should obey and go forward. He looked at me for a moment, then held out his hand. Presently, clasping his other hand over mine without speaking he bowed his head upon his breast. I shall never forget the look in his face nor the clasp of his hand when I said:—"Then, General, I shall lead my Division on.". . .

From the start the day went badly for Lee. Ewell, who was to open with an assault on Culp's Hill in co-ordination with Longstreet's attack, received too late an order to delay his action. Ewell fought with spirit, yet his failure was complete. Stuart, who finally had reached Gettysburg the night before, was expected to get behind the Union lines and disrupt their concentration but the Yankee cavalry under Alfred Pleasonton had been waiting for Stuart and handled him roughly. Meanwhile Pickett's boys moved up—with them, Private John Dooley:[27]

How long we take to gain our position, what delays, what suspense! We are soon passing over the battlefield of yesterday, and the details of burying parties are digging graves to receive the freshly fallen comrades, and, in many instances, they have only the ghastly and mangled remnants of their gallant friends to deposit in these hastily dug pits. I press very close to a headless body; the boy's head being torn off by a shell is lying around in bloody fragments on the ground.

A little further we take temporary position in the hollow of a field. Before us is a rising slope which hides the Yankee position from view. To the right of our front some quarter of a mile is a brick house near which one of our batteries now and then opens on the enemy who are generally ready to respond to the harsh greeting. Around us are some trees with very small green apples; and while we are resting here we amuse ourselves by pelting each other with green apples.

Even the debonair Colonel Freemantle was nonplused to discover that Longstreet, having his deployments completed by noon, "then dismounted and went to sleep for a short time." Over on Cemetery Ridge —across those fateful 1,400 yards, where Pickett has been ordered to charge—Haskell looked at the men dozing in the heat and lolling upon the ground: "I yawned and looked at my watch. It was five minutes before one o'clock." Then Lee was ready—all along his line the guns opened, outdoing anything at Second Bull Run, at Antietam, at Fredericksburg. In Haskell's judgment:[28]

A hundred and twenty-five rebel guns, we estimate, are now active, firing twenty-four pound, twenty, twelve, and ten pound projectiles, solid shot and shells, spherical, conical, spiral. The enemy's fire is chiefly concentrated upon the position of the Second Corps. From the Cemetery to Round Top, with over a hundred guns, and to all parts of the enemy's line, our batteries reply . . .

Who can describe such a conflict as is raging around us? To say that it was like a summer storm, with the crash of thunder, the glare of lightning, the shrieking of the wind, and the clatter of hailstones, would be weak. The thunder and lightning of these two hundred and fifty guns and their shells, whose smoke darkens the sky, are incessant, all pervading, in the air above our heads, on the ground at our feet, remote, near, deafening, ear-piercing, astounding; and these hailstones are massy iron, charged with exploding fire. And there is little of human interest in a storm; it is an absorbing element of this. . . . These guns are great infuriate demons, not of the earth, whose mouths blaze with smoky tongues of living fire, and whose murky breath, sulphur-laden, rolls around them and along the ground, the smoke of Hades. These grimy men, rushing, shouting, their souls in frenzy, plying the dusky globes and the igniting spark, are in their league, and but their willing ministers.

. . . The projectiles shriek long and sharp. They hiss, they scream, they growl, they sputter; all sounds of life and rage; and each has its different note, and all are discordant. . . . We see the solid shot strike axle, or pole, or wheel, and the tough iron and heart of oak snap and fly like straws. The great oaks there by Woodruff's guns heave down their massy branches with a crash, as if the lightning smote them. The shells swoop down among the battery horses standing there apart. A half a dozen horses start, they tumble, their legs stiffen, their vitals and blood smear the ground. And these shot and shells have no respect for men either. We see the poor fellows hobbling back from the crest, or unable to do so, pale and weak, lying on the ground with the mangled stump of an arm or leg, dripping their life-blood away; or with a cheek torn open, or a shoulder mashed. And many, alas! hear not the roar as they stretch upon the ground with upturned faces and open eyes, though a shell should burst at their very ears. Their ears and their bodies this instant are only mud. We saw them but a moment since there among the flame, with brawny arms and muscles of iron wielding the rammer and pushing home the cannon's plethoric load.

A shell tears off a man's knapsack but does not tear his coat. Like a
pagan worshiper, a man sits with his head bowed to a stone; a shell
smashes the stone into a thousand fragments, but does not touch the
man. These are freak incidents. Haskell watches the shells bursting
in the air:

. . . Their flash was a bright gleam of lightning radiating from a
point, giving place in the thousandth part of a second to a small, white,
puffy cloud, like a fleece of the lightest, whitest wool. These clouds
were very numerous. We could not often see the shell before it burst;
but sometimes, as we faced towards the enemy, and looked above our
heads, the approach would be heralded by a prolonged hiss, which always seemed to me to be a line of something tangible, terminating in
a black globe, distinct to the eye, as the sound had been to the ear. The
shell would seem to stop, and hang suspended in the air an instant,
and then vanish in fire and smoke and noise.

VI

Stretched flat on the ground, hands pointed toward the firing, Captain
W. W. Wood waited with the men in Pickett's division. Not a breath of
air stirred; in Wood's company of fifty men, the shells had killed four
and wounded fifteen; all around heads of clover had been clipped off.
Then the guns both North and South slackened their fire; soon a silence
as oppressive as the heat crept over the field. Wood scrambled up and
called his men into line:[29]

The order to go forward was given and obeyed with alacrity and
cheerfulness, for we believed that the battle was practically over, and
we had nothing to do but march unopposed to Cemetery Heights and
occupy them. The ascent of the crest of the hill, which had hitherto
concealed us from the enemy's view, was made speedily and in good
order. While making the ascent it was seen that the supports to our
left and right flanks were not coming forward, as we had been told
they would. Mounted officers were dashing frantically up and down
their line, apparently endeavoring to get them to move forward, but we
could see that they could not move. Their failure to support us was
discouraging, but did not dishearten us. Some of our men cursed them
for being cowards but still our charge was kept up and no man fell out.

Soon we were past the crest of the hill and out of sight of them. Before us stood Cemetery Heights, of which we could get glimpses

through rifts in the clouds of powder-smoke. We could not see whether or not there were troops there to defend them against us.

Somewhere further on, perhaps a hundred and fifty yards beyond the crest of the hill we had just passed, a post-and-rail fence some five feet high was encountered. This fence was quickly mounted . . . a shot, fired from somewhere to our left, struck the center company of my regiment, and . . . the smoke now lifted from our front and there, right before us stood Cemetery Heights in awful grandeur. At their base was a double line of Federal infantry and several pieces of artillery planted behind stone walls, and infantry supports were hurriedly coming up. We fully realized that Pickett's three little brigades, already greatly reduced by heavy casualties, were making alone and without possibility of succor, a desperate charge against the whole power of the Federal army.

Haskell, watching, almost unable to believe, saw "an overwhelming restless tide of an ocean of armed men sweeping upon us":[30]

. . . More than half a mile their front extends; more than a thousand yards the dull gray masses deploy, man touching man, rank pressing rank, and line supporting line. The red flags wave, their horsemen gallop up and down; the arms of eighteen thousand men, barrel and bayonet, gleam in the sun, a sloping forest of flashing steel. Right on they move, as with one soul, in perfect order without impediment of ditch, or wall or stream, over ridge and slope, through orchard and meadow, and cornfield, magnificent, grim, irresistible.

All was orderly still upon our crest; no noise and no confusion. . . . The click of the locks as each man raised the hammer to feel with his fingers that the cap was on the nipple; the sharp jar as a musket touched a stone upon the wall when thrust in aiming over it, and the clicking of the iron axles as the guns were rolled up by hand a little further to the front, were quite all the sounds that could be heard. Cap-boxes were slid around to the front of the body; cartridge boxes opened, officers opened their pistol-holsters. Such preparations, little more was needed. . . .

Doggedly up those slopes toward the waiting Yankees marched Private John Dooley:[31]

. . . Directly in front of us, breathing flame in our very faces, the long range of guns which must be taken thunder on our quivering

melting ranks. . . . The line becomes unsteady because at every step
a gap must be closed and thus from left to right much ground is
lost. . . . Capt. Hallinan has fallen and I take his place. So many
men have fallen now that I find myself within a few yards of my old
Captain. His men are pressing mine out of place. I ask him to give way
a little to the left, and scarcely has he done so, than he leaps into the air,
falling prostrate. . . . Our men are falling faster now, for the deadly
musket is at work. Volley after volley of crushing musket balls sweeps
through the lines and mows us down like wheat before the scythe.

On! men, on! Thirty yards more . . . but who can stand such a
storm of hissing lead and iron? . . . Just here—from right to left the
remnants of our braves pour in their long reserved fire; until now no
shot has been fired, no shout of triumph has been raised; but as the
cloud of smoke rises over the heads of the advancing divisions the
well-known Southern battle cry which marked the victory gained or
nearly gained bursts wildly over the blood stained field and *all that line
of guns is ours.*

Shot through both thighs, I fall.

*Haskell couldn't believe it. "Were my senses mad?" he wondered.
Yet:*[32]

. . . The larger portion of Webb's brigade—my God, it was true—
there by the group of trees and the angles of the wall, was breaking
from the cover of their works, and, without orders or reason, with no
hand lifted to check them, was falling back, a fear-stricken flock of
confusion! * The fate of Gettysburg hung upon a spider's single thread!

A great magnificent passion came on me at the instant, not one that
overpowers and confounds, but one that blanches the face and sublimes
every sense and faculty. . . . I ordered these men to "halt," and
"face about," and "fire," and they heard my voice and gathered my
meaning, and obeyed my commands. On some unpatriotic backs of
those not quick of comprehension, the flat of my sabre fell not lightly,
and, at its touch their love of country returned, and with a look at me as
if I were the destroying angel, as I might have become theirs, they
again faced the enemy. . . . This portion of the wall was lost to us,

* General Webb insisted: "What Haskell wrote, he wrote in ignorance." Bruce
Catton, editing a modern edition of Haskell's narrative, believes that Webb's
men were overpowered rather than routed.

and the enemy had gained the cover of the reverse side, where he now stormed with fire.

But Webb's men, with their bodies in part protected by the abruptness of the crest, now sent back in the enemies' faces as fierce a storm. Some scores of venturesome Rebels, that in their first push at the wall had dared to cross at the further angle, and those that had desecrated Cushing's guns, were promptly shot down, and speedy death meet him who should raise his body to cross it again. At this point little could be seen of the enemy, by reason of his cover and the smoke, except the flash of his muskets and his waving flags.

These red flags were accumulating at the wall every moment, and they maddened us as the same color does the bull. Webb's men are falling fast, and he is among them to direct and encourage; but, however well they may now do, with that walled enemy in front, with more than a dozen flags to Webb's three, it soon becomes apparent that in not many minutes they will be overpowered, or that there will be none alive for the enemy to overpower.

Webb has but three regiments, all small, the 69th, 71st and 72nd Pennsylvania . . . and he must have assistance, or this crest will be lost. Oh, where is Gibbon? where is Hancock?—some general—anybody with the power and the will to support that wasting, melting line? No general came, and no succor! I thought of Hayes upon the right, but from the smoke and war along his front, it was evident that he had enough upon his hands, if he stayed the in-rolling tide of the Rebels there. Doubleday upon the left was too far off and too slow. . . . As a last resort I had resolved to see if Hall and Harrow could not send some of their commands to reinforce Webb. . . .

Hall agreed to send his brigade, and five new colors joined Webb's embattled three. Webb had been pressed back so that he was not far from Hall's right; still, Haskell recounted:

The movement, as it did, attracting the enemy's fire, and executed in haste, as it must be, was difficult; but in reasonable time, and in order that is serviceable, if not regular, Hall's men are fighting gallantly side by side with Webb's before the all important point. I did not stop to see all this movement of Hall's, but from him I went at once further to the left, to the 1st brigade. . . . All men that I could find I took over to the right at the *double quick.*

As we were moving to, and near the other brigade of the division, from my position on horseback I could see that the enemy's right, under Hall's fire, was beginning to stagger and to break.

"See," I said to the men, "See the *chivalry!* See the gray-backs run!"

The men saw, and as they swept to their places by the side of Hall and opened fire, they roared, and this in a manner that said more plainly than words—for the deaf could have seen it in their faces, and the blind could have heard it in their voices—*the crest is safe!*

In Haskell's vivid description, "Now it was as if a new battle, deadlier, stormier than before, had sprung from the body of the old—a young Phoenix of combat, whose eyes stream lightning, shaking his arrowy wings over the yet glowing ashes of his progenitor." Wounded on the field thirty yards from the wall, Private Dooley knew—"That huzza never broke from southern throats. Oh God!" Lee saw them coming back—broken, frightened, bleeding, crippled, exhausted, crying—and more like a father than a general said gently, "Don't be discouraged. It was my fault this time." Colonel Freemantle told Longstreet, "I wouldn't have missed this for anything," and Old Pete answered, "I would have liked to have missed it very much." This was the end, yet in town Sallie Broadhead didn't know:[33]

The time we sat in the cellar seemed long, listening to the terrific sound of the strife; more terrible never greeted human ears. We knew that with every explosion, and the scream of each shell, human beings were hurried through excruciating pain into another world, and that many more were torn, and mangled, and lying in torment worse than death, and no one able to extend relief. The thought made me very sad, and feel that, if it was God's will, I would rather be taken away than remain to see the misery that would follow. Some thought this afternoon would never come to a close.

We knew that the Rebels were putting forth all their might, and it was a dreadful thought that they might succeed.

Who is victorious, or with whom the advantage rests, no one here can tell. It would ease the horror if we knew our arms were successful. Some think the Rebels were defeated, as there has been no boasting as on yesterday, and they look uneasy and by no means exultant. I hope they are correct, but I fear we are too hopeful. We shall see tomorrow. It will be the Fourth of July, and the Rebels have promised us a glorious day. If it only ends the battle and drives them off it will be glorious.

Tillie Alleman, who had taken refuge on a farm, returned to the Weikert home:[34]

I fairly shrank back aghast at the awful sight presented. The approaches were crowded with wounded, dying and dead. The air was filled with moanings, and groanings. As we passed on toward the house, we were compelled to pick our steps in order that we might not tread on the prostrate bodies. . . .

Amputating benches had been placed about the house. I must have become inured to seeing the terrors of battle, else I could hardly have gazed upon the scenes now presented. I was looking out one of the windows facing the front yard. Near the basement door, and directly under the window I was at, stood one of these benches. I saw them lifting the poor men upon it, then the surgeons cutting and sawing off legs, then again probing and picking bullets from the flesh.

Some of the soldiers fairly begged to be taken next, so great was their suffering, so anxious were they to obtain relief.

I saw the surgeons hastily put a cattle horn over the mouths of the wounded ones, after they were placed upon the bench. At first I did not understand the meaning of this, but upon inquiry, soon learned that that was their mode of administering chloroform, in order to produce unconsciousness. But the effect in some instances was not produced; for I saw the wounded throwing themselves wildly about, and shrieking with pain while the operation was going on.

To the south of the house, and just outside of the yard, I noticed a pile of limbs higher than the fence. It was a ghastly sight! Gazing upon these, too often the trophies of the amputating bench, I could have no other feeling, than that the whole scene was one of cruel butchery.

That night General Pickett wrote his wife another letter:[35]

My brave boys were full of hope and confident of victory as I led them forth, forming them in column of attack, and though officers and men alike knew what was before them—knew the odds against them— they eagerly offered up their lives on the altar of duty, having absolute faith in their ultimate success. Over on Cemetery Ridge the Federals beheld a scene never before witnessed on this continent—a scene which has never previously been enacted and can never take place again—an army forming in line of battle in full view, under their very eyes— charging across a space nearly a mile in length over fields of waving

grain and anon of stubble and then a smooth expanse—moving with
the steadiness of a dress parade, the pride and glory soon to be crushed
by an overwhelming heartbreak. . . .

Well, it is all over now. The battle is lost, and many of us are prisoners, many are dead, many wounded, bleeding and dying. Your Soldier
lives and mourns and, but for you, my darling, he would rather, a
million times rather, be back there with his dead, to sleep for all time in
an unknown grave.

After three days young Billy Bayly had learned the Rebel way:[36]

The tempers of our guests changed materially; while they insisted
that the Yanks were being whipped and driven from their defensive
position we knew to the contrary and told them so. Then the drift of the
wagon trains, stragglers and camp followers in general was back in the
direction whence they came, and inquiries as to the most direct route
to Chambersburg and Hagerstown highways were of promising por-
tent.

*History, coming to Gettysburg quite by accident, moved on. Bret Harte
wrote:*

> So raged the battle. You know the rest:
> How the rebels, beaten and backward pressed,
> Broke at the final charge and ran.
> At which John Burns—a practical man—
> Shouldered his rifle, unbent his brows,
> And then went back to his bees and cows.

VII

*Lee, who had invaded Pennsylvania to counterbalance Grant's invasion
of Mississippi, had failed. What now in Vicksburg? On that third of
July, as Pickett's shattered forces reeled back from their futile charge
at Gettysburg, Grant sent a message to Pemberton:*[37]

Your note of this date is just received, proposing an armistice for
several hours, for the purpose of arranging terms of capitulation
through commissioners to be appointed, etc. The useless effusion of
blood you propose stopping by this course can be ended at any time you
may choose, by the unconditional surrender of the city and garrison.

Men who have shown so much endurance and courage as those now in Vicksburg, will always challenge the respect of an adversary, and I can assure you will be treated with all the respect due to prisoners of war. I do not favor the proposition of appointing commissioners to arrange the terms of capitulation, because I have no terms other than those indicated above.

At three o'clock that afternoon occurred a historic meeting:

. . . Pemberton appeared at the point suggested in my verbal message, accompanied by the same officers who had borne his letter of the morning. Generals Ord, McPherson, Logan and A. J. Smith, and several officers of my staff, accompanied me. Our place of meeting was on a hillside within a few hundred feet of the rebel lines. Near by stood a stunted oak-tree, which was made historical by the event. It was but a short time before the last vestige of its body, root and limb had disappeared, the fragments taken as trophies. Since then the same tree has furnished as many cords of wood, in the shape of trophies, as "The True Cross."

Pemberton and I had served in the same division during part of the Mexican War. I knew him very well therefore, and greeted him as an old acquaintance. He soon asked what terms I proposed to give his army if it surrendered. My answer was the same as proposed in my reply to his letter. Pemberton then said, rather snappishly, "The conference might as well end," and turned abruptly as if to leave. I said, "Very well." General Bowen, I saw, was very anxious that the surrender should be consummated. His manner and remarks while Pemberton and I were talking, showed this. He now proposed that he and one of our generals should have a conference. I had no objection to this, as nothing could be made binding upon me that they might propose. Smith and Bowen accordingly had a conference, during which Pemberton and I, moving a short distance away towards the enemy's lines were in conversation. After awhile Bowen suggested that the Confederate army should be allowed to march out with the honors of war, carrying their small arms and field artillery. This was promptly and unceremoniously rejected. The interview here ended, I agreeing, however, to send a letter giving final terms by ten o'clock that night.

Grant amended his terms in the end, allowing side arms and clothing to officers, one horse each to field, staff and cavalry officers, and to "the rank and file . . . all their clothing, but no other property." Nor was his change of heart a device for saving Pemberton's face—"Had I insisted upon an unconditional surrender there would have been over thirty thousand men to transport to Cairo very much to the inconvenience of the army on the Mississippi." Pemberton "promptly accepted these terms," and on July 4 Grant and his troops had the last laugh on an old tormentor:

During the siege there had been a good deal of friendly sparring between the soldiers of the two armies, on picket and where the lines were close together. All rebels were known as "Johnnies," all Union troops as "Yanks." Often "Johnny" would call: "Well, Yank, when are you coming into town?" The reply was sometimes: "We propose to celebrate the 4th of July there." Sometimes it would be: "We always treat our prisoners with kindness and do not want to hurt them"; or, "We are holding you as prisoners of war while you are feeding yourselves." The garrison, from the commanding general down, undoubtedly expected an assault on the fourth. They knew from the temper of their men it would be successful when made; and that would be a greater humiliation than to surrender. Besides it would be attended with severe loss to them.

The Vicksburg paper, which we received regularly through the courtesy of the rebel pickets, said prior to the fourth, in speaking of the "Yankee" boast that they would take dinner in Vicksburg that day, that the best receipt for cooking a rabbit was "First ketch your rabbit.". . . The last number was issued on the fourth and announced that we had "caught our rabbit." *

---

* July 3, 1863—Lee defeated at Gettysburg with 3,903 dead, 18,735 wounded and 5,425 missing against Union losses of 3,155 dead, 14,529 wounded and 5,365 missing.

July 4, 1863—Vicksburg surrendered to Grant along with 29,491 prisoners of war.

THE ROCK OF CHICKAMAUGA

E ARLY IN THE YEAR 1863 the editors of *Harper's Weekly* asked a question which had been worrying all thoughtful Northerners —"Have We a General Among Us?" The lead editorial for January 17 began: "They say at Washington that we have some thirty-eight to forty Major-Generals, and nearly three hundred Brigadiers; and now the question is, have we one man who can fairly be called a first-class General in the proper meaning of the term?"

One by one the editors ticked them off. McDowell: "respectable . . . but no claim to the first place." McClellan: "prone rather to exaggerate than to underrate an enemy's strength; a man . . . of more science than genius." Burnside: "place . . . undetermined." Grant: will his record at Shiloh "bear the test of inquiry"? Sherman: "a capable officer and a far-seeing man." And so on through Samuel R. Curtis, James G. Blunt and Nathaniel P. Banks.

I

Only one officer drew unqualified praise:[1]

At this present moment . . . the most promising of our soldiers is William S. Rosecrans. This officer was selected by General McClellan at the outbreak of the war, and served under him in Western Virginia. He, like McClellan, had served in the army, resigned, and engaged in scientific and business pursuits. When McClellan was ordered to Washington Rosecrans succeeded him, and thoroughly accomplished his work. He drove the rebels out of Western Virginia, and enabled the people of that State to organize a State government in peace. . . . After a period of idleness, he was sent to Corinth, where he spent some weeks in necessary preparations, knowing that the enemy must attack him if he remained still. The attack came, and resulted not only in the repulse, but in the destruction of the rebel army,* and enabled General Grant to move forward to Oxford. Promoted then to the command of the Army of the Ohio, he spent six weeks at Nashville in concentrating his forces, and accumulating equipments and supplies for the campaign. He moved on 29th December, and after five days' desperate fighting, completely defeated, and "drove" the rebel army under Bragg, which, according to Richmond papers, was "to repossess Nashville within a week."

As a strategist Rosecrans has proved himself second to none. In Western Virginia his combinations were most ingenious, and his foresight wonderful. So at Corinth, where he alone of his officers foresaw the battle, and how it would end. His wonderful mathematical ability, which was remarked at West Point, stood him in good stead. At Murfreesboro he seems to have developed personal gallantry of the Grant order. Twice, at least, in the course of those five days' battles, he saved the day, and repelled the enemy, by galloping into the thick of the fight, and reanimating his troops by the spectacle of his courage. He is a man of enthusiasm, as well as a man of calculation: when his army fights, he is with them. If he pursues the enemy as briskly as he attacked them, none of our Generals will stand higher than Rosecrans.

II

But Rosecrans did not "pursue the enemy." Instead, he held the battered Army of the Cumberland in its camps at Murfreesboro. Against the proddings of the Administration he advanced a succession of arguments—he needed more supplies and forage, more cavalry, more repeating rifles for his mounted troops. Spring came, with green grass for horses and soft winds that dried up the roads; still the Federal commander waited.

Braxton Bragg, commanding the Confederate Army of Tennessee, was equally reluctant to move. Encamped at Tullahoma and Shelbyville, some thirty-five miles south of the Federal position, Bragg trained

* The Battle of Corinth, October 3–4, 1862, was a Confederate defeat, but Van Dorn's army was not demolished. Losses are given as follows: Union, 2,520; Confederate, 4,838.

and drilled his men—and at the same time smarted under the distrust
of subordinates who, he well knew, dreaded another battle under his
command.

By late June 1863, Rosecrans was at last ready. He planned to
threaten Bragg's position at Shelbyville, which Rosecrans knew to be
strongly fortified, and then slip around the right of the Confederate
army—a move which would force Bragg either to fight on ground se-
lected by the enemy, or to retreat.

Major James A. Connolly of the 123rd Illinois Regiment of Mounted
Infantry, one of the four regiments that led the advance, described the
beginning of the campaign:[2]

On the morning of June 24th, at 3 o'clock, we left camp 5 miles north
of Murfreesboro, and started to the "front," in advance of everything.
As we passed through the camps in Murfreesboro, the rattle of drums,
sounding of bugles, and clatter of wagons, told us plainly that the whole
army was to follow in our wake, and we knew full well, from the direction we were taking, that a few hours' march would bring the brigade to some of the strongholds of the enemy, so there was silence in
the column as we moved along through the mud, and every ear was
strained to catch the sound of the first gun of our advance guard that
would tell us of the presence of the enemy.

The report of the first gun echoed through the hills at noon, when the
123rd Illinois found itself a dozen miles southeast of Murfreesboro.
Connolly told the story of a sharp engagement:

We pushed ahead rapidly, for we were nearing the formidable
"Hoover's Gap," which it was supposed would cost a great many lives
to pass through, and our brigade commander determined to surprise
the enemy if possible, by a rapid march, and make a bold dash to pass
through the "Gap" and hold it with our brigade alone until the rest of
the army could get up. We soon came into the camp of a regiment of
cavalry which was so much surprised by our sudden appearance that
they scattered through the woods and over the hills in every direction,
every fellow for himself, and all making the best time they could bare-
back, on foot and every other way, leaving all their tents, wagons,
baggage, commissary stores and indeed everything in our hands, but
we didn't stop for anything, on we pushed, our boys, with their Spencer
rifles, keeping up a continual popping in front. Soon we reached the
celebrated "Gap" on the run.

This "Gap" is formed by a range of hills that run westwardly from the Cumberland Mountains, and the pike runs for about two miles through between these hills; the valley is barely wide enough to admit the passage of two wagons side by side, and the hills upon either side command the valley completely; as we swept through the valley with our 1,500 horsemen on a gallop we noticed the lines of entrenchments crowning the hills, but they were deserted; the enemy was surprised and flying before us, so we pushed onward until we passed entirely through the "Gap," when a puff of white smoke from a hill about half a mile in front of us, then a dull heavy roar, then a shrieking of a shell told us we could advance no further as we had reached their infantry and artillery force. But we had done enough, had advanced 6 miles further than ordered or expected possible, and had taken a point which it was expected would require a large part of the army to take; but the serious question with us now was: "Could we alone hold it in the presence of superior force?" We were at least 12 miles in advance of our army, and from prisoners we learned that we were confronted with 4 brigades of infantry and 4 batteries. . . .

As soon as the enemy opened on us with their artillery we dismounted and formed line of battle on a hill just at the south entrance to the "Gap," and our battery of light artillery was opened on them, a courier was dispatched to the rear to hurry up reinforcements, our horses were sent back some distance out of the way of bursting shells, our regiment was assigned to support the battery, the other three regiments were properly disposed, and not a moment too soon, for these preparations were scarcely completed when the enemy opened on us a terrific fire of shot and shell from five different points, and their masses of infantry, with flags flying, moved out of the woods on our right in splendid style; there were three or four times our number already in sight and still others came pouring out of the woods beyond. Our regiment lay on the hill side in mud and water, the rain pouring down in torrents, while each shell screamed so close to us as to make it seem that the next would tear us to pieces.

Presently the enemy got near enough to us to make a charge on our battery, and on they came; our men are on their feet in an instant and a terrible fire from the "Spencers" * causes the advancing regiment to

---

* The Spencer repeating rifle—which Lincoln had tested in person, and for which he had suggested an improved sight—began to find its way westward more abundantly after its young inventor, Christopher Spencer, dined in April 1863 with Grant. Morgan, the Rebel raider, had been an enthusiastic champion of the Spencer even earlier.

reel and its colors fall to the ground, but in an instant their colors are up again and on they come, thinking to reach the battery before our guns can be reloaded, but they "reckoned without their host," they didn't know we had the "Spencers," and their charging yell was answered by another terrible volley, and another and another without cessation, until the poor regiment was literally cut to pieces, and but few men of that 20th Tennessee that attempted the charge will ever charge again. During all the rest of the fight at "Hoover's Gap" they never again attempted to take that battery. After the charge they moved four regiments around to our right and attempted to get in our rear, but they were met by two of our regiments posted in the woods, and in five minutes were driven back in the greatest disorder, with a loss of 250 killed and wounded. . . .

We held our ground with continual fighting until 7 o'clock in the evening, when we discovered a battery coming up to our support as fast as the horses could run, and such a cheer as was sent up does one good to hear. In a few minutes our new battery was opened and we all felt better. We were nearly exhausted with the rapid march since before daylight in the morning, yet the prospect of assistance nerved the men to maintain the unequal conflict a little longer. About half past seven in the evening along came a weary, jaded regiment of infantry, trying to double quick, but it was all they could do to march at all; we greeted them with such lusty cheers as seemed to inspire them with new vigor, and they were soon in position; then came two more regiments of infantry, weary and footsore, but hurrying the best they could to the dance of death; then just at dark came our Division Commander, with his staff, and riding along our lines gave words of cheer to his brigade that had fought so long and well. In a few minutes up came General Thomas, our corps commander, his grave face beaming with delight as he grasped our brigade commander by the hand and said: "You have saved the lives of a thousand men by your gallant conduct today. I didn't expect to get this Gap for three days."

III

In nine days Rosecrans forced Bragg from his strongly fortified po-sitions in central Tennessee to Chattanooga—and lost fewer than 600 men (killed, wounded, and missing) out of almost 60,000.

Rosecrans' achievement was a masterpiece of both strategy and tactics, yet his success was due in part to the Confederate commander. Bragg had never really intended to fight unless he was attacked behind the breastworks at Shelbyville. Expecting to retreat, but expecting also

*to fight a battle somewhere in the vicinity of Chattanooga, he planned
to draw a part of the Federal army away from his front by permitting
brash John Hunt Morgan, now a brigadier general commanding a
cavalry division, to make a raid into Kentucky.*

*For the last three weeks in June, Morgan lay poised in southern
Kentucky, about seventy-five miles northeast of Nashville, Tennessee.
On July 2, as Bragg was nearing Chattanooga, Morgan, with 2,460 men
and four pieces of artillery, crossed the Cumberland River and headed
north. On the Fourth his troopers ran into a stubborn Federal regiment
stationed at Columbia near the Green River. In half an hour Morgan's
men took a sound licking, drew off, found a ford at some distance from
the town, and swung around it. Next day they had a sharp skirmish at
Lebanon but drove back the Union defenders and captured a large
quantity of rifles, ammunition, and supplies.*

*Bragg had ordered Morgan to confine his operations to Kentucky,
but the Confederate cavalryman had other ideas. Indiana and Ohio
were his real goals. A raid into Kentucky would take some of the
pressure off the retreating Bragg, but it would not help him in the battle
that would soon follow. Morgan reasoned that an invasion of the
North would create panic, and force Rosecrans to send thousands of
troops in pursuit. And what a hell of an adventure it would be!*

*After the skirmish at Lebanon, Morgan raced toward the Ohio River.
On July 8 he reached the town of Brandenburg on the Kentucky side.
An advance party had already captured two river steamers. The Confederates began to embark. A Federal gunboat tried to impede the
crossing but did little damage. By midnight Morgan's two brigades
were across.*

*Morgan headed north toward Corydon, some fifteen miles from the
river. Basil W. Duke, Morgan's brother-in-law who commanded the
Second Kentucky Cavalry, described the invasion of Indiana:*[3]

A "great fear" had fallen upon the inhabitants of that part of the
State of Indiana. They had left their houses, with open doors and un-
locked larders, and had fled to the thickets and "caves of the hills." At
the houses at which I stopped, everything was just in the condition in
which the fugitive owners had left it, an hour or two before. A bright
fire was blazing upon the kitchen hearth, bread half made up was in the
tray, and many indications convinced us that we had interrupted preparations for supper. The chickens were strolling before the door with a
confidence that was touching, but misplaced. General Morgan rode by

soon afterward, and was induced to "stop all night." We completed the preparations, so suddenly abandoned, and made the best show for Indiana hospitality that was possible under the disturbing circumstances.

MORGAN'S RAID

Morgan occupied Corydon on July 9. A local newspaper revealed how Colonel Duke took advantage of Indiana hospitality:

His men commenced pillaging the stores of Douglass, Denbo & Co., and Samuel J. Wright. Mr. W. was not at home, and they took what they pleased without let or hindrance. Mr. Denbo was sent for by Captain Charlton Morgan, the General's brother, and compelled to open his store. Everything in the shape of ready-made clothing, hats, caps, boots, shoes, etc., was taken, Captain Morgan taking a piece of fine gray cassimere, out of which to make a suit for "John." For all these goods, amounting in value to about $3,500, Mr. Denbo received the sum of $140 in Confederate scrip, some of which was dated as late as May, 1863. Mr. Wright's loss was probably somewhat larger than that of Mr. Denbo. The drug store of Dr. Reader, and several other establishments, were also relieved of portions of their contents. The hardware and drug store of Slaughter & Slemmons was saved, and is said to have been guarded, owing to the influence of a relative of Mr. Slaughter in the rebel command.

The store of the late Mr. Vance was spared, on the representation that the proprietor had been buried the day before, and nothing was taken from it.

Upon each of the three flouring-mills in Corydon a levy was made of $1,000, to be paid in consideration of Morgan's refraining to burn them. The chivalry, however, graciously condescended to receive 2,100 in greenbacks in liquidation of their claim upon the mill property.

The rebels paid no attention to the rights of private citizens or families. They robbed Mr. Hisey, Treasurer, of $750 in money; stole all the clothing of Judge F. W. Matthis, except what he had on; stole a pair of fine boots from Mr. P. B. Douglass, and committed numerous other petty thefts of a similar character. They entered private houses with impunity, ate all the victuals the ladies had cooked for the Home Guards, and compelled them to cook more.

Morgan made a feint at Cincinnati, which he had no intention of taking even had he been able, and then headed east. A correspondent of a Cincinnati newspaper recorded the raider's progress:

EAST SYCAMORE, HAMILTON COUNTY, OHIO. . . . On Tuesday, the 14th instant, at early dawn, the inhabitants hereabout were aroused from slumber by the clattering of hoofs upon the stony pike, and the clanking of *stirrups* (I suppose, as I didn't see any sabers or the like). On peeping through the window, I recognized them immediately as secesh, from their hard looks, their clothes of many colors and fashions, and their manner of riding. They did not ride in any kind of order, unless it was *disorder*. As many as could, rode abreast. Some galloped, some trotted, and others allowed their horses to walk slowly while they slept in the saddles. They were not uniformly dressed. Some wore a whole suit of the well-known blue which designates our soldiers; others had part of a suit, but most of them were arrayed in citizens' garb. Some were barefooted, some bareheaded, and one, I noticed, wore a huge green veil . . . Some wore jackets outside of their coats, as though they had dressed in a hurry. . . . Some had ladies' gaiters, dress-patterns, and the like, protruding from their pockets; and one bootless, hatless, shirtless being held his *suspenderless* pants with one hand, while he held the bridle with the other, and heeled his horse to a gallop. . . .

They were evidently very tired and sleepy, and, judging from their questions to each other, "How far do you think the blue-jackets are behind?" I should say as much frightened as we were. "How far is it to Cincinnati?" and "Have you yesterday's paper?" were the principal questions asked. In some houses of this vicinity, they turned over beds, peeped into cellars, cupboards, drawers, closets, and even babies' cradles, in search of arms, ammunition, "greenbacks," and *sich*, while others were not disturbed. They helped themselves very liberally to such eatables as could be found, besides ordering the women to prepare more. Of course, they took horses. They just *gobbled* up everybody's, except—well, perhaps his were lame, blind, or fractious. Generally, they made no distinction between the property of Copperheads and that of "Abolitionists," as they call all unconditional Union men. 'Cause why? They either did not *know* their friends, or else they considered the Northern Butternuts beneath the respect of Southern rebels, horse-thieves, freebooters, guerillas, or whatever else they may call themselves. . . .

Most persons in this part of the world considered discretion the better part of valor, and held their temper until the last invader had vanished. Like a sudden clap of thunder Morgan came among us, and passed off to the east like a meteor, leaving the natives gazing after him in stupefied horror, rubbing their eyes, and wondering whether it was all the dream of a nightmare, or a reality.

On July 19 two Federal forces, numbering 8,000, caught up with Morgan at Buffington on the Ohio River. Seven hundred Confederates were taken prisoner, but Morgan with the remaining 1,200 scurried northward on a hopeless expedition. Six days later all were captured.

Basil W. Duke, historian and apologist of the expedition, called the raid "incomparably the most brilliant of the entire war":[4]

It was not an expedition started from a point impregnably garrisoned, to dash by a well marked path to another point occupied by a friendly army. It differed from even the boldest of Confederate raids, not only in that it was vastly more extended, but also in the nerve with which the great natural obstacles were placed between the little band with which it was undertaken and home, and the unshrinking audacity with which that slight force penetrated into a populous and intensely hostile territory, and confidently exposed itself to such tremendous odds, and such overwhelming disadvantages. Over one hundred thousand men were in arms to catch Morgan (although not all employed at one time and place), and every advantage in the way of transporting troops, obtaining information, and disposing forces to intercept or oppose him, was possessed by his enemy, and yet his wily strategy enabled him to make his way to the river, at the very point where he had contemplated recrossing it when he started from Tennessee; and he was prevented from recrossing and effecting his escape (which would then have been certain) only by the river having risen at a season at which it had not risen for more than twenty years before.

The objects of the raid were accomplished. General Bragg's retreat was unmolested by any flanking forces of the enemy, and I think that military men . . . will pronounce that this expedition delayed for weeks the fall of East Tennessee, and prevented the timely reinforcement of Rosecrans by troops that would otherwise have participated in the battle of Chickamauga. . . .

To have, in our turn, been invaders, to have carried the war north of the Ohio, to have taught the people, who for long months had been pouring invading hosts into the South, something of the agony and terror of invasion—to have made them fly in fear from their homes, although they returned to find those homes not laid in ashes; to have scared them with the sound of hostile bugles, although no signals were sounded for flames and destruction—these luxuries were cheap at almost any price. It would have been an inexpiable shame if, in all the Confederate army, there had been no body of men found to carry the war, however briefly, across the Ohio, and Morgan by this raid saved us, at least, that disgrace.

Three-quarters of a century later Stanley Horn, a Southern historian justly proud of Confederate prowess, made a more realistic comment:[5]

The raid north of the Ohio was a showy affair and struck terror into Hoosier and Buckeye communities, but it was without military significance or possibilities. . . . Before the month was over Morgan and practically all his men had been captured and were locked up in various Northern prisons—Morgan himself and most of his officers in the Ohio State Penitentiary at Columbus. He escaped from prison in late November and made his way back to the Confederacy, but his days of usefulness to the Army of Tennessee were over.

IV

Morgan jabbed at the North. New York City took a belly blow that staggered the Lincoln Administration.

Behind four days of bloody rioting lay a deep, bitter resentment over the draft. The government, nevertheless, drove ahead with its conscription program. The first drawing of names took place on Saturday, July 11. Crowds gathered at the office of the provost marshal, but the people were good-natured, even jocular. Over Sunday their temper changed. As men read their names in the lists of those drawn for service, and realized that they faced three years of hardship and danger, they gave themselves up to excitement and rage.

Monday, July 13, brought the incident that led to the four bloody days. At the draft office of the ninth district, 677 Third Avenue, the drawing was resumed. Reporters for Frank Leslie's Illustrated Newspaper *were on hand:*[6]

A crowd had meanwhile assembled, and towards eleven o'clock, as the name of Z. Shay, 633 West 42 street, was called, a stone was thrown through the window, and the crowd pouring in almost in a moment destroyed the wheel, the papers, books, everything connected with the draft, and everything in the rooms, the officers barely escaping with their lives. . . .

Had it stopped here, the riot might have been regarded as a kind of spontaneous ebullition of excited men; but they proceeded to fire the building, the upper stories of which were occupied by many families, thus perilling hundreds of lives. They then cut the telegraph wires, and when the firemen arrived prevented them from extinguishing the fire. The house, with one on each side, was soon in ruins. The small force of police was powerless, and the only force sent was a squad of 40 soldiers, who were speedily attacked, and, after they had fired a volley of blank cartridges, disarmed and routed, many of them horribly beaten. The police were then attacked and, although they fought well, were similarly treated. . . .

A reporter for Harper's Weekly *captured the terrible immediacy of the riot:*[7]

MASSACRE OF A NEGRO IN CLARKSON STREET

One of the first victims to the insane fury of the rioters was a negro cartman residing in Carmine Street. A mob of men and boys seized this unfortunate man on Monday evening, and having beaten him until he was in a state of insensibility, dragged him to Clarkson Street, and hung him from a branch of one of the trees that shade the sidewalk by St. John's Cemetery. The fiends did not stop here, however. Procuring long sticks, they tied rags and straw to the ends of them, and with these torches they danced round their victim, setting fire to his clothes, and burning him almost to a cinder. The remains of the wretched negro hung there till near daylight on Tuesday morning, when they were removed by the police. This atrocious murder was perpetrated within ten feet of consecrated ground, where the white headstones of the cemetery are seen gleaming through the wooden railing.

THE MURDER OF COLONEL O'BRIEN

As I arrived at the corner of Thirty-fourth Street and Second Avenue, the rioters were dragging the body of a man along the sidewalk with a rope. It was difficult to obtain any information from the bystanders, who were terror-struck by the savage fury of the mob. I ascertained, however, that the body was that of Colonel O'Brien of the Eleventh New York. There was not a policeman or soldier within view of whom inquiry could be made. "What did they kill him for?" I asked a man leaning against a lamp-post. "Bedad I suppose it was to square accounts," replied he. "There was a woman and child kilt there below a while ago by the sojers, and in coorse a sojer had to suffer." The brutal roughs who surrounded the body fired pistols at it occasionally, and pelted it with brickbats and paving-stones. The tenacity of life of this unfortunate victim is said to have been remarkable, and those who entered the yard where the body lay some hours later state that breathing was even then perceptible.

SACKING OF A DRUG-STORE

Sated with blood, the rioters now turned their attention to plunder. A drug-store close by where Colonel O'Brien lay was completely riddled by them, the doors and windows being smashed in with clubs and stones. Women hovered upon the skirts of the crowd, and received the articles as they were thrown or handed from the store. One fellow rushed out with a closely-packed valise, which he opened in the street.

The clothes and other things contained in it were eagerly seized and contended for by boys and women standing around. There were a number of letters in it, and some documents with seals, which were probably of value to the owner; but these were savagely torn and trampled under foot by the disappointed plunderers. A woman sat upon the steps near by, and read out portions of one of the letters amidst the jeers of her ribald companions. Another passed me waving in triumph a large parchment manuscript of many pages.

ATTACK UPON THE CLOTHING-STORE OF MESSRS. BROOKS BROTHERS

From the first of the riot clothing appeared to be a great desideratum among the roughs composing the mob. On Monday evening a large number of marauders paid a visit to the extensive clothing-store of Messrs. Brooks Brothers, at the corner of Catharine and Cherry streets. Here they helped themselves to such articles as they wanted, after which they might be seen dispersing in all directions, laden with their ill-gotten booty.

THE GERMAN TAILORS

Away up in the Avenues the German tailors were sad sufferers, in consequence of the demand for confiscable apparel. I saw an able-bodied ruffian emerging from a tailor's shop with the breast of his shirt crammed full of pieces of dry-goods of all colors. His arms and shoulders were laden with clothing. He had a new soft hat stuck upon the top of his greasy cap, while in one hand he carried a "nest" of hats of assorted sizes, and a bunch of gorgeous, many-colored ties fluttered from his arm as he ran. "Why did they riddle that shop?" I asked of a woman who was standing by. "Sure the owner is a Jarman," was the reply. Here an Irishman of the non-combative type chimed in, saying, "No, it wasn't that at all; it's becase the boys wanted the clothes. But it's a shame to stale them, any how, and no good ever come of the likes." "Begorra that's thrue for you, Frank Tully," remarked his companion; and thereupon they both expressed themselves greatly in favor of virtue, and opposed to the scenes of violence passing around us. On returning down the Avenue, a quarter of a hour later, I recognized the virtuous Frank Tully and his friend, in an alley-way, busily engaged in trying on some new trowsers, which did not look as if they had been just bought and paid for.

A GORILLA AT LARGE

During the entire withdrawal of the police and military from large districts of the city many highway robberies must have been perpetrated. Coming down Third Avenue, I passed a group of young rowdies who were amusing themselves with snapping their pistols. One threw his revolver high into the air, and caught it by the barrel as it came down, bragging at the same time that it was both loaded and cocked. A few steps further on I found myself face to face with a fearful-looking desperado, who came suddenly upon me round a corner.

"Hello me buck!" cried he; "don't be in a hurry, now. Hand over your cane; and fork out all you've got."

Fortunately he was somewhat drunk, and he grasped in his right hand a bundle of "greenbacks," which seemed to embarrass him a little. As he still pressed upon me, however, I turned to the young pistoliers, saying,

"Boys, here's a fellow wants to draft me; are we going to stand that?"

This created a diversion in my favor; and when I saw that the attention of the young rowdies was attracted to the money in the desperado's hand I improved the opportunity and proceeded up a by-street, at an accelerated pace. Had I struck him with my stick, which was my first impulse, I should most assuredly have fallen a victim to the blind fury of the young pistoliers. Probably the right owner of the "greenbacks" fared much worse than I did, independent of the loss of his money.

On Tuesday, July 14, a larger, bolder mob continued the depredations of the day before. Governor Seymour hurried to the city from Long Branch, New Jersey, and from the steps of the City Hall pleaded with the crowd to disperse. At the same time, troops were ordered in—the garrisons of the forts in the harbor, a company from West Point. The police, infuriated, shot to kill. On Wednesday the suspension of the draft was announced, and New York militia regiments from the Army of the Potomac began to patrol the streets. Chaos came to an end; streetcars and omnibuses covered their routes, men returned to work. The riot had taken many lives—the estimate in killed and wounded was 1,000—and had damaged property to the extent of $1,500,000.

To what end? James Ford Rhodes answered the question:[8]

The draft was only temporarily interrupted. Strenuous precautions were taken to insure order during its continuance. Ten thousand infantry and three batteries of artillery—"picked troops including the regulars"—were sent to New York City from the Army of the Potomac; the First Division of the New York State National Guard was ordered upon duty; and the governor by proclamation counselled and admonished the citizens to submit to the law of Congress. August 19 the draft was resumed and proceeded with entire peacefulness. It went on generally throughout the country, and while it did not actually furnish many soldiers to the army, owing to the numerous exemptions under the statute and the large number of those drafted who paid the commutation money, it stimulated enlistments by inducing States, counties, cities, and towns to add to the government bounty other bounties sufficient to prevail upon men to volunteer and fill their respective quotas.

V

A month later the North suffered another brutal blow. At dawn on August 21, 1863, the guerrilla chieftain William Clarke Quantrill rode into Lawrence, Kansas, with a band of four hundred men. In his twenty-six years Quantrill had been schoolteacher, horse thief, and murderer. In 1863 he was a regularly commissioned Confederate captain, but the Union authorities had formally branded him an outlaw. Ardently proslavery, Quantrill had a grudge against Kansas, especially the antislavery center of Lawrence.

J. S. Boughton, Lawrence publisher, collected eyewitness accounts of the "massacre" for a brief history that suffers nothing in realism for having been published twenty years after the event:[9]

After . . . all fears of resistance were removed, the ruffians scattered in small gangs to all parts of the town in search of plunder and blood. The order was "to burn every house, and kill every man." Almost every house was visited and robbed, and the men found in them killed or left, according to the character or whim of the captors. Some of these seemed completely brutalized, while others showed some signs of remaining humanity. One lady said that as gang after gang came to her house, she always met them herself, and tried to get them to talking. If she only got them to talking, she could get at what little humanity was left in them. . . .

It is doubtful whether the world has ever witnessed such a scene of horror—certainly not outside the annals of savage warfare. . . . The carnage was much worse from the fact that the citizens could not believe that men could be such fiends. . . . Few expected a wholesale murder. Many who could have escaped, therefore, remained and were slain. . . .

We can only give a few of the incidents of the massacre as specimens of the whole. The scenes of horror we describe must be multiplied till the amount reaches one hundred and eighty, the number of killed and wounded.

Gen. Collamore, Mayor of the city, was awakened by their shouts around the house. His house was evidently well known, and they struck for it to prevent his taking measures for defense. When he looked out, the house was surrounded. Escape was impossible. There was but one hiding place—the well. He at once went into the well. The enemy went into the house and searched for the owner, swearing and threatening all the while. Failing to find him, they fired the house and waited round to see it burn. Mrs. Collamore went out and spoke to her husband while the fire was burning. But the house was so near the well that when the flames burst out they shot over the well, and the fire fell in. When the flames subsided, so that the well could be approached, nothing could be seen of Mr. Collamore or the man who descended into the well with him. After the rebels had gone, Mr. Lowe, an intimate friend of Gen. Collamore, went at once down the well to seek for him. The rope supporting him broke, and he also died in the well, and three bodies were drawn from its cold water.

At Dr. Griswold's there were four families. The doctor and his lady had just returned the evening before from a visit east. Hon. S. M. Thorp, State Senator, Mr. J. C. Trask, Editor of State Journal, Mr. H. W. Baker, grocer, with their wives, were boarding in Dr. Griswold's family. The house was attacked about the same time as Gen. Collamore's. They called for the men to come out. When they did not obey very readily, they assured them "they should not be harmed—if the citizens quietly surrender, it might save the town." This idea brought them out at once. Mr. Trask said, "if it will help save the town, let us go." They went down stairs and out of doors. The ruffians ordered them to get in line, and to march before them towards town. They had scarcely gone twenty feet from the yard before the whole four were shot down. Dr. Griswold and Mr. Trask were killed at once. Mr. Thorp and Mr. Baker wounded, but apparently dead. The ladies attempted to reach their husbands from the house, but were driven back. A guard was stationed just below, and every time any of the ladies attempted to go from the house to their dying friends, this guard would dash up at full speed, and with oaths and threats drive them back. After the bodies had lain about half an hour, a gang rode up, rolled them over, and shot them again. . . .

The most brutal murder was that of Judge Carpenter. Several gangs called at his house and robbed him of all he had—but his genial manner was too much for them, and they all left him alive and his house standing. Towards the last, another gang came, more brutal than the rest. They asked him where he was from. He replied, "New York." "It is you New York fellows that are doing all the mischief," one replied, and drew his revolver to shoot him. Mr. Carpenter ran into the house, up stairs, then down again, the ruffian after him and firing at him at every turn. He finally eluded them and slipped into the cellar. He was already badly wounded, so that the blood lay in pools in the cellar where he stood for a few minutes. His hiding place was soon discovered, and he was driven out of the cellar into the yard and shot again. He fell mortally wounded. His wife threw herself on to him and covered him with her person to shield him from further violence. The ruffian deliberately walked around her to find a place to shoot under her, and finally raised her arm and put his revolver under, and fired so that she could see the ball enter his head. They then fired the house. . . .

The rebels were in town from about five o'clock until nine. . . . The whole number killed was about one hundred and fifty.

VI

By holing up in Chattanooga, Bragg made that point the target of the Army of the Cumberland. Characteristically, Rosecrans planned carefully. While he threatened the Confederate position from the northwest he would put the main body of his army across the Tennessee River to the southwest. If he succeeded, Bragg would be compelled to retreat, and Rosecrans could pounce on the Confederate flank and fight a battle under conditions of his choice.

The strategy worked. The Army of the Cumberland moved forward on August 16, and Bragg acted as Rosecrans hoped he would. As the Federal army closed in, Bragg pulled out of Chattanooga, but instead of running away, he halted a few miles south of the town and gave every indication of offering battle. Rosecrans suddenly realized that his army was widely dispersed and in no position to fight a major battle. Frantically he tried to pull the scattered corps together.

Charles A. Dana, newly appointed Assistant Secretary of War and on the ground to prod Rosecrans into action—unnecessarily as it happened —described the situation of the Army of the Cumberland on the day before a bloody conflict:[10]

By noon of September 18th the concentration was practically complete. Our army then lay up and down the valley, with West Chicka-

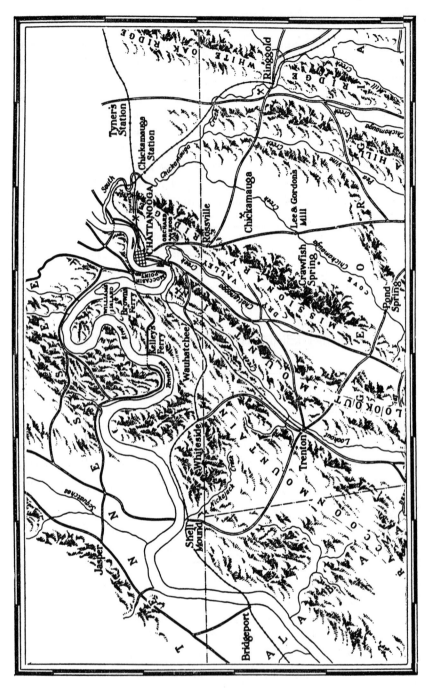

CHATTANOOGA AND CHICKAMAUGA

From *Atlas of American History*

mauga Creek in front of the greater part of the line. The left was held
by Crittenden, the center by Thomas, and the right by McCook, whose
troops were now all in the valley except one brigade. The army had not
concentrated any too soon, for that very afternoon the enemy appeared
on our left, and a considerable engagement occurred. It was said at
headquarters that a battle was certain the next day. The only point
Rosecrans had not determined at five o'clock on the afternoon of the
18th was whether to make a night march and fall on Bragg at daylight
or to await his onset.

But that night it became pretty clear to all that Bragg's plan was to
push by our left into Chattanooga. This compelled another rapid movement by the left down the Chickamauga. By a tiresome night march
Thomas moved down behind Crittenden and below Lee and Gordon's
Mills, taking position on our extreme left. Crittenden followed, connecting with Thomas's right, and thus taking position in the center.
McCook's corps also extended downstream to the left. . . . These
movements were hurriedly made, and the troops, especially those of
Thomas, were very much exhausted by their efforts to get into position.

On the next day—September 19—the battle began in earnest. Dana
summarized the fighting as it affected the Army of the Cumberland:

About nine o'clock . . . at Crawfish Spring, where the general headquarters were, we heard firing on our left, and reports at once came in
that the battle had begun there, Bragg being in command of the enemy.
Thomas had barely headed the Confederates off from Chattanooga.
We remained at Crawfish Springs on this day until after one o'clock,
waiting for the full proportions of the conflict to develop. When it became evident that the battle was being fought entirely on our left, Rosecrans removed his headquarters nearer to the scene, taking a little
house near Lee and Gordon's Mills, known as the Widow Glenn's.
Although closer to the battle, we could see no more of it here than at
Crawfish Springs, the conflict being fought altogether in a thick forest,
and being invisible to outsiders. . . .

It was not until after dark that firing ceased and final reports began
to come in. From these we found that the enemy had been defeated in
his attempt to turn and crush our left flank and secure possession of
the Chattanooga roads, but that he was not wholly defeated, for he still
held his ground in several places, and was preparing, it was believed, to
renew the battle the next day.

That evening Rosecrans decided that if Bragg did not retreat he would renew the fight at daylight, and a council of war was held at our headquarters at the Widow Glenn's, to which all the corps and division commanders were summoned. . . . Rosecrans began by asking each of the corps commanders for a report on the condition of his troops and of the position they occupied; also for his opinion of what was to be done. Each proposition was discussed by the entire council as it was made. General Thomas was so tired—he had not slept at all the night before, and he had been in battle all day—that he went to sleep every minute. Every time Rosecrans spoke to him he would straighten up and answer, but he always said the same thing, "I would strengthen the left," and then he would be asleep, sitting up in his chair. General Rosecrans, to the proposition to strengthen the left, made always the same reply, "Where are we going to take it from?"

After the discussion was ended, Rosecrans gave his orders for the disposition of the troops on the following day. Thomas's corps was to remain on the left with his line somewhat drawn in, but substantially as he was at the close of the day. McCook was to close on Thomas and cover the position at Widow Glenn's, and Crittenden was to have two divisions in reserve near the junction of McCook's and Thomas's lines, to be able to succor either. These orders were written for each corps commander. They were also read in the presence of all, and the plans fully explained. Finally, after everything had been said, hot coffee was brought in, and then McCook was called upon to sing the Hebrew Maiden. McCook sang the song, and then the council broke up and the generals went away.

This was about midnight, and, as I was very tired, I lay down on the floor to sleep, beside Captain Horace Porter, who was at that time Rosecrans' chief of ordnance. There were cracks in the floor of the Widow Glenn's house, and the wind blew up under us. We would go to sleep, and then the wind would come up so cold through the cracks that it would wake us up, and we would turn over together to keep warm.

General J. S. Fullerton, chief of staff to General Gordon Granger, commanding the Federal reserve, described the climactic fighting of September 20—a day of wild but unco-ordinated charges and counter-charges, a day of slaughter fatal to the careers of both commanding generals, a day when a Virginian who had remained loyal to the Union won the sobriquet by which he is still known:[11]

The morning of Sunday, the 20th, opened with a cloudless sky, but a fog had come up from the warm water of the Chickamauga and hung over the battle-field until 9 o'clock. A silence of desertion was in the front. This quiet continued till nearly 10 o'clock; then, as the peaceful tones of the churchbells, rolling over the land from the east, reached the meridian of Chickamauga, they were made dissonant by the murderous roar of the artillery of Bishop Polk, who was opening the battle on Thomas's front [the left or northern flank of the Federal line]. Granger, who had been ordered at all hazards to hold fast where he was, listened and grew impatient. Shortly before 10 o'clock, calling my attention to a great column of dust moving from our front toward the point from which came the sound of battle, he said, "They are concentrating over there. That is where we ought to be." The corps flag marked his headquarters in an open field near the Ringgold road. He walked up and down in front of his flag, nervously pulling his beard. Once stopping, he said, "Why the hell does Rosecrans keep me here? There is nothing in front of us now. There is the battle"—pointing in the direction of Thomas. Every moment the sounds of battle grew louder, while the many columns of dust rolling together here mingled with the smoke that hung over the scene.

At 11 o'clock, with Granger, I climbed a high hayrick nearby. We sat there for ten minutes listening and watching. Then Granger jumped up, thrust his glass into its case, and exclaimed with an oath:

"I am going to Thomas, orders or no orders!"

"And if you go," I replied, "it may bring disaster to the army and you to a court-martial."

"There's nothing in our front now but ragtag, bobtail cavalry," he replied. "Don't you see Bragg is piling his whole army on Thomas? I am going to his assistance."

. . . Thomas was nearly four miles away. The day had now grown very warm, yet the troops marched rapidly over the narrow road, which was covered ankle-deep with dust that rose in suffocating clouds. Completely enveloped in it, the moving column swept along like a desert sandstorm. Two miles from the point of starting, and three-quarters of a mile from the left of the road, the enemy's skirmishers and a section of artillery opened fire on us from an open wood. This force had worked round Thomas's left, and was then partly in his rear. Granger halted to feel them. Soon becoming convinced that it was only a large party of observation, he again started his column and pushed rapidly forward. . . .

A little farther on we were met by a staff-officer sent by General Thomas to discover whether we were friends or enemies; he did not know whence friends could be coming, and the enemy appeared to be approaching from all directions. All of this shattered Army of the Cumberland left on the field was with Thomas; but not more than one-fourth of the men of the army who went into battle at the opening were there. Thomas's loss in killed and wounded during the two days had been dreadful. As his men dropped out his line was contracted to half its length. Now its flanks were bent back, conforming to ridges shaped like a horse-shoe.

On the part of Thomas and his men there was no thought but that of fighting. He was a soldier who had never retreated, who had never been defeated. He stood immovable, the "Rock of Chickamauga." Never had soldiers greater love for a commander. He imbued them with his spirit, and their confidence in him was sublime.

To the right of Thomas's line was a gorge, then a high ridge, nearly at right angles thereto, running east and west. . . . Confederates . . . were passing through the gorge . . . ; divisions were forming on this ridge for an assault; to their left the guns of a battery were being unlimbered for an enfilading fire. There was not a man to send against the force on the ridge, none to oppose this impending assault. The enemy saw the approaching colors of the Reserve Corps and hesitated.

At 1 o'clock Granger shook hands with Thomas. Something was said about forming to fight to the right and rear.

"Those men must be driven back," said Granger, pointing to the gorge and ridge. "Can you do it?" asked Thomas.

"Yes. My men are fresh, and they are just the fellows for that work. They are raw troops, and they don't know any better than to charge up there."

Granger quickly sent Aleshire's battery of 3-inch rifle guns which he brought up to Thomas's left to assist in repelling another assault about to be made on the Kelly farm front. Whitaker's and Mitchell's brigades under Steedman were wheeled into position and projected against the enemy in the gorge and on the ridge. With ringing cheers they advanced in two lines by double-quick—over open fields, through weeds waist-high, through a little valley, then up the ridge. The enemy opened on them first with artillery, then with a murderous musketry fire. When well up the ridge the men, almost exhausted, were halted for breath. They lay on the ground two or three minutes, then came the command, "Forward!" Brave, bluff old Steedman, with a regimental flag in his hand, led the way. On went the lines, firing as they ran and bravely receiving a deadly and continuous fire from the enemy on the summit. The Confederates began to break and in another minute were flying down the southern slope of the ridge. In twenty minutes from the beginning of the charge the ridge had been carried. . . .

The enemy massed a force to retake the ridge. They came before our men had rested; twice they assaulted and were driven back. During one assault, as the first line came within range of our muskets, it halted, apparently hesitating, when we saw a colonel seize a flag, wave it over his head, and rush forward. The whole line instantly caught his enthusiasm, and with a wild cheer followed, only to be hurled back again. Our men ran down the ridge in pursuit. In the midst of a group of Confederate dead and wounded they found the brave colonel dead, the flag he carried spread over him where he fell.

Soon after 5 o'clock Thomas rode to the left of his line, leaving Granger the ranking officer at the center. The ammunition of both Thomas's and Granger's commands was now about exhausted. . . . The cartridge-boxes of both our own and the enemy's dead within reach had been emptied by our men. When it was not yet 6 o'clock, and Thomas was still on the left of his line, Brannan rushed up to Granger, saying, "The enemy are forming for another assault; we have not another round of ammunition—what shall we do?" "Fix bayonets and go for them," was the reply. Along the whole line ran the order, "Fix bayonets." On came the enemy—our men were lying down. "Forward," was sounded. In one instant they were on their feet. Forward they went to meet the charge. The enemy fled. So impetuous was this counter-charge that one regiment, with empty muskets and empty cartridge-boxes, broke through the enemy's line, which, closing in their rear, carried them off as in the undertow.

One more feeble assault was made by the enemy; then the day closed, and the battle of Chickamauga was over.

Granger, proudly recording victory, was speaking for only the fragment commanded by the intrepid Thomas. The bulk of the Army of the Cumberland had been routed. General John Beatty, whose brigade was in line not far from Granger's troops, told a different story:[12]

About four o'clock we saw away off to our rear the banners and glittering guns of a division coming toward us, and we became agitated by doubt and hope. Are they friends or foes? The thunder, as of a thousand anvils, still goes on in our front. Men fall around us like leaves in autumn. Thomas, Garfield, Wood, and others are in consultation below the hill just in rear of Harker. The approaching troops are said to be ours, and we feel a throb of exultation. Before they arrive we ascertain that the division is Steedman's; and finally, as they come up, I recognize my old friend Colonel Mitchell, of the One Hundred and Thirteenth. They go into action on our right, and as they press forward the roar of musketry redoubles; the battle seems to be working off in that direction. There is now a comparative lull in our front, and I ride over to the right and become involved in a regiment that has been thrown out of line and into confusion by another regiment that retreated through it in disorder. I assist Colonel Mitchell in rallying it, and it goes into the fight again. Returning to my old place, I find that disorganized bodies of men are coming rapidly from the left, in regiments, companies, squads, and singly. I meet General Wood and ask if I shall not halt and reorganize them. He tells me to do so; but I find the task impossible. They do not recognize me as their commander, and most of them will not obey my orders. Some few, indeed, I manage to hold together; but the great mass drift by me to the woods in the rear. The dead are lying everywhere; the wounded are continually passing to the rear; the thunder of the guns and roll of musketry are unceasing and unabated until nightfall. Then the fury of the battle gradually dies away, and finally we have a silence, broken only by a cheer here and there along the enemy's line.

"Old Pete" Longstreet, who had arrived on the field the day before with 5,000 men from the Army of Northern Virginia, also saw the battle end. His emotions were different from Beatty's:[13]

The last of my reserve, Trigg's brigade, gave us new strength, and Preston gained Snodgrass Hill. The trampled ground and bushy woods were left to those who were too much worn to escape the rapid strides of the heroic Confederates. The left wing swept forward, and the right sprang to the broad Chattanooga highway. Like magic the Union army had melted away in our presence. A few hundred prisoners were picked up by both wings as they met, to burst their throats in loud huzzas. The Army of Tennessee knew how to enjoy its first grand victory. The dews of twilight hung heavy about the trees as if to hold down the voice of victory; but the two lines nearing as they advanced joined their continuous shouts in increasing volume, not as the burstings from the cannon's mouth, but in a tremendous swell of heroic harmony that seemed almost to lift from their roots the great trees of the forest.

Before greetings and congratulations upon the success had passed it was night, and the mild beams of the quartering moon were more suggestive of Venus than of Mars. The haversacks and ammunition supplies were ordered replenished, and the Confederate army made its bivouac on the ground it had gained in the first pronounced victory in the West, and one of the most stubbornly contested battles of the war.

In midafternoon, convinced that Chickamauga was lost, Rosecrans rode off the field to Chattanooga to prepare to receive the remnants of his shattered army. To Halleck, Rosecrans sent a dismal dispatch: "We have met with a serious disaster. . . . Enemy overwhelmed us, drove our right, pierced our centre, and scattered troops there." Dana, also in Chattanooga, wired Washington: "Chickamauga is as fatal a name in our history as Bull Run."

A few hours later a future President of the United States, General James A. Garfield, Rosecrans' chief of staff, who had kept his head while his commander had panicked, put the day's fighting in proper perspective. Casualty figures confirmed Garfield's estimate of the situation. Union losses were: killed, 1,657; wounded, 9,756; missing, 4,757. Confederate losses were: killed, 2,312; wounded, 14,674; missing, 1,468:[14]

HEADQUARTERS DEPT. OF THE CUMBERLAND.
ROSSVILLE, GEORGIA, 8:40 P.M., Sept. 20, 1863

MAJOR GENERAL ROSECRANS:

I have this moment returned from the front. I wrote you a long despatch as I arrived on the field and while the battle was in progress, but it was so difficult to get communication to the rear that I fear you have not yet received it. Thomas has kept Baird's, Brannan's Raynolds' Woods' and Palmer's divisions in good order and has maintained almost the exact position he occupied this morning, except that his right has swung back nearly at right angles with the Gordon's Mills and Rossville road. Negley has stopped about six thousand men at this place. Sheridan gathered fifteen hundred of his division and reached a point three miles south of here at sunset; Davis is here with his brigade.

General Thomas has fought a most terrific battle and has damaged the enemy badly. General Granger's troops moved up just in time and fought magnificently. From the time I reached the battle-field, 3:45 P.M., till sunset the fight was by far the fiercest I have ever seen; our men not only held their ground, but at many points drove the enemy splendidly. Longstreet's Virginians have got their bellies full. Nearly every division of the field exhausted its ammunition—got supplies and exhausted it again. Turchin's brigade charged the rebel lines and took five hundred prisoners, became enveloped, swept around behind their lines and cut its way out in another place but abandoned his prisoners. Another brigade was attacked just at the close of the fight, and its ammunition being exhausted, it went in with the bayonet and drove the rebels, taking over two hundred prisoners and have got them yet. On the whole General Thomas and General Granger have done the enemy fully as much injury today as they have suffered from him, and they have successfully repelled the repeated combined attacks, most fiercely made, of the whole rebel army, frequently pressing the front and both our flanks at the same time.

The disaster on the right cannot of course be estimated now; it must be very considerable in men and material, especially the latter. The rebels have, however, done their best today, and I believe we can whip them tomorrow. I believe we can now crown the whole battle with victory. Granger regards them as thoroughly whipped tonight, and thinks they would not renew the fight were we to remain on the field. Clouds of dust to the eastward and northward seem to indicate some movements to our left. Sheridan thinks they may be projecting to come in directly on Chattanooga. I don't think so. Your order to retire on this place was received a little after sunset and communicated to Generals Thomas and Granger. The troops are now moving back and will be here in good shape and strong position before morning. I hope you will not budge an inch from this place but come up early in the morning, and if the rebels try it, accommodate them. . . .

If I am not needed at headquarters tonight, I will stay here; I am half dead with fatigue. . . .

But Rosecrans was still as thoroughly defeated as he had been in mid-afternoon. He had no stomach for the fight that might very well have turned defeat into triumph.

Braxton Bragg was in the same state of mind as the Federal commander. In fact, for most of September 20 Bragg was firmly convinced that the Army of Tennessee was being beaten. In a funk he ceased to give orders, allowing division and brigade commanders to fight their own unco-ordinated battles.

*Lieutenant General D. H. Hill, Confederate corps commander, saw
Chickamauga for what it was—a worthless victory:*[15]

Whatever blunders each of us in authority committed before the
battles of the 19th and 20th, and during their progress, the great blunder of all was that of not pursuing the enemy on the 21st. The day was
spent in burying the dead and gathering up captured stores. Forrest,
with his usual promptness, was early in the saddle, and saw that the
retreat was a rout. Disorganized masses of men were hurrying to the
rear; batteries of artillery were inextricably mixed with trains of wagons; disorder and confusion pervaded the broken ranks struggling to
get on. Forrest sent back word to Bragg that "every hour was worth a
thousand men." But the commander-in-chief did not know of the victory
until the morning of the 21st, and then he did not order a pursuit.
Rosecrans spent the day and the night of the 21st in hurrying his
trains out of town. A breathing-space was allowed him; the panic
among his troops subsided, and Chattanooga—the objective point of
the campaign—was held. There was no more splendid fighting in '61,
when the flower of the Southern youth was in the field, than was displayed in those bloody days of '63. But it seems to me that the *élan*
of the Southern soldier was never seen after Chickamauga—that
brilliant dash which had distinguished him was gone forever. . . . He
fought stoutly to the last, but, after Chickamauga, with the sullenness of
despair and without the enthusiasm of hope. That "barren victory"
sealed the fate of the Southern Confederacy.

VII

*In Richmond, J. B. Jones, the "Rebel War Clerk," made a jubilant entry
in his diary:*

"*September 22d. . . . The effects of this great victory will be elec-
trical. The whole South will be filled with patriotic fervor, and in the
North there will be a corresponding depression . . . Surely the Government of the United States must now see the impossibility of sub-
jugating the Southern people, spread over such a vast extent of territory; and the European governments ought now to interpose to put an
end to this cruel waste of blood and treasure.*"

*Had Jones known of a decision of the British government, not yet
made public, he would not have looked so hopefully to European intervention in behalf of the Confederacy.*

*The decision was the culmination of a train of events which began
in the spring of 1862, when the Confederate Navy Department ordered*

its agent in England, James D. Bulloch, to contract for at least two armored vessels for delivery at the earliest possible moment. The instructions, delayed in transmission, did not reach Bulloch until June 10. By that time he was ready with plans and specifications for two powerful armored ships which, when equipped with rams and rifles of the latest type, would be superior to anything in the Federal Navy. Bulloch acted at once and reported to his Department:[16]

On the day after the receipt of your * letter I requested the parties who had been assisting me all along to make a tender for the contract, having previously provided myself with estimates from other builders who competed for Admiralty contracts. In a few days the price was agreed upon, and I gave a verbal order for two vessels, so that no time should be lost in contracting for the large quantity of armour plate required. By giving the order for both vessels to the same builders I got a reduction of £1,250 on the cost of each, and by adopting the same size and model of ship, and a like form of engines, they can both be completed in very nearly the same time. Besides this, experience has taught me that it is far safer to keep our business as little extended as possible, as otherwise the chance of our transactions being ferreted out by the Federal spies, who abound even in this country, is greatly increased.

Later, Bulloch amplified this brief account:

I added that the contracting parties had shown great confidence in me by taking this large contract upon my assurance that the money would be forthcoming, and I hoped that the remittances would be forwarded so as to ensure prompt payment of the several instalments as they fell due. The builders with whom I contracted for the above ships were Messrs. Laird Brothers, of Birkenhead, and the whole of the arrangements were made in the same way as those for the building of the *Alabama.* They treated with me as a private individual, and the contract was a purely "commercial transaction," the agreement being that they should build and deliver the two vessels to me in the port of Liverpool, finished according to the stipulated specifications, but furnished only with such fittings and outfit as were required for an ordinary sea-voyage. In order to avoid every possible appearance of an intent to arm them within British jurisdiction, it was arranged that no

* Stephen R. Mallory, the Confederate Secretary of the Navy.

magazines were to be placed in either ship, nor any special places for stowing shells and ordnance stores.

Bulloch underestimated the astuteness of Charles Francis Adams, American Minister to England. Adams soon knew of the building of the rams, and began to present proof to the Foreign Secretary that they were intended for the Confederate service. Earl Russell, uneasy, instituted his own investigation. Bulloch made a shrewd move—he sold the ships to a French firm which engaged to resell them to him when they should be beyond British jurisdiction. So certain was he of the success of his ruse that he indulged in dreams of the destruction the rams would cause once they sailed under the Stars and Bars. On July 9, 1863, he advised the Confederate Secretary of the Navy:

I respectfully propose . . . that the ships, when ready for sea, should be ordered to proceed as quickly as possible to Wilmington, North Carolina. One could fall in with the land at New Inlet, and the other at the main "ship bar" at the mouth of Cape Fear river.

By steaming quietly in at early daylight, they might entirely destroy the blockading vessels—not one should be left to steal away and make known the fact that the iron-clads were on the coast. Crews might be ready at Smithville or Fort Caswell, to be put on board the ships as soon as they had destroyed or dispersed the blockaders, and in a very few hours afterwards the two vessels would be ready to strike a decisive blow in any direction, north or south. . . .

The Atlantic coast offers enticing and decisive work in more than one direction. Without a moment's delay, after getting their crews on board off Wilmington, our vessels might sail southward, sweep the blockading fleet from the sea-front of every harbour from the Capes of Virginia to Sabine Pass, and cruising up and down the coast, could prevent anything like permanent systematic interruption of our trade for the future. Again, should Washington still be held by the enemy, our iron-clads could ascend the Potomac, and after destroying all transports and gun-boats falling within their reach, could render Washington itself untenable, and could thus create a powerful diversion in favour of any operations General Lee might have on foot. Third, Portsmouth, New Hampshire . . . is a wealthy city in itself, and opposite the town is an important national dock and building-yard. The whole lies invitingly open to attack and destruction. Suppose our two iron-clads should steam, unannounced, into that harbour on some fine October morning, and while one proceeded to demolish the navy-yard and all it contained, the other should send a flag of truce to the mayor, to say that if $1,000,000 in gold or $5,000,000 in greenbacks were not sent on board in four hours the city would be destroyed. . . . Portsmouth could afford to pay for its existence. Philadelphia is another point open to such an attack. The river is navigable, the banks comparatively low, so that no plunging fire could be brought to bear upon the ships, and once in front of the city they could dictate their own terms. Such operations as are thus hastily sketched would inflict great damage upon the enemy, besides creating a striking effect in Europe.

Two days after Bulloch recorded his vision of conquest and ransom, William H. Seward, Secretary of State, wrote a long letter of instruction to Minister Adams. Seward granted that the officers of the crown might have interpreted British law correctly in the cases of the Alabama, Florida *and, more recently, the* Alexandra,* *but the United States still had an intolerable grievance:*[17]

If the law of Great Britain must be left without amendment, and be construed by the government in conformity with the rulings of the Chief Baron of the Exchequer, then there will be left for the United States no alternative but to protect themselves and their commerce against armed cruisers proceeding from British ports, as against the naval forces of a public enemy; and also to claim and insist upon indemnities for the injuries which all such expeditions have hitherto committed or shall hereafter commit against this government and the citizens of the United States. To this end this government is now preparing a naval force with the utmost vigor; and if the national navy, which it is rapidly creating, shall not be sufficient for the emergency, then the United States must bring into employment such private armed naval forces as the mercantile marine shall afford. British ports, domestic as well as colonial, are now open, under certain restrictions, to the visits of piratical vessels, and not only furnish them coals, provisions, and repairs, but even receive their prisoners when the enemies of the United States come in to obtain such relief from voyages in which they have either burned ships they have captured, or have even manned and armed them as pirates and sent them abroad as auxiliaries in the work of destruc-

* A gunboat constructed by the Lairds which the British government had seized on April 5, 1863. The lawsuits resulting from the seizure dragged on so long that the *Alexandra* was still the subject of litigation when the war ended.

tion. Can it be an occasion for either surprise or complaint that if this condition of things is to remain and receive the deliberate sanction of the British government, the navy of the United States will receive instructions to pursue these enemies into the ports which thus, in violation of the law of nations and the obligations of neutrality, become harbors for the pirates? The President very distinctly perceives the risks and hazards which a naval conflict thus maintained will bring to the commerce and even to the peace of the two countries. But he is obliged to consider that in the case supposed the destruction of our commerce will probably amount to a naval war waged by a portion at least of the British nation against the government and people of the United States—a war tolerated though not declared or avowed by the British government. If, through the necessary employment of all our means of national defence, such a partial war shall become a general one between the two nations, the President thinks that the responsibility for that painful result will not fall upon the United States.

Adams, aware that the presentation of this document to the British Foreign Secretary would be considered a declaration of war, kept it in his desk and continued to gather proof of the real ownership of the rams. The London Times *remarked that "ninety-nine people out of a hundred believe that these steam rams are 'intended to carry on hostilities sooner or later against the Federals,' " yet Her Majesty's law officers persisted in their refusal to advise Russell to detain the ships. On September 1 the Foreign Secretary informed Adams that the British government, though unable to interfere with the rams, would watch vigilantly for any action which could be construed as a violation of neutrality.*

Replying on September 5, Adams relied on his instructions from Seward, though he still refrained from communicating them to Russell:[18]

MY LORD,

At this moment, when one of the iron-clad war-vessels is on the point of departure from this kingdom on its hostile errand against the United States, I am honoured with the reply of your Lordship to my notes of the 11th, 16th, and 25th of July and of the 14th of August. I trust I need not express how profound is my regret at the conclusion to which Her Majesty's Government have arrived. I can regard it no otherwise than as practically opening to the insurgents free liberty in this kingdom to execute a policy described in one of their late publications in the following language:—

"In the present state of the harbour defences of New York, Boston, Portland, and smaller Northern cities, such a vessel as the 'Warrior' would have little difficulty in entering any of those ports, and inflicting a vital blow upon the enemy. The destruction of Boston alone would be worth a hundred victories in the field. It would bring such a terror to the 'blue-noses' as to cause them to wish eagerly for peace, despite their overweening love of gain which has been so freely administered to since the opening of this war. Vessels of the 'Warrior' class would promptly raise the blockade of our ports, and would, even in this respect, confer advantages which would soon repay the cost of their construction."

It would be superfluous in me to point out to your Lordship that this is war. No matter what may be the theory adopted of neutrality in a struggle, when this process is carried on in the manner indicated from a territory and with the aid of the subjects of a third party, that third party, to all intents and purposes, ceases to be neutral. Neither is it necessary to show that any Government which suffers it to be done fails in enforcing the essential conditions of international amity towards the country against whom the hostility is directed. In my belief it is impossible that any nation retaining a proper degree of self-respect could tamely submit to a continuance of relations so utterly deficient in reciprocity. I have no idea that Great Britain would do so for a moment.

After a careful examination of the full instructions with which I have been furnished in preparation for such an emergency, I deem it inexpedient for me to attempt any recurrence to arguments for effective interposition in the present case. The fatal objection of impotency which paralyzes Her Majesty's Government seems to present an insuperable barrier against all further reasoning. Under these circumstances I prefer to desist from communicating to your Lordship even such further portions of my existing instructions as are suited to the case, lest I should contribute to aggravate difficulties already far too serious. I therefore content myself with informing your Lordship that I transmit by the present steamer a copy of your note for the consideration of my Government, and shall await the more specific directions that will be contained in the reply.

Adams had issued an unnecessary ultimatum. Whether Earl Russell had finally decided to rely on what he knew but could not prove, whether the import of the smashing Union victories of Gettysburg and Vicksburg had convinced him, as they had convinced many leaders of opinion in England, that the cause of the South was hopeless, may never be known. Whatever his reason, Russell had written to his Prime Minister two days before Adams had threatened England with war:

MY DEAR PALMERSTON,—The conduct of the gentlemen who have contracted for the two iron-clads at Birkenhead is so very suspicious that I have thought it necessary to direct that they should be detained. The Solicitor-General has been consulted, and concurs in the measure, as one of policy, though not of strict law. We shall thus test the law, and, if we have to pay damages, we have satisfied the opinion, which prevails here as well as in America, that that kind of neutral hostility should not be allowed to go on without some attempt to stop it. If you do not approve, pray appoint a Cabinet for Tuesday or Wednesday next.

Palmerston did not dissent. Henry Adams, the Minister's son and secretary, wrote from London on September 16:[19]

Undoubtedly to us this is a second Vicksburg. It is our diplomatic triumph, if we manage to carry it through. . . . Whether we shall succeed, I am not yet certain. The vessels are only detained temporarily, but the signs are that the gale that has blown so long is beginning to veer about. . . . I think the discussion which is now taking place has pretty much convinced most people that this war-vessel matter is one that ought to be stopped. And if so, the mere fact that they have managed to take the first step is to me reasonable ground for confidence that they will take the others as the emergencies arise.

On October 20 Bulloch reported from Liverpool to the Confederate Secretary of the Navy:[20]

The two rams building by Messrs Laird have been virtually seized by orders from the Foreign Office, and are now in the possession of the customs officers of this port, assisted by one of her Majesty's gunboats, and a guard of marines from her Majesty's ship *Majestic*. The actual seizure took place only about a fortnight ago (October 9th), although the public has been prepared for such an event by intimations in the so-called Government organs, and discussions upon the matter in all the newspapers of the kingdom. . . .

Bulloch concluded ruefully:

Now, sir, the final issue of this affair is no longer a practical question. No amount of discretion or management on my part can effect the release of the ships.

"THE YEAR OF THE PROCLAMATION"

A<small>FTER</small> C<small>HICKAMAUGA</small>, Rosecrans fortified Chattanooga. Bragg saw an opportunity for the kind of bloodless conquest that was his concept of war. Chattanooga lies on the south side of the tortuous Tennessee River, which at this point flows from west to east. East of the city, five miles away at the closest point, Missionary Ridge extends north and south. An equal distance to the southwest lies Lookout Mountain with its northernmost shoulder touching the Tennessee. The one railroad coming in from the north—the Nashville and Chattanooga—ran so close to Lookout Mountain that, like the Tennessee River, it could be controlled by a force on the mountain. Bragg distributed his troops on Missionary Ridge, on Lookout and in the Chattanooga Valley between the two elevations, closed off the Federal communications, and waited for starvation to force his opponent to surrender.

Rosecrans, strangely bereft of the dash he had formerly shown, seemed to see as the alternative to this fate a retreat toward Nashville. Washington refused to consider the possibility. Rosecrans was relieved, and Thomas was put in command of the Army of the Cumberland. Sherman with the Army of the Tennessee was ordered to Chattanooga; Hooker brought two corps from the Army of the Potomac; and Grant was given supreme command.

I

Stanton, meeting Grant at Louisville, gave the general his orders. Grant hurried to Chattanooga, reaching there on October 23. He found the army in deplorable condition:[1]

Owing to the position of Bragg, all supplies for Rosecrans had to be hauled by a circuitous route north of the river and over a mountainous country. . . .

This country afforded but little food for his animals, nearly ten thousand of which had already starved, and not enough were left to draw a single piece of artillery or even the ambulances to convey the sick. The men had been on half rations of hard bread for a considerable time, with but few other supplies except beef driven from Nashville across the country. The region along the road became so exhausted of food for the cattle that by the time they reached Chattanooga they were much in the condition of the few animals left alive there—"on the lift." Indeed, the beef was so poor that the soldiers were in the habit of saying, with a faint facetiousness, that they were living on "half rations of hard bread and *beef dried on the hoof.*"

Nothing could be transported but food, and the troops were without sufficient shoes or other clothing suitable for the advancing season. What they had was well worn. The fuel within the Federal lines was exhausted, even to the stumps of trees. There were no teams to draw it from the opposite bank, where it was abundant. The only way of supplying fuel, for some time before my arrival, had been to cut trees on the north bank of the river at a considerable distance up the stream, form rafts of it and float it down with the current, effecting a landing on the south side within our lines by the use of paddles or poles. It would then be carried on the shoulders of the men to their camps.

At Chattanooga, Grant found General William F. Smith, recently transferred from the Army of the Potomac. Smith, an outstanding engineer, had already made plans to break Bragg's hold on the Union supply lines. Hooker, at Bridgeport on the Tennessee River twenty-five miles west of Chattanooga, would cross to the south side and fight his way if necessary to Brown's Ferry, only three miles across country from Chattanooga. There he would be met by a force which would cross the river on ferries and a pontoon bridge. Nearby heights, when seized, would cover the position.

Hooker started on October 26. The Confederates were caught nap-ping, and put up little resistance. Two days later the Union right was firmly based on Lookout Valley, south of the Tennessee, and Grant had a supply line—a "cracker line" the troops called it—by steamer and road to Bridgeport. The effect was miraculous. Grant described it:[2]

On the way to Chattanooga I had telegraphed back to Nashville for a good supply of vegetables and small rations, which the troops had been so long deprived of. Hooker had brought with him from the east a full supply of land transportation. His animals had not been subjected to hard work on bad roads without forage, but were in good condition. In five days from my arrival in Chattanooga the way was open to Bridgeport and, with the aid of steamers and Hooker's teams, in a week the troops were receiving full rations. It is hard for any one not an eye-witness to realize the relief this brought. The men were soon reclothed and also well fed; an abundance of ammunition was brought up, and a cheerfulness prevailed not before enjoyed in many weeks. Neither officers nor men looked upon themselves any longer as doomed. The weak and languid appearance of the troops, so visible before, disap-peared at once. I do not know what the effect was on the other side, but assume it must have been correspondingly depressing. Mr. Davis had visited Bragg but a short time before, and must have perceived our condition to be about as Bragg described it in his subsequent report. "These dispositions," he said, "faithfully sustained, insured the enemy's speedy evacuation of Chattanooga for want of food and forage. Pos-sessed of the shortest route to his depot, and the one by which rein-forcements must reach him, we held him at our mercy, and his destruc-tion was only a question of time."

Bragg made only one effort to "faithfully sustain" his position. Grant described a sharp engagement in which the much-abused mule played an important part:[3]

The enemy was surprised by the movements which secured to us a line of supplies. He appreciated its importance, and hastened to try to recover the line from us. His strength on Lookout Mountain was not equal to Hooker's command in the valley below. From Missionary Ridge he had to march twice the distance we had from Chattanooga, in order to reach Lookout Valley; but on the night of the 28th and 29th [of October] an attack was made on Geary * at Wauhatchie by Long-street's corps. When the battle commenced, Hooker ordered Howard up from Brown's Ferry. He had three miles to march to reach Geary. On his way he was fired upon by rebel troops from a foot-hill to the left of the road and from which the road was commanded. Howard turned to the left, charged up the hill and captured it before the enemy had time to intrench, taking many prisoners. Leaving sufficient men to hold this height, he pushed on to reinforce Geary. Before he got up, Geary had been engaged for about three hours against a vastly superior force. The night was so dark that the men could not distinguish one from another except by the light of the flashes of their muskets. In the darkness and uproar, Hooker's teamsters became frightened, and breaking loose from their fastenings stampeded directly towards the enemy. The latter, no doubt, took this for a charge, and stampeded in turn. By four o'clock in the morning the battle had entirely ceased, and our "cracker line" was never afterward disturbed.

II

Before Grant assumed command at Chattanooga, Burnside had been sent with 25,000 men to east Tennessee. The purpose of the expedition —to "protect" the loyal people of the region—was one which Lincoln cherished and continually pressed, though no important military result could be expected. Early in November, Bragg ordered Longstreet, with 20,000 troops, to follow Burnside and take care of him. Even without the menace of Longstreet, the Federal commander was in critical condition, having neither adequate supplies nor ammunition. Lincoln and Halleck urged Grant to do something, anything, for Burnside's relief. As Grant saw the situation, he could help Burnside only by attacking Bragg. If the Confederate commander could be driven from his seemingly impregnable position, he would have to recall Longstreet, and Burnside would be saved.

Yet Grant would not be strong enough to attack until Sherman and the Army of the Tennessee reached Chattanooga. While Grant waited, the President of the United States, a thousand miles away, slowly wrote the remarks he had promised to make at the dedication of the Gettysburg military cemetery on November 19. When the day came, John Hay, Lincoln's twenty-five-year-old secretary, made a short entry in his diary:[4]

* John W. Geary commanded a division in the Twelfth Corps from the Army of the Potomac.

In the morning I got a beast and rode out with the President's suite to the Cemetery in the procession. The procession formed itself in an orphanly sort of way & moved out with very little help from anybody & after a little delay Mr. Everett took his place on the stand—and Mr. Stockton made a prayer which thought it was an oration; and Mr. Everett spoke as he always does, perfectly—and the President, in a fine, free way, with more grace than is his wont, said his half dozen words of consecration, and the music wailed and we went home through crowded and cheering streets. And all the particulars are in the daily papers.

The President had said:

Four score and seven years ago our fathers brought forth on this continent, a new nation, conceived in Liberty, and dedicated to the proposition that all men are created equal.

Now we are engaged in a great civil war, testing whether that nation, or any nation so conceived and so dedicated, can long endure. We are met on a great battle-field of that war. We have come to dedicate a portion of that field, as a final resting place for those who here gave their lives that that nation might live. It is altogether fitting and proper that we should do this.

But, in a larger sense, we can not dedicate—we can not consecrate—we can not hallow—this ground. The brave men, living and dead, who struggled here, have consecrated it, far above our poor power to add or detract. The world will little note, nor long remember what we say here, but it can never forget what they did here. It is for us the living, rather, to be dedicated here to the unfinished work which they who fought here have thus far so nobly advanced. It is rather for us to be here dedicated to the great task remaining before us—that from these honored dead we take increased devotion to that cause for which they gave the last full measure of devotion—that we here highly resolve that these dead shall not have died in vain—that this nation, under God, shall have a new birth of freedom—and that government of the people, by the people, for the people, shall not perish from the earth.

III

Sherman's advance units reached Brown's Ferry on November 20, but heavy rains forced Grant to postpone his attack until the twenty-third.

Major James A. Connolly, now on the staff of division commander
Absalom Baird, described three stirring days in a letter to his wife:[5]

On Monday, Nov. 23rd our Division was ordered to move out just in
front of the fortifications. We did so, and the rebels, as they looked
down on us from Lookout Mountain and Mission Ridge, no doubt
thought we had come out for a review. But Sheridan's Division followed us out and formed in line with us. Wonder what the rebels
thought then? "Oh, a Yankee review; we'll have some fun shelling them
directly." But out came Wood's Division, then Cruft's Division, then
Johnson's Division, then Howard's entire Corps of "Potomacs." "What
can those Yankee fools mean," Bragg must have thought, as he sat at
the door of his tent on Mission Ridge and watched the long lines of blue
coats and glistening guns marching around in the valley below him,
almost within gun shot of his pickets, and yet not a gun fired. All was
peace in Chattanooga valley that day.

The sun shone brightly, the bands played stirring airs; tattered banners that had waved on battle fields from the Potomac to the Mississippi
streamed out gaily, as if proud of the battle scars they wore. Generals
Grant and Hooker, and Sherman and Thomas and Logan and Reynolds and Sheridan and scores of others, with their staffs, galloped
along the lines, and the scene that spread out around me like a vast
panorama of war filled my heart with pride that I was a soldier and
member of that great army. But what did it all mean? Bragg, from
his mountain eyrie, could see what we were doing just as well as Grant
who was riding around amongst us. The rebels thought they had us
hemmed in so that we dared not move. Two o'clock came, and all was
yet quiet and peaceful, gay as a holiday review; we could see crowds of
rebels watching us from Mission Ridge and Lookout Mountain, but
three o'clock came, and a solitary shot away over on our left, among
Wood's men, made every fellow think: "Hark!" A few moments and
another shot, then a rat-tat-tat-tat made almost every one remark:
"Skirmishing going on over there." Wood's line moved forward, a few
volleys, still Wood's line moved forward, and Sheridan's started forward, heavy work for a few minutes then all was quiet; two important
hills were gained; cheer after cheer rang out in the valley and echoed
and reverberated through the gorges of Lookout and Mission Ridge;
still it was only 5 o'clock Monday afternoon. The bands commenced
playing and the valley was again peaceful, but we all knew there was
"something up," and Bragg must have thought so too.

The men stayed where nightfall found them, sleeping on their arms. Connolly continued:[6]

Tuesday morning, Nov. 24th, broke bright and beautiful; the sun rose clear. . . . Daylight revealed the hills which Wood and Sheridan had won the day before, bristling with cannon of sufficient caliber to reach Bragg's eyrie on Mission Ridge. About 9 o'clock in the morning some 30 heavy guns opened on Mission Ridge. It appeared then that we were to advance right down the valley and attack the rebel centre, but, hark! Away off on our right—3 miles away, on the opposite side of Lookout—we hear firing. What can that mean? Suddenly the cannon, with which we have been pounding away at Mission Ridge, are silent, and all eyes are turned westward toward Lookout Mountain. The sounds of battle increase there but it is on the other side of the mountain from us and we can see nothing, but the word passes around: "Hooker is storming Lookout!" My heart grows faint. Poor Hooker, with his Potomac boys are to be the forlorn hope! What? Storm that mountain peak 2400 feet high, so steep that a squirrel could scarcely climb it, and bristling all over with rebels, bayonets and cannon? Poor boys! Far from your quiet New England homes, you have come a long way only to meet defeat on that mountain peak, and find your graves on its rugged sides! Lookout Mountain will only hereafter be known as a monument to a whole Corps of gallant New Englanders who died there for their country! But hold! Some one exclaims: "The firing comes nearer, our boys are getting up!" All eyes are turned toward the Mountain, and the stillness of death reigns among us in the valley, as we listen to the sounds of battle on the other side of the Mountain while all was quiet as a Puritan sabbath on our side of it. How hope and despair alternated in our breasts! How we prayed for their success and longed to assist them, can only be known by those of us who, in that valley, stood watching that afternoon and listening to the swelling diapason of their battle. But the firing actually did grow nearer, manifestly our men were driving them; Oh! now if they only can continue it, but we fear they cannot! I have a long telescope with which I can distinctly see everything on our side of the mountain. I scan the mountain with it closely and continuously, but not a soul can I see. After hours of anxious suspense I see a single rebel winding his way back from the firing and around to our side of the mountain.

I announce to the crowd of Generals standing around: "There goes a straggler!" and in an instant everybody's glass is to his eye, but no

more stragglers are seen, still the battle rages, and the little gleam of
hope, that solitary straggler raised in our breasts, dies out. Minutes
drag like hours, the suspense is awful, but look! look! Here comes a
crowd of stragglers! here they come by hundreds, yes by thousands!
The mountain is covered with them! They are broken, running!
There comes our flag around the point of the mountain! There comes
one of our regiments on the double quick! Oh! such a cheer as then
went up in the valley! Manly cheeks were wet with tears of joy, our
bands played "Hail to the Chief," and 50 brazen throated cannon, in
the very wantonness of joy, thundered out from the fortifications of
Chattanooga, a salute to the old flag which was then on the mountain
top. The work was done. Lookout was ours, never again to be used as a
perch by rebel vultures. Didn't we of the old Army of the Cumberland
feel proud though? It was one of the regiments that fought at Chickamauga that carried that first flag to the mountain top. It was a brigade
of the old Chickamauga army that led the storming party up the mountain. A straggling skirmish fire was kept up along our (eastern) side
of the mountain, which we could trace by the flashes of the guns, until
11 o'clock at night, but then all became quiet, and again we passed the
night in line of battle, sleeping on our arms.

*Bragg expected Hooker to press forward against the Confederate left at
the south end of Missionary Ridge. During the night of the twenty-
fourth Bragg shifted troops from the northern end of the Ridge to meet
the onslaught. The Confederate commander did not know that Sherman
with his Vicksburg veterans lay concealed north of the Tennessee River
ready to strike at the very point which Bragg had weakened.*

This day in the thick of the fighting, Connolly continued his account:[7]

Before daylight of Wednesday, Nov. 25th, Sherman had his pontoons across the river, about 3 miles north of Chattanooga, and under
cover of a dense fog, crossed his whole Corps and took possession of the
northern extremity of Mission Ridge, finding nothing there but a few
pickets, and there he fell to work fortifying. By this time Bragg saw his
mistake. The attack of Wednesday was to be on his right, at the north
end of Mission Ridge, instead of his left at the south end of the Ridge,
so he hurriedly countermarched his troops back from his left to his right.
When the fog rose, about ten o'clock in the morning, Sherman attempted to carry the summit of the Ridge but was repulsed; again he
tried it but was again repulsed, still again he tried it and was repulsed. . . .

An order came for our Division to move up the river to his support. We started. The enemy could see us from the top of the Ridge, and quickly understood (or thought they did) our design, so they commenced shelling us, as our long line of 20 regiments filed along, but we moved along until we came to where a thin strip of woodland intervened between us and the Ridge. Sheridan's Division followed us and did the same. The enemy supposed of course that we were moving on up the river to the support of Sherman, but we were not; we halted and formed line of battle in that strip of woodland, facing Mission Ridge. This, I confess, staggered me; I couldn't understand it; it looked as though we were going to assault the ridge, and try to carry it by storm, lined and ribbed as it was with rifle pits, and its topmost verge crowded with rebel lines, and at least 40 cannon in our immediate front frowning down on us; we never could live a moment in the open spaces of 600 yards between the strip of woods in which we were formed, and the line of rifle pits at the base of the mountain, exposed as we would be to the fire of the 40 cannon massed, and from five to eight hundred feet immediately above us, also to the infantry fire from the rifle pits.

I rode down along the line of our Division, and there I found Wood's Division formed on our right and facing the Ridge just as we were; I rode on and came to Sheridan's Division formed on Wood's right and facing the same. Here was a line of veteran troops nearly two miles long, all facing Mission Ridge, and out of sight of the enemy. The purpose at once became plain to me, and I hurried back to my own Division, and on asking Gen. Baird he replied: "When 6 guns are fired in quick succession from Fort Wood, the line advances to storm the heights and carry the Ridge if possible. Take that order to Col. Phelps" (commanding the third brigade of our Division) "and tell him to move forward rapidly when he hears the signal." I communicated the order at once and that was the last I saw of the brigade commander, for he was killed just as he reached the summit of the Ridge.

A few moments elapse, it is about half past three o'clock P.M., when suddenly, 6 guns are rapidly fired from Fort Wood. "Forward!" rings out along that long line of men, and forward they go, through the strip of woods, we reach the open space, say 600 yards, between the edge of the woods and the rifle pits at the foot of the Ridge. "Charge!" is shouted wildly from hundreds of throats, and with a yell such as that valley never heard before, the three Divisions (60 regiments) rushed forward; the rebels are silent a moment, but then the batteries on top of the Ridge, open all at once, and the very heavens above us seem to be rent asunder; shells go screaming over our heads, bursting above

and behind us, but they hurt nobody and the men don't notice them;
about midway of the open space a shell bursts directly over my head,
and so near as to make my horse frantic and almost unmanageable; he
plunges and bursts breast strap and girth and off I tumble with the saddle between my legs. My orderly catches my horse at once, throws the
blanket and saddle on him, gives me a "leg lift" and I am mounted
again, without girth, but I hold on with my knees and catch up with our
madcaps at the first rifle pits, over these we go to the second line of pits,
over these we go, some of the rebels lying down to be run over, others
scrambling up the hill which is becoming too steep for horses, and the
General and staff are forced to abandon the direct ascent at about the
second line of rifle pits; the long line of men reach the steepest part of
the mountain, and they must crawl up the best way they can 150 feet
more before they reach the summit, and when they do reach it, can they
hold it? The rebels are there in thousands, behind breastworks, ready
to hurl our brave boys back as they reach their works.

One flag bearer, on hands and knees, is seen away in advance of the
whole line; he crawls and climbs toward a rebel flag he sees waving before him; he gets within a few feet of it and hides behind a fallen log
while he waves his flag defiantly until it almost touches the rebel
flag; his regiment follows him as fast as it can; in a few moments another flag bearer gets just as near the summit at another point, and his
regiment soon gets to him, but these two regiments dare not go the next
twenty feet or they would be annihilated, so they crouch there and are
safe from the rebels above them, who would have to rise up to fire
down at them, and so expose themselves to the fire of our fellows who
are climbing up the mountain.

The suspense is greater, if possible, than that with which we viewed
the storming of Lookout. If we can gain that Ridge, if we can scale those
breastworks, the rebel army is routed, everything is lost for them, but
if we cannot scale the works few of us will get down this mountain side
and back to the shelter of the woods. But a third flag and regiment
reaches the other two; all eyes are turned there; the men away above
us look like great ants crawling up, crouching on the outside of the rebel
breastworks. One of our flags seems to be moving; look! look! look!
Up! Up! Up! it goes and is planted on the rebel works; in a twinkling
the crouching soldiers are up and over the works; apparently quicker
than I can write it the 3 flags and 3 regiments are up, the close fighting
is terrific; other flags go up and over at different points along the mountain top—the batteries have ceased, for friend and foe are mixed in a

surging mass; in a few moments the flags of 60 Yankee regiments float along Mission Ridge from one end to the other, the enemy are plunging down the eastern slope of the Ridge and our men are in hot pursuit, but darkness comes too soon and the pursuit must cease; we go back to the summit of the Ridge and there hold our trophies—dead and wounded rebels under our feet by hundreds, cannon by scores scattered up and down the Ridge with yelling soldiers astraddle them, rebel flags laying around in profusion, and soldiers and officers completely and frantically drunk with excitement. Four hours more of daylight, after we gained that Ridge would not have left two whole pieces of Bragg's army together.

Our men, stirred by the same memories, shouted "Chickamauga!" as they scaled the works at the summit, and amid the din of battle the cry "Chickamauga!" "Chickamauga!" could be heard. That is not *fancy* it is *fact*. Indeed the plain unvarnished facts of the storming of Mission Ridge are more like romance to me now than any I have ever read in Dumas, Scott or Cooper. On that night I lay down upon the ground without blankets and slept soundly, without inquiring whether my neighbors were dead or alive, but, on waking found I was sleeping among bunches of dead rebels and Federals, and within a few rods of where Bragg slept the night before, if he slept at all.

Private Sam Watkins of Company H, First Tennessee, saw the battle as a Confederate:[8]

About two or three o'clock, a column of Yankees advancing to the attack swept right over where I was standing. I was trying to stand aside to get out of their way, but the more I tried to get out of their way, the more in their way I got. I was carried forward, I know not whither. We soon arrived at the foot of the ridge, at our old breastworks. I recognized Robert Brank's old corn stalk house, and Alf Horsley's fort, an old log house called Fort Horsley. I was in front of the enemy's line, and was afraid to run up the ridge, and afraid to surrender. They were ordered to charge up the hill. There was no firing from the Rebel lines in our immediate front. They kept climbing and pulling and scratching until I was in touching distance of the old Rebel breastworks, right on the very apex of Missionary Ridge. I made one jump, and I heard Captain Turner, who had the very four Napoleon guns we had captured at Perryville, halloo out, "Number Four, solid!" and then a roar. The next order was, "Limber to the rear." The

Yankees were cutting and slashing, and the cannoneers were running in every direction. I saw Day's brigade throw down their guns and break like quarter horses. Bragg was trying to rally them. I heard him say, "Here is your commander," and the soldiers hallooed back, "Here is your mule."

Braxton Bragg was as befuddled as Private Sam Watkins:[9]

A panic which I had never before witnessed seemed to have seized upon officers and men, and each seemed to be struggling for his personal safety, regardless of his duty or his character. . . . No satisfactory excuse can possibly be given for the shameful conduct of our troops on the left in allowing their line to be penetrated. The position was one which ought to have been held by a line of skirmishers against any assaulting column, and whenever resistance was made the enemy fled in disorder after suffering heavy loss. Those who reached the ridge did so in a condition of exhaustion from the great physical exertion in climbing which rendered them powerless, and the slightest effort would have destroyed them. Having secured much of our artillery, they soon availed themselves of our panic, and turning our guns upon us enfiladed the lines, both right and left, rendering them entirely untenable. Had all parts of the line been maintained with equal gallantry and persistence, no enemy could ever have dislodged us, and but one possible reason presents itself to my mind in explanation of this bad conduct in veteran troops who never before failed in any duty assigned them, however difficult and hazardous: They had for two days confronted the enemy, marshaling his immense forces in plain view, and exhibiting to their sight such a superiority in numbers as may have intimidated weak-minded and untried soldiers. But our veterans had so often encountered similar hosts when the strength of position was against us, and with perfect success, that not a doubt crossed my mind.

Perhaps Private Watkins knew more about Braxton Bragg than Bragg knew about himself. Recalling Missionary Ridge, Watkins wrote:[10]

I felt sorry for General Bragg. The army was routed, and Bragg looked so scared. Poor fellow, he looked so hacked and whipped and mortified and chagrined at defeat, and all along the line, when

Bragg would pass, the soldiers would raise the yell, "Here is your mule;" "Bully for Bragg, he's h--l on retreat."

IV

When Jefferson Davis sent his annual message to the Confederate Congress on December 7, 1863, he adopted Bragg's explanation for the defeat at Missionary Ridge:[11]

This signal defeat of General Rosecrans [at Chickamauga] was followed by his retreat into Chattanooga, where his imperiled position had the immediate effect of relieving the pressure of the invasion at other points, forcing the concentration for his relief of large bodies of troops withdrawn from the armies in the Mississippi Valley and in Northern Virginia. The combined forces thus accumulated against us in Tennessee so greatly outnumbered our army as to encourage the enemy to attack. After a long and severe battle, in which great carnage was inflicted on him, some of our troops inexplicably abandoned a position of great strength, and by a disorderly retreat compelled the commander to withdraw the forces elsewhere successful, and finally to retreat with his whole army to a position some twenty or thirty miles to the rear. It is believed that if the troops who yielded to the assault had fought with the valor which they had displayed on previous occasions, and which was manifested in this battle on the other parts of the line, the enemy would have been repulsed with very great slaughter, and our country would have escaped the misfortune and the Army the mortification of the first defeat that has resulted from misconduct by the troops.

Davis had other reverses to account for. Gettysburg he blamed on a flooded river:[12]

The able commander who conducted the campaign in Virginia determined to meet the threatened advance on Richmond, for which the enemy had made long and costly preparations, by forcing their armies to cross the Potomac and fight in defense of their own capital and homes. Transferring the battlefield to their own soil, he succeeded in compelling their rapid retreat from Virginia, and in the hard-fought battle of Gettysburg inflicted such severity of punishment as disabled them from early renewal of the campaign as originally projected. Unfortunately the communications on which our general relied for receiving his supplies of munitions were interrupted by extraordinary floods, which so swelled the Potomac as to render impassable the fords by which his advance had been made, and he was thus forced to a withdrawal, which was conducted with deliberation after securing large trains of captured supplies, and with a constant and unaccepted tender of battle. On more than one occasion the enemy has since made demonstrations of a purpose to advance, invariably followed by a precipitate retreat to intrenched lines on the approach of our forces.

The major diplomatic failure of the year—Great Britain's refusal to release the Laird rams—Davis blamed on the obstinacy and partiality of a haughty nation:[13]

I regret to inform you that there has been no improvement in the state of our relations with foreign countries since my message in January last. On the contrary, there has been a still greater divergence in the conduct of European nations from that practical impartiality which alone deserves the name of neutrality, and their action in some cases has assumed a character positively unfriendly. . . .

For nearly three years this Government has exercised unquestioned jurisdiction over many millions of willing and united people. It has met and defeated vast armies of invaders, who have in vain sought its subversion. Supported by the confidence and affection of its citizens, the Confederacy has lacked no element which distinguishes an independent nation according to the principles of public law. Its legislative, executive, and judicial Departments, each in its sphere, have performed their appropriate functions with a regularity as undisturbed as in a time of profound peace, and the whole energies of the people have been developed in the organization of vast armies, while their rights and liberties have rested secure under the protection of courts of justice. This Confederacy is either independent or it is a dependency of the United States; for no other earthly power claims the right to govern it. Without one historic fact on which the pretension can rest, without one line or word of treaty or covenant which can give color to title, the United States have asserted, and the British Government has chosen to concede, that these sovereign States are the dependencies of the Government which is administered at Washington. Great Britain has accordingly entertained with that Government the closest and most intimate relations, while refusing, on its demands, ordinary amicable intercourse with us, and has, under arrangements made with the other nations of Europe, not only denied our just claim of admission into the family of nations, but interposed a passive though effectual bar to the knowledge of our rights by other powers. So soon as it had become apparent by the declarations of the British Ministers in the debates of the British Parliament in July last that Her Majesty's Government was determined to persist indefinitely in a course of policy which under professions of neutrality had become subservient to the designs of our enemy, I felt it my duty to recall the Commissioner formerly accredited to that Court, and the correspondence on the subject is submitted to you.

Davis could see no early end to the war, which continued only because of Northern perversity and degradation:[14]

The hope last year [1862] entertained of an early termination of the war has not been realized. Could carnage have satisfied the appetite of our enemy for the destruction of human life, or grief have appeased their wanton desire to inflict human suffering, there has been bloodshed enough on both sides, and two lands have been sufficiently darkened by the weeds of mourning to induce a disposition for peace.

If unanimity in a people could dispel delusion, it has been displayed too unmistakably not to have silenced the pretense that the Southern States were merely disturbed by a factious insurrection, but it must long since have been admitted that they were but exercising their reserved right to modify their own Government in such manner as would best secure their own happiness. But these considerations have been powerless to allay the unchristian hate of those who, long accustomed to draw large profits from a union with us, cannot control the rage excited by the conviction that they have by their own folly destroyed the richest sources of their prosperity. They refuse even to listen to proposals for the only peace possible between us—a peace which, recognizing the impassable gulf which divides us, may leave the two peoples separately to recover from the injuries inflicted on both by the causeless war now waged against us. Having begun the war in direct violation of their Constitution, which forbade the attempt to coerce a State, they have been hardened by crime until they no longer attempt to veil their purpose to destroy the institutions and subvert the sovereignty and independence of these States. We now know that the only reliable hope for peace is in the vigor of our resistance, while the cessation of their hostility is only to be expected from the pressure of their necessities.

The patriotism of the people has proved equal to every sacrifice demanded by their country's need. We have been united as a people never were united under like circumstances before. God has blessed us with success disproportionate to our means, and under His divine favor our labors must at last be crowned with the reward due to men who have given all they possessed to the righteous defense of their inalienable rights, their homes, and their altars.

V

One day after Davis' message was read, the Congress of the United States heard Abraham Lincoln's annual report on the state of the Union. The document was a calm recital of progress in many fields. Of one subject the President wrote with particular satisfaction:[15]

When Congress assembled a year ago the war had already lasted nearly twenty months, and there had been many conflicts on both land and sea, with varying results.

The rebellion had been pressed back into reduced limits; yet the tone of public feeling and opinion, at home and abroad, was not satisfactory. With other signs, the popular elections, then just past, indicated uneasiness among ourselves, while amid much that was cold and menacing the kindest words coming from Europe were uttered in accents of pity, that we were too blind to surrender a hopeless cause. Our commerce was suffering greatly by a few armed vessels built upon and furnished from foreign shores, and we were threatened with such additions from the same quarter as would sweep our trade from the sea and raise our blockade. We had failed to elicit from European governments anything hopeful upon this subject. The preliminary emancipation proclamation, issued in September, was running its assigned period to the beginning of the new year. A month later the final proclamation came, including the announcement that colored men of suitable condition would be received into the war service. The policy of emancipation, and of employing black soldiers, gave to the future a new aspect, about which hope, and fear, and doubt contended in uncertain conflict. According to our political system, as a matter of civil administration, the general government had no lawful power to effect emancipation in any State, and for a long time it had been hoped that the rebellion could be suppressed without resorting to it as a military measure. It was all the while deemed possible that the necessity for it might come, and that if it should, the crisis of the contest would then be presented. It came, and as was anticipated, it was followed by dark and doubtful days. Eleven months having now passed, we are permitted to take another review. The rebel borders are pressed still further back, and by the complete opening of the Mississippi the country dominated by the rebellion is divided into distinct parts, with no practical communication between them. Tennessee and Arkansas have been substantially cleared of insurgent control, and influential citizens in both, owners of slaves and advocates of slavery at the beginning of the rebellion, now declare openly for emancipation in their respective States. Of those States not included in the emancipation proclamation, Maryland, and Missouri, neither of which three years ago would tolerate any restraint upon the extension of slavery into new territories, only dispute now as to the best mode of removing it within their own limits.

Of those who were slaves at the beginning of the rebellion, full one hundred thousand are now in the United States military service, about one-half of which number actually bear arms in the ranks; thus giving the double advantage of taking so much labor from the insurgent cause, and supplying the places which otherwise must be filled with so many white men. So far as tested, it is difficult to say they are not as good soldiers as any. No servile insurrection, or tendency to violence or cruelty, has marked the measures of emancipation and arming the blacks. These measures have been much discussed in foreign countries, and contemporary with such discussion the tone of public sentiment there is much improved. At home the same measures have been fully discussed, supported, criticised, and denounced, and the annual elections following are highly encouraging to those whose official duty it is to bear the country through this great trial. Thus we have the new reckoning. The crisis which threatened to divide the friends of the Union is past.

Jefferson Davis had been unable to see an end to the conflict; Lincoln could look forward to an increasing extension of the Federal authority as the Union armies pushed into Confederate territory. Accordingly, the President had issued a proclamation, dated the same day as his message,* providing a plan for reunion. The proclamation had two basic features. The first was an oath of allegiance offered to all except those "who are, or shall have been, civil or diplomatic officers or agents of the so-called confederate government; all who have left judicial stations

* That is, December 8, 1863.

under the United States to aid the rebellion; all who are, or shall have been, military or naval officers of said so-called confederate government above the rank of colonel in the army, or of lieutenant in the navy; all who left seats in the United States Congress to aid the rebellion; all who resigned commissions in the army or navy of the United States, and afterwards aided the rebellion; and all who have engaged in any way in treating colored persons or white persons, in charge of such, otherwise than lawfully as prisoners of war, and which persons may have been found in the United States service, as soldiers, seamen, or in any other capacity."

The oath read: "I, ———, do solemnly swear, in presence of Almighty God, that I will henceforth faithfully support, protect and defend the Constitution of the United States, and the Union of the States thereunder; and that I will, in like manner, abide by and faithfully support all acts of Congress passed during the existing rebellion with reference to slaves, so long and so far as not repealed, modified or held void by Congress, or by decision of the Supreme Court; and that I will, in like manner, abide by and faithfully support all proclamations of the President made during the existing rebellion having reference to slaves, so long and so far as not modified or declared void by decision of the Supreme Court. So help me God."

The second feature of the proclamation provided for re-establishing state governments: "Whenever, in any of the States of Arkansas, Texas, Louisiana, Mississippi, Tennessee, Alabama, Georgia, Florida, South Carolina, and North Carolina, a number of persons, not less than one-tenth in number of the votes cast in such State at the Presidential election of the year of our Lord one thousand eight hundred and sixty, each having taken the oath aforesaid and not having since violated it, and being a qualified voter by the election law of the State existing immediately before the so-called act of secession, and excluding all others, shall re-establish a State government which shall be republican, and in no wise contravening said oath, such shall be recognized as the true government of the State, and the State shall receive thereunder the benefits of the constitutional provision which declares that 'The United States shall guaranty to every State in this union a republican form of government, and shall protect each of them against invasion; and, on application of the legislature, or the executive, (when the legislature cannot be convened,) against domestic violence.'"

Lincoln closed on a note of caution—and gratitude:

In the midst of other cares, however important, we must not lose sight of the fact that the war power is still our main reliance. To that power alone can we look, yet for a time, to give confidence to the people in the contested regions, that the insurgent power will not again overrun them. Until that confidence shall be established, little can be done anywhere for what is called reconstruction. Hence our chiefest care must still be directed to the army and navy, who have thus far borne their harder part so nobly and well. And it may be esteemed fortunate that in giving the greatest efficiency to these indispensable arms, we do also honorably recognize the gallant men, from commander to sentinel, who compose them, and to whom, more than to others, the world must stand indebted for the home of freedom disenthralled, regenerated, enlarged, and perpetuated.

VI

While Lincoln worked on his annual message J. T. Fields, editor of the Atlantic Monthly, *or some member of his staff, was composing a long review of the year 1863. The article, entitled "The Beginning of the End," appeared in the issue for January 1864. After reciting the record of military and domestic events and describing the diplomatic successes of the Union, the author closed with a paragraph contradicting Jefferson Davis' assumption of divine favor:*[16]

Such was the year of the Proclamation, and its history is marvellous in our eyes. It stands in striking contrast to the other years of the war, both of which closed badly for us, and left the impression that the enemy's case was a good one, speaking militarily. Our improved condition should be attributed to the true cause. When, in the Parliament of 1601, Mr. Speaker Croke said that the kingdom of England "had been defended by the mighty arm of the Queen," Elizabeth exclaimed from the throne, "No, Mr. Speaker, but rather by the mighty hand of God!" So with us. We have been saved "by the mighty hand of God." Neither "malice domestic" nor "foreign levy" has prevailed at our expense. Whether we had the right to expect Heaven's aid, we cannot undertake to say; but we know that we should not have deserved it, had we continued to link the nation's cause to that of oppression, and had we shed blood and expended gold in order to restore the system of slavery and the sway of slaveholders.

THE DEPTHS
OF SUFFERING

A̲T MISSIONARY RIDGE, for almost the only time between 1861 and 1865, war became the romantic adventure pictured by the artists of *Leslie's* and *Harper's*, with bands blaring, color-bearers advancing flags, and lines of cheering men following sword-waving officers. Much of the time war was nasty, nameless little fights. Yet the two or three men killed in such encounters were just as dead as the 1,114 (Federal, 753; Confederate, 361) who lost their lives in the spectacular storming of the heights south and east of Chattanooga.

I

Confederate Cavalry Sergeant Edwin H. Fay described a brush with the enemy which took place in western Mississippi in mid-October 1863:[1]

Last Thursday morning our scouts announced the enemy coming and all was bustle and confusion loading up our wagons and sending them to the rear. We saddled up and drew up in line of battle across our camp. Capt. Bowie of Adams Regt. was on picket and held them at bay all day but lost one man, an old Ala. acquaintance of mine, Charley Drummond from Greenville, Ala. a mess mate of Zeb. Rudulph. Poor fellow he was a good soldier and the bravest among the brave. We lay in line of battle that night and next morning the pickets falling back the enemy advanced and planted a battery within 1000 yards of ours and one of the fiercest artillery duels of the war commenced. We silenced the enemy's battery and they commenced flanking us on the right and left when we fell back about a mile and waited their approach. About 100 skirmishers held the column at bay all the rest of the day. We fell back at night some two miles and the enemy, 10,000 strong, only advanced 2 miles in two days though only opposed by 1000 cavalry and a battery of four guns. They had 30 pieces of artillery and 2500 cavalry. They took (Saturday Morn.) another road and found Gen'l John W. Whitfield and his Texans on it supported by Col. Logan's command. They skirmished all day near Livingston while we went to Canton and next morning started early to reinforce them. Loring's Division of Infantry was waiting near Canton but Sunday morning or rather Saturday night the Yanks got wind of it and started back towards Vicksburg at a double quick. We cut them off at their right flank at the Baker Creek ground but they had their wagons guarded on both sides with a double file of Infantry and our officers deemed it not prudent to attack them, so we lay still and let them pass by unmolested.

There were murmurings loud and deep from the soldiers of the brigade because the Yanks escaped us. They brought out 300 wagons some loaded with entrenching tools and telegraph wires evidently intending to take Canton and occupy it, but they met such stubborn resistance from our cavalry that they concluded west of Big Black was a safer place. They told citizens on their retreat that we had 30 thousand infantry fighting them. We lost four killed and ten wounded in our brigade, and ten or 15 graves of Yankees we have found on our battle field.

Lieutenant John Merrilies, Battery E, Illinois Light Artillery, described another of the thousands of minor expeditions in which the armies were engaged in the intervals between big battles:[2]

Dec. 2nd. 1863. Turned out at 3 o.c. Ordered to draw three days' rations of coffee and hard bread and be ready to march at daylight. Forrest reported to be in the neighborhood, evidently contemplating another raid on the R. R. Marched at 6 o.c., a brigade of cavalry and the 2nd Brigade of our division composing the expedition, Tuttle and Mowrer commanding. Followed the railroad east, marching quick. Passed thro Grand Junction and Salisbury in the forenoon, Middleton in the afternoon and by dark were within five miles of Pocahontas, which was to be our destination, the track having been torn up there yesterday. Halted here till word was brought back by the cavalry that there was no enemy in town or near it. Lay in the road all night, the horses hitched up, ordered to be in readiness at a moment's notice, notwithstanding which the men dropped asleep around the fires, worn out by the forced marching. At 2 in the morning turned out again, reversed the battery, and started back by 6 o.c. getting safely across the terrible Hatchie bottoms, which at present may be called bottomless.

Dec. 3. Reports of the rebs having got behind us last night, struck the R. R. at Salisbury, and destroyed the track. The story did not appear probable at first, but about noon skirmishing commenced ahead and the people along the road say there are about 3000 in the neighborhood of Salisbury. Marched ahead lively, but we failed to come in range, the cavalry driving them. Some artillery skirmishing commenced, continuing about an hour. Their cavalry had drawn up in two lines, but our mountain howitzers made it too hot for them, and the appearance of our column coming over the hill, admonished them to leave which they did in different directions, our cavalry pursuing. Reached La Grange at 5 o.c., horses and men badly used up, having marched over 40 miles since we left camp yesterday morning, with no better result from our journey than having the enemy double on us very handsomely, tear up our railroad six miles from camp, and get away again with little or no punishment.

II

Oftener even than little scouts and skirmishes, war was boredom, aimless marching, drudgery, disgust. Witness the diary of James Daniels, Fifth New Hampshire Volunteers, for two weeks in May 1863:[3]

May 7th. In camp near Falmouth. Fixed up our old tents. Dress-parade at night. Rained.

May 8th. In camp. Pleasant. Dress-parade.

May 9th. In camp. Pleasant.

May 10th. In camp. Inspection.

May 11th. In camp. Inspection. Dress-parade.

May 12th. In camp. Two hours' drill in forenoon. Dress-parade. Pleasant.

May 13th. In camp. No drill. Pleasant.

May 14th. In camp. Squad drill. Some rain. Dress-parade.

May 15th. In camp. Pleasant. Battalion drill in the afternoon. Dress-parade.

May 16th. In camp. Dress-parade. Pleasant.

May 17th. In camp. Was detailed on picket; was excused from duty by the doctor; abscess in the groin. Pleasant. Dress-parade.

May 18th. In camp, sick. Pleasant. Dress-parade. The colonel came back from Washington.

May 19th. Sick. Drill. Dress-parade. Pleasant.

May 20th. In camp. Moved from the old camp to a new one about a half mile in the rear. Pleasant all day.

May 21st. In camp. Detailed to dig a spring; made a good one. Pleasant all day.

In the fall of 1863 Albert Dickinson, of Taylor's Battery, Illinois Artillery, floundered around in northern Alabama:[4]

Oct. 28th. 22 years old today. Left Tuscumbia in morn & arrived at Cherokee at sundown.

29th. Heavy skirmishing Osterhaus front. We harnessed up. About noon we harnessed & went out about 2 miles & staid afternoon. Skirmishing all day in front.

30th. Started for Tennessee river, was stopped on act bad roads in front. Made about 3 or 4 miles & camped. Rained very hard during the day. . . .

31st. Marched through to Chickasaw Landing about 7 miles. Arrived in camp about 10 P.M. It was the most disagreeable days march we ever made. Marched few yards then stopped, all day long. Very cold at night. No hard bread. . . .

Nov. 1st. Stopped in Chickasaw all day. Charles B. Andrews was appointed Sergeant of Squad 4. Bill Turner appointed artificer.

Nov. 2nd. Got up at 1 A.M. & crossed Tenn River. Marched to Waterloo. Splendid springs all along the road.

Nove. 3rd. Marched to Florence. Camped mile beyond town. Splendid country. Cypress Mills. Seminary. Nice town. Had good dinner at house.

At the same time Florison D. Pitts, also an Illinois artilleryman, did nothing in Louisiana:[5]

Sunday, Nov. 1st, 1863. Put on a clean shirt. Had a pow wow in the evening. Day cloudy & rainy. Read all day.

Nov. 2nd. Had a drill in the morning. Went out as cannoneer. Mouth sore could not blow the bugle. Got a pass and went down town in afternoon. Played three games with Hugh Wilson. Day very warm. . . . Went to town in evening on my horse.

Nov. 3rd. Drilled in the morning, Cone drill master. Went out on my horse, again played coming through town. Got every body out to see what was the row. Went out and practiced Bugle in afternoon. Evening Deacon & myself took a walk in vicinity of the camp. Played flute with Roe in afternoon. Had a sing in the evening.

Nov. 4th. Drilled in the morning. Day clear & quite warm. Throop drill master. Drilled principally in the Bugle calls, fooled the Boys a good deal on them. Mail came in, got a paper from Mother & a letter from Jennie. Boys went out after cattle.

Nov. 5th. Got up at 6 o'clock in time for Breakfast. Cloudy & some rain. After Breakfast greased my Saddle & Boots. Rain came down all the afternoon. Wrote a letter to Jennie. Evening played whist with Throop & Roe. . . .

Nov. 6th. Day warm & Sultry. Read abt all day, finished *Frank Fowleigh*. In evening wrote to Mother & Charlie Pitts. No drill today, practiced Bugle in afternoon. . . .

Nov. 7th. Drilled in morning under Cone. . . . Went down town in evening. Practiced Bugle in afternoon. Day bright & warm.

A year of inactivity had reduced the Texas cavalryman Edwin H. Fay to a state of complete disgust. From Raymond, Mississippi, he wrote to his wife on September 19, 1863:[6]

This Cavalry has done nothing since a year ago. Our Co. has done nothing and worse than nothing since the fight at Corinth last Oct. Do you wonder then that I am dissatisfied when I see the Confed. losing ground daily and feel that I am so situated that I can do nothing. Our Cavalry wastes its time in grand Reviews before Hardee & Stephen D. Lee and dress parades for a few lonesome and garish young ladies. Noble employment for a band of men.

III

The soldier who had to endure only boredom and drudgery was fortunate; the wounded and the prisoners were war's pitiable victims. Sergeant Joseph F. Johnston, Company K, Nineteenth Illinois Infantry, described an experience shared by many thousands, on both sides:

FIELD HOSPITAL OPPOSITE
CHATTANOOGA TENN. Oct 1st

DEAR MOTHER

I am wounded through the left shoulder, the ball entering below
the joint of the shoulder blade & coming out just below the collar bone,
thus passing through the top of the left lung. I have to lie on my back
the only position in which I can breathe with ease. I can walk a little
ways but it makes me breathe hard. I was hit Sunday between 12 &
2 o'clock and as the regt was falling back I was carried off the field by
some of my own boys. I was left at a shanty about 7 miles from Chattanooga & two boys of my own company stayed with me to take care of
me. They did all they could until 11 AM Monday when the secesh
cavalry took them prisoners. The rebs left six nurses for 53 wounded
& the nurse who took care of me was very kind. I had cold water constantly by my side & I kept the wound cool all the time. I was bilious &
could eat little & what hunger I had was relieved by bran biscuit. There
was one small one for each meal. On Sunday the 27th the rebs came
with army wagons & moved on to Cloud Springs 5 miles. Tuesday Rosecrans sent 200 ambulances & took 800 wounded from Cloud Springs
to Chattanooga. I was dumped in an old grocery store late at night &
did not sleep a wink on the hard floor. Wednesday a lot of my boys
came to see me. One of them spoke to Dr Bogue & he sent me over here.
With so much riding I was very tired. I will not move an inch now till
I get strong enough. I am here with the wounded of our own regt, with
our own boys to wait on us & our own surgeon. I will now get the best
care the place will afford. . . .

Your affectionate son
J. S. JOHNSTON

*A month later Sergeant Johnston was still in the hospital (he was not
to be discharged until early January 1864):*

FIELD HOSP OPP CHATT
TENN. Nov 1st 1863

DEAR FATHER

The chills I spoke of in my last have gone away. The Dr ascribed it
to biliousness & gave me some "Cathartic Pills" which helped me very
much. Yesterday & the day before were cold & made me a little bilious
but today the sun shone pleasant and I put on a jacket Fred Temple

gave me and made a journey of over a quarter of a mile & back which fatigued me and gave me a little appetite.

But alas! we are reduced on rations. While the army received nothing we have half rations—*mouldy* crackers. I will have to come pretty near starving before I eat them.

The Dr says it is the diet that makes me bilious & he will send me off the first chance. The ambulance train is here but they seem to be waiting to send us *"down the river.".* . . . I have seen Elder Raymond again. He brought me a can of milk. I can get nothing of that sort after this. Army half rations is my lot. . . .

> Your Aff. Son
> J. S. JOHNSTON

Field hospitals were shambles. A correspondent of the Cincinnati Gazette, *writing from headquarters of the Army of the Cumberland on September 23, 1863, described the Union wounded and the treatment they received at Chickamauga:*[7]

A few miles' riding brought us so far on the way that we began to get glimpses of that stream of wreck, debris, mingled life and mangled humanity which always flows from a battle-field. . . .

Here is a man with an arm roughly bandaged and very bloody. The blood has dried upon it and hangs to it in great black clots. "Who are you?" "Private ———, of the Thirty-eighth Indiana." "What news have you?" "Bad enough." "Has your regiment been in the fight?" "If it has not no one has." "With what result?" "One third of its members are killed and wounded." "Were you whipped?" "Our brigade was left unsupported, overpowered by numbers, and compelled for a time to give way." "Is Colonel Scribner safe?" "So far as I know, he is."

Another with a ghastly wound in his head has upon his jacket the red stripes which show him to be an artilleryman. "Whose battery do you belong to?" "Guenther's." "Why, that is the regular battery belonging to General King's brigade; what has it been doing?" "It has been taken by the enemy." "Can that be possible?" "It is, but I have heard since that it was retaken." "How came it to be lost?" "The infantry supports gave way, and the horses being nearly all killed, of course the guns were captured."

The stream grew stronger and stronger. Stragglers were run over by wagons dashing back toward the rear. Ambulances, filled with wounded, came in long procession from toward where the battle was raging. Men with wounds of every imaginable description not affecting their locomotion, came staggering by on foot, and scores even of those who had been shot in their lower limbs, hobbled slowly on through blinding masses of dust, which at times concealed every thing from view.

At length we reached the hospital for General Brannan's division. The house had already been filled. The outhouses had been brought into requisition, and large numbers of sufferers were lying on the ground in the yard. In one corner was an operating table, beneath which lay the usual quantity of legs, arms, hands, feet, fingers, and toes. Here and there among the wounded were some cold and stiff, the seal of death upon their countenances. These had died after being carried to the yard.

Major General Carl Schurz, who commanded the Eleventh Corps at Gettysburg, watched the surgeons at work immediately after the battle:[8]

The wounded—many thousands of them—were carried to the farm-steads behind our lines. The houses, the barns, the sheds, and the open barnyards were crowded with the moaning and wailing human beings, and still an unceasing procession of stretchers and ambulances was coming in from all sides to augment the number of the sufferers. A heavy rain set in during the day—the usual rain after a battle—and large numbers had to remain unprotected in the open, there being no room left under roof. I saw long rows of men lying under the eaves of the buildings, the water pouring down upon their bodies in streams. Most of the operating tables were placed in the open where the light was best, some of them partially protected against the rain by tarpaulins or blankets stretched upon poles.

There stood the surgeons, their sleeves rolled up to the elbows, their bare arms as well as their linen aprons smeared with blood, their knives not seldom held between their teeth, while they were helping a patient on or off the table, or had their hands otherwise occupied; around them pools of blood and amputated arms or legs in heaps, sometimes more than man-high. Antiseptic methods were still unknown at that time. As a wounded man was lifted on the table, often shrieking with pain as the attendants handled him, the surgeon quickly examined the wound and resolved upon cutting off the injured limb. Some ether was administered and the body put in position in a moment. The surgeon snatched his knife from between his teeth, where it had been while his hands were busy, wiped it rapidly once or twice across his blood-stained apron, and the cutting began. The operation accomplished, the surgeon would look around with a deep sigh, and then—"Next!"

And so it went, hour after hour, while the number of expectant patients seemed hardly to diminish. Now and then one of the wounded men would call attention to the fact that his neighbor lying on the ground had given up the ghost while waiting for his turn, and the dead body was then quietly removed. Or a surgeon, having been long at work, would put down his knife, exclaiming that his hand had grown unsteady, and that this was too much for human endurance—not seldom hysterical tears streaming down his face. Many of the wounded men suffered with silent fortitude, fierce determination in the knitting of their brows and the steady gaze of their bloodshot eyes. Some would even force themselves to a grim jest about their situation or about the "skedaddling of the rebels." But there were, too, heart-rending groans and shrill cries of pain piercing the air, and despairing exclamations, "Oh, Lord! Oh, Lord!" or "Let me die!" or softer murmurings in which the words "mother" or "father" or "home" were often heard.

From battlefield stations the badly wounded and gravely ill flowed into general hospitals. Cornelia Hancock, a young Quaker woman serving as a government nurse at Letterman General Hospital, Gettysburg, wrote of her life there in letters to members of her family:[9]

Aug. 8th, 1863

. . . Our hospital is on rising ground, divided off into six avenues, and eighteen tents holding twelve men each on each avenue. We call four tents a ward and name them by a letter; mine is ward E. The water is excellent and there is order about everything. I like it a great deal better than the battlefield, but the battlefield is where one does most good. . . .

It is now about nine o'clock, every tent has a light in it, and a lot of groaning sick men. Our cook-house alone is a sight; they have meals cooked for thirteen hundred men, so you may know that they have to have the pots middling size. If you ever saw anything done on a large scale, it is done so here. There are many sights here, but the most melancholy one is to see the wounded come in in a long train of ambulances after night fall. I must be hardhearted though, for I do not feel these things as strangers do. . . .

I think we have some excellent nurses; we must have at least thirty women in the whole hospital. I have one tent of Johnnies in my ward, but I am not obliged to give them anything but whiskey. . . .

Aug. 17, 1863

. . . I do think military matters are enough to aggravate a saint. We no sooner get a good physician than an order comes to remove, promote, demote or *something*. Everything seems to be done to aggravate the wounded. They do not get any butter; there is certainly a want of generalship somewhere for there is surely enough butter in the United States to feed these brave wounded. There are many hardships that soldiers have to endure that cannot be explained unless experienced. I have nothing to do in the hospital after dark which is well for me—all the skin is off my toes, marching so much. I am not tired of being here, feel so much interest in the men under my charge. The friends of men who have died seem so grateful to me for the little that it was in my power to do for them. I saw a man die in half a minute from the effects of chloroform; there is nothing that has affected me so much since I have been here; it seems almost like deliberate murder. His friends arrived today but he had to be buried before they came. Every kind of distress comes upon the friends of soldiers. . . .

Aug. 31st, 1863

. . . All the men in my ward are doing well but two. Rufus M. is in process of dying. He belongs to the 111th New York, has keen black eyes and laid in the upper tent where thee saw him. I have taken every care of him that is possible; was determined to save him, his leg has commenced bleeding and he cannot last long. . . .

We had the medical director around yesterday, had a big inspection; he was a real alive man, went with the surgeon in charge of this hospital, went into every tent, pointed to every man, asked him the point blank question "Do you get enough to eat?" The men, of course, answered in the negative. Then in the presence of Chamberlain said: "The first thing to set your self about is feeding these men; there is nothing better, *feed them*, I say, feed them. Feed them till they can't complain." Said he had been in the service twenty-five years. Said *he* could feed men till they would not complain. Said clean avenues and clean tents would not cure a man. Things were better today and they will be, I know. The old gentleman stuck his head in every oven, in the barrels, into everything and is still on hand. . . .

Southern hospitals differed little from those in the North. Mrs. Thomas Pember, superintendent of a wing in Chimborazo Hospital, Richmond, described some of her duties in a way that throws light on the medical practices of the time:[10]

The duty which of all others pressed most heavily upon me and which I never did perform voluntarily was that of telling a man he could not live, when he was perhaps unconscious that there was any danger apprehended from his wound. The idea of death so seldom occurs when disease and suffering have not wasted the frame and destroyed the vital energies, that there is but little opening or encouragement to commence such a subject unless the patient suspects the result ever so slightly. In many cases too, the yearning for life was so strong that to destroy the hope was beyond human power. Life was for him a furlough, family and friends once more around him; a future was all he wanted, and he considered it cheaply purchased if only for a month by the endurance of any wound, however painful or wearisome.

There were long discussions among those responsible during the war, as to the advisability of the frequent amputations on the field, and often when a hearty, fine-looking man in the prime of life would be brought in minus an arm or leg, I would feel as if it might have been saved, but experience taught me the wisdom of prompt measures. Poor food and great exposure had thinned the blood and broken down the system so entirely that secondary amputations performed in the hospital almost invariably resulted in death, after the second year of the war. The blood lost on the battlefield when the wound was first received would enfeeble the already impaired system and render it incapable of further endurance.

Once we received a strong, stalwart soldier from Alabama, and after five days' nursing, finding the inflammation from the wound in his arm too great to save the limb, the attending surgeon requested me to feed him on the best I could command; by that means to try and give him strength to undergo amputation. Irritability of stomach as well as indifference to food always accompanying gun-shot wounds, it was necessary, while the fever continued, to give him as much nourishment in as small a compass as possible, as well as easily digestible food, that would assimilate with his enfeebled condition. Beef tea he (in common with all soldiers and I believe men) would not, or could not take, or anything I suggested as an equivalent, so getting his consent to drink some "chemical mixture," I prepared the infusion. Chipping up a pound of beef and pouring upon it a half pint of water, the mixture was stirred until all the blood was extracted, and only a tea-spoonful of white fibre remained; a little salt was added, and favored by the darkness of the corner of the ward in which he lay, I induced him to swallow it. He drank without suspicion, and fortunately liked it, only complaining of its being too sweet; and by the end of ten days his pulse was fairly good, and there had been no accession of fever. Every precaution was taken, both for his sake and the benefit of the experiment, and the arm taken off by the most skillful surgeon we had. After the amputation, which he bore bravely, he looked as bright and well as before, and so on for five days—then the usual results followed. The system proved not strong enough to throw out the "pus" or inflammation; and this, mingling with the blood, produced that most fatal of all diseases, pyaemia, from which no one ever recovers.

He was only one of numerous cases, so that my heart beat twice as rapidly as ordinarily whenever there were any arrangements progressing for amputation, after any length of time had elapsed since the wound, or any effort made to save the limb. The only cases under my observation that survived were two Irishmen, and it was really so difficult to kill an Irishman that there was little cause for boasting on the part of the officiating surgeons.

In the light of modern practice the surgical and hospital records of the Civil War look barbarous. Yet George Worthington Adams, whose book, Doctors in Blue, *is an able study of the medical history of the Union Army, concludes: "The medical and sanitary record of the Civil War was on the whole a good one. That this has not been generally realized is partly due to the fact that the Civil War took place at the very end of the medical 'middle ages'—immediately before bacteriology and aseptic surgery made some of the war generation's triumphs seem piddling or irrelevant." H. H. Cunningham in a companion work,* Doctors in Gray, *offers a similar but more detailed appraisal:*[11]

Confederate medical officers met the demands imposed upon them as courageously and as effectively as could have been expected. Visits to hospitals other than their own for purposes of investigation, the formation of medical societies, quiz classes, and the like all would appear to indicate the presence of a desire to improve themselves professionally; and while there was much that they did not know the restrictions to which they were sometimes subjected made it impossible for them to apply what they did know. "We did not do the best we would," explained one, "but the best we could." Some of the disadvantages under which Confederate medical officers worked was set forth concisely by one of their number: "The surgeon-general issued some valuable and useful publications, but we had no 'Medical and Surgical History of the Confederate States'; we had scarcely a journal; we had no 'Army Medical Museum'; we had no men of science and leisure to produce original work, or to record, classify and arrange the rich and abundant material gathered in the departments of either medicine or surgery. . . ."

Neither, it might be added, did they have blood plasma, x-rays, antibiotics, vitamin concentrates, vaccine to prevent typhoid fever and tetanus, and other products of recent medical and surgical research considered so essential today to the military medical officer. Nor did they have in the latter part of the war—perhaps after the battle of Chickamauga—patients whose physical condition was favorably influenced by a confident mental outlook. The men became less and less sanguine as the war entered its final stages, and the surgeons' task was rendered more difficult by the ensuing mental depression. Yet available records for the war years appear to indicate that the annual mortality and disease mortality rates throughout the conflict were less than those of other armies (except for those of the Union forces which were also relatively low) that took the field in the nineteenth century.

IV

On the morning of April 8, 1862, the day after the Battle of Shiloh, Willie Barrow, a young Confederate soldier from St. Francisville, Louisiana, found himself a prisoner of war. In the next two weeks he experienced hardships which were the common lot of hundreds of thousands, Union and Confederate, between 1862 and 1865:[12]

Wednesday, 9th. This morning I awoke early after setting up half the night with the wounded. They were all much better. They began moving them about nine o'clock to the river; about one I went with one load. Got to the river at two o'clock and a man separated me from the wounded and carried me to General Buell's quarters on the *Empress*. He had me sent to the provost-marshal and from there I went where the rest of the prisoners were.

Thursday, 10th. This morning I was up early as there was no use to attempt to sleep. We had nothing to eat until nine o'clock when they brought us a barrel of crackers and some bacon. We fried the bacon on sticks. Lord deliver me from such hardships. Sitting on the ground trying to keep warm our eyes filled with smoke and no handkerchief to blow my nose on. Sky cloudy.

Friday, April 11th. This morning it commenced to rain. We had nothing to eat but what was given to us the day before. We staid in the rain trying to keep as dry as possible before the fires. About two o'clock the provost marshal came and called us out in two ranks and called the roll to see if we were all there; they then marched us between two rows of Wisconsin troops to the river where we got aboard the *Woodford*. I slept on some straw; went to bed without anything to eat, but slept pretty sound notwithstanding the poor accommodations.

Saturday, April 12th. This morning I awoke early after a pretty sound sleep. Had for breakfast a piece of bacon, a hard cracker and a little coffee. We got out of the Tennessee in to the Ohio river about twelve o'clk. Got to Paducah about one o'clk. For dinner I had a piece of bacon and a hard cracker. This afternoon I got a paper of the 10th giving an account of the battle of Pittsburgh [Landing]. We got to Cairo about four o'clk in the morning where we staid until 10 o'clk. Weather sultry.

Sunday, April 13th. This morning I awoke bright and early as usual. Had for breakfast a hard cracker and some coffee. Got a little soap and succeeded in getting a little dirt off my hands. For dinner I had the same as for breakfast, a hard biscuit and some coffee. We were in the Mississippi river running five miles an hour. Weather cool but pleasant. I changed my bed from the straw to some hard boards.

Monday, April 14th. This morning I awoke and found myself in St. Louis, Mo.

April 23rd. We staid in St. Louis for two or three days and from there came to Chicago, Camp Douglas, where they keep all their prisoners. The reason I have not kept up my regular journal is that I have been suffering from dysinterry. The weather here is very cold and goes very hard with the boys from the south.

At Camp Douglas, Barrow found no serious cause for complaint:

Chicago, Sunday, April 27th, 1862. I am now getting over my attack of dysinterry and will commence my journal again. We are very well fixed off for prisoners. Our quarters are plenty large enough and we are permitted to go out and walk in the inclosure. Today I read and slept the day away. . . .

April 28th. This morning I was up early. After breakfast which consisted of a piece of toast and some arrow root, I read and played a game of eucre. They treat us as if we were their own soldiers, give us the same rations and everything that is necessary: for dinner we had irish potatoes and hominy. In the evening I passed the time by sleeping and reading. The weather is moderating and getting quite pleasant. . . .

Thursday, May 1st. I was up early this morning and learnt that I was to be the cook for the day. I started and made coffee for breakfast; for dinner I had beans, fried beef, and irish potatoes. After dinner I cleaned the pots and then past some of my time reading. For supper we had coffee and bread. I past the rest of my time playing whist. Weather is a little rainy. My imprisonment is beginning to pass away a little better than when I was sick. . . .

May 4th. This morning I was up a little later than usual. Blacked my shoes as it was sunday and fixed myself as nice as possible. After breakfast I read six chapters in the New Testament. Afterwards I lounged around until dinner time. After dinner I walked down in camp. . . .

May 14th. This morning after breakfast I read "Travels in Denmark & Sweden"; we got some books through the kind ladies in St. Louis, and we get books at this place through a parson (Presby) by the name of Tutle. Our dinner today was very good for prisoners-of-war; we had beef-steak, mashed-irish-potatoes, and a bread-pudding with a nice sauce. The beef-steak and potatoes was the ration but the sauce was not. . . .

June 1st. Today was a miserable day, rain, a cold wind, muddy, in fact, I have never experienced a worse one—I had to go to bed to keep warm. I tried to read—but it was too cold and disagreeable. How people can live in such a climate I cannot conceive. We received the news of the evacuation of Corinth by Beauregard. I am reading the Count of Monte Christo which is very interesting. . . .

June 4th. This morning the first thing I caught was a body louse, Ugh! Well that was strange, I did not know what kind of a louse it was. All night I was restless, scratching away at what I supposed to be the *rash*. The doctor had gave me an ointment for it but it had got no better.

In the evening I thought I would wash my neck and put on a clean undershirt. I got everything ready. I looked in my unclean shirt and lo! & behold! it was filled with lice, horrid! The whole mess profiting by my discovery we soon had a tub full of the varmints. . . .

June 13. This morning after breakfast I went to the post office. Came back and read and played a few games of draughts. After dinner I read and went to sleep; the weather is very pleasant, a little cold from the rain of last night. Reports keep coming about the exchange of prisoners. I only hope and pray that it is true and that I may soon be in my native land once again.

June 23rd. Today we had a strange proceeding. We were ordered to be in front of our quarters at one o'clock. We obeyed the cowards' orders, and were marched all into two squares, and guards placed all around us while we were in the squares. Guards around us with loaded guns. Then the brave *yanks* came with Police from Chicago, went around in the prisoners' quarters, took watches, money, Guata Percha rings, sigars, clothes etc. Then the Police robbers came through our ranks and searched us, taking pocket knives & money. The once United states giving commissions to officers who are afraid of prisoners' pocket knives. One incident is worthy of note. There was a company of Tennesseans who were thinking of taking the oath but after the proceedings of this evening they concluded that the Confederacy was the best government. . . .

June 29th . . . In the evening we received the news of our successes in Virginia.* The whole encampment was filled with the greatest enthusiasm. The men were running all over the camp for papers—but the yankees would not permit the paper boys to come in the camp. However we succeeded in getting one or two papers and received the news. Hurrah! for Seceshindom. Good! for Jackson.

A year later a prisoner, wherever confined, faced an existence far grimmer than that which Willie Barrow had endured. The South, whatever its will, lacked the resources to feed and house its prisoners in the comparative comfort which, as Union soldiers, they had enjoyed. Besides, constant contact with suffering had made even humane men callous. One result was Libby Prison, Richmond. Lieutenant Colonel F. F. Cavada, captured on the second day of Gettysburg, described the prison as he saw it on the eighteenth of July, 1863:[13]

* Confederate victories in Stonewall Jackson's Valley campaign.

The gloomy and forbidding exterior of the prison, and the pale, emaciated faces staring vacantly at us through the bars, were repulsive enough, but it was at least a haven of rest from the weary foot-march, and from the goad of the urging bayonet. . . .

We are now fairly launched upon the mysterious ocean of Libby life. . . . The room we are in is long, low, dingy, gloomy, and suffocating. Some two hundred officers are lying packed in rows along the floor, sleeping the heavy, dreamless sleep of exhaustion. But there are some who cannot sleep; they are thinking of the camp, of home, and of friends; they are quarreling with the fortune of war; they are longing for the termination of a loathsome and hateful captivity, which has only just begun. By-and-by even the most wakeful yield to the imperative demand for rest, and with one arm for a pillow, have stretched themselves out on the bare floor. . . .

Now for the Libby itself. It stands close by the Lynchburg canal, and in full view from the river. It is a capacious warehouse, built of brick and roofed with tin. It was a busy place previous to the Rebellion; barrels and bales obstructed the stone side-walk which surrounds the building on all four of its sides; barrels and boxes were being constantly hoisted in and hoisted out; numberless boats lined the canal in front of it, and loaded drays rattled over the cobbled pavement of Carey street. There was a signboard at an angle of the building, whereon you might have read in black letters on a white ground: "Libby & Sons, Ship Chandlers and Grocers." This signboard is still at its post; but a wondrous change has come over the place. There are now no bales and boxes coming in at one end, and going out at the other; no laden boats on the canal; no drays rattling over the stone pave. There is something about it indicative of the grave, and, indeed, it *is* a sort of unnatural tomb, whose pale, wan inhabitants gaze vacantly out through the barred windows on the passer-by, as if they were peering from the mysterious precincts of another world.

The building has a front of about one hundred and forty feet, with a depth of about one hundred and five. There are nine rooms, each one hundred and two feet long by forty-five wide. The height of ceilings from the floor, is about seven feet; except in the upper story, which is better ventilated owing to the pitch of the roof. At each end of these rooms are five windows.

Nothing but bread has, as yet, been issued to us, half a loaf twice a day, per man. This must be washed down with James River water, drawn from a hydrant over the wash-trough. Tomorrow, we are to be indulged with the luxury of bacon-soup.

There are some filthy blankets hanging about the room; they have been used time and again by the many who have preceded us; they are soiled, worn, and filled with vermin, but we are recommended to help ourselves in time; if we do so with reluctance and profound disgust it is because we are now more particular than we will be by-and-by.

We have tasted of the promised soup; it is boiled water sprinkled with rice, and seasoned with the rank juices of stale bacon; we must shut our eyes to eat it; the bacon, I have no doubt, might have walked into the pot of its own accord. It is brought up to us in wooden buckets, and we eat it, in most cases without spoons, out of tin cups.

Henry H. Eby, Seventh Illinois Cavalry, was captured during the battle of Chickamauga. Ten days later he and several hundred other prisoners were herded into the prison pen on Belle Isle, in the James River near Richmond:[14]

The train stopped on the south side of the river and we were ordered to alight and were conducted down to the bridge and across it to the island. The Confederate iron works were located on the island, near the bridge, it was now getting dark and as we passed them they seemed to be all aglow from the light of the fires within, and one of the boys remarked in a joking way: "Here are the iron works, and the next place will be worse." I guess the prison pen on the island, into which we were placed a few moments later, about filled the bill.

We soon arrived at the place where we were to be confined, and found it to consist of several acres of ground, surrounded by a ditch about two feet deep and three feet wide, with the soil thrown up on the outside, which formed the deadline. Outside of this the guards paced back and forth. Any person stepping upon this line would be shot down without a moment's warning. There were 7,000 or 8,000 prisoners confined on this small area of ground. Nearly one-half of them were without any shelter whatever, and many had no blankets or overcoats.

We arrived at our new quarters in the evening, and after partaking of a scanty meal looked about for a spot large enough to lie down upon to sleep. I found a place that reminded me of the garden beds we used to make at home, it being slightly raised, with a path around it. Probably this had been made by some of the prisoners, to keep the water off in case of heavy rains. We now made preparations to retire, which were very simple. As many as could crowd upon this small space of ground lay down, in spoon fashion; that is, all lying with our faces turned in the same direction, and fitted together as one would spoons in packing them away, in order to have sufficient room and keep as warm as possible. We had nothing under us except the cold, bare earth, and nothing over us except a pup tent (a piece of muslin six feet square) and the blue sky, which was rather light covering. We had advantages on the island in some respects that we did not possess at home, we were not obliged to open the windows to air our beds. My outfit of clothing consisted of shirt, pants, cavalry jacket, boots and hat. I used my hat in place of a nightcap, to keep my head from coming in contact with the ground. I generally felt quite chilly during the night, and did not sleep soundly. Got up in the morning and found that the surroundings looked very discouraging. Did not see a soul that I knew, but saw many prisoners, some of whom had been confined here for months. These appeared ragged, dirty, and discouraged to the last degree. Rations were very small, and we were hungry continually, but had plenty of river water to drink.

After six days at Belle Isle, Eby was transferred to Smith Prison, Richmond:

It had formerly been used as a tobacco factory. . . . I was confined on the third floor. . . . This was a large room, but after lying down at night the floor was about covered with men. There was scarcely room enough for a person to walk through between the rows of men. Here we were well sheltered, but suffered another extreme, being nearly suffocated on account of not having proper ventilation; not even being allowed to open a window wide enough to admit sufficient fresh air to supply the number of prisoners within. . . .

There were about three hundred of us confined within this room, for a term of about two months, and during all that time we were hardly allowed to draw a breath of fresh air. . . . This and starvation, together, weakened us to an alarming degree. Our rations were issued once a day, and we generally devoured them at one meal, and still felt hungry. It was really just enough to make one meal a day. The order to draw rations generally came in the following manner. The Confederate orderly would enter the room and cry out: "Sargin ob de floor, four men and four blankets." This announcement in the southern dialect soon became a proverb among the boys. The "sargin ob de floor" would then detail four men and four blankets (blankets were a scarce article but generally enough were found to carry the rations) to carry the rations to our room. They would hasten down the stairs, and then those left behind anxiously crowded around the windows, pale, hungry, and each one eager to catch the first glimpse of the returning four men and four blankets with the morsel of bread, and soup (the soup being carried in buckets). This was composed of small beans, some being black and others red, and nearly every one was hollow and contained several black bugs enclosed, with hard shells. When the beans were boiled the bugs separated from them, and became mixed all through the soup, and while eating it we were obliged to grind the bugs between our teeth, which made me think of chewing parched corn or grinding coffee. The ingredients of the soup except the beans and bugs were unknown to us. Some declared that there was mule meat in it, judging from the bones found in the soup. I was almost famished for a meat diet, but did not care to have it in bug form. The bread rations consisted of brown bread, which tasted good to me, but we could not tell of what it was composed. The quantity was so small that it failed to satisfy our hunger. Part of the time while in this building we received corn-bread instead of the brown bread, and occasionally a small piece of meat, the quantity being too small to be mentioned. The soup was named by some of the men "bug soup," and it was a very appropriate name, as the bugs seemed to make the biggest show.

Our beds consisted of the bare floor. For covering I had my indispensable pup tent. We remained in this building during the months of October and November, and during that time there was no fire in the room, but any quantity of foul air, which at times was so terrible that I believe it was poison to us. The closet was located at or in one corner of the room. It was nothing more than a space about six or eight feet in length and several feet wide, and extended down to the basement to the depth of twenty or twenty-five feet. It was enclosed on three sides, and the side which opened into our room or prison had no door. It remained open all the time that we were confined in this place. I do not know whether there was sufficient water at the closet to carry away all the refuse or not, but by what we saw I think not. The condition of the atmosphere was simply horrible beyond description. At times it seemed as if we would certainly suffocate. In this condition about three hundred of us lived, slept, and dined for a period of about two months.

Of all Southern prisons, Andersonville was the most feared. Sergeant S. S. Boggs, Twenty-first Illinois Infantry, described his experiences there:[15]

We learned that this was Andersonville. We were taken from the cars to an open piece of ground just east of the station, looking east about a quarter of a mile, we could see an immense stockade. The last few days of our journey we had no water, and were suffering from thirst. The car that I was in had been used as a lime car, and had a half-inch of lime dust on the floor when they loaded us in at Petersburg; they put about seventy-five men in each car; any moving around would stir up the dust. Our lips and tongues seemed parched and cracked. Two died in our car on the trip. There was a small brook within two rods of us; the guard line was between us and the water. I was pleading with the guard to let us to the water, when a little grinny-faced Rebel captain, on a sway-backed gray horse, rode up and shook a revolver in my face and said: "You Got tam Yankee! you youst vait, and you got so much vater voy you drown in booty quick!" He rode around us several times, bouncing high in his saddle, flourishing a revolver and swearing at the guards and us alternately. After satisfying himself that we did not have any thing worth robbing us of, he proceeded to form us into nineties and detachments. One of our sergeants was put over each ninety, and one over each detachment. By this time we learned that this was Captain Wirz, the commander of the interior of the prison.

We were ordered forward toward the big stockade, moving quietly and painfully along, our spirits almost crushed within us, urged on by the double file of guards on either side of our column of ragged, lousy, skeletons, who scarce had strength to run away if given the opportunity. We neared the wall of great squared logs and the massive wooden gates that were to shut out hope and life from nearly all of us forever. The uncheerful sight, near the gate, of a pile of ghastly dead—the eyes of whom shone with a stony glitter, the faces black with a smoky grime, and pinched with pain and hunger, the long matted hair and almost fleshless frame swarming with lice—gave us some idea that a like fate awaited us on the inside. The rebels knowing our desperation, used every precaution to prevent a break; the artillerymen stood with lanyard in hand at their cannister-shotted guns, which were trained to sweep the gates. All being ready, the huge bolts were drawn, the gate swung open on its massive iron hinges, and as we moved into that hell on earth we felt that we were cut off from the world and completely at the mercy of our cruel keepers.

The creek which ran through the pen was pointed out to us. A rush was made for it, as we were famishing from thirst. The water soon became cloudy; two comrades, to get the water just above the "dead line," and not knowing the danger, reached beyond it, and both dropped dead in the water, shot by the guards on the wall. We dared not move their bodies until ordered to do so by a Rebel officer, who was some time in getting around. The water running red with our comrades' blood, stopped the drinking until the bodies were removed. We had not been in the stockade ten minutes until two of our number were ready to be put on the dead pile we had seen just outside the gate, but the poor fellows missed the horrible torture which was planned for them and us, and which if I knew I had to pass through again I would cross the "dead line" and ask the guard to show me mercy by tearing my body through with the ball and buckshot from his old Queen Anne musket. . . .

The spot of ground we were to occupy was pointed out to the sergeant of our detachment, who guided us to near the northeast corner of the pen, where we arranged in rows, north and south, leaving a narrow alley between each ninety. We then commenced fixing our bedding-place, or, rather, "spooning-ground." There was yet some debris left from cutting and hewing the palisade timbers. The prisoners who had been there, some of them more than a month, had consumed nearly all of the refuse for fuel, for making huts and "dug outs." Some, with a view of speculation, had stored by many of the best poles and sticks. However, there were yet some small poles and sticks to be had along the edge of the swamp; with these, and sun-dried bricks, we made a temporary shelter, which would do in dry weather, but when it rained it seemed to rain more in the hut than it did outside, and our brick generally had to be made anew.

Our rations now consisted of a pint of coarse corn-meal and about a *gill* of stock peas per day. . . .

We tried to occupy our time in bettering our shelter and killing the lice, which had gotten a good start on us while we were being moved. When the sun shone out warm, we would take off our rags, and sitting along in a row, our hands soon were in motion, which would lead a distant observer to believe that we were having a knitting frolic, in which he might not be mistaken, and "nits" were part of the game we were after. . . .

Each detachment and ninety was counted by a Rebel sergeant every morning at eight o'clock, and about the middle of the afternoon a four-mule team drove in with a wagon-body full of coarse, chaffy corn meal. The sergeant would call for two men from each ninety to draw rations, then the man who had a pair of pants or drawers, which could be made to hold meal by tying the legs at the bottom, loaned them to the sergeant for the consideration of a spoonful of meal. The rations would be drawn in proportion to the number found in each ninety—then carried to their respective grounds, divided out, each man getting for a day's allowance nearly a pint of the meal, a tablespoonful of peas, or, instead, about one ounce of beef; a piece of bone weighing six or eight ounces being considered equal to an allowance of beef. Nearly all would eat their rations as soon as issued. Many for want of means to cook them would eat their rations raw. In all my eighteen months' prison experience, the Rebels never furnished us one item in the way of cups, cooking vessels or clothing (except water pails at Danville, Va.).

Confederate prisoners could match the Northern stories of hardship and maltreatment. This is the account of a captured Virginia infantryman:[16]

The military prison, or rather prisons, at Point Lookout [Maryland], consisted of two inclosures, the one containing about thirty, the other about ten acres of flat sand, on the northern shore of the Potomac at its mouth, but a few inches above high tide, and utterly innocent of tree, shrub, or any natural equivalent for the same. Each was surrounded by a fence about fifteen feet high, facing inwards, around the top of which on the outer face, and about twelve feet from the ground, ran a platform on which twenty or thirty sentinels were posted, keeping watch and ward, night and day, over the prisoners within. Besides these precautions, a strongly fortified palisade stretched across the tongue of land on which the prisons stood, from the bay on the northeast to the Potomac on the southwest. Within this palisade, but of course outside of the "pens," were usually two regiments of infantry, and a couple of batteries of artillery, and without the fortification two or three companies of cavalry, while, riding at anchor in the bay, one gunboat at least was always to be seen. One face of each of these "pens," the eastern, fronted the bay, and gates led from the inclosures to a narrow belt of land between the fence and the water, which was free to the prisoners during the day, piles being driven into the bay on either hand to prevent any dexterous "reb" from *flanking out.* A certain portion of the water was marked off by stakes driven into the bottom, for bathing purposes, and most of the prisoners gladly availed themselves of the privilege thus afforded; although, as the same locality precisely and exclusively was devoted to the reception of all the filth of the camp, I admit a squeamishness which deprived me of sea-bathing as long as I stayed there. . . .

I now began prison life in earnest, and none but those who have experienced it can approximate an idea of its wretchedness. This does not consist in loss of liberty, in absence from home, in subjection to others' control, in insufficient food, in scant clothing, in loss of friends, in want of occupation, in an exposed life, in the absence of all conveniences of living. God knows, all these are bad enough, and contribute in the aggregate greatly to the enhancement of the misery of a prisoner. I think, however, that the great overshadowing agony of imprisonment, to persons of any culture, is isolation—

> "——— the dreary void,
> The leafless desert of the mind,
> The waste of feelings unemployed."

The world, friends, fellow-citizens, home, are things as remote as though in another sphere. Death brings its compensation, aside from the consolations of religion, in the remembrance that it is irreversible, and we choke down and eradicate, if we cannot exalt and purify those emotions, whereof the lost were the objects, insensibly changing our social schedule to meet the new order of things. But the prisoner preserves affections and interests without being able to indulge them, and thus with straining eyes and quickening pulse, he dismisses continually the dove for the expected emblem, but it returns forever with flagging wing and drooping head, not having found whereon to rest its weary foot. Thus, there comes that despair which is the aggregate of many, or the supremacy of one disappointment—and from despair comes always degradation. Men become reckless, because hopeless—brutalized, because broken-spirited, until from disregard of the formalities of life, they become indifferent to its duties, and pass with rapid though almost insensible steps from indecorum to vice—until a man will pick your pocket in a prison, who would sooner cut his own throat at home.

From Point Lookout, the Virginian was transferred to a Federal prison at Elmira, New York:

The chief of the [medical] department was a clubfooted little gentleman, with an abnormal head and a snaky look in his eyes, named Major E. L. Sanger. On our arrival in Elmira, another surgeon, remarkable chiefly for his unaffected simplicity and virgin innocence of everything appertaining to medicine, played doctor there. But as the prisoners increased in numbers, a more formal and formidable staff was organized, with Sanger at the head.

Sanger was simply a brute. . . . He was assisted by Dr. Rider, of Rochester, one of the few "copperheads" whom I met in any office, great or small, at the North. My association was rather more intimate with him than with any of the others, and I believe him to have been a competent and faithful officer. . . . The rest of the "meds" were, in truth, a motley crew in the main, most of them being selected from the impossibility, it would seem, of doing anything else with them. I remember one of the worthies, whose miraculous length of leg and neck suggested "crane" to all observers, whose innocence of medicine was quite refreshing. On being sent for to prescribe for a prisoner, who was said to have bilious fever, he asked the druggist, a "reb," in the most *naive* manner, what was the usual treatment for that disease! Fortunately, during his stay at Elmira, which was not long, there were no drugs in the dispensary, or I shudder to picture the consequences. . . .

The whole camp was divided into wards, to which physicians were assigned. . . . These ward physicians treated the simplest cases in their patients' barrack, and transferred the more dangerous ones to the hospitals, of which there were ten or twelve, capable of accommodating about eighty patients each. Here every arrangement was made that *carpenters* could make to insure the patients against unnecessary mortality, and, indeed, a *system* was professed which would have delighted the heart of a Sister of Charity; but, alas! the practice was quite another thing. The most scandalous neglect prevailed even in so simple a matter as providing food for the sick, and I do not doubt that many of those who died perished from actual starvation.

One of the Petersburg prisoners having become so sick as to be sent to the hospital, he complained to his friends who visited him that he could get nothing to eat, and was dying in consequence, when they made application for leave to buy him some potatoes and roast them for him. Dr. S. not being consulted, the request was granted, and when, a few hours afterwards, the roasted potatoes were brought in, the poor invalids on the neighboring cots crawled from their beds and begged the peelings to satisfy the hunger that was gnawing them.

When complaint was made of this brutality to the sick, there was always a convenient official excuse. Sometimes the fault would be, that a lazy doctor would not make out his provision return in time, in which case his whole ward must go without food, or with an inadequate supply until the next day. Another time there would be a difficulty between the chief surgeon and the commissary, whose general relations were of the stripe characterized by S. P. Andrews as "cat-and-dogamy," which would result in the latter refusing to furnish the former with bread for the sick! In almost all cases the *"spiritus frumenti"* failed to get to the patients, or in so small a quantity after the various *tolls,* that it would not quicken the circulation of a canary.

But the great fault, next to the scant supply of nourishment, was the inexcusable deficiency of medicine. During several weeks, in which dysentery and inflammation of the bowels were the prevalent diseases in prison, there was not a grain of any preparation of opium in the dispensary, and many a poor fellow died for the want of a common medicine, which no family is ordinarily without—that is, if men ever die for want of drugs.

There would be, and is much excuse for such deficiencies in the South—and this is a matter which the Yankees studiously ignore— inasmuch as the blockade renders it impossible to procure any luxuries even for our own sick, and curtails and renders enormously expensive the supply of drugs, of the simplest kind, providing they are exotics; but in a nation, whose boast it is that they do not feel the war, with the world open to them, and supplies of all sorts wonderfully abundant, it is simply infamous to starve the sick as they did there, and equally discreditable to deny them medicines—indispensable according to Esculapian traditions. . . .

I ascend from pills to provender.

The commissary department was under the charge of a cute, active ex-bank officer, Captain G. C. Whiton. The ration of bread was usually a full pound *per diem,* forty-five barrels of flour being converted daily into loaves in the bake-shop on the premises. The meat-ration, on the other hand, was invariably scanty; and I learned, on inquiry, that the fresh beef sent to the prison usually fell short from one thousand to twelve hundred pounds in each consignment. Of course, when this happened, many had to lose a large portion of their allowance; and sometimes it happened that the same man got bones only for several successive days. The expedients resorted to by the men to supply this want of animal food were disgusting. Many found an acceptable substitute in rats, with which the place abounded; and these Chinese delicacies commanded an average price of about four cents apiece—in greenbacks.

I have seen scores of them in various states of preparation, and have been assured by those who indulged in them that worse things have been eaten—an estimate of their value that I took on trust.

Others found in the barrels of refuse fat, which were accumulated at the cook-house, and in the pickings of the bones, which were cut out of the meat and thrown in a dirty heap back of the kitchen, to be removed once a week, the means of satisfying the craving for meat, which rations would not satisfy. I have seen a mob of hungry "rebs" besiege the bone-cart, and beg from the driver fragments on which an August sun had been burning for several days, until the impenetrable nose of a Congo could hardly have endured them.

Twice a day the camp poured its thousands into the mess-rooms, where each man's ration was assigned him; and twice a day the aforesaid rations were characterized by disappointed "rebs" in language not to be found in a prayer-book. Those whose appetite was stronger than their apprehensions frequently contrived to supply their wants by "flanking"—a performance which consisted in joining two or more companions as they successively went to the mess-rooms, or in quietly sweeping up a ration as the company filed down the table. As every ration so flanked was, however, obtained at the expense of some helpless fellow-prisoner, who must lose that meal, the practice was almost universally frowned upon; and the criminal, when discovered, as was frequently the case, was subjected to instant punishment.

This was either confinement in the guard-house, solitary confinement on bread and water, the "sweat box," or the barrel-shirt. The war has made all these terms familiar, except the third, perhaps; by it I mean a wooden box, about seven feet high, twenty inches wide, and twelve deep, which was placed on end in front of the major's tent. Few could stand in this without elevating the shoulders considerably; and when the door was fastened all motion was out of the question. The prisoner had to stand with his limbs rigid and immovable until the jailer opened the door, and it was far the most dreaded of the *peines fortes et dures* of the pen. In midsummer, I can fancy that a couple of hours in such a coffin would inspire Tartuffe himself with virtuous thoughts, especially if his avoirdupois was at all respectable.

Jefferson Davis, in his message of December 7, 1863 to the Confederate Congress, lashed out at the North for its treatment of Confederate prisoners, ignoring the fact that conditions were at least as bad in the South. All was the fault of the Federal government's refusal to continue the exchange of prisoners under a cartel agreed upon in 1862:[17]

A systematic and concerted effort has been made to quiet the complaints in the United States of those relatives and friends of the prisoners in our hands, who are unable to understand why the cartel is not
executed in their favor, by the groundless assertion that we are the
parties who refuse compliance. Attempts are also made to shield themselves from the execration excited by their own odious treatment of
our officers and soldiers, now captive in their hands, by misstatements,
such as that the prisoners held by us are deprived of food. To this last
accusation the conclusive answer has been made that, in accordance
with our law and the general orders of the Department, the rations of
the prisoners are precisely the same, in quantity and quality, as those
served out to our own gallant soldiers in the field, and which have
been found sufficient to support them in their arduous campaigns,
while it is not pretended by the enemy that they treat prisoners by the
same generous rule. By an indulgence, perhaps unprecedented, we
have even allowed the prisoners in our hands to be supplied by their
friends at home with comforts not enjoyed by the men who captured
them in battle. In contrast to this treatment the most revolting inhumanity has characterized the conduct of the United States toward prisoners held by them. One prominent fact, which admits no denial or
palliation, must suffice as a test. The officers of our Army, natives of
southern and semi-tropical climates, and unprepared for the cold of a
northern winter, have been conveyed for imprisonment during the
rigors of the present season to the most northern and exposed situation
that could be selected by the enemy. There, beyond the reach of comforts, and often even of news from home and family, exposed to the
piercing cold of the northern lakes, they are held by men who cannot
be ignorant of, even if they do not design, the probable result. How
many of our unfortunate friends and comrades, who have passed unscathed through numerous battles, will perish on Johnson's Island,
under the cruel trial to which they are subjected, none but the Omnis-
cient can foretell.

*Clement Eaton, a present-day Southern historian, willingly admits the
existence of conditions which the Confederate President denied:*[18]

The prison camps in the South were undoubtedly places of great
suffering and death. . . . The worst condition prevailed at the huge
prison camp at Andersonville, established early in 1864 and abandoned
in September of that year as Sherman's army threatened to capture it.
In July, 31,000 prisoners were crowded into the Andersonville stock-

ade. The Confederate guards were young boys and old men who at times were afraid to go into the stockade and police it properly. Some criminals, called "raiders," from New York terrorized their fellow prisoners; but finally the Federals erected a gallows and hung six ringleaders. The food allowance was the same as that of the guards; but Northern soldiers, who came from the wheat country, were unaccustomed to a monotonous diet of corn-bread. They had to cook their rations, and often the pones would be baked so hard that they were used as footballs. Furthermore, the corn meal was coarse and unsifted, resulting in widespread diarrhea. Sanitation and hospital facilities were extremely bad. A stream flowing through the stockade became a source of great pollution; nearly all the prisoners became sick, and the mortality was frightful. By the end of the war there were 12,912 prisoners' graves at Andersonville.

Southerners have apologized for the Andersonville prison camp by pointing out that the Confederacy did not have the proper medical supplies even for its own army, and that the policy of Secretary of War Stanton and Grant of no exchange of prisoners was partly responsible for the suffering of Northern captives. Although the mortality rate of Northerners in Southern prisons was somewhat greater than that of Confederate soldiers in Northern prisons, the difference was not striking.

Fifty years before Eaton wrote, the Northern historian James Ford Rhodes reached the same conclusion:[19]

All things considered the statistics show no reason why the North should reproach the South. If we add to one side of the account the refusal to exchange the prisoners and the greater resources, and to the other the distress of the Confederacy the balance struck will not be far from even. Certain it is that no deliberate intention existed either in Richmond or Washington to inflict suffering on captives more than inevitably accompanied their confinement. Rather than to charge either section with inhumanity it were truer to lay the burden on war, recalling in sympathy with their import the words of Sophocles:—

"From wars unnumbered evils flow
The unexhausted source of every human woe."

1864

1864

CHAPTER 29

"A HIDEOUS FAILURE"

B EHIND THE SCENES in Richmond and Washington, as the year 1864 began, forces were unleashed that would bring the war into a new and final phase. North and South, men now thought and wrote as seasoned practitioners of the brutal art of killing. The blacksmith's son from Michigan on a raid up the Neuse River, or the farmer's son from Vermont riding with Averell in West Virginia, killed, plundered, and burned as matter-of-factly as in 1861 one would have shod a horse and the other plowed a field. The elation of battle had dulled; brutality had become commonplace.

I

Jefferson Davis, in his message of December 7, 1863, to the Confederate Congress, emphasized a Southern conviction that would affect the war profoundly in coming months:[1]

I cannot close this message without again adverting to the savage ferocity which still marks the conduct of the enemy in the prosecution of the war. After their repulse from the defences before Charleston, they first sought revenge by an abortive attempt to destroy the city with an incendiary composition, thrown by improved artillery from a distance of four miles. Failing in this, they changed their missiles, but fortunately have thus far succeeded only in killing two women in the city. Their commanders, Butler, McNeil, and Turchin, whose horrible barbarities have made their names widely notorious and everywhere execrable, are still honored and cherished by the authorities at Washington. The first-named, after having been withdrawn from the scenes of his cruelties against women and prisoners of war (in reluctant concession to the demands of outraged humanity in Europe,) has just been put in a new command at Norfolk, where helpless women and children are again placed at his mercy.

Nor has less unrelenting warfare been waged by these pretended friends of human rights and liberties against the unfortunate negroes. Wherever the enemy have been able to gain access, they have forced into the ranks of their army every able-bodied man that they could seize, and have either left the aged, the women, and the children to perish by starvation, or have gathered them into camps, where they have been wasted by a frightful mortality. Without clothing or shelter, often without food, incapable, without supervision, of taking the most ordinary precaution against disease, these helpless dependents, accustomed to have their wants supplied by the foresight of their masters, are being rapidly exterminated wherever brought in contact with the invaders. By the Northern man, on whose deep-rooted prejudices no kindly restraining influence is exercised, they are treated with aversion and neglect. There is little hazard in predicting that, in all localities where the enemy have gained a temporary foothold, the negroes, who under our care increased six fold in number since their importation into the colonies of Great Britain, will have been reduced by mortality during the war to not more than one half their previous number. . . .

The frontier of our country bears witness to the alacrity and efficiency with which the general orders of the enemy have been executed in the devastation of the farms, the destruction of the agricultural implements, the burning of the houses, and the plunder of every thing movable. Its whole aspect is a comment on the ethics of the general order issued by the United States on the twenty-fourth of April, 1863, comprising "instructions for the government of armies of the United States in the field," and of which the following is an example:

"Military necessity admits of all direct destruction of life or limb of armed enemies, and of other persons whose destruction is incidentally unavoidable in the armed contests of the war; it allows of the capturing of every armed enemy, and of every enemy of importance to the hostile government, or of peculiar danger to the captor; it allows of all destruction of property and obstructions of the ways and channels of traffic, travel, or communication, and of all withholding of sustenance or means of life from the enemy; of the appropriation of whatever an enemy's country affords necessary for the subsistence and safety of the army, and of such deception as does not involve the breaking of good faith, either positively pledged regarding agreements entered into during the war, or supposed by the modern law of war to exist. Men who take up arms against one another in public war do not cease on this account to be moral beings, responsible to one another and to God."

The striking contrast to these teachings and practices, presented by our army when invading Pennsylvania, illustrates the moral character of our people. Though their forbearance may have been unmerited and unappreciated by the enemy, it was imposed by their own self-respect, which forbade their degenerating from Christian warriors into plundering ruffians, assailing the property, lives, and honor of helpless noncombatants. If their conduct, when thus contrasted with the inhuman practices of our foe, fail to command the respect and sympathy of civilized nations in our day, it cannot fail to be recognized by their less deceived posterity.

Southern newspapers could always find stories and letters to support the President's charges of Yankee cruelty. One certain to inflame all Southerners came from a Confederate colonel early in 1864:[2]

HEADQUARTERS FORCES ON BLACKWATER,
FRANKLIN, VA., January 1864

GENERAL WILD, COMMANDING COLORED BRIGADE, NORFOLK, VA.:

SIR: Probably no expedition, during the progress of this war, has been attended with more utter disregard for the long-established usages of civilization or the dictates of humanity, than your late raid into the country bordering the Albemarle. Your stay, though short, was marked by crimes and enormities. You burned houses over the heads of defenceless women and children, carried off private property of every description, arrested non-combatants, and carried off ladies in irons, whom you confined with negro men.

Your negro troops fired on confederates after they had surrendered, and they were only saved by the exertions of the more humane of your white officers. Last, but not least, under the pretext that he was a guerrilla, you hanged Daniel Bright, a private of company L, Sixty-second Georgia regiment, (cavalry,) forcing the ladies and gentlemen whom you held in arrest to witness the execution. Therefore, I have obtained an order from the General Commanding, for the execution of Samuel

Jones, a private of Company B, Fifth Ohio, whom I hang in retaliation. I hold two more of your men—in irons—as hostages for Mrs. Weeks and Mrs. Mundin. When these ladies are released, these men will be relieved and treated as prisoners of war.

JOEL R. GRIFFIN,
Colonel

II

Whether General Edward A. Wild, commanding the district of Norfolk and Portsmouth, ever replied to Colonel Griffin's letter is of little importance. (No answer can be found in the Official Records.) *The material fact is the animosity toward Negro troops that Griffin revealed. In less than three months that attitude, widely prevalent in the South, would come to a point where it could be satisfied only by blood.*

On the east bank of the Mississippi River, forty miles north of Memphis in a direct line, twice that far by the meandering river, stood Fort Pillow. Originally erected by the Confederates, the fort had been in Federal hands since the early summer of 1862. In the spring of 1864 it was garrisoned by the Thirteenth Tennessee Cavalry (Union) and four companies of colored artillery—557 officers and men.

On April 12 Forrest,* with 1,500 men, attacked the fort. Striking just before dawn, his men slowly drove in the pickets. By midafternoon, after advancing cautiously and with small loss of life, they had succeeded in investing the fort on its three land sides. Under a flag of truce, Forrest sent in a demand for surrender. The defenders refused to give up. Forrest ordered an assault.

Lieutenant Mack J. Leaming, adjutant of the Thirteenth Tennessee Cavalry, described what followed:[3]

The rebel charge was immediately sounded; when, as if rising from out [of] the very earth on the center and north side, within 20 yards of our works, the rebels received our first fire, wavered, rallied again and finally succeeded in breaking our lines, and in thus gaining possession

---

* Nathan Bedford Forrest, a onetime slave dealer in Memphis, began as a private in the Confederate Army, equipped a battalion of cavalry troops at his own expense, and soon rose in reputation and rank as the best, most daring cavalry leader in the South. He escaped from Donelson and fought at Shiloh. By then neither Grant nor Sherman ever referred to him except in terms of respect for his military ability. Some credit him with originating the phrase that he who "gets there firstest with the mostest" wins the battle.

of the fort. At this juncture, one company of the Sixth U. S. Heavy
Artillery, colored troops, rushed down the bluff, at the summit of which
were our works, and many of them jumped into the river, throwing
away their arms as they fled.

Seeing that . . . the enemy had now gained possession of our
works, and in consequence that it would be useless to offer further resistance, our men threw down their arms and surrendered. For a moment the fire seemed to slacken. The scene which followed, however,
beggars all description. The enemy carried our works at about 4 P.M.,
and from that time until dark, and at intervals throughout the night, our
men were shot down without mercy and almost without regard to color.
This horrid work of butchery did not cease even with the night of
murder, but was renewed again the next morning, when numbers of
our wounded were basely murdered after a long night of pain and suffering on the field where they had fought so bravely. . . .

Of the commissioned officers of the Thirteenth West Tennessee
Cavalry . . . all were killed save First Lieut. Nicholas D. Logan, of
C Company, . . . and myself, the adjutant of the regiment.

The rebels were very bitter against these loyal Tennesseeans, term-
ing them "home-made Yankees," and declaring they would give them
no better treatment than they dealt out to the negro troops with whom
they were fighting. . . .

Of the number, white and black, actually murdered after the surrender I cannot say positively; however, from my own observation,
as well as from prisoners who were captured at Fort Pillow and afterward made their escape, I cannot estimate that number at anything less
than 300.

*Survivors added gruesome details. Hardy N. Revelle, a storekeeper at
Fort Pillow, testified under oath:*[4]

When we found there was no quarter to be shown, and that (white
and black) we were to be butchered, we . . . gave up our arms and
passed down the hill. . . . We were followed closely and fiercely by
the advancing rebel forces, their fire never ceasing at all. Our men had
given signals themselves that they surrendered, many of them throwing up their hands to show they were unarmed, and submitted to overwhelming odds.

I was about half-way down the hill, partially secreted in a kind of
ravine with Dr. Fitch, when I saw 2 men (white men) belonging to the

Thirteenth Tennessee Cavalry standing behind a stump on which they had fixed a white handkerchief, their hands thrown up. They asked for quarter. When they stood on their feet they were exposed, and I saw them shot down by rebel soldiers and killed.

A captain of the rebel troops then came where we were and ordered all the Federals (white and black) to move up the hill or he would "shoot their God-damned brains out." I started up the hill with a number of others, in accordance with the order. I was surrendered with our men. While going up I saw white men fall on both sides of me, who were shot down by rebel soldiers who were stationed upon the brow of the hill. We were at the time marching directly at the men who fired upon us. I do not know how many fell, but I remember of seeing 4 killed in this way. I also saw negroes shot down with pistols in the hands of rebels. One was killed at my side. I saw another negro struck on the head with a saber by a rebel soldier. I suppose he was also killed. One more just in front of me was knocked down with the butt of a musket.

William J. Mays, Company B, Thirteenth Tennessee Cavalry, related his experiences after the surrender. He too testified under oath:[5]

We all threw down our arms and gave tokens of surrender, asking for quarter (I was wounded in the right shoulder and muscle of the back and knocked down before I threw down my gun). But no quarter was given. Voices were heard upon all sides, crying, "Give them no quarter; kill them; kill them; it is General Forrest's orders." I saw 4 white men and at least 25 negroes shot while begging for mercy, and I saw 1 negro dragged from a hollow log within 10 feet of where I lay, and as 1 rebel held him by the foot another shot him. These were all soldiers. There were also 2 negro women and 3 little children standing within 25 steps from me, when a rebel stepped up to them and said, "Yes, God damn you, you thought you were free, did you?" and shot them all. They all fell but 1 child, when he knocked it in the head with the breech of his gun. They then disappeared in the direction of the landing, following up the fugitives, firing at them wherever seen. They came back in about three-quarters of an hour, shooting and robbing the dead of their money and clothes. I saw a man with a canteen upon him and a pistol in his hand. I ventured to ask him for a drink of water. He turned around, saying, "Yes, God damn you, I will give you a drink of water," and shot at my head three different times, covering my face with dust, and then turned from me—no doubt thinking he had killed me—remarking, "God damn you, it's too late to pray now"; then went on with his pilfering. I lay there until dark, feigning death, when a rebel officer came along, drawing his saber, and ordered me to get up, threatening to run his saber into me if I did not, saying I had to march 10 miles that night. I succeeded in getting up and got among a small squad he had already gathered up, but stole away from them during the night and got among the dead, feigning death for fear of being murdered.

Some of the survivors may have exaggerated the brutality of the captors, yet Forrest's official report gives proof that there was savagery at Fort Pillow. On April 15 the General wrote:[6]

Arrived there [Fort Pillow] on the morning of the 12th and attacked the place with a portion of McCulloch's and Bell's brigades, numbering about 1,500 men, and after a sharp contest captured the garrison and all of its stores. A demand was made for the surrender, which was refused. The victory was complete, and the loss of the enemy will never be known from the fact that large numbers ran into the river and were shot and drowned. The force was composed of about 500 negroes and 200 white soldiers (Tennessee Tories). The river was dyed with the blood of the slaughtered for 200 yards. . . .

It is hoped that these facts will demonstrate to the northern people that negro soldiers cannot cope with Southerners.

The reports from Fort Pillow inflamed the North. Lincoln, who took the news more calmly than most, was deeply concerned. Speaking at the Baltimore Sanitary Fair on April 18, he said:[7]

A painful rumor, true I fear, has reached us of the massacre, by the rebel forces, at Fort Pillow, in the west end of Tennessee, on the Mississippi River, of some three hundred colored soldiers and white officers, who had just been overpowered by their assailants. . . . We do not today *know* that a colored soldier, or white officer commanding colored soldiers, has been massacred by the rebels when made a prisoner. We fear it, believe it, I may say, but we do not *know* it. To take the life of one of their prisoners, on the assumption that they murder ours, when it is short of certainty that they do murder ours, might be too serious, too cruel a mistake. We are having the Fort Pillow affair thoroughly investigated; and such investigation will probably show

conclusively how the truth is. If, after all that has been said, it shall
turn out that there has been no massacre at Fort Pillow, it will be almost safe to say that there has been none, and will be none elsewhere.
If there has been the massacre of three hundred there, or even the tenth
part of three hundred, it will be conclusively proved; and being so
proved, the retribution shall as surely come.

Two weeks later Lincoln informed the members of his Cabinet:

*"It is now quite certain that a large number of our colored soldiers,
with their white officers, were, by the rebel force, massacred after they
had surrendered, at the recent capture of Fort Pillow. So much is
known, though the evidence is not yet quite ready to be laid before me.
Meanwhile I will thank you to prepare, and give me in writing your
opinion as to what course, the government should take in the case."*

*Some Secretaries favored retributive measures; others thought that
any punitive action would backfire against the North. In the end Lincoln
did nothing, perhaps because he became engrossed in the Wilderness
campaign, perhaps because he became convinced that the excesses
were the inevitable result of hatreds described years later by Forrest's
biographer, John A. Wyeth:*[8]

Everything considered, it may well be a matter of surprise that the
slaughter was not greater. Human life was held exceedingly cheap in
1864, and especially in west Tennessee; the scenes of bloodshed which
stained this section of the South may well suggest the reddest days of
the French Revolution.

It is difficult for those who did not live through this unhappy period,
and in this immediate section, to appreciate the bitterness of feeling
which then prevailed. Three years of civil war had passed, not without
a deplorable effect upon the morals of the rank and file of either army.
War does not bring out the noblest traits in the majority of those who
from choice or necessity follow its blood-stained paths. Too often the
better qualities hide away, and those that are harsh and cruel prevail.
Some of Forrest's men treasured a deep resentment against some of the
officers and soldiers of this garrison. They had been neighbors in times
of peace, and had taken opposite sides when the war came on. These
men had suffered violence to person and property, and their wives
and children, in the enforced absence of their natural protectors, had
suffered various indignities at the hands of the "Tennessee Tories," as
the loyal Tennesseeans were called by their neighbors who sided with

the South. When they met in single combat, or in scouting parties, or in battle, as far as these individuals were concerned, it was too often a duel to the death. Between the parties to these neighborhood feuds the laws of war did not prevail. Here, in this melee, in the fire and excitement of the assault, they found opportunity and made excuse for bloody vengeance. No official surrender; their flag still flying; some of the Federals, no matter how few, still firing back, and they shot them down regardless of the cry for quarter.

Moreover, Fort Pillow was the first prominent occasion on which Negro troops, whose free status the Confederates would not admit, came into conflict with their former owners.

But was Fort Pillow a massacre? Wyeth, a Southerner who had served two years under Forrest (though not at Fort Pillow), approached the question objectively:

To the rational mind, capable of carefully weighing the evidence on both sides, and arriving at a conclusion unbiased by prejudice, it must be clear that there was no massacre as charged. Had a wholesale and merciless slaughter been intended by General Forrest and his subordinates, it could and would have been carried out, as there was nothing to prevent it. The fact that so many escaped death is of itself a proof that a massacre was not premeditated or permitted.* It is true that more of the garrison were shot after the Southern troops were in possession of the breastworks than was necessary for the full success of the assault, but under the conditions which prevailed during the attack, it is clearly shown that an unusually large loss in killed and wounded was inevitable, even had no excesses been indulged in by the captors.

From a careful study of the subject, I am convinced that a few desperate or insanely intoxicated soldiers of the garrison resisted to the very last, and even after escape was hopeless continued to fire at the Confederates. On the other hand, notwithstanding this extreme provo-

---

* "It appears then that of the garrison of 557 there were at least 336 survivors, of whom 226 were unwounded or only slightly wounded and approximately 100 seriously wounded. The dead of the garrison may be calculated as not more than 231, which accords with the burial reports. . . . The loss of life approximated forty percent of the garrison—by no means an extraordinarily high rate for a place carried by assault as Fort Pillow was."—Robert S. Henry, *"First With the Most" Forrest*, 259.

cation, there were a number of men, both white and black, shot down, who were trying to surrender and should have been spared. About an hour before the assault was made a detachment of Forrest's command posted at the extreme left of his line broke into the quartermaster's stores which had been captured at this time, and before they could be compelled to quit the building had had access to a supply of whiskey which they discovered there. The moment Forrest learned that his men were pillaging the captured stores he rode there rapidly and put a stop to it in person.

III

While Forrest was engaged in the brief campaign that culminated in the horror of Fort Pillow, an ambitious Union expedition west of the Mississippi bogged down in the greatest fiasco of the war.

Early in 1864 Halleck ordered General Nathaniel P. Banks, then commanding at New Orleans, to invade northwestern Louisiana and nearby Arkansas and Texas. The purpose of the expedition was threefold: to seize the great stores of cotton which the farmers of the region had been unable to market; to nurture nascent reconstruction movements in Louisiana and Arkansas; and to warn the French in Mexico, by planting the Stars and Stripes in Texas, that there would come a day when the United States would be able to enforce the Monroe Doctrine.

Banks, former congressman and governor of Massachusetts, had hardly distinguished himself since he had been commissioned a major general of volunteers in the spring of 1861. Yet even he had had experience enough to realize that Halleck's venture was a hazardous one. Banks remonstrated, but Halleck overrode his objections and proceeded to put an invading army together. Banks would bring up a force from the Bayou Teche; A. J. Smith would come over from Vicksburg with 10,000 men; Frederick Steele, commanding in Arkansas, would march down from Little Rock; and Admiral D. D. Porter would ascend the Red River with a powerful fleet of gunboats. All would converge at Alexandria, Louisiana, on March 17 and then go up river to Shreveport in the northwestern corner of the state. When the expedition reached this point, Halleck apparently believed, its purposes would be achieved.

When Smith's troops arrived at the mouth of the Red River on March 11 they found Porter's flotilla already there. Two days later the soldiers disembarked from their transports and assaulted Fort de Russy, taking 260 prisoners and ten guns. Porter moved on to Alexandria, arriving there on March 14; Smith's ten thousand came in the next day. But

*Banks's contingent, sent ahead under the command of W. B. Franklin,
did not reach the concentration point until March 25. Steele, faced with
many difficulties, never even came close to the Louisiana border.*

*Meanwhile, the Confederate commander, General Richard Taylor,
erudite and peppery son of old Zachary, kept withdrawing ahead of the*

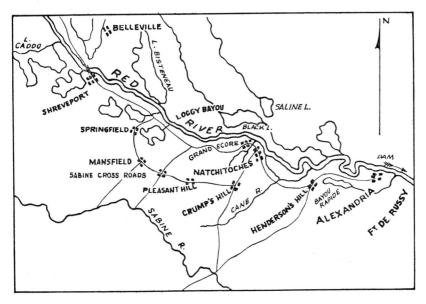

RED RIVER CAMPAIGN

*advancing Federals, harassing the invaders with frequent skirmishes
and complaining that he was expected to stop 27,000 men with hardly
more than half that number. His dispatches to Kirby Smith describe the
progress of the campaign:*[9]

IN THE FIELD, March 26, 1864.

GENERAL: . . . I am still ignorant of what disposition the enemy
has made or is making of his large force, and have no news of Green *
since I last wrote you. The difficulty of obtaining accurate intelligence
is greatly enhanced by jayhawkers.† The whole country between this
and Alexandria swarms with these outlaws, who are allied with the

* General Thomas Green, who commanded the trans-Mississippi Confederate
cavalry.
† "During the Civil War, a free-lance soldier, freebooter, or guerilla operating
in Kansas; any lawless marauder or robber." —Mathews, *A Dictionary of
Americanisms.*

enemy and acting in his interests. Several of our scouts have been murdered, and it is more dangerous for small parties to pass through the pine woods than it would be to penetrate the enemy's lines. Besides, the intimate acquaintance of the country possessed by these people renders it impossible to escape their vigilance. The arrival of one, or two even, of Green's regiments will change the whole aspect of affairs.

NATCHITOCHES, March 30, 1864—9 P.M.

GENERAL: I reached this place some two hours since. The enemy is within 12 or 14 miles in full force. He will occupy the place in the morning if he sees proper. Only one of General Green's regiments has reached here. It will go to the front in the morning. The regiment numbers 250—no very heavy re-enforcement. The next regiment numbers 350, with more than half the men reported unarmed. It will reach here tomorrow. . . .

Your dispatch of the 29th instant (No. 2460) has just come to hand. I respectfully suggest that the only possible way to defeat Steele's movement is to whip the enemy now in the heart of the Red River Valley. Price's * command could have been here on the 28th, and I could have fought a battle for the department today. To decline concentration when we have the means, and when the enemy is already in the vitals of the department, is a policy I am too obtuse to understand. There is no position short of the head of Spanish Lake, 18 miles from here, where I can undertake to do anything with my present means. In fact, Pleasant Hill, with an effort to hold the country to Blair's Landing, is the only position where I can await Green's forces and secure subsistence and forage. The enemy is in formidable numbers, prepared to overrun the Red River Valley, and he must and will succeed unless all the means at our disposal are used energetically to prevent him. I most respectfully call attention to the fact that sixteen days after the fall of Fort de Russy and the opening of the campaign by the enemy only 250 re-enforcements have reached me.

CAMPTI, March 31, 1864

GENERAL: I have the honor to report that I left Natchitoches today at 11:00 A.M., just before the head of the enemy's column reached the place. I am on the steamer *Frolic*, and shall proceed to Blair's to inspect

---

* General Sterling Price, whom Kirby Smith had ordered to oppose Steele's advance in Arkansas.

the road to Pleasant Hill, at which place the main body of my troops will encamp tonight. . . .

From all I can learn, it will be ten days before Green's command will reach me, one regiment under Major McPhaill having alone come up. The troops ordered here from Texas, excepting Green's original division, have been directed to halt in Polk County until further orders, so I am informed by Lieutenant-Colonel Herbert. If this be true, Green will bring me less than 2,000 men. Had I conceived for an instant that such astonishing delay would ensue before re-enforcements reached me I would have fought a battle even against the heavy odds. It would have been better to lose the State after a defeat than surrender it without a fight. The fairest and richest portion of the Confederacy is now a waste. Louisiana may well know her destiny. Her children are exiles; her labor system is destroyed. Expecting every hour to receive the promised re-enforcements, I did not feel justified in hazarding a general engagement with my little army. I shall never cease to regret the error.

On the day after Taylor wrote his gloomy report two divisions of infantry reached him. Green's cavalry arrived on April 6. The Confederate commander believed that he was now strong enough to offer battle. From Pleasant Hill he withdrew twenty miles in the direction of Shreveport, disposed his troops at Sabine Cross Roads near Mansfield, and waited for Banks.

The two armies probed each other on the morning of April 8, but a full-scale engagement did not take place until 4:00 P.M., when Taylor ordered his whole line forward. The Confederate cavalry advance coincided with a fainthearted Union cavalry charge. J. Russell Young, correspondent of the Philadelphia Press, *described an hour of bloody fighting:*[10]

. . . The attack of our cavalry was weak and spiritless. The firing lasted for a few minutes, the discharges of musketry became incessant, the long, thin line of clay-colored rebels began to emerge slowly from the woods, firing constantly, but always advancing at a pace that seemed like an uncertain, shuffling run. Their fire was too strong for our cavalry, and it fell back with precipitation—too much precipitation it proved; for before Ransom had his line properly formed, he was compelled to meet the onset of the whole rebel force. The retreating cavalry had partly demoralized his men, for in the heat of action, and being where they could not see the field, they could not understand why this multitude of flushed and frightened men should thus be running from the scene of battle. Many who wanted nothing but a cheerful look or nod to make them brave men, turned around without having seen a rebel, and ran likewise, so that before the battle had really opened the road presented the strange sight of hundreds of armed and unarmed men hastening to the rear, some the pictures of fright, others of abject fear, and carrying exaggerated stories to all who troubled them for information.

Four o'clock had passed, and the long shadows of the evening were darkening the pine woods. Ransom's division fought with intrepid bravery, all things considered—the sudden attack, the panic-stricken cavalry, and the number of the enemy—with a bravery that cannot be too highly commended. The rebels, however, saw their advantage, and pressed it. In the beginning of the fight General Ransom was struck in the knee, and carried from the field. This dispirited the men, for they all loved the young commander, and rejoiced to speak his praise. The fight became furious, and for a few minutes there was doubt, and gloom, and anxiety among the Federal commanders. Aid after aid galloped down the road to bring up the Third division of the Thirteenth corps, commanded by General Cameron. It was doubtful if even Cameron's men would be successful. But other troops were behind— Emory and his splendid division—and we knew that the day was ours if time only permitted us to make a proper disposition of our forces.

At three o'clock in the afternoon General William H. Emory, commanding the First Division of the Nineteenth Corps, bivouacked a mile and a half behind the Thirteenth Corps. At 3:50—Emory noted the time exactly—Franklin, the corps commander, ordered Emory to bring his infantry to the front immediately. Within fifteen minutes Emory had his men in motion:[11]

About forty minutes after commencing the march I met an aide-de-camp from the front with orders to hurry up, that the battle had commenced. After going about a mile further I met General Ransom coming back, wounded, in an ambulance, who told me that they had a pretty tough fight in front, but he did not give any very sad picture of the condition of affairs; but I thought there were a great many more men about that ambulance than looked well following him to the rear. I ordered the men to double-quick; to take a slow trot. After going about

a mile further, in all, four miles from the point of starting, I met a
parcel of servants, men and women, mounted on horses, who told us
that the day was all gone, and hallooed out to my men to turn back.
There were also a great deal of cavalry scattered among these people.
At almost the next moment a crowd of perfectly disorganized cavalry,
wagons, ambulances, and loose animals came right down the road upon
us, and all said the day was gone. I directed the leading regiments and
the flankers on each side, without halting, to fix their bayonets, and I
ordered the bands to strike up, and we had to use violence to get along
the road. There was scarcely a staff officer who did not have his sabre
bent beating people out of the road. It soon became apparent to me
that the whole cavalry was driven back and in disorder. We continued
our march; the men never broke a step, and not a man fell out of the
ranks.

In a short time we began to meet the infantry going to the rear in
disorder. About this time I received a message from either General
Banks or General Franklin, I do not remember which, to take as good
a position as I could, and form across the road, for the purpose of
checking the enemy, informing me that the advance was routed. There
was no good place where I was, and I had to continue to advance. The
ground there was not favorable for forming a line. I continued to advance for about half a mile further, still pressed on each side by infantry
and some cavalry going to the rear. Every effort to halt them or
reorganize them was impossible. I threw out regiments on each flank to
try to stop them, but they ran around them.

After marching from half a mile to a mile further I found a place
that I thought was favorable for forming a line. We also began to feel
pretty smartly the bullets of the enemy, which began to drop around us
thickly, and some of our men fell. For a moment I was afraid I had
put off forming my line too late. So I took my leading regiment, the
161st New York, under Colonel Kinsley, and led them to the front and
deployed them as skirmishers to cover my line while it was being
formed. We then found the enemy in sight and firing upon us very
rapidly. I put the first brigade directly across the road at right angles,
the second brigade on the right and a little in reserve, and the third
brigade on the left. I was still to the front with this regiment holding
the enemy. Seeing the line was formed, or nearly formed, I directed
Colonel Kinsley to rally his skirmishers and come in behind the line. It
was with great difficulty that he did so; his loss was very severe. They
had no sooner got in than the enemy appeared in three columns of at-

tack, one coming directly up the road, one on our right, and one on our left.

I directed my men to lie down and hold their fire until the enemy had got close up. The enemy came on, apparently not expecting to meet anything there. When the enemy got within about 100 yards my line opened on them. In about fifteen minutes the enemy were driven from the field with very considerable loss. By this time it was dark, and we could hear nothing in our front, except the noise of wheels, perhaps artillery or wagons going to the rear of the enemy, and the cries of the wounded men calling for water.

The stubborn stand of Emory's division had only staved off a Union rout; Mansfield would stand as a Confederate victory. Banks, convinced that he could not fight his way to Shreveport, ordered a retreat to Pleasant Hill. J. Russell Young described the Union army and its principal commanders as it lay in its new position on April 9:[12]

Pleasant Hill . . . is a clearing in the midst of these vast pine woods, about thirty-five miles from the Red River, on the road that leads from Natchitoches. It forms a plateau that rises to a noticeable elevation above the country around. It was probably intended as a settlement of more than usual importance, for I noticed an unfinished seminary, a church, a sawmill, many fine houses, and one or two that would have done credit to our Northern towns. The land was in a high state of cultivation, and every acre seemed to be traversed by ridges of ploughed soil. On the elevation where the unfinished seminary stands, a complete view of the whole field could be obtained, and with a glass, the features and the rank of men . . . could be readily seen. Here we determined to make a stand.

The day was as bright and clear and fresh as a May day in the North, and the air was so bracing that the officers found their great-coats grateful. The morning passed on. The plateau had the appearance of a parade-ground on a holiday. . . . Regiments marching to the right, and regiments marching to the left, batteries being moved and shifted, cavalry squads moving in single file through the brush, now and then an aid galloping madly, or an orderly at full speed, driving his spurs, and holding an order or despatch between his teeth, bugles sounding the different cavalry calls, and drums repeating the orders of the captains, all passed and repassed, and controlled the vision, making very much the impression that a spectator in the theatre receives as he looks upon a melodrama.

In an inclosure near the roadside was a small cluster of gentlemen to whom all this phantasmagoria had the meaning of life, and death, and power, and fame. General Banks, with his light blue overcoat buttoned closely around his chin, was strolling up and down, occasionally conversing with a member of his staff, or returning the salute of a passing subaltern. Near him was General William B. Franklin, his face as rough and rugged as when he rode through the storms of the Peninsula, the ideal of a bold, daring, imperturbable soldier. There are few braver men than this Charles O'Malley of major generals.* He had two horses shot under him the day before. His face was very calm that morning, and occasionally he pulls his whiskers nervously, as though he scented the battle afar off, and was impatient to be in the midst of the fray. General Charles P. Stone, the chief of staff, a quiet, retiring man, who is regarded, by the few that know him, as one of the finest soldiers of the time, was sitting on a rail smoking cigarettes, and apparently more interested in the puffs of smoke that curled around him, than in the noise and bustle that filled the air. There was General Smith, with his bushy, grayish beard, and his eager eye, as it looks through spectacles, giving him the appearance of a schoolmaster. General Arnold, the chief of artillery, with his high boots, and his slouched hat thrown over his head, seemed the busiest of all. The other members of the staff, colonels, and majors, and captains, completed the group; with orderlies in the distance, and servants chiding or soothing their masters' restless horses, and the body-guard dismounted and dozing under the trees. . . .

The General called for his horse and proposed to go to the front. . . . It was now eleven o'clock, and our whole army was prepared for action. The generals had determined to await the attack of the enemy, and finding it impossible to subsist the army in a country without water or forage, concluded to move the trains back to Grand Ecore, there concentrate our army, and await news from the cooperating column of General Steele, which is known to be moving through Arkansas on Shreveport. Accordingly, before our lines were formed, the trains were ordered to move, and before noon we had a clear field,

---

* An allusion far more familiar a hundred years ago than today. Charles O'Malley was the hero of Charles J. Lever's romantic novel of the same name, a story of the Peninsular War. Published in 1841, the book retained its popularity for two generations.

and were ready for the attack. . . . Noon came and passed; but beyond the slow shelling of the woods, and a stray shot from some impetuous picket, there was no sign of an engagement. Our men remained in line all day, and passed the hours by their guns; some lying down, some sleeping and dozing, others reading and eating the remnants of yesterday's ration; but all ready for the signal that would bring on the action. The day remained bright, and warm, and clear, and it began to be thought that it would close without an action, and that the enemy had withdrawn with their booty. Those in the front knew better. The rebels were there, making their dispositions and preparing for the onset.

Late in the afternoon hesitant, halfhearted sparring suddenly turned into vicious battle. Young's account continues:

On our left centre, far in the advance, was a battery of four guns, belonging to a New York regiment. It occupied an exposed position, and it had been suggested by some of the staff officers that there was danger of its capture. This battery had been making itself an object of interest to the rebels, for every ten minutes it sent a shot into their midst. About half-past four in the afternoon, a sharp volley of musketry was heard, and all eyes turned toward this battery, for over it circles of smoke were ascending, and around it men were engaged in battle. The rebel line rushed from the woods and charged the battery. The contest was sharp. The smoke obscured the sight, and for a few minutes we could only guess how the struggle was going. Finally our line was seen to retreat, but we had no fear. We knew that the men composing that line were men of the Nineteenth corps. We had seen their valor on the day before, and, although there, before our eyes, they were falling back, we felt assured it was with a purpose. So it proved. The temporary retreat was a feint, intended to draw the rebels from the woods. They came, rushed upon the battery, and surrounded it. This success brought another line of clay-colored rebels, and they cheered as though they had gained a victory. The time had come. The enemy was before us. Emory's division rallied; and one of Smith's divisions, which had been lying on the ground, arose, and sent volley after volley into the enemy's midst. This was something different from fighting an exposed division in pine woods, in the midst of baggage trains, and so the poor rebels found. Again and again they rallied, but only to fall back again and again, and finally to retreat and scamper through the woods. The battery which tempted them from their covert was retaken, and its shot and shell went plunging through their retreating column. . . .

The battle was extended along the whole line; it was nothing but charge and rally, to charge and rally again. In every point our men gained the day. The lines of Smith's division stood like the stone walls that Virginian *patois* has contributed to our military language, and every effort of the enemy to force them was futile. Thus it continued for an hour. . . . The rebels, toward the end of the engagement, tried to flank our left by sending a column over the ridge, upon which the unfinished seminary stood. The effort was more disastrous than the attempt upon the battery. They were driven back with fearful slaughter, routed from the field, leaving many hundreds of prisoners in our hands.

On April 11 General Taylor issued a flamboyant address to his troops. "Never in war," he told them, was there "a more complete victory" than Mansfield. Pleasant Hill "was emphatically the soldier's victory," where "valor and devotion triumphed over all." Kirby Smith made a more realistic evaluation. "Our repulse at Pleasant Hill," he wrote, "was so complete and our command was so disorganized that had Banks followed up his success vigorously he would have met but feeble opposition to his advance on Shreveport."

Banks, in fact, wanted to turn about and strike for Shreveport but his generals dissuaded him. Grant had stipulated that Smith's troops must be on the east side of the Mississippi by May 1. Equally important, the Red River was at an unprecedented low level and still falling. If Porter did not draw off his gunboats quickly he might well lose them. Banks gave in, and ordered a return to the starting point of the expedition.

As it was, the fleet had trouble enough in the next few days. Porter described the running battle, without equal in the war, that took place between a Confederate army and gunboats and transports:[13]

We had every reason to suppose that our return would be interrupted in every way and at every point by the enemy's land forces, and we were not disappointed. They commenced on us from high banks, at a place called Coushatta, and kept up a fire of musketry whenever an opportunity was offered them. By a proper distribution of the gunboats I had no trouble in driving them away, though from the high banks they could fire on our decks almost with impunity. As we proceeded down the river they increased in numbers, and as we only made thirty miles a day, they could cross from point to point and be ready to meet us on our arrival below. On the left bank of the river a man by the name of Harrison, with one thousand nine hundred cavalry and four or five pieces of artillery, was appointed to follow us down and annoy us. It was very fortunate for us that this person and his command were lately severely handled by a gunboat (a few weeks ago) which made them careful about coming within range. On the evening of the twelfth instant we were attacked from the right bank of the river by a detachment of men of quite another character. They were a part of the army which two or three days previous had gained success over our army, and flushed with victory, or under the excitement of liquor, they appeared suddenly upon the right bank, and fearlessly opened fire on the *Osage*, Lieutenant Commander T. O. Selfridge, (iron-clad), she being hard aground at the time with a transport (the *Black Hawk*) alongside of her, towing her off. The rebels opened with two thousand muskets, and soon drove everyone out of the *Black Hawk* to the safe casemates of the monitor. Lieutenant Bache had just come from his vessel (the *Lexington*) and fortunately was enabled to pull up to her again, keeping close under the bank, while the *Osage* opened a destructive fire on these poor deluded wretches, who, maddened with liquor and led on by their officers, were vainly attempting to capture an iron vessel. I am told that their hootings and actions baffle description. Force after force seemed to be brought up to the edge of the bank, where they confronted the guns of the iron vessel, only to be cut down by grape-shot and cannister. In the meantime Lieutenant Bache had reached his vessel, and widening the distance between him and the *Osage*, he opened a cross-fire on the infuriated rebels, who fought with such desperation and courage against certain destruction, that it could only be accounted for in one way. Our opinions were verified on inspection of some of the bodies of the slain—the men actually smelling of Louisiana rum! This affair lasted nearly two hours before the rebels fled. They brought up two pieces of artillery, one of which was quickly knocked over by the *Lexington's* guns, the other they managed to carry off. The cross-fire of the *Lexington* finally decided this curious affair of a fight between infantry and gunboats. The rebels were mowed down by her canister, and finally retreated in as quick haste as they had come to the attack, leaving a space of a mile covered with the dead and wounded, muskets and knapsacks. . . .

Night coming on, we had no means of ascertaining the damage done to the rebels. We were troubled no more from the right bank of the river, and a party of five thousand men who were marching to cut us off were persuaded to change their mind after hearing of the unfortunate termination to the first expedition. That same night I ordered the transports to proceed on, having placed the gunboats at a point where the rebels had a battery. All the transports were passed safely, the rebels not firing a shot in return to the many that were bursting over the hills. The next morning, the thirteenth instant, I followed down myself, and finding at Compte, six miles from Grand Ecore by land, that they had got aground, and would be some time in getting through, I proceeded down in this vessel [*Cricket*] to Grand Ecore, and got General Banks to send up troops enough to keep the guerillas away from the river. We were fired on as usual after we started down, but when I had the troops sent up, the transports came along without any trouble.

At Alexandria, the fleet encountered a more formidable opponent than Dick Taylor's artillery and sharpshooters—low water. Only the ingenuity of a landsman and the mighty labor of several thousand soldiers prevented an almost irreparable disaster. Admiral Porter, blithely concealing the fact that he had been the first to scoff at the expedient by which his beloved gunboats were saved, reported to Secretary of the Navy Gideon Welles:[14]

FLAG SHIP *Black Hawk*, MISSISSIPPI SQUADRON
MOUTH OF RED RIVER, May 16, 1864

SIR: I have the honor to inform you that the vessels lately caught by low water above the falls at Alexandria have been released from their unpleasant position. The water had fallen so low that I had no hope or expectation of getting the vessels out this season, and as the army had made arrangements to evacuate the country, I saw nothing before me but the destruction of the best part of the Mississippi squadron.

There seems to have been an especial providence looking out for us in providing a man equal to the emergency. Lieutenant-Colonel Bailey, Acting Engineer of the Nineteenth army corps, proposed a plan of building a series of dams across the rocks at the falls, and raising the water high enough to let the vessels pass over. This proposition looked like madness, and the best engineers ridiculed it; but Colonel Bailey was so sanguine of success that I requested General Banks to have it done, and he entered heartily into the work. Provisions were short and forage was almost out, and the dam was promised to be finished in ten days, or the army would have to leave us. I was doubtful about the time, but had no doubt about the ultimate success, if time would only permit. General Banks placed at the disposal of Colonel Bailey all the force he required, consisting of some three thousand men and two or three hundred wagons. All the neighboring steam-mills were torn down for material, two or three regiments of Maine men were set to work felling trees, and on the second day after my arrival in Alexandria from Grand Ecore the work had fairly begun. Trees were falling with great rapidity; teams were moving in all directions, bringing in brick and stone; flatboats were built to bring stone down from above; and every man seemed to be working with a vigor I have seldom seen equalled, while perhaps not one in fifty believed in the success of the undertaking.

These falls are about a mile in length, filled with rugged rocks, over which, at the present stage of water, it seemed to be impossible to make a channel.

The work was commenced by running out from the left bank of the river a tree dam, made of the bodies of very large trees, brush, brick, and stone, cross-tied with other heavy timber, and strengthened in every way which ingenuity could devise. This was run out about three hundred feet into the river; four large coal-barges were then filled with brick and sunk at the end of it. From the right bank of the river cribs filled with stone were built out to meet the barges. All of which was successfully accomplished, notwithstanding there was a current running of nine miles an hour, which threatened to sweep everything before it.

It will take too much time to enter into the details of this truly wonderful work. Suffice it to say, that the dam had nearly reached completion in eight days' working time, and the water had risen sufficiently on the upper falls to allow the *Fort Hindman, Osage,* and *Neosho* to get down and be ready to pass the dam. In another day it would have been high enough to enable all the other vessels to pass the upper falls. Unfortunately, on the morning of the ninth instant, the pressure of water became so great that it swept away two of the stone barges, which swung in below the dam on one side. Seeing this unfortunate accident, I jumped on a horse and rode up to where the upper vessels were anchored, and ordered the *Lexington* to pass the upper falls, if possible, and immediately attempt to go through the dam. I thought I might be able to save the four vessels below, not knowing whether the persons employed on the work would ever have the heart to renew their enterprise.

The *Lexington* succeeded in getting over the upper falls just in time, the water rapidly falling as she was passing over. She then steered directly for the opening in the dam, through which the water was rushing so furiously that it seemed as if nothing but destruction awaited her. Thousands of beating hearts looked on, anxious for the result. The silence was so great as the *Lexington* approached the dam that a pin might almost be heard to fall. She entered the gap with a full head of steam on, pitched down the roaring torrent, made two or three spasmodic rolls, hung for a moment on the rocks below, was then swept into deep water by the current, and rounded to safety into the bank. Thirty thousand voices rose in one deafening cheer, and universal joy seemed to pervade the face of every man present.

The *Neosho* followed next; all her hatches battened down, and every precaution taken against accident. She did not fare as well as the *Lexington,* her pilot having become frightened as he approached the abyss and stopped her engine, when I particularly ordered a full head of steam to be carried; the result was that for a moment her hull disappeared from sight under the water. Everyone thought she was lost. She rose, however, swept along over the rocks with the current, and fortunately escaped with only one hole in her bottom, which was stopped in the course of an hour.

The *Hindman* and *Osage* both came through beautifully without touching a thing, and I thought if I was only fortunate enough to get my large vessels as well over the falls, my fleet once more would do good service on the Mississippi.

The accident to the dam, instead of disheartening Colonel Bailey, only induced him to renew his exertions, after he had seen the success of getting four vessels through.

The noble-hearted soldiers, seeing their labor of the last eight days swept away in a moment, cheerfully went to work to repair damages, being confident now that all the gunboats would be finally brought over. These men had been working for eight days and nights up to their necks in water in the boiling sun, cutting trees and wheeling bricks, and nothing but good humor prevailed among them. On the whole, it was very fortunate that the dam was carried away, as the two barges that were swept away from the centre swung around against some rocks on the left, and made a fine cushion for the vessels, and prevented them, as it afterward appeared, from running on certain destruction.

The force of the water and the current being too great to construct a continuous dam of six hundred feet across the river in so short a time, Colonel Bailey determined to leave a gap of fifty-five feet in the dam, and build a series of wing dams on the upper falls. This was accomplished in three days' time, and on the eleventh instant the *Mound City, Carondelet,* and *Pittsburgh* came over the upper falls, a good deal of labor having been expended in hauling them through, the channel being very crooked, and scarcely wide enough for them. Next day the *Ozark, Louisville,* and *Chillicothe,* and two tugs also succeeded in crossing the upper falls. Immediately afterward the *Mound City, Carondelet,* and *Pittsburgh* started in succession to pass the dam, all their hatches battened down, and every precaution taken to prevent accident. The passage of these vessels was a most beautiful sight, only to be realized when seen. They passed over without an accident, except the unshipping of one or two rudders. This was witnessed by all the troops, and the vessels were heartily cheered when they passed over. Next morning, at ten o'clock, the *Louisville, Chillicothe, Ozark,* and two tugs passed over without any accident, except the loss of a man, who was swept off the deck of one of the tugs. By three o'clock that afternoon the vessels were all coaled, ammunition replaced, and all steamed down the river, with the convoy of transports in company. A good deal of difficulty was anticipated in getting over the bars in lower Red River; depth of water reported only five feet; gunboats were drawing six. Providentially, we had a rise from the back-water of the Mississippi, that river being very high at that time; the back-water extending to Alexandria, one hundred and fifty miles distant, enabling us to pass all the bars and obstructions with safety.

Union Private Larry Van Alystyne, who had come out of the peaceful Catskills to fight with New York's "Bostwick's Tigers," was aghast at the bitterness and cruelty of the war as border people knew it:[15]

Eight miles below Alexandria. The Jay-hawkers kept their promise to burn the place rather than have it go into the hands of the enemy again. About daylight this morning cries of fire and the ringing of alarm bells were heard on every side. I think a hundred fires must have been started at one time. We grabbed the few things we had to carry and marched out of the fire territory, where we left them under guard and went back to do what we could to help the people. There was no such thing as saving the buildings. Fires were breaking out in new places all the time. All we could do was to help the people get over the levee, the only place where the heat did not reach and where there was nothing to burn. There was no lack of help, but all were helpless to do more than that. Only the things most needful, such as beds and eatables, were saved. One lady begged so for her piano that it was got out on the porch and there left to burn. Cows ran bellowing through the streets. Chickens flew out from yards and fell in the streets with their feathers scorching on them. A dog with his bushy tail on fire ran howling through, turning to snap at the fire as he ran. There is no use trying to tell about the sights I saw and the sounds of distress I heard. It cannot be told and could hardly be believed if it were told. Crowds of people, men, women, children and soldiers, were running with all they could carry, when the heat would become unbearable, and dropping all, they would flee for their lives, leaving everything but their bodies to burn. Over the levee the sights and sounds were harrowing. Thousands of people, mostly women, children and old men, were wringing their hands as they stood by the little piles of what was left of all their worldly possessions. Thieves were everywhere, and some of them were soldiers. I saw one knocked down and left in the street, who had his arms full of stolen articles. The provost guards were everywhere, and, I am told, shot down everyone caught spreading the fire or stealing. Nearly all buildings were of wood; great patches of burning roofs would sail away, to drop and start a new fire. By noon the thickly settled portion of Alexandria was a smoking ruin. The thousands of beautiful shade trees were as bare as in winter, and those that stood nearest the houses were themselves burning. An attempt was made to save one section by blowing up a church that stood in an open space, but the fuse went out and the powder did not explode until the building burned down to it, and then scattered the fire instead of stopping it, making the destruction more complete than if nothing of the kind had been attempted.

The campaign ended. Transports took Smith's army back to Sherman, Banks turned over the remaining troops to General E. R. S. Canby (recently put in charge of the Military Division of the West Mississippi), Porter resumed the Mississippi patrol. The Union wrote off an inglorious failure.

At least one Confederate was no happier with the results than Washington. General Richard Taylor had protested strongly when his superior, Kirby Smith, had drawn off a part of the Confederate forces after Mansfield and Pleasant Hill and marched north to join Price in southern Arkansas. There, on April 30, the combined force had won an indecisive victory (Jenkins' Ferry) over the army which Steele was to have had at Shreveport six weeks earlier. As weeks passed, Taylor's resentment mounted, until he ended an acrimonious correspondence with as bitter and insubordinate a letter as the war produced:[16]

NEAR ALEXANDRIA, June 5, 1864

GENERAL: . . . You are mistaken in supposing that my communications were intended as complaints. I have no complaints to make. My communications were statements of facts, necessary, in my judgment, to the proper understanding of the campaign. I have not read the story of Gil Blas and the Archbishop to so little purpose as not to know that truth is often considered "objectionable by superiors," but I have not drawn the moral that it is therefore "improper in subordinates to state it."

. . . You state that the fruits of the victory of Mansfield were secured by the march of the column against Steele, and that the complete success of the campaign was determined by his overthrow at Jenkins' Ferry. After a series of engagements Banks was driven into his works at Alexandria on April 28, two days before the fight at Jenkins' Ferry, and on the day of that fight the river was completely blockaded below Alexandria against both transports and gun-boats. I am at a loss to conceive what connection the fruits of Mansfield have with the fight at Jenkins' Ferry. . . .

At Jenkins' Ferry you lost more heavily in killed and wounded than the enemy. This appears from the official report of Steele, confirmed by our officers who were present. You lost two pieces of artillery, which the enemy did not carry off because he had previously been deprived of means of transportation. . . . He burned his pontoon for the same reason, and because after crossing the Saline he had no further use for it. He marched to Little Rock after the fight entirely unmolested. He would unquestionably have gone there had the fight never occurred. We do not today hold one foot more of Arkansas than if Jenkins' Ferry had never been, and we have a jaded army and 1,000 less soldiers. How, then, was the "complete success of the campaign determined by Steele's overthrow at Jenkins' Ferry"? In truth, the campaign as a whole has been a hideous failure. The fruits of Mansfield have been turned to dust and ashes. Louisiana, from Natchitoches to the Gulf, is a howling wilderness and her people are starving. Arkansas is probably as great a sufferer. In both States abolition conventions are sitting to overthrow their system of labor. The remains of Banks' army have already gone to join Grant or Sherman, and may turn the scale against our overmatched brethren in Virginia and Georgia.

On April 24 the affair of Monett's Ferry * took place. The Federals admit that a few hours' more delay would have led to the destruction of their army. Admiral Porter in his official report states this army to be 35,000 strong. The destruction of the army would have led, of necessity, to the destruction of the fleet. These advantages were all thrown away, to the utter destruction of the best interests of the country, and in their place we have Jenkins' Ferry. Our material of war is exhausted, our men are broken down with long marches from Red River to Arkansas and from Arkansas back to Red River. About 1,000 of the best officers and men were sacrificed and no result attained. The roads to Saint Louis and New Orleans should now be open to us. Your strategy has riveted the fetters on both. . . . The grave errors you have committed in the recent campaign may be repeated if the unhappy consequences are not kept before you. After the desire to serve my country, I have none more ardent than to be relieved from longer serving under your command.

* A sharp engagement in which the Confederates tried unsuccessfully to prevent the Union forces from crossing the Cane River. The battle, which is sometimes called Cane River Crossing, took place on April 23, rather than 24, as Taylor stated.

CHAPTER 30

"CRIES AROSE OF GRANT!"

BLACKS AND WHITES slaughtered heedlessly at a minor outpost along the Mississippi, infantry and artillery fighting gunboats along the distant Arkansas—these were new aspects of a war now three years old. But the climactic event of that spring took place in Washington.

I

Horace Porter was a guest at the White House:[1]

On the evening of March 8 the President and Mrs. Lincoln gave a public reception at the White House, which I attended. The President stood in the usual reception-room, known as the "Blue Room," with several cabinet officers near him, and shook hands cordially with everybody, as the vast procession of men and women passed in front of him. He was in evening dress, and wore a turned-down collar a size too large. The necktie was rather broad and awkwardly tied. He was more of a Hercules than an Adonis. His height of six feet four inches enabled him to look over the heads of most of his visitors. His form was ungainly, and the movements of his long, angular arms and legs bordered at times upon the grotesque. His eyes were gray and disproportionately small. His face wore a general expression of sadness, the deep lines indicating the sense of responsibility which weighed upon him; but at times his features lighted up with a broad smile, and there was a merry twinkle in his eyes as he greeted an old acquaintance and exchanged a few words with him in a tone of familiarity. He had sprung from the common people to become one of the most uncommon of men. Mrs. Lincoln occupied a position on his right. For a time she stood on a line with him and took part in the reception, but afterward stepped back and conversed with some of the wives of the cabinet officers and other personal acquaintances who were in the room. At about half-past nine o'clock a sudden commotion near the entrance to the room attracted general attention, and, upon looking in that direction, I was surprised to see General Grant walking along modestly with the rest of the crowd toward Mr. Lincoln. He had arrived from the West that evening, and had come to the White House to pay his respects to the President. He had been in Washington but once before, when he visited it for a day soon after he had left West Point.* Although these two historical characters had never met before, Mr. Lincoln recognized the general at once from the pictures he had seen of him. With a face radiant with delight, he advanced rapidly two or three steps toward his distinguished visitor, and cried out: "Why, here is General Grant! Well, this is a great pleasure, I assure you," at the same time seizing him by the hand, and shaking it for several minutes with a vigor which showed the extreme cordiality of the welcome.

The scene now presented was deeply impressive. Standing face to face for the first time were the two illustrious men whose names will always be inseparably associated in connection with the war of the rebellion. Grant's right hand grasped the lapel of his coat; his head was bent slightly forward, and his eyes upturned toward Lincoln's face. The President, who was eight inches taller, looked down with beaming countenance upon his guest. Although their appearance, their training, and their characteristics were in striking contrast, yet the two men had many traits in common, and there were numerous points of resemblance in their remarkable careers. Each was of humble origin, and had been compelled to learn the first lessons of life in the severe school of adversity. Each had risen from the people, possessed an abiding confidence in them, and always retained a deep hold upon their affections. Each might have said to those who were inclined to sneer at his plain origin what a marshal of France, who had risen from the ranks to a dukedom, said to the hereditary nobles who attempted to snub him in Vienna: "I am an ancestor; you are only descendants."

. . . The statesman and the soldier conversed for a few minutes, and then the President presented his distinguished guest to Mr. Seward. The Secretary of State was very demonstrative in his welcome, and
* 1843.

after exchanging a few words, led the general to where Mrs. Lincoln was standing, and presented him to her. Mrs. Lincoln expressed much surprise and pleasure at the meeting, and she and the general chatted together very pleasantly for some minutes. The visitors had by this time become so curious to catch a sight of the general that their eagerness knew no bounds, and they became altogether unmanageable. Mr. Seward's consummate knowledge of the wiles of diplomacy now came to the rescue and saved the situation. He succeeded in struggling through the crowd with the general until they reached the large East Room, where the people could circulate more freely. This, however, was only a temporary relief. The people by this time had worked themselves up to a state of uncontrollable excitement. The vast throng surged and swayed and crowded until alarm was felt for the safety of the ladies. Cries now arose of "Grant! Grant! Grant!" Then came cheer after cheer. Seward, after some persuasion, induced the general to stand upon a sofa, thinking the visitors would be satisfied with a view of him, and retire; but as soon as they caught sight of him their shouts were renewed, and a rush was made to shake his hand. The President sent word that he and the Secretary of War would await the general's return in one of the small drawing-rooms, but it was fully an hour before he was able to make his way there, and then only with the aid of several officers and ushers.

On the following day, March 9, General Grant returned to the White House, accompanied by Fred, his eldest son. Lincoln and the members of his Cabinet greeted the distinguished visitor. The President said:

"General Grant, the nation's appreciation of what you have done, and its reliance upon you for what remains to be done in the existing great struggle, are now presented, with this commission constituting you lieutenant-general in the Army of the United States.* With this high honor, devolves upon you, also, a corresponding responsibility. As the country herein trusts you, so, under God, it will sustain you. I scarcely need to add, that, with what I here speak for the nation, goes my own hearty personal concurrence."

Grant responded:

"Mr. President, I accept the commission, with gratitude for the high honor conferred. With the aid of the noble armies that have fought

---

* The grade of lieutenant general, bestowed previously only on George Washington and Winfield Scott, was revived by act of Congress in February. Grant was nominated for this office on March 1 and confirmed by the Senate next day.

*in so many fields for our common country, it will be my earnest
endeavor not to disappoint your expectations. I feel the full weight of
the responsibilities now devolving upon me; and I know that if they are
met, it will be due to those armies, and above all, to the favor of that
Providence which leads both nations and men."*

II

In character, Grant moved swiftly:[2]

. . . My commission as lieutenant-general was given to me on the
9th of March, 1864. On the following day . . . I visited General
Meade, commanding the Army of the Potomac, at his headquarters at
Brandy Station, north of the Rapidan. I had known General Meade
slightly in the Mexican war, but had not met him since until this visit.
I was a stranger to most of the Army of the Potomac, I might say to all
except the officers of the regular army who had served in the Mexican
war. There had been some changes ordered in the organization of that
army before my promotion. One was the consolidation of five corps
into three, thus throwing some officers of rank out of important commands. Meade evidently thought that I might want to make still one
more change not yet ordered. He said to me that I might want an
officer who had served with me in the West, mentioning Sherman specially, to take his place. If so, he begged me not to hesitate about making the change. He urged that the work before us was of such vast
importance to the whole nation that the feeling or wishes of no one person should stand in the way of selecting the right men for all positions. For himself, he would serve to the best of his ability where placed.
I assured him that I had no thought of substituting any one for him.
As to Sherman, he could not be spared from the West.

This incident gave me even a more favorable opinion of Meade than
did his great victory at Gettysburg the July before. It is men who wait
to be selected, and not those who seek, from whom we may always expect the most efficient service.

Meade's position afterwards proved embarrassing to me if not to him.
He was commanding an army and, for nearly a year previous to
my taking command of all the armies,* was in supreme command of the
Army of the Potomac—except from the authorities at Washington. All
other general officers occupying similar positions were independent in

* The official order, placing Grant in command of all armies, was issued on
March 12.

their commands so far as any one present with them was concerned. I tried to make General Meade's position as nearly as possible what it would have been if I had been in Washington or any other place away from his command. I therefore gave all orders for the movements of the Army of the Potomac to Meade to have them executed. To avoid the necessity of having to give orders direct, I established my headquarters near his, unless there were reasons for locating them elsewhere. . . .

A quick trip to the West gave Grant a chance to confer with Sherman:

. . . We left Nashville together for Cincinnati. I had Sherman accompany me that far on my way back to Washington so that we could talk over the matters about which I wanted to see him, without losing any more time from my new command than was necessary. The first point which I wished to discuss was particularly about the co-operation of his command with mine when the spring campaign should commence. . . .

Some time in the winter of 1863–64 I had been invited by the general-in-chief to give my views of the campaign I thought advisable for the command under me—now Sherman's. General J. E. Johnston was defending Atlanta and the interior of Georgia with an army, the largest part of which was stationed at Dalton, about 38 miles south of Chattanooga. Dalton is at the junction of the railroad from Cleveland [Tennessee] with the one from Chattanooga to Atlanta.

There could have been no difference of opinion as to the first duty of the armies of the military division of the Mississippi. Johnston's army was the first objective, and that important railroad centre, Atlanta, the second. . . . The plan therefore was for Sherman to attack Johnston and destroy his army if possible, to capture Atlanta and hold it, and with his troops and those of Banks * to hold a line through to Mobile, or at least to hold Atlanta and command the railroad running east and west, and the troops from one or other of the armies to hold important points on the southern road, the only east and west road that would be left in the possession of the enemy. This would cut the Confederacy in two again, as our gaining possession of the Mississippi River had done before. . . .

On the twenty-third of March, Grant was back in Washington. Three days later he established his headquarters at Culpeper Court House. He believed that he understood both Lincoln and Stanton now:

* Still commanding the Department of the Gulf.

Although hailing from Illinois myself, the State of the President, I never met Mr. Lincoln until called to the capital to receive my commission as lieutenant-general. I knew him, however, very well and favorably from the accounts given by officers under me at the West who had known him all their lives. I had also read the remarkable series of debates between Lincoln and Douglas a few years before, when they were rival candidates for the United States Senate. I was then a resident of Missouri, and by no means a "Lincoln man" in that contest; but I recognized then his great ability.

In my first interview with Mr. Lincoln alone he stated to me that he had never professed to be a military man or to know how campaigns should be conducted, and never wanted to interfere in them; but that procrastination on the part of commanders, and the pressure from the people of the North and Congress, *which was always with him*, forced him into issuing his series of "Military Orders"—one, two, three, etc. He did not know but they were all wrong, and did know that some of them were. All he wanted or had ever wanted was some one who would take the responsibility and act, and call on him for all the assistance needed, pledging himself to use all the power of the government in rendering such assistance. Assuring him that I would do the best I could with the means at hand, and avoid as far as possible annoying him or the War Department, our first interview ended.

The Secretary of War I had met once before only, but felt that I knew him better.

While commanding in West Tennessee we had occasionally held conversations over the wires, at night, when they were not being used. He and General Halleck both cautioned me against giving the President my plans of campaign, saying that he was so kind-hearted, so averse to refusing anything asked of him, that some friend would be sure to get from him all he knew. I should have said that in our interview the President told me he did not want to know what I proposed to do. But he submitted a plan of campaign of his own which he wanted me to hear and then do as I pleased about. He brought out a map of Virginia on which he had evidently marked every position occupied by the Federal and Confederate armies up to that time. He pointed out on the map two streams which empty into the Potomac, and suggested that the army might be moved on boats and landed between the mouths of these streams. We would then have the Potomac to bring our supplies, and the tributaries would protect our flanks while we moved out. I listened respectfully, but did not suggest that the same streams would protect Lee's flanks while he was shutting us up.

I did not communicate my plans to the President, nor did I to the Secretary of War or to General Halleck.

III

All was not sweetness and light. Grant called Sheridan east to command the Federal cavalry in the approaching campaign against Lee. "Little Phil" had definite notions about how he wished to operate. He would not be as gratified as Grant by an early interview:[3]

At first General Meade would hardly listen to my proposition [that cavalry should be used to fight cavalry], for he was filled with the prejudices that, from the beginning of the war, had pervaded the army regarding the importance and usefulness of cavalry, General Scott then predicting that the contest would be settled by artillery, and thereafter refusing the services of regiment after regiment of mounted troops. General Meade deemed cavalry fit for little more than guard and picket duty, and wanted to know what would protect the transportation trains and artillery reserve, cover the front of moving infantry columns, and secure his flanks from intrusion, if my policy was pursued. I told him that if he would let me use the cavalry as I contemplated, he need have little solicitude in these respects, for, with a mass of ten thousand mounted men, it was my belief that I could make it so lively for the enemy's cavalry that, so far as attacks from it were concerned, the flanks and rear of the Army of the Potomac would require little or no defense, and claimed, further, that moving columns of infantry should take care of their own fronts. I also told him that it was my object to defeat the enemy's cavalry in a general combat, if possible, and by such a result establish a feeling of confidence in my own troops that would enable us after a while to march where we pleased, for the purpose of breaking General Lee's communications and destroying the resources from which his army was supplied.

The idea as here outlined was contrary to Meade's convictions, for though at different times since he commanded the Army of the Potomac considerable bodies of the cavalry had been massed for some special occasion, yet he had never agreed to the plan as a permanency, and could not be bent to it now. He gave little encouragement, therefore, to what I proposed, yet the conversation was immediately beneficial in one way, for when I laid before him the true condition of the cavalry, he promptly relieved it from much of the arduous and harassing picket service it was performing, thus giving me about two weeks in which to nurse the horses before the campaign opened.

While Sheridan and Meade were each gauging the other's peppery temper, disaster almost overtook Grant:[4]

. . . I generally visited Washington once a week to confer with the Secretary of War and President. On the last occasion, a few days before moving [from Culpeper], a circumstance occurred which came near postponing my part in the campaign altogether. Colonel John S. Mosby had for a long time been commanding a partisan corps, or regiment, which operated in the rear of the Army of the Potomac. On my return to the field on this occasion, as the train approached Warrenton Junction, a heavy cloud of dust was seen to the east of the road as if made by a body of cavalry on a charge. Arriving at the junction the train was stopped and inquiries made as to the cause of the dust. There was but one man at the station, and he informed us that Mosby had crossed a few minutes before at full speed in pursuit of Federal cavalry. Had he seen our train coming, no doubt he would have let his prisoners escape to capture the train. I was on a special train, if I remember correctly, without any guard.

IV

With the Virginia dogwoods all in bloom, Grant selected May 4 as the day to begin the movement to knock Lee out of the war. Federal effectives amounted to over 100,000, not counting Burnside's Ninth Corps held near the Rappahannock railroad bridge. Lee's army, lying west of the Rapidan, counted about 64,000 effectives. The Confederate commander knew that the hour of desperate decision approached rapidly, and tallied the tell-tale signs for his son Custis:[5]

CAMP 30 Apl '64

MY DEAR CUSTIS:

Nothing of much interest has occurred during the past week. The reports of scouts all indicate large preparations on the part of the enemy and a state of readiness for action. The 9th Corps is reported to be encamped (or rather was on the 27th) on the O & A RR between Fairfax CH and Alexandria. This is corroborative of information sent the President yesterday, but there may be some mistake as to the fact or number of corps. All their troops north of Rappahannock have been moved South, their guards called in, etc. The garrisons, provost guards, etc., in Northern cities have been brought forward and replaced by state troops. A battalion of heavy artillery is said to have recently arrived in Culpeper, numbering 3,000. I presume these are the men stated in their papers to have been drawn from the forts in N. Y. Harbour.

I wish we could make corresponding preparations. If I could get back Pickett, Hoke and R. Johnston I would feel strong enough to operate.* I have been endeavouring for the last eight or ten days to move Imboden against the B. & O. RR in its unprotected state, but have not been able. I presume he has his difficulties as well as myself. I am afraid it is too late now. I can not yet get the troops together for want of forage and am hoping for grass. Endeavour to get accurate information from Peninsula, James river, etc. My scouts have not returned from Annapolis and may get back too late.

Very affectionately your father,
R. E. LEE

GEN. G. W. CUSTIS LEE

Confederate General G. Moxley Sorrel described the real problem that confronted Lee:[6]

We were at no loss to understand Grant's intention. The Northern papers, as well as himself, had boldly and brutally announced the purpose of "attrition"—that is, the Federals could stand the loss of four or five men to the Confederates' one, and throw nice strategy into the background. It was known that we were almost past recruiting our thin ranks, and the small figures of the army as it now stood; while the double numbers of the Federals could be reproduced from the immense resources in population, not to speak of their foreign field of supplies under inducement of liberal bounties.

Grant started his march the night of May 3d [4th], via Germanna and Ely's Fords, Wilson's and Gregg's cavalry leading. Burnside also was ordered to him.

The wilderness was a wild, tangled forest of stunted trees, with in places impassable undergrowth, lying between Fredericksburg and Orange Court House, probably sixteen or seventeen miles square. Some farm clearings and a shanty or two for a few poor inhabitants might oc-

* Pickett was still in the Petersburg field; Hoke was in North Carolina on recruiting duty; Robert D. Johnston was with Early in the Valley.

casionally be seen. Two principal roads penetrated this repulsive district, the Orange Plank Road and the turnpike. The ground generally lay flat and level.

And now was to begin the last and greatest of the campaigns of the Army of Northern Virginia. The campaign of *attrition* on one side met and foiled by the fine flower of the ablest strategy of the other. It was Grant's stubborn perseverance, indifferent to the loss of life, against Lee's clear insight and incessant watchfulness. . . .

v

From a signal station on Clark's Mountain, the Confederates watched the advance of Grant's columns. A shrewd flanking movement by Lee threatened to drive a wedge between Hancock's Second Corps and the Fifth under Warren and the Sixth under Sedgwick. The skirmishing was heavy on the morning of May 5 when Meade, Warren, and Sedgwick met at Old Wilderness Tavern and decided they must attack without waiting for Hancock. By eleven o'clock the battle was becoming a bloody page in history—especially at the front where Sedgwick, coming up, soon found rebels pounding his lines. With Sedgwick traveled an unidentified eyewitness:[7]

"*Forward! by the right flank; forward!*" rings along the lines. Yonder in front are the gleaming bayonets of our first line of battle; back, just in rear, is the second line, the anxious eyes of the soldiers peering through the trees.

Was it a sadder wind than usual that swept down from the front that moment, bearing the first earnest clangor of the combat? Else why, as that wind touched the faces of the men, did such a mournful fervor blend with, but not blight the resolute curves of lips that pride forbade to tremble?

"Forward! by the right flank; forward!" again and again repeated far to right and left, until it becomes an echo.

And through a thicket, blind and interminable; over abattis of fallen trees; through swamps, and ditches, and brush-heaps; and once—a glorious breathing-space—across a half acre of open field, the obedient troops move on. . . . Sometimes the eyes of the men sink to note a by-path in the forest, like that which many a one has travelled in old days to some old spring of home-like memory. And here is the "birr" of a bullet, like that which startled one who heard it one summer afternoon, when a brother hunter was careless, and fired at a partridge as he stood

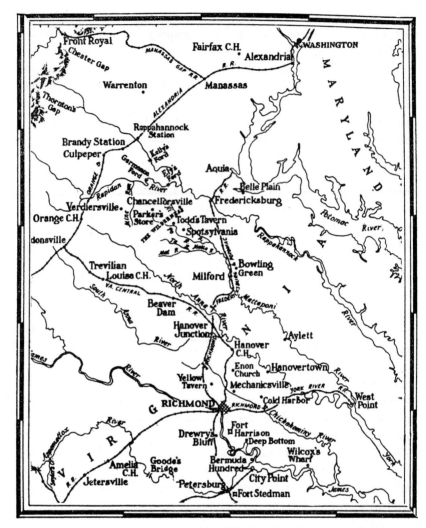

RICHMOND AND VICINITY, 1864

From *Atlas of American History*

in range. The bee-like sounds are thicker on this ridge; in the forest, a
little way ahead, there is a crackling, roaring tumult, seasoned with
wild cheers.

The Fifth corps has begun the fight in earnest—Griffin is pressing on.
Wadsworth, and Robinson, and Crawford are going in; the latter on the
left, supported by Getty, is advancing toward the enemy at Parker's
store. Behind Crawford and Getty, who are on the Orange Court-house

road, is the junction of that and the Brock road, up which, from the direction of Chancellorsville, Hancock is advancing to make connection. *That* is the vital point—that junction; to be held against all odds unto the death, else the army is severed. . . .

Here, marching through the forest with General John Sedgwick and his officers, between the first and second lines of battle of that grand old corps, which has left its mark in blood on every great battle-field in Virginia, we can hear but not see the progress of the contest in front and on the left. We hear that Griffin and Wadsworth, after gallantly charging the enemy, advancing over two lines of works, have met with superior numbers, have fought courageously, but have been pushed back. The cannon that spake a moment ago are silent. They were two guns of Captain Winslow's (Second Massachusetts) battery, the horses of which have been killed, the men of which have been sorely pressed, and which have been spiked and abandoned. We hear that Crawford's division of Pennsylvania Reserves, sent forward to Parker's store to check the surging tide of Hill's troops, pouring on to attack that junction of two roads on which so much depends, have been hurled back by the same overwhelming pressure that forces Wadsworth, and that the Seventh Pennsylvania regiment has been captured. We hear that everywhere the enemy is strongly posted, everywhere; on height, in the dense forest, using occasional open fields in the rear for artillery, but forcing us to attack in positions where the use of our own artillery is impossible. A cunning and a deceitful foe, knowing of old the splendid aim and discipline of our batteries, now compelled to silence.

The air is stifling, the sun sends its rays down through the jagged limbs of the chapparal around like red hot spears. This march is long, these bullets from an unseen foe are staining some sleeves and jackets too soon. . . .

They are there at last; the bushwhackers, thick as the sprigs and leaves that partly hide their treacherous faces. As the ponderous battle-line of the Sixth corps swings into level in their front, it sends a volley in greeting that thins those faces even as a wind of autumn rushing through an oak. General Ricketts is on the left, General Wright next, General Neill, of the Second division, whose iron brigade is made up of men who never flinched a desperate strait, holds the right of the line in support.

The fighting—who shall describe it? Not a thousand men can be seen at once, yet for miles in the front thousands are engaged. The volleyed thunders of the combat roll among the glens and ravines hoarser and higher than the voices of an Eastern jungle. The woods are alive with cries and explosions, and the shrill anvil-clatter of musketry. One cannon, pitched afar, times the wild tumult like a tolling bell. The smoke is a shroud about our heroes; there is not wind enough to lift it into a canopy.

And now, out of the concealed and awful scenery where the fight goes on, there come the ruins it has wrought, in shapes borne in blankets and on litters—maimed, tortured, writhing; with eyes dull with the stupor of coming death, or bright with delirious fire. Listen to the hell raging beyond and below; behold this silent, piteous procession, that emerges ceaselessly, and passes on. . . .

Two o'clock. In the momentary calm that sinks upon the forest in front we can hear a louder conflict gathering and growing on the left. There Crawford has been driven back; there the enemy are pressing in hordes down the turnpike, to gain the junction of the Brock road. Getty has advanced and met them. Hancock has come up at last, and Birney is going in on Getty's right. Mott and Barlow are forming on the left of the line, and Gibbon's division is coming up as a reserve. The enemy are checked, but their concentration continues. Troops are sent to the left from the Fifth corps, and by four o'clock General Hancock is in command of half the army in action.

And now, from left to right the sound of the shock of battle arises anew. Hancock is advancing, Sedgwick is advancing, Warren is in partial wait. Along the left a guttural, oceanic roar prevails, without an interval of rest. Like a great engine, dealing death, the Second corps and its supports move forward, taking equal death in return. Companies fall, regiments are thinned, brigades melt away. Stricken in the head by a bullet, General Alexander Hays, commanding the Second brigade of Birney's division, has rolled from his horse, dead. General Getty is wounded; Colonel Carroll, commanding the Third brigade of the Second division, is wounded; a host of line officers are stricken low; the enemy fights like a demon, but the fight moves on.

Sedgwick moves on, breaking the enemy's line for a moment, and taking four or five hundred prisoners. There are ripples of disaster on all the line, but they are quickly repaired.

Slowly, for the enemy is stubborn; slower yet on the extreme right, toward the river, for the enemy there has massed another force, and strives to break our flank. He finds a rock, and though he checks our advance, though hundreds of soldiers make the obeisance of death before him, he does not come on.

And as the day dies, and the darkness creeps up from the west, although no cheer of victory swells through the Wilderness from either side, we have accomplished this much at least, with much sore loss: the concentration of our army, the holding of the junction of the Orange Court-house and Brock roads; the turning back of the enemy's right flank from our path toward Richmond, and the average gain of a half mile of ground.

Colonel Theodore Lyman, who served on Meade's staff, watched his new general-in-chief that day:[8]

. . . General Grant had his station with us (or we with him); there he took his seat on the grass, and smoked his briarwood pipe, looking sleepy and stern and indifferent. His face, however, may wear a most pleasing smile, and I believe he is a thoroughly amiable man. That he believes in his star and takes a bright view of things is evident. At 4:15 P.M. General Meade ordered me to take some orderlies, go to General Hancock (whose musketry we could now hear on the left) and send him back reports, staying there till dark. Delightful! At the crossing of the dotted cross-road with the plank sat Hancock, on his fine horse—the *preux chevalier* of this campaign—a glorious soldier, indeed! The musketry was crashing in the woods in our front, and stray balls—too many to be pleasant—were coming about. It's all very well for novels, but *I* don't like such places and go there only when ordered. "Report to General Meade," said Hancock, "that it is very hard to bring up troops in this wood, and that only a part of my Corps is up, but I will do as well as I can." Up rides an officer: "Sir! General Getty is hard pressed and nearly out of ammunition!" "Tell him to hold on and General Gibbon will be up to help him." Another officer: "General Mott's division has broken, sir, and is coming back." "Tell him to stop them, sir!!" roared Hancock in a voice of a trumpet. As he spoke, a crowd of troops came from the woods and fell back into the Brock road. Hancock dashed among them. "Halt here! halt here! Form behind this rifle-pit. Major Mitchell, go to Gibbon and tell him to come up on the double-quick!" It was a welcome sight to see Carroll's brigade coming along that Brock road, he riding at their head as calm as a May morning. "Left face—prime—forward," and the line disappeared in the woods to waken the musketry with double violence. Carroll was brought back wounded. Up came Hays's brigade, disappeared in the woods, and, in a few minutes, General Hays was carried past me, covered with blood, shot through the head.

Horace Porter, on Grant's staff, found that the general, upon occasion, could lose his patience:[9]

. . . Darkness had set in, but the firing still continued. Aides came galloping in from the right, laboring under intense excitement, talking wildly, and giving the most exaggerated reports of the engagement. Some declared that a large force had broken and scattered Sedgwick's entire corps. Others insisted that the enemy had turned our right completely, and captured the wagon-train. It was asserted at one time that both Sedgwick and Wright had been captured. Such tales of disaster would have been enough to inspire serious apprehension in daylight and under ordinary circumstances. In the darkness of the night, in the gloom of a tangled forest, and after men's nerves had been racked by the strain of a two days' desperate battle, the most immovable commander might have been shaken.

But it was in just such sudden emergencies that General Grant was always at his best. Without the change of a muscle of his face, or the slightest alteration in the tones of his voice, he quietly interrogated the officers who brought the reports; then, sifting out the truth from the mass of exaggerations, he gave directions for relieving the situation with the marvelous rapidity which was always characteristic of him when directing movements in the face of an enemy. Reinforcements were hurried to the point attacked, and preparations made for Sedgwick's corps to take up a new line, with the front and right thrown back. General Grant soon walked over to his own camp, seated himself on a stool in front of his tent, lighted a fresh cigar, and there continued to receive further advices from the right.

A general officer came in from his command at this juncture, and said to the general-in-chief, speaking rapidly and laboring under considerable excitement: "General Grant, this is a crisis that cannot be looked upon too seriously. I know Lee's methods well by past experience; he will throw his whole army between us and the Rapidan, and cut us off completely from our communications." The general rose to his feet, took his cigar out of his mouth, turned to the officer, and replied, with a degree of animation which he seldom manifested: "Oh, I am heartily tired of hearing about what Lee is going to do. Some of you always seem to think he is suddenly going to turn a double somersault, and land in our rear and on both of our flanks at the same time. Go back to your command, and try to think what we are going to do ourselves, instead of what Lee is going to do."

VI

The battle, by Theodore Lyman's account, opened smartly next morning, the sixth of May:[10]

. . . General Grant ordered the attack all along the line, the next morning at 4:30; but put it off to 5 o'clock on the representation that Burnside could not get up in time. He was ordered to get in position by day-light and to go in on Hill's left flank . . . nearly parallel to the Parker's Store road. We were all up right early on that Friday the 6th of May, you may depend. "Lyman," said the General [Meade], "I want you to take some orderlies and go to General Hancock and report how things go there during the day."

It was after five when I mounted, and already the spattering fire showed that the skirmishers were pushing out; as I rode down the cross-road, two or three crashing volleys rang through the woods, and then the whole front was alive with musketry. I found General Hancock at the crossing of the plank: he was wreathed with smiles. "We are driving them, sir; tell General Meade we are driving them most beautifully. Birney has gone in and he is just cleaning them out be-au-ti-fully!" This was quite apparent from the distance of the receding firing and the absence of those infernal minié balls. "I am ordered to tell you, sir, that only one division of General Burnside is up, but that he will go in as soon as he can be put in position." Hancock's face changed. "I knew it!" he said vehemently. "Just what I expected. If he could attack *now*, we would smash A. P. Hill all to pieces!" And very true were his words.

Meantime, some hundreds of prisoners were brought in; all from Hill's troops. Presently, however, the firing seemed to wake again with renewed fury; and in a little while a soldier came up to me and said: "I was ordered to report that this prisoner here belongs to Longstreet's Corps." "Do you belong to Longstreet?" I hastened to ask. "Ya-as, sir," said grey-back, and was marched to the rear. It was too true! Longstreet, coming in all haste from Orange Court House, had fallen desperately on our advance; but he had uphill work. Birney's and Getty's men held fast and fought with fury, a couple of guns were put in the plank road and began to fire solid shot over the heads of our men, adding their roar to the other din. The streams of wounded came faster and faster back; here a field officer, reeling in the saddle; and there another, hastily carried past on a stretcher. I stood at the crossing and assisted in turning back stragglers or those who sought to go back, under pretext of helping the wounded. To some who were in great pain I gave some opium, as they were carried past me.

General Sorrel explained how the Confederates managed to spring this surprise:[11]

Longstreet had moved at 1 A.M., the march being difficult and slow in the dense forest by side tracks and deep furrowed roadways. At daylight he was on the Plank Road and in close touch with Lee when Hancock struck the two unprepared divisions [Heth's and Wilcox's of the Third Corps]. The situation when we came on the scene, that of May 6th, was appalling. Fugitives from the broken lines of the Third Corps were pouring back in disorder and it looked as if things were past mending.

But not so to James Longstreet; never did his great qualities as a tenacious, fighting soldier shine forth in better light. He instantly took charge of the battle, and threw his two divisions across the Plank Road, Kershaw on the right, Field on the left. None but seasoned soldiers like the First Corps could have done even that much. . . . Hill's men were prompt to collect and reform in our rear and soon were ready for better work.

General Lee was under great excitement immediately on the left. He wanted to lead some of our troops into action, but the Texas brigade was about him and swore they would do nothing unless he retired. A confident message from Longstreet through Colonel Venable that his line would be restored within an hour also helped him to regain his calm; and then at it we went in earnest, on both sides of the road.

Hancock's success had loosened his ranks somewhat, which helped us when we fell on him. It was a hard shock of battle by six of our brigades, three on each side of the road. No artillery came into play, the ground not being fit for it. . . .

Lyman saw that events had taken an ugly turn for Hancock:[12]

. . . Longstreet knew full well (they know everything, those Rebels) that Burnside was coming up with two divisions, on his flank; and knew too that he was late, very late. If Hancock could first be paralyzed, the day was safe from defeat, which now impended. Gathering all his forces, of both corps, he charged furiously. At a little after eleven Mott's left gave way. On the right the brigade of Stevenson, consisting of three raw Massachusetts regiments miscalled "Veterans," broke, on being brought under a tremendous fire. . . .

The musketry now drew nearer to us, stragglers began to come back, and, in a little while, a crowd of men emerged from the thicket in full retreat. They were not running, nor pale, nor scared, nor had they thrown away their guns; but were just in the condition described by the Prince de Joinville, after Gaines's Mill. They had fought all they meant to fight for the present, and there was an end of it! If there is anything that will make your heart sink and take all the backbone out of you, it is to see men in this condition! I drew my sword and rode in among them, trying to stop them at a little rifle-pit that ran along the road. I would get one squad to stop, but, as I turned to another, the first would quietly walk off.

There was a German color-bearer, a stupid, scared man (who gave him the colors, the Lord only knows!), who said, "Jeneral Stavenzon, he telled me for to carry ze colors up ze road." To which I replied I would run him through the body if he didn't plant them on the rifle-pit. And so he did, but I guess he didn't stick. Meanwhile there was no danger at all; the enemy did not follow up—not he. He was busy swinging round to oppose Burnside, and was getting his men once more in order. At half-past one I rode to General Meade and reported the state of affairs. The Provost-General went out at once and stopped and organized the stragglers. At two o'clock Burnside, who had been marching and countermarching, *did* attack. He made some impression, but it was too late, and he had not enough force to follow on. About this time I returned to General Hancock. His men were rallied along the road; but regiments and brigades were all mixed up; and we were obliged to listen to Burnside's fighting without any advance on our part. . . .

An eyewitness to the clash between Longstreet's forces and Hancock's was not surprised when shocked Federals came stumbling down the road:[13]

There, in the depths of those ravines, under the shadows of those trees, entangled in that brushwood, is no pomp of war, no fluttering of banners in an unhindered breeze, no solid tramp of marching battalions, no splendid strategy of the fields Napoleon loved to fight on. There a Saturnalia, gloomy, hideous, desperate, rages confined. That metallic, hollow rack of musketry is like the clanking of great chains about the damned; that sullen yell of the enemy, a fiendish protest and defiance. How the hours lag; how each minute is freighted with a burden that the days would have groaned to bear in other times! Still the sad, shuddering procession, emerging out of the smoke and tumult and passing on. Still the appealing eyes and clenched hands and quivering limbs of human creatures, worse than helpless, whose fighting is over. The paths are full of them; the woods are thick with them; the forest seems to take up the slow movement, and move with them, like giants hovering over the funeral of Liliputians.

Piled in ambulances, they move on further yet, while the torture of battle plies on below, making more victims. Here and there, beside some path, you shall see a heaped blanket, labelled by some thoughtful bearer with the name the corpse beneath it bore in life; here and there you shall come across a group of men bending over one wounded past help, and dying an agonized death. And often—too often—the shameful spectacle of one bearing a weapon, unhurt, pallid and fear-stricken, flits through an opening toward the rear and is gone. You shall meet with soldiers in groups of one, or two, or three, hidden in some thicket or, coolly making coffee by the roadside. And hearing the roar of the battle below, and seeing the bloody trails of the battle behind, it shall be a glad thing to see these men hunted by officers back with curses to the ranks, to share the dangers of their nobler comrades.

About this battle there is a horrible fascination. It is like a maelstrom. You feel it sucking you in, and you go nearer to see men fall like those you have seen fallen. Down through the break, underneath the edges of the smoke, where the bullets are thick and the trunks of trees, like the ranks of men, sway and fall with the smiting of shells, you have a little view of the courage and the carnage of this fight. There are the enemy, retreated to the breastworks—a ragged pile of fallen trees and heaped-up earth—hiding their heads, spitting lead and flame. Here is the Sixth corps—what you can see of it—plunging on, firing continually, tumbling over branches and limbs, sinking waist deep in swamps, fighting with its might and bleeding at every pore. The troops of the First division, under Wright, are martyred for a time in a ravine swept by musketry in front, and by a cross-fire of artillery from right and left. The few guns that we have posted to the left have funeral voices for our enemy on the ridge, perishing beneath their fire in scores.

The ridge is taken, the division breathes once more, but on come the
enemy, an avalanche of greater numbers, pushing us back. . . .

*As the Confederate assault gathered momentum, Sorrel heard Long-
street calling him:*[14]

"Colonel, there is a fine chance of a great attack by our right. If you
will quickly get into those woods, some brigades will be found much
scattered from the fight. Collect them and take charge. Form a good
line and then move forward and turning as much as possible to the
left. Hit hard when you start, but don't start until you have everything
ready. I shall be waiting for your gun fire, and be on hand with fresh
troops for further advance."

. . . The brigades of Anderson, Mahone, and Wofford were lined
up in fair order and in touch with each other. It was difficult to assemble
them in that horrid Wilderness, but in an hour we were ready. The
word was given, and then with heavy firing and ringing yells we were
upon Hancock's exposed left, the brigades being ably commanded by
their respective officers. It was rolled back line after line. I was well
mounted, and despite the tangled growth could keep with our troops in
conspicuous sight of them, riding most of the charge with Mahone's
men of the Eighteenth Virginia. . . .

A stand was attempted by a reserve line of Hancock's, but it was
swept off its feet in the tumultuous rush of our troops, and finally we
struck the Plank Road lower down. On the other side of it was James
S. Wadsworth's corps in disorder. . . . Though the old General was
doing all possible to fight it, his men would not stay. A volley from our
pursuing troops mortally wounded the gallant New Yorker and killed
his horse.

Every care was given to General Wadsworth by our surgeon. Before
they could get to him, however, some of his valuables—watch, sword,
glasses, etc.—had disappeared among the troops. One of the men
came up with, "Here, Colonel, here's his map." It was a good general
map of Virginia, and of use afterwards.

We were then so disorganized by the chase through the woods that a
halt was necessary to reform, and I hastened back to General Longstreet to press for fresh troops. There was no need with him. He had
heard our guns, knew what was up, and was already marching, happy
at the success, to finish it with the eager men at his heels.

There was quite a party of mounted officers and men riding with him

—Generals Kershaw and Jenkins, the staff, and orderlies. Jenkins, always enthusiastic, had thrown his arm around my shoulder, with "Sorrel, it was splendid; we shall smash them now." And turning back I was riding by Longstreet's side, my horse's head at his crupper, when firing broke out from our own men on the roadside in the dense tangle.

The Lieutenant General * was struck. He was a heavy man, with a very firm seat in the saddle, but he was actually lifted straight up and came down hard. Then the lead-torn coat, the orifice close to the right shoulder pointed to the passage of the heavy bullet of those days. His staff immediately dismounted him, at foot of a branching tree, bleeding profusely.

The shot had entered near the throat and he was almost choked with blood. Doctor J. S. D. Cullen, his medical director, was quickly on the spot. Even then the battle was in the leader's mind, and he sent word to Major General Charles W. Field to go straight on. He directed me to hasten to General Lee, report what had been accomplished, and urge him to continue the movement he was engaged on; the troops being all ready, success would surely follow, and Grant, he firmly believed, be driven across the Rapidan. . . .

My report to General Lee was, as instructed, immediate. I found him greatly concerned by the wounding of Longstreet and his loss to the army. . . . A new attack with stronger forces was settled on. It was to be made direct on the enemy's works, lower down the Plank Road, in the hope of dislodging him.

But meantime the foe was not idle. He had used the intervening hours in strengthening his position and making really formidable works across the road. When the Confederate troops assaulted them late in the afternoon they met with a costly repulse, and with this the principal operations on our part of the field ceased for the day; it was coming on dark.

In two days Grant's assault against Lee had cost the Union 2,246 killed, 12,037 wounded, and 3,383 missing; Confederate losses in killed and wounded were estimated at 7,750. Still, Theodore Lyman reckoned that the engagements could not be judged by comparative casualties:[15]

---

* Whereas lieutenant general was the highest rank in the U. S. Army, the Confederacy bestowed the rank of full general on Samuel Cooper, Albert Sidney Johnston, Robert E. Lee, Joseph E. Johnston, and P. G. T. Beauregard. On February 6, 1865 the Confederate Congress created the post of general in chief for Lee.

The result of this great Battle of the Wilderness was a drawn fight, but strategically it was a success, because Lee marched out *to stop our advance on Richmond*, which, at this point, he did not succeed in doing. We lost a couple of guns and took some colors. On the right we made no impression; but, on the left, Hancock punished the enemy so fearfully that they, that night, fell back entirely from his front and shortened their own line, as we shortened ours, leaving their dead unburied and many of their wounded on the ground. The Rebels had a very superior knowledge of the country and had marched shorter distances. Also I consider them more daring and sudden in their movements; and I fancy their discipline on *essential* points is more severe than our own—that is, I fancy they shoot a man when he ought to be shot, and we do not. As to *fighting*, when two people fight without cessation for the best part of two days, and then come out about even, it is hard to determine.

VII

Grant decided that he had enough of fighting Lee in this jungle. On the night of May 6 he issued new orders—with surprising results, as Horace Porter explained:[16]

Soon after dark, Generals Grant and Meade, accompanied by their staffs, after having given personal supervision to the starting of the march, rode along the Brock road toward Hancock's headquarters, with the intention of waiting there till Warren's troops should reach that point. While moving close to Hancock's line, there occurred an unexpected demonstration on the part of the troops, which created one of the most memorable scenes of the campaign. Notwithstanding the darkness of the night, the form of the commander was recognized, and word was passed rapidly along that the chief who had led them through the mazes of the Wilderness was again moving forward with his horse's head turned toward Richmond.

Troops know but little about what is going on in a large army, except the occurrences which take place in their immediate vicinity; but this night ride of the general-in-chief told plainly the story of success, and gave each man to understand that the cry was to be "On to Richmond!" Soldiers weary and sleepy after their long battle, with stiffened limbs and smarting wounds, now sprang to their feet, forgetful of their pains, and rushed forward to the roadside. Wild cheers echoed through the forest, and glad shouts of triumph rent the air. Men swung their hats, tossed up their arms, and pressed forward to within touch of their chief, clapping their hands, and speaking to him with the familiarity of comrades. Pine-knots and leaves were set on fire, and lighted the scene with their weird, flickering glare.

The night march had become a triumphal procession for the new commander. The demonstration was the emphatic verdict pronounced by the troops upon his first battle in the East. The excitement had been imparted to the horses, which soon became restive, and even the general's large bay, over which he possessed ordinarily such perfect control, became difficult to manage. Instead of being elated by this significant ovation, the general, thoughtful only of the practical question of the success of the movement, said: "This is most unfortunate. The sound will reach the ears of the enemy, and I fear it may reveal our movement." By his direction, staff-officers rode forward and urged the men to keep quiet so as not to attract the enemy's attention; but the demonstration did not really cease until the general was out of sight.

With cynicism, Theodore Lyman commented on the false optimism in the North:[17]

The newspapers would be comic in their comments, were not the whole thing so tragic. More absurd statements could not be. Lee is *not* retreating: he is a brave and skilful soldier and he will fight while he has a division or a day's rations left. These Rebels are not half-starved and ready to give up—a more sinewy, tawny, formidable-looking set of men could not be. In education they are certainly inferior to our native-born people; but they are usually very quick-witted within their own sphere of comprehension; and they know enough to handle weapons with terrible effect. Their great characteristic is their stoical manliness; they never beg, or whimper, or complain; but look you straight in the face, with as little animosity as if they had never heard a gun.

With equal cynicism, Lyman listened to Grant:

As General Grant sat under a pine tree, stoically smoking his briarwood pipe, I heard him say: "To-night Lee will be retreating south." Ah! General, Robert Lee is not Pemberton; he will retreat south, but only far enough to get across your path, and then he will retreat no more, if he can help it. In fact, orders were out for the whole army to move at dark on Spotsylvania Court House. But Lee knew it all: he could see the waggons moving, and had scouts besides. As night fell, his troops left their works and were crowding down the Parker's Store road, towards Spotsylvania—each moment worth untold gold to them! Grant had no longer a Pemberton! "His best friend," as he calls him. And we marched also. . . .

VIII

Lee guessed correctly; Grant would not retreat, but would strike for Spotsylvania Court House, on the edge of the Wilderness five miles to the southeast. On May 7 Lee began to pull back his troops; he would choose the ground where he would make a stand instead of leaving the initiative to Grant.

As the two armies converged on Spotsylvania and dug in for the coming battle, Phil Sheridan had a chance at last to use his cavalry in the way he wanted—to force Stuart to a duel in the open country behind Lee's lines. Sheridan started on May 9. For two days Stuart's troopers harassed Sheridan's long column. Then, changing tactics, Stuart swung from Sheridan's rear to his front, hoping to intercept the Union cavalry before it could ride into Richmond and commit God knew what devilry. Stuart's point of concentration was Yellow Tavern, six miles north of the Confederate capital.

Sheridan described the climax of the fighting:[18]

By forced marches General Stuart succeeded in reaching Yellow Tavern ahead of me on May 11; and the presence of his troops on the Ashland and Richmond road becoming known to Merritt as he was approaching the Brock turnpike, this general pressed forward at once to the attack. Pushing his division to the front, he soon got possession of the turnpike and drove the enemy back several hundred yards to the east of it. This success had the effect of throwing the head of my column to the east of the pike, and I quickly brought up Wilson and one of Gregg's brigades to take advantage of the situation by forming a line of battle on that side of the road. Meanwhile the enemy, desperate but still confident, poured in a heavy fire from his line and from a battery which enfiladed the Brock road, and made Yellow Tavern an uncomfortably hot place. Gibbs's and Devin's brigades, however, held fast there, while Custer, supported by Chapman's brigade, attacked the enemy's left and battery in a mounted charge.

Custer's charge, with Chapman on his flank and the rest of Wilson's division sustaining him, was brilliantly executed. Beginning at a walk, he increased his gait to a trot, and then at full speed rushed at the enemy. At the same moment the dismounted troops along my whole front moved forward, and as Custer went through the battery, capturing two of the guns with their cannoneers and breaking up the enemy's left, Gibbs and Devin drove his centre and right from the field. Gregg meanwhile, with equal success, charged the force in his rear—Gordon's brigade—and the engagement ended by giving us complete control of the road to Richmond.

Sheridan exaggerated his success at Yellow Tavern, for Stuart's stand had given Richmond's defenders time to man the fortifications and save the city. But the Confederates paid a high price. H. B. McClellan, Stuart's chief of staff, assessed it:[19]

We reached the vicinity of the Yellow Tavern that morning about ten o'clock, and found that we were in advance of the enemy's column, and in time to interpose between it and Richmond. Not knowing what force we had there, the General was uncertain whether to place himself at once between the enemy and the city, or to take a position on his flank, near the Yellow Tavern—the latter he preferred if he could be satisfied that we had a sufficient force in the trenches to defend Richmond. To ascertain this he sent me to see General Bragg. When I returned to him about two o'clock, I found that a heavy engagement had taken place, and, that after driving in a portion of our line, the enemy had been heavily repulsed. When I found the General there was a lull in the fight, and we sat quietly near one of our batteries for more than an hour, resting and talking. About four o'clock the enemy suddenly threw a brigade of cavalry, mounted, upon our extreme left, attacking our whole line at the same time. As he always did, the General hastened to the point where the greatest danger threatened—the point against which the enemy directed the mounted charge. My horse was so much exhausted by my severe ride of the morning that I could not follow him, but Captain Dorsey gave the particulars that follow.

The enemy's charge captured our battery on the left of our line, and drove back almost the entire left. Where Captain Dorsey was stationed —immediately on the Telegraph road—about eighty men had collected together, and among these the General threw himself, and by his personal example held them steady while the enemy charged entirely past their position. With these men he fired into their flank and rear, as they passed him, in advancing and retreating, for they were met by a mounted charge of the First Virginia cavalry and driven back some distance. As they retired, one man, who had been dismounted in the charge and was running out on foot, turned, as he passed the General, and, discharging his pistol, inflicted the fatal wound. When Captain Dorsey discovered that he was wounded, he came at once to his assistance and endeavored to lead him to the rear; the General's horse became so restive and unmanageable that he insisted upon being taken down and allowed to rest against a tree. When this was done Captain Dorsey sent for another horse. While waiting for this horse, the General ordered him to leave him alone and return to his men and drive back the enemy; said that he feared he was mortally wounded and could be of no more service. Captain Dorsey told him that he could not obey that order—that he would sacrifice his life rather than leave him until he had placed him out of all danger. The situation was a dangerous one. Our men were sadly scattered, and there was hardly a handful of men between that little group and the advancing enemy. But the horse arrived in time; the General was lifted onto him and led by Captain Dorsey to a safer place. There, by the General's order, he gave him into charge of Private Wheatly, of his company, and returned to rally our scattered men. Wheatly procured an ambulance, placed the General in it with the greatest care, and supporting him in his arms, he was driven from the field. As he was being brought off, he spoke to our men, whom he saw retreating, and said: "Go back! go back! and do your duty as I have done mine, and our country will be safe. Go back! go back! I had rather die than be whipped."

Stuart, mortally wounded, was carried to Richmond, where he lingered only a day. The Richmond Examiner *described his last hours:*[20]

Major-General J. E. B. Stuart, the model of Virginian cavaliers and dashing chieftain, whose name was a terror to the enemy, and familiar as a household word in two continents, is dead—struck down by a bullet from the foe, and the whole Confederacy mourns him. He breathed out his gallant spirit resignedly, and in the full possession of all his remarkable faculties of mind and body, at twenty-two minutes to eight o'clock Thursday night. . . .

We learn from the physicians in attendance upon the General, that his condition during the day was very changeable, with occasional delirium and other unmistakable symptoms of speedy dissolution. In the moments of delirium the General's mind wandered, and, like the immortal Jackson (whose spirit, we trust, his has joined) in the lapse of reason his faculties were busied with the details of his command. He reviewed, in broken sentences, all his glorious campaigns around McClellan's rear on the Peninsula, beyond the Potomac, and upon the Rapidan, quoting from his orders and issuing new ones to his couriers, with a last injunction to "make haste."

About noon, Thursday, President Davis visited his bedside, and spent some fifteen minutes in the dying chamber of his favorite chieftain. The President, taking his hand, said, "General, how do you feel?" He replied, "Easy, but willing to die, if God and my country think I have fulfilled my destiny and done my duty." As evening approached the General's delirium increased, and his mind again wandered to the battlefields over which he had fought, then off to wife and children, and off again to the front. . . .

As the evening wore on, the paroxysms of pain increased. . . . Though suffering the greatest agony at times, the General was calm, and applied to the wound with his own hand the ice intended to relieve the pain. During the evening he asked Dr. Brewer how long he thought he could live, and whether it was possible for him to survive through the night. The Doctor, knowing he did not desire to be buoyed by false hopes, told him frankly that death, that last enemy, was rapidly approaching. The General nodded and said, "I am resigned if it be God's will; but I would like to see my wife. But God's will be done." Several times he roused up and asked if she had come. . . .

At half-past seven o'clock it was evident to the physicians that death was setting its clammy seal upon the brave, open brow of the General, and told him so; asked if he had any last messages to give. The General, with a mind perfectly clear and possessed, then made dispositions of his staff and personal effects. To Mrs. General R. E. Lee he directed that his golden spurs be given as a dying memento of his love and esteem of her husband. To his staff officers he gave his horses. So particular was he in small things, even in the dying hour, that he emphatically exhibited and illustrated the ruling passion strong in death. To one of his staff, who was a heavy-built man, he said, "You had better take the larger horse; he will carry you better." Other mementoes he disposed of in a similar manner. To his young son he left his glorious sword.

His worldly matters closed, the eternal interest of his soul engaged his mind. Turning to the Rev. Mr. Peterkin, of the Episcopal Church, and of which he was an exemplary member, he asked him to sing the hymn commencing—

> Rock of ages cleft for me,
> Let me hide myself in thee—

he joined in with all the voice his strength would permit. He then joined in prayer with the ministers. To the Doctor he again said, "I am going fast now; I am resigned; God's will be done." Thus died General J. E. B. Stuart.

IX

On May 12, the day when "Jeb" Stuart's gay spirit struggled for release, the storm broke at Spotsylvania, staggering those who witnessed and survived it. At a salient in Lee's line, the "Bloody Angle," Horace Porter saw the conflict reach its peak:[21]

The battle near the "angle" was probably the most desperate engagement in the history of modern warfare, and presented features which were absolutely appalling. It was chiefly a savage hand-to-hand fight across the breastworks. Rank after rank was riddled by shot and shell and bayonet-thrusts, and finally sank, a mass of torn and mutilated corpses; then fresh troops rushed madly forward to replace the dead, and so the murderous work went on. Guns were run up close to the parapet, and double charges of canister played their part in the bloody work. The fence-rails and logs in the breastworks were shattered into splinters, and trees over a foot and a half in diameter were cut completely in two by the incessant musketry fire. . . .

We had not only shot down an army, but also a forest. The opposing flags were in places thrust against each other, and muskets were fired with muzzle against muzzle. Skulls were crushed with clubbed muskets, and men stabbed to death with swords and bayonets thrust between the logs in the parapet which separated the combatants. Wild cheers, savage yells, and frantic shrieks rose above the sighing of the wind and the pattering of the rain, and formed a demoniacal accompaniment to the booming of the guns as they hurled their missiles of death into the contending ranks. Even the darkness of night and the pitiless storm failed to stop the fierce contest, and the deadly strife did not cease till after midnight. Our troops had been under fire for twenty hours, but they still held the position which they had so dearly purchased.

X

The fighting at Spotsylvania cost Grant casualties of perhaps 17,000;
Lee's loss may have been as many as 12,000. Again, Grant "sidled to
the left," with Lee in dogged pursuit. As the Wilderness campaign
moved into its third phase, Theodore Lyman noted with wonder the
adjustments people made to the rigors of war:[22]

. . . There is, and can be, no doubt of the straits to which these
people are now reduced; particularly, of course, in this distracted region; there is nothing in modern history to compare with the conscription they have. They have swept this part of the country of all persons
under 50, who could not steal away. I have just seen a man of 48, very
much crippled with rheumatism, who said he was enrolled two days
ago. He told them he had thirteen persons dependent on him, including
three grandchildren (his son-in-law had been taken some time since);
but they said that made no difference; he was on his way to the rendez-
vous, when our cavalry crossed the river, and he hid in the bushes, till
they came up. I offered him money for some of his small vegetables;
but he said: "If you have any bread, I would rather have it. Your cavalry have taken all the corn I had left, and, as for meat, I have not tasted
a mouthful for six weeks." If you had seen his eyes glisten when I gave
him a piece of salt pork, you would have believed his story. He looked
like a man who had come into a fortune. "Why," said he, "that must
weigh four pounds—that would cost me forty dollars in Richmond!
They told us they would feed the families of those that were taken;
and so they did for two months, and then they said they had no more
meal."

What is even more extraordinary than their extreme suffering, is
the incomprehensible philosophy and endurance of these people. Here
was a man, of poor health, with a family that it would be hard to support in peacetimes, stripped to the bone by Rebel and Union, with no
hope from any side, and yet he almost laughed when he described his
position, and presently came back with a smile to tell me that the only
two cows he had, had strayed off, got into a Government herd, and
"gone up the road"—that's the last of *them*. In Europe, a man so situated would be on his knees, tearing out handfuls of hair, and calling
on the Virgin and on several saints. There were neighbors at his house;
and one asked me if I supposed our people would burn his tenement?
"What did you leave it for?" I asked. To which he replied, in a concise

way that told the whole: "Because there was right smart of bullets over thaar!"

The poorest people seem usually more or less indifferent or adverse to the war, but their bitterness increases in direct ratio to their social position. Find a well-dressed lady, and you find one whose hatred will end only with death—it is unmistakable, though they treat you with more or less courtesy. Nor is it extraordinary: there is black everywhere; here is one that has lost an only son; and here another that has had her husband killed. People of this class are very proud and spirited; you can easily see it; and it is the officers that they supply who give the strong framework to their army. They have that military and irascible nature so often seen among an aristocracy that was once rich and is now poor; for you must remember that, before the war, most of these land-owners had ceased to hold the position they had at the beginning of this century.

Sometimes Lyman was exasperated by foes who thought they were friends:[23]

To-day has been entirely quiet, our pickets deliberately exchanging papers, despite orders to the contrary. These men are incomprehensible —now standing from daylight to dark killing and wounding each other by thousands, and now making jokes and exchanging newspapers! You see them lying side by side in the hospitals, talking together in that serious prosaic way that characterizes Americans. The great staples of conversation are the size and quality of rations, the marches they have made, and the regiments they have fought against. All sense of personal spite is sunk in the immensity of the contest.

Yet when the call to battle came, they were once more bitter, unremitting enemies—a fact that Horace Porter understood:[24]

Everything was now in readiness for the memorable battle of Cold Harbor. Headquarters had been moved two miles farther to our left, and established near Old Cold Harbor, so as to be within easy reach of the main point of attack. It has been stated by inimical critics that the men had become demoralized by the many assaults in which they had been engaged; that they had lost much of their spirit, and were even insubordinate, refusing to move against the earthworks in obedi-

ence to the orders of their immediate commanders. This is a gross
slander upon the troops, who were as gallant and subordinate as any
forces in the history of modern warfare, although it is true that many
of the veterans had fallen, and that the recruits who replaced them were
inferior in fighting qualities.

In passing along on foot among the troops at the extreme front that
evening while transmitting some of the final orders, I observed an incident which afforded a practical illustration of the deliberate and desperate courage of the men. As I came near one of the regiments which
was making preparations for the next morning's assault, I noticed that
many of the soldiers had taken off their coats, and seemed to be engaged in sewing up rents in them. This exhibition of tailoring seemed
rather peculiar at such a moment, but upon closer examination it was
found that the men were calmly writing their names and home addresses on slips of paper, and pinning them on the backs of their coats,
so that their dead bodies might be recognized upon the field, and their
fate made known to their families at home.

*It was a wise precaution. William Swinton, historian of the Army of
the Potomac, understood why Cold Harbor was unique:*[25]

Next morning, with the first gray light of dawn struggling through
the clouds, the preparations began: from behind the rude parapets
there was an upstarting, a springing to arms, the muffled commands
of officers forming the line. The attack was ordered at half-past four,
and it may have been five minutes after that, or it may have been ten
minutes, but it certainly was not later than forty-five minutes past
four, when the whole line was in motion, and the dark hollows between
the armies were lit up with the fires of death.

It took hardly more than ten minutes of the figment men call time
to decide the battle. There was along the whole line a rush—the spectacle of impregnable works—a bloody loss—then a sullen falling back,
and the action was *decided*. Conceive of this in the large, and we shall
then be able to descend to some of the points of action as they individu-
alize themselves along the line.

*Colonel William Oates of the Fifteenth Alabama Infantry saw Union
troops sacrificed on a scale unparalleled since Burnside's bumbling
charges on Marye's Heights at Fredericksburg:*[26]

. . . Just before I could see the sun, I heard a volley in the woods, saw the Major running up the ravine in the direction of Anderson's brigade, which lay to the right of Law's, and the skirmishers running in, pursued by a column of the enemy ten lines deep, with arms at a trail, and yelling "Huzzah! huzzah!" I ordered my men to take arms and fix bayonets. Just then I remembered that not a gun in the regiment was loaded. I ordered the men to load and the officers each to take an ax and stand to the works. I was apprehensive that the enemy would soon be on our works before the men could load.

As Capt. Noah B. Feagin and his skirmishers crawled over the works I thought of my piece of artillery. I called out: "Sergeant, give them double charges of canister; fire, men, fire!" The order was obeyed with alacrity. The enemy were within thirty steps. They halted and began to dodge, lie down, and recoil. The fire was terrific from my regiment, the Fourth Alabama on my immediate right, and the Thirteenth Mississippi on my left, while the piece of artillery was fired more rapidly and better handled than I ever saw one before or since. The blaze of fire from it at each shot went right into the ranks of our assailants and made frightful gaps through the dense mass of men. They endured it but for one or two minutes, when they retreated, leaving the ground covered with their dead and dying. There were 3 men in my regiment killed, 5 wounded. My piece of artillery kept up a lively fire on the enemy where they halted in the woods, with shrapnel shell.

After the lapse of about forty minutes another charge was made by the Twenty-third and Twenty-fifth Massachusetts regiments, in a column by divisions, thus presenting a front of two companies only. Bryan's Georgia brigade came up from the rear and lay down behind Law's. The charging column, which aimed to strike the Fourth Alabama, received the most destructive fire I ever saw. They were subjected to a front and flank fire from the infantry, at short range, while my piece of artillery poured double charges of canister into them. The Georgians loaded for the Alabamians to fire. I could see the dust fog out of a man's clothing in two or three places at once where as many balls would strike him at the same moment. In two minutes not a man of them was standing. All who were not shot down had lain down for protection. One little fellow raised his head to look, and I ordered him to come in. He came on a run, the Yankees over in the woods firing at him every step of the way, and as he climbed over our works one shot took effect in one of his legs. They evidently took him to be a deserter. I learned from him that there were many more out there who were not wounded. This I communicated to Colonel Perry, who was again in command, General Law having been wounded in the head during the first assault; and thereupon Perry sent a company down a ravine on our right to capture them; they soon brought the colonel who led the charge, and about one hundred other prisoners. The colonel was a brave man. He said he had been in many places, but that was the worst.

Grant knew that he had made a mistake. Years later he confessed:[27]

I have always regretted that the last assault at Cold Harbor was ever made. . . . No advantage whatever was gained to compensate for the heavy loss we sustained. Indeed, the advantages other than those of relative losses, were on the Confederate side. Before that, the Army of Northern Virginia seemed to have acquired a wholesome regard for the courage, endurance, and soldierly qualities generally of the Army of the Potomac. They no longer wanted to fight them "one Confederate to five Yanks." Indeed, they seemed to have given up any idea of gaining any advantage of their antagonist in the open field. They had come to much prefer breastworks in their front to the Army of the Potomac. This charge seemed to revive their hopes temporarily; but it was of short duration. . . . When we reached the James River . . . all effects of the battle of Cold Harbor seemed to have disappeared.

Cold Harbor cost Grant 12,000 in killed and wounded against casualties for Lee of not more than 1,500. And when it was all over? Lyman found that again foes were virtually friends:[28]

To-night all the trenching tools were ordered up and the lines were strengthened, and saps run out, so as to bring them still closer to the opposing ones. And there the two armies slept, almost within an easy stone-throw of each other; and the separating space ploughed by cannon-shot and clotted with the dead bodies that neither side dared to bury! I think nothing can give a greater idea of deathless tenacity of purpose, than the picture of these two hosts, after a bloody and nearly continuous struggle of thirty days, thus lying down to sleep, with their heads almost on each other's throats! Possibly it has no parallel in history. So ended the great attack at Cool Arbor.*. . .

* Another designation of Cold Harbor.

CHAPTER 31

"BOLD OFFENSIVE"

I N MID-MARCH 1864 Grant had turned over to Sherman command of the Army of the Cumberland, the Army of the Tennessee, and the Army of the Ohio. Sherman met Grant in Cincinnati that month.

"Amidst constant interruptions of a business and social nature, we reached the satisfactory conclusion that, as soon as the season would permit, all the armies of the Union would assume the 'bold offensive' by 'concentric lines' on the common enemy, and would finish up the job in a single campaign if possible. The main 'objectives' were Lee's army behind the Rapidan in Virginia, and Joseph E. Johnston's army at Dalton, Georgia."

I

Sherman made clear his enthusiasm for Grant and his plan of operations.[1]

. . . There never was and never can be raised a question of rivalry or claim between us as to the relative merits of the manner in which we played our respective parts. We were as brothers—I the older man in years, he the higher in rank. We both believed in our heart of hearts that the success of the Union cause was not only necessary to the then generation of Americans, but to all future generations. We both professed to be gentlemen and professional soldiers, educated in the science of war by our generous Government for the very occasion which had arisen. Neither of us by nature was a combative man; but with honest hearts and a clear purpose to do what man could we embarked on that campaign, which I believe, in its strategy, in its logistics, in its grand and minor tactics, has added new luster to the old science of war. Both of us had at our front generals to whom in early life we had been taught to look up,—educated and experienced soldiers like ourselves, not likely to make any mistakes, and each of whom had as strong an army as could be collected from the mass of the Southern people,— of the same blood as ourselves, brave, confident, and well equipped; in addition to which they had the most decided advantage of operating in their own difficult country of mountain, forest, ravine, and river, affording admirable opportunities for defense, besides the other equally important advantage that we had to invade the country of our unqualified enemy and expose our long lines of supply to the guerrillas of an "exasperated people." Again, as we advanced we had to leave guards to bridges, stations, and intermediate depots, diminishing the fighting force, while our enemy gained strength by picking up his detachments as he fell back, and had railroads to bring supplies and reenforcements from his rear. I instance these facts to offset the common assertion that we of the North won the war by brute force, and not by courage and skill.

In contrast, Confederate General John Bell Hood recalled the circumstances under which he transferred from Virginia to "the Western Army":[2]

The War Department [in Richmond] had been anxious that an offensive campaign into Tennessee and Kentucky be initiated in the early Spring of 1864, and made a proposition to General Johnston to reinforce him with Polk's troops, then in Mississippi, and Longstreet's Corps, in East Tennessee. Johnston, at the appointed time, was expected to move forward and form a junction with these troops. The President and General Bragg, and also General Lee, were desirous that the offensive be assumed, and an attempt be made to drive the Federals to the Ohio river, before a large Army could be concentrated to move against us. . . .

Contending that 75,000 Confederate forces could have been mustered for this campaign, Hood told how he had come to northern Georgia under a misconception:

The President had thus agreed to afford General Johnston every facility in his power for the execution of the proposed plan of operations; and it was with the understanding we were to enter upon an active campaign that I consented to leave the Army of Northern Virginia, with which I had served since the outbreak of the war.

On the evening of my arrival at Dalton, on or about the 4th of February, I repaired to General Johnston's headquarters, and reported to him for duty. During our interview, in his room alone, he informed me that General Thomas was moving forward, and he thought it might be best for us to fall back and take up some position in rear of Dalton. I at once told him that I knew nothing of the situation or the object of General Thomas's move from Ringgold, but that we could, at least, hold our position a sufficient length of time to compel the enemy to develop his plan. The Federals, in a few days, fell back to Ringgold, having merely made a feint, in order to cover some movement then being made in Mississippi.

This was my introduction to the Army of Tennessee; albeit not calculated to inspire or encourage military ardor,—since it was proposed to retreat even before the enemy became in earnest—I nevertheless laid before General Johnston the plan to join Polk's Army and Longstreet's Corps on the march into Tennessee, gave him assurance that the authorities in Richmond would give him every assistance, and informed him, moreover, that General Lee favored the projected campaign.

General Johnston immediately took the ground that he did not very well know the country through which it was proposed to pass to the rear of the enemy; that there were difficulties to be encountered, etc., etc.; he desired Polk's and Longstreet's forces to join him at Dalton, where, this large Army being concentrated, he considered he should be left to decide and act for the best; in other words, be left to move forward, stand his ground or retreat, as might seem most expedient.

To this demand, General Lee was unwilling to accede; he was reluctant to give up Longstreet's Corps, unless for the purpose of active work and dealing hard blows, in the performance of which task it had already so often distinguished itself. The War Department objected to the withdrawal of Polk's Army from Mississippi, until active operations were to commence, as by such a movement one of the best regions of country for supplies would be abandoned to the enemy. . . .

April passed with Johnston refusing to budge from Dalton and with Hood still insisting in a letter to Braxton Bragg, who now served as military adviser to Jefferson Davis, that "to regain Tennessee would be of more value to us than a half a dozen victories in Virginia." In later years Hood retained his intense bitterness:

I cannot name one of Lee's Lieutenant Generals who would not have met this proposition from the War Department with that spirit of co-operation which is so essential in time of war. Moreover, any officer possessed of even a part of that heroic self-reliance so characteristic of Lee and Jackson, would not only have gladly accepted the ninety-one thousand (91,000) men, but, having secured a competent Quarter Master, would soon have found the necessary transportation; would have sent a dispatch to Richmond that he was moving forward, and, God willing, would take from the enemy all else needed to equip the army. Such might have been the result, instead of unremitting demands, upon the part of General Johnston, for an outfit equal to that of the United States troops, visions of insuperable difficulties, and vacillations unending.

"With the month of May," wrote an exuberant Sherman, "came the season for action." The three Western armies that he commanded—in round figures, 98,000 men and 250 guns—marched from Chattanooga without any intention of attacking Johnston at Dalton. Rather, Sherman's plan was to feint at Johnston's front and to make a lodgment in Resaca, eighteen miles to his rear, on the line of his communication and supply. The movement, Sherman admitted, was "partly, not wholly, successful"; still, Johnston was compelled "to let go Dalton and fight us at Resaca." This action, beginning on the thirteenth of May and continuing through the sixteenth, was a standoff with casualties practically even on each side. "I fought offensively and he defensively, aided by earth parapets," Sherman said succinctly. Major James Austin Connolly of the 123rd Illinois wrote his wife from the field of battle:[3]

May 15, 1864

Just as I had written the date above, I said: "Hello, the enemy are shelling us.". . . It is now about nine o'clock at night, the moon is shining with a misty light through the battle smoke that is slowly settling down like a curtain, over these hills and valleys; the mournful notes of a whippoorwill, near by, mingle in strange contrast with the exultant shouts of our soldiers—the answering yells of the rebels—the rattling fire of the skirmish line, and the occasional bursting of a shell.

Today we have done nothing but shift positions and keep up a heavy skirmish fire. Yesterday our Division and Judah's Division of Schofield's Corps, had some hard fighting. We drove the enemy about a mile and entirely within his fortifications, several of our regiments planting their colors on his fortifications, but were compelled to withdraw under a terrible fire. We, however, fell back but a short distance to the cover of the woods, where we still are, and the enemy have not ventured outside their works since. A report has just reached us that Hooker drove the enemy about a mile today. . . . We have men enough here to whip Johnston, and if he don't escape pretty soon he never will. . . .

Johnston "let go" next day, and on the twentieth of May Major Connolly wrote his wife from Kingston, Georgia:

If you will look at a map you will see that "we all" are still pushing southward, but a look at the map will give you little idea of the country we are passing through—will fail to point out to you the fields that are being reddened by the blood of our soldiers, and the hundreds of little mounds that are rising by the wayside day by day, as if to mark the footprints of the God of War as he stalks along through this beautiful country. This point is where the railroad from Rome forms a junction with the main line from Chattanooga to Atlanta. Rome is in our possession, and such has been the extraordinary rapidity with which the railroad has been repaired, as we have pushed along, that a train from Chattanooga ran into Kingston this morning about daylight, while at the same time a rebel train from Atlanta was whistling on the same road, and only two miles distant, but it is now about 9 o'clock in the morning, and the last whistle of the rebel train, north of the Etowah River, sounded some hours ago, the last rebel has undoubtedly crossed the river, the bridge across the river has been burned, I suppose, and the rebel army is wending its way, weary and dispirited, toward that mythical ditch of which we have heard so much.

General Johnston nursed a deepening resentment as he fell back across the Etowah:[4]

. . . When Brig.-General Jackson's reports showed that the head of the Federal column following the railroad was near Kingston, Lieutenant-General Hood was directed to move with his corps to a country

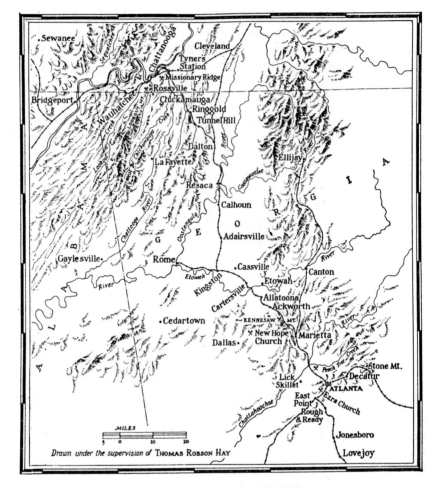

CHATTANOOGA TO ATLANTA

From *Atlas of American History*

road about a mile to the east of that from Adairsville, and parallel to
it, and to march northward on that road, right in front. Polk's corps,
as then formed, was to advance to meet and engage the enemy approaching from Adairsville; and it was expected that Hood's would
be in position to fall upon the left flank of those troops as soon as Polk
attacked them in front. An order was read to each regiment, announcing
that we were about to give battle to the enemy. It was received with
exultation.

When General Hood's column had moved two or three miles, that
officer received a report from a member of his staff, to the effect that

the enemy was approaching on the Canton road, in rear of the right of the position from which he had just marched. Instead of transmitting this report to me, and moving on in obedience to his orders, he fell back to that road and formed his corps across it, facing to our right and rear, toward Canton, without informing me of this strange departure from the instructions he had received. I heard of this erratic movement after it had caused such loss of time as to make the attack intended impracticable; for its success depended on accuracy in timing it.

Hood told another story:[5]

The three Corps Commanders, especially General Polk and myself, urged General Johnston, soon after our arrival at Cassville, to turn back and attack Sherman at Adairsville, as we had information of a portion of his Army having been sent to cross the Etowah, in order to threaten our communications south of that river. The opportunity was the more favorable, because of an open country and good roads, which would have enabled the Army to move rapidly and force the Federals, whilst divided in their forces, to accept a pitched battle, with rivers in their rear. This he declined to do. . . .

On the following day, Howard's Corps having been reported on the Ironton road (the country road referred to), I asked his authorization to march my command across an open field, and attack this detachment of the enemy, in case the report was correct. He consented.

I received no orders for battle as related by General Johnston, nor were the Corps Commanders brought together and given explicit instructions, verbal or written, as is usual and necessary upon the eve of a general engagement, although he had published, soon after our arrival at Cassville, a general order to the effect that he intended to fight. I was merely granted the privilege of doing what I had requested; the assertion, therefore, of General Johnston, that I had been ordered to move to the country road and be in readiness to attack in flank when Polk engaged the enemy in front is as erroneous as it is inexplicable.

II

Sherman, in pursuit of Johnston, could know nothing of the animosity developing between Hood and his superior, but of another source of animosity Sherman was well informed:[6]

. . . The newspapers of the South, many of which we found, were also loud in denunciation of Johnston's falling back before us without a serious battle, simply resisting by his skirmish-lines and by his rear-guard. But his friends proclaimed that it was all *strategic;* that he was deliberately drawing us farther and farther into the meshes, farther and farther away from our base of supplies, and that in due season he would not only halt for battle, but assume the bold offensive. Of course it was to my interest to bring him to battle as soon as possible, when our numerical superiority was at the greatest; for he was picking up his detachments as he fell back, whereas I was compelled to make similar and stronger detachments to repair the railroads as we advanced, and to guard them. . . .

Johnston's plan was to screen himself behind the Allatoona range. Sherman explained how a youthful experience saved him from a possible trap:

In early days (1844), when a lieutenant of the Third Artillery, I had been sent from Charleston, South Carolina, to Marietta, Georgia, to assist Inspector-General Churchill to take testimony concerning certain losses of horses and accoutrements by the Georgia Volunteers during the Florida War; and after completing the work at Marietta we transferred our party over to Bellefonte, Alabama. I had ridden the distance on horseback, and had noted well the topography of the country, especially that about Kenesaw, Allatoona, and the Etowah River. On that occasion I had stopped . . . to see some remarkable Indian mounds on the Etowah River, usually called the "Hightower." I therefore knew that the Allatoona Pass was very strong, would be hard to force, and resolved not even to attempt it, but to turn the position, by moving from Kingston to Marietta *via* Dallas; accordingly I made orders on the 20th to get ready for the march to begin on the 23d. . . .

Telegraphic communications told Sherman that Grant and Lee had met in "the bloody and desperate" battles of the Wilderness. The western armies moved from Kingston. At New Hope Church—so named from the Methodist meetinghouse there—an "accidental intersection" of the road from Allatoona to Dallas with the road from Van Wert to Marietta provided the setting for bloody fighting May 25 through 28. Sherman understood why his boys renamed New Hope the "Hell-Hole":

The night [May 25] was pitch-dark, it rained hard, and the convergence of our columns toward Dallas produced much confusion. I am sure similar confusion existed in the army opposite to us, for we were all mixed up. I slept on the ground, without cover, alongside of a log, got little sleep, resolved at daylight to renew the battle, and to make a lodgment on the Dallas and Allatoona road if possible, but the morning revealed a strong line of intrenchments facing us, with a heavy force of infantry and guns. The battle was renewed, and without success. . . .

Satisfied that Johnston in person was at New Hope with all his army, and that it was so much nearer my "objective," the railroad, than Dallas, I concluded to draw McPherson from Dallas to Hooker's right. . . . On the morning of the 28th he was fiercely assailed [and] a bloody battle ensued. . . . Meantime Thomas and Schofield were completing their deployments, gradually overlapping Johnston on his right, and thus extending our left nearer and nearer to the railroad, the nearest point of which was Acworth, about eight miles distant. All this time a continual battle was in progress by strong skirmish-lines, taking advantage of every species of cover, and both parties fortifying each night by rifle-trenches, with head-logs, many of which grew to be as formidable as first-class works of defense. Occasionally one party or the other would make a dash in the nature of a sally, but usually it sustained a repulse with great loss of life. I visited personally all parts of our lines nearly every day, was constantly within musket-range, and though the fire of musketry and cannon resounded day and night along the whole line, varying from six to ten miles, I rarely saw a dozen of the enemy at any one time; and these were always skirmishers dodging from tree to tree, or behind logs on the ground, or who occasionally showed their heads above the hastily constructed but remarkably strong rifle-trenches. . . .

By Johnston's account, Sherman's troops were roughly handled on May 27. He described an incident that revealed the stubborn nature of the combat:[7]

When the United States troops paused in their advance, within fifteen paces of the Texan front rank, one of their color-bearers planted his colors eight or ten feet in front of his regiment, and was instantly shot dead; a soldier sprang forward to his place, and fell also, as he grasped the color-staff; a second and third followed successively, and each received death as speedily as his predecessors; a fourth, however, seized and bore back the object of soldierly devotion.

Johnston saw the Federal dead piling up. Yet Major Connolly, writing his wife next day, May 28, from "in the woods, near Dallas," was singularly composed and confident:[8]

I have just sat down with my back to a sapling, to write this with pencil, on this soiled piece of paper, with a shingle on my lap, for writing desk. The adjutant of my regiment got into the enemy's lines, by some kind of mistake, a few days since, and was captured. . . . For several days our Division has not been in the front, and I have only heard the enemy's guns in the distance. . . . The weather is delightful for campaigning, and I am quite sure we will be in Atlanta by the middle of June, and we are all strongly in hope of celebrating the 4th of July at the "last ditch" of the rebellion. Some of the half hearted in our army (for we have such) are gloomy because, they say, Grant can't whip Lee, and point to the fact that gold has been rising in value ever since Grant first engaged Lee. I don't know how you folks at home feel about it, but I feel sure Grant *will* defeat Lee and that we will defeat Johnston, and that our flag will float over Richmond and Atlanta by the 4th of July, but if not by that time it will *sometime.*

We passed about 200 rebels going to the rear, this morning. They were captured in a sharp engagement last evening. We are now in the region of the Georgia gold mines, and I am told that the cripples and poor men who have not been conscripted, are out gold washing over the mountain streams, to get gold dust enough to buy corn with.

III

While Grant fought Lee and Sherman pressed Johnston closer to Atlanta, the North turned to another arena of conflict, for 1864 was a presidential election year.

By the spring of 1864 the glow of the great Union victories at Gettysburg and Vicksburg had faded. Radical dissatisfaction with the President's "soft" policy on reconstruction had mounted; conservatives looked with increasing dismay on the violation of civil rights. The distribution of patronage, always a source of trouble, had made many enemies. In some states—Missouri and New York particularly—local politicians had come to believe that their own chances of survival would be better if someone other than Lincoln headed the national ticket.

All this was political opposition. Lincoln still held the confidence of the masses, and the politicians knew it. Therefore they resorted to a flank attack—postpone the national convention from June 7, the date set by the National Committee, to September, and let the forces of discontent have time to mount.

While most of the manipulators contented themselves with behind-the-scenes maneuvering, one group of New Yorkers spoke out. The signers of an open letter to the Republican National Committee included William Cullen Bryant, editor of the New York Evening Post *(better known today as the author of "Thanatopsis" and "To a Waterfowl"); George P. Putnam, publisher; George Opdyke, millionaire merchant and former mayor of New York; William Curtis Noyes, eminent lawyer; and sixteen Union members of the New York State Senate. Calling themselves "friends of the Government and supporters of the present Administration" the signers argued:*[9]

NEW YORK, March 25

. . . The country is not now in position to enter into a presidential contest. It is very important that all parties friendly to the Government shall be united in support of a single candidate, and that, when a selection shall be made, it shall be acquiesced in by all loyal sections of the country, and by all branches of the loyal party. It is equally clear that such unanimity cannot at present be obtained, and it is not believed that it can be reached as early as the day named by you for the national convention.

Upon the result of the measures adopted by the Administration to finish the war during the present spring and summer, will depend the wish of the people to continue in power their present leaders, or to change them for those from whom they may expect other and more favorable results.

Whatever time may be gained will be an advantage to the country, inasmuch as it will allow the forming of a better informed opinion on these subjects. . . .

With a pure and patriotic desire to serve the best interests of the country, and in the belief that they will be best served by a postponement of a political convention to the latest day possible, we respectfully ask that you will reconsider your action, and name a day for the assembling of the national convention not earlier than the first day of September next.

James G. Randall, after a patient, exhaustive examination of thousands of letters exchanged by Republican politicians at this time, came to the conclusion that "a book could be made up of letters expressing distrust of the President." Thus Joseph Medill, whose Chicago Tribune *continued to support Lincoln stanchly, wrote in confidence to Elihu B. Washburne, Republican Congressman from the Galena, Illinois, district:*[10]

CHICAGO April 12.

FRIEND WASHBURNE

. . . I don't care much if the convention is put off till Aug. I oppose it in the paper moderately, but will not be distressed if the Com. postpone it a couple of months. I was opposed to calling it so early as June 7. If it should happen that Lincoln loses the nomination thereby he will have no body but himself to blame for it. If he prefers the Blairs to the Presidency why should he be deprived of his choice? I am free to say to you that if it shall be known to be his intention to continue his present cabinet I don't believe we could elect him if nominated. . . . Lincoln has some very weak and foolish traits of character. . . . If he had reasonable political sagacity and would cut loose from the semi-copperheads in his cabinet and about him, if he would put live bold vigorous radicals in their places no human power could prevent his nomination or election. The game is in his own hands: will he play it right? or has he Blair on the brain so badly that he is blinded to the true state of public feeling?

If he should be thrown overboard at Baltimore the party will in my judgment take up Grant—if he continues to be successful in battle-field. . . .

And Charles Sumner, personally friendly to the President though opposed to his reconstruction policy, could write to Charles Eliot Norton of Boston, loyal Lincoln supporter:[11]

Private, SENATE CHAMBER, 2nd May, 1864

MY DEAR NORTON,—I regret very much that the Baltimore Convention is to be at so early a day. I see nothing but disaster from mixing our politics with battle and blood. The Presidential Question should be kept back as long as possible—at least until the end of summer. On this point I have no doubt. Do not regard me as dogmatical. I should not write on this point, if you had not expressly asked my opinion.

Unless the Convention is postponed, the future seems to me uncertain. . . .

Lincoln's supporters, who dominated the Republican National Committee, had no intention of playing the game of the disaffected. On June 7, as planned, the National Union convention met at Baltimore. Here War Democrats and Republicans could join in a common cause. The official reporter noted that "a splendid band, from Fort McHenry, animated the crowded theatre with national airs, and the assemblage was graced by the presence of many ladies, who were accommodated in one of the tiers of boxes."

On the second day of the convention B. C. Cook of Illinois won the floor. "Mr. President," he said, "the State of Illinois again presents to the loyal people of this Nation, for President of the United States, Abraham Lincoln. God bless him."

William M. Stone of Iowa leaped to his feet. "In the name of the great West," he shouted, "I demand that the roll be called."

When the secretary intoned the names of the states a few minutes later, the delegations revealed the difference between private convictions and public acts:[12]

MAINE.—Maine casts her entire vote for Abraham Lincoln, of Illinois.—14 votes.

NEW HAMPSHIRE.—New Hampshire, the Granite State, in her convention on the 6th of January last, unanimously passed a resolution, nominating Abraham Lincoln for re-election as President of the United States. New Hampshire today, by her delegates, casts her ten votes, first and last, for Abraham Lincoln, of Illinois.

VERMONT.—The Green Mountain State casts her small but entire vote of ten for Abraham Lincoln, of Illinois.

MASSACHUSETTS.—Massachusetts gives her entire vote, twenty-four, to Abraham Lincoln.

RHODE ISLAND.—Rhode Island casts her entire eight votes for Abraham Lincoln.

CONNECTICUT.—Connecticut gives her twelve votes to that pure and patriotic statesman, Abraham Lincoln, of Illinois.

NEW YORK.—New York casts sixty-six votes, her entire vote, for Abraham Lincoln, of Illinois, for President of the United States.

NEW JERSEY.—New Jersey gives fourteen votes for Abraham Lincoln.

PENNSYLVANIA.—Pennsylvania gives her entire vote, fifty-two, for Abraham Lincoln, "nigger" troops, and all.

DELAWARE.—Delaware gives her vote, six, for Abraham Lincoln.

MARYLAND.—Maryland casts fourteen votes for Abraham Lincoln, of Illinois.

LOUISIANA.—Louisiana gives her fourteen votes for Abraham Lincoln.

ARKANSAS.—Arkansas casts all her votes, ten, for Abraham Lincoln.

When Missouri was called, the machinery faltered:

MISSOURI.—Mr. J. F. HUME.—Missouri comes into the Convention purified by its action, and her delegates will support the nominees made here, and do the utmost in our power to secure for them the electoral vote of the State. It is but right and proper, however, that I should state that, in the convention which designated us as delegates to this Convention, we were instructed, and we cannot, upon the first ballot, give our votes in unanimity with those who have already cast their votes. ["Order," "order."]

Mr. J. H. LANE, of Kansas.—I appeal to the Convention to hear Missouri.

The PRESIDENT.—The gentleman from Missouri is not in order unless by consent of the House.

Mr. J. H. LANE, of Kansas.—I move that consent be given.

The motion was agreed to unanimously.

Mr. J. F. HUME, of Missouri.—It is a matter of much regret that we now differ from the Convention which has been so kind to the Radicals of Missouri; but we come here instructed. We represent those who are behind us at home, and we recognize the right of instruction, and intend to obey our instructions; but in doing so, we declare emphatically that we are with the Union party of this Nation, and we intend to fight the battle through with it, and assist in carrying its banner to victory in the end, and we will support your nominees, be they who they may. [Great applause.] I will read the resolution adopted by the convention which sent us here:

"That we extend our heartfelt thanks to the soldiers of Missouri, who have been, and are now, baring their breasts to the storm of battle for the preservation of our free institutions. That we hail them as the practical Radicals of the Nation, whose arguments are invincible, and whose policy for putting down the rebellion is first in importance and effectiveness."

Mr. President, in the spirit of that resolution, I cast the twenty-two votes of Missouri for the man who stands at the head of the fighting Radicals of the nation, Ulysses S. Grant.

The roll call continued:

TENNESSEE.—The convention that sent us here instructed us to say that, in their opinion, the election by the American people to the office of President of any other man than he who now fills the Executive Chair, would be regarded both at home and abroad as a concession of something to the Rebellion, and instructed us, by all means in our power, to secure the nomination of Abraham Lincoln, and I now give him the fifteen votes of Tennessee.

KENTUCKY.—Kentucky casts her twenty-two votes for Abraham Lincoln, and will ratify that nomination in November.

OHIO.—Ohio gives her forty-two votes for "Old Abe" for President.

INDIANA.—Indiana casts her twenty-six votes for Abraham Lincoln.

ILLINOIS.—Illinois gives thirty-two votes for Abraham Lincoln.

MICHIGAN.—Michigan gives sixteen votes for Abraham Lincoln.

WISCONSIN.—Wisconsin casts sixteen votes for Abraham Lincoln, of Illinois.

IOWA.—Iowa casts sixteen votes for Abraham Lincoln.

MINNESOTA.—Minnesota casts eight votes for Abraham Lincoln.

CALIFORNIA.—California casts ten votes, all for Abraham Lincoln.

OREGON.—Oregon casts six votes, all of them, first, last, and all the time for Abraham Lincoln, of Illinois.

KANSAS.—Radical Kansas casts her six votes for "Honest Old Abe."

WEST VIRGINIA.—West Virginia remembers her friends. She casts her ten votes in this Convention, the entire vote of the State of West Virginia, representing almost the entire loyal vote of the State, for Abraham Lincoln.

NEBRASKA.—Nebraska has one man in her delegation who was never a Lincoln man, but who belongs to that proud party called the War Union Democrats, and I am requested by that delegate to say, that he submits to the Convention, and I give the six votes of Nebraska for Abraham Lincoln, whom we regard as the second saviour of the world.

COLORADO.—Colorado casts her six votes for Abraham Lincoln.

NEVADA.—Nevada gives six votes for Abraham Lincoln, of Illinois.

The PRESIDENT.—The call of the States and Territories has now been completed.

Mr. J. F. HUME, of Missouri.—The vote has not been announced, but I wish to make a motion now, without waiting for the announcement, inasmuch as it is well understood what the result of the ballot just given is. I move that the nomination of Abraham Lincoln, of Illinois, be declared unanimous.

SEVERAL DELEGATES.—Change your votes.

Mr. J. F. HUME, of Missouri.—Our vote was given under instructions, and therefore I do not know that we can change it.

The PRESIDENT.—The gentleman's motion is not in order until the vote shall have been announced.

The Secretary proceeded to announce the vote as follows: Lincoln, 484; Grant, 22.

The PRESIDENT.—The total number of votes cast is 506, of which 484 have been cast for Abraham Lincoln, and 22 for Ulysses S. Grant.

Mr. J. F. HUME, of Missouri.—I now move that the nomination of Abraham Lincoln be declared unanimous; and I do not care whether the vote of Missouri is changed or not.

SEVERAL DELEGATES.—Change the vote.

Mr. J. F. HUME.—I am authorized now to change the vote of Missouri to Abraham Lincoln, of Illinois.

The Secretaries announced that the vote was unanimous—506 for Abraham Lincoln.

The official reporter recorded that "the delegates and the audience simultaneously rose to their feet, and greeted the announcement with vociferous applause. The band struck up 'Hail Columbia' and 'Yankee Doodle,' which were rapturously received." Later in the day the convention completed its work by nominating Andrew Johnson of Tennessee for Vice President, discarding Hannibal Hamlin in favor of a War Democrat from a loyal section of the South.

Two days after the convention adjourned, crusty Edward Bates, Lincoln's Attorney General, made an entry in his diary:[13]

June 10. The Baltimore Convention (*National Union* I believe, it's called itself) has surprised and mortified me greatly. It did indeed nominate Mr. Lincoln, but in a manner and with attendant circumstances, as if the object were to defeat their own nomination. They were all (nearly) instructed to vote for Mr. Lincoln, but many of them hated to do it, and only "kept the word of promise to the ear" doing their worst to break it to the hope. They *rejected* the only delegates from Mo. who were instructed and pledged for Lincoln, and admitted the *destructives,* who were *pledged against Lincoln,* and, in fact, voted against him, *falsely alleging* that they were instructed to vote for Grant!

. . . I shall tell the Prest: in all frankness, that his best nomination is not that at Baltimore, but his nomination spontaneously, by the People, by which the convention was constrained to name him.

IV

One small segment of the Republican party—the extreme Radicals— had the courage of their convictions. In response to three calls—one representing German liberals, another disgruntled New Yorkers, a third Eastern abolitionists—the "Radical Men of the Nation" had assembled at Cleveland on May 31 for the avowed purpose of nominating John C. Frémont. Wendell Phillips, unable to attend, had sent a letter which expressed the opinions of most of the delegates:[14]

BOSTON, May 27, 1864.

. . . We have three tools with which to crush the rebellion—men, money, and the emancipation of the negro. We were warned to be quick and sharp in the use of these, because every year the war lasted hardened the South from a rebellion into a nation, and doubled the danger of foreign interference. Slavery has been our great trouble in the past, and, as every man saw, was our great danger in the future. Statesmanship said, therefore, seize at once the God-given opportunity to end it, at the same time that you, in the quickest, shortest, and cheapest manner, annihilate the rebellion.

For three years the Administration has lavished money without stint, and drenched the land in blood, and it has not yet thoroughly and heartily struck at the slave system. Confessing that the use of this means is indispensable, the Administration has used it just enough to irritate the rebels and not enough to save the State. In sixty days after the rebellion broke out the Administration suspended *habeas corpus* on the plea of military necessity—justly. For three years it has poured out the treasure and blood of the country like water. Meanwhile slavery was too sacred to be used; that was saved lest the feelings of the rebels should be hurt. The Administration weighed treasure, blood, and civil liberty against slavery, and, up to the present moment, has decided to exhaust them all before it uses freedom, heartily, as a means of battle. . . .

The Administration, therefore, I regard as a civil and military failure, and its avowed policy ruinous to the North in every point of view. Mr. Lincoln may wish the end—peace and freedom—but he is wholly unwilling to use the means which can secure that end. If Mr. Lincoln is re-elected I do not expect to see the Union reconstructed in my day, unless on terms more disastrous to liberty than even disunion would be. If I turn to General Fremont, I see a man whose first act was to use the freedom of the negro as his weapon, I see one whose thorough loyalty to democratic institutions, without regard to race, whose earnest and decisive character, whose clear-sighted statesmanship and rare military ability justify my confidence that in his hands all will be done to save the State that foresight, skill, decision, and statesmanship can do.

I think the Convention should incorporate in its platform the demand for an amendment to the Constitution prohibiting slavery everywhere within the Republic, and forbidding the States to make any distinction among their citizens on account of color or race. I think it should demand a reconstruction of States as speedily as possible on the basis of every loyal man, white or black, sharing the land and the ballot. . . .

If the Baltimore Convention shall nominate Mr. Lincoln, then I hope we shall fling our candidate's name, the long-honored one of J. C. Fremont, to the breeze, and appeal to the patriotism and common sense of the people to save us from another such three years as we have seen. If, on the contrary, the Baltimore convention shall give us the name of any man whom the Radicals of the Loyal States can trust, I hope we shall be able to arrange some plan which will unite all on a common basis and carry our principles into the Government.

In one day the Cleveland convention adopted a platform and nominated Frémont for President and John Cochrane, Attorney General of New York, for Vice President.

In Washington, Lincoln laughed. Nicolay and Hay recorded:[15]

The whole proceeding, though it excited some indignation among the friends of Mr. Lincoln, was regarded by the President himself only with amusement. On the morning after the Convention, a friend, giving him an account of it, said that, instead of the many thousands who had been expected, there were present at no time more than four hundred men. The President, struck by the number mentioned, reached for the Bible which commonly lay on his desk, and after a moment's search read these words: "And every one that was in distress, and every one that was in debt, and every one that was discontented, gathered themselves unto him; and he became a captain over them: and there were with him about four hundred men."

V

The eyes of the North focused on Grant in Virginia and Sherman in Georgia, but bloody fighting continued in other parts of the country. Nathan Bedford Forrest harried the Union forces in Tennessee and Mississippi. To dispose of the audacious Confederate cavalryman, Sherman ordered General Samuel D. Sturgis, at Memphis, to fit out an expedition, corner Forrest, and destroy him. Sturgis started in early June with nearly 9,000 men—3,300 cavalry under the now famous Grierson, 5,000 infantry (including 1,200 colored troops), 250 wagons, and 22 guns—a force three times as strong as Forrest could muster.

Rain roiled the roads and sent the creeks out of their banks. On June 8 Sturgis, oppressed by the obstacles which a perverse nature placed in his way, called a council of his senior officers to decide whether to turn back or not. All agreed that success was unlikely, but Sturgis could not forget that only a few weeks earlier he had abandoned another expedition under similar circumstances. His pride raw, he determined to move forward.

Two days later, in northern Mississippi a hundred miles southeast of Memphis, Sturgis and Forrest collided. In a few hours Sturgis's worst forebodings were realized. Lieutenant John Merrilies of Battery E, Illinois Light Artillery, recorded the Federal disaster in his diary:[16]

Friday June 10th. . . . The cavalry took the road . . . and about noon came on the enemy in force near Tishomingo Creek, bringing on heavy skirmishing. After finding the strength of the enemy Grierson sent word back to Sturgis who immediately hurried up our column, double-quicking the infantry for two miles under a broiling sun, after a march of ten miles. The 2nd Brigade got up about two o. c., or what was left of it after falling out exhausted and sun struck in squads for two miles along the road—and were immediately sent in to support the cavalry, who were being driven back and suffering from a very heavy artillery fire. Their arrival checked the advance of the enemy who had already gained the hill, and endeavored to hold Brice's Cross Roads and after severe skirmishing they succeeded in driving them [the Confederates] some distance, and holding the position.

By this time our Brigade came up, in little better plight than the 2nd, the men perfectly exhausted and entirely unfit to go into action, but there was no time to rest now, and as fast as a regiment came up it was formed and sent in—one at a time—the fighting all the time becoming harder and harder. The cavalry were now withdrawn having been fighting almost constantly since 11 o. c. and the last of our Brigade went in, by which time the 2nd Brigade was used up, or nearly so, leaving the brunt of the work to be borne by ours, for the nigger Brigade having the train to guard could not be used in front. After half an hours fighting, our 1st piece was ordered in and took position on the right, in time to assist with canister in repelling the charge the enemy soon after made in front. The ground however was not eligible for artillery, more being in position than could be used to advantage. A second time the enemy tried to carry the ridge in front, causing us severe loss, especially in the 93rd Indiana, which got into considerable confusion, a perfect storm of bullets sweeping thro them, but McMillan rallied them with great gallantry, and succeeded in again repulsing the enemy and holding his ground.

There was now a short lull in the firing, but it boded no good for us, soon springing up again, not only in front, but the bullets beginning to come over from both flanks crossing the road at almost right angles, and taking our line of battle directly in flank. It was evident now that the enemy, unable to force our position in front, were going to try their success at turning it. The Brigade was swung round as well as possible to meet this new emergency, but the nature of the ground prevented anything like a good position being obtained, and it had to fight at a great disadvantage, the enemy gradually moving round slackening their fire in front and increasing it on the flanks, their line advancing steadily and ours falling back. All hope of our being able to hold our position was given up, and the order was issued to move the artillery to the rear as fast as possible. It was not given a minute too soon, for before we could limber up our two pieces and get down the road, the enemy were on it, and one of the pieces had to go through a field, in order to get around them. The cavalry however were formed in line on one flank, and the Colored Brigade on the other, checking the onward rush of the enemy until the artillery had passed and then covering the rear of that and the ammunition train.

The supply train of over 200 wagons, with nine days' rations, had been, with astonishing carelessness, corraled within a quarter of a mile of the battle field and no effort made to get it to the rear till the troops retreating filled the road, and it became impossible to remove it. Most of the mules were unhitched at the last moment and ridden off, but not a single wagon was brought away. The column now continued moving slowly forward [away from the enemy], hard fighting going on in rear, and the enemy shelling us vigorously till darkness began to fall, when the fighting gradually ceased. The column, which had been hitherto a mass of confusion, commands being mixed up all through it, was now put in comparative order, commands united, and we continued our march steadily. All our Battery was safe with the exception of the 5th Caisson, which had the wheel horses shot and upset in the road, when there was no time left to right it.

But for Merrilies the worst was yet to come:

About 9 o. c. [on the night of June 10] the column came to a halt, and going ahead to see what the matter was, the scene that met the eye was little less than appalling. The head of the column had reached the big swamp we crossed in the morning and had commenced passing over, but no one being there to give orders, or no orders being attended to, a general rush of carriages had been made for the road which with the late rains, was in very bad order, and now after crossing it this morning was nothing but a gulf of mud and water. The whole passage soon became jammed with a confused mass of men, horses, wagons, ambulances, and artillery, plunging and floundering in the abyss, carriages dashing recklessly into each other in their frantic attempts to get away, getting smashed up and turned over, the drivers yelling, lashing, swearing, and making night hideous and soon getting the passage so hopelessly blockaded that it was impossible to get either one way or the other, except on foot or on horseback. All this was taking place long after dark, but numberless lanterns and candles twinkled all the way across, where the line of men were eagerly picking a way out, the imperfect light adding to the dismal character of the scene.

Here we lay waiting orders till half past 12, when a general council of officers was held, and it was decided—all hope of getting the column across being cut off and Sturgis having gone nobody knew where, and left us to shift for ourselves—to destroy as quickly and effectually as possible the artillery and ammunition, abandon everything and endeavor to save ourselves while the two remaining hours of darkness favored us. Accordingly after an hour spent in cutting up cartridges, chopping wheels, spiking the guns, and rendering the battery generally unserviceable, we unhitched, mounted the horses, and with some little difficulty all got safely across the dismal swamp, and followed the main column which had not three or four hours start of us. The wounded begged hard to be taken along, but that was impossible and they were left in the ambulances, with a sufficient supply of medicines. We travelled all night without being molested, but just at grey dawn while our detachment was passing a creek, where a good many of the infantry were resting and filling their canteens, a party of the enemy's cavalry dashed out of the woods and across the road, calling out Halt! Halt! and firing their pieces among the crowd. This caused considerable of a scattering, but a good many of the men had their guns loaded and returned the fire, soon making the place too hot for them, and forcing them to leave as suddenly as they had come on us.

Soon after a rear guard of cavalry was sent us, who fell in behind after we had passed, and did good service in the constant skirmishing which continued without intermission. The 59th U. S. C. was also detached to cover the rear and altho the first fighting they had seen they behaved, under very trying circumstances, with a coolness and confidence worthy of old troops. The indifference of the niggers to wounds was perfectly astonishing, numbers shot in the arms, hands, legs, their clothing soaked with blood, marching along with the rest, without a sign of pain.

VI

Brice's Cross Roads cost Sturgis 2,240 men, sixteen cannon, and his military reputation. The rumors said that Sturgis had been hoot-owl drunk; there was talk also of women—one, anyhow—over whom the general's strategy had brought tactical success. Meanwhile Sherman's solemn, plodding columns drew nearer to Atlanta as Johnston fell back into a chain of isolated hills—Pine Mountain, Lost Mountain, Kenesaw Mountain. In those June days Samuel G. French, a New Jersey Quaker turned Confederate general, was a faithful diarist:[17]

June 18.—This morning pickets and skirmishers on my left (Walker's division) gave way and let the enemy in behind Cockrell's skirmishers, and enabled them to gain the Latimer house, four hundred yards distant. Ector's skirmishers also came in. Enemy soon advanced in line of battle, and with batteries opened on the salient an enfilading and reverse fire; and all day long this fire never ceased. They could not carry my lines successfully, and we would not attack them by leaving the trenches; and so the firing went on. My loss was severe, amounting to one hundred and eighty, and as an instance of the severity of the fire on the salient, Captain Guibor had served with his battery throughout the siege of Vicksburg, yet his loss this day of thirteen men is greater than that sustained during the whole siege. Toward evening ordered to withdraw and assume a new line on Kenesaw Mountain.

June 19.—The enemy made rapid pursuit, and before my line was established on Kenesaw Mountain, skirmishing commenced, and by 12 M. artillery fire from the enemy was rapid. It ranged up and over the spur of the mountain with great fury, and wounded General Cockrell, and put thirty-five of his men *hors du combat*.

The position of our army to-day is: Hood on the right, covering Marietta on the northwest. From his left, Polk's corps (now Loring's) extends over both Big and Little Kenesaw Mountains, with the left on the road from Gilgal church to Marietta. From this road Hardee extended the line nearly south, covering Marietta on the west, the left of my division was fixed on the Marietta road; thence it ran up to the spur of the mountain called Little Kenesaw, and thence to the top of same and on up to the top of Big Kenesaw, connecting with General Walthall. Featherston was on the right of Walthall, and joined Gen. Hood's left; Walker, of Hardee's corps, was on my left; then in order came Bate, Cleburne and Cheatham.

Kenesaw Mountain is about four miles northwest of Marietta. It is over two-and-a-half miles in length, and rises abruptly from the plain, solitary and alone, to the height of perhaps 600 or 700 feet. Its western side is rocky and abrupt. Its eastern side can, in a few places, be gained on horseback, and the west of Little Kenesaw, being bald and destitute of timber, affords a commanding view of all the surrounding country as far as the eye can reach, except where the view is interrupted by the higher peak.

June 20.—Busy this morning in establishing batteries on the road, on the spur of the mountain and on the top of Little Kenesaw. In the afternoon changed the line lower down the mountain side, so as to command the ascent as far as possible. Heavy cannonading on the left of my line. Lost ten horses and a few men.

Two days later the rain ceased and Sherman established a headquarters camp close to the base of Kenesaw Mountain. Next day the cannonade was "fast and furious"; the following day nothing happened. But Sherman was getting set—French wasn't fooled:

June 25.—The everlasting "pop," "pop," on the skirmish line is all that breaks the stillness of the morning. Went early to the left of my line; could not ride in rear of Hoskins' Battery, on account of the trees and limbs felled by the shells. From top of the mountain the vast panorama is ever changing. There are now large trains to the left of Lost Mountain and at Big Shanty, and wagons are moving to and fro everywhere. Encampments of hospitals, quartermasters, commissaries, cavalry and infantry whiten the plain here and there as far as the eye can reach. Our side of the line looks narrow, poor and lifeless, with but little canvas in spots that contrasts with the green foliage.

The usual flank extension is going on. Troops on both sides move to left, and now the blue smoke of the musket discloses the line by day, trending away, far away south toward the Chattahoochee, and by night it is marked, at times by the red glow of the artillery, amidst the spark-like flash of small arms that looks in the distance like innumerable fireflies.

At 10 A.M. opened fire on the enemy from the guns on Kenesaw. Enemy replied furiously, and for an hour the firing was incessant. Received an order to hold Ector's brigade in reserve. In the afternoon considerable firing, and all the chests of one of my caissons were blown up by a shell from the enemy, and a shell from one of the chests killed a gunner. They have now about forty guns in my fronts, and when they concentrate their fire on the mountain at any one place, it is pretty severe, but owing to our height nearly harmless. Thousands of their parrott-shells pass high over the mountain, and exploding at a great elevation, the after-part of the shell is arrested in its flight, and falling perpendicularly, comes into camp, and they have injured our tents. Last night I heard a peculiar "thug" on my tent, and a rattle of tin pans, and this morning my negro boy cook put his head into my tent and said: "See here, Master Sam, them 'fernal Yanks done shot my pans last night. What am I going to do 'bout it?" A rifle ball coming over the mountain had fallen from a great height, and, perforating the pans, had entered the ground.

Except for one artillery duel, Sunday, June 26, was quiet. Flank Kenesaw or attack the center where Johnston's lines were thin—that was Sherman's problem. General Logan said that the attention the papers were giving Grant in Virginia led Sherman to remark "that his army was entirely forgotten" but "now it would fight." Up on Kenesaw, French didn't know why Sherman attacked, but French's diary made clear why, afterward, Sherman wished he had run the Rebel ends once more:

June 27.—This morning there appeared great activity among staff officers and Generals all along my front and up and down the line. The better to observe what it portended, myself and staff seated ourselves on the brow of the mountain, sheltered by a large rock that rested between our guns and those of the enemy, the infantry being still lower down the side of the mountain.

Artillery firing was common on the line at all times, but now it swelled in volume and extended down to the extreme left, and then from fifty guns burst out in my front, and thence, battery after battery following on the right, disclosed a general attack on our entire line. Presently, and as if by magic, there sprung from the earth a host of men, and in one long waving line of blue the infantry advanced and the battle of Kenesaw Mountain began.

I could see no infantry on my immediate front, owing to the woods at the base of the mountain, and therefore directed the guns from their elevated position to enfilade Walker's front. In a short time the flank fire down the line drove them back, and Walker was relieved from the attack.

We sat there, perhaps an hour, enjoying a bird's-eye view of one of the most magnificent sights ever allotted to man—to look down upon an hundred and fifty thousand men arrayed in the strife of battle on the plain below.

As the infantry closed in, the blue smoke of the musket marked out our line for miles, while over it rose in cumuli-like clouds the white smoke of the artillery. Through the rifts of smoke, or, as it was wafted aside by the wind, we could see the assault made on Cheatham, and there the struggle was hard, and there it lasted longest. So many guns were trained on those by our side, and so incessant was the roar of cannon and sharp the explosion of shells, that naught else could be heard. From the fact that I had seen no infantry in my front, and had heard no musketry near, and the elevation of my line on the mountain, I thought I was exempted from the general infantry attack; I was therefore surprised and awakened from my dreams when a courier came to me about 9 o'clock and said General Cockrell wanted assistance, that his line had been attacked in force. General Ector was at once directed to send two regiments to report to him. Soon again a second courier came and reported the assault on the left of my line. I went immediately with the remainder of Ector's brigade to Cockrell, but on joining him found the Federal forces had been repulsed. The assaulting column had struck Cockrell's works near the centre, recoiled under the fire, swung around into a steep valley where—exposed to the fire of the Missourians in front and right flank and of Sears' men on the left—it seemed to melt away or sink to the earth to rise no more.

The assault on my line repulsed, I returned to the mountain top. The intensity of the fire had slackened and no movement of troops was visible; and although the din of arms yet resounded far and near, the battle was virtually ended.

From prisoners and from papers on their persons shown us, I learned my line had, from its position, been selected for assault by General McPherson, as that of Cheatham's had been by General Thomas. . . .

The battle, in its entirety, became a pageantry on a grand scale, and barren of results, because the attacking columns were too small in numbers, considering the character of the troops they knew they would encounter.

General Cheatham's loss was one hundred and ninety-five (195); mine (French's) one hundred and eighty-six (186); all other Confederate losses were one hundred and forty-one (141), being a total of five hundred and twenty-two. What the Federal loss was I do not know. It has been variously estimated from three to eight thousand.

As nothing decisive was obtained by Sherman's attack, the firing slackened except on the skirmish line. After dark the enemy withdrew to their main trenches, the roar of guns died gradually away, and the morning of the 28th dawned on both armies in their former positions. The battle of Kenesaw, then, was a display of force and advance of troops by the enemy on the entire length of our line, that opened a furious fire of artillery and musketry, under cover of which two grand attacks were made by assaulting columns—the one on my line and the other on Cheatham's.

CHAPTER 32

FROM CHERBOURG HARBOR TO PEACH TREE CREEK

S<small>HERMAN WOULD NOT ADMIT</small> that his frontal attack on Kenesaw Mountain, which cost him 2,000 casualties as against 432 for the Confederates, was a mistake. Perhaps he was concerned about Northern morale. He need not have worried. Eight days earlier the U. S. S. *Kearsarge* had sent the Confederate raider *Alabama* to the bottom of the English Channel. When news of the victory reached the North, Sherman's one serious reverse in the Atlanta campaign was forgotten.

I

The Alabama, *commissioned by the Confederate government and built at Liverpool, slipped out of the Mersey in the early summer of 1862. During the next two years, under the command of Captain Raphael Semmes, she sank, burned or captured more than sixty ships flying the flag of the United States. In early June 1864 the* Kearsarge, *Captain John A. Winslow, caught the* Alabama *in the harbor of Cherbourg, France. Semmes's account of the battle that followed disclosed that he was living, in imagination if not in fact, in the days of chivalry:*[1]

When the *Alabama* arrived in Cherbourg, the enemy's steamer *Kearsarge* was lying at Flushing. On the 14th of June, or three days after our arrival, she steamed into the harbor of Cherbourg, sent a boat on shore to communicate with the authorities, and, without anchoring, steamed out again, and took her station off the breakwater. We had heard, a day or two before, of the expected arrival of this ship, and it was generally understood among my crew that I intended to engage her. . . .

I now addressed a note to Mr. Bonfils, our agent, requesting him to inform Captain Winslow, through the United States Consul, that if he would wait until I could receive some coal on board—my supply having been nearly exhausted, by my late cruising—I would come out and give him battle. This message was duly conveyed, and the defiance was understood to have been accepted.

We commenced coaling ship immediately, and making other preparations for battle; as sending down all useless yards and top-hamper, examining the gun equipments, and overhauling the magazine and shell-rooms. My crew seemed not only willing, but anxious for the combat, and I had every confidence in their steadiness and drill; but they labored under one serious disadvantage. They had had but very limited opportunities of actual practice at target-firing, with shot and shell. The reason is obvious. I had no means of replenishing either shot or shell, and was obliged, therefore, to husband the store I had on hand for actual conflict. . . .

As for the two ships, though the enemy was superior to me, both in size, stanchness of construction, and armament, they were of force so nearly equal, that I cannot be charged with rashness in having offered battle. The *Kearsarge* mounted seven guns:—two eleven-inch Dahlgrens, four 32-pounders, and a rifled 28-pounder. Though the *Alabama* carried one gun more than her antagonist, it is seen that the battery of the latter enabled her to throw more metal at a broadside—there being a difference of three inches in the bore of the shell-guns of the two ships.

Still the disparity was not so great, but that I might hope to beat my enemy in a fair fight. But he did not show me a fair fight, for, as it afterward turned out, his ship was iron-clad. It was the same thing, as if two men were to go out to fight a duel, and one of them, unknown to the other, were to put a shirt of mail under his outer garment. The days of chivalry being past, perhaps it would be unfair to charge Captain Winslow with deceit in withholding from me the fact that he meant to wear armor in the fight. He may have reasoned that it was my duty to find it out for myself. Besides, if he had disclosed this fact to me, and so prevented the engagement, the Federal Secretary of the Navy would have cut his head off to a certainty.

An anonymous eyewitness of the fight wrote in the London Daily News: *"The* Kearsarge *is spoken of as being iron-clad; she was no more iron-clad than the* Alabama *might have been, had they taken the precaution. She simply had a double row of chains hanging over her sides to protect her machinery. Two shots from the* Alabama *struck these chains, and fell harmlessly into the water."*

Semmes's excuses on record, he told the story of the fight:

. . . In the way of crew, the *Kearsarge* had 162, all told—the *Alabama*, 149. I had communicated my intention to fight this battle to Flag-Officer Barron, my senior officer in Paris, a few days before, and that officer had generously left the matter to my own discretion. I completed my preparations on Saturday evening, the 18th of June, and notified the Port-Admiral of my intention to go out on the following morning. The next day dawned beautiful and bright. The cloudy, murky weather of some days past had cleared off, and a bright sun, a gentle breeze, and a smooth sea, were to be the concomitants of the battle. Whilst I was still in my cot, the Admiral sent an officer off to say to me that the iron-clad frigate *Couronne* would accompany me a part of the way out, to see that the neutrality of French waters was not violated. My crew had turned in early, and gotten a good night's rest, and I permitted them to get their breakfasts comfortably—not turning them to until nine o'clock—before any movement was made toward getting under way, beyond lighting the fires in the furnaces. . . .

The day being Sunday, and the weather fine, a large concourse of people—many having come all the way from Paris—collected on the heights above the town, in the upper stories of such of the houses as commanded a view of the sea, and on the walls and fortifications of the harbor. Several French luggers employed as pilot-boats went out, and also an English steam-yacht, called the *Deerhound*. Everything being in readiness between nine and ten o'clock, we got under way, and proceeded to sea, through the western entrance of the harbor; the *Couronne* following us. As we emerged from behind the mole, we discovered the *Kearsarge* at a distance of between six and seven miles from the land. She had been apprised of our intention of coming out that morning, and was awaiting us. The *Couronne* anchored a short distance outside of the harbor. We were three quarters of an hour in

running out to the *Kearsarge,* during which time we had gotten our
people to quarters, cast loose the battery, and made all the other
necessary preparations for battle. The yards had been previously slung
in chains, stoppers prepared for the rigging, and preventer braces rove.
It only remained to open the magazine and shell-rooms, sand down the
decks, and fill the requisite number of tubs with water. The crew had
been particularly neat in their dress on that morning, and the officers
were all in the uniforms appropriate to their rank. As we were approaching the enemy's ship, I caused the crew to be sent aft, within
convenient reach of my voice, and mounting a gun-carriage, delivered
them the following brief address. I had not spoken to them in this formal way since I had addressed them on the memorable occasion of
commissioning the ship.

"OFFICERS AND SEAMEN OF THE ALABAMA!—You have, at length,
another opportunity of meeting the enemy—the first that has been presented to you, since you sank the *Hatteras!* * In the meantime, you have
been all over the world, and it is not too much to say, that you have destroyed, and driven for protection under neutral flags, one half of the
enemy's commerce, which, at the beginning of the war, covered every
sea. This is an achievement of which you may well be proud; and a
grateful country will not be unmindful of it. The name of your ship has
become a household word wherever civilization extends. Shall that
name be tarnished by defeat? The thing is impossible! Remember that
you are in the English Channel, the theatre of so much of the naval
glory of our race, and that the eyes of all Europe are at this moment,
upon you. The flag that floats over you is that of a young Republic, who
bids defiance to her enemies, whenever, and wherever found. Show the
world that you know how to uphold it! Go to your quarters."

The utmost silence prevailed during the delivery of this address,
broken only once, in an enthusiastic burst of *Never! never!* when I
asked my sailors if they would permit the name of their ship to be
tarnished by defeat. My official report of the engagement, addressed to
Flag-Officer Barron, in Paris, will describe what now took place. . . .

SOUTHHAMPTON, June 21, 1864.

SIR:—I have the honor to inform you, that, in accordance with my
intentions as previously announced to you, I steamed out of the harbor

* In January of 1863, the *Alabama,* posing as "Her Majesty's steamer *Vixen,*"
tricked the *Hatteras* into approaching. Within a hundred yards of the Federal
warship, the *Alabama* revealed her true nature by running up Confederate colors
and opening with a broadside.

of Cherbourg between nine and ten o'clock on the morning of the 19th of June, for the purpose of engaging the enemy's steamer *Kearsarge*, which had been lying off, and on the port, for several days previously. After clearing the harbor, we descried the enemy, with his head off shore, at the distance of about seven miles. We were three quarters of an hour in coming up with him. I had previously pivotted my guns to starboard, and made all preparations for engaging the enemy on that side. When within about a mile and a quarter of the enemy, he suddenly wheeled, and, bringing his head in shore, presented his starboard battery to me. By this time, we were distant about one mile from each other, when I opened on him with solid shot, to which he replied in a few minutes, and the action became active on both sides. The enemy now pressed his ship under a full head of steam, and to prevent our passing each other too speedily, and to keep our respective broadsides bearing, it became necessary to fight in a circle; the two ships steaming around a common centre, and preserving a distance from each other of from three quarters to half a mile. When we got within good shell range, we opened upon him with shell. Some ten or fifteen minutes after the commencement of the action, our spanker-gaff was shot away, and our ensign came down by the run. This was immediately replaced by another at the mizzen-masthead. The firing now became very hot, and the enemy's shot and shell soon began to tell upon our hull, knocking down, killing, and disabling a number of men, at the same time, in different parts of the ship. Perceiving that our shell, though apparently exploding against the enemy's sides, were doing him but little damage, I returned to solid-shot firing, and from this time onward alternated with shot and shell.

After the lapse of about one hour and ten minutes, our ship was ascertained to be in a sinking condition, the enemy's shell having exploded in our side, and between decks, opening large apertures through which the water rushed with great rapidity. For some few minutes I had hopes of being able to reach the French coast, for which purpose I gave the ship all steam, and set such of the fore-and-aft sails as were available.* The ship filled so rapidly, however, that before we had made much progress, the fires were extinguished in the furnaces, and we were evidently on the point of sinking. I now hauled down my colors,

* Semmes displayed a great want of generosity toward Winslow, whose seamanship had been superb. Semmes appeared to avoid close action, and Winslow forced a battle in a series of circular tracks so that Semmes was prevented from making a dash for shore. When the fight ended, the *Alabama* was nearly five miles off the coast with no chance of escaping within French jurisdiction.

to prevent the further destruction of life, and dispatched a boat to inform the enemy of our condition. Although we were now but 400 yards from each other, the enemy fired upon me five times after my colors had been struck. It is charitable to suppose that a ship of war of a Christian nation could not have done this intentionally.

Captain Semmes's "charitable" supposition was correct. Winslow, in his official report of the action, wrote: "I saw now that she [the Alabama] was at our mercy, and a few more guns well directed brought down her flag. I was unable to ascertain whether it had been hauled down or shot away; but a white flag having been displayed over the stern, our fire was reserved. Two minutes had not more than elapsed before she again opened on us with the two guns on the port side. This drew our fire again, and the Kearsarge was immediately steamed ahead and laid across her bows for raking. The white flag was still flying, and our fire was again reserved. Shortly after this, her boats were seen to be lowering, and an officer in one of them came alongside, and informed us the ship had surrendered and was fast sinking."

To the end, Semmes remained querulous:

We now directed all our exertions toward saving the wounded, and such of the boys of the ship as were unable to swim. These were dispatched in my quarter-boats, the only boats remaining to me; the waist-boats having been torn to pieces. Some twenty minutes after my furnace-fires had been extinguished, and when the ship was on the point of settling, every man, in obedience to a previous order which had been given the crew, jumped overboard, and endeavored to save himself. There was no appearance of any boat coming to me from the enemy, until after my ship went down. Fortunately, however, the steam-yacht *Deerhound*, owned by a gentleman of Lancashire, England— Mr. John Lancaster—who was himself on board, steamed up in the midst of my drowning men, and rescued a number of both officers and men from the water. I was fortunate enough myself thus to escape to the shelter of the neutral flag, together with about forty others, all told. About this time the *Kearsarge* sent one, and then, tardily, another boat. Accompanying, you will find lists of the killed and wounded, and of those who were picked up by the *Deerhound;* the remainder, there is reason to hope, were picked up by the enemy, and by a couple of French pilot boats, which were also fortunately near the scene of action.

According to the London Daily News *correspondent, "the* Kearsarge *picked up sixty-three men, one dead body, and two who died afterward on board. She also took five officers."*

But Semmes pressed his allegation that he had been unfairly treated:

At the end of the engagement, it was discovered by those of our officers who went alongside of the enemy's ship, with the wounded, that her mid-ship section, on both sides, was thoroughly iron-coated; this having been done with chains, constructed for the purpose, placed perpendicularly, from the rail to the water's edge, the whole covered over by a thin outer planking, which gave no indication of the armor beneath. This planking had been ripped off, in every direction, by our shot and shell, the chain broken, and indented in many places, and forced partly into the ship's side. She was effectually guarded, however, in this section, from penetration. The enemy was much damaged, in other parts, but to what extent it is now impossible to say. It is believed he is badly crippled. My officers and men behaved steadily and gallantly, and though they have lost their ship, they have not lost honor. . . . The enemy was heavier than myself, both in ship, battery, and crew; but I did not know until the action was over, that she was also iron-clad. Our total loss in killed and wounded, is 30, to wit: 9 killed, and 21 wounded.

Yet Semmes, essaying the difficult role of propagandist-historian, would meet his match in Gideon Welles, who wrote Winslow:[2]

NAVY DEPARTMENT, July 6, 1864.

SIR—Your very brief dispatches of the 19th and 20th ultimo, informing the Department that the piratical craft "Alabama," or "290," had been sunk on the 19th of June near meridian, by the "Kearsarge," under your command, were this day received. I congratulate you on your good fortune in meeting this vessel, which had so long avoided the fastest ships and some of the most vigilant and intelligent officers of the service; and for the ability displayed in this combat you have the thanks of the Department.

You will please express to the officers and crew of the "Kearsarge" the satisfaction of the Government at the victory over a vessel superior in tonnage, superior in number of guns, and superior in the number of her crew. The battle was so brief, the victory so decisive, and the comparative results so striking, that the country will be reminded of the brilliant actions of our infant Navy, which have been repeated and illustrated in this engagement.

The "Alabama" represented the best maritime effort of the most skilled English workshops. Her battery was composed of the well-tried 32-pounders of 57-hundred weight, of the famous 68-pounder of the British Navy, and of the only successful rifled 100-pounder yet produced in England. The crew were generally recruited in Great Britain, and many of them received superior training on board Her Majesty's gunnery ship, the "Excellent."

The "Kearsarge" is one of the first gun-boats built at our Navy Yards at the commencement of the rebellion, and lacks the improvements of vessels now under construction. The principal guns composing her battery had never been previously tried in an exclusively naval engagement, yet in one hour you succeeded in sinking your antagonist, thus fully ending her predatory career, and killed many of her crew without injury to the "Kearsarge," or the loss of a single life on your vessel.

Our countrymen have reason to be satisfied that in this, as in every naval action of this unhappy war, neither the ships, the guns nor the crew have been deteriorated, but that they maintain the abilities and continue the renown which ever adorned our naval annals.

The President has signified his intention to recommend that you receive a vote of thanks, in order that you may be advanced to the grade of commodore.

Lieutenant-Commander James S. Thornton, the executive officer of the "Kearsarge," will be recommended to the Senate for advancement ten numbers in his grade, and you will report to the Department the names of any other of the officers or crew whose good conduct on the occasion entitles them to especial mention.

Very respectfully,
GIDEON WELLES,
Secretary of the Navy.

CAPTAIN JOHN A. WINSLOW,
Commanding U. S. Steamer "Kearsarge,"
Cherbourg, France.

II

Far from the coast of France, Robert E. Lee came to a decision. He could not shake off this man Grant, but the Federal authorities might be induced to relieve the pressure. In mid-June Lee ordered Jubal A. Early to take the Second Corps of the Army of Northern Virginia with

two battalions of artillery, move up the Shenandoah Valley toward
Harpers Ferry and, if practicable, give Washington the scare of its life.

In the second week of July Gideon Welles—no friend of Secretary of
War Stanton—awoke to the fact that a powerful Confederate force was
approaching the capital, and that the capital was vulnerable:[3]

July 9, Saturday. The Rebel invasion of Maryland, if not so large or formidable as last year and year before, looks to me very annoying, the more so because I learn nothing satisfactory or reliable from the War Office, and am persuaded there is both neglect and ignorance there. It is evident there have not been sufficient preparations, but they are beginning to move. Yet they hardly have any accurate information. . . .

July 10, Sunday. When at the Department, Sunday morning, the 10th, examining my mail, one of the clerks came in and stated that the Rebel pickets were on the outskirts of Georgetown, within the District lines. There had been no information to warn us of this near approach of the enemy, but my informant was so positive—and soon confirmed by another—that I sent to the War Department to ascertain the facts. They were ignorant—had heard street rumors, but they were unworthy of notice—and ridiculed my inquiry. . . .

July 11, Monday. The Rebels are upon us. . . .

Early, on the outskirts of Washington, saw difficulties which the
panicky inhabitants overlooked:[4]

We moved at daylight on the 11th; McCausland moving on the Georgetown pike, while the infantry, preceded by Imboden's cavalry under Colonel Smith, turned to the left at Rockville, so as to reach the 7th street pike which runs by Silver Spring into Washington. Jackson's cavalry moved on the left flank. The previous day had been very warm, and the roads were exceedingly dusty, as there had been no rain for several weeks. The heat during the night had been very oppressive, and but little rest had been obtained. This day was an exceedingly hot one, and there was no air stirring. While marching, the men were enveloped in a suffocating cloud of dust and many of them fell by the way from exhaustion. Our progress was therefore very much impeded, but I pushed on as rapidly as possible, hoping to get into the fortifications around Washington before they could be manned. Smith drove a small body of cavalry before him into the works on the 7th street pike,

and dismounted his men and deployed them as skirmishers. I rode
ahead of the infantry, and arrived in sight of Fort Stevens on this road
a short time after noon, when I discovered that the works were but
feebly manned.*

Rodes, whose division was in front, was immediately ordered to
bring it into line as rapidly as possible, throw out skirmishers, and
move into the works if he could. My whole column was then moving
by flank, which was the only practicable mode of marching on the road
we were on, and before Rodes' division could be brought up, we saw a
cloud of dust in the rear of the works towards Washington, and soon a
column of the enemy filed into them on the right and left, and skir-

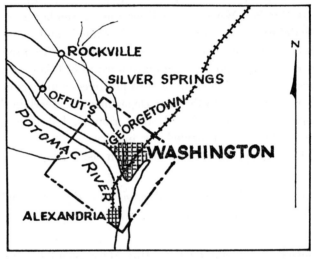

WASHINGTON AND VICINITY, 1864

mishers were thrown out in front, while an artillery fire was opened
on us from a number of batteries. This defeated our hopes of getting
possession of the works by surprise, and it became necessary to reconnoitre.

Rodes' skirmishers were thrown to the front, driving those of the
enemy to the cover of the works, and we proceeded to examine the
fortifications in order to ascertain if it was practicable to carry them by

* Welles found Lincoln at Fort Stevens. Tradition insists that Oliver Wendell
Holmes, then a captain on the staff of General Horatio G. Wright, had seen the
President peering over the parapet. Unaware of the tall man's identity, Holmes
shouted, "Get down, you damn fool, before you get shot!"

assault. They were found to be exceedingly strong, and consisted of what appeared to be enclosed forts for heavy artillery, with a tier of lower works in front of each pierced for an immense number of guns, the whole being connected by curtains with ditches in front, and strengthened by palisades and abattis. The timber had been felled within cannon range all around and left on the ground, making a formidable obstacle, and every possible approach was raked by artillery. On the right was Rock Creek, running through a deep ravine which had been rendered impassable by the felling of timber on each side, and beyond were the works on the Georgetown pike which had been reported to be the strongest of all. On the left, as far as the eye could reach, the works appeared to be of the same impregnable character. The position was naturally strong for defence, and the examination showed, what might have been expected, that every appliance of science and unlimited means had been used to render the fortifications around Washington as strong as possible. This reconnoissance consumed the balance of the day.

The rapid marching which had broken down a number of the men who were barefooted or weakened by previous exposure, and had been left in the Valley and directed to be collected at Winchester, and the losses in killed and wounded at Harper's Ferry, Maryland Heights, and Monocacy, had reduced my infantry to about 8,000 muskets. Of those remaining, a very large number were greatly exhausted by the last two days marching, some having fallen by sunstroke, and I was satisfied, when we arrived in front of the fortifications, that not more than one-third of my force could have been carried into action. I had about forty pieces of field artillery, of which the largest were 12 pounder Napoleons, besides a few pieces of horse artillery with the cavalry. Mc-Causland reported the works on the Georgetown pike too strongly manned for him to assault. We could not move to the right or the left without its being discovered from a signal station on the top of the "Soldier's Home," which overlooked the country, and the enemy would have been enabled to move in his works to meet us. Under the circumstances, to have rushed my men blindly against the fortifications, without understanding the state of things, would have been worse than folly. If we had any friends in Washington, none of them came out to give us information, and this satisfied me that the place was not undefended.

Welles visited the fortifications to see the situation for himself. He kept his head—and confided his disgust to his diary:[5]

I rode out this evening [July 11] to Fort Stevens, latterly called Fort Massachusetts. Found General Wright and General McCook with what I am assured is an ample force for its defense. Passed and met as we returned three or four thousand, perhaps more, volunteers under General Meigs, going to the front. Could see the line of pickets of both armies in the valley, extending a mile or more. There was continual firing, without many casualties so far as I could observe, or hear. . . .

I inquired where the Rebel force was, and the officers said over the hills, pointing in the direction of Silver Spring. Are they near Gunpowder or Baltimore? Where are they? Oh! within a short distance, a mile or two only. I asked why their whereabouts was not ascertained, and their strength known. The reply was that we had no fresh cavalry.

The truth is the forts around Washington have been vacated and the troops sent to General Grant, who was promised reinforcements to take Richmond. . . . Citizens are volunteering, and the employees in the navy yard are required to man the fortifications left destitute. Stanton and Halleck . . . are now the most alarmed men in Washington.

I am sorry to see so little reliable intelligence. It strikes me that the whole demonstration is weak in numbers but strong in conception. . . . I am satisfied no attack is now to be apprehended on the city; the Rebels have lost a remarkable opportunity. But on our part there is neglect, ignorance, folly, imbecility, in the last degree. The Rebels are making a show of fight while they are stealing horses, cattle, etc., through Maryland. They might easily have captured Washington. Stanton, Halleck, and Grant are asleep or dumb.

Early, sizing up the odds against him, decided that he had accomplished all that could be expected:[6]

After dark on the 11th, I held a consultation with Major-Generals Breckinridge, Rodes, Gordon and Ramseur, in which I stated to them the danger of remaining where we were, and the necessity of doing something immediately, as the probability was that the passes of the South Mountain and the fords of the upper Potomac would soon be closed against us. After interchanging views with them, being very reluctant to abandon the project of capturing Washington, I determined to make an assault on the enemy's works at daylight next morning, unless some information should be received before that time showing its impracticability, and so informed those officers. During the night a dispatch was received from Gen. Bradley Johnson from near Baltimore, informing me that he had received information, from a reliable source, that two corps had arrived from Gen. Grant's army, and that his whole army was probably in motion. This caused me to delay the attack until I could examine the works again, and, as soon as it was light enough to see, I rode to the front and found the parapets lined with troops. I had, therefore, reluctantly, to give up all hopes of capturing Washington, after I had arrived in sight of the dome of the Capitol, and given the Federal authorities a terrible fright.

Lincoln, like Welles, suspected that the defense of Washington, or at least the pursuit of the Rebels who had had the temerity to threaten the city, could have been better managed.
John Hay sketched the mood of a disgruntled President:[7]

July 13, 1864. The news this morning would seem to indicate that the enemy is retiring from every point.

The President thinks we should push our whole column right up the River Road & cut off as many as possible of the retreating raiders. . . .

July 14, 1864. Nothing of importance yet. This evening as the President started to the Soldiers' Home I asked him *quid nunc* & he said, "Wright telegraphs that he thinks the enemy are all across the Potomac but that he has halted & sent out an infantry reconnoissance, for fear he might come across the rebels & catch some of them." The Chief is evidently disgusted.

III

While Early threw Washington into panic and Grant weakened his own forces by sending a corps and two divisions to the relief of the Capital, Sherman pressed relentlessly toward Atlanta. After his repulse at Kenesaw Mountain he skirted that obstacle, only to encounter Johnston strongly intrenched in front of the Chattahoochee. Sherman's scouts found fords. Johnston, his rear endangered, took up a new line of defense along Peach Tree Creek, ten miles from Atlanta.

Suddenly the campaign took on a new aspect. Confederate Captain Thomas J. Key, who commanded a battery in Cleburne's division, noted news of moment in his diary:[8]

July 18th. This morning the whole army was surprised by the announcement that the Secretary of War had removed General Johnston from command of this army and placed it in the hands of General Hood.

Every man looked sad and disheartened at this information, and felt
that evil would result from the removal of Johnston, whom they esteem
and love above any previous commander. His address touched every
heart, and every man thought that his favorite General had been griev-
ously wronged. The cause for this procedure on the part of the President
at this eventful moment when the enemy is pressing us we have been
unable to conjecture. General Hood is a gallant man, but Johnston has
been tried and won the confidence of the soldiery. . . .

July 19th. The rumor prevailed that General Johnston was still in
command of this army. The report cheered the despondent hearts, but
I was of the impression that it was done to prevent desertions and to
cause the troops to fight with their former bravery in the now approaching conflict. So soon as I dispatched a hasty breakfast, I mounted my
horse, which I call General Longstreet, and rode with the other officers
of the battalion along the line of battle to select the commanding points
for artillery. . . . Most of Sherman's thieves are across the Chattahoochee River and are now skirmishing about two miles from the lines
of rifle pits that we are now constructing. They are making some bold
maneuvers for Atlanta, but at the same time will not come up fearlessly
and fight us on the ground of our choice. . . .

*Sherman gauged cautiously both the Confederate defenses and the
character of his new chief opponent:*[9]

During the night [July 20], I had full reports from all parts of our
line, most of which was partially intrenched as against a sally, and
finding that McPherson was stretching out too much on his left flank, I
wrote him a note early in the morning not to extend so much by his left;
for we had not troops enough to completely invest the place, and I intended to destroy utterly all parts of the Augusta Railroad to the east of
Atlanta, then to withdraw from the left flank and add to the right. In
that letter I ordered McPherson not to extend any farther to the left, but
to employ General Dodge's corps (Sixteenth), then forced out of position, to destroy every rail and tie of the railroad, from Decatur up to
his skirmish-line, and I wanted him (McPherson) to be ready, as soon
as General Garrard returned from Covington (whither I had sent him),
to move to the extreme right of Thomas, so as to reach if possible the
railroad below Atlanta, viz., the Macon road. In the morning we found
the strong line of parapet, "Peach-Tree line," to the front of Schofield
and Thomas, abandoned, and our lines were advanced rapidly close

up to Atlanta. For some moments I supposed the enemy intended to evacuate, and in person was on horseback at the head of Schofield's troops, who had advanced . . . to some open ground, from which we could plainly see the whole rebel line of parapets, and I saw their men dragging up from the intervening valley, by the distillery, trees and saplings for abatis. Our skirmishers found the enemy down in this valley, and we could see the rebel main line strongly manned, with guns in position at intervals. Schofield was dressing forward his lines, and I could hear Thomas farther to the right engaged, when General Mc-Pherson and his staff rode up. We went back to the Howard House, a double-frame building with a porch, and sat on the steps, discussing the chances of battle, and of Hood's general character. McPherson had also been of the same class at West Point with Hood, Schofield, and Sheridan. We agreed that we ought to be unusually cautious and prepared at all times for sallies and hard fighting, because Hood, though not deemed much of a scholar, or of great mental capacity, was undoubtedly a brave, determined, and rash man; and the change of commanders at that particular crisis argued the displeasure of the Confederate Government with the cautious but prudent conduct of General Jos. Johnston.

If Hood believed himself equal to his new command, he was willing nonetheless by his own testimony to offer an astonishing suggestion:[10]

. . . The order, assigning me to the command of that Army, was received about 11 P.M., on the 17th of July. My predecessor, unwilling to await even the dawn of day, issued his farewell order that memorable night. In despite of my repeated and urgent appeals to him to pocket all dispatches from Richmond, to leave me in command of my own corps, and to fight the battle for Atlanta, he deserted me the ensuing afternoon. He deserted me in violation of his promise to remain and afford me the advantage of his counsel, whilst I shouldered all responsibility of the contest.

I reiterate that it is difficult to imagine a commander placed at the head of an army under more embarrassing circumstances than those against which I was left to contend on the evening of the 18th of July, 1864. I was, comparatively, a stranger to the Army of Tennessee. Moreover General Johnston's mode of warfare formed so strong a contrast to the tactics and strategy which were practiced in Virginia, where far more satisfactory results were obtained than in the West, that I have become a still more ardent advocate of the Lee and Jackson school. The troops of the Army of Tennessee had for such length of time been subjected to the ruinous policy pursued from Dalton to Atlanta that they were unfitted for united action in pitched battle. They had, in other words, been so long habituated to security behind breastworks that they had become wedded to the "timid defensive" policy, and naturally regarded with distrust a commander likely to initiate offensive operations.

The senior Corps Commander [William J. Hardee] considered he had been supplanted through my promotion, and thereupon determined to resign, in consequence, I have no doubt, of my application to President Davis to postpone the order transferring to me the command of the Army; he however, altered his decision, and concluded to remain with his corps.

Five days after Hood assumed command, the battle for Atlanta opened across ground situated approximately halfway between the present heart of the city ("Five Points") and the town square of Decatur, five miles to the east. Captain Thomas J. Key was in the thick of the fighting that twenty-second of July:[11]

. . . About noon the enemy opened his artillery upon our advance, throwing spherical case along the road on which we were advancing. I sought an elevated spot and at once ordered one section of Goldthwaite's battery to return the fire, the Yankees being about six hundred yards distant. Simultaneously, the Captain went into action in the woods with the other section, about 100 yards to my right. Under the fire of artillery and minie balls, General Cleburne's division advanced upon the earth works of the enemy, but the fire was so galling that many faltered in the charge. The enemy's abatis was formed of saplings and bushes cut off and bent over, leaving the butt or stump two feet high.

Notwithstanding these formidable works and tangling obstructions, the brave Confederates charged over all intervening obstacles and took the dirt works together with many prisoners. The most successful movement was performed by two of General Govan's regiments which, finding a ravine across which were no fortifications, moved by the right oblique and after passing the line swung to their left, taking the Yankees in flank and rear. Here some of our men who had gone over the enemy's works were retaken. This caused the Yankees to evacuate all the fortifications protecting their rear and to abandon four pieces of

Napoleon guns. The fire of Captain Goldthwaite's battery, enfilading the enemy, caused them to go over their works to the south. . . . I at once called to the men of the battery for volunteers to go with me across the fortifications and turn the enemy's guns upon them. . . . With a cheer I led them at a double quick through the abatis to the Yankee guns. However, while my men had one gun in the road in full view of a second line of works of the enemy, and were running it up to commence firing, the Yanks from behind the second works poured such a volley of musketry upon those brave cannoneers that they were compelled to abandon the guns and leave the road. The Yanks re-enforced and came back with a charge, and I thought it advisable to retire, which we did in hasty steps and not in good order, knowing that artillerists are defenseless unless they can get their guns in an effective position. Cleburne's men met this charge manfully and in half an hour the Yankees had recrossed their works.

With Cleburne's help, Key's gunners began pounding the Yankees, and at last isolated a pocket of about four hundred that Key wanted very badly to capture:

. . . I tried to get the infantry of General Carter's brigade to charge them while I was firing, but it was impossible to get them forward. . . . I galloped back to Generals Cleburne and Hardee and informed them of . . . how we were driving them, remarking "Generals to the front," which caused a smile to play upon Cleburne's face. They sanctioned my suggestions, and in a few moments Cleburne and I were riding rapidly over the ground that I had gained with Turner's battery. As I rode I told the stragglers to rally—that the Yankees were running—and my remarks seemed to infuse new life into everyone and together we moved forward on the enemy. I also ordered forward the lieutenant commanding the section of Turner's battery and opened a fire upon the retreating foe. In a few moments General Lowrey advanced between my guns and the enemy, and knowing the direction of the Yankee lines I rode to the right and informed Generals Cleburne and Govan of the position. Then, in a few moments, a tremendous and bloody conflict followed. The battery was withdrawn, being no longer serviceable. Our forces carried a portion of the works, but night closed on the bloody tragedy.

The battle on July 22 was not so one-sided as Captain Key suggested. At noon that day Major W. H. Chamberlin of the Eighty-First Ohio

rode with General Grenville M. Dodge to a luncheon appointment at
General Fuller's headquarters:[12]

Just as General Dodge was about to dismount to accept General
Fuller's hospitality, he heard firing in a south-easterly direction, to the
rear of General Sweeney's division. He took no lunch. He was an intensely active, almost nervously restless, officer. He saw in an instant
that something serious was at hand. He gave General Fuller orders to
form his division immediately, facing south-eastwardly, and galloped
off toward Sweeney's division. He had hardly reached that command
when Hardee's line came tearing wildly through the woods with the
yells of demons. As if by magic, Sweeney's division sprang into line.
The two batteries of artillery (Loomis's and Laird's) had stopped on
commanding ground, and they were promptly in service. General
Dodge's quick eye saw the proper disposition to be made of a portion of
Colonel Mersy's brigade, and, cutting red tape, he delivered his orders
direct to the colonels of the regiments. The orders were executed instantly, and the enemy's advance was checked.* . . . The battle of
General Dodge's corps on this open ground, with no works to protect
the troops of either side, was one of the fiercest of the war. General
Dodge's troops were inspired by his courageous personal presence, for
he rode directly along the lines, and must have been a conspicuous
target for many a Confederate gun. His sturdy saddle-horse was worn
out early in the afternoon, and was replaced by another. There was not
a soldier who did not feel that he ought to equal his general in courage.
. . . We had an advantage in artillery; they in numbers. Their assaults
were repulsed, only to be fearlessly renewed, until the sight of the dead
and wounded lying in their way, as they charged again and again to
break our lines, must have appalled the stoutest hearts. So persistent
were their onslaughts that numbers were made prisoners by rushing
directly into our lines.

Even so, Dodge's left was in danger of crumbling unless he could get
support from McPherson. Lieutenant Colonel W. E. Strong, McPher-
son's chief of staff, saw troops sweep onto that open field:[13]

* Sweeney was a West Pointer, Dodge was not. In issuing orders directly to the
colonels, Dodge so hurt Sweeney's military dignity "as to bring on a personal
encounter a few days after the battle, in which he [Dodge] came near losing
his life at the hands of a hot-tempered officer."

The enemy, massed in columns three or four lines deep, moved out of the dense timber several hundred yards from Dodge's position, and, after gaining fairly the open fields, halted and opened fire rapidly on the Sixteenth Corps. They, however, seemed surprised to find our infantry in line of battle prepared for attack, and, after facing for a few minutes the destructive fire from the divisions of Generals Fuller and Sweeney, fell back in disorder to the cover of the woods. Here, however, their lines were quickly re-formed, and they again advanced, evidently determined to carry the position. The scene at this time was grand and impressive. It seemed to us that every mounted officer of the attacking column was riding at the front or at the right or left of the first line of battle. The regimental colors waved and fluttered in advance of the lines, and not a shot was fired by the rebel infantry, although their movement was covered by a heavy and well-directed fire of artillery which was posted in the woods and on higher ground, and which enabled the guns to bear upon our troops with solid shot and shell firing over the attacking column. It seemed impossible, however, for the enemy to face the sweeping, deadly fire from Fuller's and Sweeney's divisions, and the guns of Laird's 14th Ohio and Walker's batteries fairly mowed great swaths in the advancing columns. They showed great steadiness, and closed up the gaps and preserved their alignments; but the iron and leaden hail that was poured upon them was too much for flesh and blood to stand, and before reaching the center of the open field the columns were broken and thrown into great confusion. Taking advantage of this, a portion of Fuller's and Sweeney's divisions, with bayonets fixed, charged the enemy and drove them back to the woods, taking many prisoners. The 81st Ohio charged first, then the 39th and the 27th Ohio. General McPherson's admiration for the steadiness and determined bravery of the Sixteenth Corps was unbounded.

Sherman approached the grimmest moment of the day:[14]

. . . Although the sound of musketry on our left grew in volume, I was not so much disturbed by it as by the sound of artillery back toward Decatur. I ordered Schofield at once to send a brigade back to Decatur (some five miles) and was walking up and down the porch of the Howard House, listening, when one of McPherson's staff, with his horse covered with sweat, dashed up to the porch, and reported that General

McPherson was either "killed or a prisoner." He explained that when they had left me a few minutes before, they had ridden rapidly across the railroad, the sounds of battle increasing as they neared the position occupied by General Giles A. Smith's division, and that McPherson had sent first one, then another of his staff to bring some of the reserve brigades of the Fifteenth Corps over to the exposed left flank; that he had reached the head of Dodge's corps (marching by the flank on the diagonal road as described), and had ordered it to hurry forward to the same point; and then, almost if not entirely alone, he had followed this road leading across the wooded valley behind the Seventeenth Corps, and had disappeared in these woods, doubtless with a sense of absolute security. The sound of musketry was there heard, and McPherson's horse came back, bleeding, wounded, and riderless. . . .

To Sherman the death of James B. McPherson was a severe blow; he ordered the door of the Howard House wrenched from its hinges to provide a sort of table on which Dr. Hewitt examined the stricken general; and Sherman characterized McPherson as a man of "many noble qualities." Grant rated him with Sherman among "the men to whom, above all others, I feel indebted for whatever I have had of success." Major Connolly put the events of the twenty-second in a perspective somewhat different from Sherman's:[15]

. . . The rebels came out and attacked McPherson and Schofield yesterday [July 22], and gained some advantage over them, capturing several pieces of artillery, and many prisoners. McPherson was killed.

That is a severe loss, but his place can be filled; should we lose old father Thomas though, it would hurt us equal to the loss of an entire Division. We have been singularly fortunate during the entire campaign; success has crowned almost every movement, and our losses have been light, but we can't expect to get along always without some pretty tough fighting. The rebels have been more vigorous since we crossed the river than they were before, but it is only the vigor of desperation, and the more frequently they assault us, the sooner their army will be destroyed, for they *can't whip* this army; we are like the big boy, "too big to be whipped." They may gain temporary advantage here and there along our line, they may capture a few guns, but they will capture them at the expense of the blood and muscle of their army, and that they cannot replace; so I don't care how often they assault; we are here to *fight* them and *destroy* them, not to *chase* them, and if they have found their "last ditch" all right, Sherman will soon put them in it, and the oftener they attack the sooner he'll have them in it.

IV

In Virginia, Cold Harbor had convinced Grant that the direct approach to Richmond would cost more men than even the Army of the Potomac could afford to lose. He decided to move around the Confederate capital on the east and strike it through Petersburg, twenty-five miles to the south. On June 15 Grant's leading corps attacked the Petersburg fortifications, manned by sparse troops under Beauregard. The Union forces, anticipating an easy victory, went at their work in sluggish fashion; the Confederates threw everything into the battle. After three days of fighting Lee arrived, stopped the Federal advance, and the two armies settled into a siege.

A few days later Lieutenant Colonel Henry Pleasants of the Forty-eighth Pennsylvania Infantry had an idea:[16]

I was then commanding the first brigade of the second division of the 9th corps. That corps was then under the command of Major General Burnside. While commanding the brigade I frequently had occasion to go to the front line. I noticed a little cup of a ravine near to the enemy's works. I having been a mining and civil engineer many years before the war, it occurred to me that a mine could be excavated there. I examined the ground, and after I had satisfied myself that it could be done, I spoke to the officer next in rank above me, Brigadier General Potter, commanding the division. . . . He received the idea favorably, and wrote a note to General Burnside in relation to it. General Burnside sent for me, and I explained to him carefully the mode of ventilating the mine and everything about it. He seemed very much pleased with the proposition, and told me to go right on with the work.

Pleasants began his tunnel on the twenty-fifth of June. He soon discovered that apathy was a far tougher obstacle than Virginia clay:

My regiment was only about four hundred strong. At first I employed but a few men at a time, but the number was increased as the work progressed, until at last I had to use the whole regiment, non-commissioned officers and all. The great difficulty I had was to dispose of the material got out of the mine. I found it impossible to get any assistance from anybody; I had to do all the work myself. I had to remove all the earth in old cracker boxes. I got pieces of hickory and nailed on the boxes in which we received our crackers, and then iron-clad them with hoops of iron taken from old pork and beef barrels. . . .

Whenever I made application I could not get anything, although General Burnside was very favorable to it. The most important thing was to ascertain how far I had to mine, because if I fell short of or went beyond the proper place the explosion would have no practical effect; therefore I wanted an accurate instrument with which to make the necessary triangulations. I had to make them on the furthest front line, where the enemy's sharpshooters could reach me. I could not get the instrument I wanted, although there was one at army headquarters, and General Burnside had to send to Washington and get an old-fashioned theodolite, which was given to me.

Was there any reason why Headquarters could not have given Pleasants the better instrument?

I do not know. I know this: that General Burnside told me that General Meade and Major Duane, chief engineer of the army of the Potomac, said the thing could not be done; that it was all clap-trap and nonsense; that such a length of mine had never been excavated in military operations, and could not be; that I would either get the men smothered for want of air, or crushed by the falling of the earth; or the enemy would find it out, and it would amount to nothing. I could get no boards and lumber supplied to me for my operations. I had to get a pass and send two companies of my own regiment with wagons outside of our lines to rebel saw-mills and get lumber in that way, after having previously got what lumber I could by tearing down an old bridge. I had no mining picks furnished me, but had to take common army picks and have them straightened for my mining picks.

While Pleasants and his Pennsylvanians labored on their tunnel, Colonel Theodore Lyman wrote home of peaceful, lethargic days when war seemed to have gone off on a summer holiday:[17]

What shall I say of the Fourth? Our celebration could not well amount to much; the men have to stay too close in camp to do such things. The band came in the morning and serenaded, and there was saluting enough in the form of cannon and mortars from our right. This siege—if you choose to call it a siege—is a curious illustration of the customs of old soldiers. On the right—say from the Appomattox to a point opposite the Avery house—the lines are very close and more or less of siege operations are going on; so every finger, or cap, or point of a gun that shows above the works, is instantly shot at, in addition to which batteries and mortars are firing intermittently. Nothing could be more hostile! But pass to the division a little to the left of this, where our lines swing off from the enemy's, and you have a quite reversed state of things. There is not a shot! Behold the picket men, no longer crouching closely in their holes, but standing up and walking about, with the enemy's men, in like fashion, as near to them, in some places, as the length of the Brookline house. At one part, there was a brook between, and our pickets, or theirs, when they want water, hold up a canteen, and then coolly walk down to the neutral stream. All this truce is unofficial, but sacred, and is honorably observed. Also it is a matter of the rank and file. If an officer comes down, they get uneasy and often shout to him to go back, or they will shoot. The other day General Crawford calmly went down, took out an opera-glass and began staring. Very quickly a Reb was seen to write on a scrap of paper, roll it round a pebble and throw it over to our line. Thereon was writ this pithy bit of advice: "Tell the fellow with the spy-glass to clear out, or we shall have to shoot him." Near this same spot occurred a ludicrous thing, which is true, though one would not believe it if seen in a paper. A Reb, either from greenness or by accident, fired his musket, where-upon our people dropped in their holes and were on the point of open-ing along the whole line, when the Rebs waved their hands and cried: "Don't shoot; you'll see how we'll fix him!" Then they took the musket from the unfortunate grey-back, put a rail on his shoulder, and made him walk up and down for a great while in front of their rifle-pits! If they get orders to open, they call out, "Get into your holes, Yanks, we are ordered to fire"; and their first shots are aimed high, as a sort of warning. Their liberties go too far sometimes, as when two deliberately walked up to our breastwork to exchange papers; whereat General Crawford refused to allow them to return, saying very properly that the truce was not official, and that they had chosen to leave their own works and come over to ours, and that now they could carry back in-formation of our position. They expected an attack on the 4th of July— I suppose as a grand melodramatic stroke on Grant's part; but, instead thereof, the Maryland brigade brought up their band to the trenches and played "Hail Columbia"; upon which, to the surprise of everyone, a North Carolina regiment, lying opposite, rose as a man and gave three cheers!

While the army took a holiday from war, Pleasants completed the tunnel—a main gallery 511 feet long, with left and right lateral galleries of 37 and 38 feet. At the ends of the lateral galleries 8,000 pounds of powder were placed.

The explosion was set for 3:30 A.M., July 30. Burnside's Ninth Corps was to pour into the breach made by the mine and move on to Cemetery Hill, an elevation four hundred yards distant. The Fifth and Eighteenth Corps would follow, fan out, and establish a position which, when exploited, would lead to the fall of Petersburg—and Richmond.

Burnside had planned to have his one division of colored troops lead the charge. The men had not been in battle, but they had been specially trained for weeks and were burning to avenge Fort Pillow. On the night of July 29 Meade ordered a change; white divisions would go in first, the Negroes would follow. The First Division, commanded by a newcomer, General James H. Ledlie, would lead.

Before 3:30 on the morning of July 30 Ledlie's troops were in position. The hour came; nothing happened. Four o'clock; still no explosion. (The fuse had died out at a splice, and two men had gone in to make a new one.) At 4:40 the mine was sprung.

Major William H. Powell of Ledlie's staff witnessed what followed:[18]

It was a magnificent spectacle, and as the mass of earth went up into the air, carrying with it men, guns, carriages, and timbers, and spread out like an immense cloud as it reached its altitude, so close were the Union lines that the mass appeared as if it would descend immediately upon the troops waiting to make the charge. This caused them to break and scatter to the rear, and about ten minutes were consumed in re-forming for the attack. Not much was lost by this delay, however, as it took nearly that time for the cloud of dust to pass off. The order was then given for the advance. As no part of the Union line of breastworks had been removed . . . the troops clambered over them as best they could. This in itself broke the ranks, and they did not stop to re-form, but pushed ahead toward the crater, about 130 yards distant, the debris from the explosion having covered up the abatis and *chevaux-de-frise* in front of the enemy's works.

Little did these men anticipate what they would see upon arriving there: an enormous hole in the ground about 30 feet deep, 60 feet wide, and 170 feet long, filled with dust, great blocks of clay, guns, broken carriages, projecting timbers, and men buried in various ways— some up to their necks, others to their waists, and some with only their feet and legs protruding from the earth. One of these near me was

pulled out, and proved to be a second lieutenant of the battery which
had been blown up. The fresh air revived him, and he was soon able to
walk and talk. . . .

The whole scene of the explosion struck every one dumb with astonishment as we arrived at the crest of the debris. It was impossible
for the troops of the Second Brigade to move forward in line, as they
had advanced; and, owing to the broken state they were in, every man
crowding up to look into the hole, and being pressed by the First Brigade, which was immediately in rear, it was equally impossible to move
by the flank, by any command, around the crater. Before the brigade
commanders could realize the situation, the two brigades became inextricably mixed, in the desire to look into the hole.

However, Colonel Marshall yelled to the Second Brigade to move
forward, and the men did so, jumping, sliding, and tumbling into the
hole, over the debris of material, and dead and dying men, and huge
blocks of solid clay. . . . A partial formation was made by General
Bartlett and Colonel Marshall with some of their troops, but owing to
the precipitous walls the men could find no footing except by
facing inward, digging their heels into the earth, and throwing their
backs against the side of the crater, or squatting in a half-sitting, half-
standing posture, and some of the men were shot even there by the fire
from the enemy in the traverses. It was at this juncture that Colonel
Marshall requested me to go to General Ledlie and explain the condition of affairs. . . .

I found General Ledlie and a part of his staff ensconced in a protected
angle of the works. I gave him Colonel Marshall's message, explained
to him the situation, and Colonel Marshall's reasons for not being able
to move forward. General Ledlie then directed me to return at once and
say to Colonel Marshall and General Bartlett that it was General Burnside's order that they should move forward immediately. This message
was delivered. But the firing on the crater now was incessant, and
it was as heavy a fire of canister as was ever poured continuously upon
a single objective point. It was as utterly impracticable to reform a
brigade in that crater as it would be to marshal bees into line after upsetting the hive; and equally as impracticable to reform outside of the
crater, under the severe fire in front and rear, as it would be to hold a
dress parade in front of a charging enemy.

*A high command which knew nothing of the real situation continued
to send troops forward. Powell again risked death to crawl out of the
hellhole and urge Ledlie, for God's sake, to do something:*

All the satisfaction I received was an order to go back and tell the brigade commanders to get their men out and press forward to Cemetery Hill. This talk and these orders, coming from a commander sitting in a bomb-proof inside the Union lines, were disgusting. I returned again to the crater and delivered the orders, which I knew beforehand could not possibly be obeyed; and I told General Ledlie so before I left him.*

General John W. Tyler, commanding a division of the Eighteenth Corps, saw Burnside's Negro troops make their belated and hopeless charge. The time was now seven o'clock:[19]

The crater was full of men; they were lying all around, and every point that would give cover to a man was occupied. There was no movement towards Cemetery Hill; the troops were all in confusion and lying down. I asked one or two officers there if an attempt had been made to move on Cemetery Hill. They said the attempt had been made, but it had failed. I then said, "You ought to intrench your position here, and you have too many troops here already to intrench. There are so many troops here that they are in each other's way; they are only exposed to this terrific fire of the enemy," which was then growing warmer and warmer, and was a very severe fire.

While I was talking to an officer—we had sought shelter in the crater —the head of the colored division appeared at the crest of the crater, and the division commenced piling over into the crater and passing across it on the other side as well as they could. I exclaimed, "What are these men sent in here for? It is only adding confusion to the confusion which already exists." The men literally came falling right over

---

* Six months later the Joint Committee on the Conduct of the War arrived at a conclusion: "Brigadier General J. H. Ledlie, United States volunteers, he having failed to push forward his division promptly according to orders, and thereby blocking up the avenue which was designed for the passage of troops ordered to follow and support his in the assault. It is in evidence that no commander reported to General Burnside that his troops could not be got forward, which the court regard as a neglect of duty on the part of General Ledlie, inasmuch as a timely report of the misbehavior might have enabled General Burnside, commanding the assault, to have made other arrangements for prosecuting it before it became too late. Instead of being with his division during this difficulty in the crater, and by his personal efforts endeavoring to lead his troops forward, he was most of the time in a bomb-proof, ten rods in rear of the mainline of the 9th corps works, where it was impossible for him to see anything of the movements of troops that were going on."—*Report,* Vol. I, 216 (second paging).

into this crater on their hands and knees; they were so thick in there that a man could not walk. Seeing that I was going to be covered up there, and be entirely useless, I thought I would go out. As I had no control over these troops, and supposing there were officers in command, I said, "If you can get these troops beyond this line so that I can get out, I will move my division right out and cover your right flank"; and I went back for the purpose of doing so. I met General Ord on our line at the head of my division. I said, "General, unless a movement is made out of the crater towards Cemetery Hill, it is murder to send more men in there. That colored division should never have been sent in there; but there is a furor there, and perhaps they may move off sufficiently for me to pass my division out." "Well," said he, "do so if they move." A very few moments after, I thought they had started to make a rush towards Cemetery Hill, and I immediately ordered my leading brigade, which was massed by regiments, to charge to the right of the crater. The colored division by that time had nearly, if not quite, all got into the crater; had passed to the right of it by perhaps fifty yards, and were all lying down . . . trying to cover themselves the best way they could.

The gnawing fear, the hatred that caused the war in the first place now broke all bounds. George S. Bernard, Twelfth Virginia Infantry, Mahone's brigade, shuddered at what he saw:[20]

I saw Confederates beating and shooting at the negro soldiers, as the latter, terror-stricken, rushed away from them. I saw one negro running down the trench towards the place where several of us stood, and a Confederate soldier just in his rear drawing a bead on him as he ran. The Confederate fired at the poor creature, seemingly heedless of the fact that his bullet might have pierced his victim and struck some of the many Confederates immediately in its range.

A minute later I witnessed another deed which made my blood run cold: Just about the outer end of the ditch by which I had entered stood a negro soldier . . . begging for his life from two Confederate soldiers, who stood by him, one of them striking the poor wretch with a steel ramrod, the other holding a gun in his hand with which he seemed to be trying to get a shot at the negro. The man with the gun fired it at the negro, but did not seem to seriously injure him, as he only clapped his hand to his hip where he appeared to have been shot, and continued to beg for his life. The man with the ramrod continued to strike the negro therewith, whilst the fellow with the gun deliberately re-loaded it, and, placing its muzzle close against the stomach of the poor negro, fired, at which the latter fell limp and lifeless. . . . It was a brutal, horrible act, and those of us who witnessed it from our position in the trench, a few feet away, could but exclaim: "That is too bad! It is shocking!" Yet this, I have no doubt, from what I saw and afterwards heard, was but a sample of many other bloody tragedies during the first ten minutes after our men got into the trench, many of whom seemed infuriated at the idea of having to fight negroes. Within these ten minutes the whole floor of the trench was strewn with the dead bodies of negroes, in some places in such numbers that it was difficult to make one's way along the trench without stepping on them.

Tyler's men still tried to reach the objective:[21]

My leading brigade charged over our line up to the enemy's works, and took possession of about one hundred yards of it; but there were no movements of the troops in and around the crater to advance on Cemetery Hill. At the time my leading brigade charged I directed the head of my second brigade to move out through a break in our works . . . so as to join hands on the right of the first brigade and charge the enemy's lines beyond. They succeeded in getting only about half way between our lines and the lines of the enemy, when they were stopped by the enemy's fire. The first brigade . . . succeeded in reaching the enemy's works, and took possession of about one hundred yards of it, when they laid down. I immediately sent word to my first brigade commander, who was within hailing distance—within sight, probably seventy-five yards off—to take his leading regiment and charge by the right flank, so as to sweep down the enemy's lines, while I brought up the second brigade. I was in hopes to take possession of a still greater length of the enemy's line. I returned to the brigade commander of my third brigade, and ordered him to mass his troops behind our lines, and hold them in readiness for any exigency. I had but just given him his instructions when my first brigade charged by the right flank, in obedience to my orders. I immediately passed over the line to the second brigade to give the command "Forward!"

I had got, probably, half way between our line and the enemy's lines —which were perhaps only a hundred yards apart at that point, and it was a very broken country, thick underbrush and morass—when, looking to the left, I saw the troops in vast numbers come rushing back, and immediately my whole first brigade came back, and then my second brigade on my right, and everything was swept back in and around the crater, and probably all but about one-third of the original number stampeded back right into our lines.

Men huddled in the crater for hours, groaning from wounds, begging for water. As early as 9:30 A.M. Meade issued a peremptory order for withdrawal. It could not be obeyed—enemy fire was too heavy. In mid-afternoon the Confederates themselves cleared the crater, driving hundreds back to the Union lines, capturing those who remained.

Major William H. Powell summed up the casualties which the Ninth Corps had suffered in two weeks:[22]

In the engagements of the 17th and 18th of June, in order to obtain the position held by the Ninth Corps at the time of the explosion, the three white divisions lost 29 officers and 348 men killed; 106 officers and 1851 men wounded; and 15 officers and 554 men missing—total, 2903. From the 20th of June to the day before the crater fight of July 30th these same divisions lost in the trenches 12 officers and 231 men killed; 44 officers and 851 men wounded; and 12 men missing,—total, 1150. . . . In the engagement of July 30th the four divisions of the Ninth Corps had 52 officers and 376 men killed; 105 officers and 1556 men wounded; and 87 officers and 1652 men captured,—total, 3828.

CHAPTER 33

"WAR IS WAR"

THE CRATER was more than a ghastly blunder; it was proof that Richmond and Petersburg could be taken only by a long, costly siege. With Sherman apparently stalled before Atlanta, gloom enveloped the North—a gloom so oppressive that even a spectacular naval victory could not dispel it.

I

Protected by powerful forts, Mobile, Alabama remained after three years of war a safe port for blockade-runners. Moreover, during the summer of 1864, a new Confederate ram, the Tennessee, *was being ironclad here. Looking like a great turtle, the* Tennessee, *with six-inch iron plate covering her sloping sides, was considered the strongest, most powerful ironclad ever put afloat.*

One tough old Unionist who was determined that the Tennessee's *career would end where it began—in Mobile Bay—was Admiral David Farragut. A Federal assault force of 5,000 was gathered to capture the garrisons in the forts after a fleet of fourteen wooden ships and four monitors (or ironclads) had cleared the bay of Rebel vessels. On August 12, as "the gray glimmer of dawn was just beginning to struggle through a dense fog," Farragut roused his crews. A hasty repast of sandwiches and coffee was served, for the Admiral insisted that he would have breakfast inside Mobile Bay "at the regular hour." Shortly after five o'clock the Federal fleet steamed up the main channel. There disaster threatened Farragut:*[1]

. . . The vessels outside the bar . . . were all under way by forty minutes past five in the morning . . . two abreast, and lashed to-

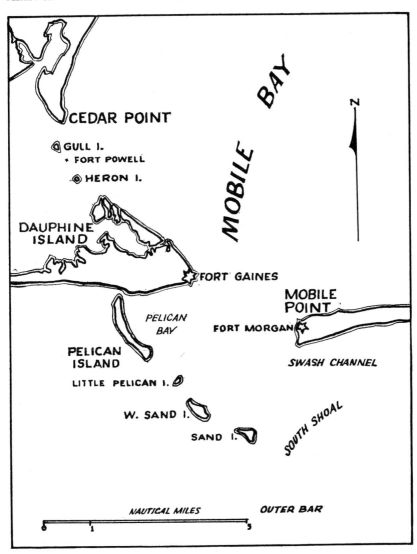

MOBILE BAY

gether. . . . The iron-clads were already inside the bar, and had been ordered to take up their positions on the starboard side of the wooden ships, or between them and Fort Morgan, for the double purpose of keeping down the fire from the water-battery and the parapet guns of the fort, as well as to attack the ram *Tennessee* as soon as the fort was passed.

It was only at the urgent request of the Captains and commanding officers that I yielded to the *Brooklyn* being the leading ship of the line, as she had four chase-guns and an ingenious arrangement for picking up torpedoes [mines], and because, in their judgment, the flag-ship ought not to be too much exposed. . . .

The attacking fleet steamed steadily up the main ship-channel, the *Tecumseh* firing the first shot at forty-seven minutes past six o'clock. At six minutes past seven the Fort opened upon us, and was replied to by a gun from the *Brooklyn,* and immediately after the action became general.

It was soon apparent that there was some difficulty ahead. The *Brooklyn,* for some cause which I did not then clearly understand, . . . arrested the advance of the whole fleet, while, at the same time, the guns of the Fort were playing with great effect upon that vessel and the *Hartford.* A moment after I saw the *Tecumseh* struck by a torpedo, dis-appear almost instantly between the waves, carrying with her her gal-lant commander and nearly all her crew. I determined at once, as I had originally intended, to take the lead, and after ordering the *Meta-comet* to send a boat to save, if possible, any of the perishing crew, I dashed ahead with the *Hartford,* and the ships followed on, their officers believing that they were going to a noble death with their commander-in-chief.

I steamed through between the buoys, where the torpedoes were sup-posed to have been sunk. These buoys had been previously examined by my Flag-Lieutenant, I. Crittenden Watson, in several nightly reconnoissances. Though he had not been able to discover the sunken torpedoes, yet we had been assured by refugees, deserters, and others, of their existence, but, believing that from their having been some time in the water, they were probably innocuous, I determined to take the chance of their explosion.

With Farragut aboard the Hartford *was J. C. Kinney, a signal officer who was to establish communication between the fleet and the army after the forts had been passed. Kinney read the signal from the* Brooklyn, *"Our best monitor is sunk." Farragut answered briefly, "Go on!" Still, "for some mysterious reason," the* Brooklyn *halted, and Kinney felt a trickling of sweat:*[2]

It was the decisive moment of the day. Owing to our position, only our few bowguns could be used, while a deadly rain of shot and shell was falling on us, and our men were being cut down by scores, unable to make reply. The sight on the deck of the *Hartford* was sickening beyond the power of words to portray. Shot after shot came through the side, mowing down the men, deluging the decks with blood, and scattering mangled fragments of humanity so thickly that it was difficult to stand on the deck, so slippery was it. The old expressions of the "scuppers running blood," "the slippery deck," etc., give but the faintest idea of the spectacle on the *Hartford*. The bodies of the dead were placed in a long row on the side, while the wounded were sent below until the surgeons' quarters would hold no more. A solid shot coming through the bow struck a gunner on the neck, completely severing head from body. One poor fellow (afterward an object of interest at the great Sanitary Commission fair in New York) lost both legs by a cannon ball; as he fell he threw up both arms, just in time to have them also carried away by another shot. At one gun, all the crew on one side were swept down by a shot which came crashing through the bulwarks. . . .

Meanwhile, the men were working the guns that could be used, as though the sight and smell of blood had sharpened their appetites. There was no skulking; in fact there was no chance to skulk, if there had been such a disposition. They stood to their work, white and black side by side. There was no thought of social differences then; and whenever a shot was believed to have been well placed, the cheers of the men rang out above the roar of the guns. As our poet laureate, the Admiral's secretary, Harry Howard Brownell, of Hartford, sang of the fight, in the most graphic and truthful description ever written of it:

> "Never a nerve that failed,
> Never a cheek that paled,
> Not a tinge of gloom or pallor.
> There was bold Kentucky grit,
> And the old Virginian valor
> And the daring Yankee wit.

> "There were blue eyes from the turfy Shannon,
> There were black orbs from the palmy Niger,
> But there, alongside the cannon,
> Each man fought like a tiger.

> One only doubt was ours,
> Only one fear we knew:
> Could the day that dawned so well
> Go down for the darker powers?
> *Would* the fleet get through?"

The fleet not only went through, but Farragut also fulfilled his boast and settled down to breakfast inside Mobile Bay at the regular hour. The meal was suddenly interrupted by a messenger-boy shouting: "The ram is coming down." J. C. Kinney, rushing onto the quarter-deck, stood beside the admiral and the fleet-captain:

The *Tennessee* fired two shots through her bow, and then kept on for the *Hartford*. The two flag-ships approached each other bow to bow. The two admirals, Farragut and Buchanan,* had entered our navy together as boys, and up to the outbreak of the war had been warm friends. But now each was hoping for the overthrow of the other, and had Buchanan possessed the grit of Farragut, it is probable that moment would have witnessed the destruction of both vessels. For had the ram struck us square, as it came, bows on, it would have plowed its way half through the *Hartford*, and, as we sank, we should have carried it to the bottom, unable to extricate itself. But the rebel admiral was not desirous of so much glory, and, just as the two vessels were meeting, the course of the *Tennessee* was slightly changed, enough to strike us only a glancing blow on the port bow, which left us uninjured, while the two vessels grated past each other. He tried to sink us with a broadside as he went by, but only one of his guns went off, the primers in all the others failing. That gun sent a shell through the berth-deck, above the water-line, killing five men and wounding eight,—the last hostile shot which has ever touched the *Hartford*. The muzzle of the gun was so close that the powder blackened the ship's side. The *Hartford* gave the ram a salute from ten heavy guns, each loaded with thirteen pounds of powder and a solid shot, but the balls merely dented her side and bounded into the air. The scene on the *Hartford* during the moment of contact was of intense excitement. The admiral coolly stood on the port quarter-rail, holding to the mizzen rigging, from which, at one time, he almost could have jumped to the deck of the ram. Flag-Lieutenant Watson, seeing him in this exposed position, secured him to the rigging by a rope's end with his own hands; so that during the day he was *twice* "lashed to the rigging." As the ships came together, Captain Drayton ran to the bow of the *Hartford*, and, as the ram sheered off to avoid striking a square blow, he shook his lorgnette at it, and exclaimed, "The cowardly rascal; he's afraid of a wooden ship!"

The *Tennessee* now became the target for the whole fleet, all the ves-

* Franklin Buchanan, former Union naval officer, who commanded the Confederate squadron.

sels of which were making toward it, pounding it with shot, and trying
to run it down. As the *Hartford* turned to make for it again, we ran in
front of the *Lackawanna*, which had already turned and was moving
under full headway with the same object. She struck us on our starboard side, amidships, crushing half-way through, knocking two port-
holes into one, upsetting two Dahlgren guns, and creating general
consternation. For a time it was thought that we must sink, and the cry
rang out over the deck: "Save the Admiral! save the Admiral!" The
port boats were ordered lowered, and in their haste some of the sailors
cut the "falls" and two of the cutters dropped into the water wrong
side up, and floated astern. But the Admiral, nearly as cool as ever,
sprang into the starboard mizzen-rigging, looked over the side of the
ship, and, finding there was still a few inches to spare above the
water's edge, instantly ordered the ship ahead again at full speed, after
the ram. The unfortunate *Lackawanna*, which had struck the ram a second blow, was making for her once more, and, singularly enough,
again came up on our starboard side, and another collision seemed imminent. And now the Admiral became a trifle excited. He had no idea
of whipping the rebels to be himself sunk by a friend. "Can you say,
'For God's sake' by signal?" he inquired. "Yes, sir," was the reply.
"Then say to the *Lackawanna*, 'For God's sake get out of our way and
anchor!' " In my haste to send the message, I brought the end of my signal flag-staff down with considerable violence upon the head of the
Admiral, who was standing nearer than I thought, causing him to wince
perceptibly but I could not apologize until I finished signaling. . . .

The remainder of the story is soon told. The ram was unable to
strike a single one of the Union vessels, while the concentration of fire
upon it tore away everything except the solid iron. First, the rebel flag-
staff fell; then the smoke-stack was shot away, and finally a well-placed
shot from the monitor *Chickasaw* broke the rudder-chain, so that the
great ram would no longer mind the helm, and she lay like a huge
monster at bay. Already a fifteen-inch solid shot from the *Manhattan*
had crushed through the iron armor and let the daylight into her, and
finally a shell exploded in one of her port-holes, and a fragment seriously wounded the rebel admiral. And then, up through the iron grat-
ing of her deck came a staff, bearing a white flag. The firing ceased, and
from vessel after vessel of the victorious fleet rang out such cheers as
are seldom heard and never forgotten—cheers which meant victory
after a hard and very doubtful struggle. And, as the cheering ceased,
a dim echo seemed to come from below, where the wounded and dying,

knowing the day was at last won, joined in the shouts of triumph, rejoiced that their sacrifice would not be in vain. So ended the fight.

For the wounded, battles never end that neatly, as Farragut knew:[3]

. . . Commander Johnston, formerly of the United States navy, was in command of the *Tennessee*, and came on board the flag-ship, to surrender his sword and that of Admiral Buchanan. The surgeon, Doctor Conrad, came with him, stated the condition of the Admiral, and wished to know what was to be done with him. Fleet Surgeon Palmer, who was on board the *Hartford*, during the action, commiserating the sufferings of the wounded, suggested that those of both sides be sent to Pensacola, where they could be properly cared for. I therefore addressed a note to Brigadier-General R. L. Page, commanding Fort Morgan, informing him that Admiral Buchanan and others of the *Tennessee* had been wounded, and desiring to know whether he would permit one of our vessels, under a flag of truce, to convey them, with or without our wounded, to Pensacola, on the understanding that the vessel should take out none but the wounded, and bring nothing back that she did not take out. This was acceded to by General Page, and the *Metacomet* proceeded on this mission of humanity. . . .

As I had an elevated position in the main rigging near the top, I was able to overlook not only the deck of the *Hartford*, but the other vessels of the fleet. I witnessed the terrible effects of the enemy's shot, and the good conduct of the men at their guns, and although no doubt their hearts sickened, as mine did, when their shipmates were struck down beside them, yet there was not a moment's hesitation to lay their comrades aside, and spring again to their deadly work.

II

The Battle of Mobile Bay and the fall of Fort Gaines and Fort Morgan soon afterward (on August 7 and August 23) gave the Union 104 guns and 1,500 prisoners, and closed one of the last remaining Southern ports; yet many thousands in the North persisted in believing that the South could not be subdued. The men of faint heart made Lincoln their target. On August 22 Thurlow Weed, shrewdest of Republican politicians, wrote to Lincoln's Secretary of State:[4]

When, ten or twelve days since, I told Mr. Lincoln that his re-election was an impossibility, I also told him that the information would soon come to him through other channels. It has doubtless, ere this, reached him. At any rate, nobody here doubts it; nor do I see any body from other States who authorises the slightest hope of success.

Mr. Raymond, who has just left me, says that unless some prompt and bold step be now taken, all is lost.

The People are wild for Peace. They are told that the President will only listen to terms of Peace on condition Slavery be "abandoned."

. . . That *something* should be done and promptly done, to give the Administration a chance for its life, is certain.

Henry J. Raymond, editor of the New York Times *and a Lincoln supporter whose loyalty could not be questioned, warned the President:*[5]

ROOMS OF THE NATIONAL UNION
EXECUTIVE COMMITTEE
ASTOR HOUSE, NEW YORK, Aug. 22, 1864

MY DEAR SIR:

I feel compelled to drop you a line concerning the political condition of the country as it strikes me. I am in active correspondence with your staunchest friends in every state and from them all I hear but one report. The tide is setting strongly against us. Hon. E. B. Washburne writes that "were an election to be held now in Illinois we should be beaten." Mr. Cameron writes that Pennsylvania is against us. Gov. Morton writes that nothing but the most strenuous efforts can carry Indiana. This State, according to the best information I can get, would go 50,000 against us tomorrow. And so of the rest.

Nothing but the most resolute and decided action on the part of the Government and its friends, can save the country from falling into hostile hands. . . .

HENRY J. RAYMOND

Raymond urged Lincoln to put Jefferson Davis on the spot by proposing a peace conference. Davis, Raymond was sure, would repel any reasonable offer and thus prove to a faltering North that the end of the war could come only through victory. Lincoln ignored the proposal, but he accepted Raymond's appraisal of public sentiment. Upon the receipt of the editor's letter Lincoln asked the members of his Cabinet to sign their names on the outside of a folded sheet of paper. Inside he had written:[6]

EXECUTIVE MANSION
WASHINGTON, Aug. 23, 1864

This morning, as for some days past, it seems exceedingly probable
that this Administration will not be reelected. Then it will be my duty
to so co-operate with the President elect, as to save the Union between the election and the inauguration; as he will have secured his
election on such ground that he can not possibly save it afterwards.

A. LINCOLN

III

*With victory almost in their possession, the Democrats met in Chicago
on August 29. Noah Brooks, correspondent of the Sacramento* Union,
*reported the temper of the convention and its choice of a candidate to
oppose Lincoln:*[7]

When the convention began to assemble in the great wigwam near
the lake shore, Vallandigham, Alexander Long, and Representative
Harris were the "stars" of the occasion. Calls for them were made at
every possible opportunity, and it was easy to see that these eminent
Peace Democrats were more popular than any other of the delegates
to the convention. It was a noisy assemblage, and it was also a Peace
Democrat convention. While Alexander Long was reading a set of
resolutions, which he proposed to have the convention adopt, asking for
a suspension of the draft until after the election, "Sunset" Cox interfered with a motion to have all resolutions referred, without reading or
debate, to the proper committee; whereupon he was roundly hissed,
and the spectators, who to the number of thousands filled the pit of the
great building, yelled, "Get down, you War Democrat!" much to his
discomfiture. The crowd of on-lookers in the pit was so great that
many of them climbed up and roosted on a fence which separated
them from the delegates, and their weight soon broke down this slender
barrier, creating the greatest confusion. Frantic ushers and policemen
attempted to preserve order; now and then a train crashing by on the
Lake Shore tracks close at hand added to the racket, and filled the
huge building with smoke and cinders.

Horatio Seymour, then governor of New York, was the president of
the Chicago convention; and it must be said that he made a much better
presiding officer than ex-Governor Dennison had proved himself in the
chair of the Republican convention at Baltimore. Seymour was tall,
fine-looking, of an imposing figure, with a good though colorless face,

bright, dark eyes, a high, commanding forehead, dark-reddish hair, and slightly bald. He had a clear, ringing voice, with a slight imperfection in his speech, and he was in the main an attractive and effective speaker, and a capital presiding officer. His opening address, which was very calm and cool, was not well received by the crowd, who evidently wanted something more heart-firing, and who incessantly shouted, "Vallandigham! Vallandigham!" But the distinguished exile, though he was not far away, was discreet enough to remain out of sight until his time came. His name was presented by the State of Ohio for membership of the committee on platform, and it was well known that the most important plank in that structure—that which related to the prosecution of the war—was his. . . . This was the famous clause which explicitly declared that "after four years of failure to restore the Union by the experiment of war, during which, under the pretense of a military necessity, or war power higher than the Constitution, the Constitution itself has been disregarded in every part . . . , the public welfare demands that immediate efforts be made for a cessation of hostilities with a view to an ultimate convention of the States, or other peaceable means to the end that at the earliest practicable moment peace may be restored on the basis of the Federal union of the States." This was the peace platform which Lincoln had expected. The war candidate, of course, was soon to be forthcoming. . . .

Although McClellan was the inevitable nominee of the convention, he did not receive the honor until one formal ballot had been taken. The first ballot gave him 150 votes; Thomas H. Seymour of Connecticut had 43 votes, and Horatio Seymour of New York received 7. There were two scattering votes cast. The roll-call had been finished, but the balloting was practically settled by the action of Missouri, which, having previously voted solidly for Thomas H. Seymour, now divided its strength, and cast 7 votes for McClellan, and 4 for Thomas H. Seymour, amid great cheering. There was then a great landslide of votes for McClellan, until all but the most uncompromising of the Peace Democrats had gone over to the inevitable nominee. Long, Vallandigham, and others held out until the last; and after all changes were made, the final vote was announced thus: McClellan, 202½; Thomas H. Seymour, 23½. Instantly the pent-up feelings of the crowd broke forth in the most rapturous manner: cheers, yells, music, and screams indescribable rent the air, and outside the wigwam a park of cannon volleyed a salute in honor of the nominee. The long agony was over, and men threw up their hats, and behaved as much like bedlamites as men usually do under such circumstances. When order was restored, Vallandigham, who until then had not spoken, mounted the rostrum, and moved that the nomination be made unanimous. It is impossible to describe the tremendous applause which greeted the appearance of the Ohio "martyr," who had only lately returned through Canada from his exile. His appearance on the platform, bland, smiling, and rosy, was the signal for a terrific outburst before he could open his mouth; and when his little speech was done, another whirlwind of applause greeted his magnanimous motion in favor of a war candidate. . . .

George H. Pendleton was nominated for vice-president without much difficulty. . . . The convention broke up in the most admirable disorder, and that night the city of Chicago seemed drunk with political excitement. Although many of the leaders had left by afternoon trains, the marching mobs halted under the windows of all the principal hotels, and demanded speeches until midnight fell, and something like silence reigned in the city.

IV

Before Atlanta, Sherman admitted that he was held in check by a stubborn defense. By late August he was convinced that Hood would hold fast though Federal artillery battered down every house. "It was evident that we must decoy him out to fight us on something like equal terms," Sherman wrote. Within Atlanta, Hood came to sense a change:[8]

The bombardment of the city continued till the 25th of August; it was painful, yet strange, to mark how expert grew the old men, women and children, in building their little underground forts, in which to fly for safety during the storm of shell and shot. Often 'mid the darkness of night were they constrained to seek refuge in these dungeons beneath the earth; albeit, I cannot recall one word from their lips, expressive of dissatisfaction or willingness to surrender.

Sherman had now been over one month continuously moving toward our left and thoroughly fortifying, step by step, as he advanced in the direction of the Macon Railroad. On the night of the 25th, he withdrew from our immediate front; his works, which at an early hour the following morning we discovered to be abandoned, were occupied at a later hour by the corps of Generals Stewart and [Stephen D.] Lee.

This movement of the Federals gave rise to many idle rumors in relation to its object. I felt confident that their plan would soon be devel-

oped; accordingly orders were issued to corps commanders to send out
scouts in their front, and to keep Army headquarters fully advised of
the slightest change in the enemy's position; to issue three days' rations and to be in readiness to move at a moment's warning. Instructions were likewise sent to General Armstrong, commanding the cavalry
in vicinity of the West Point Railroad, to be most active in securing all
possible information in regard to the operations of the enemy. . . .

ATLANTA AND VICINITY, 1864

Early [on August 28], the enemy were reported by General Armstrong in large force at Fairburn, on the West Point Road. It became at
once evident that General Sherman was moving with his main body to
destroy the Macon road, and that the fate of Atlanta depended upon our
ability to defeat this movement. . . .

On the 29th, the Federals marched slowly in the direction of Rough
and Ready, and Jonesboro. . . . Had Sherman not been doubly protected by the Chattahoochee, deep intervening creeks and ravines extending to the river, beside the wall of parapets behind which he had

thus far manoeuvered, I would have moved from East Point with our main body, and have attacked his Army whilst effecting these changes of position. This move not being practicable, I was forced to await further developments.

That Monday, August 29, Sherman was at Fairburn on the West Point Railroad, having a wonderful time:[9]

. . . The track was heaved up in sections the length of a regiment, then separated rail by rail; bonfires were made of the ties and of fence-rails on which the rails were heated, carried to trees or telegraph-poles, wrapped around and left to cool. Such rails could not be used again; and, to be still more certain, we filled up many deep cuts with trees, brush and earth, and commingled with them loaded shells, so arranged that they would explode on an attempt to haul out the bushes. The explosion of one such shell would have demoralized a gang of negroes, and thus would have prevented even the attempt to clear the road.

Meantime Schofield, with the Twenty-third Corps, presented a bold front toward East Point, daring and inviting the enemy to sally out to attack him in position. His first movement was on the 30th, to Mount Gilead Church, then to Morrow's Mills, facing Rough and Ready. Thomas was on his right, within easy support, moving by cross-roads from Red Oak to the Fayetteville Road, extending from Couch's to Renfrew's; and Howard was aiming for Jonesboro. . . . The next morning (August 31st) all moved straight for the railroad. Schofield reached it near Rough and Ready, and Thomas at two points between there and Jonesboro. Howard found an intrenched foe (Hardee's corps) covering Jonesboro, and his men began at once to dig their accustomed rifle-pits.

Hood had been outwitted, for all the brave face he put on the tale in his memoirs. Hardee with one corps was opposed by six corps under the command of Sherman. The climax came on the first of September. Tom Key, that adept Confederate artillerist, remembered:[10]

At 2 o'clock A.M. we were ordered to change base to the position occupied by General Lee, and Lee moved back to Atlanta.*. . . About

* Clearly Hood expected an attack from Sherman in front of the city. Since Lee fought with Hardee, the move gave Sherman his 6 to 1 advantage at the critical point.

3 o'clock the enemy made an attack upon General Govan's line which was facing to the north, and Key's and Swett's batteries opened such a deadly fire upon them that the line was broken. The Yankees then brought up three or four additional lines of batteries and concentrating for a desperate assault they charged up in this massed condition upon Govan's lines and against a portion of General Lewis's force which had just been thrown upon the right of Govan and, of course, had no defenses. General Govan's works were fairly strong though manned very thinly, about a rank and a half. Their fire upon the advancing enemy was steady, and that of Swett's and Key's batteries very destructive, but the immense numbers and overwhelming forces of the Yankees ran upon the works, sweeping over the right of Govan's fortifications, striking the lines at both batteries, and capturing the General and several hundred of his gallant Arkansans. The cannoneers continued to pour canister upon the enemy until they were within ten steps of their guns, and all of Key's battery were captured except twelve men. Swett's had a similar loss. . . .

The defense of the Confederates was noble, but they were too weak to contend against such numbers. . . . Night brought the bloody contest to a close, and in my opinion our opponents lost ten men to our one. . . . About midnight we reached Lovejoy Station where we halted for the night. I lay down but there was no sleep for me. The events of the day had been so unexpected and surprising that slumber could not drive sad thoughts from me.

Major James A. Connolly wrote his wife of those tense moments when "Our Corps had the honor of giving the grand finishing stroke to the campaign":[11]

. . . Oh, it was a glorious battle! But this Division suffered terribly. There was no chance of flinching there. Generals, Colonels, Majors, Captains and privates, all had to go forward together over that open field, facing and drawing nearer to death at every step we took, our horses crazy, frantic with the howling of shells, the rattling of canister and the whistling of bullets, ourselves delirious with the wild excitement of the moment, and thinking only of getting over those breast-works—great volleys of canister shot sweeping through our lines making huge gaps, but the blue coated boys filled the gaps and still rushed forward right into the jaws of death—we left hundreds of bleeding comrades behind us at every step, but not one instant did that line hesitate—it moved steadily forward to the enemy's works —over the works with a shout—over the cannon—over the rebels, and then commenced stern work with the bayonet, but the despairing cries of surrender soon stopped it, the firing ceased, and 1,000 rebels were hurried to the rear as prisoners of war.

The General rode forward with the front line despite our protests and had two horses shot under him during the charge, my tent mate . . . was shot in the right arm, why the other five of us escaped is one of the strange things found in a battle, when we were all similarly exposed to the fire. When the cheer went up I recollect finding myself in a tangled lot of soldiers, on my horse, just against the enemy's log breast-works, my hat off, and tears streaming from my eyes, but as happy as a mortal is ever permitted to be. I could have lain down on that blood stained grass, amid the dying and the dead and wept with excess of joy. I have no language to express the rapture one feels in the moment of victory, but I do know that at such a moment one feels as if the joy were worth risking a hundred lives to attain it. . . .

That night, as we lay on the ground without blankets or tents, we were aroused by sound of distant explosions away off to the North, in the direction of Atlanta, and many were the conjectures as to the cause, but the afternoon brought us the intelligence that the enemy had "evacuated Atlanta last night, blowing up 86 car loads of ammunition, and destroying large amounts of public stores." Then went up more lusty cheers than were ever heard in that part of Georgia before.

V

"I was not so much pained by the fall of Atlanta," Hood declared, "as by the recurrence of retreat, which I full well knew would further demoralize the Army and renew desertions." War has a meaning for generals that civilians may not share—a fact that little Carrie Berry could have explained:[12]

Sept. 1. Thurs. . . . Directly after dinner Cousin Emma came down and told us that Atlanta would be evacuated this evening and we might look for the federals in the morning. It was not long till the hole town found it out and such excitement there was. We have ben looking for them all evening but they have not come yet. . . . I finished my stockings to day.

Sept. 2. Fri. We all woke up this morning without sleeping much last night. The Confederates had four engenes and a long train of box cars filled with ammunition and set it on fire last night which caused a grate explosion which kept us all awake. It reminded us of the shells—of all the days of excitement, we have had it to day. Everyone has been trying to get all they could before the Federals come in the morning. They have ben running with saques of meal, salt and tobacco. They did act rediculous breaking open stores and robbing them. About twelve o'clock there were a few federals came in. They were picketed. In about an hour the cavalry came dashing in. We were all frightened. We were afraid they were going to treat us badly. It was not long till the Infantry came in. They were orderely and behaved very well. I think I shall like the Yankees very well.

Sept. 3. Sat. The soldiers have ben coming in all day. I went up to Aunties this morning and she said that she had a yankee officer to spend the night with her. We have not seen much of them. Only two of them have ben here to beg some thing to eat. We have had a rainy day and we all feel gloomy.

Mary Rawson Day, whose husband was a captain in the First Georgia Volunteers, was pleasantly surprised those first days of September:[13]

Time after time had we been told of the severity of Gen. Sherman until we came to dread his approach as we would that of a mighty hurricane which sweeps all before it caring naught for justice or humanity. Our fear of his coming did not however prevent it. The forenoon passed slowly with nothing of importance . . . with dinner time came Father, who said that the Federals had taken possession of the city. OH! What a relief for me. I had expected them to enter in disorder, exulting loudly in the success of their enterprise. The capture of Atlanta seems to have been the acme of the ambition of the Northern government.

Atlanta was taken possession of quietly. About ten o'clock in the morning [September 2] the mayor, two councilmen with the principal citizens went out to invite them in. After some hesitation they marched in under the command of Gen. Slocum. . . . Immediately upon entering the town the stars and stripes were seen floating from the flag pole on the Franklin building. Father's store was used as a signal station. The signals were given with a blue flag having a large white star in the center and in the evening they used beautiful lanterns which were moved in different directions. This day has closed and is numbered with those past and gone and the moon once more shines over sleeping, silent Atlanta.

Sherman, who believed that "the brilliant success at Atlanta" had "made the election of Mr. Lincoln certain," probably expected this congratulatory message from Washington:[14]

EXECUTIVE MANSION,

WASHINGTON, D. C., September 3, 1864

The national thanks are rendered by the President to Major-General W. T. Sherman and the gallant officers and soldiers of his command before Atlanta, for the distinguished ability and perseverance displayed in the campaign in Georgia, which, under Divine favor, has resulted in the capture of Atlanta. The marches, battles, sieges, and other military operations that have signalized the campaign, must render it famous in the annals of war, and have entitled those who participated therein to the applause and thanks of the nation.

ABRAHAM LINCOLN,
President of the United States

Next day Sherman heard from an old friend:

CITY POINT, VIRGINIA, September 4, 1864—9 P.M.
MAJOR-GENERAL SHERMAN:

I have just received your dispatch announcing the capture of Atlanta. In honor of your great victory, I have ordered a salute to be fired with *shotted* guns from every battery bearing upon the enemy. The salute will be fired within an hour, amid great rejoicing.

U. S. GRANT, *Lieutenant-General*

VI

George B. McClellan also sensed that the fall of Atlanta made a difference in the presidential campaign. How could a man be elected on a platform which called the war a failure? In accepting the Democratic nomination McClellan threw away the party creed and wrote his own:[15]

ORANGE, N. J., September 8th
To HON. HORATIO SEYMOUR AND OTHERS, COMMITTEE, &c.:

GENTLEMEN: I have the honor to acknowledge the receipt of your letter informing me of my nomination by the Democratic National Convention recently held at Chicago, as their candidate at the next election for President of the United States.

It is unnecessary for me to say to you that this nomination comes to me unsought. I am happy to know that when the nomination was made, the record of my public life was kept in view. The effect of long and varied service in the army, during war and peace, has been to strengthen and make indelible in my mind and heart the love and reverence for the Union, Constitution, laws, and flag of our country impressed upon me in early youth. These feelings have thus far guided the course of my life, and must continue to do so until its end. The existence of more than one Government over the region which once owned our flag, is incompatible with the peace, the power, and the happiness of the people. The preservation of our Union was the sole avowed object for which the war was commenced. It should have been conducted for that object only, and in accordance with those principles which I took occasion to declare when in active service. Thus conducted the work of reconciliation would have been easy, and we might have reaped the benefits of our many victories on land and sea.

The Union was originally formed by the exercise of a spirit of conciliation and compromise. To restore and preserve it, the same spirit must prevail in our councils and in the hearts of the people. The reestablishment of the Union, in all its integrity, is and must continue to be the indispensable condition in any settlement. So soon as it is clear, or even probable, that our present adversaries are ready for peace upon the basis of the Union, we should exhaust all the resources of statesmanship practised by civilized nations and taught by the traditions of the American people, consistent with the honor and interests of the country, to secure such peace, reëstablish the Union, and guarantee for the future the constitutional rights of every State. The Union is the one condition of peace. We ask no more.*

Let me add what I doubt not was, although unexpressed, the sentiment of the Convention, as it is of the people they represent, that when any one State is willing to return to the Union it should be received at once with a full guarantee of all its constitutional rights. If a frank, earnest, and persistent effort to obtain these objects should fail, the responsibility for ulterior consequences will fall upon those who remain in arms against the Union, but the Union must be preserved at all hazards. I could not look in the face my gallant comrades of the army and navy who have survived so many bloody battles, and tell them that their labors and the sacrifice of so many of our slain and wounded

* In McClellan, who was willing to restore the Union with slavery, Frémont soon saw a greater menace than Lincoln. On September 22, Frémont renounced his own candidacy in an effort to strengthen Lincoln's opposition to McClellan.

brethren had been in vain, that we had abandoned that Union for which we had so often perilled our lives. A vast majority of our people, whether in the army or navy or at home, would, as I would, hail with unbounded joy the permanent restoration of peace on the basis of the Union under the Constitution, without the effusion of another drop of blood, but no peace can be permanent without Union. . . .

VII

In Atlanta, Sherman reached a decision:[16]

. . . I took up my headquarters in the house of Judge Lyons, which stood opposite one corner of the Court-House Square, and at once set about a measure already ordered, of which I had thought much and long, viz., to remove the entire civil population, and to deny to all civilians from the rear the expected profits of civil trade. Hundreds of sutlers and traders were waiting at Nashville and Chattanooga, greedy to reach Atlanta with their wares and goods, with which to drive a profitable trade with the inhabitants. I gave positive orders that none of these traders, except three (one for each separate army), should be permitted to come nearer than Chattanooga; and, moreover, I peremptorily required that all the citizens and families resident in Atlanta should go away, giving to each the option to go south or north, as their interests or feelings dictated. I was resolved to make Atlanta a pure military garrison or depot, with no civil population to influence military measures. I had seen Memphis, Vicksburg, Natchez and New Orleans, all captured from the enemy, and each at once was garrisoned by a full division of troops, if not more; so that success was actually crippling our armies in the field by detachments to guard and protect the interests of a hostile population.

I gave notice of this purpose, as early as the 4th of September, to General Halleck, in a letter concluding with these words:

"If the people raise a howl against my barbarity and cruelty, I will answer that war is war, and not popularity-seeking. If they want peace, they and their relatives must stop the war."

Among those who discovered that Sherman meant exactly what he said were Mary Rawson Day and her family:[17]

Thursday [September 8]. The order compelling all persons to evacuate the city was today plainly written out; we could not misunderstand it. All those whose husbands were in the service were to leave on Monday, while the remainder were given fifteen days to pack and leave. Now comes a deliberation as to which home we should choose. My grandparents, aunt and cousins were to leave on Monday for the South; besides I had relations and friends down in Southwestern Georgia. This would have made it much more pleasant for us and in addition to this, the climate was much more congenial in the South. That would undoubtedly have been our choice had not one great barrier here presented itself. This was that all men of the Confederacy were conscripted and were compelled to serve in the Army. This we knew Father could stand only a short time and he had no inclination to enter the Army. But a difficulty equally as great debarred us from entering life in the "Yankee land of Canaan," the difference in the currency occasioned this embarrassment. Father's property mostly consisted in lands and Confederate money so we had not means enough to venture North unless Pa could get something for his tobacco. So we were in a vacillating condition for several days.

Friday. Father made a visit to Col. Beckworth and Col. Easton to find if no disposition could be made of the tobacco, but ill fated weed though much loved and longed for by Yankee soldiery, you seem as ever to be only a source of trouble to those who possess and use you. No success was experienced and evening found us as undecided as in the morning.

Saturday dawns and another day of continued exertion and restless anxiety slowly passes. All of this time we had been wasting our precious fifteen days. Another appeal was made today to Col. Beckworth and he promised to see Gen. Sherman and obtain a written paper allowing us to dispose of our provisions and tobacco if he could. With this assurance we prepared to spend the approaching Sabbath.*

Hood attacked Sherman's order, clearing Atlanta of its civilian population, as a measure which "in studied and ingenious cruelty" surpassed "all acts ever before brought to my attention in the dark history of war." Sherman was ready to match Hood tongue-lashing for tongue-lashing any day:[18]

In the name of common-sense, I ask you not to appeal to a just God in such a sacrilegious manner. You who, in the midst of peace and

---

* Three days later Sherman gave his consent, and Mary wrote that they had resolved "to brave the severities of the cold North West, so we immediately prepared to emigrate to the prairies of Iowa."

prosperity, have plunged a nation into war—dark and cruel war—who dared and badgered us to battle, insulted our flag, seized our arsenals and forts that were left in the honorable custody of ordnance-sergeants, seized and made "prisoners of war" the very garrisons sent to protect your people against negroes and Indians, long before any overt act was committed by the (to you) hated Lincoln Government; tried to force Kentucky and Missouri into rebellion, spite of themselves; falsified the vote of Louisiana; turned loose your privateers to plunder unarmed ships; expelled Union families by the thousands, burned their houses, and declared, by an act of your Congress, the confiscation of all debts due Northern men for goods had and received! Talk thus to the marines, but not to me, who have seen these things, and who will this day make as much sacrifice for the peace and honor of the South as the best-born Southerner among you! If we must be enemies, let us be men, and fight it out as we propose to do, and not deal in such hypocritical appeals to God and humanity. God will judge us in due time, and he will pronounce whether it be more humane to fight with a town full of women and the families of a brave people at our back, or to remove them in time to places of safety among their own friends and people.

Some residents—among them the family of Maxwell R. Berry—could not find a way of leaving Atlanta (or did not honestly try to do so). As September faded in the occupied city, his ten-year-old daughter, Carrie, preserved the tedium and dreariness of a life disrupted by war:[19]

Sat. Sept. 24. This has ben a bright day and we all have ben ironing and cleaning up. We have had so much rain that a sun shiny day seems quite pleasant.

Sun. Sept. 25. Another long and lonely day without church. So cloudy we all lay about and read until we are all tired.

Mon. Sept. 26. I have not done much to day. I have ben up to Aunties several times to see Cousin Emma and Willie for the last time. They are going off to night for the north. We all feel so sorry to see her leave for we all feel so lonesome.

Tues. Sept. 27. This has been wash day. I went up to Aunties this evening and she gave me some quilt peaces and some doll clothes.

Wed. Sept. 28. This has been another rainy day. I have ben sewing some to day. I went up to Aunties and we brushed her hair for her.

Thurs. Sept. 29. We ironed to day and we got done by two o'clock and I went up to Aunties after I was done here and she gave me some rasenes.

Fri. Sept. 30. I have ben sewing some to day on my apron. There are so many soldiers pacing backward and forward.

From May to September, inclusive, Sherman calculated that the Atlanta campaign had cost him 4,423 killed, 22,822 wounded, and 4,442 missing—an aggregate loss of 31,687. The comparative Confederate casualties, by his reckoning, were 3,044 killed, 18,952 wounded, 12,983 missing—an aggregate loss of 34,979. But even in victory Sherman found reason for concern:[20]

General Thomas occupied a house on Marietta Street, which had a veranda with high pillars. We were sitting there one evening, talking about things generally, when General Thomas asked leave to send his trains back to Chattanooga, for the convenience and economy of forage. I inquired of him if he supposed we would be allowed much rest at Atlanta, and he said he thought we would, or that at all events it would not be prudent for us to go much further into Georgia because of our already long line of communication, viz., three hundred miles from Nashville. This was true; but there we were, and we could not afford to remain on the defensive, simply holding Atlanta and fighting for the safety of its railroad. I insisted on his retaining all trains, and on keeping all his divisions ready to move at a moment's warning. All the army, officers and men, seemed to relax more or less and sink into a condition of idleness. General Schofield was permitted to go to Knoxville, to look after matters in his Department of Ohio; and Generals Blair and Logan went home to look after politics. Many of the regiments were entitled to, and claimed, their discharge, by reason of the expiration of their term of service; so that with victory and success came also many causes of disintegration.

VIII

In Virginia, while an August sun still burned, Colonel Theodore Lyman went on an excursion down the James River to the headquarters of General Benjamin F. Butler, commanding the Army of the James:[21]

This was quite a festal day for us. The General, accompanied by the Frenchies,* Rosencrantz, Bache, Biddle and myself, paid a grand

* Two French officers, Colonel de Chanal and Captain Guzman, sent as a commission to observe the campaign, were the "Frenchies" aboard.

visit to Butler. Butler was in high feather. He is as proud of all his "fixin's" as a farmer over a prime potato patch. We first got on the Greyhound, an elegant steamer (Butler believes in making himself comfortable), and proceeded down the Appomattox, past City Point, and then bore up the James, passing Bermuda Hundred, with its flotilla of schooners and steamers. . . . We had got a good bit above Bermuda Hundred and were paddling along bravely when we came in sight of two gunboats; that is, common steamers with some heavy guns on board. There are many in the river and they go up and down to keep it clear. As we drew near, I saw the men were at quarters and the guns run out. We passed between the first boat and the high wooded bank, when I beheld the gunboat captain dancing up and down on the paddle-box and roaring to us: "The left bank is lined with sh-a-a-rp-shooters!" It would have edified you to have seen the swift dignity with which General Meade and his gallant Staff stepped from the open, upper deck to the shady seclusion of the cabin! Our skipper jingled "Stop her," with his engine-room bell, and stop she did. Here was a chance for war-god Butler. "Hey? What? Sharpshooters? Pshaw! Fiddledeedee! Stop her! Who said stop her? Mr. DeRay, tell the Captain to go on, *instantly!*" And Butler danced out on the open deck and stood, like George II at Dettingen, in "an attitude of fence." I, who looked for a brisk volley of musketry, fully expected to see him get a bullet in his extensive stomach. Meanwhile the Captain went on, and, as soon as we were clear, the naval party in the rear (or "astern," we ought to say) let go one big gun, with a tremendous *whang!* and sent a projectile about the size of a flour barrel on shore, severely wounding a great many bushes and trees. The other gunboat went ahead of us and kept up a little marine combat, all on her own hook. Whether there really were sharpshooters, I know not: I only think, if there *were*, it would be difficult to say which party was the more scared. . . .

During the summer stalemate, Horace Porter greeted important guests:[22]

Mrs. Grant had come East with the children, and Colonel Dent, her brother, was sent to meet them at Philadelphia, and bring them to City Point to pay a visit to the general. The children consisted of Frederick D., then fourteen years old; Ulysses S., Jr., twelve; Nellie R., nine; and Jesse R., six. Nellie was born on the 4th of July, and when a child an innocent deception had been practised upon her by her father in letting her believe that all the boisterous demonstrations and display of fire-works on Independence day were in honor of her birthday. The general was exceedingly fond of his family, and his meeting with them afforded him the happiest day he had seen since they parted. They were com-fortably lodged aboard the headquarters steamboat, but spent most of their time in camp. The morning after their arrival, when I stepped into the general's tent, I found him in his shirt-sleeves engaged in a rough-and-tumble wrestling-match with the two older boys. He had become red in the face, and seemed nearly out of breath from the exertion. The lads had just tripped him up, and he was on his knees on the floor grappling with the youngsters, and joining in their merry laughter, as if he were a boy again himself. I had several despatches in my hand, and when he saw that I had come on business, he disentangled him-self after some difficulty from the young combatants, rose to his feet, brushed the dust off his knees with his hand, and said in a sort of apologetic manner: "Ah, you know my weaknesses—my children and my horses." The children often romped with him, and he joined in their frolics as if they were all playmates together. The younger ones would hang about his neck while he was writing, making a terrible mess of his papers, and turn everything in his tent into a toy: but they were never once reproved for any innocent sport; they were governed solely by an appeal to their affections. They were always respectful, and never failed to render strict obedience to their father when he told them seriously what he wanted them to do.

Inside the Confederate lines Sidney Lanier watched Lee:[23]

The last time I saw him with mortal eyes—for with spiritual eyes many, many times have I contemplated him since—the scene was so beautiful, the surroundings were so rare, nay, time and circumstance did so fitly frame him as it were, that I think the picture should not be lost. There was nothing melodramatic in the circumstances, nothing startling, nothing sensational—which was all the more particularly in accord with his character, for this was one of those grand but modest, sweet souls that love simplicity and shrink from all that is loud and vulgar.

It was at fateful Petersburg on a glorious Sunday morning whilst the armies of Grant and Butler were investing our last stronghold there. It had been announced to those who happened to be stationed in the neighborhood of General Lee's headquarters that religious services would be conducted on that morning by Major General Pendleton of the artillery. At the appointed time I strolled over to Dunn's Hill where General Lee's tent was pitched and found General Pendleton ensconced under a magnificent tree, and a small party of soldiers with a few ladies from the dwellings near by, collected about him. In a few moments General Lee appeared with his camp chair and sat down. The services began. That terrible battery, Number Five, was firing very slowly, each report of the great gun making the otherwise profound silence still more profound. Even Hoke's line was quiet. I sat down on the grass and gazed, with such reverence as I had never given to mortal man before, upon the grand face of General Lee.

He had been greatly fatigued by loss of sleep. As the services progressed and the immortal words of the Christian doctrine came to our hearts and comforted us, sweet influences born of the liberal sunlight that lay warm upon the grass, of the waving leaves and trembling flowers, seemed to steal over the General's soul. Presently his eyelids closed and he fell gently asleep. Not a muscle of him stirred, not a nerve of his grand countenance twitched, there was no drooping of the head nor bowing of the figure. . . . As he slumbered so, sitting erect with his arms folded upon his chest in an attitude of majestic repose such as I never saw assumed by mortal man before; as the lazy cannon of the enemy anon hurled a screaming shell to within a few hundred yards of where we sat; as finally a bird flew into the tree overhead and piped small blissful notes in unearthly contrast with the roar of the war engines; it seemed to me as if the present earth floated off through the sunlight and the antique earth returned out of the past and some majestic god sat on a hill sculptured in stone presiding over a terrible yet sublime contest of human passions.

IX

North and South, newspapers reported what was happening in and around Atlanta and Richmond. Soon a campaign in the Shenandoah Valley dominated the news. Near Winchester, armies commanded by Jubal A. Early and Phil Sheridan, newly detached from the Army of the Potomac, faced each other. Early made the fatal error of underrating an unknown opponent:[24]

The relative positions which we occupied rendered my communications to the rear very much exposed, but I could not avoid it without giving up the lower Valley. The object of my presence there was to keep up a threatening attitude towards Maryland and Pennsylvania, and prevent the use of the Baltimore and Ohio railroad, and the Chesapeake and Ohio canal, as well as to keep as large a force as possible from Grant's army to defend the Federal Capital. Had Sheridan, by a prompt movement, thrown his whole force on the line of my communications, I would have been compelled to attempt to cut my way through, as there was no escape for me to the right or left, and my force was too weak to cross the Potomac while he was in my rear. I knew my danger, but I could occupy no other position that would have enabled me to accomplish the desired object. If I had moved up the valley at all [i.e., to the southwest], I could not have stopped short of New Market, for between that place and the country in which I was there was no forage for my horses; and this would have enabled the enemy to resume the use of the railroad and canal, and return all the troops from Grant's army to him. Being compelled to occupy the position where I was, and being aware of its danger as well as apprized of the fact that very great odds were opposed to me, my only resource was to use my forces so as to display them at different points with great rapidity, and thereby keep up the impression that they were much larger than they really were. The events of the last month had satisfied me that the commander opposed to me was without enterprise, and possessed an excessive caution which amounted to timidity. If it was his policy to produce the impression that his force was too weak to fight me, he did not succeed, but if it was to convince me that he was not an able or energetic commander, his strategy was a complete success, and subsequent events have not changed my opinion.

By September 19 Sheridan was ready. Two days later a future President of the United States—Rutherford B. Hayes—wrote to his wife:[25]

CAMP NEAR STRASBURG, VIRGINIA
September 21, 1864

. . . The fighting began at daylight Monday (19th), with our cavalry. Then the Sixth Corps fighting pretty well, joined in; and about 10:30 A.M. the Nineteenth took part—some portions of it behaving badly, losing ground, two guns, and some prisoners. We in the meantime were guarding the wagons (!). Since the fight they say Crook's command was the *reserve!*

By noon the battle was rather against [us]. The Rebels were jubilant and in Winchester were cheering and rejoicing over the victory.

We were sent for. General Crook in person superintended the whole
thing. At one o'clock, having passed around on the Rebel left, we
passed under a fire of cannon and musketry and pushed direct for a
battery on their extreme flank. This division was our extreme right. My
brigade in front, supported by Colonel White's old brigade. As soon as
we felt their fire we moved swiftly forward going directly at the battery.
The order was to walk fast, keep silent, until within about one hundred
yards of the guns, and then with a yell to charge at full speed. We
passed over a ridge and were just ready to begin the rush when we

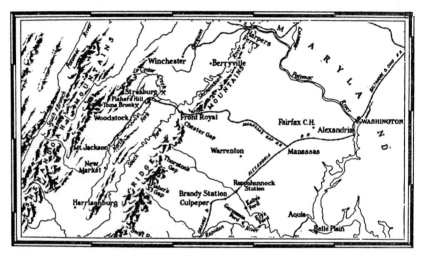

THE SHENANDOAH VALLEY, 1864

From *Atlas of American History*

came upon a deep creek with high banks, boggy, and perhaps twenty-
five yards wide.

The Rebel fire now broke out furiously. Of course the line stopped.
To stop was death. To go on was probably the same; but on we
started again. My horse plunged in and mired down hopelessly, just as
by frantic struggling he reached about the middle of the stream. I
jumped off, and down on all fours, succeeded in reaching the Rebel side
—but alone. Perhaps some distance above or below others were across.
I was about the middle of the brigade and saw nobody else, but hundreds were struggling in the stream. . . .

Soon they came flocking, all regiments mixed up—all order gone.
No chance of ever reforming, but pell-mell, over the obstructions, went
the crowd. Two cannons were captured; the rest run off. The whole of

Crook's command (both divisions) were soon over, with the general swinging his sword, and the Rebel position was successfully flanked, and victory in prospect for the first time that day.

We chased them three to five hundred yards, when we came in sight of a second line, strongly posted. We steadily worked towards them under a destructive fire. Sometimes we would be brought to a standstill by the storm of grape and musketry, but the flags (*yours* as advanced as any) would be pushed on and a straggling crowd would follow. With your flag were Twenty-third, Thirty-fourth, Thirty-sixth, and Seventy-first men, and so of all the others. Officers on horseback were falling faster than others, but all were suffering. . . .

Things began to look dark. The Nineteenth Corps next on our left were in a splendid line, but they didn't push. They stood and fired at long range! Many an anxious glance was cast that way. They were in plain sight, but no, or very little, effective help came from that handsome line. It was too far off. At the most critical moment a large body of that splendid cavalry, with sabres drawn, moved slowly around our right beyond the creek. They at a trot and finally with shouts at a gallop charged right into the Rebel lines. We pushed on and away broke the Rebels. The cavalry came back, and an hour later and nearly a mile back, the same scene again; and a third time; and the victory was ours just at sundown. . . .

We are following the retreating Rebels. They will get into an entrenched position before fighting again, and I suspect we shall not assault them in strong works. So I look for no more fighting with General Early this campaign.

Early continued to belittle his opponent, and his own losses:[26]

This battle, beginning with the skirmishing in Ramseur's front, had lasted from daylight until dark, and, at the close of it, we had been forced back two miles, after having repulsed the enemy's first attack with great slaughter to him, and subsequently contested every inch of ground with unsurpassed obstinacy. We deserved the victory, and would have had it, but for the enemy's immense superiority in cavalry, which alone gave it to him. . . .

A skillful and energetic commander of the enemy's forces would have crushed Ramseur before any assistance could have reached him, and thus ensured the destruction of my whole force; and, later in the day, when the battle had turned against us, with the immense superiority in cavalry which Sheridan had, and the advantage of the open country, would have destroyed my whole force and captured everything I had. As it was, considering the immense disparity in numbers and equipment, the enemy had very little to boast of. I had lost a few pieces of artillery and some very valuable officers and men, but the main part of my force and all my trains had been saved, and the enemy's loss in killed and wounded was far greater than mine. When I look back to this battle, I can but attribute my escape from utter annihilation to the incapacity of my opponent.

John B. Gordon, one of Early's major generals, faced facts:[27]

The pursuit was pressed far into the twilight, and only ended when night came and dropped her protecting curtains around us.

Drearily and silently, with burdened brains and aching hearts, leaving our dead and many of the wounded behind us, we rode hour after hour, with our sore-footed, suffering men doing their best to keep up, anxiously inquiring for their commands and eagerly listening for orders to halt and sleep.

Lucky was the Confederate private who on that mournful retreat knew his own captain, and most lucky was the commander who knew where to find the main body of his own troops. The only lamps to guide us were the benignant stars, dimly lighting the gray surface of the broad limestone turnpike. It was, however, a merciful darkness. It came too slowly for our comfort; but it came at last, and screened our weary and confused infantry from further annoyance by Sheridan's horsemen. Little was said by any officer. Each was left to his own thoughts and the contemplation of the shadows that were thickening around us. What was the morrow to bring, or the next month, or the next year? There was no limit to lofty courage, to loyal devotion, and the spirit of self-sacrifice; but where were the men to come from to take the places of the maimed and the dead? Where were the arsenals from which to replace the diminishing materials of war so essential to our future defence? It was evident that these thoughts were running through the brains of rank and file; for now and then there came a cheering flash of rustic wit or grim humor from the privates: "Cheer up, boys; don't be worried. We'll lick them Yankees the first fair chance, and get more grub and guns and things than our poor old quartermaster mules can pull." Distinct in my memory now (they will be there till I die) are those startling manifestations of a spirit which nothing could break, that strange commingling of deep-drawn sighs and merry songs, the marvellous blending of an hour of despair with an hour of bounding hope, inspired by the most resolute manhood ever exhibited in any age or country. . . .

When the night was far spent and a sufficient distance between the Confederate rear and the Union front had been reached, there came the order to halt—more grateful than sweetest music to the weary soldiers' ears; and down they dropped on their beds of grass or earth, their heads pillowed on dust-covered knapsacks, their rifles at their sides, and their often shoeless feet bruised and aching.

But they slept. Priceless boon—sleep and rest for tired frame and heart and brain!

Gordon saw no reason to minimize the Confederate defeat at Fisher's Hill, with which Sheridan capped his victory at Winchester:

General Sheridan graciously granted us two days and a part of the third to stop and rest and pull ourselves together for the struggle of September 22. The battle, or, to speak more accurately, the bout at Fisher's Hill, was so quickly ended that it may be described in a few words. Indeed, to all experienced soldiers the whole story is told in one word—"flanked."

We had again halted and spread our banners on the ramparts which nature built along the Shenandoah's banks. Our stay was short, however, and our leaving was hurried, without ceremony or concert. It is the old story of failure to protect flanks. Although the Union forces more than doubled Early's army, our position was such that in our stronghold we could have whipped General Sheridan had the weak point on our left been sufficiently protected. Sheridan demonstrated in front while he slipped his infantry around our left and completely enveloped that flank. An effort was made to move Battle and Wharton to the enveloped flank in order to protect it, but the effort was made too late. The Federals saw their advantage, and seized and pressed it. The Confederates saw the hopelessness of their situation, and realized that they had only the option of retreat or capture. They were not long in deciding. The retreat (it is always so) was at first stubborn and slow, then rapid, then—a rout.

THE TEST
OF FREEDOM

O CTOBER BECAME a troublesome month for Sherman. Hood, intent on restoring the "fighting spirit" in his Army of Tennessee, endeavored to turn Sherman's right flank, destroy his communications, and thus force the Federals to loosen their hold on Atlanta. On the fourth of October, Hood struck the railroad at Acworth and Big Shanty, capturing some four hundred prisoners. But Hood was playing for much bigger game—the more than a million Federal rations at Allatoona.

I

Sherman rushed down troops from Rome to save those rations, but floods had spread the railroad tracks and at least a third of a badly outnumbered Federal force never reached the field. For the Union commander, John Corse, the situation looked glum. Yet few generals could excel Corse at fighting like a bobcat:[1]

Under a brisk cannonade, kept up for near two hours, with sharp skirmishing on our south front and our west flank, the enemy pushed a brigade of infantry around north of us, cut the railroad and telegraph, severing our communication with Cartersville and Rome. The cannonading and musketry had not ceased, when, at half-past eight A.M., I received by flag of truce, which came from the north, on the Cartersville road, the following summons to surrender:

AROUND ALLATOONA, October 5, 1864
COMMANDING OFFICER U. S. FORCES, ALLATOONA:

SIR: I have placed the forces under my command in such positions, that you are surrounded, and to avoid a needless effusion of blood, I call on you to surrender your forces at once and unconditionally. Five minutes will be allowed you to decide. Should you accede to this, you will be treated in the most honorable manner as prisoners of war. I have the honor to be, very respectfully yours,

S. G. FRENCH,
Major-General Commanding Forces C. S.

To which I made the following reply:

HEADQUARTERS FOURTH DIVISION, FIFTEENTH ARMY CORPS,
ALLATOONA, GA., 8.30 A.M., October 5, 1864.
MAJOR-GENERAL S. G. FRENCH, C. S. ARMY, ETC.:

Your communication demanding surrender of my command, I acknowledge receipt of, and respectfully reply that we are prepared for the "needless effusion of blood," whenever it is agreeable to you. I am, very respectfully, your obedient servant,

JOHN M. CORSE,
Brigadier-General Commanding Forces U. S.

I then hastened to my different commands, informing them of the object of the flag, etc., my answer, and the importance and necessity of their preparing for hard fighting. I directed Colonel Rowett to hold the spur, on which the Thirty-ninth Iowa and Seventh Illinois were formed; sent Colonel Tourtelotte over to the east hill, with orders to hold it to the last, sending to me for reënforcements, if needed. Taking two companies of the Ninety-third Illinois down a spur parallel with railroad and along the brink of the cut, so disposed them as to hold the north side as long as possible. Three companies of the Ninety-third, which had been driven in from the west end of the ridge, were distributed in the ditch south of the redoubt, with instructions to keep the town well covered by their fire and watch the dépôt, where were stored over a million rations. The remaining battalion, under Major Fisher, lay between the redoubt and Rowett's line, ready to reënforce wherever most needed.

I had hardly issued the incipient orders, when the storm broke in all

its fury on the Thirty-ninth Iowa and Seventh Illinois.* Young's brigade of Texans, one thousand nine hundred strong, had gained the
west end of the ridge, and moved with great impetuosity along its crest,
till they struck Rowett's command, where they received a severe check;
but, undaunted, they came again and again. Rowett, reënforced by the
Ninety-third Illinois, and aided by the gallant Redfield, encouraged me
to hope we were safe here, when I observed a brigade of the enemy, under General Sears, moving from the north, its left extending across the
railroad.

I rushed to the two companies of the Ninety-third Illinois, which
were on the brink of the cut running north from the redoubt and parallel with the railroad, they having been reënforced by the retreating
pickets, and urged them to hold on to the spur; but it was of no avail.
The enemy's line of battle swept us like so much chaff, and struck the
Thirty-ninth Iowa in flank, threatening to engulf our little band without further ado. Fortunately for us, Colonel Tourtelotte's fire caught
Sears in flank, and broke him so badly as to enable me to get a staff-
officer over the cut with orders to bring the Fiftieth Illinois over to re-
enforce Rowett, who had lost very heavily.

However, before the regiment sent for could arrive, Sears and Young
both rallied, and made their assaults in front and on the flank with so
much vigor and in such force, as to break Rowett's line, and had not
the Thirty-ninth Iowa fought with the desperation it did, I never would
have been able to get a man back into the redoubt. As it was, their
hand-to-hand conflict and stubborn stand broke the enemy to that extent, he must stop and reform, before undertaking the assault on the
fort. Under cover of the blow they gave the enemy, the Seventh and
Ninety-third Illinois, and what remained of the Thirty-ninth Iowa, fell
back into the fort.

The fighting up to this time (about eleven A.M.) was of a most extraordinary character. Attacked from the north, from the west, and
from the south, these three regiments, Thirty-ninth Iowa, Seventh and
Ninety-third Illinois, held Young's and a portion of Sears's and Cock-
erel's brigades at bay for nearly two hours and a half. The gallant
Colonel Redfield, of the Thirty-ninth Iowa, fell shot in four places, and
the extraordinary valor of the men and officers of this regiment, and of
the Seventh Illinois, saved to us Allatoona. So completely disorganized

* Illinois had sent six volunteer regiments to the Mexican War. In the history
of the state, they were revered. Therefore, the first of the Illinois Civil War
regiments was numbered the Seventh.

was the enemy, that no regular assault could be made on the fort, till I had the trenches all filled, and the parapets lined with men.

The Twelfth Illinois and Fiftieth Illinois arriving from the east hill, enabled us to occupy every foot of trench and keep up a line of fire that, as long as our ammunition lasted, would render our little fort impregnable.

The broken pieces of the enemy enabled them to fill every hollow and take every advantage of the rough ground surrounding the fort, filling every hole and trench, seeking shelter behind every stump and log that lay within musket-range of the fort. We received their fire from the north, south, and west face of the redoubt, completely in face of the murderous fire of the enemy now concentrated upon us. The artillery was silent for want of ammunition, and a brave fellow, whose name I regret having forgotten, volunteered to cross the cut, which was under fire of the enemy, and go to the fort on the east hill and procure some ammunition. Having executed his mission successfully, he returned in a short time with an arm-load of canister and case-shot. About half-past two P.M., the enemy were observed massing a force behind a small house and the ridge on which the house was located, distant north-west from the fort about one hundred and fifty yards.

The dead and wounded were moved aside, so as to enable us to move a piece of artillery to an embrasure commanding the house and ridge. A few shots from the gun threw the enemy's column into great confusion, which, being observed by our men, caused them to rush to the parapet and open such a heavy and continuous musketry-fire that it was impossible for the enemy to rally.

From this time until near four P.M., we enfilading our ditches and rendering it almost impracticable for a man to expose his person above the parapet, an effort was made to carry our work by assault, but the battery (Twelfth Wisconsin) was so ably manned and so gallantly fought as to render it impossible for a column to live within one hundred yards of the work. Officers labored constantly to stimulate the men to exertion, and most all that were killed or wounded in the fort met their fate while trying to get the men to expose themselves above the parapet and nobly setting them the example.

The enemy kept up a constant and intense fire, gradually closing around us and rapidly filling our little fort with the dead and dying.

About one P.M., I was wounded by a rifle-ball, which rendered me insensible for some thirty or forty minutes, but managed to rally on hearing some person or persons cry, "Cease firing!" which conveyed to me the impression that they were trying to surrender the fort.

Again I urged my staff, the few officers left unhurt, and the men around me, to renewed exertion, assuring them that Sherman would soon be there with reënforcements.

The gallant fellows struggled to keep their heads above the ditch and parapet, had the advantage of the enemy, and maintained it with such success that they were driven from every position, and finally fled in confusion, leaving the dead and wounded and our little garrison in possession of the field.

Sherman pressed hard after Hood, for, as the Union general subsequently confessed, a "wild" scheme possessed him:[2]

On the sixth and seventh, I pushed my cavalry well toward Burnt Hickory and Dallas, and discovered that the enemy had moved westward, and inferred that he would attempt to break our railroad again in the neighborhood of Kingston. Accordingly, on the morning of the eighth, I put the army in motion through Allatoona Pass to Kingston, reaching that point on the tenth. There I learned that the enemy had feigned on Rome, and was passing the Coosa River on a pontoon-bridge about eleven miles below Rome. I therefore, on the eleventh, moved to Rome, and pushed Garrard's cavalry and the Twenty-third corps, under General Cox, across the Oostenaula, to threaten the flanks of the enemy passing north. Garrard's cavalry drove a cavalry brigade of the enemy to and beyond the Narrows, leading into the valley of the Chattooga, capturing two field-pieces and taking some prisoners.

The enemy had moved with great rapidity, and made his appearance at Resaca; and Hood had in person demanded its surrender. I had from Kingston reënforced Resaca by two regiments of the army of the Tennessee. I at first intended to move the army into the Chattooga valley, to interpose between the enemy and his line of retreat down the Coosa, but feared that General Hood would, in that event, turn eastward by Spring Place, and down the Federal Road, and therefore moved against him at Resaca. Colonel Weaver, at Resaca, afterward reënforced by General Raum's brigade, had repulsed the enemy from Resaca, but he had succeeded in breaking the railroad from Tilton to Dalton, and as far north as the Tunnel.

Arriving at Resaca on the evening of the fourteenth, I determined to strike Hood in flank, or force him to battle, and directed the army of the Tennessee, General Howard, to move to Snake Creek Gap, which was held by the enemy, whilst General Stanley, with the Fourth and Fourteenth corps, moved by Tilton across the mountains to the rear of Snake Creek Gap, in the neighborhood of Villanow.

The army of the Tennessee found the enemy occupying our old lines in the Snake Creek Gap, and on the fifteenth skirmished for the purpose of holding him there until Stanley could get to his rear. But the enemy gave way about noon, and was followed through the Gap, escaping before General Stanley had reached the further end of the Pass. The next day, the sixteenth, the armies moved directly toward La Fayette, with a view to cut off Hood's retreat. We found him intrenched in Ship's Gap, but the leading division (Wood's) of the Fifteenth corps rapidly carried the advanced posts held by two companies of a South-Carolina regiment, making them prisoners. The remaining eight companies escaped to the main body near La Fayette. The next morning we passed over into the valley of the Chattooga, the army of the Tennessee moving in pursuit by La Fayette and Alpine, toward Blue Pond; the army of the Cumberland by Summerville and Melville Post-Office to Gaylesville; and the army of the Ohio and Garrard's cavalry from Villanow, Dirttown Valley, and Goover's Gap to Gaylesville. Hood, however, was little encumbered with trains, and marched with great rapidity, and had succeeded in getting into the narrow gorge formed by the Lookout Range abutting against the Coosa River, in the neighborhood of Gadsden. He evidently wanted to avoid a fight.

On the nineteenth, all the armies were grouped about Gaylesville, in the rich valley of the Chattooga, abounding in corn and meat, and I determined to pause in my pursuit of the enemy, to watch his movements and live on the country. I hoped that Hood would turn toward Guntersville and Bridgeport. The army of the Tennessee was posted near Little River, with instructions to feel forward in support of the cavalry, which was ordered to watch Hood in the neighborhood of Wills's Valley, and to give me the earliest notice possible of his turning northward. The army of the Ohio was posted at Cedar Bluff, with orders to lay a pontoon across the Coosa, and to feel forward to centre, and down in the direction of Blue Mountain. The army of the Cumberland was held in reserve at Gaylesville; and all the troops were instructed to draw heavily for supplies from the surrounding country. In the mean time communications were opened to Rome, and a heavy force set to work in repairing the damages done to our railroads. Atlanta was abundantly supplied with provisions, but forage was scarce; and General Slocum was instructed to send strong foraging parties out in the direction of

South River, and collect all the corn and fodder possible, and to put his own trains in good condition for further service.

Hood's movements and strategy had demonstrated that he had an army capable of endangering at all times my communications, but unable to meet me in open fight. To follow him would simply amount to being decoyed away from Georgia, with little prospect of overtaking and overwhelming him. To remain on the defensive, would have been bad policy for an army of so great value as the one I then commanded; and I was forced to adopt a course more fruitful in results than the naked one of following him to the South-West. I had previously submitted to the Commander-in-Chief a general plan, which amounted substantially to the destruction of Atlanta and the railroad back to Chattanooga, and sallying forth from Atlanta through the heart of Georgia, to capture one or more of the great Atlantic seaports. This I renewed from Gaylesville, modified somewhat by the change of events.

II

In the Shenandoah Valley Sheridan carried out a policy which Grant had decided upon three months earlier. On July 19, a few days after Early had frightened Washington, Grant had written to Halleck: "If the enemy has left Maryland, as I suppose he has, he should have upon his heels veterans, militiamen, men on horseback and everything that can be got to follow, to eat out Virginia clear and clean as far as they go, so that crows flying over it for the balance of this season will have to carry their provender with them."

The Valley had been granted a respite until Winchester and Fisher's Hill. Then its time came. Sheridan reported to Grant:[3]

WOODSTOCK, October 7, 1864—9 P.M.

I have the honor to report my command at this point tonight. I commenced moving back from Port Republic, Mount Crawford, Bridgewater, and Harrisonburg yesterday morning. The grain and forage in advance of these points up to Staunton had previously been destroyed. In moving back to this point the whole country from the Blue Ridge to the North Mountains has been made untenable for a rebel army. I have destroyed over 2,000 barns filled with wheat, hay, and farming implements; over seventy mills filled with flour and wheat; have driven in front of the army over 4,000 head of stock, and have killed and issued to the troops not less than 3,000 sheep. This destruction embraces the Luray Valley and Little Fort Valley, as well as the main valley. A large number of horses have been obtained, a proper estimate of which I cannot now make. Lieut. John R. Meigs, my engineer officer, was murdered beyond Harrisonburg, near Dayton. For this atrocious act all the houses within five miles were burned. Since I came into the Valley, from Harper's Ferry up to Harrisonburg, every train, every small party, and every straggler has been bushwhacked by people, many of whom have protection papers from commanders who have been hitherto in this valley. From the vicinity of Harrisonburg over 400 wagonloads of refugees have been sent back to Martinsburg; most of these people were Dunkers and had been conscripted. The people here are getting sick of the war; heretofore they have had no reason to complain, because they have been living in great abundance. . . .

Tomorrow I will continue the destruction of wheat, forage, etc., down to Fisher's Hill. When this is completed the Valley, from Winchester up to Staunton, ninety-two miles, will have but little in it for man or beast.

Henry Kyd Douglas, Confederate cavalry officer, confirmed Sheridan's report:[4]

Then [October 1], . . . Sheridan set his cavalry to work on their campaign of arson, rapine, and starvation. . . .

I try to restrain my bitterness at the recollection of the dreadful scenes I witnessed. I rode down the Valley with the advance after Sheridan's retreating cavalry beneath great columns of smoke which almost shut out the sun by day, and in the red glare of bonfires, which, all across that Valley, poured out flames and sparks heavenward and crackled mockingly in the night air; and I saw mothers and maidens tearing their hair and shrieking to Heaven in their fright and despair, and little children, voiceless and tearless in their pitiable terror. I saw a beautiful girl, the daughter of a clergyman, standing in the front door of her home while its stable and outbuildings were burning, tearing the yellow tresses from her head, taking up and repeating the oaths of passing skirmishers and shrieking with wild laughter, for the horrors of the night had driven her mad. It is little wonder that General Grant in his *Memoirs* passes over this work as if he could not bear to touch it, and that no reputable historian of the North has ventured to tell the truth about it and defend it, for it is an insult to civilization and to God to pretend that the Laws of War justify such warfare.

III

While Sheridan burned and ravaged in the Valley, Early re-formed his battered troops and started after the Federals. On October 18 Sheridan

made a quick trip to Washington. The following morning, while he was
still at Winchester on his way back, Early struck. John B. Gordon re-
ported an initial Confederate victory—and an inexplicable lapse on
Early's part:[5]

The whole situation was unspeakably impressive. Everything con-
spired to make the conditions both thrilling and weird. The men were
resting, lying in long lines on the thickly matted grass or reclining in
groups, their hearts thumping, their ears eagerly listening for the orders: "Attention, men!" "Fall in!" "Forward!" At brief intervals
members of the staff withdrew to a point where they could safely strike
a match and examine watches in order to keep me advised of the time.
In the still starlit night, the only sounds heard were the gentle rustle of
leaves by the October wind, the low murmur of the Shenandoah flowing swiftly along its rocky bed and dashing against the limestone cliffs
that bordered it, the churning of the water by the feet of horses on
which sat Sheridan's faithful pickets, and the subdued tones or half-
whispers of my men as they thoughtfully communed with each other as
to the fate which might befall each in the next hour. . . .

The minute-hand of the watch admonished us that it was time to
move in order to reach Sheridan's flank at the hour agreed upon. General Payne of Virginia, one of the ablest and most knightly soldiers in
the Confederate army, plunged with his intrepid cavalry into the river,
and firing as they went upon Sheridan's mounted pickets and supporting squadrons, the Virginians dashed in pursuit as if in steeplechase
with the Union riders, the coveted goal for both being the rear of Sheridan's army. The Federals sought it for safety. Payne was seeking it to
spread confusion and panic in the Federal ranks and camps; and magnificently did he accomplish his purpose. . . .

As soon as Payne had cleared the ford for the infantry, Evans, with
his Virginians, North Carolinians, and Georgians, the old Stonewall
Brigade leading, rushed into the cold current of the Shenandoah, chilled
as it was by the October nights and frosts. The brave fellows did not
hesitate for a moment. Reaching the eastern bank drenched and cold,
they were ready for the "double quick," which warmed them up and
brought them speedily to the left flank of Sheridan's sleeping
army. . . .

The surprise was complete. The victory was won in a space of time
inconceivably short, and with a loss to the Confederates incredibly
small. Sheridan's brave men had lain down in their tents on the preced-

ing night feeling absolutely protected by his intrenchments and his faithful riflemen who stood on guard. They were startled in their dreams and aroused from their slumbers by the rolls of musketry in nearly every direction around them, and terrified by the whizzing of Minié balls through their tents and the yelling of exultant foemen in their very midst. They sprang from their beds to find Confederate bayonets at their breasts. Large numbers were captured. Many hundreds were shot down as they attempted to escape. Two entire corps, the Eighth and Nineteenth, constituting more than two thirds of Sheridan's army, broke and fled, leaving the ground covered with arms, accoutrements, knapsacks, and the dead bodies of their comrades. Across the open fields they swarmed in utter disorganization, heedless of their officers' commands—heedless of all things save getting to the rear. There was nothing else for them to do; for Sheridan's magnificent cavalry was in full retreat before Rosser's bold troopers, who were in position to sweep down upon the other Union flank and rear.

A little after sunrise we had captured nearly all of the Union artillery; we had scattered in veriest rout two thirds of the Union army; while less than one third of the Confederate forces had been under fire, and that third intact and jubilant. Only the Sixth Corps of Sheridan's entire force held its ground. It was on the right rear and had been held in reserve. It stood like a granite breakwater, built to beat back the oncoming flood; but it was also doomed unless some marvellous intervention should check the Confederate concentration which was forming against it. . . . It was at that hour largely outnumbered, and I had directed every Confederate command then subject to my orders to assail it in front and upon both flanks simultaneously. At the same time I had directed the brilliant chief of artillery, Colonel Thomas H. Carter of Virginia . . . to gallop along the broad highway with all his batteries and with every piece of captured artillery available, and to pour an incessant stream of shot and shell upon this solitary remaining corps, explaining to him at the same time the movements I had ordered the infantry to make. As Colonel Carter surveyed the position of Sheridan's Sixth Corps (it could not have been better placed for our purposes), he exclaimed: "General, you will need no infantry. With enfilade fire from my batteries I will destroy that corps in twenty minutes."

At this moment General Early came upon the field, and said:

"Well, Gordon, this is glory enough for one day. This is the 19th. Precisely one month ago today we were going in the opposite direction."

His allusion was to our flight from Winchester on the 19th of September. I replied: "It is very well so far, general; but we have one more blow to strike, and then there will not be left an organized company of infantry in Sheridan's army."

I pointed to the Sixth Corps and explained the movements I had ordered, which I felt sure would compass the capture of that corps—certainly its destruction. When I had finished, he said: "No use in that; they will all go directly."

"That is the Sixth Corps, general. It will not go unless we drive it from the field."

"Yes, it will go too, directly."

My heart went into my boots. Visions of the fatal halt on the first day at Gettysburg, and of the whole day's hesitation to permit an assault on Grant's exposed flank on the 6th of May in the Wilderness, rose before me. And so it came to pass that the fatal halting, the hesitation, the spasmodic firing, and the isolated movements in the face of the sullen, slow, and orderly retreat of this superb Federal corps, lost us the great opportunity. . . .

Sheridan heard the distant roar of artillery just in time:[6]

Toward 6 o'clock the morning of the 19th, the officer on picket duty at Winchester came to my room, I being yet in bed, and reported artillery firing from the direction of Cedar Creek. I asked him if the firing was continuous or only desultory, to which he replied that it was not a sustained fire, but rather irregular and fitful. I remarked: "It's all right; Grover has gone out this morning to make a reconnoissance, and he is merely feeling the enemy." I tried to go to sleep again, but grew so restless that I could not, and soon got up and dressed myself. A little later the picket officer came back and reported that the firing, which could be distinctly heard from his line on the heights outside of Winchester, was still going on. I asked him if it sounded like a battle, and as he again said that it did not, I still inferred that the cannonading was caused by Grover's division banging away at the enemy simply to find out what he was up to. However, I went down-stairs and requested that breakfast be hurried up, and at the same time ordered the horses to be saddled and in readiness, for I concluded to go to the front before any further examinations were made in regard to the defensive line.

We mounted our horses between half-past 8 and 9, and as we were proceeding up the street which leads directly through Winchester . . .

to the Valley pike, I noticed that there were many women at the windows and doors of the houses, who kept shaking their skirts at us and who were otherwise markedly insolent in their demeanor, but supposing this conduct to be instigated by their well-known and perhaps natural prejudices, I ascribed to it no unusual significance. On reaching the edge of the town I halted a moment, and there heard quite distinctly the sound of artillery firing in an unceasing roar. Concluding from this that a battle was in progress, I now felt confident that the women along the street had received intelligence from the battle-field by the "grape-vine telegraph," and were in raptures over some good news, while I as yet was utterly ignorant of the actual situation. Moving on, I put my head down toward the pommel of my saddle and listened intently, trying to locate and interpret the sound, continuing in this position till we crossed Mill Creek, about half a mile from Winchester. The result of my efforts in the interval was the conviction that the travel of the sound was increasing too rapidly to be accounted for by my own rate of motion, and that therefore my army must be falling back.

At Mill Creek my escort fell in behind, and we were going ahead at a regular pace, when, just as we made the crest of the rise beyond the stream, there burst upon our view the appalling spectacle of a panic-stricken army—hundreds of slightly wounded men, throngs of others unhurt but utterly demoralized, and baggage-wagons by the score, all pressing to the rear in hopeless confusion, telling only too plainly that a disaster had occurred at the front. On accosting some of the fugitives, they assured me that the army was broken up, in full retreat, and that all was lost; all this with a manner true to that peculiar indifference that takes possession of panic-stricken men. . . .

For a short distance I traveled on the road, but soon found it so blocked with wagons and wounded men that my progress was impeded, and I was forced to take to the adjoining fields to make haste. When most of the wagons and wounded were past I returned to the road, which was thickly lined with unhurt men, who, having got far enough to the rear to be out of danger, had halted, without any organization, and begun cooking coffee, but when they saw me they abandoned their coffee, threw up their hats, shouldered their muskets, and as I passed along turned to follow with enthusiasm and cheers. To acknowledge this exhibition of feeling I took off my hat, and with Forsyth and O'Keefe rode some distance in advance of my escort, while every mounted officer who saw me galloped out on either side of the pike to tell the men at a distance that I had come back. In this way the news was spread to the stragglers off the road, when they, too, turned their faces to the front and marched toward the enemy, changing in a moment from the depths of depression to the extreme of enthusiasm. I already knew that even in the ordinary condition of mind enthusiasm is a potent element with soldiers, but what I saw that day convinced me that if it can be excited from a state of despondency its power is almost irresistible. I said nothing except to remark, as I rode among those on the road: "If I had been with you this morning this disaster would not have happened. We must face the other way; we will go back and recover our camp."

John B. Gordon, bitter at Early's indecision, saw Confederate victory slip away:[7]

When the long hours of dallying with the Sixth Corps had passed, and our afternoon alignment was made, there was a long gap, with scarcely a vedette to guard it between my right and the main Confederate line. . . . Every Confederate commander of our left wing foresaw the crash which speedily came. One after another of my staff was directed to ride with all speed to General Early and apprise him of the hazardous situation. Receiving no satisfactory answer, I myself finally rode to headquarters to urge that he re-enforce the left and fill the gap, which would prove a veritable death-trap if left open many minutes longer; or else that he concentrate his entire force for desperate defence or immediate withdrawal. He instructed me to stretch out the already weak lines and take a battery of guns to the left. I rode back at a furious gallop to execute these most unpromising movements. It was too late. The last chance had passed of saving the army from the doom which had been threatened for hours. Major Kirkpatrick had started with his guns, rushing across the plain to the crumbling Confederate lines like fire-engines tearing through streets in the vain effort to save a building already wrapped in flames and tumbling to the ground. I reached my command only in time to find the unresisted columns of Sheridan rushing through this gap, and, worse still, to find Clement A. Evans, whom I left in command, almost completely surrounded by literally overwhelming numbers; but he was handling the men with great skill, and fighting in almost every direction with characteristic coolness. It required counter-charges of the most daring character to prevent the utter destruction of the command and effect its withdrawal. At the same instant additional Union forces, which had penetrated through the vacant space, were assailing our main line on the flank and rolling it up like a scroll. Regiment after regiment, brigade after brigade, in rapid succession was crushed, and, like hard clods of clay under a pelting rain, the superb commands crumbled to pieces. The sun was sinking, but the spasmodic battle still raged. Wrapped in clouds of smoke and gathering darkness, the overpowered Confederates stubbornly yielded before the advancing Federals.

There was no yelling on the one side, nor huzzahs on the other. The gleaming blazes from hot muzzles made the murky twilight lurid. The line of light from Confederate guns grew shorter and resistance fainter. The steady roll of musketry, punctuated now and then by peals of thunder from retreating or advancing batteries, suddenly ceased; and resistance ended as the last organized regiment of Early's literally overwhelmed army broke and fled in the darkness. As the tumult of battle died away, there came from the north side of the plain a dull, heavy swelling sound like the roaring of a distant cyclone, the omen of additional disaster. It was unmistakable. Sheridan's horsemen were riding furiously across the open fields of grass to intercept the Confederates before they crossed Cedar Creek. Many were cut off and captured. As the sullen roar from horses' hoofs beating the soft turf of the plain told of the near approach of the cavalry, all effort at orderly retreat was abandoned. The only possibility of saving the rear regiments was in unrestrained flight—every man for himself. Mounted officers gathered here and there squads of brave men who poured volleys into the advancing lines of blue; but it was too late to make effective resistance.

In the dim starlight, after crossing the creek, I gathered around me a small force representing nearly every command in Early's army, intending to check, if possible, the further pursuit, or at least to delay it long enough to enable the shattered and rapidly retreating fragments to escape. The brave fellows responded to my call and formed a line across the pike. The effort was utterly fruitless, however, and resulted only in hair-breadth escapes and unexampled experiences. . . .

At the point where I attempted to make a stand at night, the pike ran immediately on the edge of one of those abrupt and rugged limestone cliffs down which it was supposed not even a rabbit could plunge without breaking his neck; and I proved it to be nearly true. One end of my short line of gray-jackets rested on the pike at this forbidding precipice. I had scarcely gotten my men in position when I discovered that Sheridan's dragoons had crossed the creek higher up, and that I was surrounded by them on three sides, while on the other was this breakneck escarpment. These enterprising horsemen in search of their game had located my little band, and at the sound of the bugle they came in headlong charge. Only one volley from my men and the Federal cavalry were upon them. Realizing that our capture was imminent, I shouted to my men to escape, if possible, in the darkness. One minute more and I should have had a Yankee carbine at my head, inviting my surrender. The alternatives were the precipice or Yankee prison. There was no time to debate the question, not a moment. Wheeling my horse to the dismal brink, I drove my spurs into his flanks, and he plunged downward and tumbled headlong in one direction, sending me in another. How I reached the bottom of that abyss I shall never know; for I was rendered temporarily unconscious. Strangely enough, I was only stunned, and in no way seriously hurt. My horse, too, though bruised, was not disabled. For a moment I thought he was dead, for he lay motionless and prone at full length. However, he promptly responded to my call and rose to his feet; and although the bare places on his head and hips showed that he had been hurt, he was ready without a groan to bear me again in any direction I might wish to go. . . .

It was, perhaps, an hour or more after nightfall, and yet the vanguard of Sheridan's army had not halted. Considerable numbers of them were now between me and the retreating Confederates. The greater part of the country on each side of the pike, however, was open, and I was fairly familiar with it all. There was no serious difficulty, therefore, in passing around the Union forces, who soon went into camp for the night. Lonely, thoughtful, and sad—sadder and more thoughtful, if possible, on this nineteenth night of October than on the corresponding night of the previous month at Winchester—I rode through open fields, now and then finding squads of Confederates avoiding the pike to escape capture, and occasionally a solitary soldier as lonely, if not as sad and thoughtful, as I.

IV

With the election of 1864 drawing near, the Confederate government decided on a bold action to bring the war home to the people of the North. To lead a raid without parallel, the Rebels selected Lieutenant Bennett H. Young, twenty-one years of age and a veteran of Morgan's highly individualistic campaigns. Twice during 1864 Young had failed in attempts to release Confederate prisoners in Northern camps. When in October Young left Canada and journeyed through the night "with twenty reliable men" the little town toward which he traveled never ex-

*pected to behold a bona fide Confederate. His objective: St. Albans,
Vermont, fifteen miles south of the border.*

*Promptly at three o'clock on the afternoon of October 19, 1864,
Young and his raiders took possession of St. Albans in the name of the
Confederate States of America. John W. Headley, one of the invaders,
told a crisp story:*[8]

. . . All the citizens on the street were ordered to go into the square
and remain. This was ridiculed by a number of citizens, when the Confederates began to shoot at men who hesitated to go, and one was
wounded. The citizens now realized that the exhibition was not a joke.

The Confederates were prepared with fifty four-ounce bottles of
Greek Fire * each, and while three men went to each bank and secured
their money, the others were firing the hotels and other buildings, and
securing horses and equipments.

The citizens had been held at bay during the proceedings, which had
consumed perhaps three-quarters of an hour. But the city contained
about 5,000 inhabitants, and many men began to come into the public
square. A number of Federal soldiers appeared among them, and preparations were being made for an attack upon the Confederates, who
were now ready to go when a few more horses were equipped.

Suddenly the people began to fire from windows, and three of the
Confederates were seriously wounded. A skirmish now ensued, and one
citizen was killed. The Confederates dashed their Greek Fire against
the houses all about on the square, and began their march to escape,
with the citizens and a few soldiers, some in buggies and some on horseback, in pursuit. Lieutenant Young took the road to Shelburne, some
eight miles distant, and was beyond the reach of the pursuers until at
Shelburne he reached a bridge over a river, on which a team was found
crossing with a load of hay, for which he was obliged to wait. The pursuers approached, when the Confederates halted and opened fire, at the
same time halting the team and turning it upon the bridge set fire to the
hay, which fired and destroyed the bridge. The pursuers did not again
overtake the Confederates. Lieutenant Young and his men, however,

* Greek fire, an inflammable chemical mixture, was used by Byzantine Greeks
during the Middle Ages to set fire to enemy ships and to defend Constantinople.
The Confederate raiders knew very little about it, except that the moment it was
exposed to air it would blaze and burn everything it touched. It was a colorless
liquid.

pushed forward and reached the border line of Canada about nine
o'clock that night. . . .

*Next day Young learned that some of his men had been arrested at
Phillipsburg, Quebec. He had decided to give himself up to the Canadian authorities, but the Vermonters got there first:*

Young stopped at a farm-house, and leaving his revolvers in an adjoining room, he sat at the only fire, which was in the kitchen, to get
warm. To his surprise, about twenty-five people from St. Albans, in
pursuit of his party, learning that there was a stranger in the house,
suddenly rushed in and reached Young before he could get to his pistols, which they secured. They promptly seized him and at once proceeded to beat him with the pistols and with swords.

The American party now started with Young to return to St. Albans.
They could have killed him, but doubtless deemed it important to deliver him alive in St. Albans for several reasons. They put Young in an
open wagon with two men on each side and one in his rear, all in the
wagon. The men were excited and carried their pistols cocked, badger-
ing him with threats to shoot, while they denounced him in unmeasured
terms. Young, however, continued to protest against their proceedings,
insisting that they were in violation of British neutrality, but they said
they did not care a d--n for British law or the British nation. The front
gate was some two hundred feet from the house. The road which passed
in front of the house led from the United States to Phillipsburg. When
they reached the gate to pass out, Young suddenly knocked the men
from each side with his arms, seized the reins, and quickly turning the
horses, drove toward Phillipsburg. But his captors, who were apparently paralyzed for a moment, soon recovered, and pounced upon him
with their pistols and swords. In the midst of the melee, and fortunately
for Young, a British officer happened upon the scene. Young told him
of his character—that of a Confederate officer on British soil and entitled to protection, that his captors were Americans who proposed to
take him without any authority to the United States in violation of British neutrality and in defiance of British law.

*Assured by the British officer that other Confederate captives would be
sent to St. Albans next day, the Vermonters agreed that Young should
be taken to Phillipsburg—the last they would see of him:*

That night Lieutenant Young and his five men were carried to St. Johns, a distance of about twenty miles, and placed in jail. Here a large garrison of British Regulars was stationed, who manifested the warmest friendship for the prisoners. They went so far as to suggest to Lieutenant Young that he and his men might be rescued. They extended every courtesy, and the citizens were likewise friendly and hospitable to the prisoners. Lieutenant Young and his comrades concluded that it would be unwise now to evade the issue and preferred to await their fate in the courts of Canada, since their extradition had been demanded by the Government of the United States.*

V

Mobile Bay had been closed to the Confederacy, Atlanta had fallen, the Shenandoah Valley—granary of Lee's army—could no longer provide food for a regiment. Yet Jefferson Davis, addressing the Confederate Congress on November 7, could see no reason for discouragement in recent events:[9]

. . . At the beginning of the year the State of Texas was partially in possession of the enemy, and large portions of Louisiana and Arkansas lay apparently defenseless. Of the Federal soldiers who invaded Texas, none are known to remain except as prisoners of war. In northwestern Louisiana a large and well-appointed army, aided by a powerful fleet, was repeatedly defeated, and deemed itself fortunate in finally escaping with a loss of one-third of its numbers, a large part of its military trains, and many transports and gunboats. The enemy's occupation of that State is reduced to the narrow district commanded by the guns of his fleet. Arkansas has been recovered with the exception of a few fortified posts, while our forces have penetrated into central Missouri, affording to our oppressed brethren in that State an opportunity, of which many have availed themselves, of striking for liberation from the tyranny to which they have been subjected.

On the east of the Mississippi, in spite of some reverses, we have much cause for gratulation. The enemy hoped to effect during the present year, by concentration of forces, the conquest which he had previously failed to accomplish by more extended operations. Compelled therefore to withdraw or seriously to weaken the strength of the armies

---

* Canadian sentiment in that locality favored Young and his raiders. They were set free.

of occupation at different points, he has afforded us the opportunity of recovering possession of extensive districts of our territory. Nearly the whole of northern and western Mississippi, of northern Alabama, and of western Tennessee are again in our possession, and all attempts to penetrate from the coast line into the interior of the Atlantic and Gulf States have been baffled. On the entire ocean and gulf coast of the Confederacy the whole success of the enemy, with the enormous naval forces at his command, has been limited to the capture of the outer defenses of Mobile Bay.

If we now turn to the results accomplished by the two great armies, so confidently relied on by the invaders as sufficient to secure the subversion of our Government and the subjugation of our people to foreign domination, we have still greater cause for devout gratitude to Divine Power. In southwestern Virginia successive armies, which threatened the capture of Lynchburg and Saltville, have been routed and driven out of the country, and a portion of eastern Tennessee reconquered by our troops. In northern Virginia extensive districts formerly occupied by the enemy are now free from their presence. In the lower Valley their general, rendered desperate by his inability to maintain a hostile occupation, has resorted to the infamous expedient of converting a fruitful land into a desert by burning its mills, granaries, and homesteads, and destroying the food, standing crops, live stock, and agricultural implements of peaceful noncombatants. The main army, after a series of defeats in which its losses have been enormous, after attempts by raiding parties to break up our railroad communications, which have resulted in the destruction of a large part of the cavalry engaged in the work, after constant repulse of repeated assaults on our defensive lines, is, with the aid of heavy reënforcements, but with, it is hoped, waning prospect of further progress in the design, still engaged in an effort commenced more than four months ago to capture the town of Petersburg.

The army of General Sherman, although succeeding at the end of the summer in obtaining possession of Atlanta, has been unable to secure any ultimate advantage from this success. The same general, who in February last marched a large army from Vicksburg to Meridian with no other result than being forced to march back again, was able, by the aid of greatly increased numbers and after much delay, to force a passage from Chattanooga to Atlanta, only to be for the second time compelled to withdraw on the line of his advance without obtaining control of a single line of territory beyond the narrow track of his march, and without gaining aught beyond the precarious possession of a few fortified points in which he is compelled to maintain heavy garrisons and which are menaced with recapture.

Davis advanced a novel theory of military invincibility:

The lessons afforded by the history of this war are fraught with instruction and encouragement. Repeatedly during the war have formidable expeditions been directed by the enemy against points ignorantly supposed to be of vital importance to the Confederacy. Some of these expeditions have, at immense cost, been successful, but in no instance have the promised fruits been reaped. Again, in the present campaign was the delusion fondly cherished that the capture of Atlanta and Richmond would, if effected, end the war by the overthrow of our Government and the submission of our people. We can now judge by experience how unimportant is the influence of the former event upon our capacity for defense, upon the courage and spirit of our people, and the stability of the Government. We may in like manner judge that if the campaign against Richmond had resulted in success instead of failure; if the valor of the army, under the leadership of its accomplished commander, had resisted in vain the overwhelming masses which were, on the contrary, decisively repulsed; if we had been compelled to evacuate Richmond as well as Atlanta—the Confederacy would have remained as erect and defiant as ever. Nothing could have been changed in the purpose of its Government, in the indomitable valor of its troops, or in the unquenchable spirit of its people. The baffled and disappointed foe would in vain have scanned the reports of your proceedings, at some new legislative seat, for any indication that progress had been made in his gigantic task of conquering a free people. The truth so patent to us must ere long be forced upon the reluctant Northern mind. There are no vital points on the preservation of which the continued existence of the Confederacy depends. There is no military success of the enemy which can accomplish its destruction. Not the fall of Richmond, nor Wilmington, nor Charleston, nor Savannah, nor Mobile, nor all of them combined, can save the enemy from the constant and exhaustive drain of blood and treasure which must continue until he shall discover that no peace is attainable unless based on the recognition of our indefeasible rights.

Davis saw hope for the Confederacy in the Northern peace movement:

The disposition of this Government for a peaceful solution of the issues which the enemy has referred to the arbitrament of arms has been too often manifested and is too well known to need new assurances. But while it is true that individuals and parties in the United States have indicated a desire to substitute reason for force, and by negotiations to stop the further sacrifice of human life, and to arrest the calamities which now afflict both countries, the authorities who control the Government of our enemies have too often and too clearly expressed their resolution to make no peace, except on terms of our unconditional submission and degradation, to leave us any hope of the cessation of hostilities until the delusion of their ability to conquer us is dispelled. Among those who are already disposed for peace many are actuated by principle and by disapproval and abhorrence of the iniquitous warfare that their Government is waging, while others are moved by the conviction that it is no longer to the interest of the United States to continue a struggle in which success is unattainable. Whenever this fast-growing conviction shall have taken firm root in the minds of a majority of the Northern people, there will be produced that willingness to negotiate for peace which is now confined to our side. Peace is manifestly impossible unless desired by both parties to this war, and the disposition for it among our enemies will be best and most certainly evoked by the demonstration on our part of ability and unshaken determination to defend our rights, and to hold no earthly price too dear for their purchase. Whenever there shall be on the part of our enemies a desire for peace, there will be no difficulty in finding means by which negotiation can be opened; but it is obvious that no agency can be called into action until this desire shall be mutual. When that contingency shall happen, the Government, to which is confided the treaty-making power, can be at no loss for means adapted to accomplish so desirable an end. In the hope that the day will soon be reached when under Divine favor these States may be allowed to enter on their former peaceful pursuits and to develop the abundant natural resources with which they are blessed, let us, then, resolutely continue to devote our united and unimpaired energies to the defense of our homes, our lives, and our liberties. This is the true path to peace. Let us tread it with confidence in the assured result.

VI

Davis's reading of the Northern public mind was two months out of date. Soldiers whose states permitted them to vote in the field forecast the verdict of the North. Captain J. N. Jones, of the Sixth New Hamp-

shire, watched a lifelong Democrat succumb to some Republican elec-
tioneering:[10]

On the morning of that [election] day, at roll-call, I told the men of
my company that there would be no drill, and that at nine o'clock A.M.
opportunity to vote would be given all of them who were legal voters in
New Hampshire. The law made the three ranking officers in each company judges of election. Having no lieutenant, I invited two sergeants
to assist me. My tent was about six feet by seven, and sunk into the
ground twelve or fifteen inches for greater security against bullets that
might come straying around at any time. It was noticed, however, that
on that day the rebels were unusually quiet, firing scarcely a shot. A
cigar box answered for a ballot box. The state furnished blanks for recording each voter's name, together with that of the town he claimed to
be his residence, and for whom he voted. In case, therefore, a man
voted who had no right to do so, his vote could be thrown out. The polls
having been declared open, and both Democratic and Republican votes
placed upon the table,* the men came up, were registered, voted and
retired. There was one man, a good specimen of the New Hampshire
voter who goes to town meeting and makes a day of it. He seemed in
no hurry to vote, and I invited him to take a seat on a hard-bread box
at the mouth of the tent. He had served almost three years; had been
with the regiment in its every battle; had been slightly wounded several
times—was, indeed, a good soldier. At last he said,—"Say, captain,
what do you think of the election?" To my reply, "I guess it is all right,"
he responded, "Well, what do you think of voting? I have always been
a Democrat, and never voted anything but the Democratic ticket in my
life." "All right," said I, "there are Democratic ballots—vote just as
you please. If you can't do so after having gone through what you have,
we had better all go home. I shall vote for Lincoln, but do you vote just
as you choose." "Well," said he, "I have been thinking about voting
for Lincoln. I believe he is a pretty good man." Then taking a Republican ballot in one hand and a Democratic ballot in the other, he rested
his elbows on his knees and scanned the tickets in silence. Seeing his
dilemma, I read aloud and as impressively as I could, the following
lines of poetry printed on the back of the Republican ticket, while he
listened attentively:

* The Australian or secret ballot was still a device of the future. In 1864 a voter
registered his choice by taking the printed ballot of his party and depositing it
in the ballot box.

"What! hoist the white flag when our triumph is nigh!
What! crouch before treason—make freedom a lie!
What! spike all our guns when the foe is at bay,
With his flags and black banners fast dropping away!"

I added the response, "Not much!" and he, without saying a word, put the Lincoln ballot into the box, had his name recorded, and walked away. Company F voted solid for Lincoln, of free choice and without undue influence. And it is gratifying to record the fact that the soldiers' election was likewise a fair one throughout the army.

In Union lines before Petersburg, cheers resounded. Theodore Gerrish of the Twentieth Maine discovered why:[11]

On Tuesday, November 8th, our regiment voted for the candidates for the Presidency; Abraham Lincoln received one hundred and thirty-seven votes, George B. McClellan, thirteen. When the news of the re-election of President Lincoln by such an overwhelming majority reached the army of the Potomac, the men were wild with excitement. From the Weldon railroad, along our entire line, past Petersburgh, across the James river, in the intrenchments away round to Richmond, our men cheered until they were hoarse. The rebels heard the cheering, and supposing that we had learned of some greater victory to our arms, were anxious to know the news. At a point where the lines came within a few rods of each other, our men heard a voice from behind the rebel breastworks, "Say, Yank." "Hilloa, Johnny." "Don't fire, Yank." "All right, Johnny." "What are you'uns all cheering for?" "Big victory on our side." "What is it, Yank?" came the eager response. "Old Abe has cleaned all your fellers out up North." "You don't say so, Yank?" "Fact; gobbled the whole concern, there is not peace men enough left in the whole North to make a corporal's guard." Then there was an anxious conversation among the rebels, and the voice of the spokesman was again heard. "Well, Yank, we cheered when we heard that your little Mac was nominated, but we don't feel much like cheering now."

In Washington, John Hay sketched a President unperturbed by the uncertainties of election day:[12]

Nov. 8. The house has been still and almost deserted today. Everybody in Washington, not at home voting, seems ashamed of it and stays away from the President.

I was talking with him today. He said, "It seems a little singular that I, who am not a vindictive man, should have always been before the people for election in canvasses marked for their bitterness: always but once; when I came to Congress it was a quiet time. But always besides that the contests in which I have been prominent have been marked with great rancor."

. . . During the afternoon few despatches were received.

At night, at 7 o'clock we started over to the War Department to spend the evening. Just as we started we received the first gun from Indianapolis, showing a majority of 8,000 there, a gain of 1,500 over Morton's vote. The vote itself seemed an enormous one for a town of that size and can only be accounted for by considering the great influx since the war of voting men from the country into the State centres where a great deal of Army business is done. There was less significance in this vote on account of the October victory which had disheartened the enemy and destroyed their incentive to work.*

The night was rainy, steamy and dark. We splashed through the grounds to the side door of the War Department where a soaked and smoking sentinel was standing in his own vapor with his huddled-up frame covered with a rubber cloak. Inside a half-dozen idle orderlies, upstairs the clerks of the telegraph. As the President entered they handed him a despatch from Forney claiming ten thousand Union majority in Philadelphia. "Forney is a little excitable." Another comes from Felton, Baltimore, giving us "15,000 in the city, 5,000 in the state. All Hail, Free Maryland." That is superb. A message from Rice to Fox, followed instantly by one from Sumner to Lincoln, claiming Boston by 5,000, and Rice's and Hooper's elections by majorities of 4,000 apiece. A magnificent advance on the chilly dozens of 1862.

Eckert came in shaking the rain from his cloak, with trousers very disreputably muddy. We sternly demanded an explanation. He had slipped, he said, & tumbled prone, crossing the street. He had done it watching a fellow-being ahead and chuckling at his uncertain footing. Which reminded the Tycoon, of course. The President said, "For such an awkward fellow, I am pretty sure-footed. It used to take a pretty dextrous man to throw me. I remember, the evening of the day in 1858, that decided the contest for the Senate between Mr. Douglas and myself, was something like this, dark, rainy & gloomy. I had been reading the returns, and had ascertained that we had lost the Legis-

* In its election for state officers, October 11, Indiana had gone Republican by a safe margin.

lature and started to go home. The path had been worn hog-back and
was slippery. My foot slipped from under me, knocking the other one
out of the way, but I recovered myself & lit square, and I said to myself,
'It's a slip and not a fall.' "

The President sent over the first fruits to Mrs. Lincoln. He said, "She
is more anxious than I."

. . . Despatches kept coming in all the evening showing a splendid
triumph in Indiana, showing steady, small gains all over Pennsylvania, enough to give a fair majority this time on the home vote.
Guesses from New York and Albany which boiled down to about the
estimated majority against us in the city, 35,000, and left the result in the State still doubtful.

A despatch from Butler was picked up & sent by Sanford, saying that
the City had gone 35,000 McC. & the State 40,000. This looked impossible. The State had been carefully canvassed & such a result was impossible except in view of some monstrous and undreamed of frauds.
After a while another came from Sanford correcting the former one &
giving us the 40,000 in the State. . . .

Towards midnight we had supper, provided by Eckert. The President went awkwardly and hospitably to work shovelling out the fried
oysters. He was most agreeable and genial all the evening in fact. Fox
was abusing the coffee for being so hot—saying quaintly, it kept hot all
the way down to the bottom of the cup as a piece of ice staid cold till
you finished eating it.

We got later in the evening a scattering despatch from the West, giving us Michigan, one from Fox promising Missouri certainly, but a
loss in the first district from that miserable split of Knox & Johnson,
one promising Delaware, and one, too good for ready credence, saying
Raymond & Dodge & Darling had been elected in New York City.

Capt. Thomas came up with a band about half-past two, and made
some music and a small hifalute.

The President answered from the window with rather unusual dignity and effect & we came home.

*Two nights later, in response to a serenade, Lincoln related the mean-
ing of the election to the central issue of the war:*[13]

It has long been a grave question whether any government, not *too*
strong for the liberties of its people, can be strong *enough* to maintain
its own existence, in great emergencies.

On this point the present rebellion brought our republic to a severe test; and a presidential election occurring in regular course during the rebellion added not a little to the strain. If the loyal people, *united*, were put to the utmost of their strength by the rebellion, must they not fail when *divided*, and partially paralized, by a political war among themselves?

But the election was a necessity.

We can not have free government without elections; and if the rebellion could force us to forego, or postpone a national election, it might fairly claim to have already conquered and ruined us. The strife of the election is but human nature practically applied to the facts of the case. What has occurred in this case, must ever recur in similar cases. Human nature will not change. In any future great national trial, compared with the men of this, we shall have as weak, and as strong; as silly and as wise; as bad and good. Let us, therefore, study the incidents of this, as philosophy to learn wisdom from, and none of them as wrongs to be revenged.

But the election, along with its incidental, and undesirable strife, has done good too. It has demonstrated that a people's government can sustain a national election, in the midst of a great civil war. Until now it has not been known to the world that this was a possibility. It shows also how *sound*, and how *strong* we still are. It shows that, even among candidates of the same party, he who is most devoted to the Union, and most opposed to treason, can receive most of the people's votes. It shows also, to the extent yet known, that we have more men now, than we had when the war began. Gold is good in its place; but living, brave, patriotic men, are better than gold.

But the rebellion continues; and now that the election is over, may not all, having a common interest, reunite in a common effort, to save our common country? For my own part I have striven, and shall strive to avoid placing any obstacle in the way. So long as I have been here I have not willingly planted a thorn in any man's bosom.

While I am deeply sensible to the high compliment of a re-election; and duly grateful, as I trust, to Almighty God for having directed my countrymen to a right conclusion, as I think, for their own good, it adds nothing to my satisfaction that any other man may be disappointed or pained by the result.

May I ask those who have not differed with me, to join with me, in this same spirit towards those who have?

And now, let me close by asking three hearty cheers for our brave soldiers and seamen and their gallant and skilful commanders.

CHAPTER 35

WHILE ALL
GEORGIA HOWLED

I STOOD BY HIM when he was drunk," Sherman said.

The cause of Sherman's umbrage toward Ulysses S. Grant was a belief that the lieutenant general had hedged at Sherman's plan to march from Atlanta to the sea.

No new objection or counterproposal could daunt Sherman. He could make the march, he insisted. He would "make all Georgia howl."

I

Twenty-two years later, in a letter to R. L. Johnson, associate editor of Century Magazine, *Sherman admitted that in 1864 he had blamed the wrong man:*[1]

One single fact about the "March to the Sea" unknown to me was revealed by General Grant in his Memoirs. . . . "I was in favor of Sherman's plan from the time it was first submitted to me. My Chief of Staff, however, was very bitterly opposed to it; and as I learned subsequently, finding that he could not move me, he appealed to the authorities at Washington to stop it."

I had been acquainted with Genl. Jno. A. Rawlins, Gen. Grant's "Chief of Staff," from the beginning of the war. He was always most loyal & devoted to his Chief, an enthusiastic patriot, and of real ability. He was a neighbor of General Grant in Galena at the breaking out of the war, a lawyer in good practice, an intense thinker and a man of vehement expression: a soldier by force of circumstances rather than of education or practice yet of infinite use to his Chief throughout the war and up to the hour of his death as Secretary of War in 1869. General Rawlins was enthusiastically devoted to his friends in the Western Army, with which he had been associated from Cairo to Vicksburg and Chattanooga, and doubtless like many others at the time, October 1864, feared that I was about to lead his comrades in a "wild goose chase," and not fully comprehending the objects and also that I on the spot had better means of accurate knowledge than he in the distance. He did not possess the magnificent equipoise of General Grant, nor the confidence in my military sagacity which his Chief did, and I am not at all surprised to learn that he went to Washington from City Point to obtain an order from the President or Secretary of War to compel me with an army of sixty-five thousand of the best soldiers which America had ever produced to remain idle when an opportunity was offered such as never occurs twice to any man on Earth. General Rawlins was right according to the lights he possessed, and I remember well my feeling of uneasiness that something of the kind *might* happen, and how free and glorious I felt when the . . . telegraph was cut which prevented the possibility of orders of any kind from the rear coming to delay or hinder us from fulfilling what I knew was comparatively easy of execution and was sure to be a long stride toward the goal we all aimed at, victory and peace from Virginia to Texas. He was one of the many referred to by Mr. Lincoln, who sat in darkness, but after the event saw a great light and never revealed to me his other doubts.

Sherman believed that he had given General George H. Thomas at Nashville sufficient forces to handle Hood. On November 1 Grant wired Sherman, "If you can see a chance of destroying Hood's army, attend to that first, and make your other move secondary." Promptly Sherman replied, "No single army can catch Hood, and I am convinced the best results will follow from our defeating Jeff. Davis's cherished plan of making me leave Georgia by manoeuvring." The wire Sherman wanted came at last:[2]

CITY POINT, VIRGINIA, November 2, 1864—11.30 A.M.
MAJOR-GENERAL SHERMAN:
    Your dispatch of 9 A.M. yesterday is just received. I dispatched you the same date, advising that Hood's army, now that it had worked so far north, ought to be looked upon now as the "object." With the

force, however, that you have left with General Thomas, he must be able to take care of Hood and destroy him.

I do not see that you can withdraw from where you are to follow Hood, without giving up all we have gained in territory. I say, then, go on as you propose.

U. S. GRANT, *Lieutenant-General*

Within a week Sherman issued a special field order:

HEADQUARTERS MILITARY DIVISION OF THE MISSISSIPPI, IN THE FIELD, KINGSTON, GEORGIA, November 9, 1864.

1. For the purpose of military operations, this army is divided into two wings viz.:

The right wing, Major-General O. O. Howard commanding, composed of the Fifteenth and Seventeenth Corps; the left wing, Major-General H. W. Slocum commanding, composed of the Fourteenth and Twentieth Corps.

2. The habitual order of march will be, wherever practicable, by four roads, as nearly parallel as possible, and converging at points hereafter to be indicated in orders. The cavalry, Brigadier-General Kilpatrick commanding, will receive special orders from the commander-in-chief.

3. There will be no general train of supplies, but each corps will have its ammunition-train and provision-train, distributed habitually as follows: Behind each regiment should follow one wagon and one ambulance; behind each brigade should follow a due proportion of ammunition-wagons, provision-wagons, and ambulances. In case of danger, each corps commander should change this order of march, by having his advance and rear brigades unencumbered by wheels. The separate columns will start habitually at 7 A.M., and make about fifteen miles per day, unless otherwise fixed in orders.

4. The army will forage liberally on the country during the march. To this end, each brigade commander will organize a good and sufficient foraging party, under the command of one or more discreet officers, who will gather, near the route traveled, corn or forage of any kind, meat of any kind, vegetables, corn-meal, or whatever is needed by the command, aiming at all times to keep in the wagons at least ten days' provisions for his command, and three days' forage. Soldiers must not enter the dwellings of the inhabitants, or commit any trespass; but, during a halt or camp, they may be permitted to gather turnips,

potatoes, and other vegetables, and to drive in stock in sight of their camp. To regular foraging-parties must be intrusted the gathering of provisions and forage, at any distance from the road traveled.

5. To corps commanders alone is intrusted the power to destroy mills, houses, cotton-gins, etc.; and for them this general principle is laid down: In districts and neighborhoods where the army is unmolested, no destruction of such property should be permitted; but should guerrillas or bushwhackers molest our march, or should the inhabitants burn bridges, obstruct roads, or otherwise manifest local hostility, then army commanders should order and enforce a devastation more or less relentless, according to the measure of such hostility.

6. As for horses, mules, wagons, etc., belonging to the inhabitants, the cavalry and artillery may appropriate freely and without limit; discriminating, however, between the rich, who are usually hostile, and the poor and industrious, usually neutral or friendly. Foraging-parties may also take mules or horses, to replace the jaded animals of their trains, or to serve as pack-mules for the regiments or brigades. In all foraging, of whatever kind, the parties engaged will refrain from abusive or threatening language, and may, where the officer in command thinks proper, give written certificates of the facts, but no receipts; and they will endeavor to leave with each family a reasonable portion for their maintenance.

7. Negroes who are able-bodied and can be of service to the several columns may be taken along; but each army commander will bear in mind that the question of supplies is a very important one, and that his first duty is to see to those who bear arms.

8. The organization, at once, of a good pioneer battalion for each army corps, composed if possible of negroes, should be attended to. This battalion should follow the advance-guard, repair roads and double them if possible, so that the columns will not be delayed after reaching bad places. Also, army commanders should practise the habit of giving the artillery and wagons the road, marching their troops on one side, and instruct their troops to assist wagons at steep hills or bad crossings of streams.

9. Captain O. M. Poe, chief-engineer, will assign to each wing of the army a pontoon-train, fully equipped and organized; and the commanders thereof will see to their being properly protected at all times.

By order of Major-General W. T. Sherman,

L. M. DAYTON, *Aide-de-Camp*

II

Sherman pushed ahead with his preparations. The diary of ten-year-old Carrie M. Berry revealed the harrowing days that followed:[3]

Fri. Nov. 11. This is the last day that cars are going out to Chattanooga. We are erbliged to stay here now. Aunt Marthy went down to the carshed and I expect that she got off as she has not ben back.

Sat. Nov. 12. We were fritened almost to death last night. Some mean soldiers set several houses on fire in different parts of the town. I could not go to sleep for fear that they would set our house on fire. We all dred the next few days to come for they said that they would set the last house on fire if they had to leave this place.

Sun. Nov. 13. The federal soldiers have ben coming to day and burning houses and I have ben looking at them come in nearly all day.

Mon. Nov. 14. They came burning Atlanta to day. We all dread it because they say that they will burn the last house before they stop. We will dread it.

Tues. Nov. 15. This has ben a dreadful day. Things have ben burning all around us. We dread to night because we do not know what moment that they will set our house on fire. We have had a gard a little while after dinner and we feel a little more protected.

Wed. Nov. 16. Oh what a night we had. They came burning the store house and about night it looked like the whole town was on fire. We all set up all night. If we had not sat up our house would have ben burnt up for the fire was very near and the soldiers were going around setting houses on fire where they were not watched. They behaved very badly. They all left the town about one o'clock this evening and we were glad when they left for no body knows what we have suffered since they came in.

Carrie's assertion that the Yankees "behaved very badly" drew no denial from Major James A. Connolly of the 123rd Illinois:[4]

Our Commissaries have been busily engaged all day [November 15] in loading rations, and our Quarter Masters in issuing clothing and shoes to the troops. Up to about 3 P.M. this issuing was carried on with something like a show of regularity, but about that time fires began to break out in various portions of the city, and it soon became evident that these fires were but the beginning of a general conflagration which would sweep over the entire city and blot it out of existence;

so Quartermasters and Commissaries ceased trying to issue clothing or load rations, and told the soldiers to go in and take what they wanted before it burned up. The soldiers found many barrels of whisky and of course they drank it until they were drunk; then new fires began to spring up, all sorts of discordant noises rent the air, drunken soldiers on foot and horseback raced up and down the streets while the buildings on either side were solid sheets of flame, they gathered in crowds before the finest structures and sang "Rally around the Flag" while the flames enwrapped these costly edifices, and shouted and danced and sang again while pillar and roof and dome sank into one common ruin. The night, for miles around was bright as midday; the city of Atlanta was one mass of flame, and the morrow must find it a mass of ruins. Well, the soldiers fought for it, and the soldiers won it, now let the soldiers enjoy it; and so I suppose Gen. Sherman thinks, for he is somewhere near by, now, looking on at all this, and saying not one word to prevent it. All the pictures and verbal descriptions of hell I have ever seen never gave me half so vivid an idea of it, as did this flame wrapped city to-night. Gate City of the South, farewell!

A harrowing picture of desolated Atlanta was drawn by General W. P. Howard of the Georgia militia:[5]

The city hall is damaged but not burned. The Second Baptist, Second Presbyterian, Trinity and Catholic churches, and all the residences between Mitchell and Peters streets, running south of east, and Lloyd and Washington streets, running south of west, are safe, all attributable to Father O'Riley, who refused to give up his parsonage to the yankees, who were looking out for fine houses for quarters, and there being a large number of Catholics in the yankee army, who volunteered to protect their church and parsonage, and would not allow any house adjacent to be fired that would endanger them. As a proof of their attachment to their church, and love for Father O'Riley, a soldier who attempted to fire Colonel Calhoun's house, the burning of which would have endangered the whole block, was shot and killed and his grave is now marked. So to Father O'Riley the country is indebted for the protection of the city hall, churches, etc.

Dr. Quintard's Protestant Episcopal, the Christian and African churches were burned. The medical college was saved by Dr. D'Alvigny, who was left in charge of our wounded. The female college was torn down for the purpose of obtaining brick with which to con-

struct winter quarters. All institutions of learning were destroyed. The
African church was used as an academy for educating negroes. . . .
Very few negroes remained in the city. . . .

Many of the finest houses mysteriously left unburned were filled
with the finest furniture, carpets, pianos, mirrors, etc., and occupied
by parties, who six months ago lived in humble style.

About fifty families remained during the occupancy of the city by
the enemy, and about the same number have returned since its abandonment.* From two to three thousand dead carcasses of animals remain in the city limits.

Horses were turned loose in the cemetery to graze upon the grass and
shrubbery. The ornaments of graves, such as marble lambs, miniature
statuary, souvenirs of departed little ones, are broken and scattered
abroad.

The crowning act of all their wickedness and villainy was committed
by our ungodly foe in removing the dead from the vaults in the cemetery, and robbing the coffins of the silver name plates and tippings, and
depositing their own dead in the vaults.

*With bands playing, Sherman's army left Atlanta next morning. The
general was in exuberant spirits:*[6]

About 7 A.M. of November 16th we rode out of Atlanta by the
Decatur road, filled by the marching troops and wagons of the Fourteenth Corps; and reaching the hill, just outside of the old rebel works,
we naturally paused to look back upon the scenes of our past battles.
We stood upon the very ground whereon was fought the bloody battle
of July 22d, and could see the copse of wood where McPherson fell.
Behind us lay Atlanta, smouldering and in ruins, the black smoke
rising high in air, and hanging like a pall over the ruined city. Away
off in the distance, on the McDonough road, was the rear of Howard's
column, the gun-barrels glistening in the sun, the white-topped wagons
stretching away to the south; and right before us the Fourteenth Corps,
marching steadily and rapidly, with a cheery look and swinging pace,
that made light of the thousand miles that lay between us and Richmond. Some band, by accident, struck up the anthem of "John Brown's
soul goes marching on;" the men caught up the strain, and never be-

* General Howard's report to Governor Joseph E. Brown was dated December 7,
1864.

fore or since have I heard the chorus of "Glory, glory, hallelujah!" done
with more spirit, or in better harmony of time and place.

Then we turned our horses' heads to the east; Atlanta was soon
lost behind the screen of trees, and became a thing of the past. Around
it clings many a thought of desperate battle, of hope and fear, that now
seem like the memory of a dream; and I have never seen the place
since. The day was extremely beautiful, clear sunlight, with bracing air,
and an unusual feeling of exhilaration seemed to pervade all minds—
a feeling of something to come, vague and undefined, still full of venture and intense interest. Even the common soldiers caught the inspira-

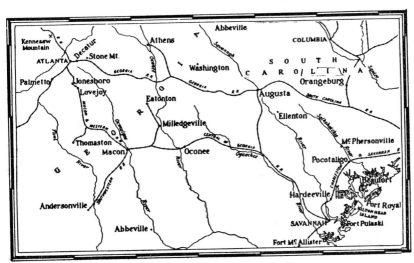

FROM ATLANTA TO SAVANNAH

From *Atlas of American History*

tion, and many a group called out to me as I worked my way past
them, "Uncle Billy, I guess Grant is waiting for us at Richmond!"
Indeed, the general sentiment was that we were marching for Richmond, and that there we should end the war, but how and when they
seemed to care not; nor did they measure the distance, or count the
cost in life, or bother their brains about the great rivers to be
crossed, and the food required for man and beast, that had to be
gathered by the way. There was a "devil-may-care" feeling pervading
officers and men, that made me feel the full load of responsibility, for
success would be accepted as a matter of course, whereas, should we
fail, this "march" would be adjudged the wild adventure of a crazy fool.
I had no purpose to march direct for Richmond by way of Augusta and

Charlotte, but always designed to reach the sea-coast first at Savannah or Port Royal, South Carolina, and even kept in mind the alternative of Pensacola.

The first night out we camped by the road-side near Lithonia. Stone Mountain, a mass of granite, was in plain view, cut out in clear outline against the blue sky; the whole horizon was lurid with the bonfires of rail-ties, and groups of men all night were carrying the heated rails to the nearest trees, and bending them around the trunks. Colonel Poe had provided tools for ripping up the rails and twisting them when hot; but the best and easiest way is the one I have described, of heating the middle of the iron-rails on bonfires made of the cross-ties, and then winding them around a telegraph-pole or the trunk of some convenient sapling. I attached much importance to this destruction of the railroad, gave it my own personal attention, and made reiterated orders to others on the subject.

The next day we passed through the handsome town of Covington, the soldiers closing up their ranks, the color-bearers unfurling their flags, and the bands striking up patriotic airs. The white people came out of their houses to behold the sight, spite of their deep hatred of the invaders, and the negroes were simply frantic with joy. Whenever they heard my name, they clustered about my horse, shouted and prayed in their peculiar style, which had a natural eloquence that would have moved a stone. I have witnessed hundreds, if not thousands, of such scenes; and can now see a poor girl, in the very ecstasy of the Methodist "shout," hugging the banner of one of the regiments, and jumping up to the "feet of Jesus."

III

Sherman found many points of interest when he reached the state capital, but his greatest fascination was reading the Southern newspapers that fell into his hands:

. . . By the 23d, I was in Milledgeville with the left wing, and was in full communication with the right wing at Gordon. The people of Milledgeville remained at home, except the Governor (Brown), the State officers, and Legislature, who had ignominiously fled, in the utmost disorder and confusion; standing not on the order of their going, but going at once—some by rail, some by carriages, and many on foot. Some of the citizens who remained behind described this flight of the "brave and patriotic" Governor Brown. He had occupied a public building known as the "Governor's Mansion," and had hastily stripped it of carpets, curtains, and furniture of all sorts, which were removed to a train of freightcars, which carried away these things—even the cabbages and vegetables from his kitchen and cellar—leaving behind muskets, ammunition, and the public archives.

On arrival at Milledgeville I occupied the same public mansion, and was soon overwhelmed with appeals for protection. General Slocum had previously arrived with the Twentieth Corps, had taken up his quarters at the Milledgeville Hotel, established a good provost-guard, and excellent order was maintained. The most frantic appeals had been made by the Governor and Legislature for help from every quarter, and the people of the State had been called out *en masse* to resist and destroy the invaders of their homes and firesides. Even the prisoners and convicts of the penitentiary were released on condition of serving as soldiers, and the cadets were taken from their military college for the same purpose. These constituted a small battalion, under General Harry Wayne, a former officer of the United States Army, and son of the then Justice Wayne of the Supreme Court. But these hastily retreated east across the Oconee River, leaving us a good bridge, which we promptly secured.

At Milledgeville we found newspapers from all the South, and learned the consternation which had filled the Southern mind at our temerity; many charging that we were actually fleeing for our lives and seeking safety at the hands of our fleet on the sea-coast. All demanded that we should be assailed, "front, flank, and rear;" that provisions should be destroyed in advance, so that we would starve; that bridges should be burned, roads obstructed, and no mercy shown us. Judging from the tone of the Southern press of that day, the outside world must have supposed us ruined and lost. I give a few of these appeals as samples, which to-day must sound strange to the parties who made them:

CORINTH, MISSISSIPPI, November 18, 1864.
TO THE PEOPLE OF GEORGIA:

Arise for the defense of your native soil! Rally around your patriotic Governor and gallant soldiers! Obstruct and destroy all the roads in Sherman's front, flank, and rear, and his army will soon starve in your midst. Be confident. Be resolute. Trust in an overruling Providence, and success will soon crown your efforts. I hasten to join you in the defense of your homes and firesides.

P. G. T. BEAUREGARD

RICHMOND, November 18, 1864.

To THE PEOPLE OF GEORGIA:

You have now the best opportunity ever yet presented to destroy the enemy. Put every thing at the disposal of our generals; remove all provisions from the path of the invader, and put all obstructions in his path.

Every citizen with his gun, and every negro with his spade and axe, can do the work of a soldier. You can destroy the enemy by retarding his march.

Georgians, be firm! Act promptly, and fear not!

B. H. HILL, *Senator*

I most cordially approve the above.

JAMES A. SEDDON, *Secretary of War*

RICHMOND, November 19, 1864

To THE PEOPLE OF GEORGIA:

We have had a special conference with President Davis and the Secretary of War, and are able to assure you that they have done and are still doing all that can be done to meet the emergency that presses upon you. Let every man fly to arms! Remove your negroes, horses, cattle, and provisions from Sherman's army, and burn what you cannot carry. Burn all bridges, and block up the roads in his route. Assail the invader in front, flank, and rear, by night and by day. Let him have no rest.

JULIAN HARTRIDGE, MARK BLAUFORD,
J. H. REYNOLDS, GENERAL N. LESTER,
JOHN T. SHOEMAKER, JOSEPH M. SMITH,
Members of Congress

Of course, we were rather amused than alarmed at these threats, and made light of the feeble opposition offered to our progress. Some of the officers (in the spirit of mischief) gathered together in the vacant hall of Representatives, elected a Speaker, and constituted themselves the Legislature of the State of Georgia! A proposition was made to repeal the ordinance of secession, which was well debated, and resulted in its repeal by a fair vote! I was not present at these frolics, but heard of them at the time, and enjoyed the joke.

Colonel William Hawley, commanding the Third Wisconsin Volunteers, gave a businesslike report of the manner in which Sherman's boys destroyed the capital of Georgia:[7]

On the twenty-second day of November, 1864, while the Twentieth army corps was approaching the city, I was directed by the Major-General commanding left wing of the army, to occupy the city as commandant of the post, with my own regiment and the One Hundred and Seventh New-York volunteers. My instructions were, to guard all public property, to maintain good order, and to perform all the duties of post commander. I immediately proceeded to establish patrols in the streets, and detailed suitable guards for the public buildings, including the State House, two arsenals, one dépôt, one magazine for powder and ammunition, and other buildings containing cotton, salt, and other contraband property. I also appointed a competent officer to take as correct an inventory of the property, contained in these and other buildings, as possible. The limited time in which I had command of the city, precluded the possibility of my getting a perfectly full and correct inventory of all the property found and destroyed, as this, in my opinion, would have required at least a week to obtain. The following is a list of the most important and valuable articles found, with the disposition made of the same:

One powder magazine, blown up; railroad dépôt and surrounding buildings, burned; two thousand three hundred muskets, smooth bore, calibre sixty-nine, burned; three hundred sets accoutrements, burned; ten thousand rounds ammunition, calibre sixty-nine, burned; five thousand lances, burned; one thousand five hundred cutlasses, burned; fifteen boxes United States standard weights and measures, burned; sixteen hogsheads salt, thrown into the river; one hundred and seventy boxes fixed ammunition, and two hundred kegs powder. Turned over all that was valuable to Major Reynolds, and threw the balance into the river. About one thousand five hundred pounds tobacco were distributed among the troops. A large quantity of cotton—say one thousand eight hundred bales—was disposed of by General Sherman; manner not made known to me. One large three-story building in the square, near the State House, was burned, together with a large number of miscellaneous articles, as parts of harness and saddles, a repair-shop, with all the necessary tools for repairing all kinds of war materials, etc.

Sherman and his marchers began to add their own idioms to the American language. A twisted railroad rail became known as "Sherman's hairpin." And "Sherman's bummers" were those deftly organized foraging parties which, operating on the flanks of his armies, kindled hatred in the hearts of plantation owners like Dolly Summer Lunt:[8]

. . . I hastened back to my frightened servants and told them that they had better hide, and then went back to the gate to claim protection and a guard. But like demons they rush in! My yards are full. To my smokehouse, my dairy, pantry, kitchen and cellar, like famished wolves they came, breaking locks and whatever is in their way. The thousand pounds of meat in my smokehouse is gone in a twinkling, my flour, my meat, my lard, butter, eggs, pickles of various kinds—both in vinegar and brine—wine, jars and jugs are all gone. My eighteen fat turkeys, my hens, chickens, and fowls, my young pigs, are shot down in my yard and hunted as if they were Rebels themselves. . . . There go my mules, my sheep, and worse than all, my boys! . . . They are not friends to the slaves. We have never made the poor cowardly Negro fight, and it is strange, passing strange, that the all-powerful Yankee nation with the whole world to back them, their ports open, their armies filled with soldiers from all nations, should at last take the poor Negro to help them out against this little Confederacy which was to have been brought back into the Union in sixty days' time!
. . . Ovens, skillets, coffee-mills, of which we had three, coffee-pots —not one have I left. . . . As the sad moments rolled on, they swept not only in front of my house, but behind; they tore down my garden palings, made a road through my back yard and lot field, driving their stock and riding through, tearing down my fences and desolating my home—wantonly doing it when there was no necessity for it.
Such a day, if I live to the age of Methuselah, may God spare me from ever seeing again!

Deep in the Georgia pine country, Major Connolly of the 123rd Illinois recounted an unusual evening:[9]

A lot of refugee negroes who are encamped near our headquarters got up a regular "Plantation Dance" to-night, and some of us went over and watched the performance which was highly amusing. The dress, general appearance, action, laughter, music and dancing of the genuine plantation negro is far more grotesque and mirth-provoking than the broadest caricatures of "Christy's Minstrels." They require neither fiddle nor banjo to make music for their ordinary plantation dances, and the dancers need no prompter, but kick, and caper and shuffle in the most complicated and grotesque manner their respective fancies can invent, while all who are not actually engaged as dancers stand in a ring around the dancers, clapping their hands, stamping their feet, swinging their bodies, and singing as loud and as fast and furious as they can, a sort of barbaric chant, unlike anything I ever heard from the lips of white mortals; I observed, however, that there is a tone of melancholy (I know of no other mode of describing it) pervading all their rude music, which was plainly discernible even when the mirth of the dancers and singers had apparently reached its highest pitch. There is more fact than fiction in the saying that a "Soldier's life is always gay," for here we are in the midst of a hostile country, engaged in a campaign which probably the whole world, at this moment, is predicting will end in our complete destruction, and yet I have spent the evening laughing at the oddities of these negroes until my head and sides are aching.

Occasionally Rebel cavalry under Joseph A. Wheeler nipped at the heels of Sherman's army; the effect was that of a military flea-bite— a nuisance. Connolly's interest remained absorbed by the Negroes:

Contrabands are still swarming to us in immense numbers. The General [Absalom Baird] is a nephew of Gerritt Smith's and is quite an abolitionist. He delights in talking with these contrabands when we halt by the roadside and in extracting information concerning their "masters and mistresses" from them. He picked up quite an original character today who calls himself "Jerry." Jerry is a lively, rollicking, fun loving fellow, with a good deal of shrewdness; about 20 years old and rather a good looking boy. Jerry got an old horse, made a rope bridle, mounted horseback and rode alongside the General all the afternoon, talking to him continually. As we rode along Jerry was silent a few minutes, then he suddenly burst into a loud laugh, shook himself all over, and turning to the General remarked: "Golly, I wish ole massa could see me now, ridin' wid de Ginrals."

After getting into camp tonight "Jerry" entertained us for two or three hours with his oddities. He told us about an old preacher in this neighborhood named Kilpatrick (Gen. Kilpatrick's headquarters are at his house tonight) and said he knew Old Kilpatrick's sermon, he had heard him preach it so often, so we got "Jerry" to preach Old Kilpatrick's sermon. I only remember part of it: "O Lord! suffer our ene*mees* to *Chaste* after us no longer, but turn *dem* gently round, O,

Lord, for we's got *notin* but our rights and our property, *an* if our ene-
mees chaste after us any longer we won't have *notin* for our *chillen.*
Bend *dar* hard hearts *an probate* necks, O, Lord, *an* suffer *dem* to
Chaste after us no longer, but turn *dem* gently round." Jerry would
roll up his eyes, and deliver this, and much more, in true ministerial
style, until we almost split our sides with laughter.

We asked "Jerry" how many "Yankees" he thought he had seen today, and he replied about "five hundred thousand." I have noticed that
it is almost universal amongst the negroes in this country, when they
first see our column come along on the road to exclaim: "Good Lord!
looks like de whole world was comin."

Camp pets—dogs and cats, a small donkey, even a raccoon—amused
Major George Ward Nichols, aide-de-camp to Sherman:[10]

. . . When the column is moving, haughty gamecocks are seen
mounted upon the breech of a cannon, tied to the pack saddle of a mule,
among pots and pans, or carried lovingly in the arms of a mounted
orderly; crowing with all his might from the interior of a wagon, or
making the woods re-echo with his triumphant notes as he rides perched
upon the knapsack of a soldier. These cocks represent every known
breed, Polish and Spanish, Dorkings, Shanghais, and Bantams—high-
blooded specimens traveling with those of their species who may not
boast of noble lineage. They must all fight, however, or be killed and
eaten. Hardly has the army gone into camp before these feathery com-
bats begin. The cocks use only the spurs with which Nature furnishes
them; for the soldiers have not yet reached the refinement of applying
artificial gaffs, and so but little harm is done. The gamecocks which
have come out of repeated conflicts victorious are honored with such
names as "Bill Sherman," "Johnny Logan," etc.; while the defeated
and bepecked victim is saluted with derisive appellations, such as
"Jeff. Davis," "Beauregard," or "Bob Lee."

Along the roadside one day Major Nichols encountered a sour-faced
old man, who was in a philosophical mood:

"They say you are retreating, but it is the strangest sort of retreat I
ever saw. Why dog bite them, the newspapers have been lying in this
way all along. They allers are whipping the Federal armies, and they
allers fall back after the battle is over. It was that ar' idee that first

opened my eyes. Our army was always whipping the Feds, and we allers fell back. I allers told 'em it was a damned humbug, and now by Jesus I know it, for here you are right on [my] place; hogs, potatoes, corn, and fences all gone. I don't find any fault. I expected it all.

"Jeff Davis and the rest talk about splitting the Union. Why if South Carolina had gone out by herself, she would have been split in four pieces by this time. Splitting the Union! Why (with a round oath) the State of Georgia is being split right through from end to end. It is these rich fellows who are making this war, and keeping their precious bodies out of harm's way. There's John Franklin went through here the other day, running away from your army. I could have played dominoes on his coat-tails. There's my poor brother sick with smallpox at Macon, working for eleven dollars a month, and hasn't got a cent of the damned stuff for a year. 'Leven dollars a month and eleven thousand bullets a minute. I don't believe in it, sir!'"

Negroes by the hundred trailing after the Federal columns, cavalry skirmishes, tightened mouths at the discovery of a prison pen at Millen —of such images was the march to the sea composed. Major Connolly was far from amused by an incident that occurred on the eighth of December:[11]

When the head of the column reached the "Ebenezer Causeway" I went ahead with one of Genl. [Jefferson C.] Davis' aids who had come back to point out our ground for camping, and as I reached the bridge, I found there Major Lee, Provost Marshal of the Corps, engaged, by Genl. Davis' order, in turning off the road, into the swamp all the fugitive negroes that came along. When we should cross I knew it was the intention that the bridge should be burned, and I inquired if the negroes were not to be permitted to cross; I was told that Genl. Davis had ordered that they should not. This *I* knew, and Genl. Davis knew must result in all these negroes being recaptured or perhaps brutally shot down by the rebel cavalry tomorrow morning. The idea of five or six hundred black women, children and old men being thus returned to slavery by such an infernal copperhead as Jeff. C. Davis was entirely too much for my Democracy; I suppose loss of sleep, and fatigue made me somewhat out of humor too, and I told his staff officers what I thought of such an inhuman, barbarous proceeding in language which may possibly result in reprimand from his serene Highness, for I know his toadies will repeat it to him, but I don't care a fig; I am determined to expose this act of his publicly, . . . I expect this will cost me my Brevet as Lieut. Colonel, but let it go, I wouldn't barter my convictions of right, nor seal my mouth for any promotion.*

IV

In mid-October, Hood had started northward toward Nashville, where he hoped to defeat Union forces under Schofield and Thomas, gain recruits, and then re-enforce Lee at Richmond.

Hood made slow progress. Not until the last day of November did he have a chance to throw his troops at Schofield, in a strong position at Franklin, twenty miles south of Nashville.

Captain Irving A. Buck, on the staff of Confederate Major General Patrick R. Cleburne—an abler officer than Hood—saw brave men in gray and butternut charge in vain against the Federal lines:[12]

At dawn, November 30, the Confederate army was put in motion towards Franklin, 18 miles distant. . . . The town is located on the south side and in a bend of the Big Harpeth River, which completely encircles it on three sides, crescent in shape. The Federal entrenchments extended from a point east to one north, in a sharp curve near the bridge of the Nashville and Decatur Railroad, thence to another curve west, both flanks resting on the river, their line crossing the neck of a peninsula. On the high ground north of the river was a strong redoubt, Fort Granger, for the protection of which and their train was stationed the Third Division of the Fourth Federal corps. Their entrenchments on the south side of the river were built in front of the now celebrated Carter house, a one-story brick building, west of the Columbia pike, and a large gin house stood on the east side of it. The pike ran through the entrenchments, while to the east side of it was the railroad. On a slope half a mile in front of the main works two brigades of Wagner's Federal division had been halted, and proceeded to throw up breastworks. . . .

General Hood formed his line of battle behind Winstead's Hill about two and a half miles from Carter's Hill, the Federal position. . . . Upon arrival General Cheatham had ridden to the top of Winstead's Hill to make observation of the Federal position, which he at once saw was very strong and well protected, and he knew that to try

* Connolly's report on the incident, addressed to his congressman, appeared in substance in the New York *Tribune.* A subsequent investigation "exonerated" Davis.

to dislodge them would be a desperate attempt. Going to General Hood he said, "I do not like the looks of this fight; the enemy has an excellent position and is well fortified." "I prefer to fight them here where they have had only eighteen hours to fortify, than to strike them at Nashville where they have been strengthening themselves for three years," replied Hood. General Forrest was also opposed to a front at-

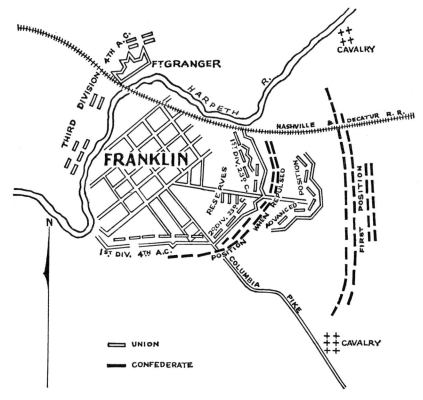

THE BATTLE OF FRANKLIN

From Lossing, *Pictorial History of the Civil War*

tack, advising that the enemy be flanked by moving to the right across the Harpeth River, which was fordable, and offered to attempt it with his cavalry if adequately supported by an infantry column. . . .

The day before the battle of Franklin the road upon which Cleburne was marching ran by Ashwood, 6 miles from Columbia, where is located the church and burial ground of the Polk family.* It was a romantic

* The family of Leonidas Polk, Episcopal bishop turned soldier, who was killed at Pine Mountain, Georgia, June 14, 1864.

place. The beautiful little Episcopal church was in the purest Gothic
style, its walls and sharp-pointed roof concealed by ivy, while the
flowers and shrubbery looked fresh and green even on this bleak November day. Cleburne reined in his horse and lingered for a moment to
admire a place of such singular beauty, and said to one of his staff that
it was "almost worth dying for, to be buried in such a beautiful spot."

. . . Upon his arrival at Winstead's Hill, whilst awaiting the formation of his command, he ascended to the summit, rested his field-glasses
upon a stump, and gazed long at the enemy's entrenchments. He simply remarked, "They are very formidable." Seating himself upon the
stump, he wrote rapidly for a few minutes in a small blank-book, which
he returned to his pocket. . . .

The ground over which the advance was to be made from the base
of Winstead's Hill was a level plain, about two and a quarter miles
across to Carter's Hill, and save for a hedge of osage orange on the
knoll near the railroad cut, and a considerable thicket of locust trees,
close to and in front of the Carter house, it was entirely unobstructed
and fenceless, and every part of the advance in plain view of the
Federals. . . . The advance was begun between half-past three and
four o'clock in the afternoon. A regiment was thrown out as skirmishers
in advance of each division. There was no halt from the time of starting
until the Confederates struck the Federal breastworks. The first was that
of the two exposed brigades of Wagner's division in the detached works
half a mile to the front of the main line. . . .

Wagner's troops broke in confusion and fled to the protection of
these works. For a long time there had existed a rivalry between
Cheatham's (Brown's) and Cleburne's division, and as the line rushed
forward, the former troops shouted to the latter, as the Federals scattered, "We will go into the works with them," and the two divisions
were pushed so rapidly that on the right of the Franklin–Columbia
pike Cleburne's reached the entrenchments almost as soon as did Wagner's demoralized men. To describe truly that which followed is beyond the power of tongue or pen. In the reckless disregard of life, and
in tenacity of purpose displayed, the attack has rarely been equalled,
never exceeded. The men fought like demons. Often the combatants
were near enough to use clubbed muskets and the bayonet. The first
desperate charge by Cheatham was repeated again and again, while
Stewart, on his right, threw his force upon the Federals in their entrenchments and fought with the same daring and determination that
Cheatham's men had shown. Inside the Federal works a new raw regi-

ment broke and ran to the rear, and into the gap thus created Brown's and Cleburne's men rushed, but from losses they were too weak to hold the ground against the reïnforcements of the seasoned and well-disciplined brigade of Gen. Emerson Opdyke. Besides, of their leaders the inspiring voice of Cleburne was already hushed in death, and Brown lay wounded on the field.

Schofield watched the battle with different emotions:[13]

General Stanley and I, who were then together on the north side of the river, rode rapidly to our posts, he to his corps on the south side, and I to the high redoubt on the north bank, overlooking the entire field.

There I witnessed the grandest display possible in war. Every battalion and battery of the Union army in line was distinctly seen. The corps of the Confederate army which were advancing or forming for the attack could also be seen, though less clearly on account of their greater distance, while the Confederate cavalry could be dimly discerned moving to the fords of the river above Franklin. Only a momentary view was permitted of this scene of indescribable grandeur when it was changed to one of the most tragic interest and anxiety. The guns of the redoubt on the parapet on which I stood with two or three staff officers had fired only a few shots over the heads of our troops at the advancing enemy when his heavy line overwhelmed Wagner's two brigades and rapidly followed their fragments in a confused mass over our light intrenchments. The charging ranks of the enemy, the flying remnants of our broken troops, and the double ranks of our first line of defense, coming back from the trenches together, produced the momentary impression of an overwhelming mass of the enemy passing over our parapets.

It is hardly necessary to say that for a moment my "heart sank within me." But instantly Opdycke's brigade and the 12th and 16th Kentucky sprang forward, and steadily advanced to the breach. Up to this moment there had been but little firing at that point, because of our own troops and the enemy coming in pell-mell; hence there was not much smoke, and the whole could be seen. But now all became enveloped in a dense mass of smoke, and not a man was visible except the fragments of the broken brigades and others, afterward known to be prisoners, flocking to the rear. A few seconds of suspense and intense anxiety followed, then the space in the rear of our line became clear of fugitives, and the steady roar of musketry and artillery and the dense volume of smoke rising along the entire line told me that "the breach is restored, the victory won"! That scene, and the emotion of that one moment, were worth all the losses and dangers of a soldier's lifetime.

Buck witnessed a curious phenomenon: a victorious army in retreat. Before the new month of December was out, the reason for this strange strategical move would be revealed:[14]

The deepening shadows of the afternoon betokening the approach of night, brought no relief to the weary but determined combatants. Darkness came, but the struggle continued. Flashes of the guns upon one side would furnish light by which a volley would be directed by the other. The opposing lines at points were within easy reach of each other, and kept up the fusillade until between 9 and 10 o'clock, when it abated, simply because both sides were actually worn out physically, and human endurance could bear no further strain. Between 11 o'clock and midnight the Federals took advantage of this cessation to slip away quietly in retreat towards Nashville.

v

That November, still stalemated in Virginia, Grant decided to enjoy a holiday. Horace Porter described a streetcar conductor who wouldn't be fooled by a cock-and-bull story:[15]

As the apprehension throughout the North had been allayed, and as there were no operations in contemplation in Virginia, General Grant started on the 17th of November, and made a short trip to Burlington, New Jersey, to see his children, who had been placed at school there, and his wife, who was with them. There went with the party an expert telegraph operator, familiar with the cipher used in official despatches, who was used in keeping up telegraphic communication with the front. On November 19 news was received at headquarters, through Confederate sources, that Lee had recalled Early's command from the valley of Virginia. This was instantly communicated to the general-in-chief. He telegraphed at once to Sheridan, mentioning this news, and saying that if he was satisfied that it was so, to send Wright's corps to City Point without delay, and move with his cavalry to cut the Virginia Central Railroad. There was destined to be no respite for the general-in-chief. Even while snatching a couple of days' rest in the quiet of his little family, he was still called on to direct important movements in the field.

Finding that there was no immediate need of his presence at the front, he decided to run over to New York for a couple of days. He had promised Mrs. Grant to go there on a shopping expedition, and he also felt some curiosity to take a look at the city, as he had not seen it since he was graduated from the Military Academy, twenty-one years before. He went with Mrs. Grant to the Astor House, quietly and unannounced, being particularly desirous of avoiding any public demonstrations. He did not realize, however, the sensation which his arrival in the metropolis would create. The news spread rapidly throughout the city, and the greatest eagerness was manifested on the part of the people to get a sight of the famous commander. The foremost citizens presented themselves at the hotel to pay their respects to him, and enthusiastic crowds filled the streets and stood for hours gazing at the windows of his rooms, in the hope of catching a glimpse of him.

Entertainments of every kind were tendered him, and invitations poured in from every quarter. He received many prominent citizens in his rooms, and had a great many interesting talks with them; but the invitations to entertainments were declined, and all public demonstrations avoided as much as possible. The next morning after his arrival the general strolled out into the streets with a former staff-officer then living in New York, and being in plain citizen's clothes, was for some time unobserved; but finally his features, which had been made known by means of the portraits everywhere displayed, were recognized, and finding a crowd surrounding him, he stepped into a street-car. The gentleman with him, finding no vacant seat, asked the conductor to have the people sit closer together and make room for General Grant. The conductor put on a broad grin, and quietly winked one eye, as much as to say, "You can't fool me with such a cock-and-bull story as that"; and the general quietly took hold of a strap, and rode throughout the trip standing with a number of others who had crowded into the car.

VI

By less than a week, Grant missed an effort by eight Confederate conspirators to burn New York City. John W. Headley, the historian of the raid on St. Albans, Vermont, recounts his part in the events of the evening of November 26, 1864:[16]

I reached the Astor House at 7:20 o'clock, got my key, and went to my room in the top story. It was the lower corner front room on Broadway. After lighting the gas jet I hung the bed-clothes loosely on the headboard and piled the chairs, drawers of the bureau, and wash-stand on the bed. Then stuffed some newspapers about among the mass and poured a bottle of turpentine over it all. I concluded to unlock my door and fix the key on the outside, as I might have to get out in a hurry, for I did not know whether the Greek Fire would make a noise or not. I opened a bottle carefully and quickly, and spilled it on the pile of rubbish. It blazed up instantly and the whole bed seemed to be in flames before I could get out. I locked the door and walked down the hall. . . .

Across at the City Hotel I proceeded in the same manner. Then in going down to the Everett House I looked over at my room in the Astor House. A bright light appeared within but there were no indications below of any alarm. After getting through at the Everett House I started to the United States Hotel, when the fire bells began to ring up town. I got through at the United States Hotel without trouble, but in leaving my key the clerk, I thought, looked at me a little curiously. It occurred to me that it had been discovered that my satchel had no baggage in it and that perhaps the clerk had it in mind to mention the fact.

As I came back to Broadway it seemed that a hundred bells were ringing, great crowds were gathering on the street, and there was general consternation. I concluded to go and see how my fires were doing. There was no panic at the Astor House, but to my surprise a great crowd was pouring out of Barnum's Museum nearly opposite the Astor. It was now a quarter after nine o'clock by the City Hall tower clock.

Presently the alarm came from the City Hotel and the Everett. The surging crowds were frantic. But the greatest panic was at Barnum's Museum. People were coming out and down ladders from the second and third floor windows and the manager was crying out for help to get his animals out. It looked like people were getting hurt running over each other in the stampede, and still I could not help some astonishment for I did not suppose there was a fire in the Museum.

In accordance with our plan, I went down Broadway and turned across to the North River Wharf. The vessels and barges of every description were lying along close together and not more than twenty yards from the street. I picked dark spots to stand in, and jerked a bottle in six different places. They were ablaze before I left. One had struck a barge of baled hay and made a big fire. There were wild scenes here the last time I looked back. I started straight for the City Hall.

There was still a crowd around the Astor House and everywhere, but I edged through and crossed over to the City Hall, where I caught a car just starting up town. . . .

Nineteen hotels were fired, yet the plot failed. Through the help of W. L. McDonald, a piano merchant, the eight conspirators escaped. Later, however, luck ran out for Robert Cobb Kennedy, as this confession, which was also his death warrant, attested:[17]

. . . After we had been in New York three weeks, we were told the object of the expedition was to retaliate on the North for the atrocities in the Shenandoah Valley. It was designed to set fire to the city on the night of the Presidential election; but the phosphorus was not ready, and it was put off until the 25th [26th] of November. I was stopping at the Belmont House, but moved into Prince Street. I set fire to four places—in Barnum's Museum, Lovejoy's Hotel, Tammany Hotel, and the New England House. The others only started fires in the house where each was lodging, and then ran off. Had they all done as I did, we would have had thirty-two fires, and played a huge joke on the fire department. I know that I am to be hung for setting fire to Barnum's Museum,* but that was only a joke. I had no idea of doing it. I had been drinking, and went in there with a friend, and, just to scare the people, I emptied a bottle of phosphorus on the floor. We knew it wouldn't set fire to the wood, for we had tried it before, and at one time concluded to give the whole thing up.

There was no fiendishness about it. After setting fire to my four places, I walked the streets all night, and went to the Exchange Hotel early in the morning. We all met there that morning and the next night. My friend and I had rooms there, but we sat in the office nearly all the time, reading the papers, while we were watched by the detectives, of whom the hotel was full.† I expected to die then, and if I had, it would have been all right; but now it seems rather hard. I escaped to Canada, and was glad enough when I crossed the bridge in safety.

I desired, however, to return to my command, and started with my friend for the Confederacy, *via* Detroit. Just before entering the city, he received an intimation that the detectives were on the lookout for us, and, giving me a signal, he jumped from the cars. I didn't notice the signal, but kept on, and was arrested in the depot.

* Kennedy was hanged in New York City a short time after this confession.
† Secretary of State Seward had been warned through the American consul at Halifax to expect plots against Northern cities on the eve of the election, and Richmond papers had openly boasted of these schemes.

I wish to say that killing women and children was the last thing thought of. We wanted to let the people of the North understand that there were two sides to this war, and that they can't be rolling in wealth and comfort, while we at the South are bearing all the hardships and privations.

In retaliation for Sheridan's atrocities in the Shenandoah Valley, we desired to destroy property, not the lives of women and children, although that would, of course, have followed in its train.

Done in the presence of

LIEUT.-COL. MARTIN BURKE,

And J. HOWARD, JR.

March 24 [1865], 10:30 P.M.

A GIFT FOR
MR. LINCOLN

———————

B Y LATE 1864 an overland telegraph between America and Europe
by way of Bering Strait and Asiatic Russia was under construction.
Since 1860, discoveries of gold, silver and cinnabar deposits in the
Sierra Nevadas and the Rockies had drawn thousands of brawling but
hard-working miners to those regions. The votes cast in the presidential
election of 1864 had demonstrated, Lincoln asserted, that "we have
more men *now* than we had when the war *began;* that we are not exhausted, nor in process of exhaustion; that we are *gaining* strength, and
may, if need be, maintain the contest indefinitely." These three events
were among those that the President emphasized on December 6, 1864,
when he reported to Congress on the state of the Union.

I

*Other paragraphs in the President's message discussed the military
situation:*[1]

The war continues. Since the last annual message all the important
lines and positions then occupied by our forces have been maintained,
and our arms have steadily advanced; thus liberating the regions left in
rear, so that Missouri, Kentucky, Tennessee and parts of other States
have again produced reasonably fair crops.

The most remarkable feature in the military operations of the year
is General Sherman's attempted march of three hundred miles directly
through the insurgent region. It tends to show a great increase of our

relative strength that our General-in-Chief should feel able to confront and hold in check every active force of the enemy, and yet to detach a well-appointed large army to move on such an expedition. The result not yet being known, conjecture in regard to it is not here indulged.

Lincoln believed that in the recent election he had heard the voice of the people:

Important movements have also occurred during the year to the effect of moulding society for durability in the Union. Although short of complete success, it is much in the right direction, that twelve thousand citizens in each of the States of Arkansas and Louisiana have organized loyal State governments with free constitutions, and are earnestly struggling to maintain and administer them. The movements in the same direction, more extensive, though less definite in Missouri, Kentucky and Tennessee, should not be overlooked. But Maryland presents the example of complete success.* Maryland is secure to Liberty and Union for all the future. The genius of rebellion will no more claim Maryland. Like another foul spirit, being driven out, it may seek to tear her, but it will woo her no more.

At the last session of Congress a proposed amendment of the Constitution abolishing slavery throughout the United States, passed the Senate, but failed for lack of the requisite two-thirds vote in the House of Representatives. Although the present is the same Congress, and nearly the same members, and without questioning the wisdom or patriotism of those who stood in opposition, I venture to recommend the reconsideration and passage of the measure at the present session. Of course the abstract question is not changed; but an intervening election shows, almost certainly, that the next Congress will pass the measure if this does not. Hence there is only a question of *time* as to when the proposed amendment will go to the States for their action. And as it is to so go, at all events, may we not agree that the sooner the better? It is not claimed that the election has imposed a duty on members to change their views or their votes, any further than, as an additional element to be considered, their judgment may be affected by it. It is the voice of the people now, for the first time, heard upon the question. In a great national crisis, like ours, unanimity of action among those seeking a common end is very desirable—almost indispensable.

* On October 13, 1864, Maryland abolished slavery by popular vote.

And yet no approach to such unanimity is attainable, unless some deference shall be paid to the will of the majority, simply because it is the will of the majority. In this case the common end is the maintenance of the Union; and, among the means to secure that end, such will, through the election, is most clearly declared in favor of such constitutional amendment.

Whither the road to peace? Lincoln thought he knew:

The public purpose to re-establish and maintain the national authority is unchanged, and, as we believe, unchangeable. The manner of continuing the effort remains to choose. On careful consideration of all the evidence accessible it seems to me that no attempt at negotiation with the insurgent leader could result in any good. He would accept nothing short of severance of the Union—precisely what we will not and cannot give. His declarations to this effect are explicit and oft-repeated. He does not attempt to deceive us. He affords us no excuse to deceive ourselves. He cannot voluntarily re-accept the Union; we cannot voluntarily yield it. Between him and us the issue is distinct, simple, and inflexible. It is an issue which can only be tried by war, and decided by victory. If we yield, we are beaten; if the Southern people fail him, he is beaten. Either way, it would be the victory and defeat following war. What is true, however, of him who heads the insurgent cause, is not necessarily true of those who follow. Although he cannot re-accept the Union, they can. Some of them, we know, already desire peace and reunion. The number of such may increase. They can, at any moment, have peace simply by laying down their arms and submitting to the national authority under the Constitution. After so much, the government could not, if it would, maintain war against them. The loyal people would not sustain or allow it. If questions should remain, we would adjust them by the peaceful means of legislation, conference, courts, and votes, operating only in constitutional and lawful channels. . . .

In presenting the abandonment of armed resistance to the national authority on the part of the insurgents, as the only indispensable condition to ending the war on the part of the government, I retract nothing heretofore said as to slavery. I repeat the declaration made a year ago, that "while I remain in my present position I shall not attempt to retract or modify the emancipation proclamation, nor shall I return to slavery any person who is free by the terms of that proclamation, or by any of the Acts of Congress." If the people should, by whatever mode or means, make it an Executive duty to re-enslave such persons, another, and not I, must be their instrument to perform it.

In stating a single condition of peace, I mean simply to say that the war will cease on the part of the government, whenever it shall have ceased on the part of those who began it.

II

The weather held fine in Georgia, and Sherman's troops joked over how by Christmas they would be feasting on oysters. The general was within reach of his goal:[2]

In approaching Savannah, General Slocum struck the Charleston Railroad near the bridge, and occupied the river-bank as his left flank, where he had captured two of the enemy's river-boats and had prevented two others (gunboats) from coming down the river to communicate with the city; while General Howard, by his right flank, had broken the Gulf Railroad. . . , and occupied the railroad itself down to the Little Ogeechee . . . so that no supplies could reach Savannah by any of its accustomed channels.

We, on the contrary, possessed large herds of cattle, which we had brought along or gathered in the country, and our wagons still contained a reasonable amount of breadstuffs and other necessaries, and the fine rice crops of the Savannah and Ogeechee rivers furnished to our men and animals a large amount of rice and rice-straw.

We also held the country to the south and west of the Ogeechee as foraging ground.

Still, communication with the fleet was of vital importance, and I directed General Kilpatrick to cross the Ogeechee by a pontoon-bridge, to reconnoitre Fort McAllister, and to proceed to St. Catherine's Sound, in the direction of Sunbury or Kilkenny Bluff, and open communication with the fleet. General Howard had previously, by my direction, sent one of his best scouts down the Ogeechee in a canoe for a like purpose. But more than this was necessary. We wanted the vessels and their contents, and the Ogeechee River, a navigable stream close to the rear of our camps, was the proper avenue of supply.

The enemy had burned the road-bridge across the Ogeechee, just below the mouth of the Camochee, known as "King's Bridge." This was reconstructed in an incredibly short time in the most substantial manner by the Fifty-eighth Indiana, Colonel Buel, under the direction of Captain Reese, of the Engineer corps, and on the morning of the thirteenth December, the Second division of the Fifteenth corps, under command of Brigadier-General Hazen, crossed the bridge to the west bank of the Ogeechee, and marched down with orders to carry by assault Fort McAllister, a strong inclosed redoubt, manned by two companies of artillery and three of infantry, in all about two hundred men, and mounting twenty-three guns, *en barbette*, and one mortar.

General Hazen reached the vicinity of Fort McAllister about one P.M., deployed his division about the place, with both flanks resting upon the river, posted his skirmishers judiciously behind the trunks of trees whose branches had been used for abattis, and about five P.M. assaulted the place with nine regiments at three points, all of them successfully. I witnessed the assault from a rice-mill on the opposite bank of the river, and can bear testimony to the handsome manner in which it was accomplished.

General William B. Hazen commanded the old division with which Sherman had fought at Shiloh and Vicksburg. These were the hard-bitten veterans who saw, three miles across a salt marsh, Rebel flags flying on Fort McAllister. By eleven o'clock on the morning of December 13, Hazen had almost closed in on the enemy:[3]

. . . About one mile from the Fort a picket was captured, revealing the whereabouts of a line of torpedoes across the road. Some time was lost in safely removing them, when, leaving eight regiments at that point, nine were carried forward to about six hundred yards from the Fort, and deployed, with a line of skirmishers thrown sufficiently near the Fort to keep the gunners from working their guns with any effect; those firing to the rear being in barbette.

The grounds to the right of the Fort being marshy, cut through by deep streams, rendered the deployment of that part of the line slow and difficult, and was not completely effected till forty-five minutes past four P.M., at which time, every officer and man of the nine regiments being instructed what to do, the bugle sounded the forward, and at precisely five o'clock the Fort was carried.

The troops were deployed in our line as thin as possible, the result being that no man in the assault was struck till they came to close quarters. Here the fighting became desperate and deadly. Just outside the works, a line of torpedoes had been placed, many of which were exploded by the tread of the troops, blowing many men to atoms; but the line moved on without checking, over, under, and through abattis, ditches, palisading, and parapet, fighting the garrison through the Fort to their bomb-proofs, from which they still fought, and only succumbed as each man was individually overpowered. Our losses were, twenty-four officers and men killed, and one hundred and ten officers and men wounded.

Meanwhile Union warships had reached the coastal sounds immediately below Savannah—Wassaw, Ossabaw, St. Catherines—and waited for a chance to help Sherman. Rear Admiral John A. Dahlgren reported to Welles how the Navy played its part as Sherman's army finally marched to the sea:[4]

On the eighteenth, General Sherman came on board the flag-ship. Having fully invested Savannah on the land side, whilst the navy held every avenue by water, General Sherman sent a summons to surrender, which was declined by General Hardee on the ground that he held his two lines of defence, and was in communication with his superior authority. General Sherman therefore prepared to attack. His army was gradually drawing closer on Savannah River, and in order to cut off the escape of the rebel forces, he concluded it would be better to send a division to reënforce the troops of General Foster, up Broad River, and make a serious attack there in the direction of the railroad, whilst that on Beaulieu would be limited to the naval cannonade, which I must not omit to mention had been begun and continued with deliberation by Lieutenant Commander Scott, in the *Sonoma*, assisted for a day or so by the mortar of the *Griffiths*, Acting-Master Ogilvie. To insure the exact concurrence of the several ports, the General went with me to Hilton Head in my steamer, and General Foster was made fully acquainted with the design. Late on Monday I put to sea, but to avoid detention from the increasing gale, the pilot preferred to follow the interior passage, and when near Ossabaw my steamer grounded. We started in the barge to pull, and were nearly in the waters of Ossabaw when a tug came along with the following telegram for General Sherman:

> FROM STATION NEAR HEADQUARTERS,
> December 4, 1864—M.

TO GENERAL SHERMAN:

General Howard reports one of General Leggett's brigades near Savannah, and no enemy. Prisoners say the city is abandoned and enemy gone to Hardeeville.

Wood captured six guns. Slocum got eight guns, and is moving on the city.

DAYTON,

Aid-de-Camp.

It was now about three P.M. General Sherman hastened to his head-quarters, and I to the division of vessels lying in front of Beaulieu. The facts of the case were soon apparent. Captain Scott, of the *Sonoma*, was in possession of Fort Beaulieu and Rosedew. I landed at the former, and after giving some brief directions, was on my way from it when I received a note from General Sherman, dated half-past six P.M., with two telegrams from General Howard, one saying, "Tatnall intends to run the blockade tonight;" the other: "Rebel boat *Savannah*, with Tatnall in, is just out of our reach."

I did not apprehend that this intention to escape could be carried into effect.

The two iron-clads which I had at Wassaw blocked the best way out, and I did not believe that the rebel ram could be brought over the shallows of Savannah River, save under the most favorable circumstances of a high tide and an easterly wind. At this time it was blowing a gale from the north-west.

Still it did not seem proper to allow the public interest to incur the least risk in a matter so important. So I ordered the *Pawnee* to tow the *Nantucket* to Savannah River, and her commander being too ill to be on deck, Fleet-Captain Bradford volunteered for the duty.

It was three o'clock on the morning of the twenty-first when I lay down for a few hours' rest; and as my steamer was still aground, got into my barge at seven A.M., pulled to Wassaw, then across the sound into the pass to the Savannah River, and had nearly reached the Savannah River when a tug came along and relieved the faithful seamen of their severe labor in a heavy gale, wet to the skin as they were. I arrived about noon, hoisted my flag in the *Wissahickon*, Captain Johnson, and proceeded up the river with the *Winona*, Captain Dana, and two tugs.

. About four P.M., the obstructions across the channel near the head of Elba Island compelled me to anchor a short distance below the city. . . .

The glorious flag of the Union once more waved over the ramparts of the forts, and the city, and the vessels of the navy on the water. Savannah has been taken in the only way probably that it was assailable. In every other the defences were complete and powerful, extending over every approach, and including the rivers that traversed the country to the southward; so that an attack in those quarters could not have succeeded. It is one of the first fruits of the brilliant campaign commencing at Atlanta, and of that fine conception—the march through Georgia.

But it is not the last, and General Sherman has but to follow out his plans in order to reap still greater advantages for the country and renown for himself.

III

In Tennessee, on the first day of December, General John Bell Hood made what seemed to him to be a logical decision:[5]

After the failure of my cherished plan to crush Schofield's Army before it reached its strongly fortified position around Nashville, I remained with an effective force of only twenty-three thousand and fifty-three. I was therefore well aware of our inability to attack the Federals in their new stronghold with any hope of success, although Schofield's troops had abandoned the field at Franklin, leaving their dead and wounded in our possession, and had hastened with considerable alarm into their fortifications. . . . I knew equally well that in the absence of the prestige of complete victory, I could not venture with my small force to cross the Cumberland river into Kentucky, without first receiving reinforcements from the Trans-Mississippi Department. I felt convinced that the Tennesseeans and Kentuckians would not join our forces, since we had failed in the first instance to defeat the Federal Army and capture Nashville. The President [Davis] was still urgent in his instructions relative to the transference of troops to the Army of Tennessee from Texas, and I daily hoped to receive the glad tidings of their safe passage across the Mississippi river.

Thus, unless strengthened by these long-looked for reinforcements, the only remaining chance of success in the campaign, at this juncture, was to take position, entrench around Nashville, and await Thomas's attack which, if handsomely repulsed, might afford us an opportunity to follow up our advantage on the spot, and enter the city on the heels of the enemy.

I could not afford to turn southward, unless for the *special* purpose of forming a junction with the expected reinforcements from Texas, and with the avowed intention to march back again upon Nashville. In truth, our Army was in that condition which rendered it more judicious the men should face a decisive issue rather than retreat—in other words, rather than renounce the honor of their cause, without having made a last and manful effort to lift up the sinking fortunes of the Confederacy.

I therefore determined to move upon Nashville, to entrench, to accept the chances of reinforcements from Texas, and, even at the risk of an attack in the meantime by overwhelming numbers, to adopt the only feasible means of defeating the enemy with my reduced numbers, viz., to await his attack, and, if favored by success, to follow him into his works. . . .

In accordance with these convictions, I ordered the Army to move forward on the 1st of December in the direction of Nashville. . . .

Grant chafed to think that Hood and his army hadn't been finished off by now. Sherman, prodded by Grant to do whatever he could to budge Thomas, admitted that he was "somewhat astonished by the attitude of things in Tennessee." Yet Sherman reminded Grant that while Thomas was "slow in mind and action" he was "judicious and brave," and in time, Sherman believed, Thomas would "outmanoeuvre and destroy Hood." Thomas also chafed under the pressure being exerted on him.

Colonel Henry Stone of Thomas' staff felt a deep sympathy for his chief:[6]

Probably no commander ever underwent two weeks of greater anxiety and distress of mind than General Thomas during the interval between Hood's arrival and his precipitate departure from the vicinity of Nashville. . . . From the 2d of December until the battle was fought on the 15th, the general-in-chief did not cease, day or night, to send him from the headquarters at City Point, Va., most urgent and often most uncalled-for orders in regard to his operations, culminating in an order on the 9th relieving him, and directing him to turn over his command to General Schofield, who was assigned to his place—an order which, had it not been revoked, the great captain would have obeyed with loyal single-heartedness. This order, though made out at the Adjutant-General's office in Washington, was not sent to General Thomas, and he did not know of its existence until told of it some years later. . . . He felt, however, that something of the kind was impending. General Halleck dispatched to him, on the morning of the 9th: "Lieutenant-General Grant expresses much dissatisfaction at your delay in attacking the enemy." His reply shows how entirely he understood the situation: "I feel conscious I have done everything in my power, and that the troops could not have been gotten ready before this. If General Grant should order me to be relieved, I will submit without a murmur." As he was writing this—2 o'clock in the afternoon of December 9th—a terrible storm of freezing rain had been pouring down since daylight, and it kept on pouring and freezing all that day and a part of the next. That night General Grant notified him that the order relieving him—which he had divined—was suspended. But he did not know who had been designated as his successor. With this threat hanging over him; with the utter impossibility, in that weather, of making any movement; with the prospect that the labors of his whole life were about to end in disappointment, if not disaster—he never, for an instant, abated his energy or his work of preparation. Not an hour, day and night, was he idle. Nobody—not even his most trusted staff-officers—knew the contents of the telegrams that came to him. But it was very evident that something greatly troubled him. While the rain was falling and the fields and roads were ice-bound, he would sometimes sit by the window for an hour or more, not speaking a word, gazing steadily out upon the forbidding prospect, as if he were trying to will the storm away. It was curious and interesting to see how, in this gloomy interval, his time was occupied by matters not strictly military. Now, it was a visit from a delegation of the city government, in regard to some municipal regulation; again, somebody whose one horse had been seized and put into the cavalry; then, a committee of citizens, begging that wood might be furnished, to keep some poor families from freezing; and, of evenings, Governor Andrew Johnson—then Vice-President elect—would unfold to him, with much iteration, his fierce views concerning secession, rebels, and reconstruction. To all he gave a patient and kindly hearing, and he often astonished Governor Johnson by his knowledge of constitutional and international law. But, underneath all, it was plain to see that General Grant's dissatisfaction keenly affected him, and that only by the proof which a successful battle would furnish could he hope to regain the confidence of the general-in-chief.

So when, at 8 o'clock on the evening of December 14th, after having laid his plans before his corps commanders, and dismissed them, he dictated to General Halleck the telegram, "The ice having melted away today, the enemy will be attacked tomorrow morning," he drew a deep sigh of relief, and for the first time for a week showed again something of his natural buoyancy and cheerfulness. He moved

about more briskly; he put in order all the little last things that remained to be done; he signed his name where it was needed in the
letter-book, and then, giving orders to his staff-officers to be ready at
5 o'clock the next morning, went gladly to bed.

The ice had not melted a day too soon; for, while he was writing
the telegram to General Halleck, General Logan was speeding his way
to Nashville, with orders from General Grant that would have placed
him in command of all the Union forces there assembled. General
Thomas, fortunately, did not then learn this second proof of General
Grant's lack of confidence; and General Logan, on reaching Louisville,
found that the work intended for him was already done—and came no
farther. At the very time when these orders were made out at Washington, in obedience to General Grant's directions, a large part of the
cavalry was unmounted; two divisions were absent securing horses and
proper outfit; wagons were unfinished and mules lacking or unbroken;
pontoons unmade and pontoniers untrained; the ground was covered
with a glare of ice which made all the fields and hillsides impassable for
horses and scarcely passable for foot-men. The natives declared that
the Yankees brought their weather as well as their army with them.
Every corps commander in the army protested that a movement under
such conditions would be little short of madness, and certain to result in
disaster.

*Hood commanded troops that were largely "confused and demoral-
ized." That redoubtable Tennessee historian, Sam Watkins, remembered that on the morning of December 15 he glanced at Hood and
recognized "how feeble and decrepit he looked, with an arm in a sling
and a crutch in the other hand, trying to guide and control his horse."
Colonel Stone watched Thomas that same morning, and saw his blue-
clad columns swarm up a hillside:*

It was not daylight, on the morning of the 15th of December, when
the army began to move. In most of the camps reveille had been
sounded at 4 o'clock, and by 6 everything was ready. It turned out a
warm, sunny, winter morning. A dense fog at first hung over the
valleys and completely hid all movements, but by 9 o'clock this had
cleared away. . . .

When . . . the sun began to burn away the fog, the sight from
General Thomas's position was inspiring. A little to the left, on Montgomery Hill, the salient of the Confederate lines, and not more than six

hundred yards distant from Wood's salient, on Lawrens Hill, could be seen the advance line of works, behind which an unknown force of the enemy lay in wait. Beyond, and along the Hillsboro' Pike, were stretches of stone wall, with here and there a detached earth-work, through whose embrasures peeped the threatening artillery. To the right, along the valley of Richland Creek, the dark line of Wilson's advancing cavalry could be seen slowly making its difficult way across the wet, swampy ground. Close in front, and at the foot of the hill, its right joining Wilson's left, was A. J. Smith's corps, full of cheer and enterprise, and glad to be once more in the open field. Then came the Fourth Corps, whose left, bending back toward the north, was hidden behind Lawrens Hill. Already the skirmishers were engaged, the Confederates slowly falling back before the determined and steady pressure of Smith and Wood.

By the time that Wilson's and Smith's lines were fully extended and brought up to within striking distance of the Confederate works, along the Hillsboro' Pike, it was noon. Post's brigade of Wood's old division . . . which lay at the foot of Montgomery Hill, full of dash and spirit, had since morning been regarding the works at the summit with covetous eyes. At Post's suggestion, it was determined to see which party wanted them most. Accordingly, a charge was ordered—and in a moment the brigade was swarming up the hillside, straight for the enemy's advanced works. For almost the first time since the grand assault on Missionary Ridge, a year before, here was an open field where everything could be seen. From General Thomas's headquarters everybody looked on with breathless suspense, as the blue line, broken and irregular, but with steady persistence, made its way up the steep hillside against a fierce storm of musketry and artillery. Most of the shots, however, passed over the men's heads. It was a struggle to keep up with the colors, and, as they neared the top, only the strongest were at the front. Without a moment's pause, the color-bearers and those who had kept up with them, Post himself at the head, leaped the parapet. As the colors waved from the summit, the whole line swept forward and was over the works in a twinkling, gathering in prisoners and guns. Indeed, so large was the mass of prisoners that a few minutes later was seen heading toward our own lines, that a number of officers at General Thomas's headquarters feared the assault had failed and the prisoners were Confederate reserves who had rallied and retaken the works. But the fear was only momentary; for the wild outburst of cheers that rang across the valley told the story of complete success. . . .

The salient at the center . . . was still firmly held. Post's successful assault had merely driven out or captured the advance forces; the main line was intact. As soon as word came of the successful assault on the

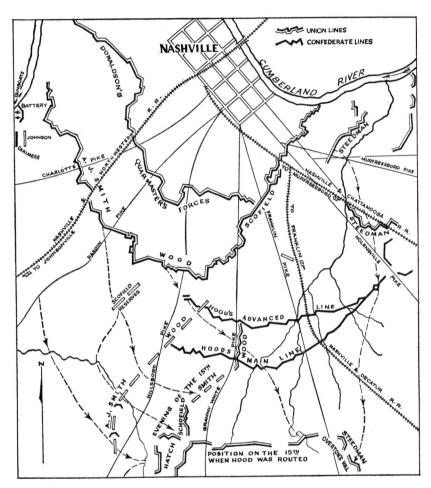

THE BATTLE OF NASHVILLE

From Lossing, *Pictorial History of the Civil War*

right, General Thomas sent orders to General Wood, commanding the Fourth Corps, to prepare to attack the salient. The staff-officer by whom this order was sent did not at first find General Wood; but seeing the two division commanders whose troops would be called upon for the work, gave them the instructions. As he was riding along the line he met one of the brigade commanders—an officer with a reputation for exceptional courage and gallantry—who, in reply to the direction to prepare for the expected assault, said, "You don't mean that we've got to go in here and attack the works on that hill?" "Those are the orders," was the answer. Looking earnestly across the open valley, and at the steep hill beyond, from which the enemy's guns were throwing shot and shell with uncomfortable frequency and nearness, he said, "Why, it would be suicide, sir; perfect suicide." "Nevertheless, those are the orders," said the officer; and he rode on to complete his work. Before he could rejoin General Thomas the assault was made, and the enemy were driven out with a loss of guns, colors, and prisoners, and their whole line was forced to abandon the works along the Hillsboro' Pike and fall back to the Granny White Pike. The retreating line was followed by the entire Fourth Corps (Wood's), as well as by the cavalry and Smith's troops; but night soon fell, and the whole army went into bivouac in the open fields wherever they chanced to be.

The Hood of Nashville was the Hood of Cassville, Kenesaw, Atlanta, Allatoona, Spring Hill, and Franklin. He accepted no blame:[7]

The 10th of December, Generals Stewart and Cheatham were directed to construct detached works in rear of their flanks, which rested near the river, in order to protect these flanks against an effort by the Federals to turn them. Although every possible exertion was made by these officers, the works were not completed when, on the 15th, the Federal Army moved out, and attacked both flanks, whilst the main assault was directed against our left. It was my intention to have made these defences self-sustaining, but time was not allowed, as the enemy attacked on the morning of the 15th. Throughout that day, they were repulsed at all points of the general line with heavy loss, and only succeeded towards evening in capturing the infantry outposts on our left, and with them the small force together with the artillery posted in these unfinished works.

Thomas sent Halleck a factual report and a promise:[8]

                                        NASHVILLE, TENN.,
                                        December 15, 1864—9 P.M.
MAJ. GEN. H. W. HALLECK,
WASHINGTON, D. C.
    I attacked the enemy's left this morning and drove it from the river, below the city, very nearly to the Franklin pike, a distance about eight

miles. Have captured General Chalmers' headquarters and train, and a second train of about 20 wagons, with between 800 and 1,000 prisoners and 16 pieces of artillery. The troops behaved splendidly, all taking their share in assaulting and carrying the enemy's breast-works. I shall attack the enemy again tomorrow, if he stands to fight, and, if he retreats during the night, will pursue him, throwing a heavy cavalry force in his rear, to destroy his trains, if possible.

Confederate Major General Carter L. Stevenson, commanding the right of Hood's line, saw Thomas' troops accept heavy punishment to fulfill their commander's promise:[9]

The enemy advanced early in heavy force in front of the new line which we had constructed late the previous night, my division extending its entire length, part of it in two and part of it in one thin rank, from a short distance to the left of the Franklin pike. The skirmishers of the right of Lee's corps (Clayton's) and mine maintained their position so well, though in small force, that in their subsequent accounts the enemy have seen fit to magnify their affair with them into a desperate assault by two corps upon our first line, which was finally successful, but attended with heavy loss. Soon afterward their forces advanced to the assault. . . . Their success the previous day had emboldened them, and they rushed forward with great spirit, only to be driven back with dreadful slaughter. Finding at last that they could make no impression upon our lines, they relinquished their attempt and contented themselves with keeping up an incessant fire of small arms at long range and an artillery fire which I have never seen surpassed for heaviness, continuance, and accuracy. This state of things continued until evening, doing, however, but little damage, my men keeping closely in the trenches and perfectly cool and confident.

General James T. Holtzclaw, commanding a Confederate brigade, testified to the bravery—and the shocking losses—of the assaulting force:

About 10 o'clock [the enemy] made a desperate charge, but was driven back, with loss. He then commenced a most furious shelling from three six-gun batteries, concentrating his fire mainly upon my right. One battery of unusually heavy guns was brought down the pike to within 600 yards of my line. The conformation of the ground prevented me sharpshooting it sufficiently to drive it away. At 12 M. the enemy made a most determined charge on my right. Placing a negro brigade in front they gallantly dashed up to the abatis, forty feet in front, and were killed by hundreds. Pressed on by their white brethren in the rear they continued to come up in masses to the abatis, but they came only to die. I have seen most of the battle-fields of the West, but never saw dead men thicker in front of my two right regiments; the great masses and disorder of the enemy enabling the left to rake them in flank, while the right, with a coolness unexampled, scarcely threw away a shot at their front. The enemy at last broke and fled in wild disorder. With great difficulty I prevented my line from pursuing; with a supporting line I should certainly have done so; but covering the pike, which would be our only line of retreat in case of disaster, I did not feel justified in hazarding the position for what might only have been a temporary success. A color-bearer of the negro brigade brought his standard to within a few feet of my line. He was shot down, and Lieutenant Knox, of the Thirty-sixth Alabama Regiment, sprang over the shattered works and brought it in. Another flag was carried off by an officer after five different bearers had fallen in the vain effort to plant it in my works. At 2 P.M. the enemy attempted a second charge, less determined than the first. Their brave officers could neither lead nor drive their men to such certain death; I noticed as many as three mounted who fell far in advance of their commands urging them forward. The shelling of the enemy's batteries between 12 and 3 P.M. was the most furious I ever witnessed, while the range was so precise that scarce a shell failed to explode in the line. The enemy seemed now to be satisfied that he could not carry my position, and contented himself by shelling and sharpshooting everything in sight.

But the weight of Union men and metal was too heavy for Confederate resistance, no matter how valiant. General Stevenson related an unexpected turn of events:

Toward evening General Lee sent me information that things were going badly on the left, and that it might be necessary to retire under cover of the approaching night. I at once hurried off orders for the artillery horses, which had been removed some distance to the rear to protect them from the fire of the enemy's artillery, under which they could not have lived half an hour, to be brought up. (It was proper to observe that about the middle of the day mist and rain arose, which entirely prevented my seeing any thing that was going on beyond my own line.) The messengers had hardly gone for the horses before the break, which, commencing some distance beyond the left of Lee's corps, extended to my line. Seeing it, the men on my left commenced leaving the works, but at the call of their officers returned at once and held the line until the enemy were within fifty steps of them on their flank and pouring a fire into them from the flank and rear. When the true situation of affairs became apparent, and it was evident that the whole army, with the exception of my division and Clayton's, had been broken and scattered, the order for their withdrawal was given, an effort being made to deploy skirmishers from my left brigade at right angles to the works to cover, in some measure, the movement. Amid the indescribable confusion of other troops, and with the enemy pouring in their fire upon their flanks and from the front—having rushed toward the break and then forward when they perceived that the troops on my left had broken—it was impossible to withdraw the command in order, and it became considerably broken and confused. Many of them were unable to get out of the ditches in time and were captured. . . . The artillery horses of Rowan's battery, on the left of my line, could not be brought up in time, and one of the guns of Corput's battery was lost by being driven at full speed against a tree and the carriage broken. The different brigade and regimental commanders had sent off their horses, there being no protection for them near the breast-works, and, being thus unable to move about more rapidly than the men, were prevented from reforming their commands as quickly as could have been desired and extricating them from the throng of panic-stricken stragglers from other commands who crowded the road. This was done at last, and the line of march taken up for Franklin.

On December 16, while the outcome of the battle was still unknown in Washington, Lincoln had wired Thomas: "You made a magnificent beginning. A grand consummation is within your reach. Do not let it slip."

Lincoln need not have worried; Thomas, as his record showed, had let few chances to win "slip." The general responded to Lincoln, Stanton, Grant and Johnson on the events of a day when, by the testimony of Sam Watkins, Hood's Army of Tennessee "degenerated into a mob . . .":[10]

HEADQUARTERS DEPARTMENT OF THE CUMBERLAND,
EIGHT MILES FROM NASHVILLE, December 16, 1864—6 P.M.
THE PRESIDENT OF THE UNITED STATES,
HON. E. M. STANTON,
LIEUT. GEN. U. S. GRANT, AND
GOVERNOR ANDREW JOHNSON, NASHVILLE:

This army thanks you for your approbation of its conduct yesterday, and to assure you that it is not misplaced. I have the honor to report that the enemy has been pressed at all points today on his line of retreat to the Brentwood Hills, and Brigadier-General Hatch, of Wilson's corps of cavalry, on the right, turned the enemy's left, and captured a large number of prisoners, number not yet reported. Major-General Schofield's troops, next on the left of cavalry, carried several heights, captured many prisoners and six pieces of artillery. Brevet Major-General Smith, next on left of Major-General Schofield, carried the salient point of the enemy's line with McMillen's brigade, of McArthur's division, capturing 16 pieces of artillery, 2 brigadier-generals, and about 2,000 prisoners. Brigadier-General Garrard's division, of Smith's command, next on the left of McArthur's division, carried the enemy's intrenchments, capturing all the artillery and troops of the enemy on the line. Brigadier-General Wood's corps, on the Franklin pike, took up the assault, carrying the enemy's intrenchments in his front, captured 8 pieces of artillery, something over 600 prisoners, and drove the enemy within one mile of the Brentwood Pass. Major-General Steedman, commanding detachments of the different armies of the Military Division of the Mississippi, most nobly supported General Wood's left, and bore a most honorable part in the operations of the day. I have ordered the pursuit to be continued in the morning at daylight, although the troops are very much fatigued. The greatest enthusiasm prevails. I must not forget to report the operations of Brigadier-General Johnson, in successfully driving the enemy, with the cooperation of the gun-boats, under Lieutenant-Commander Fitch, from their established batteries on the Cumberland River below the city of Nashville, and of the services of Brigadier-General Croxton's brigade, in covering and relieving our right and rear, in the operations of yesterday and today. Although I have no report of the number of prisoners captured by Johnson's and Croxton's commands, I know they have made a large number. I am glad to be able to state that the number of prisoners captured yesterday greatly exceeds the number reported by me last evening. The woods, fields, and intrenchments are strewn with the enemy's small-arms, abandoned in their retreat. In conclusion, I am happy to state that all this has been effected with but a very small loss to us. Our loss does not probably exceed 3,000; very few killed.

GEO. H. THOMAS,
Major-General, U. S. Volunteers,
Commanding

IV

In less than a week after Thomas triumphed at Nashville, Sherman entered Savannah:[11]

Generals Slocum and Howard moved their headquarters at once into the city, leaving the bulk of their troops in camps outside. On the morning of December 22d I followed with my own headquarters, and rode down Bull Street to the custom-house, from the roof of which we had an extensive view over the city, the river, and the vast extent of marsh and rice-fields on the South Carolina side. The navy-yard, and the wreck of the iron-clad ram *Savannah,* were still smouldering, but all else looked quiet enough. Turning back, we rode to the Pulaski Hotel, which I had known in years long gone, and found it kept by a Vermont man with a lame leg, who used to be a clerk in the St. Louis Hotel, New Orleans, and I inquired about the capacity of his hotel for headquarters. He was very anxious to have us for boarders, but I soon explained to him that we had a full mess equipment along, and that we were not in the habit of paying board; that one wing of the building would suffice for our use, while I would allow him to keep an hotel for the accommodation of officers and gentlemen in the remainder. I then dispatched an officer to look around for a livery-stable that could accommodate our horses, and, while waiting there, an English gentleman, Mr. Charles Green, came and said that he had a fine house completely furnished, for which he had no use, and offered it as headquarters. . . .

I was disappointed that Hardee had escaped with his army, but on the whole we had reason to be content with the substantial fruits of victory. The Savannah River was found to be badly obstructed by torpedoes, and by log piers stretched across the channel below the city, which piers were filled with the cobble stones that formerly paved the streets. Admiral Dahlgren was extremely active, visited me repeatedly in the city, while his fleet still watched Charleston, and all the avenues, for the blockade-runners that infested the coast, which were notoriously owned and managed by Englishmen, who used the island of New Providence (Nassau) as a sort of entrepot. One of these small blockade-runners came into Savannah after we were in full possession, and the master did not discover his mistake till he came ashore to visit the custom-house. Of course his vessel fell a prize to the navy. A heavy force was at once set to work to remove the torpedoes and obstructions in the main channel of the river, and, from that time forth, Savannah became the great depot of supply for the troops operating in that quarter.

A "shrewd" Yankee, who understood Lincoln, offered a suggestion that Sherman accepted:

Within an hour of taking up my quarters in Mr. Green's house, Mr. A. G. Browne, of Salem, Massachusetts, United States Treasury agent for the Department of the South, made his appearance to claim possession, in the name of the Treasury Department, of all captured cotton, rice, buildings, etc. Having use for these articles ourselves, and having fairly earned them, I did not feel inclined to surrender possession, and explained to him that the quartermaster and commissary could manage them more to my liking than he; but I agreed, after the proper inventories had been prepared, if there remained any thing for which we had no special use, I would turn it over to him. It was then known that in the warehouses were stored at least twenty-five thousand bales of cotton, and in the forts one hundred and fifty large, heavy sea-coast guns; although afterward, on a more careful count, there proved to be more than two hundred and fifty sea-coast or siege guns, and thirty-one thousand bales of cotton. At that interview Mr. Browne, who was a shrewd, clever Yankee, told me that a vessel was on the point of starting for Old Point Comfort, and, if she had good weather off Cape Hatteras, would reach Fortress Monroe by Christmas-day, and he suggested that I might make it the occasion of sending a welcome Christmas gift to the President, Mr. Lincoln, who peculiarly enjoyed such pleasantry. I accordingly sat down and wrote on a slip of paper, to be left at the telegraph-office at Fortress Monroe for transmission, the following:

"SAVANNAH, GEORGIA, December 22, 1864.

"To HIS EXCELLENCY PRESIDENT LINCOLN, WASHINGTON, D. C.:

"I beg to present you as a Christmas-gift the city of Savannah, with one hundred and fifty heavy guns and plenty of ammunition, also about twenty-five thousand bales of cotton.

"W. T. SHERMAN, *Major-General.*"

This message actually reached him on Christmas-eve, was extensively published in the newspapers, and made many a household unusually happy on that festive day; and it was in the answer to this dispatch that Mr. Lincoln wrote me the letter of December 26th, already
given, beginning with the words, "Many, many thanks," etc., which he
sent at the hands of General John A. Logan, who happened to be in
Washington, and was coming to Savannah, to rejoin his command.

*In 1861 Sherman had been "sadly disappointed" in Lincoln and had
damned him along with politicians generally who had "got things in a
hell of a fix." Now Sherman placed the President first among the wise
men of the country. Years later, he gave his reasons to R. L. Johnson,
associate editor of* Century Magazine:[12]

. . . Mr. Lincoln was the wisest man of our day, and now truly and
kindly gave voice to my secret thoughts and feeling when he wrote me
at Savannah from Washington under date of Dec. 26, 1864:

"When you were about leaving Atlanta for the Atlantic coast, I was
anxious if not fearful; but feeling that you were the better judge, and
remembering 'nothing risked, nothing gained,' I did not interfere. Now
the undertaking being a success, the honor is all yours; for I believe
none of us went further than to acquiesce; and, taking the work of
General Thomas into account, as it should be taken, it is indeed a great
success. Not only does it afford the obvious and immediate military
advantages, but, in showing to the world that your army could be divided, putting the stronger part to an important new service, and yet
leaving enough to vanquish the old opposing force of the whole, Hood's
army, it brings those who sat in darkness to see a great light. But what
next? I suppose it will be safer if I leave General Grant and yourself to
decide."

So highly do I prize this testimonial that I possess Mr. Lincoln's
letter, every word in his own hand writing, unto this day; and if I know
myself I believe on receiving it I experienced more satisfaction in
giving to his overburdened and weary soul one gleam of satisfaction
and happiness, than of selfish pride in an achievement which has given
me among men a larger measure of fame than any single act of my
life. . . .

v

*The month that had begun with the President promising Congress that
final victory was near now had ended. Thomas held Nashville, and in*

Savannah Negroes began dating all events from "de Time Tecumpsey was here." Above the Mason and Dixon line every song-writer seemed busy at a new ballad to commemorate the march to the sea. Among them was D. A. Warden, who produced "Sherman's on the Track":[13]

> Oh look away out yonder,
>   For de dust am rising high,
> Gen'ral Sherman's comin' 'long,
>   And Massa's goin' to die,
> He's got some nigger soldiers
>   Dat make de rebels run,
> Just hold your breff a little while,
>   And see de glorious fun,
> Just hold your breff a little while,
>   And see de glorious fun.
> Chorus.—Shout! darkies shout!
>   Old Sherman's on de track,
>   He's knock'd de breff from poor old Jeff,
>   And laid him on his back, whack!

Two stanzas later Mr. Warden composed an accurate report of the general situation:

> The railroads hab been torn to smash,
>   De lokies cannot run,
> Old Hood has got his boiler bust
>   And dat hab stopt *his* fun,
> Poor Beauregard *lies* berry sick,
>   Wid rupture and wid gout,
> While Bobby Lee begins to see
>   De game am most played out,
> While Bobby Lee begins to see
>   De game am most played out.

1865

CHAPTER 37

A KING'S CURE
FOR ALL EVILS

Ted Upson remembered a day back home in Lima, Indiana, during March 1859—Ted was going on fourteen then—when Cooper Dayton, his mother's brother from Nashville, and the Reverend Cory "got to talking right away and both got pretty mad for Preachers."

"Now, Brother Cory," Cooper Dayton asked, "if you had your own way what would you do with the slaves?"

"Free them, sir! Free them at once! You have no right to hold them a day longer in slavery."

Cooper Dayton looked at Cory. "My!" he said. "How you must love a Nigger!"

I

Almost four years of war had changed people, attitudes, circumstances.

Theodore Upson, of Company C, 100th Indiana Infantry—Ted was going on twenty now—was one of Sherman's boys who were finding the Christmas holidays in Savannah a midwinter picnic:[1]

We have been having a Christmas Jubilee. The boys raised some money and I went down into the City to get some stuff. We have a Darky cook, and he said, "You alls get the greginces and I will get you alls up a fine dinner sure." I got some chickens, canned goods, condensed milk, and a dozen eggs. These cost me pretty dear—$3.00 per doz. I wouldn't have minded so much, but when we came to use them there

was only one of the lot that was at all fit to use and that was not any
too good. But we had the dinner just the same and it was fine. Some of
the officers had a banquet—they called it. I dont know if they had egg
nog. If they did their eggs must have been better than ours, but I know
they must have had some sort of nog for the Provost Guard had to help
some of them to their Quarters.

*Major James A. Connolly, older, maturer than Upson, wrote to his wife
on January 19, 1865:*[2]

Our headquarters are in the city. My office is in a fine brick building on "Oglethorpe Square," and Captain ———, aide de camp, and
myself have private rooms in another fine residence on the same square.
We have gas light, coal fires, sofas, fine beds, bath room with hot and
cold water, and all such luxuries; so it won't do for us to remain here
long or we shall be completely spoiled for soldiering. Our beds should
be at the roots of the cypress trees of Carolina instead of the luxurious
couches of Savannah. Soldiers may *be* gentlemen but they can't *live*
like gentlemen and do soldier's duty.

I shall leave Savannah very favorably impressed with it as a city.
I have been most courteously treated by all its citizens with whom I
have come in contact, and I hope that its beautiful squares, its elegant
mansions, and its delightful streets may never hear any but peaceful
sounds. Our whole army has fallen in love with this city and we all
leave it with regret.

II

*Four hundred miles to the northeast there was action. An ominous tele-
gram sped from the fort which commanded the entrance to the Cape
Fear River and kept Wilmington, North Carolina, open to blockade
runners:*[3]

FORT FISHER,
January 12, 1865

MAJOR HILL:

There are a number of signal lights shown northeast and southeast;
they are not the blockade signals, but the old fleet signals. Today at
noon one of the blockaders ran very close down from battery Gatlin and
turned off toward the fleet; when two and a half to three miles from us
her decks seemed crowded, but not unusually so. I am just officially in-

formed that a sergeant and three men deserted from Battery Gatlin last night.

LAMB,
Colonel

Another telegram came from a nearby post:

MASONBOROUGH,
January 12, 1865

MAJ. J. H. HILL:

The lights from the fleet have increased. Thirty and more vessels in view moving toward Fisher; 10 o'clock.

T. J. LIPSCOMB,
Colonel, Commanding

General W. H. C. Whiting, commanding the Confederate garrison at Wilmington, hurried to Fort Fisher. From there he sent a series of urgent appeals to Braxton Bragg, who had a small force at Sugar Loaf, between Fort Fisher and Wilmington:[4]

FORT FISHER,
January 13, 1865

GENERAL BRAGG:

The enemy have landed in large force. Garrison too weak to resist assault and prevent their advance. You must attack them at once.

WHITING,
General

FORT FISHER,
January 13, 1865

GENERAL BRAGG:

Enemy have landed a large force. They will assault me tonight, or try to do it. You must attack.

W. H. C. WHITING,
Major-General

FORT FISHER,
January 13, 1865—8 P.M.

GENERAL BRAXTON BRAGG:

Enemy are on the beach, where they have been all day. Why are they not attacked? Our casualties about forty, after a furious bombardment. I have ordered troops from the other posts. Our submarine cable and telegraph cut by shell. Enemy ceased firing at 6 o'clock.

WHITING,
General

Next day Whiting was even more forceful:[5]

FORT FISHER,
January 14, 1865—1:30 P.M.

GENERAL BRAGG:

I send this boat, *Cape Fear,* to town for coal and wood, with the request that she return at once; she is necessary here for our communication. The game of the enemy is very plain to me. They are now furiously bombarding my land front; they will continue to do that, in order, if possible, to silence my guns until they are satisfied that their land force has securely established itself across the neck and rests on the river; then Porter will attempt to force a passage to co-operate with the force that takes the river bank. I have received dispatches from you stating that the enemy had extended to the river-bank. This they should never have been allowed to do; and if they are permitted to remain there the reduction of Fort Fisher is but a question of time. This has been notified heretofore frequently both to yourself and to the Department. I will hold this place till the last extremities; but unless you drive that land force from its position I cannot answer for the security of this harbor. The fire has been and continues to be exceedingly heavy, surpassing not so much in its volume as in its extraordinary condition even the fire of Christmas. The garrison is in good spirits and condition.

I am, general, very respectfully, your obedient servant,

W. H. C. WHITING
Major-General

Bragg, ever the optimist, reported to Lee:[6]

SUGAR LOAF,
January 14, 1865—8 P.M.

GENERAL R. E. LEE,
RICHMOND, VA.:

The enemy succeeded last night in extending his line across the peninsula, and interposed between us and Fort Fisher. His line has been closely examined by myself and General Hoke, and he considers it too hazardous to assault with such an inferior force. Fisher has been re-enforced with sufficient veterans to make it safe. The width of the river is such the enemy cannot control it from his position even with artillery, and he has yet landed none. Weather continues fine and sea smooth. Bombardment today light.

BRAXTON BRAGG

Whiting, desperate, renewed his appeals to Bragg:

FORT FISHER,
January 15, 1865.

GENERAL BRAXTON BRAGG:

Is Fisher to be besieged, or you to attack? Should like to know. The fire on the fort from iron-clads heavy, but casualties so far during the fight 3 killed and 32 wounded.

W. H. C. WHITING,
Major-General

FORT FISHER,
January 15, 1865—6:30 P.M.

GENERAL BRAXTON BRAGG:

The enemy are assaulting us by land and sea. Their infantry out-number us. Can't you help us? I am slightly wounded.

WHITING,
General

Officers at batteries near Fort Fisher reported the collapse of the defense:[7]

BATTERY LAMB,
January 15, 1865

GENERAL BRAGG:

Fort Fisher evacuated; troops rushed in confusion to Battery Buchanan. I landed at Buchanan just as the enemy was going in, and barely escaped. I will report to you tonight. There is no mistake in this information. Lieutenant Bright is here with thirty men, and wishes instruction.

A. H. COLQUITT,
Brigadier-General

BATTERY LAMB,
January 15, 1865—4:20 P.M.
(Received 4:45 P.M.)

GENERAL HÉBERT: *

Enemy still hold east part of land face of Fisher. Mound and Buchanan still firing. Flag still waving over the Mound and Buchanan.

BRIGHT,
Lieutenant

BATTERY LAMB,
January 15, 1865—10:30 P.M.
(Received 12 midnight.)

GENERAL HÉBERT:

All at once firing has ceased; also signals; and the whole fleet are now throwing rockets up—all colors. It is fully believed that the fort has surrendered. . . .

J. J. BRIGHT

Once more Bragg had the duty of announcing a result far different from what he had predicted:[8]

SUGAR LOAF,
January 16, 1865—1 A.M.

GENERAL R. E. LEE,
PETERSBURG:

I am mortified at having to report the unexpected capture of Fort Fisher, with most of its garrison, at about 10 o'clock tonight. Particulars not known.

BRAXTON BRAGG

Alexander H. Stephens, who wore no blinders, assessed the importance to the Confederacy of the loss of Fort Fisher:[9]

The fall of this Fort was one of the greatest disasters which had befallen our cause from the beginning of the war—not excepting the loss of Vicksburg or Atlanta. Forts Fisher and Caswell guarded the entrance to the Cape Fear River, and prevented the complete blockade of the port of Wilmington, through which a limited Foreign Commerce had been carried on during the whole time. It was by means of what

* General Louis Hébert, chief engineer of the Department of North Carolina.

cotton could thus be carried out, that we had been enabled to get along financially, as well as we had; and at this point also, a considerable number of arms and various munitions of war, as well as large supplies of subsistence, had been introduced. All other ports . . . had long since been closed by Naval siege. . . . Fort Sumter at Charleston, it is true, had still held out, and had never been taken, but the harbor there had been virtually closed by a strict blockade; so that the closing of the port of Wilmington was the complete shutting out of the Confederate States from all intercourse by sea with Foreign Countries.

III

Suddenly Washington and the halls of Congress became the greatest battlefield of the war. The objective to be won was the consent of Americans to a constitutional amendment abolishing slavery. When the first phase of the campaign had been fought the previous spring, the President of the United States had led the attack. Charles A. Dana had admired him greatly:[10]

Lincoln was a supreme politician. He understood politics because he understood human nature. I had an illustration of this in the spring of 1864. The administration had decided that the Constitution of the United States should be amended so that slavery should be prohibited. This was not only a change in our national policy, it was also a most important military measure. It was intended not merely as a means of abolishing slavery forever, but as a means of affecting the judgment and the feelings and the anticipations of those in rebellion. It was believed that such an amendment to the Constitution would be equivalent to new armies in the field, that it would be worth at least a million men, that it would be an intellectual army that would tend to paralyze the enemy and break the continuity of his ideas.

In order thus to amend the Constitution, it was necessary first to have the proposed amendment approved by three fourths of the States. When that question came to be considered, the issue was seen to be so close that one State more was necessary. The State of Nevada was organized and admitted into the Union to answer that purpose. I have sometimes heard people complain of Nevada as superfluous and petty, not big enough to be a State; but when I hear that complaint, I always hear Abraham Lincoln saying, "It is easier to admit Nevada than to raise another million of soldiers."

In March, 1864, the question of allowing Nevada to form a State government finally came up in the House of Representatives. There was strong opposition to it. For a long time beforehand the question had been canvassed anxiously. At last, late one afternoon, the President came into my office, in the third story of the War Department. He used to come there sometimes rather than send for me, because he was fond of walking and liked to get away from the crowds in the White House. He came in and shut the door.

"Dana," he said, "I am very anxious about this vote. It has got to be taken next week. The time is very short. It is going to be a great deal closer than I wish it was."

"There are plenty of Democrats who will vote for it," I replied. "There is James E. English, of Connecticut; I think he is sure, isn't he?"

"Oh, yes; he is sure on the merits of the question."

"Then," said I, "there's 'Sunset' Cox, of Ohio. How is he?"

"He is sure and fearless. But there are some others that I am not clear about. There are three that you can deal with better than anybody else, perhaps, as you know them all. I wish you would send for them."

He told me who they were; it isn't necessary to repeat the names here. One man was from New Jersey and two from New York.

"What will they be likely to want?" I asked.

"I don't know," said the President; "I don't know. It makes no difference, though, what they want. Here is the alternative: that we carry this vote, or be compelled to raise another million, and I don't know how many more, men, and fight no one knows how long. It is a question of three votes or new armies."

"Well, sir," said I, "what shall I say to these gentlemen?"

"I don't know," said he; "but whatever promise you make to them I will perform."

I sent for the men and saw them one by one. I found that they were afraid of their party. They said that some fellows in the party would be down on them. Two of them wanted internal revenue collector's appointments. "You shall have it," I said. Another one wanted a very important appointment about the custom house of New York. I knew the man well whom he wanted to have appointed. He was a Republican, though the congressman was a Democrat. I had served with him in the Republican county committee of New York. The office was worth perhaps twenty thousand dollars a year. When the congressman stated the case, I asked him, "Do you want that?"

"Yes," said he.

"Well," I answered, "you shall have it."

"I understand, of course," said he, "that you are not saying this on your own authority?"

"Oh, no," said I; "I am saying it on the authority of the President."

Now, in January 1865, with the Thirteenth Amendment again before Congress, Lincoln eagerly renewed the fight. James A. Rollins, a Representative from Missouri, described an interview with the President:[11]

The President had several times in my presence expressed his deep anxiety in favor of the passage of this great measure. He and others had repeatedly counted votes in order to ascertain, as far as they could, the strength of the measure upon a second trial in the House. He was doubtful about its passage, and some ten days or two weeks before it came up for consideration before the House, I received a note from him, written in pencil on a card, while sitting at my desk in the House, stating that he wished to see me, and asking that I call on him at the White House. I responded that I would be there the next morning at nine o'clock. I was prompt in calling upon him and found him alone in his office. He received me in the most cordial manner, and said in his usual familiar way: "Rollins, I have been wanting to talk to you for some time about the thirteenth amendment proposed to the Constitution of the United States, which will have to be voted on now, before a great while." I said: "Well, I am here, and ready to talk upon that subject." He said: "You and I were old whigs, both of us followers of that great statesman, Henry Clay, and I tell you I never had an opinion upon the subject of slavery in my life that I did not get from him. I am very anxious that the war should be brought to a close at the earliest possible date, and I don't believe this can be accomplished as long as those fellows down South can rely upon the border states to help them; but if the members from the border states would unite, at least enough of them to pass the thirteenth amendment to the Constitution, they would soon see that they could not expect much help from that quarter, and be willing to give up their opposition and quit their war upon the government; this is my chief hope and main reliance to bring the war to a speedy close, and I have sent for you as an old whig friend to come and see me, that I might make an appeal to you to vote for this amendment. It is going to be very close, a few votes one way or the other will decide it."

To this I responded: "Mr. President, so far as I am concerned you need not have sent for me to ascertain my views on this subject, for although I represent perhaps the strongest slave district in Missouri, and have the misfortune to be one of the largest slave-owners in the county where I reside, I had already determined to vote for the thirteenth amendment." He arose from his chair, and grasping me by the hand, gave it a hearty shake, and said: "I am most delighted to hear that."

He asked me how many more of the Missouri delegates in the House would vote for it. I said I could not tell; the Republicans of course would; General Loan, Mr. Blow, Mr. Boyd, and Colonel McClurg. He said: "Won't General Price * vote for it? He is a good Union man." I said I could not answer. "Well, what about Governor King?" I told him I did not know. He then asked about Judges Hall and Norton. I said they would both vote against it, I thought.

"Well," he said, "are you on good terms with Price and King?" I responded in the affirmative, and that I was on easy terms with the entire delegation. He then asked me if I would not talk with those who might be persuaded to vote for the amendment, and report to him as soon as I could find out what the prospect was. I answered that I would do so with pleasure, and remarked at the same time, that when I was a young man, in 1848, I was the whig competitor of King for Governor of Missouri and as he beat me very badly, I thought now he should pay me back by voting as I desired him on this important question. I promised the President I would talk to this gentleman upon the subject. He said: "I would like you to talk to all the border state men whom you can approach properly, and tell them of my anxiety to have the measure pass; and let me know the prospect of the border state vote," which I promised to do. He again said: "The passage of this amendment will clinch the whole subject; it will bring the war, I have no doubt, rapidly to a close."

Nicolay and Hay, eyewitnesses, described the critical vote in the House of Representatives:[12]

The issue was decided in the afternoon of the 31st of January, 1865. . . . The galleries were filled to overflowing; the Members watched the proceedings with unconcealed solicitude. "Up to noon," said a contemporaneous formal report, "the pro-slavery party are said to have been confident of defeating the amendment, and, after that time

* Thomas Lawson Price, elected as a Democrat in 1862.

had passed, one of the most earnest advocates of the measure said, ' 'Tis the toss of a copper.' " There were the usual pleas for postponement and for permission to offer amendments or substitutes, but at four o'clock the House came to a final vote, and the roll-call showed, yeas, 119; nays, 56; not voting, 8. Scattering murmurs of applause had followed the announcement of affirmative votes from several of the Democratic Members. This was renewed when by direction of the Speaker [Schuyler Colfax, of Indiana] the clerk called his name and he voted aye.

Colfax announced that the amendment had received the requisite two-thirds majority. According to the Washington Globe, emotions could no longer be contained:

The announcement was received by the House and by the spectators with an outburst of enthusiasm. The Members on the Republican side of the House instantly sprung to their feet, and, regardless of parliamentary rules, applauded with cheers and clapping of hands. The example was followed by the male spectators in the galleries, which were crowded to excess, who waved their hats and cheered loud and long, while the ladies, hundreds of whom were present, rose in their seats and waved their handkerchiefs, participating in and adding to the general excitement and intense interest of the scene. This lasted for several minutes.

The following night a jubilant procession marched to the White House. The band played until Lincoln appeared at a window:[13]

The President said he supposed the passage through Congress of the Constitutional amendment for the abolishment of Slavery throughout the United States, was the occasion to which he was indebted for the honor of this call. [Applause.] The occasion was one of congratulation to the country and to the whole world. But there is a task yet before us —to go forward and consummate by the votes of the States that which Congress so nobly began yesterday. [Applause and cries—"They will do it," &c.] He had the honor to inform those present that Illinois was a little ahead. He thought this measure was a very fitting if not an indispensable adjunct to the winding up of the great difficulty. He wished the reunion of all the States perfected and so effected as to remove all causes of disturbance in the future; and to attain this end it was necessary that the original disturbing cause should, if possible, be rooted out. He thought all would bear him witness that he had never shrunk from doing all that he could to eradicate Slavery by issuing an emancipation proclamation. [Applause.] But that proclamation falls far short of what the amendment will be when fully consummated. A question might be raised whether the proclamation was legally valid. It might be added that it only aided those who came into our lines and that it was inoperative as to those who did not give themselves up, or that it would have no effect upon the children of the slaves born hereafter. In fact it would be urged that it did not meet the evil. But this amendment is a King's cure for all the evils. [Applause.] It winds the whole thing up. He would repeat that it was the fitting if not indispensable adjunct to the consummation of the great game we are playing. He could not but congratulate all present, himself, the country and the whole world upon this great moral victory.

IV

With the end of slavery in sight, Lincoln made a move, though with little hope, to end the war. Early in January Francis P. Blair, Sr., an old friend of Jefferson Davis, made an unofficial visit to Richmond in a one-man effort to bring the war to a close. To Blair, Davis expressed his willingness that a conference should be held "with a view to secure peace to the two countries." Lincoln wrote of his desire that peace should come "to the people of our one common country"—a phrase that indicated no narrowing of the gap that had separated North and South for almost four years—yet he agreed to meet Confederate commissioners within the Union lines.

On February 3 Alexander H. Stephens, R. M. T. Hunter, former Confederate Secretary of State, and John A. Campbell who, though opposed to secession, had resigned as an associate justice of the United States Supreme Court when secession became a fact, were escorted to the steamer River Queen *in Hampton Roads. Stephens renewed an old friendship:*[14]

The interview took place in the Saloon of the steamer, on board of which were Mr. Lincoln and Mr. Seward, and which lay at anchor near Fortress Monroe. The Commissioners were conducted into the Saloon first. Soon after, Mr. Lincoln and Mr. Seward entered. After usual salutations on the part of those who were previously acquainted, and introductions of the others who had never met before, conversation was immediately opened by the revival of reminiscences and associations of former days.

This was commenced by myself addressing Mr. Lincoln, and alluding to some of the incidents of our Congressional acquaintance—especially, to the part we had acted together in effecting the election of General Taylor in 1848. To my remarks he responded in a cheerful and cordial manner, as if the remembrance of those times, and our connection with the incidents referred to, had awakened in him a train of agreeable reflections, extending to others. . . .

With this introduction I said in substance: Well, Mr. President, is there no way of putting an end to the present trouble, and bringing about a restoration of the general good feeling and harmony *then* existing between the different States and Sections of the country?

. . . Mr. Lincoln in reply said, in substance, that there was but one way that he knew of, and that was, for those who were resisting the laws of the Union to cease that resistance. All the trouble came from an armed resistance against the National Authority.

But, said I, is there no other question that might divert the attention of both Parties, for a time, from the questions involved in their present strife, until the passions on both sides might cool, when they would be in better temper to come to an amicable and proper adjustment of those points of difference out of which the present lamentable collision of arms has arisen? Is there no Continental question, said I, which might thus temporarily engage our attention? We have been induced to believe that there is.

Mr. Lincoln seemed to understand my allusion instantly, and said in substance: I suppose you refer to something that Mr. Blair has said. Now it is proper to state at the beginning, that whatever he said was of his own accord, and without the least authority from me. When he applied for a passport to go to Richmond, with certain ideas which he wished to make known to me, I told him flatly that I did not want to hear them. If he desired to go to Richmond of his own accord, I would give him a passport; but he had no authority to speak for me in any way whatever. When he returned and brought me Mr. Davis's letter, I gave him the one to which you alluded in your application for leave to cross the lines. I was always willing to hear propositions for peace on the conditions of this letter and on no other. The restoration of the Union is a *sine qua non* with me, and hence my instructions that no conference was to be held except upon that basis.

From this I inferred that he simply meant to be understood, in the first place, as disavowing whatever Mr. Blair had said as coming authoritatively from him; and, in the second place, that no arrangement could be made on the line suggested by Mr. Blair, without a previous pledge or assurance being given, that the Union was to be ultimately restored.

After a short silence, I continued: But suppose, Mr. President, a line of policy should be suggested, which, if adopted, would most probably lead to a restoration of the Union without further bloodshed, would it not be highly advisable to act on it, even without the absolute pledge of ultimate restoration being required to be first given? May not such a policy be found to exist in the line indicated by the interrogatory propounded? Is there not now such a Continental question in which all the parties engaged in our present war feel a deep and similar interest? I allude, of course, to Mexico, and what is called the "Monroe Doctrine,"—the principles of which are involved in the contest now waging there. From the tone of leading Northern papers and from public speeches of prominent men, as well as from *other* sources, we are under the impression that the Administration at Washington is decidedly opposed to the establishment of an Empire in Mexico by France, and is desirous to prevent it. In other words, they wish to sustain the principle of the Monroe Doctrine, and that, as I understand it, is, that the United States will maintain the right of Self-government to all People on this Continent, against the domination or control of any European power.

Mr. Lincoln and Mr. Seward both concurred in the expression of opinion that such was the feeling of a majority of the people of the North.

Could not both parties then, said I, in our contest, come to an understanding and agreement to postpone their present strife, by a suspension of hostilities between themselves, until this principle is maintained in behalf of Mexico; and might it not, when successfully sustained there, naturally, and would it not almost inevitably, lead to a peaceful and harmonious solution of their own difficulties? Could any pledge now given, make a permanent restoration or re-organization of the Union more probable, or even so probable, as such a result would?

Mr. Lincoln replied with considerable earnestness, that he could entertain no proposition for ceasing active military operations, which was not based upon a pledge first given, for the ultimate restoration of the Union. He had considered the question of an Armistice fully, and he could not give his consent to any proposition of that sort, on the basis suggested. The settlement of our existing difficulties was a question now of supreme importance, and the only basis on which he would entertain a proposition for a settlement was the recognition and re-establishment of the National Authority throughout the land.

These pointed and emphatic responses seemed to put an end to the Conference on the subject contemplated in our Mission, as we had no authority to give any such pledge. . . .

In spite of the impasse, the discussion continued, with Stephens emphasizing again the desirability of joint action against the French in Mexico. The North and South, he argued, could act together simply by adopting a military convention. Lincoln reiterated that he would take no step unless it was first agreed that resistance to national authority would cease.

The conversation turned to the status of slaves who had not been affected by the Proclamation of Emancipation. Lincoln had some comments on that subject:

He said it was not his intention in the beginning to interfere with Slavery in the States; that he never would have done it, if he had not been compelled by necessity to do it, to maintain the Union; that the subject presented many difficult and perplexing questions to him; that he had hesitated for some time, and had resorted to this measure, only when driven to it by public necessity; that he had been in favor of the General Government prohibiting the extension of Slavery into the Territories, but did not think that that Government possessed power over the subject in the States, except as a war measure; and that he had always himself been in favor of emancipation, but not immediate emancipation, even by the States. Many evils attending this appeared to him.

After pausing for some time, his head rather bent down, as if in deep reflection, while all were silent, he rose up and used these words, almost, if not quite identical:

Stephens, if I were in Georgia, and entertained the sentiments I do— though, I suppose, I should not be permitted to stay there long with them; but if I resided in Georgia, with my present sentiments, I'll tell you what I would do, if I were in your place: I would go home and get the Governor of the State to call the Legislature together, and get them to recall all the State troops from the war; elect Senators and Members to Congress, and ratify this Constitutional Amendment [the thirteenth] *prospectively*, so as to take effect—say in five years. Such a ratification would be valid in my opinion. . . . Whatever may have been the views of your people before the war, they must be convinced now, that Slavery is doomed. It cannot last long in any event, and the best course, it seems to me, for your public men to pursue, would be to adopt such a policy as will avoid, as far as possible, the evils of immediate emancipation. This would be my course, if I were in your place. . . .

Mr. Seward said, that the Northern people were weary of the war. They desired peace and a restoration of harmony, and he believed would be willing to pay as an indemnity for the slaves, what amount would be required to continue the war, but stated no amount.

After thus going through with all these matters, in a conversation of about four hours . . . , there was a pause, as if all felt that the interview should close. I arose and said that it seemed our mission would be entirely fruitless, unless we could do something in the matter of the Exchange of Prisoners. This brought up that subject.

Mr. Lincoln expressed himself in favor of doing something on it, and concluded by saying that he would put the whole matter in the hands of General Grant, then at City Point, with whom we could interchange views upon our return. Some propositions were then made for immediate special exchanges, which were readily agreed to.*

I then said: I wish, Mr. President, you would reconsider the subject of an Armistice on the basis which has been suggested. Great questions, as well as vast interests, are involved in it. If, upon so doing, you shall change your mind, you can make it known through the Military.

Well, said he, as he was taking my hand for a farewell leave, and with a peculiar manner very characteristic of him: Well, Stephens, I will re-consider it, but I do not think my mind will change, but I will re-consider.

The two parties then took formal and friendly leave of each other, Mr. Lincoln and Mr. Seward withdrawing first from the saloon together. Col. Babcock, our escort, soon came in to conduct us back to the steamer on which we came.

* On February 10 Lincoln wrote to Stephens: "According to our agreement, your nephew, Lieut. Stephens, goes to you, bearing this note. Please, in return, to select and send to me, that officer of the same rank, imprisoned at Richmond, whose physical condition most urgently requires his release."

*Stephens reported the failure of the conference to Davis. He found the
Confederate President obsessed with the conviction that in spite of ever-
mounting odds, the South could still win its independence:*

On the return of the Commissioners to Richmond, everybody was
very much disappointed, and no one seemed to be more so than Mr.
Davis. He thought Mr. Lincoln had acted in bad faith in the matter,
and attributed this change in his policy to the fall of Fort Fisher. . . .

I thought the publicity of the Mission was enough to account for its
failure, without attributing it to any bad faith, either on the part of Mr.
Blair or Mr. Lincoln; that I had expressed the opinion to Judge Campbell and Mr. Hunter, when we saw our departure announced in the
papers as it was (the whole North being in a stir upon the subject by
the time we reached City Point), that this would most probably defeat
our accomplishing anything, even if Mr. Lincoln really intended to do
anything on that line; and that it was in this view of the subject *solely,*
I had made the request of him, at the close of the interview, to *re-
consider* the matter of the Armistice.

I called Mr. Davis's attention specially to the fact, that in reply to that
request Mr. Lincoln declared he *would reconsider* it; and notwithstanding the qualification with which he made the declaration, yet I
thought if there ever had been *really* anything in the *projèt,* Mr. Davis
would still hear from it in a quiet way through the Military, after all
the then "hubbub" about Peace Negotiations had subsided. In this view
of the subject, I gave it to him as my opinion, that there should be no
written report by the Commissioners touching the Conference, especially as a full disclosure of its *real objects* could not, with propriety,
then be made; and that any report without this, however consistent
with the facts, as far as they should be set forth, would fail to give full
information upon the *exact* posture of the affairs to which it related, by
which the public mind in reference to it would be more or less misled.

He insisted that a written report should be made, and the other Commissioners concurring with him, I again yielded my views on that
point . . . , believing, as I did, that if I declined, more harm would
certainly result from a misconstruction of my course and reasons in the
matter, than would by conforming to his views and those of my Col-
leagues.

The question then was, what was next to be done?

Mr. Davis's position was, that inasmuch as it was now settled beyond question, by the decided and pointed declarations of Mr. Lincoln, that there could be no Peace short of *Unconditional Submission* on the part of the People of the Confederate States, with an entire change of their Social Fabric throughout the South, the People ought to be, and could be, more thoroughly aroused by Appeals through the Press and by Public Addresses, to the full consciousness of the necessity of renewed and more desperate efforts, for the preservation of themselves and their Institutions. By these means they might yet be saved from the most humiliating threatened degradation. In these lay the only hope left of escaping such a calamity. He himself seemed more interested than ever to fight it out on this line, and to risk all upon the issue.

By the course he proposed, I understood him to hold the opinion, that Richmond could *still* be defended, notwithstanding Sherman had already made considerable progress on his march from Savannah; and that our cause could *still* be successfully maintained, without any change in the internal policy upon the subjects referred to before.

THE HARD HAND
OF WAR

———————

A NOTHER SPRING APPROACHED—the fourth since those early days in 1861 when elderly gentlemen in Charleston enlisted as Home Guardsmen and practiced military evolutions so that they would be ready for the Negro insurrection certain to follow Mr. Lincoln's inauguration. Judge Campbell, who had accompanied Stephens to the Peace Conference at Hampton Roads, had said that spring of 1861: "Who can give self-control to Southern members [of Congress] or prevent them from showing that slavery is ordained by Heaven?" The Union armies had undertaken to give an answer in a war that now squeezed the Confederacy into an ever-diminishing stockade.

I

Ending that war quickly, effectively, had become the burning passion —with Sherman, certainly, who had no intention of lolling at ease in Savannah, or sending his army north in transports as Grant proposed. On December 24, less than two days after entering Savannah, Sherman began sketching for Grant the outline of new bold ventures:[1]

. . . I feel no doubt whatever as to our future plans. I have thought them over so long and well that they appear as clear as daylight. I left Augusta untouched on purpose, because the enemy will be in doubt as to my objective point, after we cross the Savannah River, whether it be Augusta or Charleston, and will naturally divide his forces. I will then move either on Branchville or Columbia, by any curved line that gives us the best supplies, breaking up in our course as much railroad as possible; then, ignoring Charleston and Augusta both, I would occupy Columbia and Camden, pausing there long enough to observe the effect. I would then strike for the Charleston & Wilmington Railroad, somewhere between the Santee and Cape Fear Rivers, and, if possible, communicate with the fleet under Admiral Dahlgren. . . . Then I would favor an attack on Wilmington, in the belief that Porter and Butler will fail in their present undertaking.* Charleston is now a mere desolated wreck, and is hardly worth the time it would take to starve it out. Still, I am aware that, historically and politically, much importance is attached to the place, and it may be that, apart from its military importance, both you and the Administration may prefer I should give it more attention; and it would be well for you to give me some general idea on that subject, for otherwise I would treat it as I have expressed, as a point of little importance, after all its railroads leading into the interior have been destroyed or occupied by us. But, on the hypothesis of ignoring Charleston and taking Wilmington, I would then favor a movement direct on Raleigh. The game is then up with Lee, unless he comes out of Richmond, avoids you and fights me; in which case I should reckon on your being on his heels. Now that Hood is used up by Thomas, I feel disposed to bring the matter to an issue as quick as possible. I feel confident that I can break up the whole railroad system of South Carolina and North Carolina, and be on the Roanoke, either at Raleigh or Weldon, by the time spring fairly opens; and, if you feel confident that you can whip Lee outside of his intrenchments, I feel equally confident that I can handle him in the open country. . . .

In a letter written on the same day to Halleck, Sherman advanced another argument in favor of his plan of campaign:

* A combined assault in the last week of December, 1864, which failed miserably. "Your reputation as a prophet may soon equal that as a general," Halleck wrote from Washington after Porter and Butler, in Sherman's term, "fizzled" in their attack on Wilmington. "Thank God," Halleck added, "that I had nothing to do with it, except to express the opinion that Butler's torpedo ship would have as much effect on the forts as if he should ——— at them." Sherman was no less frank, writing Halleck, "I am rejoiced that the current of events has carried Butler to Lowell where he should have stayed and confined his bellicose operations to the factory girls."

. . . I attach more importance to these deep incisions into the enemy's country, because this war differs from European wars in this particular: We are not only fighting hostile armies, but a hostile people, and must make old and young, rich and poor, feel the hard hand of war, as well as their organized armies. I know that this recent movement of mine through Georgia has had a wonderful effect in this respect. Thousands who had been deceived by their lying newspapers to believe that we were being whipped all the time now realize the truth, and have no appetite for a repetition of the same experience. To be sure, Jeff. Davis has his people under pretty good discipline, but I think faith in him is much shaken in Georgia, and before we have done with her South Carolina will not be quite so tempestuous.

I will bear in mind your hint as to Charleston, and do not think "salt" will be necessary. When I move, the Fifteenth Corps will be on the right of the right wing, and their position will naturally bring them into Charleston first; and, if you have watched the history of that corps, you will have remarked that they generally do their work pretty well. The truth is, the whole army is burning with an insatiable desire to wreak vengeance upon South Carolina. I almost tremble at her fate, but feel that she deserves all that seems in store for her. . . .

II

Grant gave his assent without reservations. Sherman had hoped to start north by mid-January but heavy rains sent the Savannah River out of its banks and made the roads impassable. Once the skies had cleared, Sherman took stock:[2]

On the 1st day of February . . . the army designed for the active campaign from Savannah northward was composed of two wings, commanded respectively by Major-Generals Howard and Slocum, and was substantially the same that had marched from Atlanta to Savannah. The same general orders were in force, and this campaign may properly be classed as a continuance of the former.

The right wing, less Corse's division, Fifteenth Corps, was grouped at or near Pocotaligo, South Carolina, with its wagons filled with food, ammunition, and forage, all ready to start, and only waiting for the left wing, which was detained by the flood in the Savannah River. . . .

The left wing, with Corse's division and Kilpatrick's cavalry, was at and near Sister's Ferry, forty miles above the city of Savannah, engaged in crossing the river, then much swollen. . . .

The actual strength of the army . . . was at the time sixty thousand and seventy-nine men, and sixty-eight guns. The trains were made up of about twenty-five hundred wagons, with six mules to each wagon, and about six hundred ambulances, with two horses each. The contents of the wagons embraced an ample supply of ammunition for a great battle; forage for about seven days, and provisions for twenty days, mostly of bread, sugar, coffee, and salt, depending largely for fresh meat on beeves driven on the hoof and such cattle, hogs, and poultry, as we expected to gather along our line of march. . . .

The enemy occupied the cities of Charleston and Augusta, with garrisons capable of making a respectable if not successful defense, but

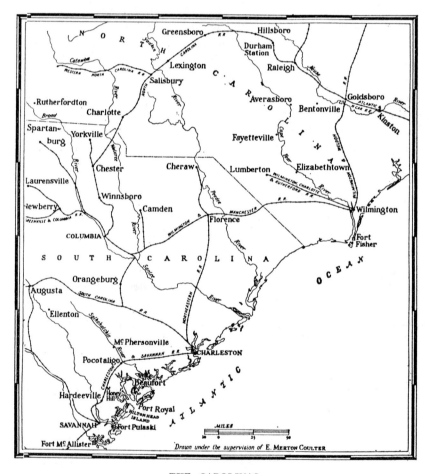

THE CAROLINAS

From *Atlas of American History*

utterly unable to meet our veteran columns in the open field. To resist or delay our progress north, General Wheeler had his division of cavalry (reduced to the size of a brigade by his hard and persistent fighting ever since the beginning of the Atlanta campaign), and General Wade Hampton had been dispatched from the Army of Virginia to his native State of South Carolina, with a great flourish of trumpets, and extraordinary powers to raise men, money, and horses, with which "to stay the progress of the invader," and "to punish us for our insolent attempt to invade the glorious State of South Carolina!" He was supposed at the time to have, at and near Columbia, two small divisions of cavalry commanded by himself and General Butler.*

. . . I knew full well at the time that the broken fragments of Hood's army (which had escaped from Tennessee) were being hurried rapidly across Georgia, by Augusta, to make junction in my front; estimating them at the maximum twenty-five thousand men, and Hardee's, Wheeler's, and Hampton's forces at fifteen thousand, made forty thousand; which, if handled with spirit and energy, would constitute a formidable force, and might make the passage of such rivers as the Santee and Cape Fear a difficult undertaking. Therefore, I took all possible precautions, and arranged with Admiral Dahlgren and General Foster to watch our progress inland by all the means possible, and to provide for us points of security along the coast. . . .

The question of supplies remained still the one of vital importance, and I reasoned that we might safely rely on the country for a considerable quantity of forage and provisions, and that, if the worst came to the worst, we could live several months on the mules and horses of our trains. Nevertheless, time was equally material, and the moment I heard that General Slocum had finished his pontoon-bridge at Sister's Ferry, and that Kilpatrick's cavalry was over the river, I gave the general orders to march, and instructed all the columns to aim for the South Carolina Railroad to the west of Branchville, about Blackville and Midway.

III

One of Sherman's aides, Major George Ward Nichols, described the progress of "the great march":[3]

February 10th.—Another important step is gained. We have crossed the south fork of the Edisto, and hold the main road beyond,

* Matthew Calbraith Butler, recently ordered to South Carolina from Richmond.

while the left wing of the army, which has been delayed so long by the Freshet that submerged the roads leading from Sister's Ferry, is at last coming into position with the remainder of the army. . . .

The crossing of the South Edisto was a feat worth mentioning somewhat in detail. It was Mower's fortune to have the lead. Upon the arrival of his division at the place known as Bennaker's Bridge, which he found burned, he was met with a sharp cannonading from the Rebels, who were in position on the other side. This was in the afternoon. He at once set to work to cross the stream. A little lower down, by dint of wading and swimming, he managed to get into the water four pontoon boats. Upon these, about eight o'clock in the evening, just as the moon was rising, he crossed his division. This night attack was something the Rebels were not prepared for, accustomed as they are to the strange doings of the "Yankees." The moon rose above the tree-tops in all her queenly splendor. Mower thought it was light enough to whip Rebels by. He was now well out of the swamp, and knew that the sooner he gained the high road the better. So, as we say in the army, he "went in," and the result was that the Rebels went out; that is, all who were not killed or captured. . . .

ORANGEBURG, February 12th.—Today another difficult task has been achieved. We have crossed the north fork of the Edisto, and occupy Orangeburg. . . .

Tonight we are encamped upon the place of one of South Carolina's most high-blooded chivalry—one of those persons who believed himself to have been brought into the world to rule over his fellow-creatures, a sort of Grand Pasha, and all that sort of thing. How the negro pioneers are making away with the evergreens and rose-bushes of his artistically arranged walks, flower-beds, and drives! These black men in blue are making brooms of his pet shrubs, with which they clear the ground in front of the tents.

We find very few wealthy planters; the inhabitants we meet, mostly women, are of the poorer class; they are frightened fearfully, and expect all sorts of outrages to be perpetrated, and appear to be correspondingly grateful that their lives and houses are spared. The stories they are told and credit are so absurd that I will not repeat them. It is enough that these foolish, ignorant people have believed them. . . .

Each day, as the army moves forward, large additions are made to the droves of cattle. Our conscription is remorseless. Every species of four-footed beast that South Carolina planters cherished among their live-stock is swept in by our flanking foragers, and the music of the animal creation mingles with the sound of the footfall of the army.

IV

As Sherman's 60,000 veterans swept northward almost unopposed, South Carolina trembled. Even before the army had moved out of Savannah the same Albert G. Magrath who, upon Lincoln's election, had ripped off the robes of a Federal judge in melodramatic rage pleaded, as governor of South Carolina, with Jefferson Davis to defend Charleston at all costs:[4]

CHARLESTON, January 22, 1865

PRESIDENT DAVIS:

I am so impressed with the belief that in the military operations in the next few days in this State the fate of the Confederation is deeply involved, that I am here to urge upon General Hardee the defense of Charleston to the last moment, in the hope that meanwhile re-enforcements will enable us to hold it. I am using all influence with Governor Brown and Governor Vance to keep our States together and each give its help to the other, but confidence is almost lost and hope is to a great extent gone. To restore these and rally the people here and elsewhere there must be a stand-point to which all should look as the place where the purposes and strength of our Government are exhibited. Circumstances have plainly made Charleston and its connections that place. The loss of these, added to our other losses, will spread dismay, and I fear that such a loss will be taken as proof that our cause is without life or hope, and any effectual resistance cannot be prolonged. My intelligence from adjoining States confirms these apprehensions most fully.

Give General Hardee the help with which he can oppose General Sherman and I assure you that the spirit of the people will rise again. Not to sustain him is to confirm the belief that our cause is already lost. . . . It is because I feel the fate of Charleston and of Branchville to a great extent will determine that of other States, and with it the cause of the Confederation, that I urge the necessity for aid upon you in the most impressive manner. Richmond will hereby fall when Charleston is lost. To retain Richmond until Charleston is lost is to sacrifice both. If Charleston can be saved, and in doing that the means of resistance for the whole Confederation can be preserved, then, although to give succor to Charleston might hasten the fall of Richmond, yet to give that succor without delay is, to me, the obvious policy. God forbid that

I should urge you to give up an inch of the soil of Virginia that can be saved; but if it must be inevitably lost, to delay that inevitable necessity at such a cost as to endanger our whole cause, is not to accomplish any good.

In mid-February Pierre Gustave Toutant Beauregard, the hero of Fort Sumter, told Jefferson Davis that Charleston would have to be evacuated. The Confederate President replied on February 16:[5]

Your telegrams of yesterday received. You can better judge of the necessity for evacuating Charleston than I can. Such full preparations had been made that I had hoped for other and better results, and the disappointment is to me extremely bitter. The re-enforcements calculated on from reserves and militia of Georgia and South Carolina, together with the troops ordered from Mississippi, must have fallen much short of estimate. What can be done with the naval squadron, the torpedo boats, and your valuable heavy guns at Charleston? Do not allow cotton stored there to become prize of the enemy, as was the case at Savannah. From reverse, however sad, if you are sustained by unity and determination among the people, we can look hopefully forward. . . .

Three weeks later the colonel of a Negro regiment pleaded for aid to the suffering residents of the cradle of secession:[6]

HEADQUARTERS POST OF CHARLESTON.
CHARLESTON, S. C., March 6, 1865
REV. JOSEPH P. THOMPSON, D.D.,
PRESIDENT OF THE AMERICAN UNION COMMISSION, NEW YORK CITY:
REVEREND AND DEAR SIR: Mr. Mahlon T. Hewitt, of your city, has called upon me in behalf of the American Union Mission to ascertain the true condition of the people of Charleston, and to devise some method by which the suffering and want occasioned by the rebellion may be most surely alleviated. We thank you for this prompt indication that the men of the North sympathize in the afflictions of their fellow countrymen, and desire to meet them when returning to loyalty in the true spirit of a Christian brotherhood. The suffering here is great, nor is it confined to the poorer classes alone. Charleston is today cut off from the back country by the presence of intervening armies. Families who have heretofore derived their income from country

estates are now, of necessity, in want. Others whose property has been gradually absorbed into rebel bonds are penniless. The rebel currency is worthless. Thus many who have been tenderly reared are now suffering. Instances of want come daily and hourly to my notice, which I am powerless to alleviate. Major-General Gilmore, commanding this department, generously turned over most of the rice captured in the city to a committee, who are distributing it for the relief of the most necessitous. But this supply can only last for a few days at the best, and does not begin to answer our wants. We need money, provisions, clothing, and medicines and delicacies for the sick. You cannot do too much for us. Your agent, Mr. Hewitt, has, at my suggestion, invited several prominent residents of Charleston, to organize as an auxiliary association to your commission, and thus insure the safe and equitable distribution of the charity which you so nobly offer. These gentlemen have accepted, and the loyal people of the North may rely upon the faithful performance of the trust. I believe that the nation will respond to the appeal which your commission makes in behalf of this great charity, and look forward hopefully to the day when the olive branch you proffer shall be planted beside hearthstones made desolate by war, and bear the golden fruitage of reconciliation and peace.

Very respectfully, your obedient servant,
STEWART L. WOODFORD,
Colonel 103d U. S. Colored Troops,
Commanding the City

v

On February 17 Sherman's forces occupied Columbia. Many a man in the Union ranks remembered that except for a sudden epidemic of smallpox the Ordinance of Secession would have been adopted here rather than in Charleston. That night fire destroyed nearly fourteen hundred residences and stores. Sherman insisted that he was not responsible for the holocaust. William Gilmore Simms, the South's favorite romantic novelist and a refugee in Columbia at the time, told another story:[7]

Among the first fires of evening was one about dark, which broke out in a filthy purlieu of low houses, of wood, on Gervais Street, occupied mostly as brothels. Almost at the same time a body of soldiers scattered over the Eastern outskirts of the city, fired severally the dwellings of Mr. Secretary Trenholm, General Wade Hampton, Dr.

John Wallace, and many others. There were then some twenty fires in full blast, in as many different quarters, and while the alarm sounded from these quarters, a similar alarm went up almost simultaneously from Cotton Town, the northernmost limit of the city, and from Main Street in its very centre . . . thus enveloping in flames almost every section of the devoted city. At this period, thus early in the evening, there were few shows of that drunkenness which prevailed at a late hour in the night, and only after all the grocery shops on Main Street had been rifled. The men engaged in this were well prepared with all the appliances essential to their work. They did not need the torch. They carried with them, from house to house, pots and vessels containing combustible liquids, composed probably of phosphorous and other similar agents, turpentine, etc., and with balls of cotton saturated in this liquid, with which they also overspread the floors and walls; they conveyed the flames with wonderful rapidity from dwelling to dwelling. Each had his ready box of Lucifer matches, and, with a scrape upon the walls, the flames began to rage. Where houses were closely contiguous, a brand from one was the means of conveying destruction to the other. . . .

Sherman placed the responsibility for the disaster upon a Confederate general:[8]

. . . In anticipation of the occupation of the city, I had made written orders to General Howard touching the conduct of the troops. These were to destroy, absolutely, all arsenals and public property not needed for our own use, as well as all railroads, depots, and machinery useful in war to an enemy, but to spare all dwellings, colleges, schools, asylums, and harmless private property. I was the first to cross the pontoon bridge, and in company with General Howard rode into the city. The day was clear, but a perfect tempest of wind was raging. The brigade of Colonel Stone was already in the city, and was properly posted. Citizens and soldiers were on the streets, and general good order prevailed. General Wade Hampton, who commanded the Confederate rear-guard of cavalry, had, in anticipation of our capture of Columbia, ordered that all cotton, public and private, should be moved into the streets and fired, to prevent our making use of it. Bales were piled everywhere, the rope and bagging cut, and tufts of cotton were blown about in the wind, lodged in the trees and against houses, so as to resemble a snow storm. Some of these piles of cotton were burning, especially one in the very heart of the city, near the Court-house, but the fire was partially subdued by the labor of our soldiers. During the day the Fifteenth corps passed through Columbia and out on the Camden road. The Seventeenth did not enter the town at all; and, as I have before stated, the left wing and cavalry did not come within two miles of the town.

Before one single public building had been fired by order, the smoldering fires, set by Hampton's order, were rekindled by the wind, and communicated to the buildings around. About dark they began to spread, and got beyond the control of the brigade on duty within the city. The whole of Wood's division was brought in, but it was found impossible to check the flames, which, by midnight, had become unmanageable, and raged until about four A.M., when the wind subsiding, they were got under control. I was up nearly all night, and saw Generals Howard, Logan, Woods, and others, laboring to save houses and protect families thus suddenly deprived of shelter, and of bedding and wearing apparel. I disclaim on the part of my army any agency in this fire, but on the contrary, claim that we saved what of Columbia remains unconsumed. And without hesitation, I charge General Wade Hampton with having burned his own city of Columbia, not with a malicious intent, or as the manifestations of a silly "Roman stoicism," but from folly and want of sense, in filling it with lint, cotton, and tinder. Our officers and men on duty worked well to extinguish the flames; but others not on duty, including the officers who had long been imprisoned there, rescued by us, may have assisted in spreading the fire after it had once begun, and may have indulged in unconcealed joy to see the ruin of the capital of South Carolina.

Little affection ever was lost between Sherman and Hampton, who soon were engaged in a brittle exchange of letters:

HEADQUARTERS MILITARY DIVISION OF THE MISSISSIPPI,
IN THE FIELD, February 24, 1865
GENERAL: It is officially reported to me that our foraging parties are murdered after capture, and labelled "Death to all foragers." One instance of a lieutenant and seven men near Chesterville, and another of twenty, "near a ravine eighty rods from the main road," about three miles from Feasterville. I have ordered a similar number of prisoners in our hands to be disposed of in like manner.

I hold about a thousand prisoners, captured in various ways, and can stand it as long as you, but I hardly think these murders are committed with your knowledge, and would suggest that you give notice to the people at large that every life taken by them simply results in the death of one of your confederates.

Of course you cannot question my right to "forage on the country." It is a war-right as old as history. The manner of exercising it varies with circumstances, and if the civil authorities will supply my requisitions I will forbid all foraging. But I find no civil authorities who can respond to calls for forage or provisions, therefore must collect directly of the people. I have no doubt this is the occasion of much misbehavior on the part of our men, but I cannot permit an enemy to judge, or punish with wholesale murder.

Personally I regret the bitter feelings engendered by this war; but they were to be expected; and I simply allege that those who struck the first blow, and made war inevitable, ought not, in fairness, to reproach us for the natural consequences. I merely assert our war-right to forage, and my resolve to protect my foragers to the extent of life for life.

I am, with respect,

Your obedient servant
W. T. SHERMAN,
Major-General United States Army

LIEUTENANT-GENERAL WADE HAMPTON,
Commanding Cavalry Forces, C.S.A.

Hampton retorted venomously:

HEADQUARTERS IN THE FIELD,
February 27, 1865

GENERAL: Your communication of the twenty-fourth inst. reached me to-day. In it you state that it has been officially reported that your foraging parties are "murdered" after capture. You go on to say that you have "ordered a similar number of prisoners in your hands to be disposed of in like manner;" that is to say, you have ordered a number of Confederate soldiers to be "murdered." You characterize your order in proper terms, for the public voice, even in your own country, where it seldom dares to express itself in vindication of truth, honor, or justice, will surely agree with you in pronouncing you guilty of murder, if your order is carried out. Before dismissing this portion of your letter, I beg to assure you, that for every soldier of mine "murdered" by you, I shall have executed at once *two* of yours, giving, in all cases, preference to any officers who may be in my hands.

In reference to the statement you make regarding the death of your foragers, I have only to say that I know nothing of it; that no orders given by me authorize the killing of prisoners after capture, and I do not believe my men killed any of yours except under circumstances in which it was perfectly legitimate and proper they *should* kill them. It is a part of the system of the thieves whom you designate as your foragers to fire the dwellings of those citizens whom they have robbed. To check this inhuman system, which is justly execrated by every civilized nation, I have directed my men to shoot down all of your men who are caught burning houses. This order shall remain in force so long as you disgrace the profession of arms by allowing your men to destroy private dwellings.

You say that I cannot, of course, question your right to forage on the country. "It is a right as old as history." I do not, sir, question this right. But there is a right older even than this, and one more inalienable—the right that every man has to defend his home, and to protect those who are dependent on him; and from my heart I wish that every old man and boy in my country, who can fire a gun, would shoot down, as he would a wild beast, the men who are desolating their land, burning their homes, and insulting their women.

You are particular in defining and claiming "war-rights." May I ask if you enumerate among these the right to fire upon a defenceless city without notice; to burn that city to the ground after it had been surrendered by the inhabitants, who claimed, though in vain, that protection which is always accorded in civilized warfare to non-combatants; to fire the dwelling-houses of citizens after robbing them, and to perpetrate even darker crimes than these—crimes too black to be mentioned.

You have permitted, if you have not ordered, the commission of these offences against humanity and the rules of war. You fired into the city of Columbia without a word of warning, after its surrender by the mayor, who demanded protection to private property; you laid the whole city in ashes, leaving amidst its ruins thousands of old men and helpless women and children, who are likely to perish of starvation and exposure. Your line of march can be traced by the lurid light of burning houses; and in more than one household there is an agony far more bitter than that of death. The Indian scalped his victim regardless of age or sex, but with all his barbarity he always respected the persons of his female captives. Your soldiers, more savage than the Indian, insult those whose natural protectors are absent.

In conclusion, I have only to request that whenever you have any of my men "murdered" or "disposed of"—for the terms seem synonymous with you—you will let me hear of it, that I may know what action to take in the matter. In the meantime I shall hold fifty-six of your men as hostages for those whom you have ordered to be executed.

I am yours, &c.,
WADE HAMPTON,
Lieutenant-General

MAJOR-GENERAL W. T. SHERMAN, U. S. A.

VI

Sherman reached Cheraw, South Carolina, on March 3 and took the town after a brisk but minor engagement. The next day Major George W. Nichols, Sherman's aide, noted in his diary:[9]

March 4th.—The capture of Cheraw is of more value than we anticipated, although the force opposed to us was not so large as had been reported. The Rebel cavalry was a division of Hampton's men, and the infantry were those who had been brought up from Charleston. Their line was first formed at Thompson's Creek, which they were driven from instantly by the impetuosity of our troops, who did not give them time to reform, but drove the entire force through the town at the double-quick. Our soldiers were at one end of the bridge while the Rebels were leaving the other, but too late to save it from the flames. We captured twenty-five cannon which had been brought to this place from Charleston; they were Blakelys, twenty-pound Parrotts, and two of Rebel manufacture. All but the Blakelys have been destroyed. These guns, used so effectively upon our fleet at Charleston, will be carried to the seacoast as trophies. General Mower fired them today in a salute in honor of the inauguration for his second term. Our honored President would have been as glad and proud as we, could he have heard the roaring of our cannon and our shouts of joy and victory. His first inauguration was not celebrated in South Carolina by loyal hearts and hands; but the glorification over the beginning of his second term goes to make up the deficiency.

Lincoln's second inauguration began less auspiciously than Nichols and the mindful Mower could have imagined. Vice President Andrew John-

son, recovering from the debilitating effect of a recent illness, had forti-
fied himself with a stiff drink of whisky—perhaps several stiff drinks
—and in consequence delivered his inaugural address and took the
oath of office with tipsy loquacity. But a day that began in gloom and
scandal turned into one of promise. Noah Brooks described the
metamorphosis:[10]

The newly chosen senators were sworn in, and the procession for the
inauguration platform, which had been built on the east front of the
Capitol, was formed. There was a sea of heads in the great plaza in
front of the Capitol, as far as the eye could reach, and breaking in
waves along its outer edges among the budding foliage of the grounds
beyond. When the President and the procession of notables appeared,
a tremendous shout, prolonged and loud, arose from the surging ocean
of humanity around the Capitol building. Then the sergeant-at-arms of
the Senate . . . arose and bowed, with his shining black hat in hand,
in dumb-show before the crowd, which thereupon became still, and
Abraham Lincoln, rising tall and gaunt among the groups about him,
stepped forward and read his inaugural address, which was printed in
two broad columns upon a single page of large paper. As he advanced
from his seat, a roar of applause shook the air, and, again and again
repeated, finally died far away on the outer fringe of the throng, like a
sweeping wave upon the shore. Just at that moment the sun, which had
been obscured all day, burst forth in its unclouded meridian splendor,
and flooded the spectacle with glory and with light. Every heart beat
quicker at the unexpected omen, and doubtless not a few mentally
prayed that so might the darkness which had obscured the past four
years be now dissipated by the sun of prosperity,

> Till danger's troubled night depart,
> And the star of peace return.

The inaugural address was received in the most profound silence.
Every word was clear and audible as the ringing and somewhat shrill
tones of Lincoln's voice sounded over the vast concourse.

Lincoln said:

At this second appearing to take the oath of the presidential office,
there is less occasion for an extended address than there was at the
first. Then a statement, somewhat in detail, of a course to be pursued,

seemed fitting and proper. Now, at the expiration of four years, during which public declarations have been constantly called forth on every point and phase of the great contest which still absorbs the attention, and engrosses the energies of the nation, little that is new could be presented. The progress of our arms, upon which all else chiefly depends, is as well known to the public as to myself; and it is, I trust, reasonably satisfactory and encouraging to all. With high hope for the future, no prediction in regard to it is ventured.

On the occasion corresponding to this four years ago, all thoughts were anxiously directed to an impending civil war. All dreaded it—all sought to avert it. While the inaugural address was being delivered from this place, devoted altogether to *saving* the Union without war, insurgent agents were in the city seeking to *destroy* it without war— seeking to dissolve the Union, and divide effects, by negotiation. Both parties deprecated war; but one of them would *make* war rather than let the nation survive; and the other would *accept* war rather than let it perish. And the war came.

One eighth of the whole population were colored slaves, not distributed generally over the Union, but localized in the Southern part of it. These slaves constituted a peculiar and powerful interest. All knew that this interest was, somehow, the cause of the war. To strengthen, perpetuate, and extend this interest was the object for which the insurgents would rend the Union, even by war; while the government claimed no right to do more than to restrict the territorial enlargement of it. Neither party expected for the war, the magnitude, or the duration, which it has already attained. Neither anticipated that the *cause* of the conflict might cease with, or even before, the conflict itself should cease. Each looked for an easier triumph, and a result less fundamental and astounding. Both read the same Bible, and pray to the same God; and each invokes His aid against the other. It may seem strange that any men should dare to ask a just God's assistance in wringing their bread from the sweat of other men's faces; but let us judge not that we be not judged. The prayers of both could not be answered; that of neither has been answered fully. The Almighty has His own purposes. "Woe unto the world because of offences! for it must needs be that offences come; but woe to that man by whom the offence cometh!" If we shall suppose that American Slavery is one of those offences which, in the providence of God, must needs come, but which, having continued through His appointed time, He now wills to remove, and that He gives to both North and South, this terrible war, as the woe due to those by whom the offence came, shall we discern therein any departure from those divine attributes which the believers in a Living God always ascribe to Him? Fondly do we hope—fervently do we pray—that this mighty scourge of war may speedily pass away. Yet, if God wills that it continue, until all the wealth piled by the bond-man's two hundred and fifty years of unrequited toil shall be sunk, and until every drop of blood drawn with the lash, shall be paid by another drawn with the sword, as was said three thousand years ago, so still it must be said, "the judgments of the Lord, are true and righteous altogether."

With malice toward none; with charity for all; with firmness in the right, as God gives us to see the right, let us strive on to finish the work we are in; to bind up the nation's wounds; to care for him who shall have borne the battle, and his widow, and his orphan—to do all which may achieve and cherish a just, and a lasting peace, among ourselves, and with all nations.

At the conclusion of Lincoln's address (Brooks wrote):

There were many cheers and many tears. . . . Silence being restored, the President turned toward Chief Justice Chase, who, with his right hand uplifted, directed the Bible to be brought forward by the clerk of the Supreme Court. Then Lincoln, laying his right hand upon the open page, repeated the oath of office administered to him by the Chief Justice, after which, solemnly saying, "So help me God," he bent forward and reverently kissed the Book, then rose up inaugurated President of the United States for four years from March 4, 1865. A salvo of artillery boomed upon the air, cheer upon cheer rang out, and then, after turning, and bowing to the assembled hosts, the President retired into the Capitol, and, emerging by a basement entrance, took his carriage and was escorted back to the White House by a great procession.

VII

Sherman pressed forward relentlessly, taking Fayetteville, North Carolina, where the Confederates had an important arsenal, on March 12 and Averysboro, on the road to Raleigh, five days later. The next day the wily general switched his objective to Goldsboro, fifty miles southeast of Raleigh.

Major General Henry W. Slocum, out in front with the left wing, described the development of a battle which neither he nor Sherman had expected:[11]

General Sherman rode with me on the 18th [of March] and left me at 6 A.M. on the 19th to join General Howard, who was marching on roads several miles to our right. On leaving me General Sherman expressed the opinion that Hardee had fallen back to Raleigh, and that I could easily reach the Neuse River on the following day. I felt confident I could accomplish the task. We moved forward at 6 A.M., and soon met the skirmishers of the enemy. The resistance to our advance became very stubborn. Carlin's division was deployed and ordered to advance. I believed that the force in my front consisted only of cavalry with a few pieces of artillery. Fearing that the firing would be heard by General Sherman and cause the other wing of the army to delay its march, I sent Major E. W. Guindon of my staff to General Sherman, to tell him that I had met a strong force of cavalry, but that I should not need assistance, and felt confident I should be at the Neuse at the appointed time.

Soon after the bearer of the message to General Sherman had left me, word came from Carlin that he had developed a strong force of the enemy in an intrenched position. About the same time one of my officers brought me an emaciated, sickly appearing young man about twenty-two or twenty-three years of age, dressed in the Confederate gray. He had expressed great anxiety to see the commanding officer at once. I asked him what he had to say. He said he had been in the Union army, had been taken prisoner, and while sick and in prison had been induced to enlist in the Confederate service. He said he had enlisted with the intention of deserting when a good opportunity presented itself, believing he should die if he remained in prison. In reply to my questions he informed me that he had formerly resided at Syracuse, New York, and had entered the service at the commencement of the war, in a company raised by Captain Butler. I had been a resident of Syracuse, and knew the history of his company and regiment. While I was talking with him one of my aides, Major William G. Tracy, rode up and at once recognized the deserter as an old acquaintance whom he had known at Syracuse before the war. I asked how he knew General Johnston was in command and what he knew as to the strength of his force. He said General Johnston rode along the line early that morning, and that the officers had told all the men that "Old Joe" had caught one of Sherman's wings beyond the reach of support, that he intended to *smash* that wing and then go for the other. The man stated that he had had no chance of escaping till that morning, and had come to me to warn me of my danger. He said, "There is a very large force immediately in your front, all under command of General Joe Johnston." While he was making his statement General Carlin's division with four pieces of artillery became engaged with the enemy. A line for defense was at once selected, and as the troops came up they were placed in position and ordered to collect fence-rails and everything else available for barricades. The men used their tin cups and hands as shovels, and needed no urging to induce them to work. I regretted that I had sent the message to Sherman assuring him I needed no help, and saw the necessity of giving him information at once as to the situation. This information was carried to General Sherman by a young man, not then twenty years of age, but who was full of energy and activity and was always reliable.

Slocum's young man was Lieutenant Joseph B. Foraker, who would one day be Governor of Ohio and a United States Senator. Slocum told him: "Ride well to the right so as to keep clear of the enemy's left flank, and don't spare horse-flesh."
Foraker never forgot his mission:

I reached General Sherman just about sundown. He was on the left side of the road on a sloping hillside, where, as I understood, he had halted only a few minutes before for the night. His staff were about him. I think General Howard was there, but I do not now remember seeing him—but on the hillside twenty yards farther up Logan was lying on a blanket. Sherman saw me approaching and walked briskly toward me, took the message, tore it open, read it, and called out "John Logan! where is Logan?" Just then Logan jumped up and started toward us. He too walked briskly, but before he had reached us Sherman had informed him of the situation and ordered him to turn Hazen back and report to you [Slocum]. It was not yet dark when I rode away. . . . It was after midnight when I got back, the ride back being so much longer in point of time because the road was full of troops, it was dark, and my "horse-flesh" was used up.

Slocum saw the Confederates drive back Carlin's division:

. . . They were handled with skill and fell back without panic or demoralization, taking places in the line established. The Twentieth Corps held the left of our line, with orders to connect with the Fourteenth. A space between the two corps had been left uncovered, and

Cogswell's brigade of the Twentieth Corps, ordered to report to General Davis, filled the gap just before the enemy reached our line.

The enemy fought bravely, but their line had become somewhat broken in advancing through the woods, and when they came up to our line, posted behind slight intrenchments, they received a fire which compelled them to fall back. The assaults were repeated over and over again until a late hour, each assault finding us better prepared for resistance. During the night Hazen reported to me, and was placed on the right of the Fourteenth Corps. Early on the next morning Generals Baird and Geary, each with two brigades, arrived on the field. Baird was placed in front of our works and moved out beyond the advanced position held by us on the preceding day. The 20th was spent in strengthening our position and developing the line of the enemy. On the morning of the 21st the right wing arrived. This wing had marched twenty miles over bad roads, skirmishing most of the way with the enemy. On the 21st General Johnston found Sherman's army united, and in position on three sides of him. On the other side was Mill Creek. Our troops were pressed closely to the works of the enemy, and the entire day was spent in skirmishing. During the night of the 21st the enemy crossed Mill Creek and retreated toward Raleigh. The plans of the enemy to surprise us and destroy our army in detail were well formed and well executed, and would have been more successful had not the men of the Fourteenth and Twentieth corps been veterans, and the equals in courage and endurance of any soldiers of this or any other country.

Bentonville was the last serious resistance which the Confederate army made to the march through the Carolinas. On March 22 Sherman entered Goldsboro. There he was joined by the armies of Schofield and Terry from New Bern and Wilmington. Thus strengthened, and with Schofield available for temporary command, Sherman set out for City Point and a conference with Grant. Arriving on March 27, he learned that Lincoln had been present for several days. The two generals proceeded to the River Queen, *the steamer on which the President had taken quarters. After extending a warm welcome, Lincoln asked many questions about Sherman's march and about military operations of the near future. More than once, Sherman remembered, the President exclaimed: "Must more blood be shed? Cannot this last bloody battle be avoided?"*

The next day Grant and Sherman, accompanied by Admiral Porter, boarded the River Queen *again. Sherman, writing seven years later, recalled the interview:*[12]

We all took seats in the after cabin, and the conversation became general. I explained to Mr. Lincoln that Admiral Porter had given me the *Bat,* a very fleet vessel to carry me back to Newbern, and that I was ready to start back then. It seemed to relieve him, as he was afraid that something might go wrong at Goldsboro in my absence. I had no such fears, and the most perfect confidence in Gen. Schofield and I doubt not I said as much.

I ought not and must not attempt to recall the words of that conversation. Of course none of us then foresaw the tragic end of the principal figure of that group, so near at hand; and none of us saw the exact manner in which the war would close; but I know that I felt, and believe the others did, that the end of the war was near. The imminent danger was that Lee seeing the meshes closing surely around him, would not remain passive; but would make one more desperate effort; and General Grant was providing for it, by getting General Sheridan's cavalry well to his left flank, so as to watch the first symptoms, and to bring the Rebel army to bay till the infantry could come up.

Meanwhile I only asked two weeks stay—the "status quo"—when we would have our wagons loaded, and would start from Goldsboro for Burkesville via Raleigh. Though I can not attempt to recall the words spoken by any one of the persons present on that occasion, I know we talked generally about what was to be done when Lee's & Johnston's armies were beaten and dispersed. On this point Mr. Lincoln was very full. He said that he had long thought of it, that he hoped the end could be reached without more bloodshed, but in any event, he wanted us to get the deluded men of the Rebel armies disarmed and back to their homes, that he contemplated no revenge—no harsh measures, but quite the contrary, and that their suffering and hardships in the war, would make them the more submissive to Law. I cannot say that Mr. Lincoln or anybody else used this language at the time but I know I left his presence with the conviction that he had in his mind, or that his Cabinet had, some plan of settlement ready for application the moment Lee & Johnston were defeated. . . .

That afternoon I embarked on the *Bat,* and we steamed down the coast to Hatteras Inlet, which we entered, and proceeded to Newbern—and from Newbern to Goldsboro by rail, which I reached the night of March 30.

CHAPTER 39

"AN AFFECTIONATE FAREWELL"

GRANT DEPARTED next morning, March 29, by railroad. The President walked down to the station to say goodbye. Horace Porter believed that Lincoln looked "more serious," with "the rings under his eyes . . . of a darker hue." Aboard the train, Grant and his staff raised their hats in a final token of respect for the President. Obviously affected, Lincoln returned the salute and called:

"Goodbye, gentlemen. God bless you all! Remember, your success is my success."

Grant sat by the train window afterward, smoking a cigar and seeming absorbed in the passing scenery. Turning to Horace Porter, the general revealed that his thoughts remained with Lincoln.

"I think we can send him some good news in a day or two," Grant said.

I

Throughout the fall and winter Grant had been hamstrung before Petersburg. With the spring of 1865 he intended to finish the war. Impatiently he waited for the end of abnormally heavy rains, and the return of Sheridan, with his magnificent cavalry, from the Valley. By late March the rains had stopped, the roads were drying, and Sheridan was back.

On the night of March 29 Grant started columns southwestward toward Dinwiddie Court House, thirty miles from City Point. Lee's troops, uneasy when they were pressed back to the vital Southside Railroad, fought sharply. Grant pushed out his lines in parallels east and west of the Southside. Clearly, he intended to sever this line and beyond it, the Richmond and Danville, on which Lee depended for supplies. Grant also meant to occupy Five Forks, ten miles north of Dinwiddie Court House.

At Five Forks, on the edge of a dry, well-watered forest, five good roads came together. To take Five Forks was to unlock all the surrounding country. Grant sent Sheridan to do the job. The talented George Alfred Townsend, who had returned to reporting battles after three years of lecturing and traveling in Europe, discovered that the war had changed during his absence. Cavalry no longer made saber charges. Even the generals had discovered that horses could take men to a point where they were needed, faster than they could march; once there, cavalrymen dismounted and fought as foot soldiers.

On April 1, at Five Forks, Townsend learned what a mighty punch Sheridan could deliver in this style of warfare:[1]

A colonel with a shattered regiment came down upon us in a charge. The bayonets were fixed; the men came on with a yell; their gray uniforms seemed black amidst the smoke; their preserved colors, torn by grape and ball, waved yet defiantly; twice they halted, and poured in volleys, but came on again like the surge from the fog, depleted, but determined; yet, in the hot faces of the carbineers, they read a purpose as resolute, but more calm, and, while they pressed along, swept all the while by scathing volleys, a group of horsemen took them in flank. It was an awful instant; the horses recoiled; the charging column trembled like a single thing, but at once the Rebels, with rare organization, fell into a hollow square, and with solid sheets of steel defied our centaurs. The horsemen rode around them in vain; no charge could break the shining squares, until our dismounted carbineers poured in their volleys afresh, making gaps in the spent ranks, and then in their wavering time the cavalry thundered down. The Rebels could stand no more; they reeled and swayed, and fell back broken and beaten. And on the ground their colonel lay, sealing his devotion with his life.

Through wood and brake and swamp, across field and trench, we pushed the fighting defenders steadily. For a part of the time, Sheridan himself was there, short and broad, and active, waving his hat, giving orders, seldom out of fire, but never stationary, and close by fell the long yellow locks of Custer, sabre extended, fighting like a Viking, though he was worn and haggard with much work. At four o'clock the Rebels were behind their wooden walls at Five Forks, and still the cavalry pressed them hard, in feint rather than solemn effort, while a battalion dismounted, charged squarely upon the face of their breastworks which lay in the main on the north side of the White Oak road. Then, while the cavalry worked round toward the rear, the infantry of Warren, though commanded by Sheridan, prepared to take part in the battle.

Townsend believed that the "genius" with which Sheridan now disposed his infantry "should place him as high in infantry tactics as he has heretofore shown himself superior in cavalry." Townsend watched as Sheridan, extending his lines, drove the Rebels into their breastworks. Dismounting his cavalry, he charged on front and flank:

. . . At last, every Rebel was safe behind his intrenchments. Then the signal was given, and the concealed infantry, many thousand strong, sprang up and advanced by echelon to the right. Imagine a great barn door shutting to, and you have the movement, if you can also imagine the door itself, hinge and all, moving forward also. This was the door:

AYRES—CRAWFORD—GRIFFIN

Stick a pin through Ayres and turn Griffin and Crawford forward as you would a spoke in a wheel, but move your pin up also a very little. In this way Ayres will advance, say half a mile, and Griffin, to describe a quarter revolution, will move through a radius of four miles. But to complicate this movement by echelon, we must imagine the right when half way advanced cutting across the centre and reforming, while Crawford became the right and Griffin the middle of the line of battle. Warren was with Crawford on this march. Edgar M. Gregory commanded the skirmishers. Ayres was so close to the Rebel left that he might be said to hinge upon it; and at 6 o'clock the whole corps column came crash upon the full flank of the astonished Rebels. Now came the pitch of the battle.

We were already on the Rebel right in force, and thinly in their rear. Our carbineers were making feint to charge in direct front, and our infantry, four deep, hemmed in their entire left. All this they [the Confederates] did not for an instant note, so thorough was their confusion; but seeing it directly, they, so far from giving up, concentrated all their energy and fought like fiends. They had a battery in position, which belched incessantly, and over the breastworks their musketry made one unbroken roll, while against Sheridan's prowlers on their left, by skirmish and sortie, they stuck to their sinking fortunes, so as to win unwilling applause from mouths of wisest censure.

It was just at the coming up of the infantry that Sheridan's little band was pushed the hardest. At one time, indeed, they seemed about to undergo extermination; not that they wavered, but that they were so vastly overpowered. It will remain to the latest time a matter of marvel that so paltry a cavalry force could press back sixteen thousand infantry; but when the infantry blew like a great barn door—the simile best applicable—upon the enemy's left, the victory that was to come had passed the region of strategy and resolved to an affair of personal courage. We had met the enemy; were they to be ours? To expedite this consummation every officer fought as if he were the forlorn hope. Mounted on his black pony, the same which he rode at Winchester, Sheridan galloped everywhere, his flushed face all the redder, and his plethoric but nervous figure all the more ubiquitous. He galloped once straight down the Rebel front, with but a handful of his staff. A dozen bullets whistled for him together; one grazed his arm, at which a faithful orderly rode; the black pony leaped high, in fright, and Sheridan was untouched, but the orderly lay dead in the field, and the saddle dashed afar, empty. . . .

Townsend wrote with the enthusiasm of a reporter to whom such scenes were new: "Imagine along a line of a full mile, thirty thousand men struggling for life and prestige; the woods gathering about them —but yesterday the home of hermit hawks and chipmunks—now ablaze with bursting shells, and showing in the dusk the curl of flames in the tangled grass, and, rising up the boles of the pine trees, the scaling, scorching tongues."

Yet Townsend missed the real story of Five Forks. Orders from Robert E. Lee to Fitzhugh Lee and Pickett had urged: "Hold Five Forks at all hazards." Then General Tom Rosser had arrived with a mess of fresh shad. Pickett and Fitzhugh Lee were picking the bones clean when Sheridan came storming down, catching the three Confederate commanders flat-footed. In a letter home Pickett accepted his rout philosophically:[2]

Well, I made the best arrangements of which the nature of the ground admitted. . . . About two o'clock in the afternoon, Sheridan made a heavy demonstration with his cavalry, threatening also the right flank. Meantime Warren's corps swept around the left flank and rear of the infantry line . . . and the attack became general. . . .

I succeeded in getting a sergeant and enough men to man one piece, but after firing eight rounds the axle broke. Floweree's regiment fought hand to hand after all their cartridges had been used. The small cavalry force, which had gotten into place gave way, and the enemy poured in. . . . We were completely entrapped. . . .

My darling, overpowered, defeated, cut to pieces, starving, captured, as we were, those that were left of us formed front and north and south and met with sullen desperation their double onset. With the members of my own staff and the general officers and their staff officers we compelled a rally . . . enabling many of us to escape capture. . . .

The birds were hushed in the woods when I started to write, and now one calls to its mate, "Cheer up—cheer up." Let's listen and obey the birds, my darling.

II

Sunday, April 2, 1865—a beautiful day in Richmond. That morning Jefferson Davis attended services in St. Paul's Church. There a messenger brought him the grim news that Lee's lines had broken and his troops were in full retreat toward Danville. President Davis, going to his office, assembled the heads of departments and bureaus "as far as they could be found" to plan an orderly transfer of government from doomed Richmond to Danville. Quickly the streets filled with wagons of every description as the race to quit the city gained momentum. The last uniformed Confederate to leave Richmond was Captain Clement Sulivane, who "saw few sleeping eyes during the pandemonium of that night":[3]

The division of General G. W. C. Lee, of Ewell's corps, at that time rested in the trenches eight miles below Richmond, with its right on the James River, covering Chaffin's Bluff. I was at the time its assistant adjutant general, and was in the city on some detached duty connected with the "Local Brigade" belonging to the division—a force composed of the soldiers of the army detailed on account of their mechanical skill to work in the arsenals, etc., and of clerks and other employes of the War, Treasury, Quartermaster and other departments.

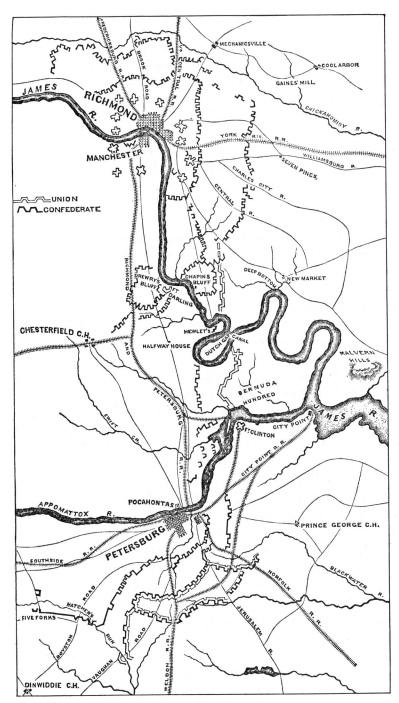

RICHMOND AND PETERSBURG

From Lossing, *Pictorial History of the Civil War*

Upon receipt of the news from Petersburg I reported to General Ewell (then in Richmond) for instructions, and was ordered to assemble and command the Local Brigade, cause it to be well supplied with ammunition and provisions, and await further orders. All that day and night I was engaged in this duty, but with small result, as the battalions melted away as fast as they were formed, mainly under orders from the heads of departments who needed all their employes in the transportation and guarding of the archives, etc., but partly, no doubt, from desertions. When morning dawned, fewer than 200 men remained, under command of Captain Edward Mayo.

Shortly before day General Ewell rode to my headquarters and informed me that General G. W. C. Lee was then crossing the pontoon at Drewry's; that he would destroy it and press on to join the main army; that all the bridges over the river had been destroyed except Mayo's, between Richmond and Manchester; and that the wagon bridge over the canal in front of Mayo's had already been burned by Union emissaries. My command was to hasten to Mayo's bridge and protect it and the one remaining foot-bridge over the canal leading to it, until General Gary of South Carolina should arrive.

I hurried to my command and fifteen minutes later occupied Mayo's bridge, at the foot of 14th street, and made military dispositions to protect it to the last extremity. This done, I had nothing to do but listen for sounds and gaze on the terrible splendor of the scene. And such a scene probably the world has never witnessed. Either incendiaries or (more probably) fragments of bombs from the arsenals, had fired various buildings, and the two cities, Richmond and Manchester, were like a blaze of day amid the surrounding darkness. Three high arched bridges were in flames; beneath them the waters sparkled and dashed and rushed on by the burning city. Every now and then, as a magazine exploded, a column of white smoke rose up as high as the eye could reach, instantaneously followed by a deafening sound. The earth seemed to rock and tremble as with the shock of an earthquake, and immediately afterward hundreds of shells would explode in air and send their iron spray down far below the bridge. As the immense magazines of cartridges ignited, the rattle as of thousands of musketry would follow, and then all was still for the moment except the dull roar and crackle of the fast-spreading fires. At dawn we heard terrific explosions about "The Rockets," from the unfinished iron-clads down the river.

By daylight on the 3rd a mob of men, women and children, to the number of several thousands, had gathered at the corner of 14th and

Cary streets and other outlets in front of the bridge, attracted by the vast commissary depot at that point; for it must be remembered that in 1865 Richmond was a half-starved city, and the Confederate government had that morning removed its guards and abandoned the removal of the provisions, which was impossible for the want of transportation. The depot doors were forced open and a demoniacal struggle for the countless barrels of hams, bacon, whisky, flour, sugar, coffee, etc., raged about the buildings among the hungry mob. The gutters ran whisky, and it was lapped as it flowed down the streets, while all fought for a share of the plunder. The flames came nearer and nearer, and at last caught in the commissariat itself.

At daylight the approach of the Union forces could be plainly discerned. After a little came the clatter of horses' hoofs galloping up Main street. My infantry guard stood to arms, the picket across the canal was withdrawn, and the engineer officer lighted a torch of fat pine. By direction of the Engineer Department barrels of tar, surrounded by pine knots, had been placed at intervals on the bridge, with kerosene at hand, and a lieutenant of engineers had reported for the duty of firing them at my order. The noisy train proved to be Gary's ambulances, sent forward preparatory to his final rush for the bridge. The muleteers galloped their animals about half-way down, when they were stopped by the dense mass of human beings. Rapidly communicating to Captain Mayo my instructions from General Ewell, I ordered that officer to stand firm at his post until Gary got up. I rode forward into the mob and cleared a lane. The ambulances were galloped down to the bridge, I retired to my post, and the mob closed in after me and resumed its wild struggle for plunder.

A few minutes later a long line of cavalry in gray turned into 14th street and, sword in hand, galloped straight down to the river. Gary had come. The mob scattered right and left before the armed horsemen, who reined up at the canal. Presently a single company of cavalry appeared in sight, and rode at headlong speed to the bridge. "My rearguard," explained Gary. Touching his hat to me, he called out, "All over! Good-bye! Blow her to h--l!" and trotted over the bridge. That was the last I ever saw of General Gary of South Carolina.

In less than sixty seconds Captain Mayo was in column of march, and as he reached the little island about half-way across the bridge, the single piece of artillery loaded with grape-shot that had occupied that spot arrived on the Manchester side of the river. The engineer officer, Dr. Lyons, and I walked leisurely to the island, setting fire to the provided combustible material as we passed along, and leaving the north section of Mayo's bridge wrapped in flame and smoke. At the island we stopped to take a view of the situation north of the river, and saw a line of blue-coated horsemen galloping in furious haste up Main street. Across 14th street they stopped, and then dashed down 14th street to the flaming bridge. They fired a few random shots at us three on the island, and we retreated to Manchester. I ordered my command forward, the lieutenant of engineers saluted and went about his business, and myself and my companion sat on our horses for nearly half an hour watching the occupation of Richmond. We saw another string of horsemen in blue pass up Main street, then we saw a dense column of infantry march by, seemingly without end; we heard the very welkin ring with cheers as the United States forces reached Capitol Square, and then we turned and slowly rode on our way.

A fretful Stanton wired Lincoln at City Point not to expose himself. The President replied in a gay mood, "Thanks for your caution; but I have already been to Petersburg." Horace Porter saw him there:[4]

Mr. Lincoln soon after arrived, accompanied by Robert, who had ridden back to the railroad-station to meet him, and by his little son, "Tad," and Admiral Porter. He dismounted in the street, and came in through the front gate with long and rapid strides, his face beaming with delight. He seized General Grant's hand as the general stepped forward to greet him, and stood shaking it for some time, and pouring out his thanks and congratulations with all the fervor of a heart which seemed overflowing with its fullness of joy. I doubt whether Mr. Lincoln ever experienced a happier moment in his life. The scene was singularly affecting, and one never to be forgotten. He said: "Do you know, general, I had a sort of sneaking idea all along that you intended to do something like this; but I thought some time ago that you would so manoeuver as to have Sherman come up and be near enough to co-operate with you." "Yes," replied the general; "I thought at one time that Sherman's army might advance far enough to be in supporting distance of the Eastern armies when the spring campaign against Lee opened; but I had a feeling that it would be better to let Lee's old antagonists give his army the final blow, and finish up the job. If the Western troops were even to put in an appearance against Lee's army, it might give some of our politicians a chance to stir up sectional feeling in claiming everything for the troops from their own section of country. The Western armies have been very successful in their campaigns, and it is due to the Eastern armies to let them vanquish their old enemy single-handed." "I see," said Mr. Lincoln; "but I never thought of it in that light. In fact, my anxiety has been so great that I didn't care where the help came from, so that the work was perfectly done." "Oh," General Grant continued, "I do not suppose it would have given rise to much of the bickering I mentioned, and perhaps the idea would not have occurred to any one else. I feel sure there would have been no such feeling among the soldiers. Of course I would not have risked the result of the campaign on account of any mere sentiment of this kind. I have always felt confident that our troops here were amply able to handle Lee." Mr. Lincoln then began to talk about the civil complications that would follow the destruction of the Confederate armies in the field, and showed plainly the anxiety he felt regarding the great problems in statecraft which would soon be thrust upon him. He intimated very plainly, in a conversation that lasted nearly half an hour, that thoughts of leniency to the conquered were uppermost in his heart.

Meanwhile his son Tad, for whom he always showed a deep affection, was becoming a little uneasy, and gave certain appealing looks, to which General Sharpe, who seemed to understand the mute expressions of small boys, responded by producing some sandwiches, which he offered to him, saying: "Here, young man, I guess you must be hungry." Tad seized them as a drowning man would seize a life-preserver, and cried out: "Yes, I am; that's what's the matter with me." This greatly amused the President and the general-in-chief, who had a hearty laugh at Tad's expense.

Safely back at City Point, the President gave Stanton no peace of mind. Lincoln's wire to the Secretary continued: "It is certain now that Richmond is in our hands, and I think I will go there tomorrow. I can take care of myself."

Thomas Thatcher Graves, on the staff of General Godfrey Weitzel, who commanded the troops occupying Richmond, could hardly believe his eyes on the morning of April 4:[5]

On passing out from Clay street, from Jefferson Davis's house, I saw a crowd coming, headed by President Lincoln, who was walking with his usual long, careless stride, and looking about with an interested air and taking in everything. Upon my saluting he said: "Is it far to Presi-

dent Davis's house?" I accompanied him to the house, which was occupied by General Weitzel as headquarters. . . .

At the Davis house, he was shown into the reception-room, with the
remark that the housekeeper had said that that room was President
Davis's office. As he seated himself he remarked, "This must have
been President Davis's chair," and, crossing his legs, he looked far off
with a serious, dreamy expression. At length he asked me if the housekeeper was in the house. Upon learning that she had left he jumped
up and said, with a boyish manner, "Come, let's look at the house!"
We went pretty much over it; I retailed all that the housekeeper had
told me, and he seemed interested in everything. As we came down
the staircase General Weitzel came in, in breathless haste, and at once
President Lincoln's face lost its boyish expression as he realized that
duty must be resumed. Soon afterward Judge Campbell, General Anderson (Confederates), and others called and asked for an interview
with the President. It was granted, and took place in the parlor with
closed doors.

I accompanied President Lincoln and General Weitzel to Libby
Prison and Castle Thunder, and heard General Weitzel ask President
Lincoln what he (General Weitzel) should do in regard to the conquered people. President Lincoln replied that he did not wish to give
any orders on that subject, but, as he expressed it, "If I were in your
place I'd let 'em up easy, let 'em up easy."

*That afternoon A. W. Bartlett, of the Twelfth New Hampshire, saw
the wild enthusiasm of Richmond's Negroes:*[6]

When it became certain that it was really "Marsa Abraham" that
was in their midst, there was such a rush to see and speak with him
that it was almost impossible, at times, for his carriage to move. A number of bright eyed and woolly headed urchins, taking advantage of
this delay, climbed upon the top of the carriage and took a peep at him
over the rim, greatly to the amusement of the President. His reception
in a city which, only a day or two before, had been the headquarters
and centre of the Rebellion, was most remarkable; and more resembled the triumphant return from, than an entry into the enemy's capital. Instead of the streets being silent and vacated, they were filled with
men, women, and children, shouting and cheering wherever he went.

"I'd rather see him than Jesus," excitedly exclaims one woman, as
she runs ahead of the crowd to get a full view of his benign counte-

nance. "De kingdom's come, and de Lord is wid us," chants another. "Hallelujah!" shouts a third; and so on through a whole volume of prayers, praises, blessings, and benedictions showered down upon him, the great emancipator of a race, and the saviour of his country, thus redeemed, as he walked slowly forward with smiling face and uncovered head. . . .

But it was not the colored population alone which welcomed the Union troops and their great commander-in-chief into the city of Richmond. Thousands of the white citizens were glad to be again under the protection of the flag of their fathers; and some, who had been true to it from the first, keeping it safely hidden away as a sacred emblem of their loyalty, were more happy, if possible, though less demonstrative, than the negro, as they once more were allowed the privilege of spreading its bright folds to the free air of heaven.

Another early visitor to Richmond, George Alfred Townsend, revealed to readers of the New York Herald *that not all Southerners had supported the Confederacy. At Castle Thunder, the state prison, an abandoned record book made him shudder:*[7]

These are some of the entries:

"George Barton,—giving food to Federal prisoners of war; forty lashes upon the bare back. Approved. Sentence carried into effect July 2.

"Peter B. Innis,—passing forged government notes; chain and ball for twelve months; forty lashes a day. Approved.

"Arthur Wright,—attempting to desert to the enemy; sentenced to be shot. Approved. Carried into effect, March 26.

"John Morton,—communicating with the enemy; to be hung. Approved. Carried into effect, March 26."

In an inner room are some fifty pairs of balls and chains, with anklets and handcuffs upon them, which have bent the spirit and body of many a resisting heart. Within are two condemned cells, perfectly dark—a faded flap over the window peep-hole—the smell from which would knock a strong man down.

For in their centre lies the sink, ever open, and the floors are sappy with uncleanliness. To the right of these, a door leads to a walled yard not forty feet long, nor fifteen wide, overlooked by the barred windows of the main prison rooms, and by sentry boxes upon the wall-top. Here the wretched were shot and hung in sight of their trembling comrades.

The brick wall at the foot of the yard is scarred and crushed by balls and bullets which first passed through some human heart and wrote here their damning testimony. The gallows had been suspended from a wing in the ledge, and in mid-air the impotent captive swung, none daring or willing to say a good word for him; and not for any offence against God's law, not for wronging his neighbor, or shedding blood, or making his kind miserable, but for standing in the way of an upstart organization, which his impulse and his judgment alike impelled him to oppose. This little yard, bullet-marked, close, and shut from all sympathy, is to us the ghastliest spot in the world. Can Mr. Davis visit it, and pray as he does so devoutly afterward? When men plead the justice of the South, and arguments are prompt to favor them, let this prison yard rise up and say that no such crimes in liberty's name have ever been committed, on this continent, at least.

Charles Dana also had reached Richmond:[8]

Immediately upon arriving I began to make inquiries about official papers. I found that the records and documents of the departments and of Congress had generally been removed before the evacuation, and that during the fire the Capitol had been ransacked and the documents there scattered. In the rooms of the Secretary of the Senate and of the Military Committee of the House of Representatives in the State House we found some papers of importance. . . .

General Weitzel told me that he had found about twenty thousand people in Richmond, half of them of African descent. He said that when President Lincoln entered the town on the 4th [5th] he received a most enthusiastic reception from the mass of the inhabitants.* All the members of Congress had escaped, and only the Assistant Secretary of War, Judge John Archibald Campbell, remained in the fallen capital of the Confederacy. Most of the newspaper editors had fled, but the Whig appeared on the 4th as a Union paper, with the name of its former proprietor at its head. The night after I arrived [that is, April 6th] the theater opened.

There was much suffering and poverty among the population, the rich as well as the poor being destitute of food. Weitzel had decided to issue supplies to all who would take the oath. In my first message to Mr. Stanton I spoke of this. He immediately answered: "Please ascer-

* Judith Brockenbrough McGuire insisted, however, that those who greeted Mr. Lincoln so warmly represented the "low, lower, lowest of creation."

tain from General Weitzel under what authority he is distributing rations to the people of Richmond, as I suppose he would not do it without authority; and direct him to report daily the amount of rations distributed by his order to persons not belonging to the military service, and not authorized by law to receive rations, designating the color of the persons, their occupation, and sex." Mr. Stanton seemed to be satisfied when I wired that Weitzel was working under General Ord's orders, approved by General Grant, and that he was paying for the rations by selling captured property.

The important question which the President had on his mind when I reached Richmond was how Virginia could be brought back to the Union. He had already had an interview with Judge Campbell and other prominent representatives of the Confederate Government. All they asked, they said, was an amnesty and a military convention to cover appearances. Slavery they admitted to be defunct. The President did not promise the amnesty, but he told them he had the pardoning power, and would save any repentant sinner from hanging. They assured him that, if amnesty could be offered, the rebel army would be dissolved and all the States return.

III

Lee's one idea, falling back from Petersburg, was to join with Joe Johnston's troops in North Carolina. Foreseeing some such emergency as now happened, Lee, days before, had instructed Richmond to send supplies to Amelia Court House, forty miles southwest of Richmond, on the Richmond and Danville Railroad. On the fourth of April he led his hungry, gaunt-eyed soldiers into this depot on their route to Danville. There were no supplies. Francis Lawley, correspondent for the London Times, *watched the Army of Northern Virginia stumble forward:*[9]

The country through which we were passing was a tract of straggling woods and pine barrens with occasional little patches of clearings. The foraging parties had to go so far afield in quest of food that they were taken prisoners by wholesale. In the face of such suffering as they left behind, it cannot be wondered at if some of the poor fellows courted capture.

Those foragers who returned to Lee brought little or nothing with them. The sufferings of the men from the pangs of hunger have not been approached in the military annals of the last fifty years. But the

sufferings of the mules and horses must have been even keener; for
the men assuaged their craving by plucking the buds and twigs of trees
just shooting in the early spring, whereas the grass had not yet started
from its winter sleep and food for the unhappy quadrupeds there was
none. As early as the morning of the 4th, Lee sent off half his artillery
toward the railroad to relieve the famished horses. This artillery
making slow progress, thanks to the exhaustion of the horses, was captured by the Federals on the 8th, but not until General Lindsay Walker
had buried many of his guns, which were of course subsequently ex-
humed (70 of them at one haul) by their captors.

It is easy to see that the locomotion of an army in such a plight must
have been slow and slower. The retreat was conducted in the following
fashion: About midnight the Confederates slipped out of their hasty
works, which they had thrown up and held during the previous day,
and fell back until ten or eleven o'clock the next morning. Then they
halted, and immediately threw up earthworks for their protection during the day. It was not long before the wolves were again at their heels,
and from their earthworks the Confederates exchanged a heavy fire

FROM RICHMOND TO APPOMATTOX

From *Atlas of American History*

with their pursuers throughout the day. Delayed by the necessity of
guarding a train from thirty-five to forty miles in length, enfeebled by
hunger and sleeplessness, the retreating army was able to make only
ten miles each night. This delay enabled the active Sheridan to get
ahead with his cavalry and destroy the depot of provisions along the
railroad between Burkeville and Danville.

Upon the 5th, many of the mules and horses ceased to struggle. It
became necessary to burn hundreds of wagons. At intervals the enemy's cavalry dashed in and struck the interminable train here or there,
capturing and burning dozens upon dozens of wagons. Toward evening

of the 5th, and all day long upon the 6th, hundreds of men dropped from exhaustion and thousands let fall their muskets from inability to carry them further.

The scenes of the 5th, 6th, 7th and 8th were of a nature which can be apprehended in its vivid reality only by men who are thoroughly familiar with the harrowing details of war. Behind and on either flank an ubiquitous and increasingly adventurous enemy—every mud-hole and every rise in the road choked with blazing wagons, the air filled with the deafening reports of ammunition exploding and shells bursting when touched by the flames, dense columns of smoke ascending to heaven from the burning and exploding vehicles—exhausted men, worn-out mules and horses lying down side by side—gaunt famine glaring hopelessly from sunken lack-lustre eyes—dead horses, dead mules, dead men everywhere—death many times welcomed as God's blessing in disguise—who can wonder if many hearts, tried in the fiery furnace of four years' unparalleled suffering and never hitherto found wanting, should have quailed in presence of starvation, fatigue, sleeplessness, misery, unintermitted for five or six days and culminating in hopelessness.

Riding hard on the heels of the retreating Confederates, Colonel Theodore Lyman knew Lee's flight was hopeless:[10]

> HEADQUARTERS ARMY OF POTOMAC
> RICHMOND AND BURKEVILLE R.R.
> 10 MILES NORTH OF BURKEVILLE
> April 6, 1865

We are pelting after Old Lee as hard as the poor doughboys' legs can go. I estimate our prisoners at 16,000, with lots of guns and colors. At six A.M. the three infantry corps advanced in line of battle, on Amelia Court House; 2d on the left; 5th in the centre; and 6th on the right. Sheridan's cavalry, meantime, struck off to the left, to head off their waggon-trains in the direction of the Appomattox River. We did not know just then, you perceive, in what precise direction the enemy was moving. Following the railroad directly towards Amelia C.H., General Meade received distinct intelligence, at nine o'clock, that the enemy was moving on Deatonsville, intending probably to cross the Appomattox at High Bridge. Instantly General Meade gave orders for the 6th Corps to face about and move by the left flank and seek roads in the direction of High Bridge, with the idea of supporting the cavalry in their attempt to head off the enemy; the 2d Corps were turned into the left-hand road nearest Jetersville, and directed to push on and strike the enemy wherever they could. At nine we got to the left-hand road lying some way beyond Jetersville, and here the 5th Corps was turned in, with orders to follow the road through Paineville and attack whatever they found. These prompt dispositions ensured the grand success of the day, which the newspapers have gracefully handed over to General Sheridan!

Here I may as well say that Lee was trying to escape with his large artillery and waggon trains. At first he thought to move directly along the railroad, through Burkeville, to Danville. Cut off by the 5th Corps and the cavalry, he *now* was trying to march "cross lots" and get to the Danville road, somewhere below us. . . . At ten, we got back to Jetersville, a collection of half-a-dozen houses with a country church. From the second story of a house I witnessed a most curious spectacle —a fight, four miles off in a straight line! At that point was a bare ridge, a little above Deatonsville, and there, with my good glass, I could see a single man very well. It was just like a play of marionettes! and the surrounding woods made side scenes to this stage. At first, I saw only the Rebel train, moving along the ridge towards Deatonsville, in all haste: there now goes a pigmy ambulance drawn by mouse-like horses, at a trot. Here come more ambulances and many waggons from the woods, and disappear, in a continuous procession, over the ridge. Suddenly—*boom! boom!* and the distant smoke of Humphreys' batteries curls above the pine trees. At this stimulus the Lilliputian procession redoubles its speed (I am on the point of crying "bravo!" at this brilliant stroke of the gentleman who is pulling the wires). But now enter from the woods, in some confusion, a good number of Rebel cavalry; they form on the crest—but, *boom! boom!* go the cannon, and they disappear. Ah! here come the infantry! Now for a fight! Yes, a line of battle in retreat, and covering the rear. There are mounted officers; they gallop about, waving their tiny swords. Halt! The infantry form a good line on the crest; you can't scare *them*. What are they carrying? Spears? No, *rails;* that's what it is, rails for to revet a breastwork. They scramble about like ants. You had better hurry up, Yanks, if you want to carry that crest! (The stage manager informs me the Yanks *are* hurrying and the next act will be—Enter Duke Humphrey, in haste.) Hullo! There come six fleet mice dragging something, followed by more: yes, a battery. They unlimber: a pause: Flash!—(count twenty-two seconds by Captain Barrows's watch) then, *bang! bang!*

There come in their skirmishers! running for their lives; certainly the Yanks are in those woods. Now they turn their guns more to the left; they are getting flanked. Their officers gallop wildly. You seem to hear them shout, "Change front to the rear!" anyhow they do so, at a double-quick. Then one volley of musketry, and they are gone, guns and all! The next moment our skirmishers go swarming up the hill; up goes a battery, and down goes the curtain.

There is no rest for the wicked. All day long the peppery Humphreys, glaring through those spectacles, presses hotly in their rear; the active Sheridan is felling trees across their front; on their right is the Appomattox, impassable; and now, as the afternoon closes, here comes the inevitable Wright, grimly on their left flank, at Sailor's Creek. The 6th Corps charges; they can't be stopped—result, five Rebel generals; 8600 prisoners, 14 cannon; the Rebel rear-guard annihilated! As we get to our camp, beyond Deatonsville, there comes a Staff officer with a despatch. "*I* attacked with two divisions of the 6th Corps. *I* captured many thousand prisoners, etc., etc. P. H. Sheridan." "Oh," said Meade, "so *General Wright wasn't there.*" "Oh, yes!" cried the Staff officer, as if speaking of some worthy man who had commanded a battalion, "Oh, yes, General Wright *was* there." Meade turned on his heel without a word, and Cavalry Sheridan's despatch proceeded—to the newspapers!

The uneven contest at Sailor's (Saylor's) Creek, that saw a Confederate corps terribly hacked and General Ewell captured, ended on April 7. Horace Porter described another memorable event of that day:[11]

A little before noon on April 7, 1865, General Grant, with his staff, rode into the little village of Farmville, on the south side of the Appomattox River, a town that will be memorable in history as the place where he opened the correspondence with Lee which, two days later, led to the surrender of the Army of Northern Virginia. He drew up in front of the village hotel, a comfortable brick building, dismounted, and established headquarters on its broad piazza. News came in that Crook was fighting large odds with his cavalry on the north side of the river, and I was directed to go to his front and see what was necessary to be done to assist him. I found that he was being driven back, the enemy (Munford's and Rosser's cavalry divisions, under Fitzhugh Lee) having made a bold stand north of the river. Humphreys was also on the north side, isolated from the rest of our infantry, confronted by a large portion of Lee's army, and having some heavy fighting. On my return to general headquarters that evening, Wright's corps was ordered to cross the river and move rapidly to the support of our troops there. Notwithstanding their long march that day, the men sprang to their feet with a spirit that made every one marvel at their pluck, and came swinging through the main street of the village with a step that seemed as elastic as on the first day of their toilsome tramp. It was now dark, but they spied the general-in-chief watching them with evident pride from the piazza of the hotel as they marched past. Then was witnessed one of the most inspiring scenes of the campaign. Bonfires were lighted on the sides of the street; the men seized straw and pine-knots, and improvised torches; cheers arose from their throats, already hoarse with shouts of victory; bands played, banners waved, and muskets were swung in the air. A regiment now broke forth with the song of "John Brown's body," and soon a whole division was shouting the swelling chorus of the popular air, which had risen to the dignity of a national anthem. The night march had become a grand review, with Grant as the reviewing officer.

Ord and Gibbon had visited the general at the hotel, and he had spoken with them, as well as with Wright, about sending some communication to Lee that might pave the way to the stopping of further bloodshed. Dr. Smith, formerly of the regular army, a native of Virginia, and a relative of General Ewell, now one of our prisoners, had told General Grant the night before that Ewell had said in conversation that their cause was lost when they crossed the James River, and he considered that it was the duty of the authorities to negotiate for peace then, while they still had a right to claim concessions, adding that now they were not in condition to claim anything. He said that for every man killed after this somebody would be responsible, and it would be little better than murder. He could not tell what General Lee would do, but he hoped that he would at once surrender his army. This statement, together with the news that had been received from Sheridan, saying that he had heard that General Lee's trains of provisions, which had come by rail, were at Appomattox, and that he expected to capture them before Lee could reach them, induced the general to write. . . .

Grant detailed the historic correspondence that followed:[12]

Feeling now that General Lee's chance of escape was utterly hopeless, I addressed him the following communication from Farmville:

"April 7, 1865

"GENERAL: The result of the last week must convince you of the hopelessness of further resistance on the part of the Army of Northern Virginia in this struggle. I feel that it is so, and regard it as my duty to shift from myself the responsibility of any further effusion of blood, by asking of you the surrender of that portion of the Confederate States army known as the Army of Northern Virginia.

"U. S. GRANT,
"*Lieutenant-General*

"GENERAL R. E. LEE."

Early on the morning of the eighth, before leaving, I received at Farmville the following:

"April 7, 1865

"GENERAL: I have received your note of this date. Though not entertaining the opinion you express on the hopelessness of further resistance on the part of the army of Northern Virginia, I reciprocate your desire to avoid useless effusion of blood, and therefore, before considering your proposition, ask the terms you will offer on condition of its surrender.

"R. E. LEE,
"*General*

"LIEUTENANT-GENERAL U. S. GRANT."

To this I immediately replied:

"April 8, 1865

"GENERAL: Your note of last evening, in reply to mine of same date, asking the condition on which I will accept the surrender of the army of Northern Virginia, is just received. In reply I would say that, *peace* being my great desire, there is but one condition I would insist upon, namely: That the men and officers surrendered shall be disqualified for taking up arms again against the Government of the United States until properly exchanged. I will meet you, or will designate officers to meet any officers you may name for the same purpose, at any point agreeable to you, for the purpose of arranging definitely the terms upon which the surrender of the army of Northern Virginia will be received.

"U. S. GRANT,
"*Lieutenant-General*

"GENERAL R. E. LEE."

Early on the morning of the eighth the pursuit was resumed. General Meade followed north of the Appomattox, and General Sheridan, with all the cavalry, pushed straight for Appomattox Station, followed by General Ord's command and the Fifth corps. During the day General Meade's advance had considerable fighting with the enemy's rear guard, but was unable to bring on a general engagement. Late in the evening General Sheridan struck the railroad at the Appomattox station, drove the enemy from there, and captured twenty-five pieces of artillery, a hospital train, and four trains of cars loaded with supplies for Lee's army. During this day I accompanied General Meade's column, and about midnight received the following communication from General Lee:

"April 8, 1865

"GENERAL: I received at a late hour your note of to-day. In mine of yesterday I did not intend to propose the surrender of the Army of Northern Virginia, but to ask the terms of your proposition. To be frank, I do not think the emergency has arisen to call for the surrender of this army; but as the restoration of peace should be the sole object of all, I desired to know whether your proposals would lead to that end. I cannot, therefore, meet you with a view to surrender the Army of Northern Virginia; but as far as your proposal may affect the Confederate States forces under my command, and tend to the restoration of peace, I should be pleased to meet you at ten A.M. to-morrow on the old stage road to Richmond, between the picket lines of the two armies.

"R. E. LEE,
"General

"LIEUTENANT-GENERAL U. S. GRANT."

Early on the morning of the ninth I returned him an answer as follows, and immediately started to join the column south of the Appomattox:

"April 9, 1865

"GENERAL: Your note of yesterday is received. I have no authority to treat on the subject of peace; the meeting proposed for A.M. to-day could lead to no good. I will state, however, General, that I am equally anxious for peace with yourself, and the whole North entertains the same feeling. The terms upon which peace can be had are well understood. By the South laying down their arms they will hasten that most desirable event, save thousands of human lives, and hundreds of millions of property not yet destroyed. Seriously hoping that all our difficulties may be settled without the loss of another life, I subscribe myself, &c.,

"U. S. GRANT,
"*Lieutenant-General*

"GENERAL R. E. LEE."

On the morning of the ninth General Ord's command and the Fifth corps reached Appomattox station just as the enemy was making a desperate effort to break through our cavalry. The infantry was at once thrown in. Soon after a white flag was received, requesting a suspension of hostilities pending negotiations for surrender.

Before reaching General Sheridan's headquarters, I received the following from General Lee:

"April 9, 1865
"GENERAL: I received your note of this morning on the picket line, whither I had come to meet you, and ascertain definitely what terms were embraced in your proposal of yesterday with reference to the surrender of this army. I now ask an interview in accordance with the offer contained in your letter of yesterday for that purpose.

"R. E. LEE,
"*General*

"LIEUTENANT-GENERAL U. S. GRANT."

IV

Colonel Theodore Lyman described a truce that upset two Union generals:[13]

. . . At 10.30 came, one after the other, two negroes, who said that some of our troops entered Lynchburg yesterday; and that Lee was now cut off near Appomattox Court House. This gave us new wings! An aide-de-camp galloped on, to urge Humphreys to press the pursuit, and all waggons were ordered out of the road, that the 6th Corps might close in immediately on his rear. Away went the General again, full tilt, along the road crowded by the infantry, every man of whom was footing it, as if a lottery prize lay just ahead! A bugler trotted ahead, blowing to call the attention of the troops, while General Webb followed, crying, "Give way to the right! Give way to the right!" Thus we ingeniously worked our way, amid much pleasantry. "Fish for sale!" roared one doughboy. "Yes," joined in a pithy comrade, "and a tarnation big one, too!" The comments on the General were endless. "That's Meade." "Yes, that's him." "Is he sick?" "I expect he is; he looks kinder wild!" "Guess the old man hain't had much sleep lately."

The heavy artillery firing we had earlier heard, now had suddenly ceased, and there was a perfect stillness—a suspicious circumstance that gave us new hope. Somewhat before noon we got to General Humphreys, some five miles east of the Court House and at the very head of his men. He reported that he had just struck the enemy's skirmish line, and was preparing to drive them back. At that moment an officer rode up and said the enemy were out with a white flag. "They shan't stop *me!*" retorted the fiery H.; "receive the message but push on the skirmishers!" Back came the officer speedily, with a note. General Lee stated that General Ord had agreed to a suspension of hostilities, and he should ask for the same on this *end* of the line. "Hey! what!" cried General Meade, in his harsh, suspicious voice, "I have no sort of authority to grant such suspension. General Lee has already refused the terms of General Grant. Advance your skirmishers, Humphreys, and bring up your troops. We will pitch into them at once!" But lo! here comes now General Forsyth, who had ridden through the Rebel army, from General Sheridan (under a flag), and who now urged a brief suspension. "Well," said the General, "in order that you may get back to Sheridan, I will wait till two o'clock, and then, if I get no communication from General Lee, I shall attack!" So back went Forsyth, with a variety of notes and despatches. We waited, not without excitement, for the appointed hour. Meantime, negroes came in and said the Rebel pickets had thrown down their muskets and gone leisurely to their main body; also that the Rebels were "done gone give up." Presently, the General pulled out his watch and said: "Two o'clock—no answer—go forward." But they had not advanced far, before we saw a Rebel and a Union officer coming in. They bore an order from General Grant to halt the troops. Major Wingate, of General Lee's Staff, was a military-looking man, dressed in a handsome grey suit with gold lace, and a gold star upon the collar. He was courageous, but plainly mortified to the heart. "We had done better to have burnt our whole train three days ago," he said bitterly. "In trying to save a train, we have lost an army!" And there he struck the pith of the thing.

The reporter Sylvanus Cadwallader was at Appomattox Court House on that historic ninth of April, 1865:[14]

. . . The news of the pending negotiations for the surrender spread rapidly through both armies. As we came out on the open ground near the village, both armies were in plain view. The soldiers of each were in line of battle, and ready to renew the contest on short notice. Officers were galloping in all directions, colors were flying, and it had more the appearance of a grand review of troops, than of contending hosts. A nearer view, however, disclosed dirty, tattered, ranks of soldiers, none of them well clad, and nearly all officers in fatigue dress.

We struck the upper or south end of the principal street of the village, and turned northward to the Court House. Lee's army still lay north and east of the town. A close lookout was kept for Gen. Lee. When nearly in front of a two-story brick house on the right, or east side of the street, an orderly in rebel uniform was seen holding a couple of horses near the north end of the building. One was a dapple-gray, with a Grimsley saddle and plain single-reined bridle on him, without anything to denote rank.

A staff officer dashed across the open blue grass yard and inquired whose horses they were. The orderly said they belonged to Gen. Lee, who was in the house. The house stood back several rods from the street. The front fence was wholly down, and mostly carried away. So Gen. Grant rode across the yard to the front entrance to a long porch which extended the whole length of the house, dismounted, ascended a half dozen steps onto the porch, and was about to enter the half-open door of a wide hall which separated the ground floor into two suites of rooms, when Gen. Lee met him, exchanged salutations, and conducted him into the front room on the left side of the hall. The staff all remained on their horses. In a few minutes Gen. Grant came to the front, and beckoned to us to come in. . . .

Grant remembered his emotions when he shook the hand of Lee:[15]

What General Lee's feelings were I do not know. As he was a man of much dignity, with an impassible face, it was impossible to say whether he felt inwardly glad that the end had finally come, or felt sad over the result, and was too manly to show it. Whatever his feelings, they were entirely concealed from my observation; but my own feelings, which had been quite jubilant on the receipt of his letter, were sad and depressed. I felt like anything rather than rejoicing at the downfall of a foe, who had fought so long and valiantly, and had suffered so much for a cause, though that cause was, I believe, one of the worst for which a people ever fought, and one for which there was the least excuse.

With Grant in the McLean House that day was Horace Porter:[16]

The contrast between the two commanders was singularly striking, and could not fail to attract marked attention as they sat, six or eight feet apart, facing each other. General Grant, then nearly forty-three years of age, was five feet eight inches in height, with shoulders slightly stooped. His hair and full beard were nut-brown, without a trace of gray in them. He had on his single-breasted blouse of dark-blue flannel, unbuttoned in front and showing a waistcoat underneath. He wore an ordinary pair of top-boots, with his trousers inside, and was without spurs. The boots and portions of his clothes were spattered with mud. . . . His felt "sugar-loaf," stiff-brimmed hat was resting on his lap. He had no sword or sash, and a pair of shoulder-straps was all there was about him to designate his rank. . . .

Lee, on the other hand, was six feet and one inch in height, and erect for one of his age, for he was Grant's senior by sixteen years. His hair and full beard were a silver-gray, and thick, except that the hair had become a little thin in front. He wore a new uniform of Confederate gray, buttoned to the throat, and a handsome sword and sash. . . . His top-boots were comparatively new, and had on them near the top some ornamental stitching of red silk. Like his uniform, they were clean. On the boots were handsome spurs with large rowels. A felt hat which in color matched pretty closely that of his uniform, and a pair of long, gray buckskin gauntlets, lay beside him on the table. . . .

Grant recalled, with a hint of chagrin, "I must have contrasted very strangely with a man so handsomely dressed." The two generals talked for a time of old army days until, Grant admitted, "General Lee called my attention to the object of our meeting":[17]

. . . I called to General Parker, secretary on my staff, for writing materials, and commenced writing out the following terms:

APPOMATTOX C.H., VA.,
Ap'l 9th, 1865

GEN. R. E. LEE,
COMD'G C. S. A.

GEN.: In accordance with the substance of my letter to you of the 8th inst., I propose to receive the surrender of the Army of N. Va. on the following terms, to wit: Rolls of all the officers and men to be made in duplicate. One copy to be given to an officer designated by me, the other to be retained by such officer or officers as you may designate. The officers to give their individual paroles not to take up arms against the Government of the United States until properly exchanged, and each company or regimental commander sign a like parole for the men of their commands. The arms, artillery and public property to be parked and stacked, and turned over to the officer appointed by me to receive them. This will not embrace the side-arms of the officers, nor their private horses or baggage. This done, each officer and man will be allowed to return to their homes, not to be disturbed by United States authority so long as they observe their paroles and the laws in force where they may reside.

Very respectfully,
U. S. GRANT,
Lt.-Gen.

When I put my pen to the paper I did not know the first word that I should make use of in writing the terms. I only knew what was in my mind, and I wished to express it clearly, so that there could be no mistaking it. . . .

Grant's letter was handed to Lee. Horace Porter watched intently:[18]

Lee pushed aside some books and two brass candlesticks which were on the table, then took the book and laid it down before him, while he drew from his pocket a pair of steel-rimmed spectacles, and wiped the glasses carefully with his handkerchief. He crossed his legs, adjusted the spectacles very slowly and deliberately, took up the draft of the terms, and proceeded to read them attentively. When he reached the top line of the second page, he looked up, and said to General Grant: "After the words 'until properly' the word 'exchanged' seems to be omitted. You doubtless intended to use that word."

"Why, yes," said Grant; "I thought I had put in the word 'exchanged.'"

"I presumed it had been omitted inadvertently," continued Lee; "and, with your permission, I will mark where it should be inserted."

"Certainly," Grant replied.

Lee felt in his pocket as if searching for a pencil, but he did not seem to be able to find one. Seeing this, I handed him my lead-pencil. . . .

To Grant, receiving a surrender was part of the business of war. He continued his narrative without embellishment:[19]

No conversation, not one word, passed between General Lee and myself, either about private property, side arms, or kindred subjects. He appeared to have no objections to the terms first proposed; or if he had a point to make against them he wished to wait until they were in writing to make it. When he read over that part of the terms about side arms, horses and private property of the officers, he remarked, with some feeling, I thought, that this would have a happy effect upon his army.

Then, after a little further conversation, General Lee remarked to me again that their army was organized a little differently from the army of the United States (still maintaining by implication that we were two countries); that in their army the cavalrymen and artillerists owned their own horses; and he asked if he was to understand that the men who so owned their horses were to be permitted to retain them. I told him that as the terms were written they would not; that only the officers were permitted to take their private property. He then, after reading over the terms a second time, remarked that that was clear.

I then said to him that I thought this would be about the last battle of the war—I sincerely hoped so; and I said further I took it that most of the men in the ranks were small farmers. The whole country had been so raided by the two armies that it was doubtful whether they would be able to put in a crop to carry themselves and their families through the next winter without the aid of the horses they were then riding. The United States did not want them, and I would, therefore, instruct the officers I left behind to receive the paroles of his troops to let every man of the Confederate army who claimed to own a horse or mule take the animal to his home. Lee remarked again that this would have a happy effect. . . .

The much talked of surrendering of Lee's sword and my handing it back, this and much more that has been said about it is the purest romance.

V

The two generals signed the papers. Then Lee shook hands with Grant, bowed to the other officers, and left the room. Waiting on the porch for his horse, Lee three times struck the palm of his left hand with his right fist. At a slow trot, he rode back to his army. Horace Porter described the jubilant scene inside the McLean House:[20]

Mr. McLean had been charging about in a manner which indicated that the excitement was shaking his nervous system to its center; but his real trials did not begin until the departure of the chief actors in the surrender. Then relic-hunters charged down upon the manor-house, and began to bargain for the numerous pieces of furniture. Sheridan paid the proprietor twenty dollars in gold for the table on which General Grant wrote the terms of surrender, for the purpose of presenting it to Mrs. Custer, and handed it over to her dashing husband, who galloped off to camp bearing it upon his shoulders. Ord paid forty dollars for the table at which Lee sat, and afterward presented it to Mrs. Grant, who modestly declined it, and insisted that Mrs. Ord should become its possessor. General Sharpe paid ten dollars for the pair of brass candlesticks; Colonel Sheridan, the general's brother, secured the stone inkstand; and General Capehart the chair in which Grant sat. . . . A child's doll was found in the room, which the younger officers tossed from one to the other, and called the "silent witness."

Colonel Charles Marshall, who had accompanied Lee on his meeting with Grant, described a different scene and mood:[21]

On the night of April 9th after our return from McLean's house General Lee sat with several of us at a fire in front of his tent, and after some conversation about the army and the events of the day in which his feelings towards his men were strongly expressed, he told me to prepare an order to the troops.

The next day it was raining and many persons were coming and going, so that I was unable to write without interruption until about 10 o'clock, when General Lee finding that the order had not been prepared, directed me to get into his ambulance, which stood near his tent, and placed an orderly to prevent anyone from approaching us. I made a draft in pencil and took it to General Lee who struck out a paragraph, which he said would tend to keep alive the feeling existing between the North and the South, and made one or two other changes. I then returned to the ambulance, recopied the order and gave it to a clerk in the office of the Adjutant General to write in ink.

After the first draft of the order had been made and signed by General Lee, other copies were made for transmission to the corps commanders and the staff of the army. All these copies were signed by the General and a good many persons sent other copies which they had made or procured and obtained his signature. In this way many of the orders had the General's name signed as if they were originals.

The full text of the order follows:

GENERAL ORDER NO. 9

HEADQUARTERS ARMY OF NORTHERN VIRGINIA, 10th April 1865

After four years of arduous service marked by unsurpassed courage and fortitude the Army of Northern Virginia has been compelled to yield to overwhelming numbers and resources.

I need not tell the survivors of so many hard fought battles, who have remained steadfast to the last, that I have consented to this result from no distrust of them. But feeling that valor and devotion could accomplish nothing that could compensate for the loss that would have accompanied the continuance of the contest, I determined to avoid the useless sacrifice of those whose past services have endeared them to their country.

By the terms of the agreement Officers and men can return to their homes and remain there until exchanged. You will take with you the satisfaction that proceeds from the consciousness of duty faithfully performed and I earnestly pray that a merciful God will extend to you his blessing and protection.

With an unceasing admiration of your constancy and devotion to your country and a grateful remembrance of your kind and generous consideration of myself, I bid you all an affectionate farewell.

R. E. LEE
General

Meade, obviously satisfying his curiosity, took Colonel Theodore Lyman on a fascinating ride next morning:[22]

. . . Monday April 10 is a day worthy of description, because I saw the remains of our great opponent, the Army of Northern Virginia. The General proposed to ride through the Rebel lines to General Grant, who was at Appomattox Court House; and he took George and myself as aides; a great chance! for the rest were not allowed to go, no communication being permitted between the armies. At 10.30 we rode off, and, passing along the state road, soon got to the picket line, where a row of our men were talking comfortably with an opposite row of theirs. There the General sent me ahead to see some general of theirs who might give us a guide through the lines. I rode a little beyond a wood, and came on several regiments, camped there. The arms were neatly stacked and the well-known battle-flags were planted by the arms. The men, looking tired and indifferent, were grouped here and there. I judged they had nothing to eat, for there was no cooking going on. A mounted officer was shown me as General Field, and to him I applied. He looked something like Captain Sleeper, but was extremely moody, though he at once said he would ride back himself to General Meade, by whom he was courteously received, which caused him to thaw out considerably. We rode about a mile and then turned off to General Lee's Headquarters, which consisted in one fly with a campfire in front. I believe he had lost most of his baggage in some of the trains, though his establishment is at all times modest. He had ridden out, but, as we turned down the road again, we met him coming up, with three or four Staff officers. As he rode up General Meade took off his cap and said: "Good-morning, General." Lee, however, did not recognize him, and, when he found who it was, said: "But what are you doing with all that grey in your beard?" To which Meade promptly replied: "You have to answer for most of it!" Lee is, as all agree, a stately-looking man; tall, erect and strongly built, with a full chest. His hair and closely trimmed beard, though thick, are now nearly white. He has a large and well-shaped head, with a brown, clear eye, of unusual depth. His face is sunburnt and rather florid. In manner he is exceedingly grave and dignified—this, I believe, he always has; but there was evidently added an extreme depression, which gave him the air of a man who kept up his pride to the last, but who was entirely overwhelmed. From his speech I judge he was inclined to wander in his thoughts. You would not have recognized a Confederate officer from his dress, which was a blue military overcoat, a high grey hat, and well-brushed riding boots.

As General Meade introduced his two aides, Lee put out his hand and saluted us with all the air of the oldest blood in the world. I did not think, when I left, in '63, for Germantown, that I should ever shake the hand of Robert E. Lee, prisoner of war! He held a long conference with General Meade, while I stood over a fire, with his officers, in the rain. Colonel Marshall, one of his aides, was a very sensible and gentle-manly man, and seemed in good spirits. He told me that, at one time during the retreat, he got no sleep for seventy-two hours, the conse-quence of which was that his brain did not work at all, or worked all wrong. A quartermaster came up to him and asked by what route he should move his train: to which Marshall replied, in a lucid manner: "Tell the Captain that I *should* have sent that cane as a present to his baby; but I could not, because the baby turned out to be a girl instead of a boy!" We were talking there together, when there appeared a great oddity—an old man, with an angular, much-wrinkled face, and long, thick white hair, brushed *à la* Calhoun; a pair of silver spectacles and a high felt hat further set off the countenance, while the legs kept up their claim of eccentricity by encasing themselves in grey blankets, tied somewhat in a bandit fashion. The whole made up no less a person than Henry A. Wise, once Governor of the loyal state of Virginia, now Brigadier-General and prisoner of war. By his first wife he is Meade's brother-in-law, and had been sent for to see him. I think *he* is punished already enough: old, sick, impoverished, a prisoner, with nothing to live for, not even his son, who was killed at Roanoke Island, he stood there in his old, wet, grey blanket, glad to accept at our hands a pittance of biscuit and coffee, to save him and his Staff from starvation! While they too talked, I asked General Lee after his son "Ronnie," who was about there somewhere. It was the "Last Ditch" indeed! He too is punished enough: living at this moment at Richmond, on the food doled out to him by our government, he gets his ration just like the poorest negro in the place! We left Lee, and kept on through the sad remnants of an army that has its place in history. It would have looked a mighty host, if the ghosts of all its soldiers that now sleep between Gettysburg and Lynchburg could have stood there in the lines, beside the living.

CHAPTER 40

"WHERE I LEFT OFF"

T HE PEOPLE ARE FULL OF REJOICING," the editors of *Harper's Weekly* commented in their lead article for April 22, 1865. "The war for the Union has been *their* war, fought in their interest, sustained by their patriotism—a patriotism that has withheld neither property nor life. Let the people rejoice, then, in the final triumph, with a consciousness of their own strength, but especially with a conviction of the righteousness of their victory and a sense of overwhelming gratitude to the God of Battles. Their *Hail Columbia* is fitly accompanied by their *Te Deums.*"

I

On March 27, 1865, Secretary of War Edwin M. Stanton had ordered: "That at the hour of noon on the 14th of April 1865 Brevet Maj. Gen. Anderson will raise and plant upon the ruins of Fort Sumter in Charleston harbor the same United States flag which floated over the Battlements of that fort during the rebel assault and which was lowered and saluted by him and the small force of his command, when the works were evacuated on the 14th day of April 1861." Dr. F. Milton Willis witnessed this restoration of national authority:[1]

Sergeant Hart, who had replaced the flag after it had been shot away in the first assault, stepped forward with the Fort Sumter mail-bag in his hand. As he quietly drew forth from its long seclusion the same old flag of '61, the wildest shouts went up. The old symbol of union was quickly attached to the halyards by three sailors from the fleet who were in the first fight, and crowned with a wreath of evergreen set with clusters of rosebuds and orange blossoms. . . .

General Robert Anderson, the hero of the day, stepped forward and with uncovered head and voice trembling with emotion, said:

"I am here, my friends, my fellow-citizens and fellow-soldiers, to perform an act of duty to my country dear to my heart, and which all of you will appreciate and feel. Had I observed the wishes of my heart it should have been done in silence; but in accordance with the request of the Honorable Secretary of War, I make a few remarks, as by his order, after four long, long years of war, I restore to its proper place this dear flag, which floated here during peace before the first act of this cruel rebellion. (Taking the halyards in his hands, he said:) I thank God that I have lived to see this day, and to be here, to perform this, perhaps the last act of my life, of duty to my country. My heart is filled with gratitude to that God who has so signally blessed us, who has given us blessings beyond measure. May all the nations bless and praise the name of the Lord, and all the world proclaim, 'Glory to God in the highest, and on earth peace, good-will toward men.' "

"Amen! Amen!" the multitude responded. Then the old veteran grasped the halyards with firm and steady hand and drew aloft the starry banner; and as, all tattered by shot and shell, it rose above the battlements into its native air, a loud and prolonged shout, from fort and fleet, greeted it. The whole audience sprang to their feet. Bands began to play their most inspiring music. Men swung their hats and grasped each other by the hand; women and children waved their handkerchiefs, and many wept for joy. As it rested at length in its old place at the top of the staff, and waved its victorious folds toward the recovered city which had first disowned it, the enthusiasm became tumultuous and overpowering, till at last it found relief in the national song:

> "The star spangled banner, O long may it wave,
> O'er the land of the free, and the home of the brave!"

II

After Appomattox the complete collapse of the Confederacy ·became inevitable. Official telegrams and newspaper dispatches charted the wave of surrenders. The Secretary of War to Major General John A. Dix, commanding the Department of the East:[2]

WAR DEPARTMENT, WASHINGTON, D. C.
April 28, 1865—3 o'clock P.M.

MAJOR-GEN. DIX: A dispatch from Gen. Grant, dated at Raleigh, 10 P.M., April 26, just received by this Department, states that "Johnston surrendered the forces in his command, embracing all from here to the Chattahoochie, to Gen. Sherman on the basis agreed upon between Lee and myself for the Army of Northern Virginia."

EDWIN M. STANTON

General E. R. S. Canby to Military Headquarters at Memphis:

HDQRS. MILITARY DIVISION OF WEST MISSISSIPPI,
CITRONELLE, May 4

Lieut-Gen. Taylor has this day surrendered to me with the forces under his command, on substantially the same terms as those accepted by Gen. Lee.

The New York Tribune, May 29:

PEACE!
KIRBY SMITH SURRENDERS
THE OLD FLAG WAVES FROM MAINE TO THE RIO GRANDE!
OFFICIAL ANNOUNCEMENT

WAR DEPARTMENT,
WASHINGTON, Saturday, May 27, 1865

MAJOR-GEN. DIX: A dispatch from General Canby, dated at New Orleans, yesterday, the 26th inst., states that arrangements for the surrender of the Confederate forces in the Trans-Mississippi Department have been concluded. They include the men and materiel of the army and navy.

EDWIN M. STANTON, *Secretary of War*

III

Alexander H. Stephens, Vice President of the Confederate States of America, had reached a decision as early as the Hampton Roads conference. He would be the first of the captains and the kings to depart:[3]

I saw nothing to prevent Sherman himself from proceeding right on to Richmond and attacking Lee in the rear, to say nothing of any movements by Grant, who then had an Army in front of not much, if any, under 200,000 men. Lee's forces were not over one fourth of that number. Sherman's army, when united with Schofield's and Terry's, who were joining him from Wilmington, North Carolina, would be swelled to near 100,000. To meet these, the Confederates had in his front nothing but the fragments of shattered armies, amounting in all to not one half the number of the Federals.

When the programme of action, thus indicated by Mr. Davis [resistance to the end] . . . was clearly resolved upon, I, *then*, for the first time, in view of all the surroundings, considered the Cause as utterly hopeless.

It was then that I withdrew from Richmond. . . . He [Davis] inquired what it was my purpose to do? I told him it was to go home and remain there. I should neither make any speech, nor even make known to the public in any way my views of the general condition of affairs, but quietly abide the issues of fortune, whatever they might be. Differing as we did, at that time, upon these points, as we had upon others, we parted in the same friendship which had on all occasions marked our personal intercourse. . . .

I, therefore, left on the 9th of February, and reached home the 20th, where I remained in perfect retirement, until I was arrested on the 11th of May.*

James Russell Lowell remembered a "startled April morning" when the news flashed across the country:[4]

WASHINGTON, Friday, April 14, 1865

The President was shot in a theater tonight, and perhaps mortally wounded.

(Later)

WASHINGTON, Friday, April 14, 1865

Like a clap of thunder out of clear sky spread the announcement that President Lincoln was shot while sitting in his box at Ford's Theater. The city is wild with excitement. A gentleman who was present thus describes the event: At about $10\frac{1}{2}$ o'clock, in the midst of one of the acts, a pistol shot was heard, and at the same instant a man leaped upon the stage from the same box occupied by the President, brandished a

* Stephens was confined in Fort Warren, Boston harbor, for five months and then released on his own parole.

long knife, and shouted, *"Sic semper tyrannis!"* then rushed to the rear of the scenes and out of the back door of the theater. So sudden was the whole thing that most persons in the theater supposed it a part of the play, and it was some minutes before the fearful tragedy was comprehended. The man was pursued, however, by some one connected with the theater to the outer door and seen to mount a horse and ride rapidly away.

WAR DEPARTMENT,

WASHINGTON, April 15, 1865

MAJOR-GENERAL DIX: Abraham Lincoln died this morning at twenty-two minutes after 7 o'clock.

EDWIN M. STANTON, *Secretary of War*

Walt Whitman wrote: "Mother prepared breakfast—and other meals afterward—as usual; but not a mouthful was eaten all day by either of us. We each drank half a cup of coffee; that was all. Little was said. We got every newspaper morning and evening, and the frequent extras of that period, and passed them silently to each other."

Whitman began at once Lincoln's greatest eulogy:

O Captain! my Captain! our fearful trip is done,
The ship has weathered every rack, the prize we sought is won,
The port is near, the bells I hear, the people all exulting,
While follow eyes the steady keel, the vessel grim and daring;
   But O heart! heart! heart!
     O the bleeding drops of red,
       Where on the deck my Captain lies,
         Fallen cold and dead.

O Captain! my Captain! rise up and hear the bells;
Rise up—for you the flag is flung—for you the bugle trills,
For you bouquets and ribboned wreaths—for you the shores
          a-crowding
For you they call, the swaying mass, their eager faces turning;
   Here Captain! dear father!
     This arm beneath your head!
       It is some dream that on the deck
         You've fallen cold and dead.

My Captain does not answer, his lips are pale and still,
My father does not feel my arm, he has no pulse nor will,

The ship is anchored safe and sound, its voyage closed and done,
From fearful trip the victor ship comes in with object won;
  Exult O shores, and ring O bells!
    But I, with mournful tread,
      Walk the deck my Captain lies,
        Fallen cold and dead.

While Whitman grieved in New York, another great American, unaware of the President's death, reached home:[5]

General Robert E. Lee, lately commanding the rebel armies, arrived in Richmond yesterday afternoon, at half-past three o'clock. The first intimation of the arrival of the General was the call made upon Lieutenant H. S. Merrell, Post Quartermaster of Richmond, for forage and stabling for twenty horses in behalf of General Lee. Shortly after three o'clock General Lee arrived on the pontoon bridge that spans the James between Richmond and Manchester, an opposite town. Here an immense crowd had collected to receive him, and he was greeted with cheers upon cheers, the acclamations of the people, so generously and heartily bestowed, visibly affecting him. Whenever he passed Union officers they raised their caps. . . . As he proceeded along the streets to his residence in Franklin Street the crowd increased in numbers, and the cheers grew louder.

The General was accompanied by five members of his staff, General Lee and all wearing swords. As he dismounted at his residence the thousands of people who surrounded him again greeted him with acclaims, and so many as could get near his person shook him heartily by the hand. . . . The good feeling in relation to General Lee was common to both Unionists and rebels, and was fully shared in by all.

A month later the war ended for Jefferson Davis. The Secretary of War wired Major General Dix:[6]

WAR DEPARTMENT, WASHINGTON, May 13

The following dispatch, just received from Gen. Wilson, announces the surprise and capture of Jefferson Davis and his staff, by Col. Pritchard and the Michigan Cavalry, on the morning of the 10th inst., at Irwinsville, in Irwin County, Georgia.

"MACON, GA., May 12, 1865—11 A.M.

"LIEUT. GEN. U. S. GRANT AND HON. SECRETARY OF WAR,

WASHINGTON, D. C.:

"I have the honor to report that at daylight of the 10th inst., Col. Pritchard, commanding 4th Michigan Cavalry, captured Jeff. Davis and family, with Reagan, Postmaster-General; Col. Harrison, Private Secretary; Col. Johnson, A. D. C.; Col. Morris, Col. Lubbeck, Lieut. Hathaway and others. Col. Pritchard surprised their camp at Irwinsville, in Irwin County, Ga., 75 miles southeast of this place. They will be here tomorrow night, and will be forwarded under strong guard without delay.*. . .

"J. H. WILSON, *Brevet Major-General*"

Harper's Weekly *told how, in Virginia, history completed a cycle:*[7]

Edmund Ruffin, the father of secession in Virginia, and who fired the first gun on Fort Sumter, committed suicide June 17, 1865. A memorandum was found among his papers stating that he preferred death to living under the United States Government. He was upward of seventy-four years old when he committed this act of self-murder. At the time of his death he was staying in Amelia County, Virginia. The suicide was a deliberate act, the deluded man taking a musket loaded with buckshot, and placing the muzzle in his mouth, with the aid of a stick touched the trigger. The first cap failed to explode, when he replaced it with a better one, fired the piece, and was instantly killed. The upper portion of his head was entirely blown off.

. . . His death seems a fit close to that stage of his life which he devoted to rebellion against his Government. He that taketh the sword must perish by the sword, even though it be through madness and by his own act.

IV

Since the summer of 1864, in countless homes, North and South, families had gathered around the parlor piano to sing:

"The men will cheer, the boys will shout,
The ladies they will all turn out,

---

* Davis was confined in Fortress Monroe, off Hampton Roads, for two years. On May 13, 1867, on a writ of habeas corpus, he was admitted to bail in the amount of $100,000. The first name on the bail bond was that of Horace Greeley.

And we'll all feel gay,
When Johnny comes marching home."

Yet for Emma Florence LeConte, a seventeen-year-old girl who had lived through the burning of Columbia, South Carolina, the promise of the song was not fulfilled:[8]

The troops are coming home. One meets long-absent, familiar faces on the streets, and congregations once almost strictly feminine are now mingled with returned soldiers. Our boys—Cousin Johnny and Julian —have come home, too. It was pleasant to see them again, but the meeting was more sad than glad. We would have waited many years if only we could have received them back triumphant. For four years we have looked forward to this day—the day when the troops would march home. We expected to meet them exulting and victorious. That was to be a day of wildest joy, when the tidings of peace should reach us, and the thought of that time used to lighten our hearts and nerve us to bear every trial and privation. Then we determined, after our independence was acknowledged and the time came for Gen. Lee to disband his army, to go on to Richmond to see the glorious sight, to see the hero take leave of his brave victorious men. The army is disbanded now—oh! Merciful God!—the hot tears rush into my eyes and I cannot write.

Captain S. H. M. Byers, rescued by Sherman in February 1865 after fifteen months in Confederate prisons, found that he stood alone:[9]

At last my accounts were ready. "But your regiment," said the Assistant War Secretary, "does not exist. What was left of them were all put into a cavalry troop long ago. *You are the last man of the regiment.*" Across the face of my paper he wrote: "Discharged as a supernumerary officer."

Henry Kyd Douglas, whose brigade was the last to lay down its arms at Appomattox, left Fort Delaware where he had been imprisoned for parole violation:

On the 23rd of August, the General issued Special Order No. 328 saying that as my sentence had expired—I think I had only been there about a month or a little over—I would be discharged and furnished transportation to my home at Shepherdstown. On that day, accompanied by his wife and daughter and staff, he took me to Wilmington on his boat and gave an excellent dinner on board. At Wilmington I took my leave of them, with sincere expressions of thanks for their uniform courtesy, one and all, while I was the unwilling guest of the Government at Fort Delaware.

For me, the War was over, at last!

Leander Stillwell, Sixty-first Illinois, received his discharge at Springfield and made his way home:[10]

I arrived at the little village of Otterville about sundown. It was a very small place in 1865. There was just one store, (which also contained the postoffice,) a blacksmith shop, the old stone school-house, a church, and perhaps a dozen or so private dwellings. There were no sidewalks, and I stalked up the middle of the one street the town afforded, with my sword poised on my shoulder, musket fashion, and feeling happy and proud.

I looked eagerly around as I passed along, hoping to see some old friend. As I went by the store, a man who was seated therein on the counter leaned forward and looked at me, but said nothing. A little further up the street a big dog sprang off the porch of a house, ran out to the little gate in front, and standing on his hind legs with his forepaws on the palings, barked at me loudly and persistently—but I attracted no further attention. . . .

I now had only two miles to go, and was soon at the dear old boyhood home. My folks were expecting me, so they were not taken by surprise. There was no "scene" when we met, nor any effusive display, but we all had a feeling of profound contentment and satisfaction which was too deep to be expressed by mere words.

When I returned home I found that the farm work my father was then engaged in was cutting and shocking corn. So, the morning after my arrival, September 29th, I doffed my uniform of first lieutenant, put on some of my father's old clothes, armed myself with a corn knife, and proceeded to wage war on the standing corn. The feeling I had while engaged in this work was sort of queer. It almost seemed, sometimes, as if I had been away only a day or two, and had just taken up the farm work where I had left off.

CHAPTER 1

1. John G. Nicolay and John Hay, *Abraham Lincoln: A History* (New York, 1890), II, 306–07; hereafter cited as Nicolay and Hay.
2. Nicolay and Hay, II, 307–14.
3. New York *Tribune*, Nov. 12, 1860; in Herbert Mitgang (ed.), *Lincoln as They Saw Him* (New York, 1956), 212–14.
4. Samuel W. Crawford, *The Genesis of the Civil War* (Hartford, Conn., 1887), 12–13.
5. Mary Boykin Chesnut, *A Diary from Dixie* (New York, 1905; reissued, Boston, 1949), 3.
6. *War of the Rebellion . . . Official Records of the Union and Confederate Armies* (Washington, D. C., 1880–1901), Ser. 1, I, 74–76; hereafter cited as *Official Records*.
7. Daniel E. H. Smith, Alice R. H. Smith and Arney R. Childs (eds.), *Mason Smith Family Letters, 1860–1868* (Columbia, S. C., 1950), 3–4.
8. *Official Records*, Ser. 1, I, 90.
9. Crawford, *The Genesis of the Civil War*, 48–55.
10. Abner Doubleday, *Reminiscences of Forts Sumter and Moultrie in 1860–'61* (New York, 1876), 64–67.
11. Frank Moore (ed.), *The Rebellion Record: A Diary of American Events* (New York, 1861–1868), I, 8–9; hereafter cited as *Rebellion Record*.

CHAPTER 2

1. *The Crime Against Kansas, Speech of Hon. Charles Sumner,* 19th and 20th May, 1856 (Washington, D. C., 1856. Pamphlet).
2. Paul M. Angle (ed.), *Created Equal? The Complete Lincoln-Douglas Debates of 1858* (Chicago 1958), 110–11, 112–13.
3. Angle, *Created Equal?*, 267–68.
4. Angle, *Created Equal?*, 332–33.
5. *Report of Select Committee of the Senate on the Harper's Ferry Invasion* (Washington, D. C., 1860), 40.
6. Quoted in "The Hanging of John Brown" by Boyd B. Stutler, *American Heritage*, No. 2, 6–9.
7. Allan Nevins, *The Emergence of Lincoln* (New York, 1950), II, 98–107.

CHAPTER 3

1. Roy P. Basler (ed.), *The Collected Works of Abraham Lincoln* (New Brunswick, N. J., 1953), IV, 195–96; hereafter cited as *Collected Works*.
2. Dunbar Rowland (ed.), *Jefferson Davis Constitutionalist, His Letters, Papers and Speeches* (Jackson, Miss., 1923), V, 47–48; hereafter cited as *Davis Constitutionalist*.
3. Rowland, *Davis Constitutionalist*, V, 49–53.
4. *Collected Works*, IV, 255–61.
5. Nicolay and Hay, III, 378–79.
6. Nicolay and Hay, III, 380–81.
7. Thomas C. DeLeon, *Four Years in Rebel Capitals* (Mobile, Ala., 1890), 24–26.
8. *Official Records*, Ser. 1, I, 13–14.
9. *Official Records*, Ser. 1, I, 29.
10. Robert Underwood Johnson and Clarence Clough Buell (eds.), *Battles and Leaders of the Civil*

War (New York, 1884–1888), "Inside Sumter in '61," I, 66–69; hereafter cited as *B. & L.*

11. *Official Records*, Ser. 1, I, 11.

12. Katherine M. Jones (ed.), *Heroines of Dixie* (Indianapolis, 1955), 17–22.

13. Crawford, *The Genesis of the Civil War*, 435–37.

14. *Official Records*, Ser. 1, I, 12.

15. Jones, *Heroines of Dixie*, 20–22.

16. Quoted in Roy F. Nichols, *The Disruption of American Democracy* (New York, 1948), 395–96.

17. Stephen Vincent Benét, *John Brown's Body* (New York, 1927), 71–72.

CHAPTER 4

1. Nicolay and Hay, IV, 71.

2. Nicolay and Hay, IV, 76–77, 79–80.

3. Associated Press dispatch, April 15, 1861.

4. *Official Records*, Ser. 3, I, 70–87.

5. *Official Records*, Ser. 3, I, 70–83.

6. *Official Records*, Ser. 4, I, 225–35.

7. Chicago *Tribune*, April 17, 1861.

8. *Rebellion Record*, I, 28.

9. Chicago *Tribune*, April 17, 1861.

10. John Beauchamp Jones, *A Rebel War Clerk's Diary* (Philadelphia, 1866), I, 21–23.

11. Henry Kyd Douglas, *I Rode With Stonewall* (Chapel Hill, N. C., 1940), 5.

12. Capt. Robert E. Lee, *Recollections and Letters of General Robert E. Lee* (New York, 1904), 26–27.

13. S. H. M. Byers, *With Fire and Sword* (New York, 1911), 11–13.

14. Jessie Grant Cramer (ed.), *Letters of Ulysses S. Grant* (New York, 1912), 24–26.

15. William G. Stevenson, *Thirteen Months in the Rebel Army* (New York, 1862), 35–39.

16. Mary Anna Jackson, *Memoirs of Stonewall Jackson* (Louisville, Ky., 1895), 145–46.

17. William Tecumseh Sherman, *Memoirs of General W. T. Sherman, written by himself* (New York, 1875; corrected, 1876), I, 167–68.

18. Samuel L. Clemens, *Works* (Hartford, Conn., 1899), XXI, 236–39.

19. John W. Hanson, *Historical Sketch of the Old Sixth Regiment of Massachusetts Volunteers* (Boston, 1866), 23–29, 31–32.

20. Helen Nicolay, *Lincoln's Secretary, A Biography of John G. Nicolay* (New York, 1949), 95–96.

21. Nicolay and Hay, IV, 156–57.

22. Tyler Dennett (ed.), *Lincoln and the Civil War, In the Diaries and Letters of John Hay* (New York, 1939), 20–21.

23. Jefferson Davis, *The Rise and fall of the Confederate Government* (New York, 1881), I, 328–30.

CHAPTER 5

1. Judith Brockenbrough McGuire, *Diary of a Southern Refugee During the War* (New York, 1867), 17–18.

2. *Collected Works*, IV, 385–86.

3. Benjamin F. Butler, *Butler's Book* (Boston, 1892), 256–60.

4. *Official Records*, Ser. 1, II, 719–21.

5. Joseph E. Johnston, *Narrative of Military Operations, Directed, during the Late War Between the States* (New York, 1874), 33–34.

6. *Report of Committee on the Conduct of the War*, Senate Document, 37th Congress, 3rd Session, 1862–1863, Pt. II, 56–57; hereafter cited as *C.C.W.*

7. Johnston, *Narrative of Military Operations*, 36–38.

8. Sherman, *Memoirs*, I, 180–81.

9. George W. Bicknell, *History of the Fifth Regiment Maine Volunteers* (Portland, 1871), 28–30.
10. *B. & L.*, I, 209–10.
11. Davis, *The Rise and Fall of the Confederate Government*, I, 349–50.
12. *B. & L.*, I, 212–13.
13. Josiah M. Favill, *The Diary of a Young Officer* (Chicago, 1909), 34–36.
14. *Official Records*, Ser. 1, II, 320–21.
15. Lyman Trumbull to Mrs. Lyman Trumbull, Washington, D. C., July 22, 1861, in Horace White, *The Life of Lyman Trumbull* (Boston, 1913), 166–67.
16. *C.C.W.*, Pt. II, 76.

CHAPTER 6

1. Quoted in G. F. R. Henderson, *The Civil War, A Soldier's View* (Chicago, 1958), 121–22.
2. Ulysses S. Grant, *Personal Memoirs* (New York, 1885), I, 243, 246–50.
3. Clemens, *Works*, XXI, 256–57.
4. Grant, *Memoirs*, I, 138–39.
5. George Brinton McClellan, *McClellan's Own Story* (New York, 1887), 57–62.
6. Sherman, *Memoirs*, I, 194–97.
7. McClellan, *Own Story*, 84–92.
8. Walter H. Taylor, *Four Years with General Lee* (New York, 1878), 24.
9. Capt. Robert E. Lee, *Recollections and Letters*, 39–41.
10. John Beatty, *Memoirs of a Volunteer* (New York, 1946), 60.
11. *The Annals of the War* (Philadelphia, 1879), 89–90.
12. Capt. Robert E. Lee, *Recollections and Letters*, 44–46.
13. J. F. C. Fuller, *Grant and Lee* (reissued, Bloomington, Ind., 1957), 117–29.
14. Sherman, *Memoirs*, II, 406–08.
15. Capt. Robert E. Lee, *Recollections and Letters*, 105–06.

CHAPTER 7

1. *B. & L.*, I, 264–66.
2. *B. & L.*, I, 267–68.
3. *B. & L.*, I, 269–71.
4. *B. & L.*, I, 282.
5. *Rebellion Record*, II, 516–17.
6. *Rebellion Record*, II, 497–98.
7. *Rebellion Record*, II, 517–18.
8. *Collected Works*, IV, 506.
9. *Collected Works*, IV, 531–32.
10. Cramer, *Letters of Ulysses S. Grant*, 64–67.
11. Grant, *Memoirs*, I, 274–77.
12. *Rebellion Record*, III, 299.
13. *Rebellion Record*, III, 232–33.

CHAPTER 8

1. *Collected Works*, V, 544–45.
2. *B. & L.*, I, 675–76.
3. *B. & L.*, I, 684–86.
4. McClellan, *Own Story*, 173–74.
5. Quoted in Lloyd Lewis, *Sherman, Fighting Prophet* (New York, 1932), 201.
6. Henry Adams, *The Education of Henry Adams* (Privately printed, 1906; Boston, 1918), 122–23.
7. Sarah Agnes Wallace and Frances Elma Gillespie (eds.), *The Journal of Benjamin Moran 1857–1865* (Chicago, 1949), II, 912–17; hereafter cited as *Moran Journal*.
8. Donaldson Jordan and Edwin J. Pratt, *Europe and the American Civil War* (Boston, 1931), 29–31.
9. *Moran Journal*, II, 925.
10. *Proceedings of the Massachusetts Historical Society*, Nov., 1911, 128–29.
11. *Collected Works*, V, 29–30.
12. *Rebellion Record*, Supplements: II, 31, 47, 71, 87, 99; III, 9, 24, 36, 37, 48.

CHAPTER 9

1. *Annals of the War*, 76–79.
2. *Collected Works*, V, 96–97.
3. *Rebellion Record*, IV, 30.
4. *Rebellion Record*, IV, 41–42.

5. *Rebellion Record*, IV, 43, 47.

6. *Rebellion Record*, IV, 73–74.

7. *Rebellion Record*, IV, 75.

8. *Rebellion Record*, IV, 75–76.

9. Grant, *Memoirs*, I, 294–99.

10. *Rebellion Record*, IV, 173, 174.

11. *Rebellion Record*, IV, 185–86.

12. *Rebellion Record*, IV, 207–09.

13. *Rebellion Record*, IV, 210.

14. McClellan, *Own Story*, 215–17.

15. McClellan, *Own Story*, 195–96.

16. Edward Younger (ed.), *Inside the Confederate Government, The Diary of Robert Garlick Hill Kean* (New York, 1957), 23–24.

17. Julia Ward Howe, *Reminiscences of Julia Ward Howe, 1819–1899* (Boston, 1899), 274–75.

18. *The Atlantic Monthly*, Feb., 1862, 145.

CHAPTER 10

1. *Annals of the War*, 20.

2. *Rebellion Record*, IV, 273–74.

3. *Rebellion Record*, IV, 467.

4. *Rebellion Record*, IV, 275–76.

5. *Annals of the War*, 24–25.

6. *Rebellion Record*, IV, 267–68.

7. *Rebellion Record*, IV, 270–71.

8. *Moran Journal*, II, 971–72.

9. *Annals of the War*, 679–80.

10. *Annals of the War*, 682–83.

11. *Rebellion Record*, IV, 381–82.

12. *Rebellion Record*, IV, 388.

13. *Rebellion Record*, IV, 388; Stevenson, *Thirteen Months in the Rebel Army*, 115–16; *Iowa Journal of History*, July, 1954, 242, 251, 254, 265.

14. *Rebellion Record*, IV, 393–94.

15. *Rebellion Record*, IV, 382–83.

16. J. F. C. Fuller, *The Generalship of Ulysses S. Grant* (New York, 1929), 108–11.

17. Sherman, *Memoirs*, I, 254–55.

18. Grant, *Memoirs*, I, 368–69.

CHAPTER 11

1. *B. & L.*, II, 710–11.

2. *Rebellion Record*, Supplement I, 286–87.

3. *B. & L.*, II, 713–14.

4. *Rebellion Record*, Supplement I, 287–88.

5. *Rebellion Record*, Supplement I, 280–82.

6. *B. & L.*, II, 14–15.

7. *B. & L.*, II, 16–17.

8. *B. & L.*, II, 18.

9. *B. & L.*, II, 19–21.

10. Edward A. Pollard, *The Second Year of the War* (New York, 1865), 19–21.

11. Quoted in Richard B. Harwell (ed.), *The Confederate Reader* (New York, 1957), 105.

12. Pollard, *Second Year of the War*, 21.

13. Benjamin F. Butler, *Private and Official Correspondence of Gen. Benjamin F. Butler during the Period of the Civil War* (Privately issued [Norwood, Mass.] 1917), II, 35–36.

14. Butler, *Private Correspondence*, II, 36–37.

15. Butler, *Private Correspondence*, II, 70–71.

16. *Rebellion Record*, VI, 270–71.

CHAPTER 12

1. *Collected Works*, V, 157–58.

2. George Alfred Townsend, *Rustics in Rebellion* (Chapel Hill, 1950), 36–38 [original title: *Campaigns of a Non-Combatant* (New York, 1866)].

3. McClellan, *Own Story*, 306–17.

4. *Collected Works*, V, 185.

5. Townsend, *Rustics*, 93–95.

6. McClellan, *Own Story*, 306–17.

7. Chesnut, *Diary from Dixie*, 216–17.

8. *Rebellion Record*, V, 6.

9. Pollard, *Second Year of the War*, 29–31.

10. Pollard, *Second Year of the War*, 31 n–32 n.

11. Thomas W. Hyde, *Following the Greek Cross or, Memories of the Sixth Army Corps* (Boston, 1894), 50–53.

12. McClellan, *Own Story*, 352–57.
13. George C. Gorham, *Life and Public Services of Edwin M. Stanton* (Boston, 1899), I, 400.
14. David Donald (ed.), *Inside Lincoln's Cabinet, The Civil War Diaries of Salmon P. Chase* (New York, 1954), 84–86.
15. McClellan, *Own Story*, 352–57.
16. Jones, *Rebel War Clerk's Diary*, I, 123–25.
17. Townsend, *Rustics*, 58–60.
18. Townsend, *Rustics*, 67.
19. *Collected Works*, V, 216; McClellan, *Own Story*, 394–402.
20. Townsend, *Rustics*, 86–89.
21. William Child, *A History of the Fifth Regiment New Hampshire Volunteers* (Bristol, N. H., 1893), 82–84.
22. *Rebellion Record*, V, 88.
23. Rebellion Record, V, 97.
24. McClellan, *Own Story*, 394–402.

CHAPTER 13

1. Earl Schenck Miers, *Robert E. Lee, A Great-Life-in-Brief* (New York, 1956), 73–75.
2. *B. & L.*, II, 442–45.
3. *Rebellion Record*, V, 192–93.
4. *Rebellion Record*, V, 196–97.
5. *B. & L.*, II, 347.
6. Pollard, *Second Year of the War*, 311.
7. McClellan, *Own Story*, 441.
8. *Rebellion Record*, V, 238.
9. Pollard, *Second Year of the War*, 315–16.
10. *Southern Bivouac*, II, 655.
11. Stanley F. Horn, *The Robert E. Lee Reader* (Indianapolis, 1949), 190–91.
12. McClellan, *Own Story*, 424–25.
13. *Rebellion Record*, V, 242–43.
14. *Rebellion Record*, V, 244.
15. *Rebellion Record*, V, 244–45.
16. Robert Stiles, *Four Years under Marse Robert* (New York, 1903), 97.
17. Pollard, *Second Year of the War*, 321–24.

18. Comte de Paris, *History of the Civil War in America* (Philadelphia, 1876), II, 144–46.
19. Jones, *Rebel War Clerk's Diary*, I, 142.

CHAPTER 14

1. *Rebellion Record*, V, 179–80.
2. James D. McCabe, *Life and Campaigns of General Robert E. Lee* (Philadelphia, 1870), 644.
3. Townsend, *Rustics*, 206, 220, 224–26.
4. Roebling Papers, Ms., Rutgers University Library.
5. *Rebellion Record*, V, 402–03.
6. Roebling Papers.
7. W. W. Blackford, *War Years With Jeb Stuart* (New York, 1946), 132–34.
8. Blackford, *War Years*, 123.
9. Blackford, *War Years*, 120–22.
10. Joseph T. Durkin (ed.), *John Dooley, Confederate Soldier* (Washington, D. C., 1945), 20–22, 23–24.
11. Roebling Papers.
12. William Butler Papers, MS., Chicago Historical Society.
13. *Rebellion Record*, V, 615–16.
14. *Collected Works*, VI, 6–7.

CHAPTER 15

1. *Official Records*, Ser. 1, XIX, Pt. 2, 600, 601–02.
2. *B. & L.*, II, 604.
3. *Rebellion Record*, V, 606–07.
4. *War Talks in Kansas* (Kansas City, 1906), 250.
5. G. Moxley Sorrel, *Recollections of a Confederate Staff Officer* (Jackson, Tenn., 1958), 101.
6. *Rebellion Record*, V, 432–33.
7. Blackford, *War Years*, 144–45.
8. *Rebellion Record*, V, 447.
9. *Rebellion Record*, V, 467–69.
10. *Rebellion Record*, V, 467–69.
11. Blackford, *War Years*, 150–51.
12. Durkin, *John Dooley*, 45–48.
13. Rufus R. Dawes, *Service with the Sixth Wisconsin Volunteers* (Marietta, Ohio, 1890), 90–92.

14. Charles Francis Adams, Jr., "Historians and Historical Societies," *Proceedings of the Massachusetts Historical Society,* Second Series, XIII, 105–06.
15. *B. & L.,* II, 690–93.
16. *B. & L.,* II, 681.

CHAPTER 16

1. *Rebellion Record,* Supplement I, 305–306.
2. *Rebellion Record,* Supplement I, 308.
3. *Rebellion Record,* Supplement I, 317.
4. *Rebellion Record,* Supplement I, 321–22.
5. *Collected Works,* V, 144–46.
6. Davis, *Rise and Fall of the Confederate Government,* II, 180.
7. *Collected Works,* V, 169, 222–23.
8. *Collected Works,* V, 278–79.
9. David Homer Bates, *Lincoln in the Telegraph Office* (New York, 1907), 138–41.
10. Francis B. Carpenter, *Six Months in the White House with Abraham Lincoln* (New York, 1866), 20–22.
11. *Collected Works,* V, 317–19.
12. Davis, *Rise and Fall of the Confederate Government,* II, 184–86.
13. *Collected Works,* V, 388–89.
14. *Collected Works,* V, 419–21.
15. *Collected Works,* V, 423–24.
16. *Collected Works,* V, 425; Chase Diary, *Annual Report, American Historical Association, 1902,* Vol. II. (Washington, D. C., 1903), 87–89.
17. Davis, *Rise and Fall of the Confederate Government,* II, 190–91.
18. *Collected Works,* V, 438–39.
19. *Harper's Weekly,* Oct. 4, 1862.

CHAPTER 17

1. Grant, *Memoirs,* I, 408–12.
2. Grant, *Memoirs,* I, 412–13.
3. Grant, *Memoirs,* I, 416–17.
4. Grant, *Memoirs,* I, 417–19.

5. Philip Henry Sheridan, *Personal Memoirs* (New York, 1904), I, 190–92.
6. Sheridan, *Memoirs,* I, 193–95.
7. Sheridan, *Memoirs,* I, 195–98.
8. *Rebellion Record,* VI, 23–24.
9. *Moran Journal,* II, 1063–64.
10. Adams, *Education,* 154–56.
11. Grant, *Memoirs,* I, 426–27.
12. Ulysses S. Grant, *Headquarters Records,* Ms., Library of Congress.
13. Cadwallader Ms., Illinois State Historical Library, Springfield.
14. Grant, *Memoirs,* I, 429.
15. Lewis, *Sherman, Fighting Prophet,* 257–59.

CHAPTER 18

1. *Collected Works,* V, 505–06.
2. *Collected Works,* V, 514–15.
3. *Collected Works,* V, 531–32, 537.
4. *Rebellion Record,* VI, 94–95.
5. *Rebellion Record,* VI, 95–96.
6. *Rebellion Record,* VI, 103.
7. *Rebellion Record,* VI, 97.
8. *Rebellion Record,* VI, 97–98.
9. *Rebellion Record,* VI, 105.
10. *Rebellion Record,* VI, 98–99.
11. *Rebellion Record,* VI, 103–04.
12. *Rebellion Record,* VI, 110–11.
13. *Rebellion Record,* VI, 111.
14. Eugene A. Cory, *A Private's Recollections of Fredericksburg* (Providence, 1884), 24–25.
15. *B. & L.,* III, 78.
16. Capt. D. P. Conyngham, *The Irish Brigade* (Boston, 1869), 346.
17. *Rebellion Record,* VI, 79.
18. *Collected Works,* VI, 13.
19. Sherman, *Memoirs,* I, 291–92.
20. John Beatty, *Memoirs of a Volunteer* (New York, 1946), 152.
21. *Rebellion Record,* VI, 118–19.
22. *Rebellion Record,* VI, 158–59.
23. *Rebellion Record,* VI, 165.
24. Beatty, *Memoirs,* 155–56.
25. *Rebellion Record,* VI, 166; Beatty, *Memoirs,* 156–57.
26. *Rebellion Record,* VI, 166.

27. *Rebellion Record*, VI, 161.
28. Pollard, *Second Year of the War*, 183–86.

CHAPTER 19

1. Nicolay and Hay, IV, 421, 429–30.
2. *Collected Works*, VI, 29–30.
3. Thomas Wentworth Higginson, *Army Life in a Black Regiment* (Boston, 1870), 39–42.
4. Rowland, *Davis Constitutionalist*, V, 409–11.
5. *Rebellion Record*, VI, 343–44.
6. *Rebellion Record*, VI, 357–58, 360–61.
7. Emma Martin Maffitt, *The Life and Public Services of John Newland Maffitt* (New York, 1906), 267–69.
8. *Rebellion Record*, VI, 430–31.
9. James Russell Soley, *The Blockade and the Cruisers* (New York, 1885), 156–60.
10. Thomas Taylor, *Running the Blockade* (New York, 1896), 44–54.
11. *Harper's New Monthly Magazine*, Sept., 1866, 498–99; *Official Records*, Navies, Ser. 1, VIII, 417; Soley, *The Blockade*, 165–66.
12. *Official Records*, Navies, Ser. 1, VIII, 417, 459, 471.
13. Soley, *The Blockade*, 165–66.

CHAPTER 20

1. *Official Records*, Ser. 1, XXI, 916–18.
2. *Official Records*, Ser. 1, XXI, 944–45.
3. *Official Records*, Ser. 1, XXI, 953–54.
4. *Rebellion Record*, VI, 398–400.
5. *Collected Works*, VI, 78–79.
6. Regis de Trobriand, *Four Years with the Army of the Potomac* (Boston, 1889), 413–14.
7. Charles Francis Adams, Jr., *An Autobiography* (Boston, 1916), 161.
8. *C.C.W.*, I, Pt. 2, 112–13.

9. *B. & L.*, IV, 35–41.
10. *B. & L.*, III, 155–56.
11. *B. & L.*, III, 203.
12. *B. & L.*, III, 205.
13. John O. Casler, *Four Years in the Stonewall Brigade* (Guthrie, Okla., 1893), 216–22.
14. *B. & L.*, III, 211–14.
15. *B. & L.*, III, 165–71.
16. *Official Records*, Ser. 1, XXV, 805.
17. *B. & L.*, III, 214.
18. G. F. R. Henderson, *Stonewall Jackson and the American Civil War* (London, 1898), II, 579.

CHAPTER 21

1. Quoted in Henry Adams, *The Great Secession Winter of 1860–61 and Other Essays* (New York, 1958), 146–47, 152.
2. *Harper's Weekly*, Feb. 3, 1863.
3. Charles W. Ramsdell, *Behind the Lines in the Southern Confederacy* (Baton Rouge, 1944), 12–13.
4. *Rebellion Record*, VIII, 272, 273.
5. Quoted in Jones, *Rebel War Clerk's Diary*, I, 250, 252–53.
6. Quoted in Ramsdell, *Behind the Lines*, 47–48.
7. *Harper's Weekly*, Feb. 21, 1863.
8. Jones, *Rebel War Clerk's Diary*, I, 284–86.
9. Bell Irvin Wiley, *The Plain People of the Confederacy* (Baton Rouge, 1944), 54–55, 56–57, 60–62, 65–66.
10. Charles A. Dana, *Recollections of the Civil War* (New York, 1898), 18–19.
11. *Annals of the War*, 706–07, 709, 713, 719–21.
12. Charles S. Winslow, "Historical Events of Chicago," Ms., Chicago Historical Society.
13. New York *Times*, June 17, 1863.
14. *Rebellion Record*, XI, 23–24.
15. Edward Dicey, *Six Months in the Federal States* (London, 1863), II, 220–23.

16. Francis Trevelyan Miller (ed.), *The Photographic History of the American Civil War* (New York, 1912), IX, 132, 176, 351.

CHAPTER 22

1. *Harper's Weekly*, Mar. 14, 1863.
2. *The American Annual Cyclopaedia and Register of Important Events*, 1863, 271, 273–74.
3. James L. Vallandigham, *A Life of Clement L. Vallandigham* (Baltimore, 1872), 224–26.
4. Vallandigham, *Life*, 458–59, 464.
5. Vallandigham, *Life*, 250–52.
6. Vallandigham, *Life*, 255–59.
7. *The Trial of Clement L. Vallandigham by a Military Commission* (Cincinnati, 1863), 13–16.
8. *Collected Works*, VI, 266–69.
9. James Ford Rhodes, *History of the United States from the Compromise of 1850 to the Final Restoration of Home Rule at the South in 1877* (New York, 1892–1906), IV, 251–52.
10. Chicago *Times*, June 5, 1863.
11. New York *Tribune*, June 4, 1863.

CHAPTER 23

1. *Official Records*, Ser. 1, XVII, 710.
2. *Official Records*, Ser. 1, XVII, 780–81.
3. *Collected Works*, VI, 48–49.
4. Grant, *Memoirs*, I, 442–44.
5. Benjamin P. Thomas (ed.), *Three Years with Grant as Recalled by War Correspondent Sylvanus Cadwallader* (New York, 1955), 54–55 [Ms. in Illinois State Historical Library, Springfield].
6. John Q. Anderson (ed.), *Brokenburn: The Journal of Kate Stone 1861–1868* (Baton Rouge, 1955), 168–73.
7. David D. Porter, *Naval History of the Civil War* (Hartford, Conn., 1886), 303–04.
8. Porter, *Naval History*, 305–06.

9. Thomas, *Three Years with Grant*, 61–62.
10. Dana, *Recollections*, 30–32.
11. James Harrison Wilson, *Under the Old Flag* (New York, 1912), I, 163–64.
12. Dana, *Recollections*, 37–38.
13. Porter, *Naval History*, 311.
14. *Transactions of the Illinois State Historical Society*, 1907, 127–29.
15. *Trans., Ill. St. Hist. Soc.*, 1907, 129–30.
16. Porter, *Naval History*, 313–15.
17. Grant, *Memoirs*, I, 477–81.
18. Grant, *Memoirs*, I, 490–93.
19. Dana, *Recollections*, 48–50.
20. *B. & L.*, III, 486–87.
21. Thomas, *Three Years with Grant*, 69–70.
22. Thomas, *Three Years with Grant*, 70–72.
23. *B. & L.*, III, 478–79.
24. Thomas, *Three Years with Grant*, 73–75.

CHAPTER 24

1. *Official Records*, Ser. 1, XXVII, Pt. 3, 882.
2. Jones, *Rebel War Clerk's Diary*, I, 327–28.
3. *War Sketches and Incidents, as Related by Companions in the Iowa Commandery, Military Order of the Loyal Legion* (Des Moines, 1893), 208–14.
4. Grant, *Memoirs*, I, 515–17.
5. *Annals of the War*, 343–46.
6. Grant, *Memoirs*, I, 519–20.
7. *Rebellion Record*, X, 572.
8. Grant, *Memoirs*, I, 529–31.
9. McClernand Papers, Illinois State Historical Library, Springfield.
10. Thomas, *Three Years with Grant*, 90–92.
11. Dickey Papers, Illinois State Historical Library, Springfield.
12. Tupper Papers, Illinois State Historical Library, Springfield.
13. *Rebellion Record*, X, 576.
14. *Century Magazine*, Sept., 1885, 771–73.

15. Lord Journal, Manuscript Division, Library of Congress.
16. Vicksburg *Daily Citizen,* July 2–4, 1863.
17. Clemens, *Works,* IV, 280–82.
18. William Ward Orme, *Civil War Letters of Brigadier General William Ward Orme—1862–1866* (Springfield, Ill. 1930. Pamphlet); reprinted from *Journal of the Illinois State Historical Society* (Vol. XXIII), 280–81.
19. *B. & L.,* III, 540–42.
20. Wilbur F. Crummer, *With Grant at Fort Donelson, Shiloh and Vicksburg* (Oak Park, Ill., 1915), 137–42.
21. Michael Jacobs, *Notes on the Rebel Invasion of Maryland and Pennsylvania and the Battle of Gettysburg* (Philadelphia, 1864), 15–18.

CHAPTER 25

1. Broadhead Ms., Library, National Parks Service, Gettysburg, Pa.
2. Mrs. Tillie (Pierce) Alleman, *At Gettysburg, or What a Girl Saw and Heard of the Battle* (New York, 1889), 19–20.
3. Bayly Ms., Library, National Park Service, Gettysburg, Pa.
4. *Annals of the War,* 208.
5. Blackford, *War Years,* 224–25.
6. Durkin, *John Dooley,* 98–99.
7. Alleman, *At Gettysburg,* 21–22.
8. Broadhead Ms.
9. Bayly Ms.
10. Oliver Otis Howard, *Autobiography* (New York, 1908), I, 412, 413–14.
11. Miller, *Photographic History,* II, 211.
12. Bret Harte, *The Lost Galleon* (San Francisco, 1867), 27–28.
13. Charles Carleton Coffin, *The Boys of '61, or Four Years of Fighting* (Boston, 1896), 293–95.
14. Alleman, *At Gettysburg,* 43–45.
15. Frank Aretas Haskell, *The Battle of Gettysburg* (Wisconsin

History Commission, 1910), 18–30. [Earlier editions, privately issued, were dated "about 1880," 1898 and 1908.]
16. *Annals of the War,* 420–22.
17. Alleman, *At Gettysburg,* 49–50.
18. Arthur James Lyon Freemantle, *Three Months in the Southern States* (London, 1863), 257–60.
19. Haskell, *Gettysburg,* 41–43.
20. Haskell, *Gettysburg,* 42, 43–4.
21. *Rebellion Record,* X, 179.
22. William C. Oates, *The War Between the Union and the Confederacy and Its Lost Opportunities* (New York, 1905), 216, 221–22, 228–29.
23. Ziba B. Graham, *On to Gettysburg, Two Days from My Diary of 1863* (Detroit, 1889), 12.
24. Haskell, *Gettysburg,* 54–57.
25. *B. & L.,* III, 313–14.
26. George Edward Pickett, *The Heart of a Soldier* (New York, 1913), 94–95, 98–99.
27. Durkin, *John Dooley,* 101–02.
28. Haskell, *Gettysburg,* 97–103.
29. Philadelphia *Weekly Times,* Aug. 11, 1877.
30. Haskell, *Gettysburg,* 113–14.
31. Durkin, *John Dooley,* 105–07.
32. Haskell, *Gettysburg,* 119–26.
33. Broadhead Ms.
34. Alleman, *At Gettysburg,* 71–74.
35. Pickett, *The Heart of a Soldier,* 99–100.
36. Bayly Ms.; Harte, *The Lost Galleon,* 28.
37. Grant, *Memoirs,* I, 557–59, 563–64.

CHAPTER 26

1. *Harper's Weekly,* Jan. 17, 1863.
2. James A. Connolley, *Three Years in the Army of the Cumberland* (Bloomington, Ind., 1959), 89–90, 90–94.
3. Basil W. Duke, *History of Morgan's Cavalry* (Cincinnati, 1867), 434–35; F. Senour, *Morgan and His Captors* (Cincinnati, 1865), 124–25, 155–59.

4. Duke, *Morgan's Cavalry*, 458–61.
5. Stanley F. Horn, *The Army of Tennessee* (Norman, Okla., 1953), 233.
6. *Frank Leslie's Illustrated Newspaper*, July 25, 1863.
7. *Harper's Weekly*, Aug. 1, 1863.
8. Rhodes, *History of the U. S.*, IV, 330.
9. [J. S. Boughton], *The Lawrence Massacre by a Band of Missouri Ruffians under Quantrell* (Lawrence, Kans., n.d. Pamphlet).
10. Dana, *Recollections*, 110–11, 111–14.
11. *B. & L.*, III, 666–67.
12. Beatty, *Memoirs of a Volunteer*, 250–51.
13. James Longstreet, *From Manassas to Appomattox* (Philadelphia, 1896), 455–56.
14. Thomas B. Van Horne, *The Life of Major-General George H. Thomas* (New York, 1882), 148–49.
15. *B. & L.*, III, 662.
16. James D. Bulloch, *The Secret Service of the Confederate States in Europe* (London, 1883), I, 385–86, 409–12.
17. George E. Baker (ed.), *The Works of William H. Seward* (Boston, 1884), V, 387–88.
18. *Diplomatic Correspondence of the United States*, 1863, Pt. I, 367.
19. Worthington Chauncey Ford (ed.), *A Cycle of Adams Letters, 1861–1865* (Boston, 1920), II, 82–83.
20. Bulloch, *Secret Service*, I, 420–22.

CHAPTER 27

1. Grant, *Memoirs*, II, 24–25.
2. Grant, *Memoirs*, II, 38–39.
3. Grant, *Memoirs*, II, 40–41.
4. Dennett, *Lincoln and the Civil War*, 121; *Collected Works*, VII, 21.
5. Connolly, *Three Years*, 151–52.
6. Connolly, *Three Years*, 152–55.

7. Connolly, *Three Years*, 155–59.
8. Sam R. Watkins, *"Co. Aytch," Maury Grays, First Tennessee Regiment* (Nashville, 1882), 104–05.
9. *B. & L.*, III, 727.
10. Watkins, *"Co. Aytch,"* 105.
11. Rowland, *Davis Constitutionalist*, VI, 95–96.
12. Rowland, *Davis Constitutionalist*, VI, 94–95.
13. Rowland, *Davis Constitutionalist*, VI, 96, 104–05.
14. Rowland, *Davis Constitutionalist*, VI, 127–28.
15. *Collected Works*, VII, 48–53.
16. *Atlantic Monthly*, Jan., 1864, 122.

CHAPTER 28

1. Bell Irvin Wiley (ed.), *This Infernal War, The Confederate Letters of Sgt. Edwin H. Fay* (Austin, Tex., 1958), 346–47.
2. Merrilies Diary, Ms., Chicago Historical Society.
3. Child, *The Fifth Regiment New Hampshire Volunteers*, 193.
4. Dickinson Diary, Ms., Chicago Historical Society.
5. Pitts Diary, Ms., Chicago Historical Society.
6. Wiley, *This Infernal War*, 329; Johnston Ms., Chicago Historical Society.
7. *Rebellion Record*, VII, 411.
8. Carl Schurz, *The Reminiscences of Carl Schurz* (New York, 1908), III, 339–40.
9. Henrietta Stratton Jaquette (ed.), *South After Gettysburg, Letters of Cornelia Hancock from the Army of the Potomac 1863–1865* (Philadelphia, 1937), 17, 19, 23, 24.
10. Phoebe Yates Pember, *A Southern Woman's Story* (New York, 1879), 133–36.
11. H. H. Cunningham, *Doctors in Gray: The Confederate Medical Service* (Baton Rouge, 1958), 264–66.

12. "Civil War Diary of William Micajah Barrow," *Louisiana Historical Quarterly*, Oct., 1934, 722–23; *Ibid.*, 723–29.
13. F. F. Cavada, *Libby Life: Experiences of a Prisoner of War* (Philadelphia, 1864), 19–27.
14. Henry H. Eby, *Observations of an Illinois Boy in Battle, Camp and Prisons, 1861–1865* (Mendota, Ill., 1910), 137–44.
15. S. S. Boggs, *Eighteen Months a Prisoner under the Rebel Flag* (Lovington, Ill., 1887), 17, 22–24, 26–27.
16. Virginia Confederate, *In Vinculis, or The Prisoner of War* (Petersburg, Va., 1866), 58–63, 138–47.
17. Rowland, *Davis Constitutionalist*, VI, 122–23.
18. Clement Eaton, *A History of the Southern Confederacy* (New York, 1954), 106.
19. Rhodes, *History of the U. S.*, V, 508.

CHAPTER 29

1. *Rebellion Record*, VIII, 278–79.
2. *Rebellion Record*, VIII, 304–05.
3. *Official Records*, Ser. 1, XXXII, Pt. 1, 561–62.
4. *Official Records*, Ser. 1, XXXII, Pt. 1, 528–29.
5. *Official Records*, Ser. 1, XXXII, Pt. 1, 525–26.
6. *Official Records*, Ser. 1, XXXII, Pt. 1, 610.
7. *Collected Works*, VII, 302–03.
8. John A. Wyeth, *Life of General Nathan Bedford Forrest* (New York, 1899), 367–68.
9. *Official Records*, Ser. 1, XXXIV, Pt. 1, 510, 514–15.
10. *Rebellion Record*, VIII, 546–47.
11. *C.C.W.*, II, 217–18.
12. *Rebellion Record*, VIII, 549–50.
13. *Rebellion Record*, VIII, 521.
14. *Rebellion Record*, VIII, 529–31.
15. Lawrence Van Alstyne, *Diary of an Enlisted Man* (New Haven, Conn., 1910), 320–21.

16. *Official Records*, Ser. 1, XXXIV, Pt. 1, 546–48.

CHAPTER 30

1. Horace Porter, *Campaigning with Grant* (New York, 1897) 18–21.
2. Grant, *Memoirs*, II, 116–23.
3. Sheridan, *Memoirs*, I, 355–56.
4. Grant, *Memoirs*, II, 141–42.
5. Letter owned by Stanley F. Horn, Nashville; quoted in Stanley F. Horn, *The Robert E. Lee Reader* (Indianapolis, 1949), 362–63.
6. Sorrel, *Recollections*, 226–27.
7. *Rebellion Record*, XI, 440–41.
8. George R. Agassiz (ed.), *Meade's Headquarters 1863–1865, Letters of Colonel Theodore Lyman from the Wilderness to Appomattox* (Boston, 1922), 91–92.
9. Porter, *Campaigning with Grant*, 68–70.
10. Agassiz, *Meade's Headquarters*, 93–94.
11. Sorrel, *Recollections*, 230–31.
12. Agassiz, *Meade's Headquarters*, 95–97.
13. *Rebellion Record*, XI, 442–43.
14. Sorrel, *Recollections*, 231–35.
15. Agassiz, *Meade's Headquarters*, 98–99.
16. Porter, *Campaigning with Grant*, 78–79.
17. Agassiz, *Meade's Headquarters*, 100, 102.
18. Sheridan, *Memoirs*, I, 377–78.
19. H. B. McClellan, *Southern Historical Society Papers*, VII, 142–43.
20. McClellan, *Southern Hist. Soc. Papers*, VII, 107–09.
21. Porter, *Campaigning with Grant*, 110–11.
22. Agassiz, *Meade's Headquarters*, 132–33.
23. Agassiz, *Meade's Headquarters*, 106.

24. Porter, *Campaigning with Grant,* 174–75.
25. William Swinton, *Army of the Potomac* (New York, 1866), 495.
26. Oates, *The War Between the Union and the Confederacy,* 366–67.
27. Grant, *Memoirs,* II, 276–77.
28. Agassiz, *Meade's Headquarters,* 147–48.

CHAPTER 31

1. *B. & L.,* IV, 250.
2. John Bell Hood, *Advance and Retreat* (New Orleans, 1880), 89, 91–92, 95.
3. Connolly, *Three Years,* 208–09.
4. Johnston, *Narrative of Military Operations,* 321–22.
5. Hood, *Advance and Retreat,* 99.
6. Sherman, *Memoirs,* II, 39, 42, 44–45.
7. Johnston, *Narrative of Military Operations,* 330–31.
8. Connolly, *Three Years,* 213–14.
9. *Annual American Cyclopaedia,* 1864, 785.
10. Washburne Ms., Library of Congress.
11. *Proceedings of the Massachusetts Historical Society,* Vol. 58, 135.
12. D. F. Murphy, *Proceedings of the National Union Convention* (New York, 1864), 63–66.
13. "Diary of Edward Bates," *Annual Report, American Historical Association,* 1930, Vol. 14, 374.
14. Edward McPherson, *The Political History of the United States . . . during the Great Rebellion* (Washington, D. C., 1865), 412.
15. Nicolay and Hay, IX, 40–41.
16. Merrilies Diary, Ms., Chicago Historical Society.
17. Samuel G. French, "Kennesaw Mountain," *The Kennesaw Gazette* (n.d.).

CHAPTER 32

1. Raphael Semmes, *Memoirs of Service Afloat* (Baltimore, 1869), 752–59.
2. Porter, *Naval History,* 655.
3. Gideon Welles, *Diary of Gideon Welles* (Boston, 1911), II, 70–71.
4. Jubal A. Early, *A Memoir of the Last Year of the War for Independence* (Lynchburg, Va., 1867), 56–58.
5. Welles, *Diary,* II, 72–73.
6. Early, *Memoir,* 58–59.
7. Dennett, *Letters and Diary of John Hay,* 209–10.
8. Wirt Armistead Cate (ed.), *Two Soldiers: The Campaign Diaries of Thomas J. Key, C.S.A. and Robert J. Campbell, U.S.A.* (Chapel Hill, 1938), 89–90.
9. Sherman, *Memoirs,* II, 74–75.
10. Hood, *Advance and Retreat,* 161–62.
11. Cate, *Two Soldiers,* 94–97.
12. *B. & L.,* IV, 326.
13. *B. & L.,* IV, 327–28.
14. Sherman, *Memoirs,* II, 76–77.
15. Connolly, *Three Years,* 240.
16. *C.C.W.,* I, 112–13 [second paging].
17. Agassiz, *Meade's Headquarters,* 181–82.
18. *B. & L.,* IV, 551–54.
19. *C.C.W.,* I, 120–21 [second paging].
20. George S. Bernard, *The Battle of the Crater* (Petersburg, Va., 1892), 159–60.
21. *C.C.W.,* I, 120–21 [second paging].
22. *B. & L.,* IV, 559.

CHAPTER 33

1. *Rebellion Record,* VIII, 101–02.
2. *Scribner's Monthly,* May, 1881, 204–05, 207–08 [ownership actually had passed to *Century Magazine*].
3. *Rebellion Record,* VIII, 102.

4. Robert Todd Lincoln Papers, Library of Congress.
5. Robert Todd Lincoln Papers.
6. *Collected Works*, VII, 514.
7. Noah Brooks, *Washington in Lincoln's Time* (New York, 1896), 182–88.
8. Hood, *Advance and Retreat*, 202–04.
9. Sherman, *Memoirs*, II, 105–06, 107.
10. Cate, *Two Soldiers*, 126–28.
11. Connolly, *Three Years*, 257–59.
12. Carrie Berry Diary, Ms., Atlanta Historical Society. .
13. Rawson Diary, Ms., Atlanta Historical Society.
14. Sherman, *Memoirs*, II, 110.
15. *Annual American Cyclopaedia*, 1864, 794.
16. Sherman, *Memoirs*, II, 110–11.
17. Rawson Diary.
18. Sherman, *Memoirs*, II, 120–21.
19. Berry Diary.
20. Sherman, *Memoirs*, II, 130.
21. Agassiz, *Meade's Headquarters*, 204–05.
22. Porter, *Campaigning with Grant*, 283–84.
23. Ethel Armes, *Stratford on the Potomac* (Greenwich, Conn., 1928), 5.
24. Early, *Memoir*, 79–80.
25. Charles Richard Williams (ed.), *Diary and Letters of Rutherford B. Hayes* (Columbus, O., 1922), II, 508–11.
26. Early, *Memoir*, 90–91.
27. John B. Gordon, *Reminiscences of the Civil War* (New York, 1904), 323–26.

CHAPTER 34

1. *Rebellion Record*, IX, 179–80.
2. *Rebellion Record*, IX, 2–3.
3. *Official Records*, Ser. 1, XLIII, 30–31.
4. Douglas, *I Rode With Stonewall*, 314–16.
5. Gordon, *Reminiscences*, 337–42.
6. Sheridan, *Personal Memoirs*, II, 68–80.

7. Gordon, *Reminiscences*, 347–51.
8. John W. Headley, *Confederate Operations in Canada and New York* (New York, 1906), 259–61.
9. Rowland, *Davis Constitutionalist*, VI, 384–98.
10. Lyman Jackman, *History of the Sixth New Hampshire Regiment* (Concord, N. H., 1891), 344–46.
11. Theodore Gerrish, *Army Life: A Private's Reminiscences of the Civil War* (Portland, Me., 1882), 219–20.
12. Dennett, *Diaries and Letters of John Hay*, 232–36.
13. *Collected Works*, VIII, 100–01.

CHAPTER 35

1. Ms., Collection of Alfred M. Stearn, Chicago.
2. Sherman, *Memoirs*, II, 166, 174–76.
3. Berry Diary.
4. Connolly, *Three Years*, 301–02.
5. W. P. Howard, Official Report, *Macon (Ga.) Telegraph*, Dec. 10, 1864.
6. Sherman, *Memoirs*, II, 178–80, 188–90.
7. *Rebellion Record*, IX, 147.
8. Lunt, Dolly Sumner, *A Woman's Wartime Journal* (New York, 1918), 25, 29–42.
9. Connolly, *Three Years*, 332–33, 339–40.
10. George Ward Nichols, *The Story of the Great March, from the Diary of a Staff Officer* (New York, 1865), 74–77.
11. Connolly, *Three Years*, 354–55.
12. Irving A. Buck, *Cleburne and His Command* (New York, 1908), 326–33.
13. John A. Schofield, *Forty-Six Years in the Army* (New York, 1897), 177–79.
14. Buck, *Cleburne and His Command*, 333.
15. Porter, *Campaigning with Grant*, 325–26.

16. Headley, *Confederate Operations*, 274–76.
17. Benn Pitman, *The Assassination of President Lincoln and the Trial of the Conspirators* (New York, 1865), 54.

CHAPTER 36

1. *Collected Works*, VIII, 148–49, 151–52.
2. *Rebellion Record*, IX, 5.
3. *Rebellion Record*, IX, 175.
4. *Rebellion Record*, IX, 202–03.
5. Hood, *Advance and Retreat*, 299–300.
6. *B. & L.*, IV, 454–60.
7. Hood, *Advance and Retreat*, 302.
8. *Official Records*, Ser. 1, XLV, Pt. 2, 194.
9. *Official Records*, Ser. 1, XLV, Pt. 1, 694–95, 705–06.
10. *Official Records*, Ser. 1, XLV, Pt. 2, 210–11.
11. Sherman, *Memoirs*, II, 217–19, 231–32.
12. Ms., Collection of Alfred Stearn, Chicago.
13. Broadside, Emory University Library, Emory University, Ga.

CHAPTER 37

1. Theodore F. Upson, *With Sherman to the Sea* (Bloomington, Ind., 1958), 145.
2. Connolly, *Three Years*, 374–75.
3. *Official Records*, Ser. 1, XLVI, Pt. 2, 1043.
4. *Official Records*, Ser. 1, XLVI, Pt. 2, 1048.
5. *Official Records*, Ser. 1, XLVI, Pt. 2, 1056.
6. *Official Records*, Ser. 1, XLVI, Pt. 2, 1053, 1064–65.
7. *Official Records*, Ser. 1, XLVI, Pt. 2, 1071.
8. *Official Records*, Ser. 1, XLVI, Pt. 2, 1078.
9. Alexander H. Stephens, *Constitutional View of the Late War between the States* (Philadelphia, 1868–70), II, 619–20.
10. Dana, *Recollections*, 174–77.

11. I. N. Arnold, *The Life of Abraham Lincoln* (Chicago, 1885), 358–59.
12. Nicolay and Hay, X, 85–86.
13. *Collected Works*, VIII, 254–55; Stephens, *Constitutional View*, II, 599–602, 613–14, 618–23.

CHAPTER 38

1. Sherman, *Memoirs*, II, 225, 227–28.
2. Sherman, *Memoirs*, II, 268–72.
3. Nicholas, *Story of the Great March*, 145–51.
4. *Official Records*, Ser. 1, XLVII, Pt. 2, 1035–36.
5. *Official Records*, Ser. 1, XLVII, Pt. 2, 1201.
6. *Official Records*, Ser. 1, XLVII, Pt. 2, 711.
7. *Who Burnt Columbia?* (Charleston, S. C., 1875. Pamphlet).
8. *Rebellion Record*, XI, 377, 387–88.
9. Nichols, *Story of the Great March*, 198–99.
10. Brooks, *Washington in Lincoln's Time*, 238–40.
11. *B. & L.*, IV, 692–93, 695.
12. Letter to Isaac N. Arnold, Nov. 28, 1872, Ms., Chicago Historical Society.

CHAPTER 39

1. Townsend, *Rustics*, 252–55.
2. Pickett, *The Heart of a Soldier*, 172–75.
3. *B. & L.*, IV, 725.
4. Porter, *Campaigning with Grant*, 450–52.
5. *B. & L.*, IV, 727–28.
6. A. W. Bartlett, *History of the Twelfth Regiment New Hampshire Volunteers* (Concord, N. H., 1897), 271–73.
7. Townsend, *Rustics*, 270–71.
8. Dana, *Recollections*, 265–67.
9. *Confederate Veteran* (Atlanta, Ga.), Vol. I, 211.
10. Agassiz, *Meade's Headquarters*, 348–51.

11. Porter, *Campaigning with Grant*, 458–59.
12. *Rebellion Record*, XI, 356–57.
13. Agassiz, *Meade's Headquarters*, 356–58.
14. Thomas, *Three Years with Grant*, 325–26.
15. Grant, *Memoirs*, II, 489.
16. Porter, *Campaigning with Grant*, 473–74.
17. Grant, *Memoirs*, II, 491–92.
18. Porter, *Campaigning with Grant*, 477–78.
19. Grant, *Memoirs*, II, 492–94.
20. Porter, *Campaigning with Grant*, 486–87.
21. Maj.-Gen. Sir Frederick Maurice (ed.), *An Aide-de-Camp of Lee* (Boston, 1927), 275.
22. Agassiz, *Meade's Headquarters*, 359–62.

CHAPTER 40

1. Dr. F. Milton Willis, "Replacing the Flag upon Sumter," *Fort Sumter Memorial* (New York, 1915), 37–39.
2. New York *Tribune*, April 29, May 12 and May 29, 1865.
3. Stephens, *Constitutional View*, II, 624–26.
4. New York *Tribune*, April 15 and April 17, 1865.
5. New York *Weekly Herald*, April 22, 1865.
6. New York *Tribune*, May 15, 1865.
7. *Harper's Weekly*, July 29, 1865.
8. Earl Schenck Miers (ed.), *When the World Ended: The Diary of Emma LeConte* (New York, 1957), 98–99.
9. Byers, *With Fire and Sword*, 202; Douglas, *I Rode with Stonewall*, 349.
10. Leander Stillwell, *The Story of a Common Soldier, or Army Life in the Civil War* (Erie, Kans., 1917), 154.

PAUL M. ANGLE *is the country's foremost living scholar on Abraham Lincoln. He has been more influential than any other man in throwing new light on Lincoln's thought and activity and in documenting the importance of the Middle West in the Civil War. He was for many years executive secretary of the Abraham Lincoln Association; since 1945 he has been director of the Chicago Historical Society, which has been called "the Athenaeum of mid-America." A graduate of Miami University in Oxford, Ohio, he has been awarded four honorary degrees. He is the author of a long list of important monographs on the Civil War, including* The Lincoln Reader, Created Equal *and* Mary Lincoln, Wife and Widow, *which he wrote with Carl Sandburg. In 1959, the sesquicentennial year of Lincoln's birth, he was sent by the State Department to lecture on Lincoln in Japan.*

EARL SCHENCK MIERS, *who lives in Edison, New Jersey, left a career in publishing to become an independent scholar and writer, also specializing in the Civil War period. He has only one honorary degree, from Rutgers, where he also did his undergraduate studying. He has also written many specialized books on the Civil War, including* The Great Rebellion, The General March to Hell, The Web of Victory: Grant at Vicksburg *and* Robert E. Lee. *Most recently he has served as editor-in-chief of* Lincoln Day by Day, *the three-volume product of the Lincoln Sesquicentennial Commission. In reviewing this work, Carl Sandburg called Mr. Miers "one of the more free-going and vivid writers on Lincoln and the Civil War."*